English Drama: A Cultural History

# English Drama:
## A Cultural History

*Simon Shepherd and Peter Womack*

**BLACKWELL**
*Publishers*

First published 1996

2 4 6 8 10 9 7 5 3 1

Blackwell Publishers Ltd
108 Cowley Road
Oxford OX4 1JF
UK

Blackwell Publishers Inc.
238 Main Street
Cambridge, Massachusetts 02142
USA

*British Library Cataloguing in Publication Data*

A CIP catalogue record for this book is available from the British Library.

*Library of Congress Cataloging-in-Publication Data*
Shepherd, Simon.
English drama, a cultural history / Simon Shepherd and Peter Womack.
p.    cm.
Includes bibliographical references and index.
ISBN 0-631-16812-5. – ISBN 0-631-19938-1 (pbk.)
1. English drama–History and criticism.   2. National characteristics, English, in literature.
3. Literature and history–England–History.   4. Theater and society–England–History.
I. Womack, Peter, 1952– .   II. Title.
PR625.S54   1996
822.009–dc20                                                    95-32852
                                                                      CIP

Typeset in 10½ on 12pt Garamond
Typeset by Best-set Typesetter Ltd., Hong Kong
Printed in Great Britain by T.J. Press Ltd, Padstow, Cornwall
This book is printed on acid-free paper

# Contents

# Acknowledgements

The following people have helped out with this book, by reading and talking and sharing their intelligence:

Sarah Carpenter, Jon Cook, Janette Dillon, Tony Gash, Andrew Gurr, Andrew McNeillie, Gyuri Sárossy, Laura Scott, Mick Wallis.

Thank you for your work and support.

## Note to the Reader

The User's Guide and chapters 1, 4, 5, 9 and 11 were written by Peter Womack; chapters 2, 3, 6, 7, 8, 10 and 12 were written by Simon Shepherd.

# User's Guide

The books on the English drama shelf run in meaningless order from John Arden to William Wycherley, the uniformity of their spines concealing a vast range of dramatic conventions and purposes. Picking them out at random, and confronting the difference between a medieval miracle play and a Victorian social comedy, a heroic tragedy and a feminist revue, it starts to feel as if giving all these things the common name of 'play' is simply misleading. How to make genuine sense of this lavish and shambling repertoire – even of any of it?

This book has been shaped by a clear, not to say dogmatic, answer to that question: that plays make sense only in relation to the historically actual practice of theatre. What makes dramatic texts similar to one another is that each one is a script for a show, for a meeting of some kind between a performer and an audience. And what makes them unlike one another is that this meeting is not a fixed form, but an event which can come about in various ways, with various assumptions, for various reasons. To read a play intelligently, we need to understand what kind of show it is the script for.

So what determines, in a particular case, what kind of show is to go on? The intentions of a dramatist, certainly – but not just that: a show is never simply the product of the writer, always of the writer together with the actors. Writer and performer have to negotiate; and the course of the negotiations is not purely a matter of their personalities – it also depends on the way the theatre is run. In some theatres the writer has been a kind of craftsman, producing dialogue to the actors' specifications, while in others the writer has been defined as an artist, and actors as the servants of his controlling conception. The relationship is not constant over time, but changes in response to changing ideologies and modes of theatrical organization: in other words, it is historically conditioned. And the negotiations do not end there. Writer and performer alike make their decisions in the light of their relations with the audience. Who is the show for? Who forms the intended audience, and who forms the actual audience (they are not always the same)? What is the show expected to do for its spectators – to amuse them, indoctrinate them, offend them? In any case, its relationship with them is not always direct: in many theatres, it is mediated and regulated by patrons, managers, critics, censors. Theatre, in short, is inescapably social in character: the show is produced, always, not as the innocent realization of somebody's ideas, but as the outcome of a dense network of interests, needs, desires, habits, authorities. The convenient name for this network is 'culture'. The making and interpreting of plays in English culture, then, is the subject of this book.

In exploring this subject, we immediately encountered an interesting problem: namely, that the cultural life of a play is a double one. First it lives in the theatre in and for which it is written; and then, if it is not forgotten, it lives all over again, differently, in the theatres where it is revived and the editorial and critical processes which mediate it. The Corpus Christi drama which plays in the streets of fifteenth-century York is not the same thing, cannot have the same meaning, as the relic of English culture which is rediscovered by populist scholars in the early nineteenth century, and the play which is performed for an audience of tourists in the grounds of York Minster in the late twentieth century is different again. In a way, this second life of plays makes them all contemporary: a Jacobean tragedy, a Victorian melodrama and a modern realist play can all come together in the work of the same actors, in the same week, on the stage of a repertory theatre. But then, in performance, their incompatible historical and theatrical origins are still felt, as kinds of resistance: the doubleness is irreducible.

What we have done, therefore, is to divide the book into six *pairs* of chapters, devoting each pair to one of the phases of English dramatic production which are of interest to students and practitioners of theatre. The first two chapters are about medieval drama, then come the Renaissance, the Restoration, the melodramatic theatre of the nineteenth century, the establishment of naturalism in the late nineteenth and early twentieth centuries, and finally the post-war era up to about 1990.

The first chapter in each pair is an essay in the history of drama, reading selected plays in the light of the theatrical culture which produced them, and also analysing the culture by means of the plays. In each case, as it has turned out, the history is that of a period of sixty years or so – roughly a lifetime – and in each case, over that time, the conditions and practices of dramatic production changed in important ways. It is the scope of these changes that we have set out to describe: our interest is not in the character of a theatrical 'age' imagined as complete and homogeneous, but precisely in incompleteness, contradiction, uneven development. In all these historical chapters, then, the approach to what might be called the data is frankly selective: rather than writing a continuous narrative of English drama, we have entered its history through a limited number of decisive moments; and within those moments we have highlighted a limited number of plays, not because we are trying to construct a new dramatic canon, but because these particular texts best illustrate the forces and developments we are seeking to understand.[1]

The second chapter in each pair investigates the 'second life' of the drama whose history appeared in the first – to complement the story of how it *was produced* with the story of how it *is reproduced*. These secondary stories are more diffuse and complicated to tell, spreading across several centuries and media and often interrupted by phases of cultural invisibility. They should be used, therefore, not as chapters in a history but rather as studies in a set of concurrent cultural themes: 'naturalistic', 'Elizabethan', 'melodramatic' and the rest are loaded – not to say overloaded – terms in the theatrical discourse of our own time, our own inheritance; and what we have sought to do here is to unpack this baggage so that we can, so to speak, see what we've got.

The intended effect of this dual structure is that the book can be used in different ways. A reader who wants to know about the historical conditions of English play-writing will concentrate on the odd-numbered chapters, which add up to an account of the making of scripts from the late fifteenth century to the present, though not, as we have said, a seamless or continuous account. Alternatively, the analysis of the cultural reproduction of drama can be grasped by reading the even-numbered chapters. And thirdly, we have in mind a student who may be concerned with only one of the theatrical moments we have chosen to concentrate on; this reader should pick out the relevant pair of chapters and treat them as a short book which introduces her object of study from several different points of view. The fourth and last possibility is to read the whole thing. We don't assume this response: each chapter has been designed to make sense on its own. But every chapter is informed by the same coherent set of arguments, and to engage fully with these arguments it is of course necessary to take the book as a whole.

A moment's thought will make it obvious that the gap between the first and second chapters in each pair gets narrower as the book goes on. The reproducers of medieval drama, discussed in chapter 2, struggle with the products of a culture unassimilably different from their own; whereas the relationship between chapters 9 and 10 is almost one of continuity, since, as we argue, 'naturalism' has not yet relinquished the hegemonic position it established a century ago. In the final pair of chapters, the time difference disappears altogether, because we are still living in the configuration they describe. We have nevertheless kept to something like the same pattern: chapter 11 is an essay in the history of the post-war theatrical establishment, and chapter 12 departs from both the history and the establishment to investigate the nature of late-twentieth-century theatricality.

Having explained what we mean by 'drama', 'cultural' and 'history', we should say something about the other big word in the title of this book, 'English'. It is a suspect category in this kind of context because of the long and disreputable tradition of criticism which assimilates Scottish, Welsh, Irish, American and 'Commonwealth' writing into a fantastic imperial unity called 'English Literature'. We have used the adjective advisedly, not in an attempt to do the same for the stage, but in acknowledgement of the necessary limitations of this study. In Ireland and Scotland, especially, there are and have long been connected but autonomous theatrical cultures whose complexities and determinations we have neither the space nor the experience to talk about. A title page which billed 'British Drama' would in that sense be a fraudulent one. At the same time, English culture has been so materially dominant within the United Kingdom that its theatre has inevitably pulled in actors, writers and plays from the peripheries – from Ireland mainly but more recently also from Scotland. These immigrants are essential to any understanding of 'English' drama, precisely because their ambiguous presence, their half-incorporated outsideness, is a vital part of what makes it what it is.[2]

As far as the theatre is concerned, this is a question not primarily of national identity but rather of metropolitan domination. Since the late sixteenth century, theatrical production in Britain has been organized in an increasingly unitary system whose centre, socially, economically and politically, is London. Of course, this hierarchy has been continually deplored and resisted, from the attempts of the people of Chester to keep their urban drama in the 1570s[3] to the aggressive marketing of Glasgow as a theatre capital in the 1980s. But although there are times – arguably we are living in one now – when theatre is more inventive, popular and energetic at the edges than it is at the centre, that fact doesn't shift the structural relation itself. It is therefore possible to speak, as on the whole we have done, about 'English drama', meaning the drama of the London-centred theatrical system, bearing in mind that it has been, and is, a system at once strong and strongly contested.

These problems of definition are, in any case, less pressing here than they are in literary criticism. 'Literature', according to an influential critique of the 1980s, 'is what gets taught': it is an entity which is not reflected but constituted by the study of it. However true this may be, the same cannot be said of the theatre. Few of the practices which are explored in this book are beholden to the academy for their existence; if anything, they have flourished in spite of it. Whatever we say, some people go on playing, and other people go on coming to watch them. This book comes out of long reflection on that ineradicable habit, which in our opinion is a very good one. The reader should feel free to play with the results.

## NOTES

1 The continuous narrative may be found, done on a grand scale, in the seven volumes of *The Revels History of Drama in English* (London: Methuen, 1975–83), and more recently and compactly in Trussler 1994.

2 At certain times a decisive part. There would not be much left, for example, of a history of either English play-writing or English theatrical production in the late nineteenth century which decided to exclude, as extraneous figures, Dion Boucicault, George Bernard Shaw, Oscar Wilde and W. B. Yeats.

3 See H. C. Gardiner 1967: 82; also Clopper 1978: 236–40.

# 1

# Medieval Drama

## 1  The Birth of the Author

From the start, the history of English theatre has been punctuated by official announcements that there is to be no more of it. In 1545, for example, a royal 'Proclamation for the Abolishment of Interludes' notes that drama in London is currently being 'more commonly and besylye [= busily] set foorth and played than heretofore hathe bene accustomed', and commands everybody to stop. However, the document seems to have been drafted by a committee, for it goes on to specify an interesting set of exemptions. Playing in the capital is forbidden

> Onles it be in the houses of noble men or of the lorde Maire Shryves or aldermen of the same his highnes Citie for the time beinge Orels in the houses of gentelmen or of the substancyall & sad [= sober, serious] Comminers or hed parissheners of the same Citie or in the open stretes of the said citie as in tyme paste it hathe been used & accustomed or in the commen halles of the Companyes felowshipps or brotherheddes of the same Citie. (Wickham 1963: 327)

At first sight, these qualifications seem to bring the proclamation close to nullity. If you can play in great men's houses, or in the open street, or in common halls, then where can you not play? (There were, of course, no purpose-built theatres at this time.) But the order is not just talking about physical playing spaces. What it is really concerned with is authorization.

The theatrical events which it is seeking to permit are of three kinds:

1   performances commissioned by citizens whose prominence and status
    make it easy to hold them accountable for what happens;
2   street performances authorized by custom;
3   performances sponsored by one of the guilds of the City of London (this is
    what 'Companyes' means, and it implies an association whose status
    guarantees its corporate respectability).

What the proclamation forbids, then, is playing which is not under the
auspices either of a recognized tradition or of a recognized member of society.
Drama is legitimate unless it is freelance.

The significance of this list of acceptable forms of theatre is inseparable
from its date. It appeared two years before the death of Henry VIII. A decade
before, in the early 1530s, Henry had set in motion the legislative and cultural
upheaval which appears in the history books as the English Reformation.
Under the administration of Thomas Cromwell, the King's principal minister
from 1534 to 1540, the English State broke with the Roman Catholic Church,
expropriated the monasteries, and oversaw the first phase of the transformation
of England into a Protestant country.[1] Among the weapons of this struggle
was the stage: in the words of the most influential Reformation ideologue,
John Foxe, 'Players, Printers, Preachers be set up of God as a triple bulwark
against the triple crown of the Pope, to bring him down' (P. W. White 1993:
2). Cromwell maintained an acting company, run by the militants' leading
playwright, John Bale, to promote Protestant ideas, and there were clearly
many other propagandizing troupes at less elevated levels of the patronage
network (1993: 12–41). In 1540, however, for complex political and factional
reasons, Cromwell was ousted and executed, Bale went into exile, and the
ideological career of the Reformation was drastically braked, even in places
reversed.

Our proclamation, then, is part of the State's attempt to re-establish control
over a cultural revolution which it had initiated, but which now appeared to
be getting out of hand. The chosen strategy is doubly interesting.

Firstly, it is clear that what the document is trying to do is to return drama
to the status quo ante. Relatively few pre-Reformation drama scripts have
survived, but the ones which are extant fall into three broad categories.[2] There
are the urban cycles of pageants depicting the creation, fall, redemption and
judgement of mankind – the so-called 'mysteries' or 'Corpus Christi plays'.
There are the shorter individual plays about biblical or legendary saints and
miracles. And there are the moral plays – allegorical contests between personi-
fied forces of good and evil. All three of these theatrical forms were flourishing
in the 1540s, and all were being staged in one or other of the contexts
permitted by the proclamation. The pageants were performed in the open
street, on the occasion of an annual festival, according to a tradition going back
about two centuries; they were produced by the companies and fellowships of
the town. Miracle plays seem to have been done either by touring semi-

professionals or local amateurs under the auspices of a parish or group of parishes. And moral drama, at least in its relatively courtly sixteenth-century form, was the theatre of the great house, domestic entertainment hospitably presented by wealthy, noble or royal individuals. Thus in reining in the doctrinal and organizational innovations of a period of crisis, the authorities are not trying to abolish theatre, but to re-normalize it, to put it back into the times and places and institutional frameworks which are, as they put it, 'convenient' – that is, fitting and proper. The forms of what we call medieval theatre were not archaic or residual in 1545; indeed, there are quite strong reasons for thinking of the early sixteenth century as the high point of 'medieval' drama's extent and creativity. Rather, they were the forms which powerful people could recognize as convenient.

Secondly, it is striking, for a modern reader used to later forms of theatrical control, that the proclamation distinguishes between acceptable and unacceptable drama on the basis of the circumstances of performance, rather than by asking about the plays' content. Whoever wrote the document thinks of a play, not as something written by a dramatist, but as something done by a group of actors; not as a text, but as a certain kind of social behaviour. The type of regulation he sets up reflects this assumption: just as if he were controlling a non-literary activity such as gambling or holding a public meeting, he lays down when, where and by whom playing may be carried on.

State regulation of drama was a new thing at this point – it became necessary precisely because the State had just dismantled the previous regulator, the medieval Church – and it seems clear that functionaries were still learning how to do it. Wickham suggests plausibly that this proclamation is designed to reinforce an Act of Parliament of 1543, which forbids actors to engage in the interpretation of Scripture or to do anything tending to tumult and schism, while encouraging them to set forth interludes 'for the rebuking and reproaching of vices' (Wickham 1963: 352). Clearly this attempt to prescribe a certain type of play in advance is virtually unenforceable. The 1545 proclamation is a legislative advance on that, since it at least provides for matters which can be unambiguously demonstrated in a court. The trouble with it, on the other hand, is that it produces the desired effect only if all the noblemen, substantial commoners, fellowships and so on can be relied upon not to countenance the wrong kind of play. In the divided polity of Henry VIII's last years, this was not a well-founded assumption.

The solution to the lawmakers' problem, which seems to have been discovered during the following decade or so, is prelicensing: instead of trying to preset the limits of acceptability, the law simply requires the actors to obtain permission for each new show, and bans everything which is not allowed (Wickham 1963: 72–3). But then a further step follows from this device. What the licensing authority needs, in order to decide whether or not to allow a proposed performance to go ahead, is a reliable indication of what it is going to be like – in other words, a script. Thus a regulatory system of this kind entails dramatic *authorship* both as a condition and as a consequence: it does not work unless a play can be considered as emanating primarily from its written text, and to the extent that it does work, it strengthens that very primacy by making the text into a sort of promise which the performers are legally bound to keep.

These documents indicate, then, that in the mid sixteenth century there were two models of theatre. According to one, theatre was a kind of social activity, and it was the responsibility of the person or persons who *authorized* it. According to the other, it was a kind of text, and it was the responsibility of the person or persons who *authored* it. These versions of what is happening are not in principle incompatible, and there is no neatly identifiable historical moment at which the one gives way to the other. But it is not too much to say that the second version, the authorial model, looks forward towards modern conventions, to our own theatre of dramatists and their censors, whereas the first one, the authority model, takes us back towards a culture in which a play is not the utterance of a playwright but an act performed within communal institutions, and where it is the requirements of those institutions, rather than anyone's individual intentions, which effectively dictate its form. Of course, medieval plays had scripts, and these were written by somebody (though until the very end of the fifteenth century there is no record of any dramatic writer's name). But the writer has no rights or responsibilities in relation to the text: it is not his thought, but the social occasion of the performance, which confers unity and significance on the words that are spoken.

Take for example the pageant cycle known as the 'N-town play', one of the four cycles which survive in more or less complete form.[3] It is a manuscript from some time in the second half of the fifteenth century, and it contains forty-two pageants, beginning with the creation of heaven and ending with the Day of Judgement. It owes its name to its opening proclamation, which is a long rhymed announcement of what the show will contain, ending:

> A Sunday next, yf that we may,
> At vj of the belle we gynne oure play
> In N-town . . .
>
> (Spector 1991: I, 21)

This presumably means that the script was to be used for performance in several places, and 'N-town' is a blank to be filled by the actor. Either there was a touring production, or, more likely, the script was lent out to various towns to enable them to stage their own performances. Reading the proclamation, it is natural to expect that the rest of the manuscript will contain the text of the play that was actually performed. However, the 'N-town play' has been shown to be a sort of anthology, put together from several different originals.[4] The proclamation describes the pageants one by one, and the first seven pageants do indeed follow the order which it announces. But the next seven, which are all about the apocryphal doings of the Virgin Mary, do not correspond to anything in the proclamation. They add up to a semi-independent saint's play which has been inserted into the cycle at the appropriate moment (just before the Annunciation). Then, later on, there are ten pageants devoted to the events of Holy Week; they have stage directions which make it clear that the action is continuous between many of them, so that they amount to a single long, complexly structured Passion play – or rather to two, because at the beginning of the fourth of these pageants we find, confusingly, a prologue which refers to the events of the first three as matters which were performed 'last year' (Spector 1991: I, 296). This suggests that the drama was designed for performance on an annual festival day, and that its two parts were done alternately, an arrangement which is evidently incompatible with the unified cycle described in the proclamation. There are similar unconformities within individual pageants, some of which have alternative endings. In short, the 'play', as we have it, is what its makers would have called a *compilatio*, 'written' by someone whose main activity was copying out text from other manuscripts, but who also felt free to stitch these together into a new whole by arranging them and adding stage directions. It is likely that the source manuscripts themselves had the same character, and almost certain that the product was never staged word for word in its entirety. Made, itself, by an active process of selecting, revising and combining, the script offers itself for the same kind of use by actors. It is not at all simply a ragbag; it is a highly structured and intellectually ambitious dramatic text. But its genesis is a process of transmission rather than creation; the work of its writer was not authorial but scribal; its totality has not so much been created as accumulated.

We can see some of the implications of this distinction by returning to a figure who undeniably was a dramatic author: John Bale. His work for the stage, produced in the late 1530s, was very much the kind of thing the regulators of the 1540s were trying to suppress. In its strident anti-Catholicism, it certainly sets out to provoke schism, if not tumult; and its engagement with the interpretation of Scripture is detailed and intense. Many of his scripts are lost, but the surviving ones include several dramatizations of biblical episodes which correspond closely to those staged in the urban pageants, and which are evidently fragments of a project to 'reform', in the full sense, the drama of the Catholic Church.

For example, both Bale and the N-town cycle present the temptation of Christ in the wilderness. The events of the two short plays are identical, since both follow the scriptural narrative given in Matthew 4: 1–11. Jesus fasts for forty days in the wilderness, and then the devil comes to him with three suggestions – that he should turn the stones of the desert into bread; that he should throw himself from the pinnacle of the temple in the confidence that angels will bear him up; and that he should fall down and worship the devil himself in return for the possession of all the kingdoms of the world. Jesus turns back each temptation with a quotation from Mosaic law, and on the third, identifies the tempter as Satan. The devil departs from Christ, and angels minister to him.

Because the two plays share the same scriptural ground, the differences in interpretation are revealing. In the N-town play, the three temptations are explicitly identified with three distinct sins – gluttony, vainglory and covetousness. The implicit point, derived from patristic commentary on the Gospel, is that these are the three sins which came into the world when Eve ate the forbidden fruit; the play enacts Christ's freedom from original sin and so, by looking back to the Fall and forward to the Passion, establishes him as the spotless sacrifice which the redemptive scheme of the whole cycle requires. Bale is not concerned with this itemizing of individual sins. What his Satan is doing with all three temptations is arguing with Christ about whether he is really the Son of God: the first temptation turns on the idea that Christ's life would be a great deal more comfortable if he agreed to abandon this role; the second is proposed as a sort of test to establish whether God is really with him; and the third is a direct attack on Christ's allegiance to God:

> Forsake the beleve    that ye have in Gods worde,
> That ye are hys sonne,    for it is not worth a torde.
> Is he a father    that se hys sonne thus famysh?
> If ye beleve it    I saye ye are to folysh.
> (Bale 1986: II, 60, ll. 293–6)

This temptation, then, is not an incitement to the general sins of humanity, but a specific attempt to undermine Christ's faith and his commitment to his mission on earth.

This new note of religious controversy is particularly pronounced in the second temptation, where St Matthew has Satan citing the Bible:

> And he saith unto him, If thou be the Son of God, cast thyself down: for it is written, He shall give his angels charge concerning thee: and in their hands they shall bear thee up. (Matt. 4: 6)

The devil's reference is to Psalm 91, verses 11–12:

> For he shall give his angels charge over thee, to keep thee in all thy ways. They shall bear thee up in their hands.[5]

Bale seizes on the opportunity offered by this diabolic misuse of Scripture. His Satan is disguised as a religious man, and talks like a friar; moreover, his Christ pounces on the quotation and points out that Satan has cut the phrase 'to keep thee in all thy ways', which he minutely interprets to show that by quoting selectively, Satan has perverted the sense of the verse. Thus, without changing the story, but with a new kind of intellectual excitement, the traditional Temptation play turns into a polemic about scriptural interpretation, setting priestly manipulation (Satan) against a Protestant reappropriation of the true Word (Christ).

The same shift can be seen more crudely in the play's insistence that the story of Christ in the wilderness is not a divine injunction to fast. Bale not only offers his own different interpretation of the forty days; he goes out of his way to denounce what he evidently regards as a popish misinterpretation of the story. The denunciation is issued not only through the words of Christ in the play, but also through a figure called Baleus Prolocutor (Bale as spokesman), who introduces and concludes the performance in direct address to the audience. This expository device is not unprecedented: some of the N-town pageants include a comparable figure called Contemplacio, who commands silence, does bits of linking narrative, and concludes the action by drawing a moral and blessing the public. But Bale adapts this convention in two striking ways. For one thing, his expositor is a controversialist, identifying incorrect doctrine and distancing himself from it: whereas Contemplacio formally represents Christian humanity as a whole, Baleus Prolocutor is frankly speaking for some people as opposed to others. And for another, Bale's spokesman is explicitly a dramatization of the author: in fact, since we know that Bale organized the performances as well as writing the scripts, we can presume that Baleus Prolocutor *is* the author in person.

In Roland Barthes's famous and mischievous announcement of it, 'the death of the author' occurs at the hands of the text (Barthes 1986). What with the pre-existing linguistic and rhetorical codes which flow into any act of writing the moment the writer takes up his pen, and the multiplication of ironic and fictive voices which overtakes him as soon as he begins to 'say' anything, the author dies because he is diffused throughout a textual field, undone by the sheer proliferation of signifying impulses. He can no longer be invoked as the determining origin or limit of the text's meaning, because he is too caught up in its insidious play of possibilities himself. In Bale's revision of pre-Reformation biblical drama, we can see something like this process in reverse. The iconoclastic playwright moves in on a pre-existing scene which belongs not to another playwright but to an institutional set of functions: its rhythms are dictated by the words of Scripture, by a long and almost canonical tradition of scriptural commentary, by the allegorical correspondences which constitute its place in the cycle as a whole, and by the performance requirements of a customary social and devotional event. He does not necessarily wish to be anything but the latest link in the chain of this transmission: his name appears on the title page of the printed edition, but only as the person who 'compiled' the text; and certainly he wants it to be understood that the origin and limit of the play's meaning is not Bale, but God. However, his non-authorial status, so to speak, is fatally compromised by his conscious position in the middle of an ideological struggle. God can no longer be represented as speaking unambiguously: a gap has opened up between his Word and its interpretation. Into this gap come the Prolocutor, arguing with the audience about the meaning of the play itself, and, within the play, Christ and Satan, arguing about the meaning of certain verses from the Old Testament.

Within this argument, it is Christ who adopts what might be called the *authorialist* position: whereas Satan, as a caricatured Catholic, regards the Bible as a diffuse anthology of quotations from which one selects at will, Bale–Christ insists, like a modern English teacher, on reading for meaning:

> In no wyse ye ought    the scriptures to deprave,
> But as they lye whole    so ought ye them to have.
> Nomore take ye here    than serve for your vayne purpose,
> Leavynge out the best    as ye shuld tryfle or glose.
>
> (ll. 215–18)

Reading, on this view, is not an open-ended play of selection and interpretation; ingenuity must be limited by the duty to seek out honestly the sense of the whole thing – to discover, as best one can, God's meaning. That is to say, Christ (but, understandably, not Satan) thinks of the Bible as a book which has an author.

Moreover, it is clear that once these arguments have broken out, the actors need a more or less implicit way of saying to the audience: 'and this is what *we* think.' It is as the subject of that expression, the one who claims the right to decide what is meant, and accepts the responsibility for avoiding misunderstanding, that the author makes his appearance in the theatre. Bale, who breaks with precedent by representing Christ's resistance to temptation as a personal commitment, constitutes himself as a dramatic author by virtue of his own. The schism which the authorities are struggling to suppress turns out to be the matrix which forms the figure of the dramatist.

## 2   In the Open Streets

To consider theatrical life before the author, we can begin with a fact about urban cycle drama which, although it is quite well known, is so extraordinary as to have provoked some scholarly incredulity. It has to do with the scale of the performance. The York play, which is the largest and best documented of the surviving cycles, has forty-eight pageants, which were played on movable wagons drawn through the streets. The actors did not play on the move: there was a set sequence of about twelve stopping places ('stations') arranged on a route around the city. The people responsible for the first pageant ('The Fall of the Angels') began proceedings by performing it at the first station, then moved their wagon to the second station, where they performed it again, while the next wagon moved into position at the first station and performed 'The Creation'. By the time 'The Fall of the Angels' got to the twelfth station for its final performance, 'The Annunciation' was being played for the first time, back at the beginning of the route, and the whole of the Old Testament section of the cycle was being performed simultaneously in twelve different places a few hundred yards apart from one another.[6] By the end of the day, if this plan was carried out in its entirety, the total number of performances given in the streets of York works out at 576.

We do not know for certain that this astonishing figure was ever actually reached. Numerous detailed qualifications have to be added to that schematic account. The extant script, known as the 'Register', was prepared as the City Corporation's official record of the cycle in the second half of the fifteenth century. By this time the play had been presented annually for about a century; it is possible that the manuscript contains all the pageants that were ever included, and that what was played in any particular year was a selection. The same logic might conceivably mitigate the number of stations. But the conjectural adjustments which can be made to the arithmetic do little to alter the essential conception. The *idea* of the York play has a theatrical extravagance unparalleled by any dramatic practice that has arisen since the Reformation.

The common-sense modern reaction to it is clearly summarized by A. C. Cawley:

> It is sometimes argued that convenience and economy of staging, as well as unity of dramatic effect, would be better served by a performance of all the cyclic plays in one fixed location than by their performance in succession at several different acting stations. . . . At first glance, the processional performance of the Corpus Christi play at York, with its twenty-seven different actors playing the part of Jesus in the twenty-seven different plays in which the part occurs, does seem to be intolerably wasteful and fragmented. (Cawley et al. 1983: 30)

The alternative is not at all inconceivable: possibly the Towneley cycle, and almost certainly the N-town play, were indeed performed in a single location. The evidence of processional staging is mostly from York and Chester. It appears, then, that the citizens of these places organized things in this way not because it was all they knew how to do, but because they chose to. Why? Cawley continues: 'Practical and artistic considerations did not necessarily decide how the plays were performed: tradition and the vested interests of the guilds were likely to be just as important.' This comment refers to the peculiar socio-economic structure of the plays, which we must briefly consider.

The play was performed once a year, and was attached to the feast of Corpus

Christi. This was the last in the sequence of annual festival days leading up to and away from Easter – Shrove Tuesday at the beginning of Lent, the Annunciation, Palm Sunday, Easter itself, the Ascension, Pentecost, Trinity Sunday – which turned the first half of the medieval year into a ritual cycle, rehearsing each spring the phases of the birth, death, resurrection and ascension of Christ.[7] Corpus Christi was a relatively late addition to this ceremonial repertoire, promulgated in 1264 and adopted in England during the early fourteenth century. It was dedicated to the real presence of the body of Christ in the Host – that is, unlike most of the other feasts, which celebrated biblical events, this one was focused on the doctrine, liturgy and central symbol of the Church. The main event was not the play, but a procession in which the Host – the consecrated bread and wine of the Mass – was carried through the town, attended by the leading ecclesiastical and secular dignitaries. This public dimension to the festival, whereby the Host was, unusually, brought out of the Church and venerated in the open streets, gave it the character of a civic as well as a devotional ritual: by a conscious and intentional metaphor,[8] the body of Christ signified the body of the community, and served to reaffirm its hierarchical unity.

The play arguably served a similar ideological purpose in a slightly different way. Under the oversight of the City Corporation, the pageants were paid for and staged by the guilds, which were at once trade organizations and religious fraternities. Each guild had its own pageant, assigned to it on the basis of its specialism (the Shipwrights built the Ark, the Bakers produced the Last Supper) or its resources (the wealthiest group, the Mercers, staged the spectacular Last Judgement pageant), by an order which changed only slightly over decades as individual trades prospered or failed. Thus the annual performance, for any particular guild, was a regular opportunity to reassert its distinctive identity – its wealth, its piety, and its status in the intricate pecking order of the town – while at the same time the massively centripetal organization of the play as a whole enacted the ultimate integration of all these sectional interests under the sign of Corpus Christi, the sacred body of which everyone is supposed to be a member.[9]

Thus when Cawley speaks of the determination of the dramatic form by 'tradition and the vested interests of the guilds', it is not difficult to see what he means. 'Convenience and economy' were not paramount considerations; on the contrary, conspicuous display was one of the aims of the production. And as for 'dramatic unity', the social conditions of performance suggest at least two qualifications to this historically questionable criterion.

One is that, as we have just seen, the meaning of the play as a ceremonial event turns on a complex equilibrium of unity and heterogeneity. Certainly unity is important, but it is given anyway by the narrative and typological structuring which links every word spoken on every stage to the play's only determining event: the Passion of Christ. And it is equally vital that it should be a unity *of* the greatest possible diversity: the sections must have space to register their relative autonomy, otherwise the cumulative wholeness would be insubstantial and abstract.

Secondly, the notion of dramatic unity overlooks the different form, the differently constituted unity, of the procession. We saw that an ecclesiastical procession was the central event of the feast of Corpus Christi itself, and although the processional performance of the play is not the same thing (they presumably happened on successive days), the two spectacular journeys through the same streets are evidently analogous. The coherence of the form consists of its juxtaposition of levels of existence: the sacred imagery (whether in the vestments and furniture of the liturgy or in the narrative enactment of the drama) is deliberately taken round the common spaces where people live and work. The object of the exercise, you could say rather schematically, is to consecrate the everyday environment – both the physical environment of the shops and houses before which the spectacle passes, and the institutional environment whose representatives take their allotted, status-determined places in the procession. This can be seen in the York Skinners' pageant, 'The Entry into Jerusalem'. Christ rides on an ass – presumably in the street in front of the pageant wagon   and is greeted by eight 'burgesses', who deliver formal and choric speeches expressing the 'welcome of all abowte / To owre ceté' (Beadle 1982: 219). They speak as official representatives of the Jerusalem crowd, and at the same time they are surrounded by the York crowd in the real street: the scene closely resembles a royal visit to the city, and there is a very clear sense, as the play's modern editors point out, that Christ is being welcomed into York (Beadle and King 1984: 106). This is an exceptionally self-conscious statement of the principle of the show as a whole. The proliferation of imitation Christs, twenty-seven of them a dozen times each, preaching, blessing, suffering, judging, all day, on every corner, represents a total *permeation* of the town by the divine body whose originating oneness their very multiplicity denotes.

But in spelling out the implications of 'tradition and vested interests', we find that the distinction between social and institutional requirements on the one hand, and 'practical and artistic considerations' on the other, has broken down. It all depends what practice, what art, we are talking about. The communal and ritual syntax of an event like this means, precisely, that the artistic and the institutional do not merely constrain one another, but interpenetrate. Compare Cawley's comments with an account by Joyce McMillan of a community play performed in Dundee in 1988:

It takes a long time to make your point under the kind of conditions faced by Dundee's great community show Witch's Blood II on Saturday night. By the time the 300-strong cast, panting and mud-streaked under the brilliant floodlights and fine drizzling rain in the courtyard of old Dudhope Castle, had belted out their final chorus, the audience had been on its feet for the best part of four hours. We had been bussed in convoy from Dudhope Park to a mud-and-dung-strewn millyard in the old Markets district . . . and then to a bleak municipal dump-site on the banks of the Tay; we were wet, we were cold, we were angry at the Scottish weather. (*Guardian*, 11 July 1988)

The Dundee play clearly resembles the York play at several points. It involves an amateur cast of hundreds; it moves the action between several locations in the town, at least partly so as to engineer an act of communal self-realization, though in the 1980s this is done in terms of the city's mercantile and industrial past rather than in religious terms. And the critique is also effectively the same in both cases: that this is an extraordinarily uneconomical way to do a play ('making your point' is the journalist's equivalent of 'achieving unity of dramatic effect'), but that nevertheless, somehow, the cumbersome and fragmented mode of the production is worth it – Cawley is a champion of cycle drama, and the review of *Witch's Blood* is an enthusiastic recommendation.

One sense of that 'nevertheless', of course, is the sentimental one: it may be a failure 'artistically', but it is redeemed by the artless community involvement it generates. Bad drama is revalorized through the revelation of simple faith and the excited faces of children. No doubt this is an element in literary scholars' taste for both medieval and modern 'community' drama; McMillan's cosy nationalization of the weather is indicative of the tone. But she goes on to say something more specific than that: several times, on the point of losing patience with the whole clumsy business, she was drawn back into it by some arresting piece of *acting* by one or another of the untrained cast. Primarily a reviewer of professional theatre, she concludes that 'good acting has frighteningly little to do with technique.' What these actors have instead of the techniques of the contemporary professional, it is implied, is a performing context in which the techniques are not needed. The distinctive features of the community play – the sheer numbers, the complicated real mobilization of bodies and objects, the appropriation of non-theatrical space, the multiple playing configurations which place actors and audience in unpredictable relationships – combine to give the drama the weight and rootedness of an *event* (as opposed to the representation of an event). Within this event, the energies and skills and gestures of ordinary social living suddenly become theatrically significant; this is a peculiarly defined space where many people turn out to be 'cunning, discreet and able players';[10] it is not a play about the community, but the community playing itself. That theatricalization of the social sphere is one 'artistic' prize of the determination of dramatic form by tradition and vested interests: we should perhaps think of Corpus Christi as, in this special sense, an actors' theatre.

However, putting it like that – in terms of the ownership of the spectacle – raises a further question which the transhistorical invocation of 'community' risks blurring. Take, almost at random, the York pageant of Christ's interrogation by Annas and Caiaphas, presented by the craft guild of Bowers and Fletchers. Caiaphas opens the play by commanding silence – a frequent and obvious opening move in street performance – and parading his power and knowledge:

> Pees, bewshers, I bid no jangelyng ye make,
> And sese sone of youre sawes, & se what I saye,
> And trewe tente unto me this tyme that ye take,
> For I am a lorde lerned lelly in youre lay. . . .
>
> There is nowder lorde ne lady lerned in the lawe,
> Ne bisshope ne prelate that preved is for pris,
> Nor clerke in the courte that connyng will knawe,
> With wisdam may were hym in worlde is so wise.
>
> I have the renke and the rewle of all the ryall,
> To rewle it by right als resoune it is,
> All domesmen on dese awe for to dowte me,
> That hase thaym in bandome, in bale or in blis,
> Wherfore takes tente to my tales and lowtis unto me.
>
> (Beadle 1982: 243)

(*Silence, fine sirs, I command that you make no babbling, and stop your speech soon, and see what I say, and truly pay attention to me now, for I am a lord truly learned in your law. . . .*

*There is neither lord nor lady learned in the law, nor bishop nor prelate whose worth is proven, nor clerk in court who has knowledge, that may bear himself in the world with such great wisdom.*

*I have the reign and rule of all royalty, to govern by right, as reason dictates, all the judges on the bench ought to fear me, who have them in my control, in suffering or in joy, so pay attention to my words and bow down to me.*)

There are, you could say, two distinct ways of speaking about this character, this stage voice. The first is this: it is the occasion of a remarkable, savage travesty of the bases of social authority. The speaker is a local craftsman; the writing is skilfully designed, with its forceful alliterative beats, so that an amateur and possibly illiterate performer can both learn it and project it in the open air. The audience is socially miscellaneous, freely assembled in the street, but not very large: as modern reconstructions have suggested, one of the incidental advantages of processional performance is that it breaks a big crowd up into small groups so that the conditions of any one performance are surprisingly intimate. Since medieval York is a fairly small place, with not more than two or three thousand households, the actor is quite likely to be known to some of the spectators. It is a holiday: no one is working, and occasional records of drunkenness and disturbance suggest that part of the point of Corpus Christi is to have a good time.[11] The actor stands on the wagon, dominating the relaxed little crowd, splendidly dressed, and probably looking like a bishop.[12] He uses his temporary and playful authority to command silence, and then lays claim to all the advantages of the ruling class: rank, law, learning, civil and ecclesiastical power. As with almost all such vaunting speeches in the medieval theatre, the claims are total – he says he is the *most* powerful, the *most* learned of all[13] – and this has a double effect: on the one hand it universalizes the image, making the particular potentate the emblem of earthly sovereignty as such; and on the other it makes the speaker sound hysterically boastful. In combination, then, it amounts to a cheerful, festive representation of all human authority as ridiculous. In this case, the claims are comic anyway, because the spectators know that in the story Caiaphas is not the ruler of rulers but a murderer of Christ and the blind instrument of a divine purpose he knows nothing about; and also because the extremely anti-illusionist circumstances of performance foreground the fact that the speaker is not the ruler of anything, but is playing at it. These two different mechanisms of demystification reinforce one another in practice, and arrive at their full point at the end of the pageant, when the soldiers blindfold the silent, ragged Christ and play a brutal game in which he is supposed to guess which of them has just hit him. So the logic of the spectacle is that the staged bishop is really a blind fool, and the staged blind fool is really God. What is the relationship between a show like this and the official display of civil and ecclesiastical power in the Corpus Christi procession of the previous day?

The second way of speaking about Caiaphas includes an answer to that question. Certainly the actor is playing, but he is doing so under authority – the authority of his guild and, over the guild, the City Corporation, which checks the performance against the master copy of the script and imposes fines for failures to comply with the day's arrangements; but also the authority which can be traced in the script itself. It is itself a compilation of authorities, combining details from the different Gospels into a single sequence of action; and the sureness with which it does this is informed by doctrinal and didactic intentions. For example, the reason for stressing that Caiaphas is a master of the law is that the transcendence, or fulfilment, of the Old Testament law by divine grace is the action of the entire drama; this pageant is one of a long sequence, including Abraham and Isaac, the Flood, the Woman Taken in Adultery, the Betrayal, the Crucifixion, and the Harrowing of Hell, which figure and refigure the mystery whereby God visits the scene of punishment and translates it into the language of forgiveness. As the guardian of that mystery in the form of the Host which is the object of the Corpus Christi celebration, the Church renews its authority through these enactments. In this context, the demonization of the bishop, and the deification of the beggar, are impeccably orthodox: they show Christ despised and rejected, and implicitly counsel the public to look for salvation not in the shows of the world but only in Christ. There is no hard evidence, but the theological and biblical facility of this structure strongly suggests clerical authorship of the plays, and they do, consciously and effectively, promulgate the Church's doctrine and the Church's discipline. Their vigorous anti-establishment moves have always a pre-ordained place within the larger ideology of the establishment: their utopian mockery of the mighty in their seats is startling only to a modern reader who is not taking their religious framework seriously.[14]

What emerges, for us, in the gap between these two descriptions of the vaunt of Caiaphas, is the spaciousness of the collectively produced performance text. The cycle as a whole may represent a disciplinarian closure, but the concern to diffuse that totality through the physical and social structure of the town accords the parts a great deal of autonomy. The events of the Passion are horrific, and seem to have been staged with gruesome literalism, but without abandoning a tone of festive and anachronistic comedy.[15] The action continually privileges the poor, the unlocated, the meek who shall inherit the earth, while never ceasing to be a parade of the corporate wealth of the town and its trades. This paradox rises to a climax in the final play, when Christ in glory identifies himself with the poor, the sick and the imprisoned, blesses those who helped him and casts those who neglected him into the fire.[16] This apotheosis of the unprivileged needs to be read alongside the surviving props list for the play (Beadle 1994: 94), whose extravagance shows how much the York Mercers were prepared to spend on their privileged situation at the top of the Corpus Christi bill.

Underlying these contradictions is not so much anybody's mental ambivalence as the poised material structure of the annual event: the sense in which it belonged simultaneously to the Church, to the incorporated town and to the crowd.[17] A functionalist sociology would say that this simultaneity was precisely the point of the exercise – that through the performance and the veneration of the omnipresent body of Christ the competing and stratified elements of the community were ritually harmonized. Without having to make things quite that neat, we can at least say that the energy and invention of this theatre comes not from its reflection of the unity, but from its negotiation of the plurality, of the community that made it.

## 3   Miracles Playing

We speak for convenience about morality plays, mystery plays, saints' plays; but these distinctions probably had little force in the fifteenth century. As we have seen, theatrical practices were more likely to be classified by the auspices under which they took place than sorted out into a scheme of dramatic genres. To take one spectacular example, the late-fifteenth-century play of *Mary Magdalen* features first a scene in which Magdalen's castle is besieged and infiltrated by the World, the Flesh and the seven deadly sins; then the story of her meeting with Jesus, the raising of Lazarus and the death and resurrection of Christ, all dramatized much as it would be in a Corpus Christi cycle; and then, after the ascension of Christ, a legendary sequence in which she sails to Marseilles, converts the king and queen of Marseilles to Christianity, and is the means of their miraculous protection on their voyage to the Holy Land (D. C. Baker et al. 1982: 24–95). So far as we can tell from the script, the action is continuous; the play cannot be said to cross generic boundaries because it does not even recognize them. Moral allegory, biblical narrative and hagiographic fantasy all inhabit a single dramatic world.

One possible name for this world can be found in one of the few pieces of sustained criticism of theatre which survive from medieval England: the late-fourteenth-century *Tretise of Miraclis Pleyinge* (Davidson 1981). The anonymous author of this tract invariably calls acting in a religious context 'miraclis pleyinge', and his argument makes clear from the outset that what he means by this is literally the playing of miracles:

> sithen miraclis of Crist and of hise seintis weren thus effectuel, as by oure bileve we ben in certein, no man shulde usen in bourde and pleye the miraclis and werkis that Crist so ernystfully wroghte to oure helthe. (p. 35)

(*since the miracles of Christ and of his saints were thus effectual, as we know for certain by our faith, no man should use in jest and play the miracles and works which Christ wrought so much in earnest for our health.*)

We can return to the polemic later; what is immediately interesting is this writer's sense of what is happening on the medieval religious stage. Truly to perform a miracle, as Christ and the saints did, is to make an intervention in the natural course of things (curing an incurable sickness, walking on the water, raising the dead) so astonishing that the beholders are seized by an apprehension of the grace of God. In a sense, then, miracles are already theatrical: they are visible actions carried out for the sake of their effect upon spectators. To perform a miracle in play is to simulate this effect by means of a device; the debate is then about whether such a substitution is permissible. So when the writer says 'miracles playing' he is talking not exactly about a dramatic genre ('miracle plays') but rather about a devotional practice (playing – as opposed, say, to *working* – miracles). A Cistercian abbey in Kent had an image of the crucified Christ which nodded its head, moved its eyes, and shed tears in response to the prayers of pilgrims (G. M. Gibson 1989: 15); this spectacle, which was produced by 'certain engines and old wires', was also a kind of 'miracles playing', and, like the more recognizably dramatic kinds, it was denounced and destroyed by agents of the Reformation. This way of looking at the question defines medieval drama as one element in a larger repertoire of religious theatricality. What is the place of the stage in this diverse culture?

The cycles include a curious semi-biblical episode which modern critics call 'Joseph's Doubts'. It usually begins with a long speech in which Joseph, the husband of the Virgin Mary, confides in the audience. He is troubled: he is an old man, he has taken a young wife, he has never slept with her, but she is pregnant. If he does not punish her as an adultress, he will be scorned as an old cuckold; and yet he cannot bring himself to see her as unchaste:

> I knew nevyr with here, so God me spede,
> Tokyn of thynge in word nor dede
> That towchyd velany.
> Nevyrtheles, what forthy,
> Thow she be meke and mylde,
> Withowth mannys company
> She myght not be with childe!
> (Spector 1991: I, 127)

*(As God is my help, I never knew with her any sign of anything in word or deed that touched on wickedness. Nevertheless, for all that, though she be meek and mild, she couldn't be with child unless she had been with a man!)*

Those last two lines, with their common-sense insistence on the physical bottom line of the question, place Joseph squarely in the ignoble, material world of the *fabliau*, the comic and ethical tale of domestic mishap familiar to us from Chaucer. So when Mary replies, as she must, that she has been impregnated not by a man but by the archangel Gabriel, Joseph's exasperation is entirely in keeping with the style of the play. A rich vein of medieval anti-feminist anecdote has taught him what to make of cock-and-bull stories like *that*.

Humanist critics have praised the realistic quality of this sequence; but it is a curious kind of realism, because it is clear throughout that Joseph is entirely wrong. Mary is, after all, the holy Mother of God, venerated throughout Christendom: it is inconceivable that the little play could engineer such a dramatic suspension of belief that the spectators are induced to share, even temporarily, Joseph's uncertainty. There is no real dilemma: in the end, an angel appears to Joseph to explain the true position, and all is well. What the play does by delaying this resolution for a hundred lines or so is to present the naturalistic *fabliau* world as a prison. Inside it, Joseph is stuck; his wife cannot possibly be unchaste, but cannot possibly be chaste either; there is no way out.

The door is unlocked only by the miracle: the Virgin Birth. So the effect of this comic method of dramatizing the story is to enact the defeat of the empirical. The bases of Joseph's misunderstanding – the evidence of his senses, his knowledge of the world, his reasonable logic of cause and effect – are mockingly relegated to the sphere of illusory appearance by the knowledge of the truth which is shared by the angel and the audience. As Stephen Medcalf has neatly said, paraphrasing Boetius, medieval thought tended to assume that 'the true view of the universe is perceived not from where we are but from where God is' (Medcalf 1981: 60). 'Joseph's Doubts' is a rather ingenious dramatization of that assumption.

The N-town play reinforces the effect with a legendary supplement, 'The Trial of Mary and Joseph'. In this version, Mary's virginity is not a chance circumstance but a religious commitment which Joseph has promised to honour in marrying her. Her pregnancy therefore places the legal authorities in a double bind analogous to Joseph's: either she is an adultress, or else he has broken his promise. Two 'Detractors' accuse them in a sort of ecclesiastical court; Mary and Joseph both protest their innocence, and the judge, who is a bishop, imposes a magical test to establish which of them is lying. Each of them has to drink from 'the bottle of God's vengeance' and walk round the altar: this ritual will have no effect on the innocent, but the guilty person who performs it will be struck down in some way. First Joseph, and then Mary, is vindicated by the test: the divine bottle seems to be producing contradictory results. Finally one of the Detractors takes the test, is afflicted with terrible pains and confesses his falsehood. It is not explained to the court how the statements of Mary and Joseph can both be true: the whole forensic structure is simply blown away by the wordless divine intervention.

Strikingly, 'The Trial of Mary and Joseph' takes the motifs of the 'Joseph's Doubts' plays and externalizes them. The unpleasantly sceptical part of Joseph's attitude becomes two nasty and cynical characters who are punished in the end; the incompatible stories which are nevertheless both true are rendered spatially actual by being attached to two different people; the reasonableness of Joseph's earthly criteria of truth is dramatized as a legal hearing; and the underlying spiritual truth is made concrete by embodying it in the drink and the ritual perambulation. The result is much less congenial to a realist conception of drama: the antics in this courtroom seem bizarre and frivolous by comparison with the more restrained staging of 'Joseph's Doubts'. But then, arguably, that grotesque dislocation of a merely human procedure is precisely the point. The evidential categories of the material world are in an absolute sense invalid, because of the underlying assumption that the view 'from where we are' is false. Since playing is a merely human practice, it can of course not show the view from where God is. But what it can do is to present the human perspective in such a way that it is constantly running into blind spots, losing coherence, being revealed as imperfect. Miracles are the mechanisms of this sabotage of the visible: directly staged, they nevertheless function as abrupt intimations of the unstageable truth.

This is perhaps how to read the extraordinary *Play of the Sacrament*, an entirely non-biblical play associated with Croxton in East Anglia, dating from the second half of the fifteenth century. It tells the story of a group of Jews who get hold of the Host, the consecrated bread of the Mass which, according to the doctrine of the Church, is the body of Christ. The leading Jew, Jonathas, derides this doctrine on naturalistic grounds:

> The beleve of these Cristen men ys false, as I wene;
>     For the beleue on a cake – me thynk yt ys onkynd.
>     And all they seye how the preste dothe yt bynd,
> And be the myght of his word make yt flessh and blode –
> And thus be a conceyte the wolde make vs blynd.
>                 (Davis 1970: 58–89, ll. 199–203)

*(The belief of these Christian men is false, I think; for they believe in a cake – it seems unnatural to me. And they all say how the priest binds it and makes it into flesh and blood by the power of his word – and so by an idea they seek to make us blind.)*

'Make us blind' implies, I think, 'make out that we are blind': we can *see* that it is a cake, so the assertion that it is really flesh and blood is an absurd denial of the obvious.

Apparently provoked by this, the Jews set out to test the Host. They prick it with their daggers and cut it in pieces. It bleeds and, terrified and demented, Jonathas holds it up while they nail it to the wall; but when he tries to let go of it his hand comes off and remains attached to the bread. They pull the nails out with pincers and throw the Host and the hand together into a cauldron of boiling oil, which bubbles over red with blood. Finally they cast the whole thing into an oven; the oven also bleeds and bursts open, and the figure of Christ appears from the wreckage with its five wounds. At this point the Jews all pray to Christ, who restores Jonathas' hand. They convert to Christianity and send for a bishop, who petitions Christ for their forgiveness, after which the figure turns back into bread.

It seems fairly clear that this lurid show is polemical in a specific sense. It was staged at a time when Lollardy was an active force in the religious life of East Anglia. The Lollards were critics of the doctrinal and institutional power of the Church, and one focus of their opposition was precisely the question of the transubstantiation of the Host (Beckwith 1992: 66–7). The play's Jews, then – who have no dramatic specificity as Jews (like most medieval theatrical villains, they worship 'Machomete so myghty') – really represent Christian heretics who deny the miracle of the Mass. The action constitutes an assertion, not just of orthodox doctrine, but specifically of the authority of the Church:

the magical powers displayed by the piece of bread have been conferred on it by a priest, and its terrifying metamorphoses are brought to a peaceful end only by the arrival of the bishop.

But this polemical project does not have the effect, as Bale's does, of carving out an argumentative space for authorial identity, because, paradoxically, the play denies the possibility of the theological position it denounces. In theory, as we saw, the Jews believe that the Host is only a cake. But they pay a large sum of money to obtain it, they are fascinated by it, they persecute it with obsessive violence – it is obvious that they do not so much disbelieve in it as believe in it and hate it. That the Host is the body of Christ is affirmed in the play not only through its spectacular physical manifestations but also through the fact that there is not really anybody in the cast who thinks otherwise. In 'The Trial of Mary and Joseph', disbelief in the Virgin Birth was projected on to malicious detractors who eventually confessed their falsehood; here, similarly, disbelief in the Mass is attributed to destructive buffoons who are not intellectually propounding a different interpretation but pathologically resisting the truth. This incorporation is carried out in narrative terms by so arranging matters that the Jews unconsciously re-create their communal role in the original Passion of Christ: torturing him, nailing him up, consigning him to hell and sealing him up in a tomb, only to be dumbfounded by his resurrection. Just as the persecutors in the original Passion story imagine they are defeating and suppressing Christ when in truth they are conforming to a divine plan which will lead to his ultimate triumph, so in this play, again, eternally, those who set out to disprove the original story end up re-enacting it in spite of themselves. In so far as the play is responding to theological opponents, it does so not by debating with them, but by constructing a stage world in which they appear as walking contradictions, monstrous and unsustainable. The decisive refutation is performed, not by authorial discourse, but by the silent, suffering Host.

Formally, then, the show plays to an audience which, like the congregation at the Mass itself, is taken to be united in a single faith. Actually, the play is aware of division – as we have seen, it is its *raison d'être* – but it represses that contradiction by projecting it on to the demonized figures of the Jews. However, this strategy of containment is not completely successful. One sign of the tension is the fact that the miracle is produced, not by love and faith, but by malice and incredulity. It is the cruelty of its tormentors that elicits from the Host the spectacular manifestation of its true nature: without their shocking transgression, there would be no revelation. Within a community of believers who all *knew* that the bread is truly flesh, it would simply be free to continue to look like bread; and it is to bread that it reverts when that community is established at the end of the play. Its miraculousness, so to speak, is wrung from it by torture. This irony enables us to make sense of the grotesque violence of the spectacle. The miracle is violent in the sense that it aggressively confronts and disrupts the order of things in the world: in unredeemed mankind, then, it is shown as producing horror and dismay. The literal violence done to the Host, and the retaliatory terrorism of the Host itself, dramatize that raging division of worlds, substantiating the role of miracles as the saboteurs of the empirical. The unity of Christendom is a contested and forcible one (maintained, for example, by burning heretics to death on various doctrinal grounds including this one); staged miracles have an edge of violence because they are skirmishes in a necessarily undeclared war.

And it is also contradictory, in a different, formal sense, that a theatre so extremely dedicated to the invalidation of the visual should be so grossly illusionistic. The bleeding cake, the detachable hand, the exploding oven – these are the devices of a conjuror's theatre: like the trick Christ in the Cistercian abbey, they depend for their effectiveness on the concealment of the mechanism. It is integral to the logic of the show that the spectators are meant to believe their eyes. This appeal to the senses is at the heart of the objections in the *Tretise*:

> pleyinge, for it is fleysly, never bedyn of God, shulde not be don with the mervelouse werkis of God, for they ben gostly. . . . [P]leyinge of miraclis benemeth men ther bileve in Crist and is verre goinge bacward fro dedis of the spirit to onely signes don after lustis of the fleysh that ben agenus alle the deedis of Christ. . . . And thefore we schal nevere findyn that miraclis pleying was usid among cristene men but sithen religious onely in tokenes shewiden ther religioun and not in dedis, and sithen pristis onely in signes and for money schewiden ther pristhode and not in dedis. (Davidson 1981: 49)

(*playing, because it is fleshly, never commanded by God, should not be done with the marvellous works of God, because they are spiritual. . . . The playing of miracles takes away men's belief in Christ, and is truly going backwards from deeds of the spirit to mere signs, done according to the lusts of the flesh, which is contrary to all the deeds of Christ. . . . And therefore we shall never find that miracles playing was a custom among Christian men, but it has developed since there were religious men who showed their religion only in tokens and not in deeds, and since there were priests who showed their priesthood only in signs and for money and not in deeds.*)

Belief in Christ is of the spirit; religious playing takes it away because it seduces the spectators into basing their faith on physical objects and actions instead; theatricality for this writer means, exactly, signs substituted for the realities they are supposed to signify. On this view, then, the devotional theatre centred on the playing of miracles is the victim of an internal irony. It sets out to destroy the coherence of the sensory world, but in its voracity for ever more incontrovertible mechanisms to achieve this destruction, it becomes, itself, sensational. It is like a man who is so anxious to convince us of the existence of invisible substances that he resorts to assuring us that he has seen them.

The last sentence of the quotation offers a historical explanation for that self-defeating anxiety: that the authority of the invisible substances is in decay. According to the writer, the growth of a theatre of miracles is part of a general, decadent theatricalization of devotion: players are like the monks and priests of these latter days whose religious observances are empty tokens. That way of putting it reminds us that the treatise as a whole is an anti-clerical and reforming text – in other words, it denounces theatre from precisely the Lollard point of view which the theatrical devices of *The Play of the Sacrament* are designed to demonize. The late medieval staging of miracles, then, is not the naive expression of a unified cosmos: rather, it is a sophisticated icono-graphic attempt to assemble, or reassemble, such a unity in the face of its felt disintegration. The spectacular legendary theatre of East Anglia in the late fifteenth and early sixteenth centuries, and the anti-spectacular scriptural theatre of Bale, do not in any simple way stand in the relation of old to new. Rather, they both bear equally the marks of a polarization of image and word, sign and doctrine, which is generated by the crisis of the religious culture as a whole.

# 4   History

'Miracles playing' will not do as a description of all late medieval acting. The most obvious exception is moral drama – the theatrical convention of which the oldest surviving complete example is the spectacular early-fifteenth-cen-tury *The Castle of Perseverance*, and by which the actors represent, not the persons of sacred stories, but abstract principles such as Mankind, the World, Mercy, Covetousness, and so on.

We could say that if the fundamental gesture of miracles playing is the performance of an action, the fundamental gesture of moral drama is the dramatization of a word. Thus in *The Castle of Perseverance* the principal forces contending for dominion over Mankind – God, the World, the Flesh and the Devil – are all located, each occupying its own painted mansion in a different quarter of the acting area. In one scene, two of the World's servants, Lust-Liking and Folly, persuade Mankind to enter their master's service, dress him in rich clothes, and lead him to the mansion of the World. The World responds:

> Now, Foly, fayre the befall,
> And Luste, blyssyd be thou ay!
> Ye han browth Mankynde to myn hall

Sertys in a nobyl aray. . . .
Mankynde, I rede that thou rest
Wyth me, the Werld, as it is beste.
(M. Eccles 1969: ll. 725–35)

(*Now, Folly, good luck to you, and Lust, bless you forever! You have brought Mankind to my hall, nobly dressed for sure. . . . Mankind, I advise you to stay with me, the World, as it is best.*)

If we write out a literal description of an action of this kind, the result is a statement which can also be read as an ethical maxim. 'Mankind is led to live with the World by Folly and Lust'; 'Mankind's rich clothes show that he serves the World'; 'As Mankind approaches the World, he turns his back on God.'[18] The drama takes the flat proposition, as it were, and projects it into three dimensions, so that its verbs become physical actions, its nouns actors, its adjectives costumes and its prepositions spatial and social relationships. The process which generates the theatrical event has the effect of a systematic series of puns. The drama is essentially an animated sentence, a play on words.

This form is therefore logically exempt from the Lollard and Protestant attack on theatre as a type of idolatry. Its discursive mode is not ritual or revelation, but exposition. It cannot be accused of playing with sacred persons and events, because it does not undertake to represent persons and events at all. The sentences it animates are all in the present tense. And it cannot be tainted by the association of theatrical playing with deception, because it depends for its very intelligibility on the transparency of the illusion: the spectators need to bear in mind that Pride is not a real person, but an actor embodying the meaning of a word. In short, it is an oddity in the history of drama – perhaps because the basic idea of it is familiar to us, we sometimes fail to notice how odd – a type of narrative theatre which is neither sacred nor historical nor fictional.

It is not surprising, then, that moral drama came most strongly into its own in the sixteenth century, in the decades around the English Reformation. At a time of iconoclasm, a time when the privileged medium of religious truth was, with increasing insistence, the word rather than the image, a theatre with such a rigorously verbal base appeared both more useful and less suspect than most other medieval dramatic modes. It was not new – fragmentary evidence takes its history in England well back into the fourteenth century, and there are much older European scripts – but it was newly central: of the seventy-odd allegorical play-texts which survive, all but five are from the sixteenth century. However, it is at just this point of its greatest scope that we can see moral drama colliding and negotiating with the secular forms of representation which it defines itself by excluding: history and fiction.

The negotiation is virtually allegorized, itself, in a strange scene in the Henrician biblical drama *Godly Queen Hester*. The play tells the story from the Book of Esther of the rise and fall of Aman ('Haman' in the Authorised Version). The Children of Israel are living in one of their periods of exile in the realm of the great King Ahasuerus. The king has an overweening minister, Aman, who plots their destruction, but fortunately a Jewish girl, Hester, attracts the king by her virtue and wisdom, and becomes his new queen. She pleads with him on behalf of her people, and eventually Aman is discredited and executed. During the phase of Aman's supremacy, the play's three vices – Pride, Adulation and Ambition – come together on stage to complain that they have no occupation because Aman has absorbed into himself all the pride, adulation and ambition that are going. Pride, who would conventionally be gorgeously costumed, comes on 'poorly arrayed' because Aman has bought up all the good cloth and is using the law to stop anyone else dressing as well as him. Ambition, meanwhile, has discovered that all the avenues of advancement in the State are under the control of this one man:

> So that I repent, that ever I went,
> 　Unto the scoles:
> For his large commission, maketh me Ambition
> 　To dwell amonge fooles.
> 　　　　　　　　　　　　　　　　(Greg 1904: 21)

Aman has taken over their dramatic role, leaving them with nothing to *be*. With extinction thus staring them in the face, the vices make their will: in formal speeches they bequeath all their vice to Aman and wish him a bad life. Then they go off singing to the tavern, and take no further part in the play. The only subsequent mention of them comes when Aman meets a wise fool called Hardydardy, who says he has heard about the vices' testament, and adds that they prophesied, reliably in his opinion, that Aman would be hanged. They sound, in his description, like famous local characters who are not around any more. Astonishingly (and rather precociously: moral allegory would hold the stage for a few more decades yet), a genre of religious drama has acted out its own secularization.

　　What is distinctive about this sequence is not the mere interaction of allegorical and historical characters. Morality convention had always been capable of sharing the stage with other forms. We have already seen how the siege of an allegorical castle, which is the central action of *The Castle of Perseverance*, is also one of the incidents of the Digby *Mary Magdalen*. Another example is the scene of the 'Parliament of Heaven', in which Mercy, Righteousness, Truth and Peace are depicted as the four daughters of God, who debate whether or not mankind should be punished for his misdeeds; this scene appears both in the purely allegorical *Castle* (ll. 3129–228) and in the eleventh pageant of the cyclical N-town play. Clearly the morality convention is something in the nature of a theatrical resource, which may function as the only communicative code for an entire play, but can also interact with the persons of sacred history.

Rather, the startling thing about *Godly Queen Hester* is the conscious, metatheatrical gesture with which the vices consent to their own redundancy. Most obviously, it is a satirical conceit: the pride of Aman is hyperbolically shown as beggaring Pride itself. But the effect of enacting this trope is to fill the stage with paradoxes. Strictly speaking, the vices ought to be praising and manipulating Aman: that is the scenario which would conform to a sentence such as 'Aman is governed by Pride, Adulation and Ambition.' But actually they appear as quite negligible figures who watch his irresistible rise to power from the sidelines, and complain about it in the tone of minor losers in a Court power struggle. The diabolical energy of the old universal enemies of mankind has been siphoned off into the new dynamism of one wicked character, who is not 'mankind', but a historical individual. On the other hand, this individual is not at all the uncategorizable subjectivity which realist criticism expects a 'character' to be; on the contrary, he is constituted precisely by his *characterization* at the hands of the vices; he actually does acquire what they relinquish, and so *is*, in more than a merely impressionistic sense, Pride, Adulation and Ambition. But he cannot entirely be that either, because his role has a biographical shape (a *past* tense narrative sentence), ending with his execution, an event which does not signify (as the death of a vice would have to) the disappearance of those bad qualities from the world, but only their just punishment in this particular person. The universal categories of pure allegory have not collapsed, but they have fallen into history.

The history in question is not so much biblical as contemporary. The play was not published until 1561, and its date and occasion have been a matter of dispute, but Alistair Fox has made a convincing case for seeing it as an anti-Protestant celebration of the fall of Cromwell in 1540 (Fox 1989: 240–5). Thus the different weighting of the allegorical signs, in comparison with *The Castle of Perseverance*, is partly a matter of performing context. *The Castle* was a large-scale open-air spectacle, coming out of the intense ecclesiastical and monastic theatre culture of fifteenth-century East Anglia;[19] probably it was designed for repeated performance over many years to entire rural communities, rather like the N-town play (and conceivably in the same venues). *Godly Queen Hester* is a *pièce d'occasion*, written for semi-private performance in the house of a great patron, presumably a member of the Howard faction, and for an audience primed to read the action topically. Ahasuerus is Henry VIII, Aman is Cromwell, Hester, the new queen who defeats him, is the king's fifth wife, Catherine Howard, and the Children of Israel whom she thereby saves are the adherents of the old religion who had been losing ground rapidly under Cromwell's regime. Thus, as with Bale but at a different level of the dramatic text, the forcing house for the mutation of dramatic form is schism. Aman cannot be accorded the general validity of a representative figure (such as Mankind, Pride, or even Herod) because it is precisely his individual agency which is politically in question, and which the universal typology is being deployed to nail. The invited audience is supposed to read the character, not as the meaning of a word, but as somebody in particular. The bizarre formal separation whereby the vices divest themselves of their defining qualities and disappear to the pub (*who are they* as they leave the stage?) is like a witty farewell to the cultural and religious unity which had sustained their dramatic identity. Not that either Court factionalism or doctrinal dispute were anything new; but now, as national politics organized itself round irreconcilable confessional opposition, they implied divided audiences, divided heroes and villains, divided ways of staging meaning. It was Cromwell's conservative opponents who were behind the attempt of 1543 to restrict drama to 'the rebuking and reproaching of vices' – that is, to the restoration of the unitary meanings of a historically innocent allegory. *Godly Queen Hester* wryly acknowledges that even their own playwrights cannot manage it.

It is not possible to attribute that loss of innocence to the work of any one theatrical innovator, but if it were, the prime candidate, once again, would be John Bale. His most ambitious surviving play, *King Johan*, does not so much consent to the historicization of its allegory as force it through with savage inventiveness. The title role represents the thirteenth-century English King John, whose historical conflict with the papacy over the taxation of the Church is interpreted as a foreshadowing of the Henrician Reformation. In staging John's moral and political predicament, Bale exploits two closely related features of the morality form as he found it: disguise and doubling. Disguise is a conventional means used by vices to lure the central 'mankind' figure to his ruin; for example in Skelton's Court morality *Magnyfycence* (*c.*1520), Courtly Abusion presents himself to Magnificence as Pleasure, Cloaked Collusion as Sober Sadness, and so on. The referent of this device is obviously hypocrisy; but it also has the effect of complicating the theatricality of the spectacle, since the spectator must now connect the dramatic character with two antithetic words at once. This is made still more elaborate by a heavy use of doubling: for reasons of economy, the plays which were designed to be staged by professional troupes in the service of royal or aristocratic patrons were written so that they could be played by a small company. *King Johan*, with a cast of thirteen, is written for a company of five (Bale 1986: 1, 22 and 152–3).

Bale's use of these resources is ingenious enough to require a diagram. His hero is assailed by four vices: Sedition, Usurped Power, Private Wealth and Dissimulation. And as king, he is supported – or rather should be supported: they are very fallible – by his three estates: Clergy, Nobility and Civil Order. But then Bale is also concerned to present John's historical struggle with the Church, and the main characters in that story are the Pope, the Papal Legate

Pandulph, the Cardinal Archbishop of Canterbury Stephen Langton, and Simon of Swinsett, the monk who, according to the chronicles Bale was using, murdered the king by poison. The structure of the play resolves all these figures into the work of four actors:

| | | | |
|---|---|---|---|
| 1 | **Clergy** doubled with | **Usurped Power** disguised as | **The Pope** |
| 2 | **Nobility** doubled with | **Private Wealth** disguised as | **Pandulph** |
| 3 | **Civil Order** doubled with | **Dissimulation** disguised as | **Simon** |
| 4 | | **Sedition** disguised as | **Langton** |

The effect of the disguises is extraordinarily complex. To present the Pope as Usurped Power in disguise is, at the most elementary polemical level, to accuse him of usurpation. But it is also, secondly, to suggest that his identity as Pope is a piece of theatrical trickery, which is exactly what Bale wants to say about the pomp and ritual of the Catholic hierarchy in general. At one point, for example, Dissimulation is bringing a letter to Usurped Power / the Pope, and in the middle of a characteristic scene of scatological horseplay between the vices, hesitates to approach him:

USURPID POWRE:   Late me se those wrytynges.   Tush, man, I pray the
                        cum nere.
DISSYMULACYON:   Yowre horryble holynes   putth me in wonderfull
                        fere.

(ll. 888–9)

The rough mutual teasing places the Pope's holiness in the ribald, game-playing world of the vices: it is just fooling about. But then the document is read, and turns out to be a letter from the English bishops asking for the Pope's support in their dispute with King John – that is, it is part of the political plot, seriously presented as such. So this clownish pretend-Pope is immediately presented as someone who really does *act as* the Pope in the practical world. The third and most radical effect of the disguises, then, is to set out a historical narrative in terms which show its chronicled facts as a mere surface: underneath, all along, there are the universal categories of the morality play, of which the historical individuals are only the temporary embodiments. Temporal events are no more than instances of an eternal schema: in other words, the historical paradigm (consistently with Bale's practice as a non-dramatic historian and exegetist) is apocalyptic.

It is this third, non-satirical type of doubleness which is developed by the formal doubling. After the death of King John, the actor who was playing him reappears as Imperial Majesty, a complete figure of royal authority who (unlike John) is not outmanœuvred by the vices but exposes and banishes them. He is clearly, if optimistically, meant to represent Henry VIII; but this identification only works because the two English kings are both local instances of the transcendent principle which the role names. It is in so far as Henry can *be* Imperial Majesty that he will be able to deliver the play's happy ending in the real world. Under Imperial Majesty's direction, the fallible estates reform themselves: Clergy promises to exile Usurped Power, Nobility undertakes to drive Private Wealth from the monasteries, and Civil Order sees to it that Dissimulation is hanged. So in a final *coup de théâtre*, Reformation is expressed as the victory of each of the three actors over his bad other role. The proliferation of disguises appears in retrospect as itself an emblem of corruption: the play is complete when everyone on the stage has become what they ought to be.

This is a much more powerful historicization of the allegory than the ironic gesture of the vices in *Godly Queen Hester*, because the universal principles, so far from being hollowed out by the historical narrative, are identified as its essential content. This in turn reflects the fact that Bale conceives of God's purposes as working themselves out, not independently of historical contingency, but through it. To put it crudely, the reforming playwright, writing at a moment of high revolutionary confidence, *wants* to get history into his theatre because he is sure it is on his side. Conservative drama, by contrast, breaks the eternal present tense of allegorical theatre reluctantly, as in *Godly Queen Hester*, or formally resists it, as in *Respublica* (1553), a sophisticated Court moral interlude from the reign of the Catholic Queen Mary, which stages the Reformation as the temporary ascendancy of a quartet of vices: Avarice, Insolence, Oppression and Adulation. They gain influence over Respublica (the commonwealth) for a time by passing themselves off as Policy, Authority, Reformation and Honesty, but are arbitrarily exposed and defeated by the descent from heaven of Mercy, Peace, Justice and Nemesis, so that 'the old good estate' of the realm can be restored (Greg 1952: l. 1922). What lends conviction to this optimistic dismissal of the events of the preceding twenty years is that the morality convention leads the audience to expect that the reign of the vices will be short-lived and, in the last analysis, illusory: the unchanging scenario of temptation, sin and redemption is deployed to negate the historicity of the play's real subject matter. Both sides in the schism are engaged, whether they want to be or not, in the struggle to appropriate the authority of the moral stage.

We must not forget that all these plays were being produced at the apex of the social pyramid, in or near the Court: at the same time, in East Anglian villages and northern and midland towns, the 'medieval' repertoire – the supra-historical drama of the whole world – continued to be performed and extended. The division and mutation of the allegorical sign system was not part of a breakup of the pre-existing dramatic order so much as a discovery of its latent capacities in response to pressures which were mostly experienced by the political elite. Bale himself, a metropolitan propagandist from an East Anglian monastic background, represents continuity in the midst of fierce cultural change in his use of the schemata of moral drama. He is a medieval playwright: his allegories are not a concession to old convention, but the vital language in which he stages historical meaning.

## 5 Fiction

Unlike miracles playing, moral drama has no necessary formal commitment to religion: as we have seen, the dramatized words can denote secular concepts, such as Civil Order or Measure,[20] as well as theological virtues and vices. Virtually no secular medieval drama has in fact survived, but a late exception is *Fulgens and Lucres*, an interlude played in the household of Henry VII's Archbishop of Canterbury at some time in the 1490s. Although the characters have non-allegorical names, and the action is presented as having taken place in ancient Rome, the plot is essentially a 'present tense' disputation. Lucres, the daughter of the senator Fulgens, has two suitors – Publius Cornelius, who is recommended by his high birth, and Gaius Flaminius, a plebeian who is recommended by his virtue. Their competitive courtship is therefore a debate about the relative claims to advancement of rank and merit: it is understood that Lucres has no personal predilections, but will award herself to the more deserving candidate. After a somewhat episodic comedy plot, the two suitors come together with Lucres to make their formal speeches of self-recommendation; Lucres hears the claims of patrician and plebeian, and decides in favour of the latter.

The classical setting, the quasi-legal display of rhetoric, the elements of formal comedy, the secular problematic – many features of this text identify it with a humanist literary culture, and so place it apart from all the theatrical modes discussed in this chapter so far. It is also differentiated by being unambiguously authorial: it is perhaps the earliest English dramatic text to record the dramatist's name,[21] and it ends with one of the actors conveying a message from the author to the spectators:

> Yet the auctor therof desyrith
>   That for this season
> At the lest ye will take it in pacience.
> And yf ther be ony offence
> (Show us wherein or we go hence)
>   Done in the same,
> It is onely for lack of connynge,
> And not he but his wit runnynge
>   Is thereof to blame.
>           (Medwall 1980: part II, ll. 907–15)

This entry of the dramatist is strikingly different from the one we saw in Bale's *Temptation* play. There, it seemed that the author appeared in order to register a commitment, to take responsibility for the play's meaning. Here it is exactly the opposite: the author draws attention to himself only to make it clear that anything which is not satisfactory is due to incompetence or looseness of invention, and is not intentional. *He* takes no responsibility for any of it.

This graceful evasiveness is characteristic of the play as a whole. From a theatrical point of view, the most interesting thing about it is the two roles simply headed A and B; these unlocated characters start out as supposed members of the audience, and then progressively become involved in the play, gaining employment with the two suitors and trying to make love to Lucres' maid, while never losing their freedom to talk to the audience in the time and place of the performance rather than the play. This fluid status gives rise to a teasing series of metatheatrical jokes: for example, A, announcing the interval, explains that it is needed both to give Gaius and Cornelius time to prepare their arguments and to allow the company in the hall to have the next course of their meal. The events are occurring in ancient Rome *and* at a feast in 1490s England; they are happening spontaneously in front of us *and* they are a prepared and scripted entertainment. In other words, the ambiguous status of the performed action is adopted – appropriately for a festive interlude – as a kind of game.

It is by cultivating the ambiguity in this way that the author maintains his freedom to say 'it's not me.' Just before the suitors launch on their arguments, Lucres adds her own disclaimer:

> . . . what so ever sentence I gyve betwyxt you two
> After myne owne fantasie, it shall not extende
> To ony other person: I wyll that it be so! . . .
> It may not be notyde for a generall precedent,
> All be it that for your partis ye do therto assent.
>                                             (part II, ll. 428–33)

This is a remarkable sideways move. The choice which Lucres is about to make obviously *is* exemplary: it is the point of the performance that in coming down on the side of plebeian merit, it compliments the commoners whom Henry VII had promoted to powerful positions as a counterweight to the baronial dynasties, and in particular the master of the feast itself, the Archbishop Henry Morton. Lucres is not an unconditional individual but a discursive signifier of a fairly well-defined kind: in making her assert that she is *not* a signifier, the play lays claim to the provisional space of fiction, where it is possible to advance a specific and topical opinion without being held accountable for it. This is of course not an unprecedented cultural space in itself: it could be said to be Chaucer's chosen territory. But it is foreign to what were then the prevalent forms of drama. By introducing literature into the theatre, humanism opens up a genuinely new playground.

## NOTES

1  For a clear outline of these political events, see Cross 1976: 60–80.
2  These are surveyed in the many introductions to medieval drama. See, for example, Beadle 1994 or Cawley et al. 1983.
3  The others are those belonging to York and to Chester, and the Towneley play, which is possibly but not certainly associated with Wakefield.
4  See the introduction and notes to Spector 1991, and also the essay on N-town by Alan J. Fletcher in Beadle 1994: 163–88.
5  Quotations from the Authorised Version. The translation current at the time of the play, Tyndale's 1534 New Testament, is not significantly different.
6  For a clear and authoritative account of processional staging, see Meg Twycross in Beadle 1994: 38–55.
7  For a study of this cycle in anthropological terms, see Phythian-Adams 1972.
8  See the prologue to the Ordinances of the York Corpus Christi guild, printed in Lozar 1976.
9  This logic is brilliantly set out in James 1986.
10  The phrase is from a York ordinance of 1476, quoted in Beadle and King 1984: xxiii.
11  See for example the report of a friar, William Melton, who saw the York play in 1426, quoted in Cawley et al. 1983: 89.
12  Caiaphas patronizingly attributes Christ's muteness to timidity at the splendour of his appearance (l. 289), and a soldier refers to him as 'our bishop' (l. 327). The N-town Passion, which has more stage directions than York, makes it clear that Annas and Caiaphas are to appear as bishops (Spector 1991: I, 267, play 27, l. 76 (stage direction)).
13  The main exponent of this style in the cycle plays is Herod, but it is equally found in other types of medieval play – for example, the merchant in the Croxton *Play of the Sacrament*, and the pride-before-a-fall protagonist of *Magnyfycence*.
14  I discussed this issue from a slightly different point of view in Womack 1992: 98–103.
15  The best-known instance of this doubleness is the York Crucifixion play, which combines physical torment and slapstick farce in a single grotesque image. On staging, the most reverberant record is the interview from the 1640s with an old man who remembered seeing Corpus-Christ's play in Kendal when he was young: 'there was a man on a tree and blood run down.' (Cawley et al. 1983: 3–4).
16  'The Last Judgement', in Beadle 1982: 413–15 (ll. 277–364). It dramatizes Matthew 25: 31–46. In the more vigorously written Towneley version of the same idea, it is still clearer that the condemned souls, who never helped the Son of Man, are richly dressed.
17  A proclamation from Chester (1531–2) almost brings the different elements into syntactic connection, stating that the performance is mounted 'not only for the augmentacion and incres of the holy and Catholick faith of our Savyour Jesu Crist

and to exort the myndes of the common people to good devotion and holsome doctryne therof, but also for the commenwelth and prosperitie of this Citie' (quoted in Cawley et al. 1983: 39).

18 The literal truth of this last one is proved by the staging plan for the play, which shows a circular acting area with a mansion at each point of the compass: World is in the east, and God in the west. The plan is reproduced in most books on medieval drama, and is exhaustively if controversially analysed in Southern 1957.

19 The concept of an 'East Anglian tradition' is argued by John C. Coldewey in Beadle 1994: 189–210. For the case for monastic involvement, see G. M. Gibson 1989: 107–36.

20 The personification of moderation in *Magnyfycence* – an *earthly* virtue.

21 Henry Medwall, whose name appears on the title page of the first edition. The book is undated, but was probably produced in about 1515, which would mean that *Fulgens and Lucres* is also the earliest English printed play. The two 'firsts' are obviously not coincidental: the fixing of text by the new technology tends to promote authorial definition.

# 2

# The Beginning of the Story of Drama

## 1 Adam and Eve

In the beginning was nakedness. The first people, the sacred book tells us, were created naked, and God then clothed them. When, however, those first people are transferred from the book's pages to a stage, when there are other people already there watching, the work of Creation gets a little more vexed. And the questions begin. When Adam and Eve appeared on stage at the start of a cycle of medieval mystery plays, were they naked? Or had the stage created them clothed? How did the watching people see what the stage showed them? Can such a thing as a performance ever be really innocent or sacred or simple?

Inextricably built into the religious story of the mystery cycle plays, the first appearance of the first human beings presents a problem for later ages. For once it gets on a stage, Creation seems to raise all sorts of issues that relate less to nature than to politics, less to God than to theatre. These all began to surface as soon as the modern period started to inquire into the beginnings of English drama. The interest in the staging of the first people was part of a fantasy about origins, stages and people.

It was in the early 1820s that the image of the medieval Adam and Eve attracted scholarly concern. An essay on 'Mysteries, Moralities, and the other early drama' appeared in the first issue of *The Retrospective Review* (1820).[1] Commenting on the stage direction that Adam and Eve should be naked, the anonymous author argues that such stage directions 'certainly contain a singular display of primitive simplicity'. Our 'unlettered' ancestors, we have been told, were 'guiltless of any knowledge of the rules by which the drama is governed in more critical times' (*Retrospective Review* 1820: 338, 333). The attitude to the past here is double-edged: its simplicity is primitive, innocent but also 'unlettered' – without a need for the rules of more modern, more civilized times.

From another angle the clash between simplicity and rules turns into a critique of modern times. Being unlettered, our ancestors 'were strangers indeed to delicacy of taste; they beheld the broad and unformed delineations of nature, and thought no harm: while we, on the most distant approach to freedom of thought and expression, turn away in disgust, and vehemently express our displeasure.' The 'extraordinary spectacle' of an apparently naked Adam and Eve 'was beheld by a numerous company of both sexes with great composure' (Hone 1823: 220).

When we move from the beginnings of the interest in medieval theatre in the 1820s forward to the 1980s, the sense of a modern culture without sufficient 'composure' is firmly apparent: 'I suspect that modern productions, which present an actress as Eve in the semi-nakedness of a leotard, and thus force the sexual side upon us, are introducing an irrelevant distraction.' In her explorations of what might have been authentic medieval staging, the teacher Meg Twycross warns against thinking of Eve as naked: 'Eden is not a Carry On nudist camp.' The way to avoid the distractions which come with a debased culture is to be more rigorously medieval: 'Played by a boy in a suit of whitleather and a long blonde wig, Eve could be a representation of naked femininity without any of its distracting actuality: we could concentrate on the role. She would I think come over a lot less frivolous than our modern sexy Eves: less of a simpleton, more of an innocent' (Twycross 1983: 160).

The ambiguity in the concept of ancestral simplicity is now sorted out: a simpleton is bad, an innocent is good. Being unlettered is not being underdeveloped, but being in a state untouched by modern cultural debasement, still having *spiritual* force: 'I saw her face clearly; she was illuminated from within, rapt with the tremendousness of the story now moving to its climax.' This is the journalist Bernard Levin, and the rapt woman moving to climax is courtesy of the National Theatre *Mysteries*, the most successful of modern restagings of medieval cycle drama. It broke many of the medieval rules that Twycross was exploring, but in that sense, for Levin, succeeded: 'I wish there were another word for performance, for it diminishes the thing that has been created, which far transcends any idea of a theatre . . . and of a play' (*Making* 1985). Medieval drama here becomes a medium in which performance can shake free of the debasement of theatre, making contact with the yearnings of raw spirituality.

Medieval drama, like Eden, is not a Carry On film. Its performance promises access to something more transcendent, something less frivolous, than what is available in contemporary culture. In this sense the 'medieval' is not just a contrast with, but a challenge to, a debased present. In the opinions we have noted so far, the terms of the contrast shift in their importance and value.

Medieval culture may be defined as primitive and unlettered, or earnestly spiritual, or, in William Hone's view of 1823, a people's culture constrained by the control of Church and monarchy. In other words, the discussion of Adam and Eve's nakedness is not so much about medieval stagings of, but competing modern searches for, Eden.

## 2    A False Glare

The most polemical of the attitudes to Adam and Eve is that of William Hone. Who was he? An antiquarian who collected and published examples of medieval culture, he gathered carols, early dramas, descriptions of folk festivals and popular clowning. This scholarly activity was typical of the way the past had been explored, both in England and Europe, since about the middle of the previous century. By 1825 Thomas Sharp, a Coventry hatter and antiquarian, felt justified in describing his own time as 'an age peculiarly characterised by a spirit of research into our national antiquities' (Sharp 1825: 174). The keyword here is 'national': it was explicitly a nationalist feeling which informed scholarly interest in earlier cultures and language. When in 1839 Thomas de Quincey called for a history of the English language – indeed, such a thing as the Oxford English Dictionary – he claimed it would be 'a monument of learning and patriotism' (Crowley 1989: 39).

The research into national antiquities had two strands. The first was a form of local history which grew out of and added to the already well-established volumes of county histories. John Stevens's *History of the Antient Abbeys* included four N-town pageants; a York sheriff, John Croft, printed a York pageant in his *Excerpta antiqua* (1797) (Lancashire 1977: 60–1). Thomas Sharp's work aimed also to commemorate the culture of a specific *locality* by printing the dramatic records of medieval Coventry's mystery plays. The second strand of research was what we could call anthropological. Joseph Strutt argued in *The Sports and Pastimes of the People of England* (1801) that the study of sports and pastimes was a way of estimating the 'character' of a people. From this, in 1838, William Marriott suggested that through a study of mystery plays we 'are perhaps better enabled to judge of the state of civilisation in which they were, than from other sources' (W. Marriott 1838: vi). Theatre history begins to emerge as a discipline by promising to offer a unique way of understanding the *character of people*.

But neither locality nor anthropology gave the primary meaning to the word 'people' in Hone's work: for him it was class. He was a fierce political opponent of, and polemicist against, the authority of Church and State. He wrote (and was prosecuted for) political tracts such as as: *The Political House that Jack Built* (1819), an attack on soldiers, taxation, clergy, law, courtiers; *The Queen's Matrimonial Ladder* (1820) defending Queen Caroline as an enemy of establishment corruption, and describing the owner of the 'folly' at Brighton as 'an old fat Mandarin'; *The Right Divine of Kings to Govern Wrong!* which is self-explanatory. Together with his political parodies of liturgy, his publication of *The Apocryphal New Testament* (1820) was seen as an attack on the Church, and thus of a piece with his other political tracts. His 'shimble-shamble' collection of 'illustrations' of ancient customs (1823) is similarly inhabited by an anti-religious rhetoric: 'From the manifold corruptions of religion resulted the gross practices and delusions which are noticed in the ensuing pages without comment' (p. x).

Defining people's culture *against* the manifestations of ecclesiastical or secular rule, Hone wrote of a division not acknowledged in histories of counties.[2] So too he differed from anthropologists in seeing the people and their activities as an arena of contest, always in process. In his account of the origin of mysteries, Hone constructs an idea of a popular culture that has religion foisted upon it. He follows the historian Warton's account of how the clergy failed to proscribe entertainments at fairs 'and determined to take these recreations into their own hands. They turned actors; and instead of mummeries presented stories taken from legends or the bible. This was the origin of sacred comedy' (Hone 1823: 200). The mysteries were thus a part of, and parasitic upon, the already existing popular entertainments: 'there is no room for surprise that all writers concur in attributing the performance of these Mysteries to that body who were the authors of the Feast of Fools and the Feast of the Ass' (p. 169).

By Hone's account the invention of the mystery plays has, then, a political function. They are the products of a conservative religious establishment which sought to oppose and contain the threat of religious reforms emanating from Wycliffe and his Bible translation: 'All arts were used to suppress it, and to enliven the slumbering attachment of the people to the "good old customs" of the church. There is abundant evidence of studious endeavours to both these ends in the Coventry Mysteries' (Hone 1823: 204). The attack on the social and political function of the mysteries shares the concerns of other contemporary radicals for the damaging effects of illusion, fantasy or mystification – what Percy Shelley called superstition and Marx was later to term 'inverted consciousness'. The monkish author of the Coventry mysteries was, says Hone, 'likely to conceive that a false glare might obscure the dawnings of the human mind' (p. 203).

Hone's opposition of conservative Church to forward-looking people re-emerges in more modern accounts of medieval feasts: 'Its official, ecclesiastical face was turned to the past and sanctioned the existing order, but the face of the people of the market-place looked into the future and laughed.' 'False glare', roughly translated, is ideology: 'laughter in the Middle Ages remained outside all official spheres of ideology and outside all official strict forms of social relations.' These remarks come from Bakhtin (1984: 81, 73), who began working on Rabelais and medieval culture in 1934, leading to publication of *Rabelais and his World* in 1965. Bakhtin knew the work of anthropologists such as James Frazer and also drew on Flögel's work on 'comic grotesque' (1788) and court jesters, which has similarities with Hone's study of medieval folk festivals. Just as Hone attacked Regency rule, Bakhtin's description of the medieval is polemically pointed at the repressive regime of Stalin. Against official, nationalist definitions of 'folk', Bakhtin stressed sensuality and blasphemy; against the productive worker's pectorals of official socialist art, there gurgled the lower bodily stratum in the medieval market-place; against fear, laughter is emphasized. The important point about this pre-bourgeois world is that it is, again, always in process of development: 'The material bodily principle is contained not in the biological individual, not in the bourgeois ego, but in the people, a people who are continually growing and renewed.' The relationship of language and community is thus dynamic: the speech forms of the market-place 'liberated from norms, hierarchies, and prohibitions of established idiom, become themselves a peculiar argot and create a special collectivity'. In the 'ambivalence' of medieval language usage Bakhtin discovers what becomes a key concept, its 'organic and spontaneous character' (1984: 19, 188, 165).

The notion of a character that can be called 'organic' takes us somewhere different from the descriptions of ideological struggle for the minds of a divided people. This comes about because, pressing on Bakhtin's account of the Middle Ages, there is a strong sense of a chronological division between capitalism and what precedes it. Capitalism, he suggests, inaugurated an existence which felt fragmented, individualist – where people became alienated from each other and their work. What is lost in capitalism is the sense of the energy, the communal, the laughter. The conflict between authoritarian Church and people is thus transposed into a conflict between capitalist bourgeois and people. That move is clear in the work of English Marxists contemporary with Bakhtin: 'the cathedrals were bourgeois and not feudal . . . the bourgeois play begins in the cathedrals as the mystery play frowned on by the Church authorities.' The effect of this bourgeois order on personal life is described by Christopher Caudwell in 1937 as a harnessing of the instincts to the 'needs of the harvest' through 'the group festival, the matrix of poetry, which frees the stores of emotion and canalises them in a collective channel' (Caudwell 1946: 284, 34). The image of emotion already existing in stores, waiting to flow into a channel, has a physical, organic materiality. The language is that of organism. Pre-capitalist work, in the Marxist accounts, is not alienated, is bodily fulfilled. As Alick West put it, again in 1937: 'Rhythm, and poetry and music together with it, developed out of the regularly repeated movements of the body in work (which, with this accompaniment of poetry and music, was very different from work under capitalism)' (West 1975: 79).

The possibility of bodily fulfilment in the days of capitalism was witnessed by the folklorist, Ralph Tiddy: 'There is an ostler at the village Inn . . . a graceless boy, who reads disreputable pink novels and spends his share of the Whit-Monday takings of his Morris side in getting scandalously drunk; but when he is dancing he is transfigured' (Tiddy 1923: 21). As an army officer in the First World War (which killed him), Tiddy taught folk dances to his soldiers, and danced for an 'entranced' audience of them with his friend (and lover) Ralph Honeybone. Tiddy was associated with Cecil Sharp's revival of folk dance and song, which he valued as an untaught expression, predating State education, of something specifically indigenous to the rural working class. But his delight with the ostler also recalls Levin, tucked into the National Theatre audience, gazing at Eve. Transfigured by the spirit of 'medieval' performance, the class division between ostler and artiste dissolves, replaced by the glow of the fresh-faced *organic*.

One of the problems about the 'organic' is that it blurs together not only different class positions but also false and true consciousness – the glow of the organic may be composed of both a false glare and the light of dawn. So, while as an *institution* the Church may be separated from, indeed seen as oppressive to, the people, at the same time religious *feeling* can produce the same bodily energy as can the rhythm of collective work. This sense of a religion that can be separated from institution is articulated by a Communist contemporary of Caudwell and West, Ralph Bates, in his novel *The Olive Field* (1936) set in modern Spain:

> the carrying of the statues was not only a mere pageant but an intensive heightening of the magic they exercised. The cries and the bowings, the animosities and fierce excitements . . . all of this did not come from belief in the remote and mystical Trinity but a close blood-pulsing, heart-stirring magic. . . . A Church which abolished its images or pictures would abolish itself. To cut away that drama would be as stupid as saying mass in Spanish. (Bates 1936: 201)

The attraction of the magic, for the novelist as for the peasants, is that however mystificatory it might be, it is organic not alienated, ancient not modern. The people whose lives are deadened in modern society will not be fulfilled by cultural modernity or avant-gardism: their blood will only pulse through old, *pre-capitalist* forms of expression. As Malcolm Lynch put it in 1983, 'the natural heartcry of the people can be effective if presented in an ancient way.'[3] For many artists who support the people's cause there is a commitment to *recovering* – in an alienated modernity – the forms which will make the heartcry effective.

For Lynch those forms included folk song and, pre-eminently, the mystery play (defined as an amalgamation of mummers' play and medieval 'workers' drama). He consciously used the mystery play as a model for a pageant he wrote in 1967 for the United Textile factory workers. But the connection between ancient forms and heart-stirring magic becomes more difficult when Lynch cites the mystery as a direct precursor for his work on the early TV soap opera *Coronation Street*. The struggle to make the heartcry 'effective' ends up always finding itself compromised in the meeting between archaic religious forms and the deadening culture of capitalism. Something of the organic life of people constantly slips from the grasp. A couple of examples can suggest what happens.

In 1946 Merseyside Unity Theatre, a theatre of 'the left', incorporated *The Second Shepherds Play* into a political revue, *Unity Fare*. The opening peasant complaint against conditions had a relevance that could be echoed 'even by British workers in factories streamlined for profit'. But as important as protest was the figure of Mak, 'the archetypal rogue . . . undermining authority with anarchic mischief'. As the 'first English secular comedy' in a 'long tradition' (Dawson 1985: 55), the play could make a link back to an authentic pre-capitalist people's voice. But in defining it as secular, Merseyside Unity cut out the religious ending of the play which staged Christ's nativity. Alongside the protest and anarchy there was no place for mystificatory – indeed magical – solutions to social problems; and it is magic which is blood-pulsing.

Religion is, by contrast, the starting point for Benjamin Britten's experiments with the format of religious cantata. In this work he challenged and rethought some of the dominant musical modes, especially nineteenth-century English choral music with its characteristic institutions and political resonances. Britten also employed theatrical forms that were outside the dominant: *Curlew River* (1964) draws upon Japanese Noh drama; the Chester mystery play of Noah became the libretto for *Noyes Fludde* (1957). This cantata was a part of the process of discovering English roots for English music, where these roots lay in the activities of the 'people' rather than in the institutions of an imperial State, in folk song rather than anthem. *Noyes Fludde* was a product of welfare state Britain, and shares some of its contradictions. The ancient mystery play is fused with the familiar institution of the church choir, so that there is less comic anarchy than parish procession, with key roles in the enactment of sacred events taken by children. At crucial moments hymns to traditional tunes are sung – as it were democratically – by the whole audience, in their role as congregation. A feeling of organic, heart-stirring community is thus established. But the tradition of protest has been obliterated by the new-found sense of what we might call spiritual welfare.

Once you duck out of the glare of religion it is possible to find a less compromising form of popular culture. Robert Weimann's *Shakespeare and the Popular Tradition in the Theater* argues that the Bard's work got its peculiar power from a tradition of popular culture: 'a remarkable continuity of play-fully inverted conceptions of the world which extends from the Roman

Saturnalia down to the rural May games . . . and the urban mummings and masques in England'. While he may not draw on this tradition as a direct source, 'Shakespeare made use of structural and verbal elements comparable to those of the folk play' (Weimann 1987: 21, 39). The connection between popular culture and what's called 'festive release' spread as an idea after Bakhtin's work appeared in English. But it was being circulated before this, contained – ironically enough – in studies of the national Bard. C. L. Barber's work on Shakespeare's 'festive' comedy, published in 1959, described how 'setting up a mock lord and demanding homage for him are playfully rebellious gestures, into which Dionysian feeling can flow' (Barber 1959: 29).

Some analysts argue that what is playfully rebellious is not really rebellious, that the voice of the people is never separable from dominant ideologies, that what is apparently subversive is also misguided, that topsy-turvy remains mystified. The Marxist Weimann, by contrast, insists on the oppositional quality of that voice:

> processional topsy-turvydom and the attitudes of festive release were not at all incompatible with some sort of communal consciousness and some elements of social criticism. In fact the traditions of popular myth, ritual, and disguise seemed to provide a favourable vehicle for a naively rebellious expression of the common man's sense of the world and his [*sic*] position in it. (Weimann 1987: 24)

The definition of the common man's sense of the world – or, as the Jacobin Hone put it, the dawning of the human mind – is something for which study of medieval culture has provided a favourable vehicle. But it keeps bumping up against obstacles every time it returns to the modern world: that dawn is never quite not a false glare; the organic is perhaps not so much collective as mystified. Can the non-alienated medieval people ever be the same as the modern proletariat? Can a voice which is authentic ever escape historical mutation? Is the prospect of Eden ever unhedged?

The strands of the 'organic' popular are now bound up with the modern proletariat. Popular expression is seen to be continually reinterpreted, debased, denied, even commercialized. It thus becomes politically important for those on the side of the people to try and pin down the *real* uncompromised organic. And it falls to the modern artistic and educational elite to disentangle the threads. Thus, paradoxically, the medieval 'popular' voice comes to be guarded by, and depends for its very expression on, the discourse – so to speak – of the academy. Even Tiddy was a don, in English Literature.

This contradiction in what we might call the officially recognized organic is very strikingly apparent in the National Theatre's 1970s project to stage *The*

*Mysteries*. The souvenir booklet for the production locates itself within a familiar academic tradition when it quotes G. W. Matthew (1924): 'The Mystery Plays may be regarded as the most democratic thing in English literature. Whatever may have been their original conception, they became in fact in the Middle Ages, of the people, by the people, for the people.' In the booklet members of the company speak of a return to a culture and art form that are outside, and more real than, the debased present. John Tams, the music director, describes the search for a 'non-bourgeois' organic popular music; the production, said Peter Hall, had to rediscover a 'lost technique'. That which is lost is found by theatre workers committed to an authentic performance. In the name of the popular, they perform a cultural rescue: 'our purpose to throw out all the scholarship and bring the plays back to a popular audience.'

Those who throw out the scholarship include the poet Tony Harrison, a trained classical scholar – but in this circumstance qualified by his working-class roots, which he shares with the director. The booklet, which has an almost horticultural seriousness about roots, makes a parallel between the guildsmen who originally performed the mysteries and the modern workmen (that is, professional actors) at the National Theatre. It was the proximity of the sweat of these workmen that apparently gave the audience – 'willing members of a biblical throng' – a particular thrill. Sweat marks the distance from scholarship. The basic opposition here is clinched in a famous publicity photo: actors on Easter Sunday carry a crucifix on the National Theatre terrace, while in the background sits the dome of St Paul's. Contrasting sharply with the monumental façade of the institutional Church is the authentic spirituality now only able to be spoken as drama and poetry.

In that photo there is an opposition, echoing back through 1930s Marxists to William Hone, between people and State institution. But if we deflect the false glare we see that the people are really actors, and one of the State institutions is a theatre. Members of the National Theatre, authorized by their own roots in the 'people', become the representatives of a people's culture, acting on behalf of a State-subsidized institution in a social democratic society. Rosy as it might seem from the other side of the Tory-dominated 1980s, that social democracy was then dying in the hands of a reactionary Labour government. But the rediscovery of the 'medieval' worked to produce faith which overrode endemic contradictions. In the National Theatre performance it was not so much the people who were organic as the *theatre workers*. With a social place that had negotiated the move from working to middle class, their radical commitment embracing a love of poetry, the theatre workers were the bearers of a true authenticity. An organic once supposedly located in street carnival is rediscovered in a custom-built theatre. The force of National mysteries, in short, produces social democracy as the voice of the people.

## 3   A Phoney Tree

In Hone's radical reading of medieval mysteries 'there can be no doubt that Adam and Eve were naked.' The presence of the revealed body is a sign, as much as it is in the work of Blake, for a standpoint that is against repression. By contrast, many academic commentators want to draw a veil over what Bakhtin would call the lower bodily stratum. W. A. Davenport argues that the two major types of medieval drama, mystery cycles and moralities, meet in the sense that Christ's 'human body on the Cross is the most powerful image of mortality and reminder of the separability of flesh and spirit' (Davenport 1982: 6). Rather than meeting in the presence of actors' bodies, the dramas meet only in that unique body which is celebrated for its escape from the corporeal.

Published in 1982 – near the start of what could be called a significantly un-popular decade – Davenport's account confidently stifles the idea of a 'popular voice'. After describing the received model for the origins of medieval drama, he concludes that the 'family tree always looked phoney and it is a relief to be able to discard it and accept the more plausible modern view that the English mystery cycles were created by educated literary men . . . out of a combination of existing traditions of drama and religious material' (p. 1). While for Hone, say, the popular elements of mysteries might give them their importance, their artistic quality as seen by Davenport is achieved under the guidance of an educated elite. In the years between Hone and Davenport, despite a temporary blip when it was thrown out of the National Theatre, scholarship sustains its claim on the mysteries, and in doing so defines its changing relation to what it designates popular.

Something of this process may be illustrated from the accounts of the discovery of the mysteries. In 1831 Collier's *History of English Dramatic Poetry* analysed the Towneley, Chester and Coventry plays; in 1840, in his edition of *The Harrowing of Hell*, J. O. Halliwell-Phillipps suggested that Collier had left nothing to be said on the history of the plays. The next year, in his edition of the Coventry Mysteries, Halliwell-Phillipps noted that three collections of the plays had descended to modern times: Markland's 1818 Chester Mysteries, Hunter's Towneley plays of 1836 and Marriott's collection (of Chester, Coventry and Towneley plays) of 1838. Sharp's seminal publication of the Coventry *Pageant of Shearmen and Taylors* had appeared in 1825. Before this period, descriptions of the York and Coventry plays had been contained in the county histories written, respectively, by F. Drake (1736) and Dugdale (1656), where they fell into line as a part of civic history, along with mayors' proclamations and genteel genealogies. The plays were first treated as art-works by Warton, *History of English Poetry* (1774–81) and Percy (1765): in the latter case they came to be valued specifically as 'simple' products of the people, a part of a late-eighteenth-century cult of the rustic.

The name that is missing from Halliwell-Phillipps's survey of materials in 1841 is that of Hone. His *Ancient Mysteries Described* (1823) tells how he found the text of the Coventry plays in the British Library in 1817–18. He also read about the York plays in Drake's history and read the Chester Mysteries in the British Library Harleian manuscripts. But the plays themselves were not the object of his interest. They are merely the quarries for examples of Apocryphal material. He downplays his own scholarship, as shaped more by enthusiasm than rigour, and claims no aspiration to be 'antiquarian'. Nevertheless, apart from Markland's work on Chester in 1818, Hone's attention to medieval drama in 1823 was a forerunner of the scholarly discoveries that happened a decade or so later. His work on carols is clearly methodical and his history of theatrical representation, starting from Matthew Paris in 1240, predates Collier.

That disavowal of scholarship may be seen, yet again, as a political move. Hone's account of medieval literature runs against the scholarly evaluation of the self-appointed literary authority of *The Retrospective Review* (1820), which thinks the plays are 'as inartificial, as rude and jejune, as can well be imagined' (p. 332). The author concludes that the only explanation for their popularity was that the people lacked any other drama, and that they were ignorant: 'They thirsted for the living springs of immortality, and, not being able to obtain access to the sacred fountains themselves, they drank in with delight the vapid waters, which were brought thence by those who had been more fortunate' (p. 337). Although Hone suggested an explicitly scholarly and ancient derivation for the plays, his deliberate disclaimer about his own work indicates how far he was sceptical of the role of scholars with regard to the people: he refused to see scholars as those simply 'more fortunate' in enlightenment.

Against Hone's, the preferred account of the mysteries is a story of the doings of the 'more fortunate'. These doings consist of offering that which is sacred to spectators who are essentially ignorant 'in times of intellectual slavery' (Halliwell-Phillipps 1840: 4). In such times as those of Reform and then Chartist agitation, an art form which can serviceably affect ignorant minds has an interest. In his edition of the Towneley plays Hunter notes there was 'much not only to entertain, but to affect seriously and serviceably the minds of the simple rustics who, on these occasions, were wont here to congregate, as well as to give them, in the way in which they could best receive it, information concerning the principal events of sacred history' (J. Hunter 1836: xvi). The editors of the 1830s set about effacing the presence of an already extant 'simple rustic' culture; they start to chop down the phoney tree. When Marriott slotted the mysteries into place as a continuation of sacred dramas 'written since the first centuries' (W.

Marriott 1838: x), they gained a literary pedigree untouched by popular culture.

The modern offspring of that pedigree is the bustling scholarly industry which studies medieval religious drama. The break with folk culture has been completed. Festivals of Fools tend to be forgotten as elements of medieval culture, consigned to a pop anthropology less 'serious' than scholarship. Much of the work on mysteries is now conducted under the institutional or ideological aegis of the Records of Early English Drama, or REED. This project aims to collect, rather than interpret, documents of theatrical activity, where civic records – as in county history – are as important as fictional texts. REED scholars stress method, rigour, organization in a modern version of the language by which the first 'discoverers' of medieval drama identified themselves. REED continues the work begun by Sharp and Halliwell-Phillipps. As much as for the decade 1830–40, the modern scholarship is itself predicated on value judgements. These are summarized in Theresa Colletti's account of REED, which shows how REED 'inherits its historical method from the nineteenth century', where that method may be called 'unexamined positivism'. 'Theory' and 'theorizing' become dirty words, the antitheses of 'fact'. The evidence of documents is said to be able to speak for itself. Yet REED's collection of records is also selection: 'The records present both local and methodological problems in the state in which they survive and the manner in which they are appropriated, problems that fundamentally belie REED's aspiration to neutrality and to exhaustiveness of recovery.' For example, some sort of dramatic activity is recorded only because it involved infringing the law (Colletti 1990: 266–7). Records of dramatic activity are frequently selected out of longer documents, a procedure which both excludes material and assumes it knows what a 'relevant' dramatic document is. This means that the records recovered are radically decontextualized, and the effect of the scholarly research is thus to cut away mysteries, lumberjack-fashion, from a sense of the whole town life which gives deep meaning to their images and function.

REED-influenced academics tend to imply that only their research establishes the real facts of the mysteries. But when the National Theatre's team reached for what they saw as the real spirit of medieval drama, they threw out scholarship. In its place they put their own social and spiritual community with the plays. But so too, according to Colletti, 'REED projects its own ideal myth of community. Its participants join forces in the shared purpose of finding and preserving records of early drama' (1990: 281). There are, then, two 'communities' making their own different distinctions between authentic and phoney trees: on one hand the authentic is the documentary history discovered by scholars of facts; on the other hand the authentic is the dramatic event performed by those who are moved by the spirit of the original. The opposition may be said to be between the 'official historical account' and the 'official organic experience'. One lot aims to know the historically real; the other lot aims to be in touch with the real organic.

## 4   Hearing Voices

The division between the two communities is not between scholars and theatre workers. For REED also has a theatrical component to its project. Dramatic records can suggest how a play was staged. This historical reality can then be embodied, perhaps even 'experienced', in dramatic production. Thus the staging of a play may function as a research tool, apparently offering a way of discovering how it was done and how it was seen. Theatre academics at the Universities of Toronto and Lancaster have aimed to make productions that work with and within the constraints of historical authenticity. In 1977, the same year that the National Theatre team were discovering and sharing their 'spirit of faith' with their audience, 'the University of Toronto Center for Medieval Studies produced the entire York cycle on pageant wagons in an effort to stage the cycle "as closely as possible" to the conditions the records describe' (Colletti 1990: 262). The REED approach to drama connects with, and academically institutionalizes, the belief that practitioners must learn to listen to the play, that they must, in the words of one of the Medieval Players, let the plays 'speak with their own voice'.

Hearing voices can sometimes lead to social embarrassment. William Marriott, who struck at the folk roots of the phoney tree, had cause to ponder the Chester Adam and Eve:

> the direction in the margin is, that Adam and Eve shall cover genitalia sua cum foliis, whereas until then stabunt nudi, et non verecund-abuntur. Perhaps our forefathers thought it no indecency to give such representations . . . but it must nevertheless strike us as not a little extraordinary, that at least as late as the close of the sixteenth century such scenes were to be found in England. (W. Marriott 1838: lxii)

If you share Marriott's conviction that those bodies really were naked, he assumes you will find the imagined sight extraordinary, indecent, primitive, something we have grown out of. Yet mysteries were 'very useful in the civilisation of the people, from their bringing together all classes, and giving them a taste for other amusements than those which required only strength and prowess' (p. lxiii). It is in fact the lower class which benefits, since the educated already have a taste for the amusements which comprise plays. By refocusing working-class bodily activities into a taste for religious drama, that class becomes civilized. Plays will replace amusements merely requiring strength and prowess. Thus the mysteries will civilize, or control, the embarrassingly honed musculature. Lurking in this view of mysteries is an unspoken contrast with the popular but apparently less elevating drama of the 1820s. The scholars who were discovering the drama of the Middle Ages were doing so in the context of a contemporary drama which dangerously provoked and exhibited popular enthusiasms. The crucial decade that edited medieval plays was also the decade that saw the activities of politically aware artisans organizing themselves around the issue of Chartism. The Middle Ages offered to scholarly gentlemen a preferred version of an innocent, primitive people.

That innocence is in turn protected by responsible 'medieval' performances – even where the original material may be recalcitrant, as, say, in the case of the figure of Lechery in *The Castle of Perseverance* which displays 'the Playboy view of sexuality. There is nothing much in it that a female actor could identify with.' This remark comes from Meg Twycross's account of her project to investigate what happens when modern performance adopts the medieval convention of men playing women's parts. As the rigorous parade of documentary evidence suggests, this project is REED in the rehearsal room. One of its results is that the matter of Adam and Eve's nakedness has now at last been settled. But this doesn't prevent Twycross coming up against – even as Marriott did – a certain sort of worrying exhibitionism. Men in women's clothes, she says, 'fall into two categories: the pantomime dame and the drag queen'. This remark omits to recognize a major strand of gay performance, from the Brixton Faeries and Bethnal Rouge through to Bloolips, where men in dresses disrupt the straightforward cultural opposition between masculine and feminine. What it does recognize, by contrast, is that drag queens are – apparently – associated with 'exhibitionism'; and, furthermore, that Renaissance schoolmasters were legitimately concerned about cross-dressing confusing their pupils 'at an impressionable age about their own sex-roles, especially if they were exposed to potential sollicitation [*sic*] from homosexual members of their audience'.

Where the scholarly medieval restaging is vigilant about the dangers of homosexual exposure, the mysteries are conscientiously continuing their cultural role of being 'very useful in the civilisation of the people'. Twycross's project works to affirm the correct responses, the civilization, as it were, of a particular community of watchers: 'when I have talked about it [transvestism] to my friends, the women have reacted to the whole concept much more positively than the men: possibly because they feel less threatened by the subject.' A responsible performance is one which regards threat and strangeness as improper: 'when the women played Mary and Elizabeth, they came over as two individuals, each with their own character, history, and experiences . . . It was easy to relate to the warmth of their feeling for each other, and the naturalism of the situation came to the fore. They were "people like us". The men communicated none of this' (Twycross 1983: 159, 135, 156, 136, 150).

The academically approved medieval performance discovers that those far-off people are innocent warm people, like us.

It seems, here, to be the response of the audience which establishes the authenticity of the performance. Thus the academic investigation of how to perform mysteries is actually a statement about how to watch them. This has been an accepted part of medieval drama studies since at least 1966 when V. A. Kolve's *The Play Called Corpus Christi* appeared. This book is not part of the REED project, in that it is concerned predominantly with interpreting the mysteries as text. Kolve uses the concept of a theatre of game, where laughter has a spiritual function and meaning. The theatre of game is most famously to be found in certain modernist practices – plays by Ionesco or Beckett – but 'the cycles can give us the thing itself in its first flowering.' That means we need to 'read them, stage them, and understand them properly'. Part of the process of understanding properly entails a rejection of 'popular' culture: 'If we would get inside these plays, we must renounce certain oversimple conceptions of their audience and their purpose. The plays were neither written by the unlearned nor staged exclusively for them' (Kolve 1966: 23, 7). The learned response knows that the comic action, the routines of play and game, even the response of laughter are nothing to do with Bakhtin's carnival: they are all doctrinally legitimated parts of the feast of celebration which is Corpus Christi. No other corpus is relevant: the argument is about how to watch, not about who watches; about interpretation, not reception. By insisting on the criteria for proper watching, whether by being one of the learned or her female friend, the study of medieval mysteries sustains their civilizing mission.

That mission is made much easier when the expert – the researcher, scholar, director – has a position of power. The obvious example is that of a professional teacher working with students. It is a feature of a great deal of the modern stagings of medieval plays that they happen within these sorts of power relations: the expert gives instructions to those who are, as it were, amateur. Those instructions can be literally enforced where the teacher is assessor. But frequently the relation is more open, as where the expert teaches at a local college but directs, on a regular basis, for and with the community of the city, as Keith Ramsay did in Lincoln. Thus in the staging of the Lincoln plays the college of education and the cathedral are linked, as it were organically, within a civic project. On a grander level again, there is the example of E. Martin Browne staging the York cycle in York in 1951. Browne was a national, not a local, scholar: as director of the British Drama League he had been campaigning since the late 1940s for a theatre research centre, negotiating with the Society for Theatre Research and the Arts Council. Browne was an expert at the centre of expertise. And the year of his production of the York cycle was the Festival of Britain. So when God's voice opens the cycle, the medieval cathedral city, institutionalized theatre history and reaffirmed national identity together speak.

Each level of staging of mysteries enacts the relationship of academy, town and nation to history, finding in it, after all, like the county historians did, county people, people like us. The plays are most amenable to this enactment because medieval mysteries are, uniquely, under almost total control by teachers and textual scholars. So that when the plays speak with their own voice it comes through a mesh of documents fine enough to filter out those indecent tendencies towards unlearned laughter and exhibitionism. Drama is made civilized.

## 5   Dramatic Animals

So where have the folk gone? In British education and civic life medieval drama means guild cycle drama and morality plays. Folk rituals and mumming plays have the status of bizarre antiquities, confined to cultural margins, while cycle plays become serious art, seriously studied.

Or rather, folk culture has come to occupy the space vacated by cycle plays. The jockeying for academic position may be highlighted if the process of 'medieval discovery' is arranged, however grossly, into periods. The first, say 1800–40, is the enquiry into national antiquities, developed by bibliographers and philologists, at a time when 'English' was not a university subject and had no methodology of interpretation. Guild plays existed as documents and could be catalogued as real by historical scholarship. Folk customs might be practised, but they didn't have texts and therefore couldn't, so to speak, be saved.

The second period, say 1890–1930, concerns itself with cultural evolution. E. K. Chambers's *The Medieval Stage*, first published in 1903, grew out of a desire to describe the cultural conditions which led to Shakespearean drama. Thirty years later, Young produced, in *The Drama of the Medieval Church* (1933), a model for the transition from ritual to drama. In these versions, Church practices evolve into guild drama, guild drama into Renaissance theatre, while society as a whole evolves towards civilization. Alongside this rather crude Darwinian model of cultural evolution, there were more hard-headed influences on Chambers, namely Nietzsche's theory of drama and James Frazer's researches in anthropology. As English emerged as a university subject, it looked for models by which to define its own role and practice, as distinct from the already existing subjects of Latin and Theology. There were Matthew Arnold's ideas about the civilizing role of art, but these came with moral and religious baggage which Chambers didn't want. In Frazer he found a model which allowed him to escape simple ideas of evolution towards 'civilized' society within a uniform framework of Christian moral thought. Chambers's work coincided with, and was part of, a widespread interest in folk music and drama. Elsewhere in Europe this interest in folk roots derived from the resistance of the culturally dispossessed against alien dominant cultures. In

Britain that feeling was part of the motivation that drove Cecil Sharp and Ralph Tiddy to collect and revive examples of folk culture. But the inter-relation between folk culture and guild drama, as proposed by Chambers, was refused by others. The phoney tree had, after all, been cut down in the 1830s. Coinciding with a peculiarly totalitarian, not to say fascist, moment in the Europe of 1933, the interest of Young's book fixed itself upon the controlling institutional power of the Catholic Church.

The third period, say 1950–90, attended to the specific artistic quality of medieval drama. The title of Waldo F. McNeir's essay on 'The Corpus Christi Passion plays as Dramatic Art' makes clear this approach: the plays are not 'primitive works of art' but 'the final outcome of a slowly developed growth' (McNeir 1951: 602). The year before, Rossiter, following Chambers, had written a study of this drama as one part of a range of forms, which were all defined as exponents of the anti-sacred. But the dominant practice in the now well-established discipline of 'English' was so-called New Criticism, which sought to describe the formal features of art-works which were conceived as autonomous. Thus major revaluations of mysteries which appeared in the 1960s discovered principles of internal unity, thematic or structural coher-ence, literary competences: ritual form is considered not so much as social interaction but artistic unifying structure; repentance is considered not as psychic process but as unifying theme; the lived mess of religious activity is smoothly streamlined into what may be dealt with as typology and iconogra-phy. The increasing emphasis on the autonomy of medieval guild drama as artefact, where 'art' is defined in a very specific way, formed the ideological legitimation for REED's concentration on dramatic records divorced from wider historical process or contemporary mediation. Rossiter's interest in the staged expression of the anti-sacred was a dead end; the developing scholarly *practice* narrowed its focus onto guild plays, which meant that there was no theoretical framework for thinking of folk drama alongside cycles. One insti-tutional practice of a period was thus privileged above others.

Once extracted, the study of medieval cycle drama on its own has an attraction which, as several of its historians have noted, comes from the appearance of a full development to the genre, with a beginning, middle and end. Intellectual pleasure derives from the promise of being able to account for the origins of the form and the joy of knowing where a culture has come from, which in turn gives the analysts a sense of their own competence and cultural security. Furthermore, the form is now a *finished* practice: its institutional end was officially marked by Elizabethan legislation, and its modes of articulation ceased to be effective in Renaissance religious and cultural change. By con-trast, the drama of the Renaissance remains in process, reshaped by new theatrical explorations and political agendas, championed by non-specialists and theatre folk, and hence continually compromising itself with non-literary liaisons and promiscuous experimentations. Medieval drama – that's to say, cycle plays – has to be kept intact if it is to carry its particular promise of making knowable a whole, completed art form.

Chambers, Rossiter and others in the so-called pagan school undid the work of the 1830s by writing about mysteries as a dramatic practice entangled with and crossed over by other cultural practices. For them, cycle plays were mainly distinguished by their *institutional* specificity, being performed by guilds. So when in 1965 Hardison challenged the authority not only of Chambers but also of Young he accused them of having inadequate theories of drama, if any: 'At no point in *The Medieval Stage* is there a discussion of what constitutes drama' (Hardison 1965: 17). Hardison's own view of drama emerges in his critique of Young. He quotes a passage from Young, including the sentence: 'In some external and recognizable manner the actor must pretend to be the person whose words he is speaking, and whose actions he is imitating.' Hardison then comments:

> Young is clearly not thinking of literary texts but of performances, not of what appears in manuscripts but of what would presumably occur if the manuscript were acted out. Whatever else it may be, this is an extremely limiting view of drama. Discussions of drama are often weakened by ignorance of stagecraft, but acting and staging procedures are certainly not essential elements of the theory of drama. (pp. 30, 31)

No longer the tentative discipline of Chambers's day, 1960s English demonstrated that what could work for books could work for plays. And where these plays, without the protection of proper authors, threatened to slide back into a tangled cultural mess, the modern literary scholar could step in to identify their specific artistic coherence and insist upon the rules of interpretation by which they were governed. Thus the fortuitous conjunction of New Criticism and medieval drama produced for 'English' a satisfactorily tidy theory of drama – by the neat ploy of ditching the dramatic.

The focus on mysteries concentrates on the products of the institutional nexus of medieval guilds and Church, both in positions of economic and cultural power. To theorize dramatic practice on the basis of mysteries alone is to replace the whole cultural activity of a community with a privileged part of it. 'English' engages itself with privileged art-works not only because it is interested in books, but also because it needed, historically, to define itself against anthropology (as it did later against sociology). Part of the reason why Hardison cannot find a 'proper' theory of drama in Chambers's work is that Chambers was writing under the influence of anthropology. For drama theorists, unlike 'English' scholars, anthropology (and indeed sociology) have remained empowering disciplines. Medieval drama scholars became much occupied with the distinctions between ritual and drama; an anthropological theory of performance produces instead a dialectical unity, where ritual and drama have the potential to transform, in either direction, into each other (see Schechner 1983: 124–63). Similarly, the attempt to make clear-cut distinctions between comic and serious, which raise all sorts of literary questions about genre and interpretation, may be rethought using a model where, to use Schechner's terms, what is communally 'efficacious' and what is 'entertaining' are in continual negotiation with, and interpenetration of, each other.

While documents and authors have interested the literary scholar, anthropologists have been interested in processes and 'people'. Within the history of scholarship these divergent interests have not been politically disinterested. James Frazer was a rationalist for whom Christianity amounted, in the main, to a 'barbarous superstition' (Hardison 1965: 14). Hardison criticized Chambers's work for being 'affected by anti-clericalism to such a degree that the dramatic elements in religious drama are treated as a rebellion against religion rather than as attempts to express it' (p. 18). The thinking here attributed to Chambers reaches back to Hone, and through him to Joseph Strutt, whose *The Sports and Pastimes of the People of England* (1801) was reprinted by Hone in 1833. Strutt observed, dispassionately: 'Notwithstanding the Seriousness of the Subjects that constituted these mysteries, it seems clear that they were not exhibited without a portion of pantomimical fun to make them palatable to the vulgar taste; and indeed the length and the dulness of the speeches required some such assistance to enliven them, and keep the spectators in good humour' (Strutt 1801: 118). It was the 'amateur' enthusiast Ralph Tiddy who warned that: 'The anthropologist may discredit his science if he fails to recognize that man at a very early period indeed was an artistic and a dramatic animal and not merely a religious one' (Tiddy 1923: 76).

Tiddy's own cultural analysis situated itself in the social history of Britain: 'The growth of commerce and the consequent growth of towns were perpetually dragging the classes apart.' This history is always in process, no point of rest is available. Furthermore the organic folk culture just doesn't exist: 'the modern survival of peasantry' is not 'a fair representative of the folk that made traditional poetry and drama and dance. . . . He is, for one thing, merely a survival, not part of a really living community. He is probably rather a degenerate survival: for he has suffered, through some generations at least, by the decay of his industry, by comparative neglect and isolation, and perhaps from worse things than that' (pp. 64, 65). There is a particular strand in political thought which values the apparent evidence of cultural continuities. Such 'evidence' might be Hardin Craig's assertion that Macbeth and Everyman are connected by 'a community of race and purpose' (H. Craig 1955: 389). Tiddy's own example is Yeats's statement that 'Folk poetry . . . binds the unlettered . . . to the beginning of time.' To which Tiddy rejoined: 'When I read these words, I smell a mystic in the wind' (Tiddy 1923: 61).

Through Tiddy's work the anthropologists can be linked to Marxist accounts of medieval culture. The same emphasis falls on social process, a culture negotiated and produced within a set of economic and social power relations. Art-works are seen as products of a society that make sense of or challenge social values. And in the same way the academic discovery of those art-works is also part of a process of making sense and challenging. The quest for the authentic and the organic is, in one respect, a quest to find some resting point outside cultural process. 'English', in shutting out the dramatic animals, puts – as the phrase goes – its own house in order.

By way of conclusion we might contrast two geographically close, but different, events. In the dark country lanes around Antrobus in Cheshire, at the time of year of All Souls' Day, there are suddenly streams of cars moving from one pub to another. They are following the performance of the Antrobus soul-caking play. In the play King George is killed and resurrected by a doctor; there is also Beelzebub and a horse which shits potatoes. The mummers perform in about three pubs in one evening. In the nearby city of Chester, every four years, there are performances of the Chester mystery plays. The two sets of events are very unlike. Financially the mystery cycle is more expensive than the mumming play to mount, and to watch. In social terms, the 'mumming' play is done by the villagers of Antrobus (of mixed class status) and hosted by local pubs, whereas in the city the civic, tourist and educational structures organize around the staging of the cycle. Antrobus has its following of cultural studies academics (which it used to resent); the Chester cycle has its tourists and scholars. Neither event is medieval: the mumming play is probably an eighteenth-century corruption or reworking, the mysteries are a modern production based on a late-sixteenth-century written text. The Antrobus play is still guarded by the performers, who hide the horse's head and orally transmit the text through generations; a very local custom. The Chester cycle is a known set of texts, staged by scholarship, civic community and tourist industry; a national heritage artefact. As versions of our knowledge of the 'medieval', we might say that the mumming play derives from and defines the official organic community and the mystery cycle derives from and defines the organic official community.

## NOTES

1   *The Retrospective Review* defined itself as 'an attempt to recall the public from an exclusive attention to new books, by making the merit of old ones the subject of critical discussion' (p. viii).
2   Hone (1823) notes, at this time, Francis Dance's paper on Feasts of Fools given to the Society of Antiquaries on 10 May 1804.
3   The information about Lynch comes from Mick Wallis, for whose pioneering work on pageantry in Britain see Wallis 1994a and Wallis 1995.

# 3

# Renaissance Drama

## 1  The Purpose of Playing

At a time very nearly halfway between the opening of the commercial theatre in London and the official order to stop playing, a cultured aristocrat told a group of professional performers how to act.

> Suit the action to the word, the word to the action, with this special observance, that you o'erstep not the modesty of nature. For anything so o'erdone is from the purpose of playing, whose end, both at first and now, was and is to hold as 'twere the mirror up to nature. (Shakespeare 1982: 288)

That playing should have anything to do with natural modesty would have come as some surprise to those moralists who, only a handful of years earlier, had described the theatre as sinful and sensual. Audiences, they said, tended not to censure but to delight in staged villainies and bawdy; a response that was only to be expected when people were distracted from the virtuous practices of work and worship. Play, for the legislators of London, was not work. Playing was done by those who had been legally classed with non-workers and casual labour, in buildings that had little claim to a licensed place within the boundaries of the respectable city. Represented diagrammatically, the relations between playing and civic government look like a map of a city under siege, with the theatres clustered to the north – in Clerkenwell and Shoreditch – and in Southwark to the south, poised like siege engines around a wealthy citadel. And in one of those siege engines, in 1601, in an imaginary Denmark a fictional prince with an obviously serious project claims that the purpose of playing is now and has always been 'to show virtue her feature, scorn her own image, and the very age and body of the time his form and pressure' (p. 288).

To show the body of the time on stage might not seem virtuous to all points of view (for instance, a corrupt ruler might not like it). But Hamlet's story is staged in such a way that most watchers of it feel the disaffected prince is emotionally and morally, if not politically, central. When you look with the prince's eyes an apparently orderly state looks corrupt, founded on a criminal act. This situation gives a more aggressive edge to the purpose of playing. For Hamlet is going to use a staging of his father's murder to reveal the guilt of a ruler, his uncle. Where virtue is shown her feature, current orderliness might well be disrupted.

Not all playing is so morally purposeful. For instance, clowns make people laugh just when the play gets onto 'some necessary question'. If you want to reveal the guilt of kings, Hamlet says, you have to resist the temptation to please 'barren spectators'. A clown who upstages the seriousness shows 'pitiful ambition'. Hamlet's remarks have particular point since they are addressed to a newly arrived group of players that have recently fallen out of fashion. Their acting has been parodied by a company of child performers who are now 'tyrannically clapped' (p. 255). When he learns of this shift in theatrical taste, Hamlet is unsurprised. It is similar, he suggests, to the way that the people who once mocked his uncle now flatter him as king. Seen in this political light, playing shows itself willing to replace 'necessary' questions with its own 'ambition', seeking an applause which might be called tyrannical. In circumstances, then, where theatre selects its subject matter in order to fit with dominant taste, the purpose of playing is to make money.

The news about theatrical fashion that reached Elsinore was already common knowledge to the real actors and audience of *Hamlet*. That's what gives the prince's response its particular force. The imaginary Danish castle temporarily dissolves into the real Globe Theatre as its actors gesture to the north side of the river where, less than a mile away, a company of boy actors known as the Children of the Revels was performing. And when the Danish prince shows himself so knowledgeable about the fashions and pitfalls of playing, his opinions are spoken with all the experience of one of the leading actors of the company at the Globe, Richard Burbage. A sensitivity to the child actors had rather more relevance in Burbage's personal history than in Hamlet's, in that Burbage's father, James, had tried, a few years before, to build the theatre in Blackfriars which now housed the children. James had been seeking to capitalize on the success of his theatre in Shoreditch by making the next logical move: the acquisition of a site in the heart of the city's wealthy sector. But the citadel withstood the siege engine's advance. Thus prevented, Burbage fell back on a second best – Southwark. It was a suburban area of popular entertainments and its theatrical potential had already been proven by James's rival, Philip

Henslowe. So, just along the river from Henslowe's Rose Theatre, the theatrical timbers that had been brought down from Shoreditch were reconstructed by James Burbage's sons into the family's new, and most famous, enterprise, the Globe Theatre. That move, in a sort of entrepreneurial chess game, provoked Henslowe, who looked north, in the direction Burbage had come from. With a gesture that neatly shows that enterprise wants to own skills as much as fabric, Henslowe bought the services of James Burbage's own architect to shape for him his new enterprise in Clerkenwell, the Fortune Theatre. The siege engines are also chess pieces. Or rather, because we need something with less romance and more than two players, the game is Monopoly. For now, within the city, in the suburbs of which Burbage and Henslowe were moving, there in the prime site for attracting and making wealth, were the child actors, news of whom eventually reached Elsinore.

Which triggers in Hamlet a concern motivated less by aesthetics than economics: 'What, are they children? Who maintains 'em? How are they escotted?' (p. 256). The assumption that they are 'maintained' – that is to say, financially patronized – by somebody connects with the observation that they are very ready to please fashionable taste. The man who scripted the question and the man who spoke it were neither of them maintained by anybody. Both were 'sharers' (shareholders) in their own company. Their livelihood came from the surplus profit on sales of the company's product. They were owners, investors and indeed paymasters, employing journeymen, hired hands, to do the lesser acting and stage management tasks. They may have been known as the Lord Chamberlain's – or later the King's – Men, but they played in the theatre the Burbages built. To have a name which paid lip-service to the arrangements of patronage was of course useful in the political-cum-legal dealings with civil authorities. But it was not a substantial source of money. And while the Lord Chamberlain may have politically protected his 'Men', it is unlikely he interfered artistically as Hamlet does with the visiting players. When Rosencrantz introduces those players he calls them the 'tragedians of the city', because there is no other way of identifying them. The real London companies, by contrast, were not 'of the city'. Indeed they were resented by the London authorities. They were thus defined *against* the culture of the city, as autonomous entities seeking to make money. Their names give them corporate identities in their own right.

At this period it was the acting company rather than the theatre which was the unit of business. That is clearly displayed when, eight years after Hamlet's discussion of playing, the same company walked onto that fashionable stage at Blackfriars. The King's Men had played frequent performances at Court; but it is their acquisition of a second theatre, and especially that theatre – at the heart of the city – that is the real evidence of their unique success as a company. The commercial push from the margins to the centre was re-enacted, eight years later again, in 1617, from suburban unfashionable

Clerkenwell southwards to the moneyed Drury Lane. But this time a rather
different story is told.

The man who made that move south was Christopher Beeston. He had
himself begun as an actor, rather than property developer, performing alongside *Hamlet*'s author in the late 1590s. Attached to the new theatre in
Clerkenwell, the Red Bull, he came to manage its business affairs. In 1617 he
acquired a property in Drury Lane, known both as the Phoenix and the
Cockpit. To launch his new theatre, he drew on the repertory, and capital
assets, of the Red Bull company. A number of costumes and playbooks were
transferred from Clerkenwell to Drury Lane. This seems to have been regarded
by some as more a social than a geographical move, for on Shrove Tuesday
1617 the traditional riot by London apprentices destroyed Beeston's new
house, together with those costumes and playbooks. It seems that this was not
an attack on theatre itself but, as Andrew Gurr argues, a class anger directed
specifically at Beeston's attempt to remove from the Red Bull something that
should remain there, to entertain an audience that expected to see shows in
Clerkenwell and not in Drury Lane. The polarization between these two
theatres in 1617 was much more intense than that between the Globe and
Blackfriars in 1609. The Red Bull was supposedly 'rougher' than the Globe,
and Drury Lane, being to the west of Blackfriars, was closer to Whitehall and
government than to the commercial city. But also we are now talking about
the entrepreneurial activities of one man rather than a company.

And that man made and broke companies. With a speculative eye on
changes in regime and fashion, Lady Elizabeth's Men were reorganized into
Queen Anne's Company, who in turn were broken up to form a new boys'
company. This is the work not of an investor in property but of a theatre
manager. He built a family business which, following the model of all such
businesses, could be handed on to his son. He ensured he was sole owner of his
capital assets, having his theatre's plays protected from publication by the
Lord Chamberlain. The State machinery that was meant to regulate theatres
was manipulated into servicing Beeston's enterprise. At various times, Beeston
gives the censor's wife a pair of gloves; makes the censor a shareholder in the
theatre; offers to keep an eye on what his poets were writing – in short, to take
over the censor's function. The bribing gloves go from theatrical margin to
government centre; by becoming a shareholder the centre is drawn into the
margin's quest for profit; the margin assumes its own place on the moral high
ground. The testing of the State's control over their theatrical activities is a
new stage in the process that began with the gathering of those theatrical siege
engines around the citadel. During that process, the terminology changes
significantly. The powerful people in the King's Men were known as 'sharers'
(shareholders); when Richard Heton became a manager in the late 1630s he
defined his relation to his company as that of 'governor'.

At the moment Beeston tries to absorb into himself the function of State censor, his story gives a new twist to the State's definition of an actor as 'masterless man'. Between the 1590s and 1630s the men who were building playhouses and making shows created a transformation of their own profession: 'vagabond' turns into 'governor'. But Beeston's story is not quite over, and its final spasm suggests that the transformation still has a theatrical quality of impermanence about it. Beeston's business passed to his son William. In May 1640, William put on a play which was politically risky; he was arrested and imprisoned. In his absence the censor appointed as 'governor' a courtier, William Davenant. There are contemporary hints that Davenant engineered the furore. Whether true or not, at that critical time the courtier replaced the well-heeled son of the self-made man. The business that began in marginal Clerkenwell, and moved speculatively into the centre, ends up being absorbed by that centre. When his theatre was taken over by Davenant it passed into the control of one whose social class Beeston was always, finally, outside. To Davenant the business was attractive for everything Beeston had established: independent enterprise and managerial power, built from and – crucially – tested against central administration. As a successful courtier, Davenant would have already been in possession of a sharp nose for a juicy windfall.

When theatre management becomes something which courtliness might take on, the concept of playing has changed. Back towards the beginning of this story, Philip Henslowe had been given a title that recognized his artistic achievement: 'Master of the Royal Game of Bears'. Playing is made equivalent to the sport for which there is official recognition. Thus for the map-makers of Renaissance London the same symbol served for animal-baiting arenas as for theatres. In some theatres indeed, such as the Hope, human and animal performers shared the same venue – which would confirm a general feeling that playing occupied the same cultural space as savage sports. For stage performances seemed to make a similar appeal to irrational excitements, a similar invitation to passionate excess. The audience, 'being but an assemblie of Tailors, Tinkers, Cordwayners, Saylers, Olde Men, yong Men, Women, Boyes, Girles', were already predisposed. Youths cruise the auditorium, looking for women. They are not worried about making an exhibition of themselves: 'yong ruffins' and 'harlots' 'presse to the fore-front of the scaffoldes, to the end to showe their impudencie, and to be as an object to al mens eies' (in Gurr 1987: 207, 206). If you want to display yourself to all men's eyes, you behave like an actor:

> Onlie the filthines of plaies, and spectacles is such, as maketh both the actors & beholders giltie alike. For while they saie nought, but gladlie looke on, they al by sight and assent be actors. (in Barish 1981: 80)

The stage absorbs its audience into itself, by simply encouraging them to look: 'delight being mooved with varietie of shewes, of eventes, of musicke, the longer we gaze, the more we crave' (in Gurr 1987: 207). Using non-verbal means – laughter, music and spectacle – the stage encourages an audience that is not craven, but craving. Years later, in 1632, a Presbyterian divine, William Prynne, resurrected the antagonism to theatre. He described music – 'effeminate lust-provoking' – in terms similar to those he used of clothing: 'Those Playes which are usually acted and frequented in over-costly effeminate, strange, meretricious, lust-exciting apparell, are questionlesse unseemely' (in Barish 1981: 86). The wicked apparel is not only shown on stage but also frequents the auditorium. The audience dresses up for the play: in doing so it seems to want to incorporate itself imaginatively in the event of the enactment, itself to become the show.

To exempt any form of drama from such attacks, it has to be defined as different from 'show'. The anti-theatricalist pamphleteer Philip Stubbes makes exception for 'very honest and very commendable exercyses' (in Barish 1981: 83). The word 'exercise' had recently come into use as a term for a sort of religious practice, drawing on an older sense of training of mind and spirit. Religious exercise develops an active commitment to belief. When drama is exercise, it still has the show's power to stir and engage; but now it activates towards moral ends. So the most famous early defence of 'serious' drama, by Philip Sidney, argues that when an audience are engaged by the activities of a noble hero, they themselves want to perform noble deeds, and are thus morally elevated. Such a response was apparently witnessed for real by Thomas Nashe at a performance of one of Shakespeare's *Henry VI* plays:

> How would it have joyed brave Talbot (the terror of the French) to thinke that after he had lyne two hundred yeares in his Tombe, hee should triumphe againe on the Stage, and have his bones newe embalmed with the teares of ten thousand spectators at least . . . who, in the Tragedian that represents his person, imagine they behold him fresh bleeding! (in Gurr 1987: 209)

When it produces tears, drama is very different from those activities with which it is meant to be morally equivalent: 'gameing', harlots, etc. The performance of Talbot is legitimate and functional because it is, most simply, patriotic. To enjoy his heroism is to enjoy Englishness terrorizing the French. And the form of enjoyment is itself particularly English. As Nashe says later, 'our representation honourable, and full of gallant resolution, not consisting, like theirs, of a Pantaloun, a Whore, and a Zanie' (E. K. Chambers 1923: IV, 239). By contrast with the *commedia dell'arte* masks, the heroic performance is straightforward, with an authenticity vouched for by a sense of the living joy of the dead hero.

Nashe's defence of theatre works by taking the things that are bad about drama – sex and laughter – and claiming that they are not native, that they're characteristics of *foreign* drama. Tales of our English forefathers' valiant acts are, in fact, a useful reproof to the present. Thus the moral attack on drama is not so much refuted as absorbed, and hence adapted to work in conjunction with an already existing national myth of a 'plainness' which is quintessentially English. Talbot thus contrasts not only with the decadent French but also with the 'effeminate' Henry VI. The same thing happens in a contemporary play, *Thomas of Woodstock*, where the titular hero, an aristocrat who prides himself on his plainness, is critically contrasted with Richard II and his favourites. Plainness is able to oppose monarchy because it speaks from a powerful conjunction of qualities: being purposeful, suspicious of sensuality, English. Hence, for Nashe, it was the *opponents* of theatre who showed themselves 'shallow-braind', 'not the depest serchers into the secrets of government'. Later on, one such searcher advised his performers to be purposeful in putting on a play that was going to reveal the guilty secrets of monarchy.

The purposeful theatre is deeply suspicious of showiness, and it thus tends to designate as showy anything to which it is opposed. So, for example, in the chronicle play which tells of the early life of the man who will be Henry V, once Prince Hal appears the traditional heroics of Hotspur begin to feel like bluster. Hal, in a most unprincely way, participates in a world of petty criminality, which contrasts with Hotspur's aristocratic virtue. That contrast is, however, less important than the opposition between Hal's authenticity and Hotspur's theatricality, for Hotspur's performance feels as if it has wandered in from another play, such as Marlowe's *Tamburlaine*. When that's clear, 'Hotspur' becomes something which derives itself from theatrical cliché rather than historical reality. The distinction here is one of the purposeful play's specialities, for, every time it makes it, it defines its own non-showiness – much as Hamlet does to the spectacle of royal power when he chooses to wear black.

So it is completely logical that the seriousness of Hamlet's purpose leads him to warn the players not to perform like those actors who 'strutted and bellowed', the style associated with the *Tamburlaine* performances. The style was attractive to performers because it had its willing audience, even if Hamlet didn't like it: 'O, it offends me to the soul to hear a robustious periwig-pated fellow tear a passion to tatters, to very rags, to split the ears of the groundlings, who for the most part are capable of nothing but inexplicable dumb-shows and noise' (p. 287). When he calls that audience 'groundlings', the contrast of purpose and showiness gains a new dimension. 'Groundlings' is a jokey word that seems to designate those watching in the cheapest part of the cheaper theatres. It is this lot, the poorest theatre-goers, that supposedly like shows and noise. So, by Hamlet's argument, purposeful theatre can not only be separated from purposeless theatre, but the distinction between the two reflects economic and social division. Thirty years later Hamlet's views had become the accepted opinion of fashionable society – purposeless sensuality was explained away as a perversion of theatre insisted upon by a social class who knew no better. What seems to have happened, then, is that purposeful theatre came into being in a world where all theatre was suspected of being sensual (and thus potentially un-English). Its 'plainness' was made up of a suspicion of anything which might turn out to be showy, sensual and, hence, theatrical. Hence it defined itself by asserting what it was not – not cliché, not established practice, not common taste. When the entrepreneurial activity moves from suburb to wealthy centre, it measures itself against what it once was: the suburban practice is what purposeful theatre has to deny.

Hamlet's thoughts come back to the pleasure, specifically laughter, of a different audience. *His* purpose, unlike the capability of groundlings and ambition of clowns, wants explicable dumbshows. But dumbshows don't have to be explicable to have effect. The *power* of theatre is not the same as purpose. This can be demonstrated by someone who was less particular about virtue than Hamlet. When he has sold his soul to the devil to achieve worldly power, Faustus thinks he can display that power effectively by putting on shows. The more purposeless the show is, the more powerfully it works as a bit of showing off (as a moralistic audience will note). When Faustus provides the Emperor with a show of Alexander the Great and his paramour, the Emperor is so excited by the spectacle that he leaves his throne, attempts to hug Alexander. Faustus has to remind him that this is not really Alexander, that these are 'shadows', not substantial. So he can't touch. At most, to satisfy the excitement produced by the show, he can inspect the wart on the neck of Alexander's lover.

If you thought theatre was dangerously sensual, you would note that this show produces a deep desire, which causes a ruler to leave his throne; and that this desire can neither be fully satisfied nor put into words; and that the potential opportunity to admire a classical hero (which Sidney would approve) is diverted into – and satisfied by – the inspection of a wart on a woman's neck. You would note, also, that these 'shadows' might either be actors or devilish spirits; in neither case the real thing, although they produce real excitement. Putting on shows thus seems peculiarly appropriate to someone who aims to better himself as an individual, who doesn't play by the rules, who doesn't as it were bring proper goods to the market. Furthermore, you might be uncer- tain as to the different ways in which the show is 'explicable'. For instance, the Emperor is moved to lose all sense of himself and his State, behaving like a groundling. He then is watched by Faustus, for whom the show is explicable as a demonstration both of his own power and of the magic of theatre. He is in turn, presumably, watched by Mephistophilis, for whom the show is explicable as part of the project to distract, and retain, Faustus. These watchers in their turn are watched by an audience who see both a show and a moral commentary on show. In understanding the moral, they are supposedly free of the sensual trap. But what if the gaze of Mephistophilis also strays across the audience, dangerously implying that, however they respond, they are always subject to the devil's look? The ability to do moral commentary is then only an illusory freedom from the operation of theatre power.

When the distinction between explicable and inexplicable dumbshows collapses, it takes with it the division between sensuality and morality. Enacting a revenge of show upon exercise, *Dr Faustus* claims to derive from the genre of Morality play, and then doesn't behave like one. But it doesn't not behave like one either, just as show never shakes free of exercise. Deeply distrustful of the purposes of Morality, *Dr Faustus* finds itself saying that its shadows can only be important when they are *not* substantial. This is what Hamlet also worries about:

> Is it not monstrous that this player here,
> But in a fiction, in a dream of passion,
> Could force his soul so to his own conceit
> That from her working all his visage wann'd,
> Tears in his eyes, distraction in his aspect,
> A broken voice, and his whole function suiting
> With forms to his conceit? And all for nothing!
> For Hecuba!
>
> (p. 270)

When a player does it, it's done with his soul – the tears appear – and yet at the same time it's all a conceit, a fiction.

By contrast with a player, Hamlet, who really does have a motive and 'cue for passion', cannot strut and bellow, cannot drown the stage with tears. His emotional expression thinks of itself as real by being different from show. For an audience, however, a distinction between conceit and motive, show and expression, is less easy to keep hold of. Claudius and Polonius set up a meeting between Hamlet and Ophelia in order to learn from Hamlet's behaviour if love is the reason for his conduct. They plant Ophelia so Hamlet will come across her as if by chance. Polonius organizes her to look like an image of piety:

> Read on this book
> That show of such an exercise may colour
> Your loneliness.
>
> (p. 276)

The men withdraw, to spy unseen upon Hamlet and so learn about his character, much like a theatre audience. Hamlet enters and, while Ophelia does her silent show of exercise, he speaks his thoughts: 'To be or not to be'.

Then he confronts her, denying the love that she had believed he once felt. His soliloquy is written as if the person is arguing through a sequence of thoughts for himself. Its manner differs from the formalized arrangements of a public speech; it is produced as the expression of a psychic interior rather than emblematic show (Wallis 1994b). But, even if the sorts of performance are distinguishable, the play doesn't prioritize one over the other, nor does it keep them fully separate. Does Hamlet move from expression to show when he 'notices' Ophelia? And, although she is doing an arranged show, is she not psychically engaged? The staged confrontation between suffering and show produces no reliable conclusion for the on-stage audience. Nor, therefore, does it produce clarity for the real audience, themselves also 'seeing unseen'. What is dramatized by the whole sequence is the urge to have contact with reliably real, and hence communicative, expression.

Alexander's paramour's wart won't do as a substitute. Those who stand as the 'lawful espials', the real audience, of *Hamlet* are worked upon so that they too share the deep need for some purposeful expression which Hamlet himself talks of, something which will hold the mirror up to nature. When Hamlet attacks the efforts of actors who strutted and bellowed, it's possible to hear the voice of the new star, Richard Burbage, and the rising company, the Chamberlain's Men, as they turn their backs on the older stars such as Alleyn, who made his name strutting Tamburlaine. Where the old actors seem made by Nature's journeymen, without accent or gait of Christians, Hamlet wants something respectable, independent from its theatrical past, a playing which is – of all things – godly and natural. But wanting is not having. There is something so seductive about that player's performance that weeps for nothing, for Hecuba, yet it is ultimately a monstrous fiction; if you really were connected, it would be less fictional, more purposeful, but eventually less satisfying. Caught between fiction and frustration, Hamlet finds he can say nothing, can't do the performance. And that, of course, *is* the performance. The rising company had made a show of that want which constituted so much of their contemporary theatre, the want for something that was both purposeful and playing.

## 2  Two – or Three – Truths are Told

In 1607 two citizens at Blackfriars theatre wanted something so strongly that they interrupted the prologue. They wanted a hero who was himself a citizen, who would do 'admirable', wondrous, things, like killing a lion 'with a pestle'. During the play they ask that other performances be curtailed, to make space for more exhibitions of heroic deeds.

These heroic deeds are done in that strutting style that Hamlet disliked. But they're done by those very boys that caused such comment in Elsinore.

Indeed some of the heroics are a pastiche of the verse of one of the King's Men's own strutters, Hotspur. References to other theatres, parodies of performing styles: these are signs of a commercial battle between contemporary companies. Whereas at a basic level theatres may have seemed all the same, in that they were in the business of offering plays to paying audiences, the competition for those audiences drove each theatre towards differentiating its own product from that of its rivals. In short, they were developing their own clearly delineated product identities. So the citizens who demand those heroics, without seeing them as funny, are making a mistake about the *product identity*. They have, quite literally, walked into the wrong theatre. For although rich citizens did go to the Blackfriars, that theatre didn't specialize in shows 'in honour of the commons of the city'. To see the sort of performance they wanted, they should have gone to the Red Bull in Clerkenwell. The fact that the biggest mistake of the citizens is simply to be in the wrong place is an indication that the product identity was founded not so much on plays or players – who moved around and changed their styles – but on the theatre building itself.

As you've guessed, those embarrassing citizens aren't real. They were invented as part of a play that aims to define theatrical product identity. The play, *The Knight of the Burning Pestle*, was a failure at its first performance, but was later much more successfully revived. In other words, the movement towards product identity – especially the relationship between fashionable and unfashionable theatre – is still only in process in 1607, not yet finished. Hence there is a lot of self-consciousness about performing here rather than there, performing this way rather than that, which tells us clearly about a key element in achieving the product identity: namely, the development of a particular performance–audience relationship.

In general terms, that relationship is physically structured by the dimensions of a theatre building and its characteristic disposition of spaces. Less tangibly, it is also affected by a sense of the theatre's cultural location – whether its entertainment was on a par with sports like bear-baiting, or whether it was expensive, exclusive and precious. Developing from here is the part played by repertoire in not only contributing to the theatre's identity but also shaping the audience's sense of itself. An audience learns to be treated, by performances, as if it has specific expectations and demands: the Citizens at *Knight* are meant to be a joke because they haven't learnt to want what a Blackfriars audience wants. This dislocation between the two sets of wants is characterized as theatrical incompetence.

For example, when Mistress Merrythought enters, she is prevented from speaking by the Citizen's Wife, who asks her 'to refrain your passion a little till Rafe have dispatched the giant'. Mistress Merrythought, having stood on stage acting nothing for ten lines, goes off. A Boy enters, and the Citizen instructs him to go and bring Rafe on. To which the Boy replies: 'In good faith, sir, we cannot. You'll utterly spoil our play, and make it to be hissed, and it cost money; you will not suffer us to go on with our plot' (Beaumont 1969: 69). By treating the performers as their economic clients, the Citizens force the performance not only to abandon acting and plot but, most embarrassingly, to declare its own profit-motive. This happens not because the Citizens are anti-theatrical but because they have no competence in the conventions and protocols of the performance. When they prefer to see Rafe's fight rather than have Mistress Merrythought's passion, it's not really a choice of spectacle over characterization, because to them Mistress Merrythought isn't even acting, she is real. And they want a proper *show* for their money.

Everything that can't be defined as show, it seems, has to be real. The Wife is especially funny because, as a woman, she sides with characters, replays stage arguments with her husband, sees things that don't exist. She sees a lump on the head of someone who has acted a fight, and offers him medication. She allows herself to be taken over by the play: ''a has put me into such a fright that I tremble, as they say, as 'twere an aspen leaf. Look o' my little finger, George, how it shakes. Now, i'truth, every member of my body is the worse for't' (Beaumont 1969: 63). Her literal-mindedness is funny, firstly, because it is theatrically incompetent, and, secondly, because it unintentionally reveals information about her body. The more intense the focus that the performer can put onto that little finger, the more it becomes – unlike, say, Alexander's paramour's wart – a joke. The audience of *Knight* is expected to find funny the inappropriateness of the Citizens in that they are at the wrong theatre, looking for the wrong show. But they also respond wrongly. They are both insufficiently engaged and too engaged; making a muddle of what is real or not. The woman says, 'I would have something done, and I cannot tell what it is' (p. 51). She is funny because she doesn't know what she wants, unlike the Blackfriars audience. She has to learn the propriety of only wanting what is offered.

The Citizen's Wife would have fitted in better at the theatres which performed seriously what *Knight* parodied – specifically this would have been at the Globe's *Macbeth* (1606) or the Red Bull's *Rape of Lucrece* (1607). At the first play she would even have seen a woman of similar status watching a 'performance' that had to be taken as real, and being put in a fright about it. A waiting-gentlewoman has seen Lady Macbeth sleepwalk, attempting to wash blood from her hands. She has heard things which she cannot tell, so she invites a Doctor to watch with her. For him, likewise, the effect of what he has seen is that 'I think, but dare not speak' (Shakespeare 1964: 146). Although the 'sleeping' performer reveals a great deal about herself as it were unintentionally, particularly through the intense focus on a small part of her body, her performance doesn't make its audience feel secure. Indeed in the tyrannical conditions of Macbeth's rule, watching becomes more risky in proportion to the amount of real 'passion' which is expressed. The performance is thus dangerous to the extent that it not only takes its watchers into unfamiliar territory, beyond their 'practice', as they say, but also inhibits a sharing of response: the Doctor can't help the waiting-woman, both must lock up in their own selves what they have seen.

The problems of spectating here are relevant to the play as a whole. For instance, its hero is given lines that cue a sort of strutting in the manner of Tamburlaine: 'wither'd Murther . . . thus with his stealthy pace, / With Tarquin's ravishing strides, towards his design / Moves like a ghost' (Shakespeare 1964: 50). He is doing, if only for himself, a sort of performance. When he sees a dagger which obviously isn't there – like seeing a bump on the head of an actor who has simulated a fight – he is somebody whose viewpoint is clearly deluded, excessively engaged with a fiction. But then he also speaks lines which are to be understood, like Hamlet's, as real thought-process expressing itself. And when he sees the ghost of the murdered Banquo, although nobody else on stage can see it, the audience does. We begin looking through the eyes of the person whom everybody else might regard as deluded; his risky viewpoint is shared. And the *naturalness* of sharing it is nowhere more clearly marked than at the moment when the audience agrees to accept from him an image of an actor as someone who merely struts and frets, an image that signifies the emptiness of human life, a tale of sound and fury. That image of the actor as empty is offered – and heard – as a point of high tragic emotion, from someone whose own status as strutter, indeed even as actor, has vanished from view: it's like learning to treat Mistress Merrythought as a real person.

It is characteristic of the difference between the Globe's sort of watching as against that of Blackfriars that the moment when the audience is made to share the deluded viewpoint as if it were real – the entry of the ghost – is the moment which is specially selected for parody in *Knight*. The risky watching in which *Macbeth* is interested becomes mere joke when the text reaches Blackfriars. Before it gets there, however, it travels further north, to the Red Bull, where it is incorporated by Heywood into a drama about another vicious couple, Tarquin and Tullia, in his *Rape of Lucrece*. On his way to the rape, their son Sextus is equipped with drawn sword, lighted taper and chunks of pastiche *Macbeth*: 'Cynthia, mask thy cheek, / And, all you sparkling elemental fires, / Choke up your beauties' etc. He then pauses, to 'weigh' his sin (Heywood 1888: 389). Although this is doing something very different from *Macbeth*, it isn't a joke. Whereas in *Macbeth* this sort of thinking moment is designed to produce, against the odds, engagement, a sense of access to a mind in process, here it is a moral emblem. Because they are pastiche, recognizable from elsewhere, the lines function – as much as the sword and taper – as a *sign* for the quality of murderous power: its brutality has a specific theatricality.

When the opponents of Tarquin discuss how to live under tyranny, they are advised that it is safer not to 'yield so much to passion'. We have now had three different people trying to restrain 'passion': the Citizen's Wife to Mistress

Merrythought, Lady Macbeth to her ghost-fearing husband, and now the Roman Collatine. Although 'passion' is the same thing each time, the audience is invited to take very different attitudes to its expression. Here Collatine suggests that by appearing to be 'offenceless' they can live securely in dangerous times, until they have an opportunity for revenge. Brutus, who himself survives by playing the clown, agrees with him, and invites them all to sing. This frivolity is actually a serious image which gives a _political_ twist to the business of expressing emotion. Thus: it's only tyranny which claims the space, and indulgence, to make a performance of its desires; so the best way of resisting this sort of personal rule is to refuse its language, to refuse engagement; so the private person can stay safe by playing a role.

Heywood's play is much less powerful, as an experience, than _Macbeth_ precisely because it is interested in a _political discussion of_, rather than _emotional engagement with_, inner persons. The avant-garde theatricality being developed at the Globe is here balanced against the sort of clowning-around that Hamlet despised. In short, a very different product identity is defining itself against what is going on not only south of the river but also in Blackfriars. This is marked when Brutus asks his confederates to sing. He advises they choose no topics that touch on tyranny but instead do 'a song of the pretty suburbians' (Heywood 1888: 361). So on the stage of the unfashionable Red Bull, in the red-light district of Clerkenwell, a group of performers sing about suburban whores. It looks, out of context, like a 'metatheatrical' joke – aware of theatre's reputation for being immoral entertainment. But, in the context of the play, it's to be understood as a serious image of discontent, purposefully biding its time under tyranny by clowning – which amounts to a political choice to refrain from emotional expression.

Our three theatre buildings are thus offering their audiences different ways of viewing, different points of engagement. Those differences may be felt most keenly if we juxtapose, briefly, three characters. One of Tarquin's opponents is called Valerius: he survives by singing, and then plays a major part in the overthrow of the monarchy. As a character, he gets absorbed into the text of _Knight_, which abandons the anti-monarchism, but has fun with an old man who sings, laughs at disasters, infuriates his family and is utterly ineffectual. Which makes him sound rather like another old man, a tragic king who ran round the stage of the Globe with flowers in his hair, shouting obscenities. All three men respond to disaster in ways which seem improper. In the Globe's old man – King Lear – it's called madness; in the Blackfriars old man it's called humour, in the sense of a perverse caprice; in Valerius it's humour in the sense of a mask of jollity. Each man's condition requires, and grows out of, a specific relationship with an audience; each is staged within a few months and a few miles of the others; each excludes the possibility of the others. Similar material is being revisited and radically differentiated within a narrow world. Those humorous men don't displace each other; none of them is a more developed form of the others. Part of their force, indeed, derives from their grating coexistence.

Within the construction of theatrical product identities, characterization is a key area of contest. These old men were presumably interesting to the various theatres because they focus attention on the verbal expression of 'humour' or temperament on stage, which was one of the major elements in the depiction and definition of the person in drama. The other major element was to do with how the person occupied *space*. Ben Jonson described Edward Alleyn's strutting as 'scenical'. The strutting not only made a display of itself but produced an attitude towards, and use of, scenic space. If we had to explain why Macbeth doesn't feel like a strutting and fretting player, we might say that it was because he not only spoke, but occupied space, differently. How does this work?

The behaviour of characters is connected with the constraints of the space in which they find themselves; or, put more accurately, the actor constructs for the audience a sense of specific place by having the character respond to it. That spatial construction took place on an empty platform which shared the same light and air as the audience. If it was ranged round three sides of that platform, that audience could see itself framing the action, could see itself watching a man talking to an imaginary dagger. It also became implicated in that action at the moment when it agreed to imagine whatever fictional location was proposed – like imagining that a king sleeps in a nearby room – while the space in fact remains, at the same time, so obviously both empty and shared. In this sense the space is *fluid* – being whatever it is imagined at will. The alternative to the fluid sense of space here is to *fix* meaning, by using real objects, a table say, that define location and, consequently, set limits to a body's range of movements.[1] That fixing makes a sort of picture for the audience to look at – a ghost sitting at a table, say – and its visual pleasure creates a response that is very different from the feeling of the fluid empty space, in which someone might talk aloud to himself about the ghost. When the actor moves between fixed and fluid spaces he produces different feelings in an audience – not only because of conventions around the closeness or distance of the performer, and space which is special or shared, but also because of the different sorts of sensory engagement and pleasure which are offered. So it is due to space as much as to language that Macbeth feels different from Tamburlaine: not so much scenical strutting as, perhaps, scenical fretting.

Now in *Knight of the Burning Pestle* that movement between fixed and fluid spaces is curtailed. The play's effect depends on watching the Citizens watch the show. As performers they are in that fluid space which shares itself with the audience, and is separate from fixed fictional locations. The events of the play-within-the-play are never to be engaged with directly, since they're always the object of the Citizens' attention: pictures to be looked at. While the Citizens invite direct engagement from the audience, it's done with a deliberate imaginative poverty which is symptomized by them being confined, in that fluid space, to their stools. There's a paradox here: the play ostensibly blames the Citizens for pushing themselves into that space; but of course the play put them there in the first place, and in doing so itself opted to *limit* its own use of the most imaginatively fluid area of the Renaissance stage. It's as if it keeps an eye on itself to ensure that it never becomes like a female citizen who forgets that a stage is a stage.

A mistake like that in Blackfriars can cost you dear. If you enter a building run by a con man, a whore and an impertinent servant, as in any other theatre, you are to treat with suspicion their claims about the reality of what they show you. If you are either too greedy or too literal-minded to remain vigilant, you will end up disappointed, fleeced or, perhaps worse, laughed at. Such a monitory tale, about a house in Blackfriars run by tricksters, was acted at Blackfriars theatre by the very company – the King's Men – who in the not so distant past, in another place, had invited an audience to imagine that a wooden theatre was a battlefield. As a test of credibility that invitation is not so very different from persuading someone that the practice of alchemy can turn base metals into gold. To make an analogy between theatrical creation and the activities of an alchemist is to designate such creation specious, charming and fake. One of the jokes of Ben Jonson's play *The Alchemist* is that it leads you to expect that when the owner of the misused building returns, there will be an end to the tricks and disguises. But if your landlord is called Lovewit, you open up the possibility for a negotiation between his use of the building and its previous, witty, abuse. The impertinent servant can thus re-establish his relations with his master in a way which suits both their interests.

Excluded by these interests are the people who had visited the house as customers of the alchemist. These are the ones who are tricked, and they fall for it because they want to believe in what they have bought. The real audience, by contrast, knows that the appearance of, say, a queen of fairies has to be an illusion. The important thing about illusions is that, if they're to work, the desire to believe in them has to be real. And the more absurd the illusion is, the more forcefully real must be the desire that requires, say, a fairy queen to exist. The visitors are thus tricked because they are too preoccupied with their desires to know that what they're paying for is a pretence. The roles of customer and spectator are separate.

The more the customers become self-centred, the more comical the play gets, as the tricksters move faster to deal with the demands. This comic plotting depends on qualities of knowledge, awareness and wit. These are not the same pleasures as those of the wild but ignorant fantasizings. As lovers of wit themselves, the real spectators of that house in Blackfriars have a different relationship with it from its customers, just as the audience's pleasure at *Knight* was meant to come from its sense of its own distinction from the citizen-customers. Each play offers its audience a viewpoint that is consciously based on a particular version of theatre in which illusion is the opposite of truth. A true desire for illusion is itself laughable; people who suffer from such desires don't belong in theatrical houses in Blackfriars. For 'lovers of wit' – those who would be proper Blackfriars audiences – the distinction between customers and spectators is as follows: customers bring to the theatre their own conspicuous needs, but spectators conspicuously have no needs; the truth they know is that other people's truths are false. While the Citizen's Wife wants something without knowing what it is, lovers of wit might claim to know things without having wants.

Yet Lovewit also materially gains. Spectator at some level is customer, and without those hilarious desires the spectacle would not happen. In blurring these roles together, Jonson's play shows that it both depends on and is yet troubled by one particular feature of the performance–audience relationship. That relationship we have seen constructed through the expression of passion and the use of space. These will often be specific to particular theatres, promoting their product identity. Each form of audience engagement produces a need to distinguish what we have called customer and spectator: a need to separate sorts of desire and truth. Here then we find perhaps what's troubling Jonson: the theatrical product identity works powerfully because it gives the audience a sense of itself, as against others who are outsiders, by identifying correct and incorrect responses to theatre, normal and abnormal desires. Its work is thus *ideological*, and that's why there are so many insistent, various, claims to know truth from falsity. In the sprawling market-place of London theatres this ideological work is repeated time and again. In the competition of product identities there could be no overall agreed way of doing things. For *one theatre's truth is another theatre's lie*; one person's alchemy is another's witchcraft. Truth ceases to exist outside of a series of various rival propositions. The desire for something single that can be called theatrical truth defines itself, variously, as loving wit, or holding a mirror to nature, or just wanting. As the Scottish recipient of a real set of magical illusions might say, two truths are told . . . or three or four.

So while a fairy queen at Blackfriars in 1610 is a hilarious fake, the apparent resurrection of a dead queen the next year at the Globe feels as if it comes from sincere longing. The penitent King of Sicilia has, at the end of *The Winter's Tale*, been taken to the house of a woman called Paulina. There, in the company of his returned daughter, Perdita, Paulina will discover to him a statue of his dead wife. Leontes finds the art to be so lifelike that it is almost real. When he touches it, he discovers that it does indeed breathe. This act of touching is not here a substitute for the real thing. The spectacle is itself real, the grim gap between art and life doesn't exist. As it is organized by the scene, the emphasis doesn't fall on Paulina's trickery (for that's what it is), but on the wondering discovery that the shadow has substance, the statue is real. The sense of wonder comes from a belief in an impossible truth, in a narrative which values trust and belief as interpersonal qualities. The final scene has no place for the play's clown figure, a cheating ballad-seller. Kingly theatre, if we may so call it, has a specialness that separates it from pedlar's trifles. Much of that quality of specialness derives from the scene being set in the only space in the play-world specifically designated female. At the centre of its image of truth is a triangle of woman, female friend and daughter, all positioned so that the natural bonding comes to feel *sacramental* – like officiant, statue and kneeling supplicant. Leontes, a new-made man, faces the theatre of the future.

We would have to change theatres (though not company or author) in order to hear the father's voice sardonically break through the wonder with the riposte: ''tis new to thee.'

## 3   A Mortal God

It is probable that the actor who expressed wonder at a statue coming alive was the same man who, in a different hat, advised players to imitate nature. As a star, however, his fame was associated not so much with the sharp-tongued persona of the philosophic prince as with the performing that displayed a penitent king submitting himself to a woman.

Richard Burbage was famous for submerging himself in each role that he took. In thus allowing a variety of fictions to take him over, he would have confirmed the worst fears of an early critic of actors: 'Are they not variable in hart, as they are in their part?' (in Barish 1981: 104). For even in the year that he played such affecting royal submission, Burbage helped to organize the theatrical penetration into Blackfriars of the King's Men. With two houses to play in, the company consolidated its success by willingly adapting itself to the different identities of each theatre. Precisely by being variable in heart the company, like its star, gained advantage in the market-place. This apparent paradox was something which a defender of theatre, rather than any of its critics, could understand. Writing about Richard Perkins, the star who succeeded Burbage, Thomas Heywood praised his modesty and industry. The royal submission, the staged submergence of the self, is for Heywood not a sign of promiscuous variability but of hard work.

Seen from the time of Burbage and Perkins, earlier performers showed too much attention to the self. The Elizabethan comedian Richard Tarlton was described as a 'self-resembling' performer: his acting seemed to have insisted that you remain aware of the clown Tarlton behind the roles he took. Similarly there's a suggestion that the technique of his contemporary, Edward Alleyn, worked continually, through his 'scenical strutting', to insert himself at the centre of the scene. Indeed that emphasis on centrality was specifically engineered in the role with which Alleyn was closely associated. Tamburlaine first appears as a shepherd-bandit who has taken captive a princess of Persia, her train and treasure. The scene is organized so that Tamburlaine dominates it vocally and is visually at its centre: captured treasure moves from the edge to the middle of the stage, where the shepherd dresses himself as knight. The visual power of this transformation is confirmed when the Persian commander who has been sent to attack Tamburlaine is won over to him by the effect of his presence. That presence, carefully built by vocal and muscular rhythms (including 'strutting'), has the feel of a personal charisma that naturally draws all eyes towards it. We could say a stare is born.

In the performance of a star like Alleyn, centrality ceases to be a mere matter of position and becomes transformed into a quality, centredness. This centredness is for the dramatist Webster the defining quality of an actor: 'sit in a full Theater, and you will think you see so many lines drawn from the circumference of so many ears, whiles the Actor is the Centre' (in Bruster 1992: 6). The interest here in sound is explored in Webster's play *The Duchess of Malfi*: at the end of the fourth act the Duchess is strangled by order of her brother Ferdinand. *Visually* the focus isn't completely held on the Duchess. She has knelt between her executioners, making herself the centre of a picture of martyrdom. Pulling us away from that picture is the presence of the disguised agent, Bosola – unknown to the Duchess but known to the audience, in a fluid space that is outside, but threatens, the Duchess's specialness. By contrast, *vocally*, the uninterrupted rhythms of the Duchess's valediction make her central, which in turn gives tragic grandeur to her righteousness. Between the visual and the vocal, centredness is fragile yet strained for. When at the end of the next act the Duchess's brothers die, any sense of centredness is missing. The stage is visually divided between a group of courtiers and the Cardinal's death-struggle with Bosola; the sound is chaotic because his cries are treated as fake. Into the struggle comes the now mad Ferdinand, brandishing his sword over his head in a gesture that is both grandly heroic and a total misrecognition of the scene in front of him. It's a grim joke about centredness.

The design of the part of Ferdinand, especially in its closing moments, is such that the more forcefully it is played, the more dangerously unpredictable he becomes, both thrilling and decentred. The part was taken by Burbage, the very man who specialized not in self-centring but in submerging the self. Thus in the contrast between the death of the Duchess and the death of Ferdinand there's a movement from self-centring tragic grandeur to grimly jokey decentredness, and that movement is felt as loss, as a world which dwindles from personal bravery to the Court of the sick prince. In her death scene, the Duchess, in a moment of temporary resurrection, has a moral effect on Bosola which is powerful enough to turn him from cynical malcontent into active revenger. It assimilates him into her picture. The image is of woman as moral and spiritual authority, recalling the feeling of Leontes in the presence of his resurrected wife. But in Webster's play that image is not the end point: there is a post-Duchess world that now has neither reverence nor centre. In such a world the impression of centredness can only be supplied by something as fake as theatre.

To see it that way is to find another meaning in Webster's definition of the actor. The Duchess's death partly owes its force to the reaction to it of Bosola, just as it's Leontes' reaction which gives a feeling of the power of the living statue. If the actor is at the centre of a full theatre, it's that fullness which gives power to the centre. When a theatre fills in order to see an actor perform, the audience volunteers to accept the totally fictional authority of the actor. Which means that Burbage was not just self-submerging but was also, to his fans, a 'mortal god'.

Shadowing this discussion of acting there is a larger question about theatre's relation to society. As *The Duchess of Malfi* sees it, a world was coming into being in which the staging of personal grandeur was neither possible nor appropriate. From this it follows that when people willingly accept the authority of someone who has no real grandeur, they lose possession of their own individuality. This development of Webster's point comes from the dramatist who noted Burbage's godlike standing with his fans: in an early 1620s play, Middleton made the moment of adoring spectatorship into a crucial narrative twist. Two women watch the procession of the Duke of Florence, and the younger one says, 'Methought he saw us.' To which her mother-in-law replies, 'That's everyone's conceit that sees a duke' (Middleton 1975: 33). The younger one is right, and, as she finds out to her cost, by looking at him she has empowered him not only to look at her but also to take sexual possession of her: as he says to her later, 'You know me, you have seen me; here's a heart / Can witness I have seen thee' (p. 63). The Duke justifies his personal desires by invoking the accepted norms of business and courtesy; he fulfils his individual wants by apparently submerging his individuality into society. Bianca, his victim in the ambivalently titled *Women Beware Women*, learns that it will also suit her best to accept the norms of the world.

Middleton's vision of a world which demands submergence, if not loss, of self leads him to develop a form of theatre writing and playing which will be appropriate to this world. The explorations of centredness in Webster's work are thus developed, a decade later, into a mode of what we might call decentred characterization. A good example of this at work is provided by another woman whose personal life is mapped out for her. While Isabella is being inspected by the foolish Ward whom she is destined to marry, she speaks aside:

> But that I have th' advantage of the fool,
> As much as woman's heart can wish and joy at,
> What an infernal torment 'twere to be
> Thus bought and sold, and turned and pried into; when alas
> The worse bit is too good for him! And the comfort is

'Has but a cater's place on't, and provides
All for another's table.

(p. 112)

The stage picture, of a woman treated like a horse at market, forces an agreement with Isabella's anger, and hence with her adulterous project to cheat the fool. But her speech feels strangely detached, not a direct expression of feeling: she speaks as 'woman' in general as much as 'I' in particular; what is happening isn't a torment but could be; the 'I' thinks of itself in terms of 'advantage', learnt competition. Over half the speech is an extended metaphor wittily describing the Ward's sexual inadequacy. Within the metaphor Isabella's own body is food, moving from one man to another, in a world of shopping and service. And the fool is stupid because he doesn't know how to enjoy the food. He is mocked within a scheme of male heterosexual pleasure from which Isabella's self, if not her body, is effaced. Yet she is there, of course, speaking the satire, inviting us to watch how the men look at her even while she is looked at. But we have come some distance since Tamburlaine so fully, satisfyingly, placed himself at the centre of attention. Here the inspected woman encourages us to look at the men looking at her; at the same time her speech deflects any sense of centred self; so she becomes like an object, looked at by a look she mocks. This mode of performing restrains itself from full expressivity, so it is an appropriate ending when Middleton does the tragic deaths as a court masque gone wrong: the climax of blood-letting is, as it were, a failed performance.

The play's scepticism about the pleasure of being looked at connects with its interest in relating the shape of self to the organization of society; in short, how will interlocks with rule. This combination of elements returns us to the idea that something larger is shadowing the explorations of acting modes. We can focus on it more sharply by using Burbage once again, at his death. Middleton noted, somewhat provocatively, that his funeral drew larger crowds than the other major funeral in 1619, that of Queen Anne. The observation gives a new twist to the idea of acting star as a mortal god, for the only official claim on that title may be said to be that of the king: James I rather heavy-handedly insisted that his attempt at personal rule was justified by his special relationship with God. By 1619, however, James was quite widely unpopular and the ceremonies of kingship were hard put to it to sustain the magic of monarchy. He was an actor at the centre of, so to speak, an empty theatre. The notion of a royal actor has a truth to it, in the sense that for would-be absolutist rulers, as for performers, their career prospects are apparently bound up with the successful promotion of their personal charisma. On the other hand, monarchs, however unpopular, still have huge resources of power which are not available to actors. So that while Burbage might have a more authoritative 'godlike' presence than James I, he was in fact much more vulnerable. Performance was used by authority and it told lies about authority; but it also clearly had a power that was somehow separate from authority. These circumstances mean that, for theatre workers in the early decades of the seventeenth century, questions about acting lead into questions about rule.

These questions provided the whole substance of a play put on during one of those tense hiccups in royal rule, the transition from one monarch to another. James I died in 1625; in 1626 the King's Men performed Philip Massinger's *The Roman Actor*. The play, set in Roman times, is an extended exploration of the relationship between theatre and authority. It opens with a company of actors defending their profession under the tyrannical rule of the emperor, Domitian. Ancient arguments about the moral power of drama are put: drama encourages its audience to emulate heroic acts, it touches the guilty. When an actor recalls 'In a tragedy of ours' a 'guilty hearer's' conscience being pricked, it's like the King's Men remembering back twenty-five years to *Hamlet*. Later on, the action restages one of the classic instances of drama's power: the Empress has become so erotically obsessed with the star actor, Paris, that she forgets she is watching a performance; she leaves her seat, like the Emperor in *Faustus*, to prevent the character killing himself. But while in *Faustus* – or *Knight of the Burning Pestle* – the joke is on the moved spectator, here the actors are clearly the clients of a powerful audience, highly vulnerable to the audience's desires. So Paris is threatened when the Empress insists 'Thou must be really, in some degree, / The thing thou dost present. – Nay, do not tremble; / We seriously believe it' (Massinger 1887–9: II, 26, 62). At first sight this moment is a restatement of the idea that drama and society are necessarily separate: that it's not the fault of actors if their performance touches the guilty, that they have no control over an audience that chooses to watch sinfully. But the Empress isn't wholly wrong. The changes to the real lives of actors, evident in success stories like the King's Men, show that, over time, the business of performing can alter the status if not the identity of those who perform. And increasingly that performing was specializing in such effects as silent 'trembling'. To produce such an effect the actor must really be taken over by a learnt muscular discipline so that, however it is motivated, the body actually trembles. So in that silent moment drama concedes what it officially denies: far from being disinterested and emblematic, performance really is what it presents. Which is what makes it successful, and answerable to rulers.

Like his Empress, Domitian has an interest in performance. He forces a political enemy to listen to his former wife singing, commanding that he listen in silence, and then makes the silence permanent by beheading him. Later he presides over a public torture, giving instruction that the crowd – and hence audience – be watched to ensure no one expresses sorrow. This control over audience response is not only a repressive action: it also sets up the tyrant as organizer as much as performer. The theatre of rule stages the ruler; the Roman emperor is also the Roman Actor, a performer who watches himself watched. But in the torture scene Domitian himself becomes the most disturbed, frustrated by the victims' refusal to express pain. He *needs*, psychically and politically, a performance of feeling. This need causes him to enter the actors' drama. Domitian loves Paris as a performer; but when he discovers the Empress's lust for the actor, honour requires that Paris be killed. The contradiction between the demands of love and honour is solved by a performance. Domitian takes the place of one of the actors, but refuses to use a stage sword, so at the correct moment in the imitated action he inflicts real death. If it makes the actor special, this mode of killing, designed 'to distinguish / My Paris from all others' (p. 70), makes the ruler special too. In this way performance enables the absolute ruler apparently to solve contradictions which arise from his manner of ruling.

That is to put it much more abstractly than Domitian feels it. He describes his method of killing as something which protects Paris' body from the hangman's hook and keeps his limbs whole. The death enables him to possess that body for himself while at the same time giving it distinction. This is not so much artistic patronage of a favoured performer as *erotic investment*. Which is why an imitation won't do: it has to be a real body, really dying. The actor knows this. When he is asked if he is ready, Paris replies that Death's 'cold embraces should not bring an ague / To any of my faculties, till his pleasures / Were served and satisfied' (p. 69). In the picture of an actor who is so special that he satisfies the ruler's pleasure even as he dies, the theatre has produced a remarkably ambivalent image of its own achievement. It consciously sets itself apart from the nasty performances organized by tyrants, and it admits that its success doesn't come from moral emblems and historical tales but from the production of *feeling*. Paradoxically, however, by producing feeling it becomes more, rather than less, interesting to those people who wield real power in the specific conditions that are described as 'personal rule'. For those conditions produce anxieties about guaranteeing that feeling is real – that people are what they present – and fantasies about completely possessing those who are looked at with favour. As the Roman actors of 1626 grimly see it, theatre owes its success to the production of pleasures which are not separate from, but shaped by, the contradictions and needs of personal rule.

They had no need to be too grim about it, from a commercial point of view, since over the previous fifteen years plays offering these pleasures had become very popular. We can take further our account of modes of performing, and the linked matter of theatre and rule, by looking at a typical example. At around the time when the most popular dramatist with the King's Men was heading into retirement, the two dramatists who would inherit his status wrote for the company a play called *A King and No King*. It was a provocative title for 1611, when James I was outshone in many eyes by the charisma of his eldest son, and sure enough Beaumont and Fletcher's play takes for its hero an unstable absolute ruler, called Arbaces. He finds himself desiring Panthea, whom he thinks is his sister, and although he decrees that she is not his kin he can't stick by his decision. He may, as an absolute ruler, be able to make law; but he is also in the grip of something more absolute, a desire or fate that operates beyond his control: 'who does know / But that my loathed fate may turn about' (Beaumont and Fletcher 1964: 73). That consternation at a turning-about which happens to oneself is a key state in this sort of play. It's as if the interest is not in Macbeth plotting, but in Macbeth amazed to find himself plotting – character seems to have become split. The unpredictable turnings-about are the workings of what is emotionally rather than politically absolute, and have the effect of dislocating individuals from commonly agreed norms of social interaction. They are pushed towards what they can't name or categorize: as Panthea says, 'in myself I find – I know not what / To call it, but it is a great desire' (p. 99). Passions grow with a force of their own, watched by the subjects they take over. This leads to capricious, obsessive and inconstant behaviour. It typically produces scenes like the one in which Panthea welcomes her brother Arbaces back from Armenia: he suddenly refuses to recognize her, so she kneels in silence, eight other people stand silently, and Arbaces and the Armenian king speak separate asides. Set up like this, the more fully expressive the asides are, the more embarrassing they feel to the audience.

Performance becomes the time when nothing happens, when disagreements or contradictions are held in stasis, potent but without solution. Thus Panthea looks at her impossible turnings-about:

> should I excuse
> My mother's fault, I should set light a life
> In losing which a brother and a king
> Were taken from me. If I seek to save
> That life so lov'd, I lose another life
> That gave me being – I shall lose a mother.
>
> (pp. 28–9)

The substance of the drama is, in short, not the imitation of action but the formulation of paradox. Hence there is an interest, typically, in brother–sister story-lines which neatly bring natural feeling and legal inhibition into insoluble contradiction. The job of the performance, which is perhaps its appeal, in these paradoxically named 'tragicomedies' is to restate continually the terms of a contradiction, to explore their variants, to sharpen them into paradox, to replay them fetishistically – but not to imagine any way of abolishing them. Thus Panthea's only solution seems to be death, until, right at the end of the play and from somewhere outside of it, a hitherto hidden fact makes an ending possible. So what was so dizzyingly 'turning about' can at last be held still. The sudden new twist or discovery at the end of a tragicomedy became one of the genre's most notorious features. But the genre can't do without it –

precisely because it is the only way of ending a play that is so remorselessly organized around the eternal to-and-fro movement of paradox. That continual movement and its abrupt termination produce an overall sensation that's far from cosily complete. As Arbaces describes it, and he should know, 'the whole story / Would be a wilderness to lose thyself / Forever' (p. 130).

If this sense of performance-as-wilderness is just emerging with *A King and No King* in 1611, let's see where it got to by moving forward twenty years, into the closing decade of licensed theatres, in a play called, aptly enough, *The Traitor*. The story-line is fairly standard, involving lust and treachery in Florence. But the play takes time off to make an image of what it's doing: when the paranoid Depazzi wants to rehearse his defence in the event of being arrested, he instructs his servant Rogero to imagine himself as prosecutor. Rogero, as an inferior, naturally has problems with this, so Depazzi threatens: 'I will beat you if you wo'not imagine at my bidding' (Shirley 1965: 38). Once he gets started, however, Rogero discovers his part as the State's 'nimble tongu'd orator' and begins to speak at great length, inventing elaborate crimes of which to accuse Depazzi and not allowing him to interrupt. He has become, says his master, 'transported'. Depazzi can only get his servant to stop imagining by beating him, which is where Rogero started: 'I ha' done. Imagine I ha' done. I but obey'd your lordship, whose baton I find stronger than my imagination. My lord, you will answer this, to strike i'th'court thus!' (p. 42). Even as Rogero's performance is officially ending, the imagined court is still there, coexisting with Depazzi's 'real' space. It is as if, in his relation with his master, once Rogero is transported he cannot return to where he began.

Depazzi learns that a master may order a performance to take place but, once it starts, it will not necessarily follow an expected shape, nor will his relation to it remain under his control. It will exceed the function of serving the master's interest and the transported servant will no longer be in his right place. The performance not only brings into being an imaginary courtroom but it enables a servant to feel himself fully possessed with the authority of religion and commonwealth: 'I will speak truth and I will be heard, and no man else in this place' (p. 42). At the moment of its delivery it is impossible to say that the servant doesn't have that authority. Which means that the *real problem with performance* is, in brief, and as Hamlet knew, that it imagines *too much*. It gets out of control.

There are other performances besides Rogero's: a scheme to spread rumours of the duke's death and a moral masque which indicts the duke. Both use performance for political purpose, to make things happen; each is more interesting as politics than as performance. In their contrast with Rogero the play is perhaps articulating its sense of drama's relation to a world which in 1631 was already full of political image-making. Rogero's performance is engaging because he becomes transported and excessive and ceases to be answerable. The play chooses to – maybe has to – make its statement about

performance in a 'comic scene', a scene set apart from tragic decorum, without
narrative purpose. But that sense of the *purposeless* is deeply important to its
tragic imagery. The death of the heroine, Amidea, at the hands of her brother,
Sciarrha, is organized as a picture. She kneels and veils her face; he stabs her;
she unveils and looks at the wound. The effect is produced by the methodical
manner of the violence in conjunction with the excessive – purposeless – detail
of the veil. Its meaning, however, can't be precisely fixed. There are a number
of associations in circulation: a woman veiling herself, making herself 'head-
less', in order to be penetrated by the knife; lifting her veil, reclaiming her
identity, not to look at the man but to contemplate her wound. What would
be simply a scene of tragic confrontation between brother and sister is moved,
precisely by the veil – the purposeless detail – into a playing out of something
psychically deep which pertains to men's relations to women. Its methodical
organization gives it the artifice of 'play', but it is very serious play, necessarily
inscrutable. Unlike the political performances, but like Rogero, this performance is powerful because it has nothing purposeful to say. The play is thus not
only a wilderness where a king is no king, but it is an imagining which is
necessarily traitorous.

   The drama which so inscrutably veils its head is far from being on the
cultural margins. *The Traitor* was done by Queen Henrietta's Men, managed
by the entrepreneur Christopher Beeston. Having reached the centre of the
citadel, this drama denies its capacity to teach, refuses to have a purpose. It has
brought with it a favourite stage gesture: it was there at the close of *A King* and
it occurs again between Sciarrha and Amidea: 'The duke, thou know'st, did
love thee.' 'Ha!' 'Nay do not start already' (p. 84). A 'start' is an involuntary
movement, caused by the force of feeling that responds to a revelation. It is
often treated as something that is unnecessary to the process of the action ('do
not start'); and it shows the body in the grip of feeling, a spasm outside
consciousness. As a way of staging the person these starts may be contrasted to
Alleyn's strutting, with its presence and centredness. Which suggests a nice
irony about the development of Renaissance drama, for when it was culturally
emerging it strutted and when it got to the centre it started.


# 4   The Crack in the Works

In recognition of his work, *The Traitor's* author, James Shirley, was granted the
office of Valet of the Chamber – which makes something of a contrast with
Henslowe's position all those years ago in regard to bears. Rewards were
forthcoming in the early 1630s from a monarchy that had interests in theatre.
The queen liked play-acting, and the king collected plays, read them, and
drew bits to the censor's attention. Play-writing was no longer the preserve of
jumped-up craftsmen's sons and students. It was an acceptable demonstration

of one's courtly accomplishment. It was also a useful source of money and, as we have seen, the courtier Davenant, for one, learnt a lesson from all those less than genteel people who had got rich through theatre.

So in 1633, when William Prynne, the Presbyterian cleric, attacked the theatre, for all the old reasons, it was now readily taken as an attack on monarchy. Prynne himself was brutally punished, but his arguments were also answered in a deliberately public way. The answer consisted of a procession and masque, involving large numbers of, mainly, lawyers and students of the four London law schools, the Inns of Court. The event staged the interconnectedness of ruling institutions and groups, showing off their wealth and taste, in a display of what we might call a confident hegemony. The name of this event early in February 1634 was *The Triumph of Peace*, and its author the same who wrote *The Traitor*. To assist him he had the composer William Lawes, who later that year worked with Milton on his *Masque . . . at Ludlow Castle*, and the masque designer Inigo Jones. For some years Jones had been using masques for avant-garde experiments with the use of scenic perspective in performance. He found that audiences could be given considerable pleasure from the illusion that they were able to survey a space which both extended for a great distance and yet was satisfyingly ordered. Furthermore that pleasure could be given by degrees, so that when the perspective sightlines were extended into the audience the most eminent spectator would get a visual effect that was not available to anyone else, seeming to direct the show at him alone. This was clearly very different from the mêlée around the Globe platform. The visual effect, taken together with the fact that a masque was done for one performance only, in front of a selected audience, at a huge cost, gave the whole event the magic of being unrepeatable, ineffable. By contrast, the procession was done a second time because it was so successful, which made it a somewhat cruder display of wealth and power. Prynne – who might be seen as the event's only begetter – was also mutilated twice, which makes for an even cruder display of the same things.

That procession was, in part, a symbolic attempt by the four Inns of Court to disavow their embarrassing Presbyterian member. What is also significant about it is that the Inns students were one of the main consumer groups of theatre, not only as spectators but now, in a much newer way, as purchasers of playbooks. It was indeed a proper part of the event that it itself became a successful book, being printed three times in one year. In earlier decades, while the State might have commemorated its ceremonials in published form, plays themselves had not been printed on any regular basis, since the companies which owned them wanted to protect their repertoires from pirating and rival performance. But towards the end of the 1620s plays were circulating – having a cultural existence – as books. This circulation gave them a profitable economic afterlife. Thus, for example, in 1623 there seems to have been an unusual amount of theatrical activity, involving company reorganizations, and the

Palsgrave's Men put on a number of new plays. In a rival company the business manager and an important 'sharer' decided to arrange publication that year of the works of one of their most successful dramatists, now dead. So the book of Shakespeare's plays appeared. Twenty years afterwards, with the theatres closed, some actors found an afterlife as booksellers.

Playbooks came to be officially recognized as part of the capital assets of the company. In June 1637 the King's Men, on a second attempt, apparently secured their ownership of their plays, in a rapidly developing and cutthroat market-place. The Lord Chamberlain instructed that none were to be printed unless there was 'some Certificate in writing under the handes of John Lowen & Joseph Taylor for the Kings servantes & of Christopher Bieston for ye Kings & Queenes young Company' (in Bentley 1941: I, 54). Lowin and Taylor were leading actors; as Domitian and Paris in *The Roman Actor* they had explored the erotics of theatre. The other name is, as we know, the person whose sharp practices turned management into a profession. By the time his son succeeded him, managerial control of art-works had become endearingly aesthetic: the writer Francis Kirkham remembered that 'to the admiration of the whole Company' William Beeston had 'judiciously discoursed of Poësie' (Bentley 1968: VI, 71).

After the theatres had closed, drama lived on, legitimately, as books. Of these, one of the most celebrated was the collected works of Beaumont and Fletcher, published in 1647. In it we find again John Lowin's name, heading a list of theatrical signatures to the volume's dedication. The name of the man without whom no King's Men's play could be published appears in a volume printed by a professional bookseller–publisher. This publisher, Humphrey Moseley, had by this date become a specialist in drama. By 1646 he had bought up thirty-eight of the protected King's Men's plays; by 1653 he had bought another thirteen. The King's Men, who had taken seriously the ban on performing, needed to sell off assets. Their purchase by Moseley was, as Maureen Bell has shown, a considerable economic gamble. He was counting on the fact that there had developed a readership for plays and that this readership had disposable income. His gamble paid off, and he went on to a successful publishing career, specializing in drama and poetry. In the process he developed a form of publisher's catalogue: so we might say that the pioneer of drama collections was also a pioneer of advertising.

The Beaumont and Fletcher volume, on which so much was gambled, was carefully put together. As a collection it was an unusual, and very expensive, format for play printing. But it also had extensive prefatory material written by friends and patrons of the dramatists and actors associated with the plays. This material is conspicuously royalist in feel, and it links together celebrated writers and public figures. The volume is dedicated to Philip, Earl of Pembroke and Montgomery, the Lord Chamberlain who protected the King's Men's plays, specifically named here as patron of the 'sweet Swan of Avon' –

which links back to another famous collection. Shirley's preface notes that 'It is not so remote in Time, but very many gentlemen may remember these authors.' The author of *The Triumph of Peace* had, as we know, a nose for hegemonic display. The reader, he says, ought to 'congratulate thy own happiness, that in the silence of the Stage thou hast a liberty to read these inimitable plays.' In the act of reading, a lost hegemony may be re-found: not so much a substitute for watching plays, reading is a way of circumventing government repression, a way of rediscovering 'liberty'. With this inside it, Moseley's gamble is more than a collected edition. In a world fluttering with political pamphlets it is an expensive printed object which in its very collectedness invokes a network of hegemonic interest. As a publisher Moseley was transforming what may be remembered into what could be owned; and in owning this drama the culture of the class with a disposable income could apparently express and preserve its own wholeness – which had the mutually obliging effect of expressing and preserving businessmen like Moseley.

If the drama we've looked at seems rather recalcitrant to preservation in print, its transition to it becomes more possible – indeed more *appropriate* – when you follow Shirley's identification of the significant effects of Beaumont and Fletcher:

it cannot be denied but that the young spirits of the Time, whose Birth and Quality made them impatient of the sowrer wayes of education, have from the attentive hearing these pieces, got ground in point of wit and carriage of the most severely employed Students. (in McLuskie 1989: 206)

The plays provide education both through and of *wit*. It is wit which distinguishes – supposedly – one class's entertainment from another's. In a prologue written for the Globe, Shirley makes show of distress that the play is not on at Blackfriars:

Our Author did not calculate his Play,
For this Meridian; The Bank-Side he knowes
Is far more skilful at the ebbes and flowes
Of water then of Wit.
(in Gurr 1987: 189)

'Wit' is not only one of the main criteria now for assessing drama but it also marks cultural divergence. Shirley's witty play will include 'No shews', 'no Target fighting', 'No Bawd'ry, nor no ballads', 'No clown, no squibs, no divells' (p. 189). These proscribed items had their home in the Red Bull, notorious for clowning and fight scenes, noisy devils, drums and trumpets.

Setting itself meticulously apart from visual and aural pleasures, from an over-insistent physicality, wit found a home in the written. As far back as 1619 a new company at the Red Bull, conscious perhaps of changes happening around them, had tried to modify the repertoire by offering the audience 'Sence and Words', to make the stage 'reform'd, and free / From the loud Clamors it was wont to bee' (in Bentley 1968: VI, 242). When wit offers to reform the stage, to define drama against clamours, and thus to carry the banner of freedom, there's a sense of a literary theatre culture discovering itself – taking pleasure in commenting on drama, practising choice, displaying discrimination, giving its interest physical form in the collection of playbooks. Shirley put it this way:

> we are
> In this wits Market, furnish'd with all ware,
> But please your selves, and buy what you like best,
> Some deep commodities mingle with the rest.
>
> (in Butler 1987: 104)

Wit doesn't just enable plays to become commodities. It exercises itself in the freedom to shop.

The practising of choice can sometimes amount to articulating dissent. The dramatist Richard Brome mocked Suckling's play *Aglaura* (1637) for its format as a printed object:

> By this large Margent did the Poet mean
>   To have a Comment writ upon his Scene?
> Or is it that the Ladies, who ne're look
>   On any but a Poeme or Play-book,
> May, in each page, have space to scribble down
>   When such a Lord, or Fashion comes to Town.
>
> (Brome 1873: preface)

Far from preserving drama in fashionable society, the book allows that society to stamp itself onto the play, turning play into fashion accessory. The expensive format removed the play from a 'sociable' existence: *Aglaura* 'by her Giant-bulk this only gaines, / Perchance in Libraries to hang in chaines' (1873: preface). The rage at the commodity had wider implications: Brome attacked Suckling, who was a courtier, a second time in May 1640, in a play which seemed to criticize royal policies. This led to the closing of the Cockpit Theatre, the arrest of the actors and the eventual replacement of the manager, whom Brome admired, by another courtier, Davenant.

These political tensions within fashionable theatre culture insisted on themselves even at the supposed centre of control. Charles I had come across a passage in a play by Massinger that he wanted cut out. It's about enforcing arbitrary taxation. The Master of the Revels, Sir Henry Herbert, copied it into his office book and commented: 'This is a peece taken out of Phillip Messengers play, called *The King and the Subject*, and entered here forever to bee remembered by my son and those that cast their eyes on it, in honour of Kinge Charles, my master' (in Edwards et al. 1981: 113). The play itself is now lost: so, ironically, Herbert had honoured his monarch by preserving for posterity the very lines that Charles wanted to lose for posterity. But Herbert and his family had some experience of brushing up against the arbitrariness of the Stuarts. He had given a licence to a play which in 1624 – the year after the Shakespeare First Folio – caused one of the greatest theatrical sensations of the period. It was Middleton's *Game at Chesse*, which attacked the plan to marry Prince Charles, as he was, to a Spaniard. Theatre censorship existed, supposedly, to keep plays like this off the stage. But the Herbert family was, historically, sympathetic to the militant Protestant politics expressed by the play – as were Middleton's moneyed contacts in the mercantile city. When it finally arrives at the cultural centre, then, commercial drama finds itself walking on an already political stage.

That political stage could also be called 'wit's market', since everybody, whatever their faction, had the money to shop. In the wealth display produced as the artistic answer to William Prynne it's very clear who the outsiders are. The figures of Peace, Law and Justice have sixteen sons, male masquers – 'No foreign persons' – who are presented to the royal audience: 'The children of your reign, not blood' (Shirley 1888: 460). They do a dance, a song is sung, and the masquers dance again:

> after which they again retire to the scene; at which they no sooner arrive, but there is heard a great noise, and confusion of voices within, some crying, 'We will come in,' others 'Knock 'em down, call the rest of the guard;' then a crack is heard in the works, as if there were some danger by some piece of the machines falling; this continued a little time, there rush in a Carpenter, a Painter, one of the Black guard, a Tailor, the Tailor's Wife, an Embroiderer's Wife, a Feather maker's Wife, and a Property man's Wife. (p. 462)

The people who've burst in think they have a right to see the masque since they have supplied the scenery and props: as the Painter says, 'let us challenge a privilege; those stairs were of my painting' (p. 462). Privilege is, as it were, challenged on the grounds of moral equality: 'what though we be no ladies, we are Christians in these clothes, and the king's subjects, God bless us' (p. 463). But they are laughed at, and, as the Tailor observes, the masquers won't perform while the intruders are present. So they need to find a way of getting off: they decide the appropriate thing is to do a dance, and after it, 'let us go off cleanly, and somebody will think this was meant for an antimasque' (p. 463). When they've gone the masque starts again.

The point about the market-place, as people were coming to realize, is that just because you've contributed to it that doesn't necessarily give any rights in regard to it. And, on this occasion when not even the market can be left to itself, the masque defines a space that isn't for sharing, even by the most loyal subjects. With their pride in craftsmanship and their respect for artistic decorum, it is the enthusiastic tradesfolk rather than the anti-theatrical Prynne who threaten the ineffable flow of the masque. They know all about performance in terms of its spectacle and rules, everything – except for its magic, that thing we might call its hegemonic place. The presence of the masque will only – or can only – exist in the intruders' absence. In its need to *stage* that exclusion, rather than silently to assume it, Shirley's masque may have constructed for a particular social group a Triumph that can't at the same time be Peace.

Indeed it's the lack of peace – the noise, the bawdy, the jigging, all the Red Bull antics of the intruders – which constitutes one of the high points of the entertainment. When a performance high point consists of embarrassment about being on stage, you can hear the sound of cracking in the cultural works. That sound gets louder when it is insiders like you, rather than outsiders, who are the ones embarrassed. For instance, it is red faces all round in a scene from Richard Brome's 1641 play, *A Jovial Crew*. At one point the forces of law enter, to put a stop to an illegal performance done by a group of social outsiders, beggars. What they find instead is that it is a group of insiders, genteel young people dressed up as beggars. To make matters worse, two of these insiders – the women – are really trying to be beggars. They are doing this because they feel their lives are stifled and their liberty limited 'in our father's rule and government'; they want for themselves the 'absolute freedom, such as the very beggars have'. So they resolve to become beggars, not as play-acting but for real. And, as happens in this sort of drama, the role takes them over and compels their male lovers to go along too. The women's attempt to escape their place in patriarchal rule expresses a yearning for something authentic, for a freedom that is 'absolute' in that it is outside of a familiar, repressive social structure, the thing represented by real outsiders.

But while the women's yearnings may be real, their attempts to change their social class are a comical failure. Which leads them to where we first found them, dressed up as beggars under the gaze of their own class's agents of law, hilariously exposed, while the real beggars have slipped away. By now, however, the play's audience has found that what it thinks is real has a habit of slipping away, of not being there when you expect it. When the would-be beggars try to use real beggar language, they compulsively repeat their re-hearsed phrases; it is as if, like so many of the other characters, they are trapped into the very language they use, subjected to its verbal patterns and social attitudes. This means that the main pleasure offered by a very funny play doesn't come from the adventure of characters and story going somewhere new, but from the precision with which they remain meticulously the same. So the whole thing feels artificial, rehearsed, self-conscious. The play repeatedly refers to its own project and ends up, appropriately, by restaging its own story of gentlefolk as enacted by beggars. As part of the enactment the two would-be beggar women act themselves: it's at this point we realize that reality, far from slipping away, has been in front of us all the time and what it consists of is repetition, rehearsal, replay.

This makes things rather complicated. For when reality and play are clearly separate, you can keep play under control by preventing it or prosecuting it. The Justice of the Peace who watches the beggars' play is certainly on the look-out for any mockery of justice; and there will have been more people besides the JP whose ears will have pricked up when the beggars' Prologue uses those words which in 1641 were so highly charged – Court, city and country. But the Prologue disarmingly abjures any interest in these things, and the JP falls asleep. He wakes when he hears the word 'justice', but he is assured that the play is now over. Which is only half true, for the beggars' play has ceased to be clearly separate. It has begun to blur into the rest of the play, which is still going on. So the attempt to police references to such things as justice becomes complicated when reality and play get tangled together. It's a tricky tangle, because while you might assume that reality's power to prosecute makes it more powerful than play, play has an ancient capacity to make reality mutate, into play. Thus, for example, when law tries to prevent a performance – which is where we came in on *The Jovial Crew* – it says: 'A many counterfeit rogues! . . . You were acting a play but now. We'll act with you. Incorrigible vagabonds' (Brome 1968: 109). When law acts, does it take action or take a role? Both; law acts *by* taking a role. To say that, however, is to wipe out – disarmingly – the crucial distinction between law and play which insists that law takes its authority from something authentic.

When drama refuses to make things authentic, defining reality as play, it is not only refusing to fulfil its audience's wants but also refusing to create them. Brome's play offers us a description of drama's activity at the cultural centre in 1641: those beggars who so inspired the trapped women's dreams of authentic freedom are first presented as a stage picture, like a discovery scene in a masque when the scenic shutters open. This is repeated for their second appearance: the audience sees an aristocrat and his friend watching some beggars feasting; while the beggars remain unaware, the aristocrat compares his state to theirs. The on-stage audience fantasizes about a picture, projecting his own feelings into it. But his contemplation is disrupted when the beggars become aware that they are watched: they 'look out' from the picture – as if the watcher's secure survey meets at the vanishing point a pair of eyes staring back. The tense moment is defused when the beggars learn that the audience is their

patron: they exit praising him. Caught up in that theatrical hiatus are the
social and aesthetic characteristics of late Renaissance drama. In so far as plays
are performed by beggars, we might say, the only reliable thing about drama
is that it can be bought.

Brome is thinking about more than the late 1630s. There's something
stirring here from a long way back, a history that is explicitly spoken in a
previous play of Brome's, *The Antipodes* (1638). Here an arts-loving lord called
Letoy gives some advice to a group of players: he asks them to avoid sawing
gestures and deafening delivery, and 'holding out your bum in a set speech':

> I'll none of these absurdities in my house,
> But words and action married so together
> That shall strike harmony in the ears and eyes
> Of the severest, if judicious, critics.
>
> (Brome 1966: 39)

You can hear the echo of another voice, from thirty-five years ago. Hamlet
wanted drama to imitate nature; he wanted to use a play to reveal a guilty man.
But there's a crucial difference in 1641. On the brink of social revolution the
theatre's images of its own activity seem pretty sceptical about trying to get
close to nature, truth, reality. When someone gives advice on playing, he
seems himself to be replaying something said somewhere before. Instead of
holding the mirror up to nature, this drama seems to hold the mirror up to
culture. As such it can't – or won't – do anybody's moral detective work for
them. Its tangle of reality and play, its suspicions about authenticity and
freedom, insist on theatre as an irresponsible space – the sort of place where,
when you think you've discovered something, it looks back at you.

Our final image of this theatre sees it dragged back into the street, but even
there compulsively holding its mirror up in such a way that the reflection
never stops being in play. At the end of January 1649, the king was beheaded;
earlier that month the Salisbury Court performers had been taken off under
arrest, and on the way 'they oftentimes tooke the Crowne from his head who
acted the King, and in sport would oftentimes put it on again' (Bentley 1968:
VI, 114).

## NOTES

1   What I am calling fixed and fluid space relates to, but is not the same as, Robert
    Weimann's concept of *locus* and *platea*. These terms are derived from medieval
    playing, where the *locus* is the scaffold or house, an emblematically labelled
    location; the *platea* is playing space that is more open – open to different uses,
    various actions, various interpretations at will, metaphoric. See Weimann 1987.

# 4

# The Image of Elizabethan Drama

## 1 'The Age of Shakespeare'

'There have been two great periods of British drama – the Elizabethan and that of the present day' (J. B. Marriott 1929: 5). That was written in 1929, but it could equally have been thirty years earlier, when it was possible to hail 'the Renascence of the English Drama' (H. A. Jones 1895), or thirty years later, when Osborne, Wesker, Pinter and their contemporaries were figuring as the 'new Elizabethan' dramatists. For Dryden in the 1670s, ambiguously comparing himself with 'the giant race before the flood' (Dryden 1987: 455), the same proposition would be self-evidently true; and it also seems to have applied to the 1830s, when the dramatic genius of Sheridan Knowles, maker of verse tragedies for Macready, could appear as 'the greatest and most undoubted that the world has seen since the age of Elizabeth' (Foulkes 1986: 164). Each new English theatre defines itself by direct comparison with the Globe, overlooking, as it gazes back towards that remote splendour, all the less distant predecessors who did the same thing. It is *always* the case that there have been only two great periods of British drama: the Elizabethan, and that – whenever it happens to be – of the present day.

The most obvious cause of this effect is the anomalous status of the best-known Elizabethan dramatist, William Shakespeare. Shakespeare is unique, because his plays have always been in the repertoire – often selectively and in heavily adapted forms, but nevertheless continuously. *Hamlet*, for example, apart from being the object of a famously large quantity of literary criticism, is also, no less remarkably, the occasion of an unbroken oral tradition. That is, according to the story (P. Holland 1979: 66), Shakespeare taught the role to Joseph Taylor, who was seen in it by William Davenant, who taught it to the

Restoration actor-manager Thomas Betterton, who played it for nearly fifty years and made it a stock play, which it remained throughout the eighteenth century. By the time the stock company system finally expired around the middle of the nineteenth century, the role of Hamlet was well established as an almost obligatory *rite de passage* for aspiring classical actors, and so it has remained; almost every season produces at least one fresh Hamlet (one survey counts sixty-seven productions in London alone in the period 1900–79). It is therefore fairly safe to say that since its first performance in 1600 or 1601, the play has never once ceased to be part of the living repertoire of the English theatre; a sort of apostolic succession affiliates the latest Prince to the author himself. This is of course not true of very many Shakespeare plays; but it is not true of any other dramatist at all.

Consequently, Shakespeare appears in each theatrical generation as a kind of contemporary – not because some mysterious textual elixir ensures his inexhaustible 'relevance', but because his plays are always being done on the same stages, and by the same companies, as the newly written ones. Macready in the 1830s did Sheridan Knowles's Virginius and Bulwer's Richelieu – and Lear and Henry V; half a century later Irving established his legendary reputation with Mathias in *The Bells* – and Hamlet and Shylock; Olivier in the 1950s is remembered for Béranger in *The Rhinoceros* and Archie Rice in *The Entertainer* – and Coriolanus and Titus Andronicus. Sheridan Knowles, Edward Bulwer, Leopold Lewis, Eugène Ionesco and John Osborne are entirely heterogeneous figures: no playbill in theatre history could imaginably feature them all. But Shakespeare goes with everything. When a drama student, today, puts together her standard audition kit – one modern speech, one Shakespeare – she is acknowledging the continuing stability of a binary structure which is at least 200 years old. If, then, each new generation sees a dramatic universe which contains nothing but the Elizabethan theatre and itself, this recurrent historical vision is understandable as the projection of an always current institutional reality.

The Elizabethan theatre, then, has consistently been accorded the highest prestige within dramatic culture. But the terms of its authority are oddly distorted by the fact that its representative is so gigantic and so single. Even its name is misleading: the period it really denotes includes only the last third of the reign of Elizabeth I, and the whole of her successor's, because the real centre of interest is the two decades (roughly 1590–1610) when Shakespeare was writing. It is Shakespeare's theatre; its audiences inhabited Shakespeare's London; other people who were writing plays for it were Shakespeare's contemporaries, and today their work is likely to be revived, if at all, by the Royal Shakespeare Company. The effect of this monarchical structure is that Renaissance drama is diminished and amplified at the same time – dwarfed, on the one hand, by the colossus which bestrides it and, on the other hand, aggrandized by its association with him. To unravel this paradox we need a brief narrative of its formation.

When the theatres reopened in 1660, Shakespeare was not yet the name of a period. He was one of the old dramatists – the others were Jonson, Beaumont and Fletcher – whose plays were still admired, and were also available in reasonably good collected editions. Those that were thought worth reviving were taken up and rewritten for the changed conventions of the Restoration stage, with little more concern about which bits of the script were original and which were new than Shakespeare had shown when adapting from dramatic sources himself (Dobson 1992). His scripts were still theatrically current, which meant that they continued to change. He belonged, without ambiguity, to the theatre of the present.

In their printed form, of course, the plays had more fixity and a stronger code of authorship. But even here there is a parallel story. The 1623 Folio was followed by three more in the course of the century, each one based on its immediate predecessor; and the first editor of Shakespeare's works, Nicholas Rowe in 1709, took his text from the last of them. Rowe's successors in the early part of the eighteenth century did the same thing: Pope (1725) based his text on Rowe, Theobald (1733) and Hanmer (1744) on Pope, Warburton (1747) on Theobald, and so on (G. Taylor 1990:69–99). The text thus moved steadily further away from the 1623 starting point, not only because of the multiplication of errors through so many layers of copying, but also because the editors themselves believed that the earliest printings were in any case hopelessly corrupt and untrustworthy; consequently, whenever they encountered a line which failed to make sense, they attributed the lapse to textual corruption and altered it, each editor drawing on his intuition about what Shakespeare would have intended. The intuitions, together with the criteria for what counted as making sense, were thus the vehicle of an ongoing remake of the Shakespearean text in the image of its editors' culture.

On the page as well as the stage, then, Shakespeare was being steadily updated. He was performed in the same manner, and interpreted by the same canons, as a new playwright; his presence in the culture, which by the early decades of the eighteenth century was an increasingly dominant one, was not at all the presence of 'Elizabethan theatre'. At this point, however – roughly in the period between the 1730s and the 1760s – the situation was radically altered by his deification. This was a complex event with no single explanation. It is clearly associated with the acting career of David Garrick, an enormously talented self-publicist who established himself as the new god's prophet. And the heroicization of both Garrick and Shakespeare was shaped, more generally, by a striking new individualism in the language of aesthetics, as the theory of the genius, the free entrepreneurial creator, challenged the neo-classical conception of art as a rule-governed activity.[1] Moreover, all this was happening during a particularly intense phase of the struggle for global hegemony between Britain and France: the cultural high ground of neo-classicism was indisputably in French hands, and the discovery of Shakespeare as a native counter-classic was perhaps a strategic requirement. However it came about – by whatever combination of ideological, aesthetic and adventitious factors – it was a *fait accompli* by the late 1760s; Shakespeare emerged from the Seven Years War (1756–63) in a position of absolute literary supremacy which he has not relinquished since. The triumphs were held, only a little belatedly, in 1769 at Stratford, where Garrick organized his Shakespeare Jubilee, an elaborate programme of concerts, dinners and rituals in honour of the great Warwickshire and England player (Deelman 1964).

This affected Shakespeare's historical positioning in complicated ways. On the one hand, apotheosis had the effect of cutting his last links with his contemporaries. He was now placed in the company of Homer, Aeschylus and Milton, not of Jonson, Beaumont and Fletcher – whose plays, not coincidentally, were finally dropping out of the repertoire of the London theatres at just this time. It was part of the orthodoxy of Shakespeare's praise to say, as Garrick's friend Samuel Johnson says in the most influential eighteenth-century appreciation of all, that his characters 'are not modified by the customs of particular places . . . or by the accidents of transient fashions and temporary opinions: they are the genuine progeny of common humanity, such as the world will always supply, and observation will always find' (Vickers 1979: 57).[2] Shakespeare is the transhistorical exponent of humanity in general, so very little hangs on the question of the particular time and place where he happened to live. But then, on the other hand, this newly classic status meant a newly reverent attitude to the words. The casual remaking of the text to fit changing theatrical and literary conventions now seemed like an appalling carelessness; if Shakespeare was, as Garrick's Jubilee oration flatly declared, the greatest dramatic poet the world had ever seen (Vickers 1979: 355–60), then every scrap of his writing was valuable if only by virtue of its being his. The cult of individual creativity produced an anxiety about textual authenticity; the accretions of editorial and stage traditions now looked like adulteration rather than improvement. As a result, the drama's point of origin acquired a special interest as the moment of an original purity. Editors started using the earliest rather than the latest copies (A. Walker 1964: 136–40), and theatres began advertising the plays 'as written by Shakespeare'. Paradoxically, then, as the genius of Shakespeare was raised above history, it was also identified, more specifically than before, with its particular historical time. His writings became universal; but then the universality prompted a new minuteness of attention to them, which revealed how local they also were, how full of theatrical devices and linguistic expressions which no modern writer would ever use.

The Shakespeare cult, in fact, led to the general diffusion of a printed text which partially failed to confirm the deity of the cult's own object. SHAKE-SPEARE, as bardolatrous typesetters preferred to call him, was undoubtedly immortal, but somehow not everything written by Shakespeare was SHAKE-

SPEARE. The rhetorical struggle to deal with this central instability is a rich source of eighteenth-century critical metaphor: gold and ore, flowers and weeds, jewels and rubbish, sun and clouds. Most of these images implicitly recommend a programme of purification, and this is what the theatre of Garrick did. The scripts were adapted to fit the mid-eighteenth-century theatre's production values, literary conventions and canons of decency. But this policy sat uneasily with the claim to be performing the plays as written by Shakespeare; there was something awkward about a position which on the one hand made it an article of faith that Shakespeare was the poet of common humanity, and on the other hand doctored his works to remove traces of those transient fashions and temporary opinions which he was supposed to have transcended for himself. In 1773, when the acting editions were printed, the editors made the best of it; they had, they said, preserved Shakespeare's beauties while expunging his deformities, in order 'to render what we call the essence of SHAKESPEARE, more instructive and intelligible, especially to the ladies and to youth' (Dobson 1992: 209). But this is not convincing: if the 'essence' is suited to the ladies and the young, then adult males are presumably reading uncut versions, which makes nonsense of the suggestion that cutting produces the more genuine text. If SHAKESPEARE is to be established, a more robust construction is needed.

It involved the deployment of Elizabethan dramatic culture. Here is a representatively fashionable voice, Elizabeth Montagu's, in 1769 (the same year as Garrick's Stratford Jubilee):

> Shakespeare's plays were to be acted in a paltry tavern, to an unlettered audience just emerging from barbarity. . . . Shakespeare wrote at a time when learning was tinctured with pedantry, wit was unpolished and mirth ill-bred. . . . By contagion, or from complaisance to the taste of the public, Shakespeare falls sometimes into the fashionable mode of writing. But this is only by fits, for many parts of all his plays are written with the most noble, elegant, and uncorrupted simplicity.   (Vickers 1979: 329)

Here the two Shakespeares are the noble one who is the object of modern veneration, and the contaminated one who deferred to the bad taste of his time. The mythic narrative is that only the first one is essential: the historically located Shakespeare appears 'only by fits' – that is, when he was not himself – or only in so far as 'his poverty and the low condition of the stage . . . obliged him to this complaisance' (p. 331). It seems that if circumstances had allowed him to please himself, Shakespeare's work would have conformed entirely to the taste of the later eighteenth century; it was with pain and reluctance that he fitted himself to the Procrustean bed of his own age. Thus the things about

Shakespeare which seem unworthy of SHAKESPEARE need not be emended or cut; instead, they can be understood as historical and therefore external to Shakespeare's true, supra-historical being.

This is a much more powerful solution, because instead of suppressing historical difference in the text, it organizes it into a stable binary opposition. As the national genius, Shakespeare is us; but in reading his works we constantly encounter things whose obscurity or impropriety advertise them as sharply not-us, thus disturbing the identification. Trying to remove the not-us elements would be a surreptitious and in any case endless labour; so what we do instead is to call the Shakespeare-who-is-us Shakespeare, and the Shakespeare-who-is-not-us His Age.

Montagu's version of His Age is extremely negative: she takes it for granted that the aesthetic values of her own culture are universally applicable. Despite her invocation of the idea of differing times, her historicism is really limited to the projection of Shakespeare's faults on to a faulty age. The same structure appears in enormously more extended and subtle form in the work of Edmond Malone. His edition of Shakespeare, in preparation from the mid-1770s and published in 1790, was an antiquarian one, supplementing the text with encyclopaedic amounts of information about Shakespeare's life, language, sources and theatre. The effect of this, as a recent study of Malone points out (De Grazia 1991: 123), was to situate Shakespeare not in the same world as the editor and the reader, but in the different world memorialized in the collected records and documents. The editor's task, having established the text, is therefore not to condemn or to correct Shakespeare's 'faults', but to provide explanations of anything that appears obscure or absurd, which he does by referring it, non-evaluatively, to the 'manners, and habits, and prejudices' of the age.

The effect of this massive accretion of contemporary detail is that it makes a limited segment of the past into a unitary object of knowledge. His Age is now not just a relatively barbaric or ignorant past, defined only by its failures to be now, but a distinctive 'period', with its own positive character. All the same, the negative origin of the concept, its function as not-us, is still active. For one thing, this construction of the 'period' makes it an *aspect* of Shakespeare. Its miscellaneous records form a unitary object because his presence unites them; it is as the Age of Shakespeare that it is grasped (and subsequently reproduced in a thousand book titles); so that, for example, to suggest that the most noteworthy poet in the Age of Shakespeare was someone other than Shakespeare is now not just a minority opinion, but a contradiction in terms. His Age *annotates* him: it is not so much that Shakespeare appears as a part of Elizabethan culture, but rather that Elizabethan culture appears as a part of Shakespeare (the other parts, as we know, being not for an age but for all time). And what is more, it is still the case that Elizabethan culture is the part of Shakespeare which is not us. In the editorial process, the notion of the Age and its customs is triggered, as it were, only by those points which would appear anomalous, tasteless or unintelligible without it. A line which strikes everybody as fitting, tasteful and intelligible doesn't require the supplement of history. The Age itself is therefore constructed out of everything which transgresses the prevailing canons of fitness, taste and intelligibility – that is, the Elizabethans are set up to be what we are not. This does not necessarily set them up to be what we dislike – on the contrary, as we shall see, it can make them particularly attractive. But it does involve the cultural appropriation of 'Elizabethan' drama in the logic of the Other, that figure which, securing my identity by being what I am not, appears as both the antithesis and the reflection of what I am. We shall look at three themes of this logic: that our stage is pictorial and theirs is verbal; that ours is prose and theirs is poetry; and that ours is middle class and theirs is popular. Already we have come far enough with the argument to expect that in all three cases, it is our differences with ourselves that the Elizabethans will mostly be talking about.

## 2　Making Pictures

In 1773, when Malone was just beginning his career as a Shakespearean scholar, the classical actor Charles Macklin mounted a controversial new production of *Macbeth*, in which he appeared in a tartan plaid (Nicoll 1980: 170–2). This novelty represented an application to the play of a fairly new concept in staging – historical accuracy. Until the mid eighteenth century, Elizabethan plays had been performed in a rather arbitrary mixture of costumes, with conventional theatrical outfits, such as 'Roman', 'Persian' or 'Spanish', appearing on the same stage as the dress of the actors' own time and place. An individual's appearance was differentiated as far as it concerned character type and social rank – thus Garrick, for example, dressed like a tobacconist for Drugger in *The Alchemist* and like a general for Macbeth. But regarding both these figures as universal human types, he would not have been concerned to ask what a tobacconist would have worn in London in 1610, or a military leader in Scotland in 1040. Conversely, Macklin, by wearing a supposedly authentic costume, was projecting not a generic type but a historically actual individual – that's to say, the point of the innovation was to enhance the effect of reality for the audience. This new convention grew in power through the early nineteenth century, and led ultimately to Shakespeare productions whose every visual detail was based on research into the place and time where the action was supposed to be set. By the 1850s, the researches of the actor-manager Charles Kean could lead to his election as a Fellow of the Society of Antiquaries; his *Macbeth* rejected the tartan plaid as wrong for the eleventh century, and opted for a neo-Saxon look, which was defended by a scholarly essay published in the playbill (Foulkes 1986: 19–20, 61). In 1871 Charles Calvert, outdoing even Kean, brought a real gondola back from Italy for *The Merchant of Venice*. And by the end of the century, Shakespeare at

Irving's Lyceum or Beerbohm Tree's Her Majesty's was an elaborate spectacle with scores of drilled extras producing an image of life in republican Rome (*Julius Caesar*), medieval London (*Henry V*), a sixteenth-century Jewish–Italian ghetto (*The Merchant of Venice*), and so on (Mazer 1981: 7–48).

So as Malone and his successors assembled their documentary reconstruction of the Age of Shakespeare, the same antiquarian impulse was forming a theatrical style of comprehensive scenic illusion. Everything within the frame of the proscenium arch was to be consistent with the chosen historical setting; no sign of either the nineteenth century or the theatre was to interfere with the spectators' delight at being transported back to Elizabethan times, or their feeling that 'the veritable Richard [II] stood, moved, and spoke' before their eyes (Booth 1991: 48). In both cases, this project of total period authenticity was at the same time an exhibition of distinctively modern technique. The editors were sweeping away the archival and textual amateurism of their predecessors. And the makers of historical spectacle in the theatre were using the characteristic methods of industrialization: mechanization (which made it possible to move more and heavier scenery), the co-ordinated application of mass labour power (a big Lyceum show of the 1890s had a work-force of over 500), and technological innovation (which in this period was above all a matter of lighting). The magic which brought some bygone age to life was itself insistently an achievement of the present. It therefore dramatized the remoteness of the past in the same breath as executing its spectacular recovery. Even as these people moved and spoke, you realized that they had been dust for centuries; that was what was exciting. Consequently, the more triumphantly authentic the rendition of the past became, the more conclusively it was objectified, homogenized, resolved into a picture.

This pictorial unity is the real point of what is sometimes called 'archaeological' Shakespeare. After all, the pursuit of historical authenticity would in itself be rather futile, given the unembarrassed anachronisms of the text itself (which were of course much remarked upon by historicist editors). What the antiquarian research actually produces is not an interpretation of the play, but an inexhaustible repertoire of objects which, since they all come from the same real life, are all guaranteed to be visually and culturally compatible with each other. These objects can then combine with human figures to make up a synthetic *world*. It is a world which is, so to speak, full; every square foot is characteristic; the spaces in between the people are all made good with things. Pictorial, in fact, in the specific sense that it is the same version of reality as that which informs the academic tradition of oil-painting. Everything, especially including the impression of depth, is combined in a single surface with no excess and no gaps, such that the frame is totally filled but no more. The significance of this plenitude, in the theatre as in painting, is the reciprocal adequacy of consciousness and its object. Mind and world form a perfect fit, and the received name for this happy stability is Nature.

It is to make pictures in this sense that the improvements in lighting are needed. In the old theatre, lit by chandeliers, the stage and the auditorium essentially form a single room, and the point of maximum visibility is the middle of the room. This spatial logic naturally keeps the actors out in the middle, away from the scenery, since moving back to the painted flats would be like retreating to a weak and shadowy position against the wall. With each technical advance (the optical intensification of candle-light and oil lamps in the eighteenth century, then gas in the early nineteenth, and finally electrification shortly before 1900), it becomes more and more possible to light the scenery and darken the auditorium (Bergman 1977: 215–19, 256, 286–97). The actor can therefore, without loss of power and visibility, go upstage and *inhabit the set*. By degrees he leaves the social space of the audience and becomes one, instead, with the fictive space of the play. Actor and setting cease to be two discrete signifiers and form a single totality, a world.

Pictorial historicism, in other words, was not just a theatrical fashion; it was the theatrical form of a particular version of reality. This appears very clearly in the work of one of Malone's followers, Nathan Drake. His thousand-page survey, *Shakespeare and His Times*, which appeared in 1817, is perhaps the earliest substantial attempt to combine the Author and the Age in a single study. In his introduction, Drake explains the relationship between the two: the idea is 'to place Shakespeare in the fore-ground of the picture, and to throw around him, in groups more or less distinct and full, the various objects of his design; giving them prominency and light, according to their greater or smaller connection with the principal figure' (N. Drake 1817: I, iii). Here the illusionist grammar of grouping and lighting seems to be the natural way to express Drake's sense of his scholarly task. Shakespeare poses in front of a 'view of the Times'; pictorial composition is the paradigm for historical understanding.

It is also, not surprisingly, the criterion of dramatic mastery. Following Schlegel, Drake defines Shakespeare as the great romantic and picturesque dramatist, in opposition to the classical and sculptural genius of Sophocles. That's to say, the formal principles which govern the painterly style of production are also attributed to the plays themselves: Shakespeare paints character to the life, highlights some figures while relegating others to the background, and so on. This synthetic power is one of the qualities which substantiate the newly harsh critical distinction between Shakespeare and his contemporaries. For example, Drake suggests that one reason for Ben Jonson's fall into obscurity is his 'laboured and indiscriminate finishing' (II, 577) – that is, he has no chiaroscuro, but works up each of his characters with equal and as it were mechanical intensity regardless of their importance in an overall scheme. Consequently there is no pictorial harmony, no 'tact'; the 'classical' principle of separation blocks the 'romantic' principle of combination. Drake finds that in these plays he cannot resolve all the surfaces of the dramatic text into a single plane as he can in Shakespeare. Jonson fails to make a picture; and so cannot be (and in fact never was) accommodated on the pictorial stage.

In this perceptive but drastic judgement there is a whiff of displacement. Fitting Shakespeare into the pictorial theatre is not after all quite a smooth matter: to take an extreme example, the fourth act of *Antony and Cleopatra* appears to require fourteen scene changes in about forty minutes' playing time, an insane way to write for a scenic stage, and one which limited the play's Victorian popularity despite its romantic and spectacular possibilities. Despite such tensions, Shakespeare is confirmed as picturesque through a formal contrast with Jonson, who is not (elsewhere, a similar logic constructs Shakespeare as regular and natural in contrast with the barbaric and fitful genius of Marlowe (II, 245–8)). Thus once again, 'the Age' does service as an alibi, easing the assimilation of Shakespeare by projecting his awkward angles on to his contemporaries.

What lies behind this particular awkwardness is the fact that Shakespeare's theatre was not pictorial at all. Ironically, this was established by the researches of Malone: that is, the scholarly reconstruction of Elizabethan England demonstrated that 'authentic' staging was itself inauthentic. Authenticities collided. Drake's reaction to this difficulty is striking: he simply refuses to take Malone's word for it that there were no 'moveable painted scenes' on the Elizabethan stage. He quotes an earlier dissenting editor, George Steevens:

> without characteristic discriminations of place, the historical dramas of Shakespeare in particular would have been wrapped in tenfold confusion and obscurity; nor could the spectator have felt the poet's power, or accompanied his rapid transitions from one situation to another, without such guides as painted canvas only could supply. – But for these, or such assistances, the spectator, like Hamlet's mother, must have bent his gaze on mortifying vacancy. (II, 212)

Drake himself adds that since painted canvas backgrounds featured in pageants well before Shakespeare's time, there was nothing to prevent their use in the theatre, whose machinery was demonstrably quite sophisticated in other ways. Then he goes on: 'Nor can we, indeed, conceive, as Mr Steevens has remarked, how the minute inventory of Imogen's bedchamber, and the accurate description of the exterior of Inverness Castle, could have been rendered intelligible or endurable without such assistance.'

Steevens and Drake between them make three important assumptions here. Firstly, they find it inconceivable that a theatre which was *able* to have painted scenery would *choose* not to; the absence of 'such assistance' could only mean that the company had not thought of it, or lacked the materials. Secondly, they assume that if spectators are not told where a scene is meant to be taking place, they will be bewildered. And thirdly, they require that any object which a character mentions as present must be always represented on the stage, otherwise the character's words will be incomprehensible or absurd.

Considered as universal propositions, all these assumptions are false; what is interesting is the critical project which is so wedded to them that rather than relinquish them it overrides precisely the kind of evidence it usually respects. If the three assertions could be boiled down to a general rule, it would be that stage representation is *inherently* pictorial. (Thus, for example, we see a stage with no image of a castle upon it. According to the rule, the stage cannot be non-pictorial; so it must be presenting a picture of a place where there is no castle. If therefore a man stands on that stage and says he can see a castle, he must be understood to be hallucinating. And since Duncan and Banquo, in the sixth scene of *Macbeth*, are obviously meant to be in their right minds, it follows that Shakespeare must have intended there to be a picture of a castle.) This rule is confirmed when Drake deals with the indications, also available to him via Malone, that the Elizabethan stage was decorated with black drapes when a tragedy was performed. This was clearly a ceremonial mark of the genre, analogous to the decor of a royal funeral; Drake, however, takes it that Shakespeare associated tragedy with darkness, and that the black hangings, covering the painted sky on the ceiling of the Elizabethan stage, were intended to represent a gloomy and starless night (II, 214). This argument forcibly converts a non-representational message into a representational one; the forcing shows how far Drake is prepared to go in defence of the pictorial rule. If he were to entertain the possibility that the black drapes were not a picture of the night sky but a way of saying 'This play is a tragedy', he would be admitting *different kinds of sign* to the same theatre text, and so destroying the continuity of consciousness and object. What is at stake, in other words, is the unity of Nature.

All the same, Drake's incredulity was not the only possible attitude. Coleridge, for instance, mentions the Elizabethans' scenic penury in his lectures of 1811–12, and so far from disbelieving it, he lists it among Shakespeare's historical advantages:

> All may be delighted that Shakespear did not anticipate [the scenic stage], & write his plays with any conception of that strong excitement of the senses, that inward endeavour to make everything appear reality which is deemed excellent as to the effort of the present day.
>
> Surely we may be grateful that we may take Shakespeare out of the rank of mere stage-writers to place him among the Miltons, the Homers, the Dantes. (Coleridge 1987: I, 229)

Although Coleridge is flatly disagreeing with Drake, the same conception of theatre dominates the thinking of both of them. Drake cannot imagine a visual theatricality which works other than by making pictures – and neither can Coleridge. But instead of concluding that Shakespeare's theatre must therefore have made pictures in spite of the evidence, Coleridge concludes that it was somehow scarcely theatrical at all – that, as he puts it in a later lecture, 'Shakespeare found the stage as near as possible a closet' (p. 254). He imagines a stage so devoid of visual or tangible character that it is virtually immaterial, a theatre which says 'we appeal to your imaginations', and which presents 'the idea of the poet . . . not of the actors, not of the thing to be represented' (p. 229). Thus in a characteristic sideways move, Coleridge makes the historical Elizabethan stage into an *anti-theatrical idea*, an impossible theatre whose purity reproves the sensuality and externality of the real institution. Inward, ideal, a mere medium between the imagination of the poet and the imaginations of the audience, Coleridge's Globe is essentially an allegory of reading. He is therefore surprisingly close to maintaining, as his friend Charles Lamb maintained in an essay published in the same year (1812), that Shakespeare's tragedies are not suitable for representation on the stage.

Today, when Shakespeare's suitability for the stage is a truth universally acknowledged, Lamb's opinion is well known only for being wrong. Even so, it is interesting to see how he defends the indefensible. He maintains that Shakespeare's language, in its incomparable metaphoric richness, is not a representation of people speaking, but is the poet's means of communicating to us the inner workings of their minds. To put it into the mouths of actors is to turn the *medium* of representation into an *object* of representation and so to present the audience, absurdly, with the doings of a group of people who all seem to be orators. Instead of the idea we get the verbal display; instead of passion, a copy of the usual external signs of passion. The same anomaly affects the costumes. For example, when Macbeth becomes king, he appears in a lavish coronation robe:

> And if things must be represented, I see not what to find fault with in this. But in reading, what robe are we conscious of? Some dim images of royalty – a crown and sceptre, may float before our eyes, but who shall describe the fashion of it? Do we see in our mind's eye what Webb or any other robe-maker could pattern? This is the inevitable consequence of imitating everything, to make all things natural. Whereas the reading of a tragedy is a fine abstraction. (Lamb 1980: 100)

The robe diminishes the tragedy, not because its particular form is inappropriate, but merely because it does have a particular form, whose inert and external fixity cannot embody the 'fine abstraction' of Macbeth's usurped royalty as can the shadowy images which float before the mind's eye in reading.

All this can be read simply as a refusal of the material dimension of the theatre – an attempt to lift Shakespeare entirely out of that gross element which is composed by the robe-maker, and the wig-maker, and the carpenter and the gas-man and the actor, and install him, as Coleridge suggests, alongside Milton and Dante, in a realm sullied by nothing more sensual than ink and paper. And certainly the texts of the Renaissance theatre were being redefined as Literature at roughly this point – Shakespeare because of his national and international role as a culture hero of the Romantic poets, and the other playwrights because of their almost complete absence from the nineteenth-century stage. The development of pictorial historicism even ironically contributed to the process of abstraction, because the mechanics of the spectacle were so time-consuming that the texts had always to be heavily cut for performance, which meant that the devoted Shakespearean had to resort to the 'closet' for anything resembling a complete play. All the same, it is not clear that a wholesale rejection of theatre as such is the necessary consequence of Coleridge and Lamb's arguments.

Lamb, after all, was not a reclusive poet who detested the theatre. He was an enthusiastic and perceptive reviewer of acting, and was also extremely widely read in the neglected drama of the seventeenth century. At odd moments in his anthology *Specimens of English Dramatic Poets* (1808), the theatrical sense and the antiquarianism come acutely together. For instance, he comments on a comic scene by Marston which turns on a character's being unconventionally dressed. The indecorum, he says, would have been much more striking in 1602 than in 1808:

> The blank uniformity to which all professional distinctions in apparel have been long hastening, is one instance of the Decay of Symbols among us, which whether it has contributed to make us a more intellectual, has certainly made us a less imaginative people. Shakespeare certainly knew the force of signs – 'a malignant and a turban'd Turk'. (Lamb 1980: 120)

Elsewhere, a scene in an obscure play by Rowley provokes this:

> The old play-writers are distinguished by an honest boldness of exhibition, they shew every thing without being ashamed. If a reverse in fortune be the thing to be personified, they fairly bring us the prison-grate and the alms-basket. (p. 123)

In both these comments, typically, the old play is used as a stick to beat the culture of Lamb's own time, which is made to seem pallid and euphemistic in contrast with the visual directness of a lost mode of expression. His mistrust of the material life of the stage seems to have disappeared; instead, he is implicitly complaining that modern drama is not visual *enough*. But then what resolves the apparent contradiction is that in these instances, Lamb is talking about *signs*. The citizen's flat cap, the Turk's turban, the prison-grate and the alms-basket are theatrically exciting because they are visible things which

firmly signify invisible ideas (social status, or religious affiliation, or misfor-
tune). Lamb takes it for granted that the essential truth of drama is a truth of
feeling and imagination, an inward truth; that is what impels him towards the
inward reception of solitary reading. But if the outward appearances of
the stage could work like a metaphoric language, not imitating but symbol-
izing or personifying, then drama could communicate the immaterial
despite its own materiality. So what he finds stupefying about Shakespeare in
performance is not strictly speaking the presence of things and people on the
stage, but the relentless commitment to the unity of Nature which means that
things represent only things, and people only people. In other words, it is on
the *pictorial* stage that Shakespearean drama fails; Lamb expresses that by
saying that Shakespeare is unsuitable for the stage in general because, for him,
the pictorial stage is the only possible kind. But it is not the only imaginable
kind: on the contrary, he imagines an older stage, a theatre of the symbol
which *has become* impossible because of the escalating illegibility of the social
world, the diminishing visibility of our real lives. In that sketchy
historicization of the critic's discontent, we can just make out the image of an
alternative.

For unexpectedly, 'the opinion that Shakespeare's plays are written for the
reader and not for the stage' is firmly endorsed in the twentieth century by one
of the godfathers of modern theatre, Edward Gordon Craig. In an extraordinary essay on *Macbeth* (1908), Craig argues that the power of the play all comes
from the unseen spirits whose influence is felt at every turn of the action. As
Macbeth and Lady Macbeth move hypnotically upon their fate, unlocatable
voices whisper to them, invisible hands pluck them by the sleeve.

> And who are these mysterious three who dance gaily without making
> any sound around this miserable pair as they talk together in the dark
> after the dark deed? We know quite well as we read; we forget altogether
> when we see the play presented on the stage. There we see only the weak
> man being egged on by the ambitious woman who is assuming the
> manners of what is called the 'Tragedy Queen'; and in other scenes we
> see the same man, having found that the same ambitious lady does not
> assist him, calling upon some bogies and having an interview with them
> in a cavern. . . . how can we show this thing properly if we take as the
> main and primary point for our consideration Macbeth and his wife,
> Banquo and his horse, and the thrones and the tables, and let these
> things blind us to the real issues of the drama? (E. G. Craig 1983:
> 173–6)

This is exactly the tone and emphasis of Lamb: still, a century later, the dark
interior of the drama is felt to be blocked off by the coronation robe, the flatly
positive presence of people and things. But the implications are different,
because when Craig discusses what is seen on the stage he is speaking as,

precisely, a stage designer. In a deliberate paradox, he is reflecting on the impossibility of staging the play and at the same time sketching a production of it. The point of this devious procedure is to force a transformation of the theatre. For Craig, putting on plays which *are* suitable for presentation on the stage is a pointless activity because the suitability means that there is no need to change anything; the theatre is. left as it is; nothing has *happened*. The impracticability of Shakespeare is his value: together with Ibsen, he is Craig's lever for prising open the 'natural' closures of the pictorial stage. Lamb's mild and essayistic provocation is belatedly brought home, and the realization makes it into an attack on the whole idea of representing nature. The Shakespeare Craig is concerned with is the supernatural one – the witches in *Macbeth*, the ghost in *Hamlet*, the island in *The Tempest* – because it is there that he finds spirits by whose aid the theatre can liberate itself from the dismal task of imitating life.

Thus the Romantics' Shakespeare, having been confined in the closet for the whole of the nineteenth century, is returned at last to the theatre so that his heady immateriality can be used to dismantle the scenery. The configuration was first theorized, not by Craig himself, but by W. B. Yeats, who saw Craig's staging of Purcell's *Dido and Aeneas* in the spring of 1901 before going on to Stratford to see the Shakespeare Festival performances of the history plays. He would like, he says, to see Craig's scenery at Stratford:

> As we cannot, it seems, go back to the platform and the curtain, and the argument for doing so is not without weight, we can only get rid of the sense of unreality, which most of us feel when we listen to the conventional speech of Shakespeare, by making scenery as conventional. Time after time his people use at some moment of deep emotion an elaborate or deliberate metaphor, or do some improbable thing which breaks an emotion of reality we have imposed upon him by an art that is not his, nor in the spirit of his. . . . We set these cloudy actions among solid-looking houses, and what we hope are solid-looking trees, and illusion comes to an end, slain by our desire to increase it. In his art, as in all the older art of the world, there was much make-believe, and our scenery, too, should remember the time when, as my nurse used to tell me, herons built their nests in old men's beards! ('At Stratford-on-Avon', Yeats 1961: 101)

Just as in Lamb's remarks about the Decay of Symbols, the banality of the pictorial stage is here treated as a symptom of the historical loss of a metaphorical and imaginative language: the insistent primitivism of the structure of feeling, as Yeats looks back to childhood, or to a folk world, or to the origins of art, gathers up into itself the supposed conventional simplicity of Elizabethan staging. He goes on to discuss *Richard III*, Act V, Scene 3, which directly raises the question of naturalness, not only because, once again, it contains spirits and so breaks the unity of nature, but also because it is one of the few scenes in Shakespeare where the script actually dictates a non-naturalistic setting, since the two armies' tents, which must be supposed to be a mile or so apart, have to be on the stage at the same time:

> Mr Benson did not venture to play the scene in *Richard III* where the ghosts walk as Shakespeare wrote it, but had his scenery been as simple as Mr Gordon Craig's purple back-cloth that made Dido and Aeneas seem wandering on the edge of eternity, he would have found nothing absurd in pitching the tents of Richard and Richmond side by side. Goethe has said, 'Art is art, because it is not nature!' (p. 101)

Quoting Goethe so that he defends the stage conventions of the 1590s while sounding like a symbolist of the 1890s, Yeats neatly wraps the complicated play of old and new up in a single intertextual slogan. Aestheticist design links up with Elizabethan drama to banish nature from the theatre.

Too uncompromisingly modernist to influence the theatrical mainstream directly, Craig and Yeats were avant-garde also in the strict sense that they spoke for the future. In 1901 the consensual wisdom was still that only a fanatic would deny the need to adapt Shakespeare for the scenic theatre, and that the texts which appear in the *Complete Works* 'belong to literature, not to the stage' (S. Jones 1899: 122–3); but the consensus was already crumbling. William Poel had been mounting experimental reconstructions of 'Elizabethan' staging since 1881 (R. Speaight 1954); and in 1912–14 Harley Granville Barker produced *A Midsummer Night's Dream, Twelfth Night* and *The Winter's Tale* in non-representational settings which cunningly synthesized Elizabethan revivalism with fashionable decorative abstraction to produce a style which W. Bridges Adams neatly and accurately called 'Poel *de luxe*' (Bridges Adams 1954: 10). Between the wars Barker's influence, diluted by convention but supplemented by limited production budgets, unravelled the tradition of Victorian pictorialism at the main houses of classical revival, Lilian Baylis's Old Vic and Bridges Adams's Stratford Memorial Theatre. And in the 'new Elizabethan' 1950s, throwing out the proscenium arch became the touchstone of progressive Shakespearean production: in 1951 Bernard Miles constructed in his garden the open stage which later became the Mermaid Theatre, and in 1957, after various experiments, Tyrone Guthrie and Tanya Moiseivitsch opened the arena theatre in Stratford, Ontario, which is best known in England as the model for the Chichester Festival Theatre (1962) (Styan 1977: 193ff). These theatrical developments were both reflected and ratified by scholars such as C. Walter Hodges, Leslie Hotson and Richard Southern, who recovered the unadorned Renaissance stage in passionate detail as an exemplar of anti-naturalistic drama. Finally, the opening of Chichester coincided with the foundation of the Royal Shakespeare Company, whose initial production style, formed by Peter Hall and John Bury, took it for granted that the bare stage was the natural default setting for Shakespeare. The fanatics of fifty years earlier had come to power.

Since then, ironically, researches even more minute than Malone's have suggested that the Elizabethan stage may have used a great deal more canvas and paint than he supposed. Perhaps there were pictures after all; the point is debatable (Hattaway 1982: 36–40). If the received version for most of the twentieth century has been the bare platform, austerely non-representational, open to the rushing wind of Shakespeare's imagination, this is not a simple matter of the weight of evidence. Rather, it represents the continuing authority of the Romantic conception of Shakespeare as an unconditional creative genius who, like the Protestant God, is most purely present in the barest and least pictorial places of worship. Theatre got Elizabethan drama back from Literature, but on Literature's terms.

## 3   A Poetical Age

It is 1716, and two men of letters are visiting Kenilworth Castle, the seat of Queen Elizabeth I's great courtier the Earl of Leicester. One is Joseph Addison, the revered representative of Augustan civility; the other is John Arbuthnot, the convivial friend of Swift and Pope. As they walk around the ruins, they compare the time of Elizabeth with their own. They agree that the eighteenth-century political constitution is superior to the autocratic rule of the Tudors, but what about the state of poetry? Arbuthnot points to the remains of the canal where Leicester staged a floating masque to entertain his sovereign, and declares that the present age must yield precedence to that of Shakespeare and Spenser. Addison demurs: Shakespeare, he maintains, would have done great things in any age, and as for the spectacles of the banqueting hall and the tiltyard, and the extravagant fictions of a poet such as Spenser – surely these are the symptoms of barbarism rather than the triumphs of cultivation? Arbuthnot half-accepts the accusation, but subtly adds that barbarism, at least in moderation, is not necessarily the enemy of literature:

> There is, I think, in the revolutions of taste and language, a certain point, which is more favourable to the purposes of poetry than any other. . . . it lies somewhere between the rude essays of unconnected fancy, on the one hand, and the refinements of reason and science, on the other. (Hurd 1911: 71)

This posits a conflict of interest between poetry and civilization. Addison, the supreme literary Whig, offers a consistent vision of progress, a historical journey from tyranny towards liberty, from barbarism towards refinement, from the fantastic towards the reasonable. Arbuthnot accepts this grand narrative unreservedly, but adds that as we benefit from the increasingly secure victory of liberty, refinement and reason, what suffers is poetry. His story is a kind of tragedy: like a romantic villain-hero, fancy has to be sacrificed for something which has more utility but less energy than itself; its passing leaves the world safer and more comprehensible, but less authentically alive.

The conversation is itself a fiction, a sort of Socratic dialogue composed by Richard Hurd in 1759. By projecting his romanticization of the reign of Elizabeth back by forty years or so, Hurd gives it an almost mythic reverberation: the leading English Augustans, at the height of their civilizing mission, suspect for a pregnant moment that there is something they have overlooked. The suspicion is neatly dramatized by the setting: once upon a time, Kenilworth was the scene of colour and action; now two literary gentlemen exchange theories among the ruins. This is not a drama, after all – only a dialogue. Where there had been fantastic display, there is sober reasoning; where poetry used to be spoken, now only prose is heard.

Hurd stops short of stating this elegy as a historical fact; his whimsical literary form renders the idea playful and provisional. Its inheritors, for the most part, showed no such caution as, over the following years, the opposition between poetical past and prosaic present grew into an orthodoxy. A short history will suggest at once its consistency and its variants.

It turns up significantly in the first national literary history with any claims to comprehensiveness: Thomas Warton's *History of English Poetry* (1774–81). For Warton, the Elizabethan period is categorically 'the most POETICAL age of these annals' (Warton 1781: 490), a time when even the prose was poetic, whereas now (the mirroring structure is typical) even poetry is written in prose. The context for this judgement is the same as Hurd's – the story of a fortunately transitional moment: 'Every goblin of ignorance did not vanish at the first glimmerings of the morning of science. Reason suffered a few demons to linger, which she chose to retain in her service under the guidance of poetry. . . . Prospero had not yet *broken and buried his staff* (p. 496).

The imagery of night and morning is plainly progressivist: Warton is not about to argue the superiority of ignorance over science. But by introducing Prospero he adds, in the language of the poetry itself, that enlightenment is also disenchantment. The time of *The Tempest* – the protracted point at which Prospero is about to renounce his magic but has not yet done so – represents the Age of Shakespeare, the brief happy time when the demons no longer enslaved us but had not yet abandoned us. Another generation later, in 1819, we find William Hazlitt in his *Lectures on the Dramatic Literature of the Age of Elizabeth* deploying the same topic of transition in different terms:

> The accidents of nature were less provided against; the excesses of the
> passions and of lawless power were less regulated, and produced more

strange and desperate catastrophes. . . . They were borderers on the savage state, on the times of war and bigotry, though in the lap of arts, of luxury, and knowledge. They stood on the shore and saw the billows rolling after the storm: 'they heard the tumult, and were still.' (Hazlitt 1931: 189–90)

The idea of the Elizabethans as 'borderers', living between the realms of barbarism and civility, is from Hurd and Warton. But whereas their opposition had been mentalistic, aligning barbarism with fancy and civility with reason, Hazlitt makes it a matter of social experience, so that barbarism means war and lawlessness, and civility means peace and regulation. The ambivalence of the figure remains the same: lawlessness and war are being put forward as both destructive of society and productive of poetry. Today, human passions and convictions are mediated by the institutions of society, instead of erupting into immediate action; we therefore lead safer lives, but the price of our safety is that the elements of poetry no longer happen to us; we have to get them from books. Our protectedness cuts us off from a violent directness of expression with which Elizabethan drama had *just enough* contact. This is a drastic extension of the theory. Before, civilization was only depriving us of the imaginary, and forcing us to live in a world of plain truth; now, it is depriving us of concreteness, and forcing us to live in a world of abstractions.

The implications of such a shift can be seen at our next stopping point: Edward Dowden's book, *Shakspere: A Critical Study of His Mind and Art*, which appeared in 1875. In Dowden's version of 'the Age', Elizabethan drama appears as, precisely, a talisman against abstraction. Sounding disturbingly but misleadingly like Mr Gradgrind, he says that all a dramatist needed in those days was an appetite for facts:

> He needed not, as each of our poets at the present time needs, to have a doctrine, or a revelation, or an interpretation. The mere fact was enough, without any theory about the fact; and this fact men saw more in its totality, more in the round, because they approached it in the spirit of frank enjoyment. It was not for them attenuated into an aspect, or relegated to a class.
>
> In the Renascence and Reformation period life had grown a real thing. (Dowden 1892: 9–10)

The would-be decisive words recur through the whole characterization of the drama – positive, concrete, real, fact, life, vitality – as if Dowden is half-conscious of the philosophical inanity of his point and is trying to browbeat it into significance. The reason for his persistence emerges a little later, in a statement of cultural need so naked that it's almost touching. He wants the drama of 'the fact' as a corrective to the spiritual malady of his own age, which he calls 'lethargy of heart'. Many of us, he says, have moments when all our knowledge seems sterile:

> The persons we know seem to shrivel up and become wizened and grotesque. The places we have loved transform themselves into ugly little prisons. The ideals for which we lived appear absurd patterns, insignificant arabesques, devoid of idea and of beauty. . . . To this mood of barren world-weariness the Elizabethan drama comes with no direct teaching, but with the vision of life. Even though death end all, these things at least *are* – beauty and force, purity, sin, and love, and anguish, and joy. These things are, and therefore life cannot be a little whirl of dust. (pp. 29–30)

This is still the polarity of science and poetry, but now restated in psychological terms, and conflated with the Victorian problematic of faith and doubt. The language of science, whatever its utility, desolates the heart and dries up the world because it names only dead concepts which no longer vibrate with what Dowden nostalgically calls 'the joyous energy of a faith'. The Elizabethan drama ministers to this joyless condition because of the pre-scientific directness of its engagement with reality; its language, too passionate and picturesque to conceptualize, merely and gloriously affirms; it is the prelapsarian speech of immediate presence.

It is worth emphasizing that this extraordinary projection comes from the heart of the Victorian cult of Shakespeare. By this time, Shakespeare was a well-organized national institution, served by numerous clubs and societies dedicated to his greater glory. It was the most active of these, the New Shakspere Society (Benzie 1983: 178–220), which effectively commissioned Dowden's *Shakspere* (hence the odd spelling, which was the Society's preferred form). The book was much reprinted over the next two or three decades, and can be read as the official programme of late Victorian bardolatry. The years of its dominance were also, as it happens, the theatrical nadir of non-Shakespearean Renaissance drama: from 1850 until the 1890s, revivals were largely confined to one or two scripts which had been kept alive through an accident of theatrical tradition; and by the 1880s – the years of sumptuous and successful Shakespeare productions at Irving's Lyceum – no other Renaissance plays were being done at all (Griswold 1986: 223).

Dowden reflects and probably reinforces this pattern by virtually ignoring every dramatist except Shakespeare; so when he refers expansively to 'the Elizabethan drama', it is natural to suspect that this is only another way of talking about his individual hero. But actually the point is not that simple. Certainly Dowden finds his 'Elizabethan' spirit in Shakespeare – in his alleged qualities of emotional directness, genial linguistic energy, vigorous and unanxious enjoyment of 'the fact'. But Dowden's Shakspere is also a Hamlet –

the idealist, the 'rebel against the fact', drawn to infinite profundities of passion and speculation – in short, he is a Romantic poet. This sentimental figure is clearly incompatible with the naively positive Elizabethan – as, of course, is the state of self-division itself. In other words, the cultural need which Dowden is expressing is not only intense but also contradictory: if Shakespeare is to save us from abstraction and doubt, he must be like us (otherwise we could not identify with him) and at the same time not like us (otherwise we could not believe that he has what we lack). The contradiction is organized in the way we have already encountered: when Shakespeare saves us through our identity with him, he is called Shakspere, but when he saves us through his difference from us, his name is 'Elizabethan drama'.

Elizabethan drama therefore entered the twentieth century with a set of mythic oppositions already firmly attached to it: it connoted a pre-scientific wholeness and concretion, as opposed to the scientific abstraction of post-Enlightenment knowledge; a violent directness of engagement with passion, as opposed to the bloodlessly mediated discourse of civilization; and a poetic quality as opposed to the prose of modernity. This last opposition is not simply a reflection of the fact that Renaissance plays are usually written in verse; it is informed by the belief, central to the whole construction, that Elizabethan *life* was poetic – that, as Hazlitt put it, 'The surface of society was embossed with hieroglyphics, and poetry existed "in act and complement extern"' (Hazlitt 1931: 191). It is a literary critic's idyll: in those days, one did not merely read poems, one lived them.

After 1900, the non-Shakespearean repertoire began to reappear, though its position in both the literary and the theatrical canon has remained marginal. Revivals by the Phoenix Society in the 1920s filled out the concept of 'Elizabethan drama' with some actual plays by Marlowe, Jonson, Webster and others (Griswold 1986: 223); and at the same time T. S. Eliot, in a two-pronged campaign as poet and critic, set out to install the Jacobean tragedists among his literary ancestors (Eliot 1951: 109–233). Despite this, the mythic oppositions showed remarkable stability. For example, the idea of ordinary life as poetic dominates what is perhaps the most influential twentieth-century characterization of 'the Age', E. M. W. Tillyard's *The Elizabethan World Picture* (1943). This very readable and much read book is a sort of tourist guide to the universe as it was supposedly conceptualized by the Elizabethans. The universe which emerges is one in which, you could say, to exist is to signify: a complicated system of classifications and correspondences brings everything, including the human mind, into a syntactic and metaphoric relationship with everything else. The world is a meaningful composition made out of symbols – that is, a poem. The tone in which Tillyard expounds this 'world picture' has an odd provocative tranquillity: on the one hand, he insists that it is all very 'queer', and fundamentally different from the world picture of any sane person today; while on the other hand, he enjoys repeating that it would all have been perfectly familiar to an educated man of the age – that the strange forms of connectedness he describes are not Elizabethan inventiveness, but Elizabethan normality. What this double emphasis does, as Hugh Grady has pointed out, is to discover in Elizabethan England a fantastic grounding for symbolist poetics (Grady 1991: 182): in those days, it seems, everybody was Baudelaire – or, more exactly, everybody *inhabited*, as a matter of course, the world which Baudelaire aberrantly *imagines*.

So metaphors are real and reality is metaphoric: you can have it both ways, and that fantasy connects with another strand of the myth – the story of the fortunately transitional moment. As in the whole Romantic tradition, the Elizabethan stage stands on the very threshold between medieval and modern worlds, and gets the best of both:

> Modern astronomers, hating the asteroids for being so many and so obstructive, have named them the vermin of the sky. To us this is no more than a metaphor with an emotional content. To the Middle Ages the observation would have been a highly significant fact, a new piece of evidence for the unity of creation: the asteroids would hold in the celestial scale of being the position of fleas and lice in the earthly. The Elizabethans could take the matter either or both ways. (Tillyard 1943: 121)

The Middle Ages are enslaved, as it were, by an order of truth which firmly includes the celestial vermin; while we are no less oppressed by an order of truth which excludes them. Only the Elizabethans, lucky borderers, are allowed to mix and match cosmologies. No wonder they could write better plays than we can.

Contemporary academic work tends for institutional reasons to exaggerate its novelty and deny its continuities; nevertheless, it is clear that the myths whose formidable stability we have been sketching have not yet lost their power to shape the image of Renaissance drama. Take for example this reflection on Jacobean tragedy, from Francis Barker's *The Tremulous Private Body* (1984):

> That the body we see is so frequently presented in fragments, or in the process of its effective dismemberment, no doubt indicates that contradiction is already growing up within this system of presence, and that the deadly subjectivity of the modern is already beginning to emerge and to round vindictively on the most prevalent emblem of the discursive order it supersedes. But despite the violence unleashed against the body, it has not yet been quenched. However much it has been subsequently ignored, it remains in the texts themselves as a vital, full materiality. . . . In the fullest sense which it is now possible to conceive,

from the other side of our own carnal guilt, it is a *corporeal* body, which, if it is already touched by the metaphysic of its later erasure, still contains a charge which, set off by the violent hands laid on it, will illuminate the scene, incite difference, and ignite poetry. (F. Barker 1984: 24–5)

This labyrinth of relative clauses is actually full of unambiguous markers of time – 'already', 'not yet', 'still', and so on – through which the passage *implies*, though it teasingly refrains from *telling*, a quite linear story. The story is this. Once upon a time, the world was organized as a system of presence whose prevalent emblem was the body, which was then fully alive, present and corporeal. Then this unitary world was disrupted by the deadly subjectivity of the modern, which violently attacked the body and later ignored and erased it. Now, after the end of that vengeful process, we look back on the body's materiality across the barrier of our guilt, and cannot fully conceive it. The moment of Jacobean tragedy is the crucial midpoint of this story, the exciting juncture when the body was under attack but not yet effaced, and in whose texts there is enough of the lost plenum to inspire us, but not so much that its totality baffles us. The mixing of the two worlds at this critical point is explosive, and the explosion is poetry. Thus despite the book's aggressively post-structuralist manner, its account of Renaissance drama is intensely traditional. There is the fortunate transition from a primitive to a civilized state, providing the optimum moment for poetry. There is the poetic Elizabethan world, in which the practical and the symbolic have not yet come apart. And, as in Dowden, there is the elegy for a world which used to be full and real, but which has now been disembodied by a deadly subjectivity.

The mythic oppositions seem, indeed, to be present here in purer form than before – Barker's narrative has none of the trappings of empiricist historiography (such as evidence), and the psychoanalytic overtones of his language tend if anything to draw attention to the classically Oedipal shape of his story. Consistently in a way, Renaissance drama is being treated as a set of symbols, capable of focusing historical, political and psychic themes all at once through a sort of allegorical layering. This interpretive licence, or licentiousness, is baldly set out in a less subtle book, Steven Mullaney's *The Place of the Stage* (1988). Mullaney's allegory is declared in the title: the book is about the geographical situation of the theatres in the suburbs and liberties of Elizabethan London, and also, in the same breath, about the place of drama in the culture. By a punning use of terms – place, space, distance, margin, liberty and so on – the place of the stage comes to stand for the marginal yet strategic role of literature in the social order. The supposedly ritual and symbolic character of the early modern city licenses a move whereby every fragment of its social history may be read as a poetic image. Before long, the Globe is acting out the argument of Plato's *Republic* and, observing this, Mullaney remarks, 'History at times reveals an acute capacity for literalizing the metaphors of its past' (Mullaney 1988: 56). The air of surprise with which he unearths this capacity is unconvincing because it is too clear that he is the one who buried it there in the first place. The Romantic conception of a 'poetical' Elizabethan age has arrived at its caricature: history is now fully fictionalized, and placed at the disposal of the critic–fantasist to fashion into whatever pattern he can render rhetorically coherent. Explicitly, the past is a medium in which the mediated preoccupations of the present can acquire immediate material forms – that is, if the age of Shakespeare is being produced as poetic, the poetic genre in play is *pastoral*. Which brings us to the vital question of the swains.

# 4   Groundlings

In the summer of 1993, a small but typical Shakespearean controversy escaped from the Arts reservation and appeared in the news. It concerned the company Northern Broadsides, who were doing a version of *The Merry Wives of Windsor* in Yorkshire dialect. Somebody attacked this decision, and then somebody else defended it on the radio by saying that the company were 'giving Shakespeare back to the groundlings'. This slogan is both reverberant and recurrent: it was used, for example, to praise Olivier's film of *Henry V* in 1945; it underlay the artistic policies of the RSC in its modestly iconoclastic 1960s phase (Sinfield 1985: 170); it hovered over the strange impromptu festival, part community politics and part showbiz glamour, which marked the campaign to save the remains of the Rose Theatre from property developers in the summer of 1989. On this last occasion, Robbie Barnett, a street entertainer involved in the campaign, reportedly said that the Elizabethan Rose 'was a theatre where the working class sweated into the armpits of the middle class. The Rose was not about the RSC's po-faced performances' (C. Eccles 1990: 239). Barnett's conception of the Elizabethan audience is hard to visualize, but its ideological thrust is clear: the Rose stands for a theatrical experience which is warm, physical and popular, as opposed to the RSC, which he implicitly denounces as cool, mental and socially exclusive. And he also implies, like all the versions of the slogan, that Shakespeare originally belonged to the warm popular theatre, and was stolen at some point by the cool exclusive one. Shakespeare and the groundlings, it seems, have a kind of right to each other.

On the other hand, it appears that we cannot – or at any rate that we do not – give Shakespeare back to the groundlings. The *Henry V* film imitates popular cinema, but it has had the career of an art-house and schools matinée film. The RSC's sense of its audience mutated rapidly from 'popular' to 'young' (largely young graduate). Northern Broadsides' phonetic iconoclasm, like Michael Bogdanov's studious populism, doesn't really impugn Shakespeare's high-cultural status; indeed, it depends on that status for its power to provoke. Thus the slogan recurs, not only because it encapsulates a recurrent aspiration, but also because it is ineffective: it never happens, it always has to be urged again. We are constantly saying it because we are unable to do it – how has this contradiction arisen?

The word itself can fairly be described as Victorian. Critics found it, of course, in *Hamlet*, in the scene where the Prince, lecturing the actors, deplores the kind of performer who seeks 'to split the ears of the groundlings, who for the most part are capable of nothing but inexplicable dumb-shows and noise' (III ii 10). But Hamlet's use of the word is clearly a joke; if 'groundling' was in ordinary Elizabethan use at all, it seems to have meant a kind of fish; by applying it to the people standing on the ground in the theatre, Shakespeare is inviting the actor to tease them, just as Jonson teases them, more deviously, by calling them 'under-standing gentlemen'. And the word showed little early sign of passing into the mainstream of Shakespeare reception. Malone cites it as part of the evidence about the structure of the Shakespearean playhouse, but he does not use it himself; and Hazlitt quotes the line several times, but always in connection with actors who shout too much, never in order to make a point about Elizabethan spectators. By degrees, however, the word moved out of its joking context and began to be adopted as the *ordinary term* for a section of the Elizabethan audience. Thus by 1849, G. H. Lewes could refer to people who always say that if Shakespeare 'wrote trash sometimes, it was to please the groundlings' (Lewes 1964: 143). This is a highly typical context. There is no satiric intonation – the implication is that there simply *were* people called groundlings – but at the same time they are being invoked only as people with low tastes which we (writer and reader) don't share. The word, and the prejudice it expresses, have become naturalized.[3]

By the end of the century groundlings were firmly established in critical discourse. In 1904, for example, A. C. Bradley, discussing the Porter in *Macbeth*, concedes casually, 'I dare say the groundlings roared with laughter at his coarsest remarks' (Bradley 1965: 333). The context here is the same insistence on the different, finer taste of the writer: Bradley is arguing that the Porter is a sinister and disturbing figure, and that it is crass to react to him as merely comic. Countless critics in the first half of this century adopt the same assumption: to pick one more example at random, W. J. Lawrence, in his whimsical essay *Those Nut-Cracking Elizabethans* (Lawrence 1935: 1–8), takes it for granted that his readers will understand what is meant by 'writing down to the level of the groundlings' (the original punning conflation of physical and mental levels as now an unconscious one). The tradition is not dead yet: I still meet students who have learnt, while studying Shakespeare for A level, that he put the gross bits in to please the groundlings. A whole class of Elizabethan spectators has come into existence on the basis of a couple of contemporary references: educated people in the twentieth century apparently

know intuitively what these spectators were like, how they behaved, and –
despite the fact that, being *ex hypothesi* illiterate, they left no record of themselves – exactly which scenes they enjoyed.

In short, what we have here is a class myth, whose structure has as much to
do with the period of its formation (the nineteenth century) as with the period
on to which it is projected (the sixteenth). In particular, the rise of the
groundlings as an explanatory category in Shakespeare criticism coincides
with the long drawn out decline and fall of a related English theatrical
institution: the pit.

The pit was a central feature of all English theatres from 1660 until the late
nineteenth century. It was the ground-floor area directly in front of the stage,
where there were no seats, but unreserved places on backless benches. It was an
ambiguous part of the house – privileged, because it had the most immediate
relationship with the stage, and because it could be seen from many of the
other seats; but also *low*, not only literally, but also in its traditions of
exhibitionism, jostling and noise. A box *contains* its occupants – that is, it both
affords them a protected space and prevents them from invading other people's
space; in the pit, on the other hand, you are out in the open, at once less
protected and less constrained. In this sense, the pit was the direct descendant
of the Elizabethan playhouse yard or 'ground' which gave the groundlings
their name.

A structural opposition, then, defines the pit as low and the adjacent boxes
as high. But this does not translate directly into the terms of class. The pit was
never simply a working-class preserve: it was not the cheapest place in the
house, and at some points in its history it appeared as the high-fashion zone,
or as the place where the expert critics sat. So the operative dualisms are
subtler: the boxes are mature and established, the pit is young and mobile; the
boxes are individual patrons, the pit is a crowd; the boxes are socially defined,
the pit is socially confused; the boxes are decorous, the pit is rowdy. Thus the
pit represents, not a lower-class audience, but rather a *mixed* audience: it was
a place where gentry, workers, apprentices, poets and prostitutes could all sit
jumbled up together in a sort of brief collective holiday from their respective
social determinations. This is the idea of a popular audience in the older sense
– not a class audience, but an audience which is in some loosely metonymic
way *the people*.

The heroic period of the pit's history was the Regency – the epoch when its
power was asserted in unmistakably political terms by the extraordinary events
known as the Old Price Riots. These were an organized response to the policies
of John Philip Kemble when he was the actor-manager of Covent Garden in
1809. To meet the cost of rebuilding the theatre after a fire, Kemble raised
ticket prices and increased the number of boxes at the expense of space in the
gallery. Sixty-seven nights of rioting in the theatre followed, at the end of
which Kemble was forced to give in to most of the rioters' demands, and

recognize formally 'the antient and indisputable right of the pit' (Donohue 1975: 54). It was a triumph for the mixed audience: the most recent historian of the crisis has shown by an analysis of the occupations of those arrested in the theatre that the rioters included gentlemen, business and professional men, clerks, tradesmen, apprentices, and skilled and unskilled workers. Kemble was defeated by a remarkably heterogeneous coalition, and what held it together was a shared self-description: the audience were the people, and 'King John' was encroaching on their rights. With elusive but appropriate theatricality, the drama's patrons assumed the authority of a sovereign assembly, entitled to enter the theatre on the terms authorized by custom, and claiming, as a matter of free speech, the right to express its approval or disapproval of the entertainment submitted to its judgement (Baer 1992: 65–88).

However, as often happens, these rights were being proclaimed in such ringing tones only because they were already under threat. Kemble, after all, was behaving like any rational exponent of political economy – he was seeking, within the law, to maximize the return on his capital. He ran into difficulties because Covent Garden was not a simple business proposition, but a Patent theatre with a long institutional accumulation of customary privileges and practices. But already new, unofficial theatres were opening all over London; and once the old Patent system was formally abolished in 1843, all managers were free to run theatres on purely commercial lines. The pit had claimed its 'antient and indisputable right' on the basis of custom; liberal Victorian reform removed that basis.

And then the commercial objections to the pit were very obvious. It made little sense to sell the best places in the house at middle prices; and in so far as the pit kept up its customs of noise and disorder, it was putting off the respectable patrons on whom the theatre's future depended. There was evidence that this was really happening – that 'the higher and more civilized classes' were deserting the theatre in favour of the opera or the novel (Booth et al. 1975: 23), and that playgoing was increasingly perceived as uncomfortable, unfashionable and vulgar. This apparent drift down market was a source of anxiety not only to box-office managers, but also to critics of drama. To mid-Victorian theatre enthusiasts such as George Lewes and Henry Morley, the stage seemed to be stuck in a vicious circle: because the serious-minded middle-class public stayed away, the managers were obliged to pander to popular taste, which meant that the shows were mostly foolish and vulgar, which meant that the serious-minded middle-class public stayed away. The important thing to realize about this logic is that it implies a loose alliance between commercial and artistic interests: it proposes that a better class of audience will lead to a better class of play, and vice versa.

Late-nineteenth-century theatre management, then, conducted a deliberate campaign against the pit. Literally, the space was invaded by orchestra stalls – that is, top price seats at the front – which first appeared in London in the

1820s, and became an increasingly regular feature after about 1850, pushing the 'pittites' back under the lower gallery, away from direct contact with the stage. Famously, this process was first taken to its logical conclusion by Marie and Squire Bancroft, an immensely successful managerial couple who took over the Haymarket in 1880. When they opened – with Bulwer's *Money*, aptly enough – it transpired that the pit, with its unreserved places at two shillings, had been entirely replaced by stalls seats at ten shillings each (*The Theatre* 1880: 1, 175–9). Demonstrators on the opening night shouted, 'Where's the pit?'; they may have had a faint folk memory of 1809, but they could not reproduce that level of passion and organization, because there was no longer a popular ideology which could legitimate a riotous defence of custom. The change was quite widely disliked, but even those who disliked it accepted that the Bancrofts were entitled to conduct their business as they saw fit. In other words, the final abolition of the pit represented, not just a move up market, but also, at the same time, a decisive privatization of theatrical space. It closed down the public sphere of the pit; it enormously increased prices so as to attract fashionable spectators by a guarantee of social exclusiveness; it established the downstairs audience in individually reserved seats; it proscribed all direct communication between the stage and the auditorium; and in claiming the right to make these changes, it denied that the audience had any *collective* rights of its own, instead offering spectators the individual rights of customers.

In completing these transformations, the Bancrofts appear as the founders of the modern West End, where there is no crowd ethos, where the seats nearest the stage are also the most comfortable and expensive ones, and where theatre, considered as a social event, is dominated by the upper middle class. The foundation was an undeniable success, in the sense that it produced a much more stable, respectable and profitable institution than the mid-Victorian theatre had been, but the price of this success, quite directly, was the expulsion of the latter-day groundlings, who were sent off to the gallery, to the East End houses, to the music-hall, and rather later to the cinema.

Even among the social and cultural elite, this was not a price that everyone was happy to pay. For it was not simply a matter of economic health, or even of class hegemony. It was something also about the *internal* dynamics of the theatre: 'The pit once removed or curtailed, the pit once banished upstairs, the pulse of interest which once vibrated through the theatre ceases to beat. The hum is hushed. The applause is deadened. The entertainments cease to fizz' (*The Theatre* 1880: 1, 140).

That was the drama critic Clement Scott in 1874, and he returned passionately to the fray in response to the Bancrofts' innovation in 1880. For him and his supporters, the pit was the space of audience involvement, of true theatrical passion. This argument was tied up in their minds with the memory of the legendary master of passionate acting, Edmund Kean, who died in 1833 but was still being talked about fifty years later.

According to one popular anecdote, a friend is supposed to have met Kean one night and asked him what Lord Essex thought of his performance. Kean replied: 'Damn Lord Essex! The pit rose at me' (S. Jones 1899: 135). One of the Bancrofts' opponents, H. J. Byron, comments:

> When the pit 'rose' at Kean, there can be no doubt that it did him good. As the pit at that time was the haunt of the critical, no doubt the applause was judicious. *And there was plenty of it.* A languid collection of fashionable stall-occupiers would have probably sent him back broken-hearted to the provinces. (*The Theatre* 1880: 1, 134)

Both the story and the response combine a romantic taste for emotional immediacy (Kean values the spontaneous response more than the considered judgement) with a sentimental but aggressive populism (Kean isn't the posh people's actor, he's *our* actor). In something like the same tone, George Lewes, writing in the 1870s, recalls Kean's performance in *Othello* as 'irradiated with such flashes that I would again risk broken ribs for the chance of a good place in the pit to see anything like it' (Lewes 1875: 5). He implies that the pit, despite or because of its danger and discomfort, is the only place from which you would want to see such an actor. Evidently Kean, on his night, was raising and riding constant bursts of applause like a circus performer; his act, as Othello or Richard III, was not a solo but a duet with the pit; this was perhaps the last time that the performance of Shakespearean tragedy was a form of popular entertainment. So the comparison with him which hangs over every leading actor until the rise of Irving is not only the rose-tinted memory of a great individual star, but also nostalgia, as the pit declines, for the years of its power and glory. The demise of the popular audience was experienced by many middle-class playgoers, certainly, as a gain in decorum, comfort, individual freedom to concentrate on the play; but it also felt like a loss of energy. Theatre was no longer an active encounter between the actor and the crowd – in Robbie Barnett's terms, it ceased to be sweaty and became po-faced.

The groundlings had been got rid of; and it is easy to see that their appearance in the accepted picture of Elizabethan theatres is an ideological reflex of their expulsion from Victorian ones. The uneducated groundling, who threatens Shakespeare's art (but in vain) with his misbehaviour and coarse appetites, at once demonizes the popular audience and neutralizes it by removing it to a remote age. This distancing was neatly dramatized in the 'Shakespeare's England' event mounted at Earl's Court in 1912 (O'Connor 1987). The exhibition, which in its mixture of faking, heritage and profiteering now seems like an early theme park, featured a replica Globe Theatre, where Shakespearean playlets were regularly performed. Visitors sat in the galleries and looked down not only at the stage but also at the 'pit', where 'prentices and orange-wenches cavorted in supposedly authentic garb. The rehearsed behaviour of these picturesque groundlings was naive and disorderly: this was a caricature of the sociable popular audience, which sealed its exclusion from the modern auditorium by making it, on the contrary, part of the antique show.

Told like that, the story invites an easy identification with the 'pittite' rearguard. The silencing of the theatre crowd seems part of the middle-class respectability that covers nineteenth-century England like a wet Sunday, suppressing an older, carnivalesque popular culture. Thus in 1880 Frank Marshall, another of Clement Scott's friends, protests about people who 'glare furiously at you if you venture to applaud': 'Such an open and robust mode of conveying to the actors that you are amused or delighted by their efforts shocks the delicate modesty of these persons, who do not think it proper or respectable to express their feelings at all' (*The Theatre* 1880: 2, 71).

Who does not take the side of the robust and delighted against the delicate and squeamish? Today, when all expression of feeling is suppressed by the hushed auditoria of our respectable palaces of culture, Marshall's plea for the freedom to applaud and hiss reads like a voice from a more open world. However, it is a particular kind of openness. He goes on to champion hissing, in particular, as a way of policing the propriety of the dialogue; and he concludes: 'I hope that the time is long distant when any indecent or blasphemous sentence will fail to meet with instant reprobation, in the shape of hearty hissing, from the majority of an English audience.'

This rousing declaration reminds us that Clement Scott was also the critic who, a decade later, led the chorus of frightened outrage which greeted Ibsen's *Ghosts* (Egan 1972: 187–93); and that the genial conservatives who stuck up for the pit were also, in many cases, the opponents of any kind of moral or intellectual daring in the new drama of the 1890s, and supporters of the Lord Chamberlain's censorship of plays in the most narrow and timid period of that institution's history. In short, it raises the possibility that in the closing decades of the nineteenth century, populism in the theatre was inescapably aligned with ideological reaction.

That was certainly how it looked, for example, to William Archer, the leading proponent of the new drama. According to Archer, the reappearance of serious drama in London was heralded by the Bancrofts in the 1860s and 1870s, and broke decisively through in the early 1890s, with the arrival of Ibsen around 1890, with the foundation in 1891 of the Independent Theatre, a society devoted to the presentation of uncommercial or unlicensed plays, and with the beginnings of a serious native realism in plays by Shaw in 1892 and Pinero in 1893 (Archer 1923). It seemed, almost suddenly, that after nearly a century of derivative and vulgar play-writing, England once again had a dramatic literature as capable as the modern novel of holding an intelligent person's attention. As that language implies, however – serious literature versus vulgar play-writing – this upsurge of dramatic intelligence was intimately connected with the formation of an elite audience; not only in the sense that domestic realism presupposed the quietened auditorium, but still more in the sense that the new drama required the formation of something like an organized avant-garde – a system of theatrical societies, literary coteries and little magazines which could support ventures too heterodox to stand a chance of commercial backing (Stokes 1972: 111–80). Drama was entrusting its future to the progressive minority, as the opposition took shape – in the theatre as elsewhere in the culture at just this point – between true art on the one hand and mass entertainment on the other. In this frame of reference, the groundlings appeared as the enemies of everything challenging and exper-imental. It is not a coincidence that Archer himself took the grimmest possible view of the Elizabethan audience, repeatedly attacking the dramatists (other than Shakespeare) for pandering to the appetites of a barbarous mob. Review-ing a revival of *The Duchess of Malfi* in 1892, for example, he finds the horrors of the fourth act gross and unmeaning: it is evident, he declares, 'that Eliza-bethan audiences found a pleasurable excitement in the crude fact of seeing little children strangled on the stage, and that Webster, to say the least of it, had no insuperable objection to gratifying that taste' (Hunter and Hunter 1969: 83).

Here is the most unpleasant notion of what popular theatre might be: the spectators have base and ugly tastes, and the dramatist prostitutes his talent to them. Good writers are those who rise above this demeaning relationship, as Shakespeare himself must presumably have done, aiming at an independent idea of excellence and not responding to the crowd.

But there is a historical irony here. The production which Archer was reviewing was by William Poel, the founder of the Elizabethan Stage Society and, as we have seen, pioneer of the 'authentic' staging of Renaissance plays. Poel's career, from his production of the First Quarto *Hamlet* in 1881 to Peele's *David and Bethsabe* in 1932, was a relentless campaign to prove that the Elizabethan stage, without scenery or scene breaks, was the right medium for the performance of poetic drama. And since this was an uncommercial idea, on the whole, Poel got his productions on to the stage only by making use of exactly the same network of stage societies and subscription performances which supported the development of new writing – the institutions of the progressive minority. *The Duchess of Malfi*, in fact, was presented by the Independent Theatre, the same society which had upset Scott the year before by presenting *Ghosts*, in Archer's translation. Nor was Poel's identification with the advanced drama an accidental one: though others called him an archaeologist, he described himself as a modernist (R. Speaight 1954: 90); he was hailed as a fellow innovator by Lugné-Poe, the director of the avant-garde Théâtre de l'Oeuvre in Paris; like Shaw and Granville Barker, he was a Fabian whose hostility to commercial theatre was a matter of political principle as well as immediate circumstances. His productions were intellectually self-conscious: they were designed to illustrate and test a theory, and tended to attract an audience of theatrical and academic specialists. Thus the auspices under which Shakespeare and his contemporaries arrived on the twentieth-century stage were thoroughly elitist. Indicatively, when Poel himself put Elizabethan spectators on the stage for a production of *Measure For Measure* in 1893, he made them staid, decorous and attentive – not at all the jolly groundlings of the Earl's Court exhibition, which he visited and loathed (Poel 1968: 208–16).

This is important because Poel's influence on Renaissance revival in the twentieth century has been very great. As we saw earlier, a clear line runs from him through Granville Barker, the Stratford Memorial Theatre, and the experiments of the 1950s to the modern RSC. In other words, Renaissance drama in this century has been revived, on the whole, within an anti-commercial and anti-populist ideology. Barker focuses the ideology into a myth in his extraordinary British Academy Shakespeare lecture 'From *Henry V* to *Hamlet*' (1925). In the myth, there are two Shakespeares – the 'complaisant' popular playwright, who is supremely good at producing what the public wants; and 'the other, the daring, the creative Shakespeare', who saves the complaisant one from the vulgarity of success by reasserting his genius at crucial and commercially inconvenient moments. The conclusion is that the plays written by this second Shakespeare, the reckless and daemonic one, could be adequately staged only by a serious, non-commercial company whose inflexible rule would be 'that the work should be done for its own sake' (H. G. Barker 1974: 167). This is a programme for emancipating drama, not only from the low taste of the groundlings, but from the influence of any audience whatever. It is also, explicitly and polemically, a programme for a National Theatre.

Here is the contradiction which stalks the subsidized classical theatre of the post-war period and ensures that Shakespeare always should, and never can, be given back to the groundlings. The project of this state-funded theatre is to develop a national repertoire, centred on Shakespeare, and present it to the people: that is what, in some ultimate sense, justifies its subsidy, and it is also what is implied by the socialist and anti-commercial artistic culture out of which it came. But as we have seen, this same culture also took the form of a struggle for serious, independent and progressive drama which was in practice a struggle against a residual popular theatre. So its integrity is defined, historically, by opposition to the groundlings whom it nevertheless exists to serve. In this situation, the Elizabethan theatre takes on the character of a compensatory projection, a place which managed, as we somehow fail, to practise high and low culture at the same time. That is what it means in the Olivier *Henry V*, where the image serves as a model of wartime national unity; but it also informs the assumptions of modern students through such critical books as C. L. Barber's *Shakespeare's Festive Comedy*, or Michael Hattaway's

*Elizabethan Popular Theatre*, which make the 1590s Bankside into a sort of Arts Council idyll, drawing patrician and plebeian harmoniously together in the enjoyment of a single fabulously multivalent text. In other words, the Globe comes to carry the dream of a common culture, transcending the divisiveness of society.

Whatever the fantastic form of the common culture, its real institutional form in the twentieth century is very clear: it is the state education system, briefed as it repeatedly is, from the Newbolt Report to the National Curriculum, to inoculate the social order with the best of the nation's literary heritage. English classical theatre throughout this time has been formed in symbiosis with the educational institutions. Barker's is a representative career: having revolutionized English staging in his ten years as a leading director (1904–14), he retired from the theatre and turned into a Shakespeare critic, in which role he influenced several strategic academics, such as John Dover Wilson, G. B. Harrison (with whom Barker wrote the first *Companion to Shakespeare Studies* in 1934), and also George Rylands and Nevill Coghill, who both crossed the same frontier in the opposite direction to direct Shakespeare productions for Gielgud in 1944–5. Already, when Barker was addressing the British Academy in 1925, London schools had begun to send groups of children to performances of Shakespeare (Styan 1977: 67); today, this audience is built into the operation of any theatre doing Renaissance drama, fostered by party bookings, company education officers, schools workshops, and programmes that look like GCSE coursebooks.

At the RSC, in particular, where an estimated 10 per cent of ticket sales are to school pupils, the interchange between the stage and the classroom happens on a national scale. Take, for example, the strange history of *The Revenger's Tragedy*. Unrevived for centuries, it had been praised, and enticingly quoted from, by T. S. Eliot in 1930 (Eliot 1951: 189–92); and from there found its way into the 1950s Anglo-American literary canon, which led to its inclusion in the main paperback Renaissance drama series in the mid-1960s. There, presumably, it was discovered by the RSC and given a low-budget end of season try-out in 1966. This was a critical hit, and was revived in 1967 and again in 1969–70. This led directly to an increase in the play's exposure on student reading lists, first in universities, but soon afterwards in schools. As an A level text twice over (for English Literature and also for Theatre Studies), the play now had a position in the schools market which easily justified revival, and it was given a successful second production by the RSC in 1987. In the twenty years between its first and second Stratford productions, the play had developed from a marginal curiosity to an established dramatic classic; indicatively, a lavish photograph from the second production adorns the cover of a summative student textbook, *The Cambridge Companion to English Renaissance Drama* (Braunmuller and Hattaway 1990). This brief career is representative in the way it shuttles between theatre, education, and academic publishing, with each institution contributing to the momentum in the others. The repertoire shapes the syllabus, which returns the compliment.

This is a question not just of canon-formation, but of inner structure. On the one hand, classroom practice is influenced by theatrical methods of work; this is the keynote of the 'Shakespeare and Schools' project which was influentially developed by the Cambridge Institute of Education in the mid-1980s (R. Gibson 1990). Not content with taking the class to the theatre, this movement seeks to bring the theatre into the classroom, devising workshop exercises which encourage the pupils to play at being actors, directors, designers. The constant theme of its in-service material is that Shakespeare can speak to children of all ages and abilities so long as they experience him practically and somatically, rather than critically and cerebrally; in other words, it deploys an idealization of the theatre in the service of an idealization of the comprehensive school. In a direct echo of the myth of the classless Globe, Shakespeare becomes the topic and symbol of the ultimate mixed ability education. It was as such that he made his way into the early, liberal version of the National Curriculum for English: riven by incompatibilities of class, language and ideology, we could all at least unite around and within this universally approachable drama (National Curriculum 1989: chapter 7, section 16). Like most such moments of transcendence, this one proved politically ambiguous: as the curriculum was dragged to the right, Shakespeare became the symbol of the forcible imposition of high culture *regardless* of class, language and ideology. 'Give Shakespeare back to the groundlings' coarsened into 'Make the groundlings do Shakespeare'; the travesty was made possible, of course, by the real overlap between the two propositions; the participatory model of Shakespeare in schools always had involved a degree of ideological blindness to the issue of authority. (The groundlings who don't *want* Shakespeare back fail the exam.)

And conversely, the theatre has absorbed, during this long partnership, the priorities of education. However pleasurable it is, a revival of a Renaissance play always carries the mark which was stamped upon the entire pre-1642 repertoire by the circumstances of its entry into the modern theatre: the sign of *seriousness*. As Allon White once pointed out, 'the social reproduction of seriousness is a key process in education', marking off, through the controlling opposition of classroom and playground, what counts as knowledge from what counts only as messing about (A. White 1993: 131). Within that opposition, Renaissance revivals have been firmly aligned, institutionally and stylistically, with the classroom: Shakespeare at Stratford is a form of knowledge, and everything about the experience confirms that it is serious – the informative programme, the tasteful decor and lighting, the RP *gravitas* of the voices, the attention which is evidently being paid, as in a good essay, to character, theme and language. The audience – again this resembles a classroom – is quiet, attentive, and often mildly bored; one does not necessarily expect the accumulation of cultural capital to be exciting.

This pedagogic co-option of Renaissance drama in performance brings undeniable advantages: we see fuller, more coherent, more thoughtfully worked out productions of the plays than perhaps any previous generation. Or at any rate, if these advantages are not undeniable, still, we are hardly the ones to deny them – me writing this, you reading it, both thoroughly implicated in the academic–theatrical symbiosis. Whatever the calculus of theatrical satisfactions, it remains evident that these scripts come to us across a decisive historical discontinuity: we can reconstruct their conventions, but not reassume the stage–audience relationship which those conventions infer. The groundlings, grinning, sweating, making a noise, are like grotesque effigies of our ancestors, haunting our improvement with an image of the energies we have sacrificed to secure it.

## NOTES

1   The most concentrated statement of this critical revision is Edward Young's *Conjectures on Original Composition* (1759), which is full of illuminating entrepreneurial metaphors for the creation of literary value. The application to Shakespeare was made in the 1760s by, for instance, William Duff; there is an extract in Vickers 1979: 367–73.

2   This is from the preface to Johnson's edition of Shakespeare, which appeared in 1765. The edition itself was superseded by the scholarship of the later eighteenth century, but the critical prestige of Johnson was such that the preface had a long independent life.

3   One revealing exception to this rough chronology of adoption is Maurice Morgann, who published his pioneering experiment in 'psychological' criticism, *An Essay on the Dramatic Character of Sir John Falstaff*, in 1777. Morgann continued to revise the essay after its publication, and in a late addition (probably 1789–90) he blames the 'groundlings' for the moment, offensively farcical in his opinion, when Falstaff carries off the dead Hotspur on his back (Morgann 1972: 282). If, as I think, this is a historically precocious deployment of the idea, then it tells us something about its cultural function. Morgann is concerned to rescue Falstaff, as both a sympathetic individual and a profound character study, from the coarse clowning associated with the role in the theatre. Encountering a fragment of the authentic text which appears to him to *dictate* coarse clowning, he dissociates it from Shakespeare by attributing it to the groundlings. They come into existence, then, as a function of the process of literarization: preparing the play for consumption as literature, the critic needs this waste bin to contain its indigestible scraps of theatricality.

# 5

# Restoration Comedy

*Charles II was famous for his wit and his inventions. Among the latter was an unbridled and merry way of behaving and writing plays, called the Reformation. This was a Good Thing in the end as it was one of the earliest causes of Queen Victoria's determination to be good.*

W. C. Sellar and R. J. Yeatman, *1066 And All That*

## 1 Virtue in Danger

'Restoration' drama is the slightly unsatisfactory label for the work of the London theatres which were set up on the accession of Charles II in 1660 and whose distinctive conventions then dominated the stage for the next fifty years or so. Most of its scripts disappeared from the repertoire in the course of the eighteenth century, reappearing – very selectively – only after about 1920. The reason for this eclipse was that 'Restoration' drama rapidly came to seem, in retrospect, unspeakably licentious. As everyone knew, it was in the last third of the seventeenth century that the theatre had touched the nadir of profaneness and immorality.

The phrase is from the title of Jeremy Collier's tract on the subject, *A Short View of the Profaneness and Immorality of the English Stage*, which appeared in 1698 and provoked the most concentrated moral panic in English theatrical history. This was not created out of nothing; rather, Collier was the indicator and beneficiary of a wider ideological shift. But anxiety about the moral state of the theatre instantly acquired his name; subsequent attacks honoured him, and it was against him that the playwrights defended themselves in print.

What were the theatrical conditions which produced immorality and profaneness in such profusion that even a short view of them took up nearly three hundred pages? We can begin to answer this question by considering the playhouse itself, using as a vehicle one of Collier's principal targets: Vanbrugh's comedy *The Relapse; or, Virtue in Danger.*

It opened in November 1696 at the theatre in Drury Lane, built about twenty years earlier by Sir Christopher Wren. This was the best space for spoken drama in London, stylishly combining grandeur and intimacy. Its most striking feature, from a modern point of view, is the scale of the forestage. Scholarly work on the surviving evidence (Hume 1980: 41, 62) gives an apron depth of 21 feet, and an auditorium depth of only 32 feet and 6 inches – that is, well over a third of the area in front of the curtain is occupied by the stage. When *The Relapse* opened, this immense platform had just been cut back in order to increase the audience capacity. This is an unsurprising move given the precarious economics of the theatre at the time; what is surprising is that the building was so extravagantly designed in the first place. Upstage from the curtain is an extended space for changeable scenery, going back about 45 feet; so the total depth of the stage is exactly double that of the auditorium. If an actor comes right down to the front, he is 65 feet away from the back wall of the stage and only 35 feet from the back wall of the auditorium, and is closer to most of the spectators than he is to most of the scenery. The downward thrust of the acting area, its invitation to the actors to come out and meet the audience, is extreme.

As this forestage shrank progressively through the eighteenth century, its diminution was theorized by the increasingly dogmatic view that the meeting which it facilitated was an undramatic and disruptive one. An essay of 1767 puts it very clearly:

> The actors, instead of being so brought forwards, ought to be thrown back at a certain distance from the spectator's eye, and stand within the scenery of the stage, in order to make a part of that pleasing illusion for which all dramatic exhibitions are calculated. But by such a preposterous inversion of things, the very intent of theatric representation is destroyed; and the proposed effect defeated, by thus detaching actors from the precincts of the decoration, and dragging them forth from the scenes into the midst of the parterre. (Hume 1980: 45n)

This writer assumes that a theatrical performance is supposed to be imitating nature: he wants a separation of actor and spectator, and a unity of actor and scene, in order to produce a convincing illusion. To drag the actors forth from the scenes, into the midst of the space occupied by the public, is 'preposterous' because it wrecks the illusion, inverting the subordination of actor to role and drawing attention to the performers *as performers*. Conversely, the deliberate projection of the show out on to the forestage, which a design such as Wren's promotes, suggests the presence of a different model of drama, in which acting is an imitation of nature only secondarily. It *is* that, certainly; but before that, it is a kind of rhetoric, an act of communication with an audience.

On the forestage, the actors are very obviously in *the same room* as the spectators. We see them amongst us as we see one another, lit by the same candles, audible within the same acoustic, communicating through the same gestural repertoire. There is even a sense in which they compete with the other spectators for our attention. Take, for example, the moment when Lord Foppington excuses the pains he takes over his appearance by remarking that 'a man must endeavour to look wholesome, lest he make so nauseous a figure in the side-bax, the ladies should be compelled to turn their eyes upon the play' (Vanbrugh 1989: 72–3). The actor, Colley Cibber, says this standing a few feet from the side-boxes themselves, which form the side walls of the forestage, so that the actual gentlemen sitting in them are effectively part of the decor. Foppington's ornate clothes and artificial manners are a direct parody of theirs; his words invite a comparison of their appearance with his. The stage performance interacts with the life on view in the boxes, which themselves resemble little stages. In a similar way the pit, traditionally the place for the most vocal section of the audience, shares space with the forestage and is a secondary object of spectatorship for the boxes and galleries which surround it (D. Roberts 1989: 27–8). It is not surprising that Cibber, in his memoirs, mourns the extra ten feet of downstage space (Cibber 1968: 224–6): he had lost some of the ambivalent zone between the scenery and the crowd which was the spatial and social medium of the fops that made him famous.

This complex of specular relations is informed not only by the architecture, but also by the fact that the theatre is a meeting place. The metropolitan landed and financial elite which calls itself 'Town' conducts much of its social life in a series of public spaces – the Mall, the Exchange, some select coffee-houses and restaurants – of which the playhouse is one. These locations have some of the characteristics of what Norbert Elias calls 'court society' (Elias 1983) – that is, they are privileged assemblies in which membership and status are articulated through a code of manners. Civility, as both a social ideal and a practical means of class distinction, takes the form of a disciplining of the body, its movements, poses, functions and proximities, which is not highly internalized but is rather a conformity to external rules. A meticulous regime of deportment governs the movements of well-bred persons in public space. As an eighteenth-century tutor of this art puts it:

> Let us imagine ourselves, as so many living pictures drawn by the most excellent masters, exquisitely designed to afford the utmost pleasure to beholders; and indeed, we ought to set our bodies in such a disposition,

when we stand in conversation, that, were our actions or postures delineated, they might bear the strictest examination of the most critical judges. (Kellom Tomlinson in Styan 1986: 67)

Beholders, delineators, critical judges: the characterization of good posture infers the gaze of a discriminating spectator at every point. Social behaviour is inherently theatrical – that is, it is formed by a consciousness of being watched, and an intention of affording pleasure. And because sociability is in this sense a kind of performance, the performance on the stage is not a purely mimetic practice, removed from society in a transcendent artistic space, but rather is itself a kind of social behaviour.

This sense of the theatre as a rule-governed social encounter is heightened further by the familiarity between the actors and a large part of the audience. The spectators are a fairly small group of Londoners who come often (*The Relapse*, for example, expects them to have seen Cibber's *Love's Last Shift*, to which it is a sequel). They react noisily and effectively: a new play can be hailed as a success or hissed into oblivion in a single night. They know the company, who greet them in prologues and epilogues as old acquaintances. The stars appear in every show, under names which are deliberately insubstantial: the ones in this show (Loveless, Fashion, Worthy) are typical in that they are both generalizing (they are the names of *characters*, not of people) and formulaic (the same group of words is recycled and recombined from play to play). Roles, in other words, are quite lightly worn: they are not unique self-grounded individuals, and not pretending to be, but are explicitly discursive categories, signs in use in the continuing conversation between the actors and the audience. All this tends to disconnect the actor's body from the pseudo-substance of the fictional world, and connect it, instead, to the responses of the spectators.

It is not surprising, then, that writers and audiences are drawn to this front-of-house centre of theatrical energy, and in particular to metatheatrical scenes which make the fiction bend round and join up with the playhouse itself. One such sequence precipitates the relapse of Vanbrugh's title. Loveless, the re-claimed husband from *Love's Last Shift*, is in town for the first time since his reformation, and on his honour not to be tempted back into his former debauchery. He goes to the theatre and has an experience which he dutifully reports to his wife:

LOVELESS: Know then, I happened in the play to find my very character, only with the addition of a relapse; which struck me so, I put a sudden stop to a very harmless entertainment, which till then diverted me between the acts. 'Twas to admire the workmanship of nature in the face of a young lady that sat some distance from me, she was so exquisitely handsome.

AMANDA: So exquisitely handsome?

LOVELESS: Why do you repeat my words, my dear?

AMANDA: Because you seemed to speak 'em with such pleasure, I
thought I might oblige you with their echo.

LOVELESS: Then you are alarmed, Amanda?

AMANDA: It is my duty to be so, when you are in danger.

LOVELESS: You are too quick in apprehending for me; all will be well
when you have heard me out. I do confess I gazed upon her; nay,
eagerly I gazed upon her.

AMANDA: Eagerly? That's with desire.

LOVELESS: No, I desired her not; I viewed her with a world of admiration, but not one glance of love.

AMANDA: Take heed of trusting to such nice distinctions.

(Vanbrugh 1989: II i 39–57)

The uneasy argument continues until it is interrupted by the announcement of
Berinthia, whose arrival is the punch-line for the sequence:

AMANDA: O dear! 'tis a relation I have not seen these five years. Pray her
to walk in.

(*Exit* SERVANT.)

(*To* LOVELESS) Here's another beauty for you. She was young when
I saw her last; but I hear she's grown extremely handsome.

LOVELESS: Don't you be jealous now; for I shall gaze upon her too.

(*Enter* BERINTHIA.)

(*Aside*) Ha! By heavens, the very woman!

(ll. 104–9)

Loveless's astonishment is funny because nobody else in the theatre will have
been even mildly surprised. It is virtually a rule of the genre that an exchange
of glances in a theatre leads to an intrigue: Loveless's experience, which he
fondly imagines to be particular to him, is already established as a *conventional
sign* of virtue in danger.

This convention, which is common to the writers and the enemies of
Restoration comedy, has literary origins. In Dryden's translation of Ovid, for
example, the predatory lover is told not to bother, here, with the subtler codes
of courtship:

> But boldly next the fair your seat provide,
> Close as you can to hers, and side by side.
> Pleased or unpleased, no matter, crowding sit,
> For so the laws of public shows permit.
>
> (*Ars Amatoria*, Dryden 1987: 417)

Dramatic and non-dramatic descriptions of the Restoration playhouse are indeed full of flirtations, assignations and prostitution. It is hard to decide how far this evidence reflects actual practice, and how far it is conditioned by classical imitation and satiric decorum. On the one hand, there is plenty of evidence that respectable gentlewomen went to plays unescorted, which they would hardly have done had the theatre been the continuous saturnalia it appears in some of the more heated accounts. On the other hand, the record includes, not only literary satire, but also serious attempts to ban masks from the auditorium because they were encouraging both professional and amateur soliciting (Styan 1986: 115; Thomas 1989: 189). It seems unlikely that all this smoke was from a fire that had been extinguished before the fall of Rome. One contributory factor, crudely enough, is that the audience were packed into a very small space. Apart from the places in boxes, the seating was all on benches, and in a full house (upwards of 500) the spectators, dressed in the rather bulky fashions of the 1690s, will have been jammed together in a manner which a twentieth-century theatre audience would find physically and psychologically uncomfortable. The effect was a suspension of the normal rules of social distance. And whatever may have been the literal consequences of this combination of physical proximity and social promiscuity, the cultural definition of the space clearly interprets its 'laws' as a kind of sexual licence. In other words, the social and sociable network of gazes, linking boxes, pit, stage and galleries, is eroticized; the dialectics of playgoing – seeing and being seen, spectatorship and sartorial display – are specified as exchanges of sexual energy.

It is within precisely this network that Loveless's story wittily situates itself. He interprets the play he saw, not as a pseudo-reality, but as a form of communication: when he says he found his 'very character' in the play, he is not talking about an encounter with his double in a Romantic sense; he means that the role 'characterized' him, defined the typical features of his situation in such a way as to render them knowable. The actor is therefore offering Loveless himself as just such a typifying figure (since it is obvious to all but him that he too is about to acquire 'the addition of a relapse' and so make his identity with the stage character complete). But at the same time, by standing on the stage and describing himself as a spectator in the auditorium who was watch-ing, not only the play, but also one of the other spectators, the character identifies himself with those who are watching him. He inserts himself in the complex of specular relations that radiate out from him as he speaks, and comments ironically on their dynamics.

The irony is this. For Loveless, the point of his little story is that it demonstrates the power of drama to check the wanderings of desire by holding up a salutary mirror to them. But his telling of this improving tale is fatally contradictory. For one thing, he is *also* trying to say that his gazing on the young lady in the audience was a 'harmless entertainment' – an assurance which is incompatible with his having been alerted to its dangers by the play. And for another, as Amanda points out, the enthusiastic language in which he recounts the incident revives the pleasure which it is supposed to have suppressed. Thus, while he is *saying* that watching and representing are forms of control over sexual appetite, what he is *showing*, in the same breath, is their power to incite.

He is trying to sustain a 'nice distinction' between looking with admiration and looking with desire. The undignified collapse of this distinction articulates the ambiguities of the audience's own 'gaze'. Berinthia's entrance completes the circle. The unknown object of Loveless's vainly denied desire emerges from her narrated place in the auditorium and appears on the stage – turning out, by the way, to be the actress who in real life is married to the actor playing Loveless (P. Holland 1979: 69). He turns and, behind his fictional wife's back, confides in the audience. They are thus invited to laugh at the *coup de théâtre*, certainly, but at the same time to look through his eyes at the woman who has just arrived on stage; *their* distinction between the pleasures of 'admiration' and 'desire' is compromised as well as his.

The condition of this complex effect is, once again, the conspicuous presentness of Restoration theatre, its lack or refusal of mechanisms for distancing the performers and confining them within the scene where they would appear as mere embodiments of imaginary characters. By appearing in social space, explicitly performing in front of a crowd which is conscious of its own presence, the actor accepts the relations with a spectator as an open social transaction. She – or he – is not just an image in an ethical mirror, but is really being looked at and enjoyed. In all theatre there is perhaps an implicit voyeurism; but this particular theatre makes it ingeniously and scandalously explicit. One trace of this awareness is the coarse and recurring joke, in prologues and epilogues, about the sexual availability of the actresses. Some actresses literally were prostitutes, but the joke is not so much recording a social fact as expressing a cultural attitude: that to make a living by exhibiting one's body in public is a kind of prostitution in itself. In this context, Jeremy Collier begins to look as if he does not altogether deserve the patronizing footnotes he usually gets from the twentieth-century admirers of Vanbrugh or Congreve. He has grasped the point which eludes all the critics who abstract the art of drama from the social practice of theatre: that when this stage depicts whores, it is not an isolated incident, but a trace of the sense in which it *is* one.

## 2   Smut

This conclusion roughly accords with the sense that Restoration theatre has something uniquely sexy about it (Stafford-Clark 1989: 61). To specify this vague feeling, we can start from that sign of sexual immorality which Collier most reductively identifies: immodest language spoken on the stage, or, as he flatly terms it, smut.

The offensiveness of smut is a long-lived theme of dramatic censorship, persisting vigorously, for instance, in the rules governing broadcast drama today. On the face of it, it seems a critically unproductive obsession, since it wrenches individual words and phrases out of any meaningful context in order to try them separately at the bar of moral propriety. But for our purposes, this procedure does at least have the merit of restoring dramatic dialogue to its place on the stage. Collier refuses to naturalize the expressions he condemns; he overrides their fictional occasion and considers them as words spoken in a public place; just as the bodies of the performers are really on view, so these things are really to be said.

Moreover, innuendo, which is what Collier is mostly talking about, is a structural idea. It means, not just talking dirty, but talking in two senses at once, one sense being socially acceptable, and the other referring illicitly to sex. The point of *double entendre* is its doubleness. Take a typical example, not a particularly flagrant one, from George Etherege's comedy *The Man of Mode*, first produced in 1676, but still in the repertoire at the end of the century. The heroine, Harriet, has been insisting to Dorimant, the rake-hero, that she is not the easy lay he is used to, and he has replied with assurances that he doesn't despair of her and is prepared to wait.

> HARRIET: To men who have fared in this town like you, 'twould be a great mortification to live on hope. Could you keep a Lent for a mistress?
> DORIMANT: In expectation of a happy Easter; and though time be very precious, think forty days well lost to gain your favor.
> (Etherege 1966: III iii 73–82)

Everything said here has a double meaning, and both senses are clear enough. What is interesting is the relation between them: the respectable sense covers up the illicit one, but is also the medium by which it is communicated, not only gesturing towards sexual feeling in a general way, but also carrying out very specific sexual negotiations. However, this paradox of concealment and expression is not quite all that is happening.

The exchange was condemned for smut and profanity, and received this unsatisfactory defence from one of Collier's opponents, Edward Filmer:

> Now, tho' the first hint be here given by a Woman; and both Question, and Answer, are at Bottom Smutty and Prophane, yet is there nothing in either, so plain and gross, as may seem to border, in the least, on Rusticity, or ill Manners. (in Hawkins 1972: 104)

Whether out of naivety or disingenuousness, Filmer reads the double meanings in the exchange as if they were *euphemisms* – that is, verbal devices for
protecting the tone of well-bred conversation from the latent indecency of its
content. There is a genuine example of such a usage in Dorimant's phrase 'to
gain your favor': in the context, 'your favor' can only mean 'your agreement
to have sex with me', and Dorimant is using the pallid and courtly expression
in conformity to the ordinary rules of politeness. There is no 'point' being
made: this is merely the way gentlemen in this society really talk. Certainly it
is concealing and conveying its real meaning at the same time; but it is
obviously not the same kind of thing as the *double entendres* proper – the thread
of mutual understanding running through 'fared', 'keep a Lent', 'happy
Easter'.

The difference is not hard to see. Both figures involve the substitution of
one term for another. In the case of euphemism, the intention is to avoid the
direct expression of an indecent idea; consequently, the hope is that the
substitution itself will pass unnoticed, since if it draws attention to itself, it
also draws attention to the indecency it was meant to veil. *Double entendre*, on
the other hand, parades the substitution (and therefore the indecency); the
incongruity between the polite words and the impolite meaning is not an
incidental difficulty, but is the very point of the joke. It is therefore heightened by choosing discourses whose applicability is a matter of ingenuity and
surprise: sex in Restoration plays is discussed in the terms of theology, military strategy, finance, field sports, medicine and, in at least one case, geology.
(According to Berinthia in *The Relapse*, the amorous posers of the Town 'have
a torrent of love to dispose of . . . but 'tis like the rivers of a modern philosopher (whose works, though a woman, I have read): it sets out with a violent
stream, splits in a thousand branches, and is all lost in the sands' (II i 467–
71).) This kind of impudent misappropriation is like euphemism reversed:
denied its own language, sexuality colonizes all the others; the thing which
cannot be talked about becomes the thing which the things which can be
talked about are about.

The central significance of this form can be seen in the way it shapes, not
only passages of dialogue, but also plots. In *The Country Wife* (1675), for
example, one plot concerns the affair between the rake Horner and the wife of
the title; and it is so designed that they are brought together entirely by the
misdirected efforts of the jealous husband, Pinchwife. There is an even more
programmatic example of the same conceit in Otway's *The Soldier's Fortune*
(1680): Beaugard, the rake hero, makes advances to a young wife, who responds by telling her husband all about it and requesting him to return the
ring which, she says, Beaugard has insolently sent her. Beaugard never sent her
a ring: the message is in code. Decoding it correctly, Beaugard accepts the ring
with assumed shame and confusion, and asks the husband to tell his wife that
he is conscious of having offended her, and is anxious to satisfy her in any way

he can (Otway 1932: vol. II, 126–32). Sequences like this are mechanisms for generating innuendo in the dialogue, but they also constitute a sort of dramatic *double entendre* in themselves. The ring has two meanings, and so does the husband's action: just as the word 'satisfy' doubles its honourable and sexual senses, so the precautions of marital propriety double as pimping.

A third and more extreme example of the device will clarify its theatrical logic. In Aphra Behn's *The False Count* (1682), the jealous husband is the victim of an elaborate conspiracy to make him believe that he and his entire family have been captured by the Turks, that his wife has been chosen for the Grand Turk's harem, and that if he fails to co-operate with this arrangement he will be garrotted. The husband protests for a while, but is then so intimidated that he not only withdraws his objections, but apologizes for having presumed to advance them in the first place, and begs the Grand Turk to ratify his pardon by taking the wife off to bed at once. To this humble petition the Grand Turk, who is the wife's lover in disguise, graciously accedes. Here the scam amounts to a play within a play, an orientalist fantasy in which gallant and cuckold are transformed into sultan and slave; and the doubleness of meaning extends to every single stage sign in the whole of Acts IV and V. What this exuberant silliness reveals is the complicity between sexual innuendo and theatrical invention. In pursuit of their satisfaction, the lovers resort to illusions and transformations which form the substance of the comedy; their more or less abject expedients take them ever further into a space where every appearance is false, where what seems natural is posed, what seems fortuitous is contrived, and what seems a matter of life and death is a trick which one unguarded moment would reveal to be nothing. A space, in short, which manifests the real conditions of the theatre itself.

The unusual extravagance of *The False Count* is a heightened typicality. The identity games of masquerade, the pretexts to get unwanted husbands out of the way, the routines in which the heroine tests the hero by tempting him in disguise, the charades that exploit the superstition or snobbery of the guardian-figure – all over the comic theatre, in various kinds of beaux' stratagems, the pursuit of love triggers a flight into a false reality whose basic structure is that of *double entendre*. The flight is euphoric, and occasionally alarming, because it suspends contingency, placing the world explicitly (as dramatic form places it implicitly) at the disposal of the irresponsible imagination. Conversely, dramatic form is shown to be the *product* of desire: the play-making impulse, so to speak, is sexual.

This produces a coincidence of interests between the 'immoral' characters and the audience; the appetite for sexual pleasure within the play rhymes with the appetite for theatrical pleasure which has brought people to see it; and the gulled husbands and fathers, who would restore a coercive world of single *entendre* if they could, appear as the enemies of the show. But in reality they are *constitutive* of the show, since an unopposed progress to sexual consummation would of course be dramatically null. By endangering and retarding the liaison, they produce the dramatic structure, and the pleasure. So the material of the spectacle itself – what is literally shown and said on the stage – has a fetishistic character: in it, the sexual aim is diverted and delayed, and at the same time elaborated and adorned. From the point of view of theatrical representation, after all, the centrality of sex goes with its *sameness*: like death in classical tragedy (to which it is linked by the commonest seventeenth-century *double entendre* of all), it is the off-stage absolute, the undifferentiated point which representation endlessly leads up to and always stops short of. (The point, to put it another way, at which sexual pleasure becomes a matter of satisfaction instead of excitation, and therefore ceases to be theatrically productive.) In this sense, innuendo appears not just as a tactic for evading a law of propriety, but as a prismatic means of multiplying discourse around a signified which remains basely and lightlessly itself. In the end, there is nothing to be said – but the resources of culture, wit and morality are poured into the voluptuous project of postponing that end for five whole acts.

## 3   An Evening's Love

So theatre is eroticized: almost any Restoration play, regardless of its plot, could be given the title of Dryden's 1668 comedy, *An Evening's Love* (Dryden 1970b).

It is a showy piece set in Madrid on the last evening of carnival. Don Alonzo's establishment consists of his two daughters, Jacinta and Theodosia, and their *précieuse* cousin, Aurelia. Aurelia is beloved of young Don Lopez; Don Melchor is in love with both Aurelia and Theodosia and, unable to choose between them, has gone into hiding, telling everyone except Theodosia that he has gone to the war in Flanders. Jacinta is simply out for a good time before Lent sets in. The two English visitors, Wildblood and Bellamy, make a play for Jacinta and Theodosia respectively, and, after various intrigues, that is how it ends: Jacinta with Wildblood, Theodosia with Bellamy, Aurelia with Don Lopez, Don Alonzo tricked, and Don Melchor exposed. A supplementary couple – the sisters' woman, Beatrix, and the gallants' man, Maskall – completes the design.

The carnival setting is central to the conception. It provides a pretext for the extensive use of masks and disguises. And because it is about to end, it organizes the time of the action in a theatrical fashion: the evening in Madrid, like the evening in the theatre, is a time of irresponsibility which will come to an end at a fixed hour. This metatheatrical dimension is further extended by the play's most conspicuous device, which is that Bellamy spends much of the time, for reasons too complicated to explain, pretending to be an astrologer;

which not only adds a further layer to the tissue of disguises, but is also the occasion of a series of faked visionary phenomena. The wildest and most implausible of these comes in the last act, when several illicit couples are crowded into a summerhouse, where Don Alonzo is about to go and look for them. In desperation, Bellamy gets them all to come out and passes them off as apparitions called up by his mystical art. Plainly visible, they hide by pretending to be illusory, which of course at another level is what they really are. The show revels in its own conscious artificiality; every facet of its action reflects and celebrates theatrical invention.

Its values, accordingly, are amoral and formal ones. Don Melchor is the villain in the sense that it is his duplicity which retards the *dénouement*, but he is indecisive rather than malevolent. The reason for his expulsion from the happy ending is really that by being attached to two women instead of one, and being present for one and absent for the other, he has disturbed the pattern of couples unacceptably. He is blamed, you could say, not for moral turpitude but for structural solecism. A similar aestheticism marks the other plot, in which Jacinta plays a series of tricks on Wildblood, seducing him in various disguises and luring him into disastrous plunges at the gaming table. Her ostensible object is to test his constancy – a virtue he barely even claims to possess. The real point of the tricks is to permit her to occupy multiple positions in relation to him and so elaborate the design. In their best scene, an entire quarrel and reconciliation is staged in a single sequence of dialogue, accompanied by a self-conscious parallel manœuvre between Beatrix and Maskall. The form is thoroughly musical, like an extended ensemble number in a Mozart *opera buffa*. This is quite typical of the dramatic style: from the casual and *ad hoc* nature of the ethical characterization, and the detailed brilliance of the patterns of symmetry, repetition and variation, it is evident that Dryden is not interested in mimesis, but in devising something like a fast-moving and complicated dance.

That is not merely an impressionistic way of putting it. In the dialogue essay 'Of Dramatic Poesy', published in the same year, the same analogy appears in the course of an argument about rhyme in drama. Crites argues that rhyme destroys the illusion of spontaneity in dialogue by making it clear that the speakers 'perform their tricks like fortune-tellers, by confederacy' (Dryden 1970a: 65). Neander replies:

> Suppose we acknowledge it, how comes this confederacy to be more displeasing to you than a dance which is well contrived? You see there the united design of many persons to make up one figure: after they have separated themselves in many petty divisions, they rejoin one by one into a gross. The confederacy is plain amongst them; for chance could never produce anything so beautiful, and yet there is nothing in it, that shocks your sight. (p. 73)

In the immediate context, this is not a very good argument. Crites was saying, not that visible confederacy is shocking *per se*, but that it is shocking in drama, which is supposed to make its characters seem like autonomous individuals. A dance has no such mimetic purpose, so there is no contradiction in its bearing the marks of 'united design'. What Neander is actually but inexplicitly doing is denying the premise that the illusion of unplanned interaction is the proper aim of dramatic dialogue. He is happy to spoil that illusion for the sake of producing something *beautiful* – and the explanation of that point turns into an elegant description of the structure of *An Evening's Love*.

This formalism, however, is not at all the same thing as abstraction. Dryden's critical preface to *An Evening's Love* itself is committed to the assumption that the chief end of comedy is 'divertisement and delight' (Dryden 1970a: 105); and the proposed non-mimetic theatrical pleasure is unequivocally sensuous. Dancing, after all, is a sexual as well as a mathematical activity. The point is made with startling clarity in the theatre prologue, which is worth quoting in full.

At the time of the first performance, Dryden had just become the King's Theatre's resident playwright, contracted to do three scripts a year. The prologue reflects on this uniquely well-established position:

> When first our Poet set himself to write,
> Like a young Bridegroom on his Wedding-night
> He layd about him, and did so bestir him,
> His Muse could never lye in quiet for him:
> But now his Honey-moon is gone and past,
> Yet the ungrateful drudgery must last:
> And he is bound, as civil Husbands do,
> To strain himself, in complaisance to you:
> To write in pain, and counterfeit a bliss,
> Like the faint smackings of an after-kiss.
> But you, like Wives ill pleas'd, supply his want;
> Each writing *Monsieur* is a fresh Gallant:
> And though, perhaps, 'twas done as well before,
> Yet still there's something in a new amour.
> Your several Poets work with several tools,
> One gets you wits, another gets you fools:
> This pleases you with some by-stroke of wit,
> This finds some cranny, that was never hit.
> But should these janty Lovers daily come
> To do your work, like your good man at home,
> Their fine small-timber'd wits would soon decay;
> These are Gallants but for a Holiday.
> Others you had who oftner have appear'd,

Whom, for meer impotence you have cashier'd:
Such as at first came on with pomp and glory,
But, overstraining, soon fell flat before yee.
Their useless weight with patience long was born,
But at the last you threw them off with scorn.
As for the Poet of this present night,
Though now he claims in you an Husbands right,
He will not hinder you of fresh delight.
He, like a Seaman, seldom will appear;
And means to trouble home but thrice a year:
That only time from your Gallants he'll borrow;
Be kind to day, and Cuckold him to morrow.

> > > > > > > > (Dryden 1970b: 214–15)

The prologues and epilogues of Restoration theatre are often flirtations; this one goes further and makes sexual intercourse a complete and remarkably detailed model of the relationship between the writer and his audience. It is a striking metaphor because while, on the one hand, it makes communication central to the business of writing plays, on the other hand it gets rid of the question of *what* is to be communicated. This civil poet, valiantly striving to please his insatiable public one more time, is not imagined as having anything to 'say' to us; the whole emphasis of the equivocal verbs – 'strain', 'do', 'work', 'get', 'find' – is on what he wishes and is expected to *do* to us. Thus, if a writer comes up with a new idea – building in an astrologer, as here, or making the cuckold an amateur scientist, as in Shadwell's *The Virtuoso* (1676) – this is not (according to this model) because he has any comments to make on astrology or science. It is rather 'some cranny, that was never hit' – a new caress, a surprising touch amid the familiar satisfactions. Theatrical pleasure is not instrumental to the representation of manners or morals or any other extra-theatrical reality; on the contrary, the representations are instruments of pleasure.

Dramatic realism – to generalize the point – tends constantly to dematerialize the stage. It takes its speech, bodies, personalities, costumes, movements, rhythms – in one word its substance – and subordinates all that to the function of portraying the world. Only nature is allowed to be material; the elements of theatrical spectacle count as mere reflections of that prior materiality, themselves not real but (on the contrary) realistic. What Dryden's sexual model brings into view, against that suppression, is the 'reality' of the theatre itself. Doing a play appears, like sex, as an act whose meaning is not derived from some external referent which it is to denote, but develops through the vigour and inventiveness with which the connection itself is made. The model does read like formalism in its reduction of 'content' to the status of a mere function of the autotelic form. But it is a coarse and bawdy formalism, because the 'form' is the whole social, material and erotic encounter of live theatre, in which the speaker is explicitly and practically involved. Its 'radical inversion of the priorities of the work of art' (Jameson 1972: 82) claims no general validity, but merely reflects, with provocative amorality, the immediate life of the show.

It is tempting, then, to elect Dryden as an exponent of what would now be called performance theatre – graceful, material, autonomous and sexy – against the grey authority of literary referentiality. However, this will not quite do. It is true that the imagery of the prologue sketches a persuasive erotics of theatrical 'divertisement and delight'. But its argument is something else: a sardonic exposition of the author's *economic* relations with the public.

The spectators appear to the writer as insatiably demanding, moving faithlessly from one 'writing *Monsieur*' to the next in search of fresh satisfactions. This fickleness places Dryden, as the theatre's resident play-wright, in the position of a complaisant cuckold, resenting the new lovers who supplant him, but forced to accept them because it is impossible for him to do it all himself. That is to say, his fellow playwrights are at once his colleagues in the interminable task of keeping the audience happy, and his rivals, whom he is professionally obliged to depreciate by way of advertising his own services. The real humiliation, which is figured in the persona of the humble husband, is that of the poet in the commercial theatre, studying to hit off the capricious taste of the Town, obsequiously hoping that the public will allow his play at least the three performances which he needs to make any money out of it, and aware that no amount of excellence in the writing can guarantee him against the risk of simply going out of fashion tomorrow. The way the relationship is gendered registers the humiliation as subversive of a norm: in theory the poet–male is sovereign, but in fact the audience–female is the sole judge of whether the labouring pen has successfully 'done her work'. From her verdict, however whimsical, there is no appeal to classical canons of taste, or literary reputation, or critical demonstration, or moral excellence: here in the theatre, these imposing male institutions are nothing more than props for the vulnerable poetical ego. What matters is that the audience should keep coming: if it does, the props are redundant, and if it does not, they are cold comfort.

The phrase 'commercial theatre' suggests something like the West End or even Hollywood; but we need to be rather more historically specific about this. It was a commercial theatre, certainly – absolutely and immediately dependent on the income from ticket sales. The right to present plays in London, granted by royal patent in 1660, was a piece of private property which could be owned, inherited and transferred like any other; to buy into it was a straightforward commercial investment which was supposed to pay a dividend. However, the official framework within which this nakedly monetary criterion operated was not a 'free market'. On the contrary, it was designedly and artificially limited.

The grant of 1660 set up two theatre companies, and made it illegal for anyone to perform plays in London except under the aegis of one or the other of them (Thomas 1989: 11–12). The theatrical diversity of the pre-1642 period – and in particular its popular theatre – was thus deliberately closed off in order to make the stage more controllable. There were to be no more than two companies, owing their existence to the king's pleasure and operating under the eye of a Court official such as the Lord Chamberlain or the Master of the Revels. This was indeed the situation over the next fifty years (and in fact for much longer), except that for some of the time the two companies merged so that there was only one.

The effect of this duopoly was even more restrictive in practice than it looks on paper. Each of the companies was naturally concerned to secure its position against its only competitor; neither could contemplate yielding the social and cultural high ground to the other. Thus both studied the taste of the Court, invested heavily in architectural splendour and movable scenery, and sought to draw their core audience from the fashionable elite. It used to be thought by theatre historians that they were wholly successful in this project: that the Restoration theatre was essentially Court entertainment. It has since been shown that actual audiences were a good deal more diverse than that, with foreign visitors, domestic servants and the London middle class all significantly represented (Loftis et al. 1976: 13–25). But the core of truth in the 'courtly' stereotype is that the culturally dominant group, the leading patrons both in the politics of company management and the socially interactive milieu of the playhouse itself, were the privileged elite known to social observers of the time as the 'quality'. This ascendancy can be seen very directly in the biographies of the writers: some, like Sedley and Etherege, themselves belonged to the 'quality', while many others, like Wycherley and Congreve, used their theatrical and literary success to join it.

The relation between the two theatres was consequently a competition for the *same* audience. If either house had a big success, it instantly and directly dented the takings at the other; and when this happened, the response of the loser was not to seek new audiences (since that would be to accept second-class status by going down market), but to try and repair its fortunes with a successful show that matched its rival's and won the audience back. From a capitalist point of view, you could say that this form of competition, though periodically intense, was not *progressive*: it remained essentially a zero-sum game. The impasse is not only a matter of attitude: it became institutionally fixed as companies organized themselves to play the game as effectively as possible. The repertoire, for example, had to be extremely flexible to meet short-term audience demand; so a very large number of stock plays was kept in readiness, and new plays were custom-written and typecast so that they could join the stock with the minimum of disruption. These tactics for keeping a grip on the existing audience tended to lock the theatre into a closed system which made radical experiment impracticable. Paradoxically, the incessant search for novelty precluded innovation. The business was not organized for growth.

The theatre's development into an authentically commercial institution was being arrested half-way by a residual aristocratic hegemony. Its artists had the autonomy, but not the respectability, of independent commodity producers, and they had the privileges, but not the security, of servants. The complicated frustrations of their transitional position can be heard in the way they address the audience, in the disrespectful servility and self-deprecating aggression of prologues and epilogues. Another example from Dryden catches the many-layered tone. In the prologue to *Secret Love* (1667) he tells the customers:

> you think yourselves ill us'd,
> When in smart Prologues you are not abus'd. . . .
> Your Fancy's pall'd, and liberally you pay
> To have it quicken'd, e're you see a Play.
> Just as old Sinners, worn from their delight,
> Give money to be whip'd to appetite.
>                                    (Dryden 1966: 120)

The audience, it seems, are constantly on the point of getting jaded, and decadently require fresh and perverse stimulation. Equally, the poets are continually at risk of running out of ideas: at this point, less than seven years after the reopening of the theatres, flattering prologues have already been replaced by abusive ones, and the abusive ones have already become a cliché, which Dryden artfully dusts off by abusing the audience for liking abuse. What is he going to do for his next prologue? This is the complaisant husband again, striving to come up with a new variation on what can only be the same old transaction. The writer's inventiveness and the spectator's appetite are both imagined, like Horner's china in *The Country Wife*, as finite stocks, which have to be carefully eked out if the trade is to continue.

But then what relieves that closed circle of anxiety, and even gives the tone a sort of grubby geniality, is the flat knowingness of the references to money. The economics of the encounter are flamboyantly on show: the mode of address says, 'this is what you are fool enough to pay for, and what we are unscrupulous enough to purvey.' This is the point on which the style most obviously separates itself out from twentieth-century show business. Fully commercial theatre characteristically affirms immaterial values – love, altruism, the indomitable human spirit, finding one's true self, and so on. It is on its honour to do so: the customers have paid for an experience which transcends the sordid business of making a living, and it would be a breach of commercial ethics to take their money and not deliver the goods. No such discretion is incumbent upon the Restoration theatre. Trapped in the residual honour code of its patrons, it fails or refuses to recognize any moral imperative that is founded upon trade, and regards its own inescapable exchange relationships as uniformly degrading. The dramatic poet, turning out wit for money, is something like a prostitute or a gamester, and the paying audience are his gulls. In short, he is a professional entertainer who lacks an ideology to cover his case, and so cannot attain the innocence which such an ideology would afford.

Thus the meeting between the actors and the audience has the character of an unsecured deal – not an official engagement, but an evening's love. The ethical rationales for comedy – the mirror held up to nature, the salutary ridicule of folly, and the rest – are really beside the point; which is why the playwrights' own retorts to Collier are so evasive and unconvincing (Congreve 1964; Vanbrugh 1927). In practice, the theatre has no legitimate account of itself to offer. Historically suspended between a residual courtly authorization which is incompatible with its economic position, and an emergent bourgeois authorization which is incompatible with its social position, it takes the fool's option and accepts the disreputable privileges of living with no authorization at all. Its only justification is pleasure: that ideological penury is the basis of its sexual metaphors, and also the source of its vitality.

## 4  Profaneness

For Collier, as for other reformers at the turn of the century, the profanity of the theatre is at least as offensive as its sexual licence – if not more so, since it offends God as well as man. One plausible context for this line of attack is the long divorce, noted by Glynne Wickham among others, of drama and the sacred (Wickham 1963: 96). The English stage – so the argument runs – was predominantly a religious one until Elizabethan Protestantism forced a separation between theatre and the central concerns of faith; even then, the drama kept in touch with its sacred roots down to 1642; but after 1660 it went through a further phase of secularization which cut acting off from its ritual origins and restricted it, thematically and formally, to a rationalistic imitation of 'manners'. Theatre had been desacralized by the same cultural shift which had suppressed the theatricality of religion: in Collier's denunciations of the profaneness of the stage, we are hearing a religious man's reaction to what had become a fundamentally secular type of representation.

This cultural narrative covers a good deal of the evidence. When Collier objects to dramatic characters casually saying 'Gad' the whole time, and Vanbrugh replies that contemporary Englishmen do in fact say this, and that drama takes no responsibility for the manners it portrays (Vanbrugh 1927: 197–8), this is clearly a secular defence against a religious attack. The implication is that theatre, like science, is neither sacred nor profane, but refuses metaphysics altogether and unpretentiously records whatever phenomena fall under its observation. This beguiling argument, however, does less than justice to the theatrical tradition which Vanbrugh is opportunistically defending.

In particular, it speaks as if there were no distinction, within the theatre, between genres. And in practice, the difference between comedy and tragedy was very clearly marked. Under the typecasting system, an individual actor had two specialist 'lines', one for comedy and one for tragedy; they were not necessarily similar. Comedy was in prose or a loose, colloquial verse; tragedy in blank verse or heroic couplets. Comedy was set in the present and in London or a city with recognizably similar social conventions; tragedy was historically and geographically exotic. Comedy was dressed in costumes which referred, sometimes in great detail, to the fashions on view in the auditorium; tragedy with a fantastic splendour which denoted not so much the clothes of the notionally depicted society as the dignity of the genre itself. Theoretical discussions of drama were neo-classical in their frame of reference: that is, it was genre which formed the basis of detailed judgements about the propriety of actions, language or characters in a particular play. None of this is to say that comic elements were absolutely banned from tragedies or vice versa; the point, really a much more significant one, is that audiences possessed two different grammars for the enjoyment of theatre, and were educated to expect that the meaning of any given dramatic sign would change if it was moved from one to the other.

So this is a theatre in which the relation between the two significant genres is an *organized* one – they are distinct, but their distinctness is itself a form of connection, such that the identity of each is informed by the presence of the other. This gives a special value to early plays like Dryden's *Secret Love* (1667) and Sedley's *The Mulberry Garden* (1668), in which the two dramatic languages are not merged, but alternated in a binary dramatic structure. This baroque combination was a fairly short-lived form, not developing beyond the early 1670s, but it constitutes a paradigm for the general relationship, doing within one play what the theatre was doing, less immediately, in its repertoire as a whole. The best-known example is probably Dryden's *Marriage à-la-Mode* (1671).

The comic half is a libertine quartet: a husband and wife who are tired of each other attempt to have affairs, fixing by chance on two people who are engaged to be married to each other on parental instructions. This neat cat's-cradle alternates with the romance of Leonidas and Palmyra, a noble couple brought up in humble circumstances who appear at Court and discover, in a series of misleading revelations, first that only Palmyra is royal and so that they are unable to marry, then that only Leonidas is royal and they are still unable to marry, and finally that they are both royal but unrelated and can marry with general approval.

Both these plots are machines for producing crises as often, as forcefully and as lucidly as possible. Moreover, both are powered by the same three sources of energy: love, paternal injunction and marriage. For Leonidas and Palmyra, all three are sacred: Palmyra will always be faithful to Leonidas because she will not profane her love, but she will not marry him because she will not profane a father's authority, and if he marries someone else she will not contemplate adultery because she will not profane the marriage tie. All three principles are raised to the height of refinement by the mathematical perfection of their incompatibility. The image of filial duty is particularly exalted because the apparent identity of the father changes at each new twist of the plot, which makes it clear that it is not a question of personal affection. It is pure duty, unmixed with the slightest coinciding feeling. This purity is exactly the point: the play manipulates the situations in order to produce the sharpest possible realization of the abstract principles it is seeking to stage. In this rather specialized sense, it is, like much heroic tragedy of the Restoration, a form of sacred drama, structured by the effort to make absolute metaphysical ideas visible in action. It is in this context of consciously strained values that we should consider the play's stylish opening image. Doralice, the discontented wife, appears for a moment and then withdraws to try out a new song. Palamede, the reluctant fiancé of the other woman, enters in travelling clothes and listens unseen. She sings:

> Why should a foolish Marriage Vow,
>   Which long ago was made,
> Oblige us to each other now
>   When Passion is decay'd?
> We lov'd, and we lov'd, as long as we cou'd,
>   Till our love was lov'd out in us both:
> But our Marriage is dead, when the Pleasure is fled:
>   'Twas Pleasure first made it an Oath.
>
> (Dryden 1978: 315)

The lightness of the versification and the nicety of the emotional tone – somehow cheeky and melancholy at the same time – almost disguise the lyric's hard structure, which is that of an argument. It is putting the case that an oath is no more than the expression of an intention, and so that if the intention is overtaken by time, the oath no longer constitutes an obligation. The argument is profane in the sense that it refers the vow, naturalistically, back to the desires of the individuals who made it, ignoring the proposition that it is binding because it invoked heaven. It is a topical issue, in a way: legal practice was painfully adapting, at just this historical point, to a cultural desacralization of juridical swearing (Staves 1987: 191–251). But in the 'serious' world, of course, that secularization of oaths was leading to their redefinition as legally binding contracts, rather than to the pleasantly anarchic state of affairs which is envisaged in the song. The contention that, since 'pleasure first made it an Oath', the oath dies at the same time as the pleasure, is a sophism, a consciously *illicit* argument – as is made clear in the second verse, which applies the theory to a justification, not of divorce, but of guilt-free adultery. So there are two things to be said at once about the comic *Marriage à-la-Mode*'s profanation of what the 'serious' *Marriage à-la-Mode* holds sacred, both vital if somewhat contradictory.

One is that it is *not* the innocent flouting of abstract rules by real (still less by realistic) behaviour. The two worlds are equally highly patterned, equally aware of the theoretical implications of particular choices, equally initiated in that generalizing discourse in which speakers universalize their actions, argue their case and situate themselves in relation to impersonal laws. When Palamede and Doralice travesty the code which governs Leonidas and Palmyra, they know what they are doing; their witty and irreverent use of the language of moral and religious law places them firmly in the same speech world as their exalted counterparts. This parodic connection applies to beliefs in actual society as well: Palamede ends one scene with a neat summary of his philosophy:

> Rogues may pretend Religion, and the Laws;
> But a kind Mistris is the *Good old Cause*.
>
> (IV iii)

The Good Old Cause was the name given to the religious and political beliefs underlying the Parliamentary resistance to Charles I: this misappropriation of the phrase defines the mistress as not merely a girl one fancies but an alternative belief system. The comic style, within the double structure, is not casually profane, but studiously *profaning*. Palamede's vice is a semiotic activity.

But then the other thing which equally needs to be said is that these conscious and considered acts of profanation are performed within the enclosure created for them by the generic organization itself. It is above all a hierarchical organization. Following Aristotle, the critical commonplace of the age is that tragedy is the stage equivalent of epic poetry, in which serious-minded poets represent noble actions and the doings of noble persons, while comedy, written by the more trivial-minded and concerning the meaner sort of people, corresponds to lampoon (Aristotle 1965: 35–6). Comedy is thus inferior to tragedy in several superimposed senses: it is socially low instead of high, it depicts base actions instead of noble ones, and it encodes a non-serious attitude to life instead of a serious one. This is a historically quite specific selection from the various grounds of differentiation offered by the *Poetics*. It distributes the language, ideas and characters of the stage in terms of *vertical stratification* – the essential opposition is not so much that between pity and laughter, say, or death and marriage, as that between high and low. The opposition is therefore radically relational, because 'low' is conceptually necessary to 'high', as 'laughter' is not necessary to 'pity'. It is thus not quite accurate to see the profane figures of Restoration comedy – the inversion of obligation and pleasure, the sensual 'devotions' – as *attacks* on the elevated code of tragedy and heroic drama, or on the tenets of Christianity either. Rather, the profanity *complements* the heroic, completing its image of a dualistic world which is material as well as ideal, creatural as well as intellectual, appetitive as well as juridical, and so on. The relation is antithetic, definingly so; but the antithesis is stable; there is no demand that either version should ultimately destroy the other. Palmyra and Palamede both obey their fathers – Palmyra because the name of father is sacred, Palamede because he wants to inherit the old man's money. The two versions of filiality coexist, just as, for example, the human form is noble in history painting and base in tavern painting.

The ground of this stability, crucially, is social and political. The characters of tragedy are 'noble' – that is, proud, publicly honourable, magnanimous, visually splendid, and so on, but also, anchoring these subjective qualities in a social signifier, they are princes. Not, of course, that Restoration comedy has a corresponding interest in low life: the difference that matters is that the interactions of serious drama happen at Court, whereas the characters of comedy are leading private lives. This distinction is particularly striking in *The Mulberry Garden* (1668), where the comic plot takes place in the contemporary Town locations – private houses, London parks – which had already been established in 1630s comedy and would remain much the same for the next fifty years, while the heroic one concerns two cavaliers, proscribed under the Protectorate, whose love tangles eventually get sorted out by the return of Charles II in 1660. Of the two plots, then, one takes place in history and the other outside it. Or, to put it more rigorously, the locus of serious drama is the State, whereas that of comedy is civil society. The clarity of the distinction is thus politically absolutist: the superiority of the State-as-serious over civil-society-as-comic is total and schematic. The relation between them is like master and slave, or king and fool: the values of the latter are licentious only because they are *licensed*, their apparent rebelliousness really only part of a composite sign which denotes their absolute subordination. In short, the profanity of Restoration comedy, its insouciant endorsement of faithlessness and impiety, makes sense inside monarchic ideology.

The subordination is a kind of turning loose, of course. Spared the tribulations of importance, the fine ladies and gentlemen inhabit the liberty of the sub-plot where they play safely like bad children with the swords and sceptres of the grown-ups. In *The Mulberry Garden*, for example, one of the ladies agrees to a proposal to go and eat syllabubs on condition that the gentlemen say nothing but what they think. Her sister objects:

Faith, Sister, let's bate 'um that circumstance, Truth is a thing meerly
necessary for witnesses, and Historians, and in these places doth but curb
invention, and spoil good Company; We will only confine 'um to what's
probable. (Sedley 1928: 122)

Her opposition between truth and probability is a light allusion to Aristotle's
opinion that historians are required, as she says, to be truthful, poets only to
be probable. 'In these places' – the secondary and provisional spaces of comedy
– it is possible to choose to count as a poet. The libertinism is characteristic,
but then so is the awareness of it: the witty misapplication of theory *knows* that
it is indefensible (the speaker is also signalling her awareness that the gentlemen are going to tell lies), and makes dramatic room for itself by not asking
to be 'taken seriously'. The freedom – of speech and movement – is not the
freedom of liberalism, but the freedom of privilege under authority.

This is also the freedom of the theatre, another enclosed space, patronized
and licensed by the State, avowedly a diversion for the Town, its entertainments always securely framed by the familiar ironic disclaimers of the prologue and epilogue. The comic drama's addiction to metatheatrical devices
indicates its awareness that theatricality itself was a formula for its indulged
liberty, its artificially allowed refusal to let truth curb invention and spoil
good company. But the condition of this circumscribed irresponsibility was
the absolute stability of the hierarchy which gave it its place: only if the
utopian stage of heroic drama retained its ideal purity could the sphere of the
profane be purely playful; civil society could be represented as entirely
unpolitical only so long as the State's monopoly of politics could be represented as total. And in practice, this transcendent separateness could only be
sustained for a few years after 1660.

We can see the strains on it by returning for a moment to *Marriage à-la-
Mode*. It was staged by the King's company in 1671, and a few months later
the rival company, the Duke's, reacted to its success with a play called *The
Reformation*. This unconvincing satire has a Venetian setting and features an
English tutor, clearly a portrait of Dryden himself, who assures his charges
that English society is characterized by a complete absence of restrictions on
sexual behaviour, and encourages them to launch the reformation of the title
to bring Venice to the same anarchic state. The young reformers echo
Palamede's joke about Puritanism in a song:

> Away with all things that sound like to Laws,
> In this our new *Reformation*;
> Let the Formalists prate, the good old cause
> Is a general toleration.
>
> (*Reformation* 1986: 19)

Here, perhaps insincerely but at least in intention plausibly, the 'licensed' character of Dryden's libertine comedy is ignored, and the play is understood as propaganda for the lifestyle which could be deduced by taking Palamede's paradoxes as pieces of advice. Conversely, an essay of 1674, vindicating matrimony, interprets the same scenes as satire, in which 'What is either wicked or silly in modish colours [is] so well painted, as would divert any person that is owner of the least ingenuity from both' (H. Brooks 1935). In both these readings, the playfulness of Dryden's play is not received, and its dual structure is rendered monologic and didactic. The doubleness survives only in the incompatibility of the two single interpretations. Neither reader allows Dryden to keep comedy in unresolved equilibrium with 'seriousness'. For both, he must either be advocating his modish marriages, or else satirizing them.

Although we cannot legitimately elect these two spectators as representative, it is interesting that both appear to come from outside the elite audience which Dryden was seeking to please. The author of *The Reformation* was probably Joseph Arrowsmith, an Oxford student shortly to take holy orders; and the anonymous essayist identifies himself as a 'Country Gentleman', a character which conventionally signifies decent independence of the sophistical values of the Court. Their outsiders' readings, then, suggest how a diversity of viewpoints in the playhouse could scramble the schematic hierarchy of serious and comic, true and privileged, State and civil society. The imagined societies of these split-plot shows, in which private life happens on the fringes of the Court and is directly determined by events at the centre, are fantasies of royal cultural hegemony which no longer correspond to the reality of London. The increase in population, the growing wealth of the City, the development of a non-courtly West End, the unofficial culture of the coffee-houses, the very high number of temporary residents in the capital, the political splits within Court circles themselves – a whole complex transformation was tending to diversify the theatre's constituency and confirm it as a free-standing commercial venture: an institution of civil society, and not an organ of the State. (Whereas Charles I's actors had been summoned to Court, Charles II went to the theatre.) The stage was thus oriented towards multiple social and ideological centres, which pulled its meanings in different directions, troubling the clear-cut generic distinctions which underlie Dryden's gay and ultimately innocuous inversions of value.

Thus the generic container in which profanity is theoretically sealed is in practice imperfectly shut; there is always a danger that comic decorum will be misread as subversion, so that the irresponsible scepticism of the licensed jester leaks into the real world. For the writer, this is an ambiguous mishap: it is after all the danger of being taken seriously, which is also a kind of opportunity.

In *The Provok'd Wife* (1697), Lady Brute, the wife of the title, is considering with her niece whether she should react to the provocations of her husband by cuckolding him:

> LADY BRUTE: Why, after all, there's more to be said for't than you'd imagine, child. I know according to the strict statute law of religion I should do wrong; but if there were a Court of Chancery in heaven, I'm sure I should cast him.
> BELLINDA: If there were a House of Lords you might.
> LADY BRUTE: In either I should infallibly carry my cause. Why, he is the first aggressor, not I.
> BELLINDA: Ay, but you know, we must return good for evil.
> LADY BRUTE: That may be a mistake in the translation.
>                                    (Vanbrugh 1989: 161, I i 84–96)

Chancery was the court of equity, to which a litigant could turn if denied justice by courts operating under 'strict statute law'. Collier finds Lady Brute's witticism blasphemous on two counts: it supposes that there is no equity in heaven, and it suggests that, if there were, adultery would not be punished (J. Collier 1972a: 83). Defending himself a few months later, Vanbrugh admits that the line may seem 'liable to exception' at first:

> Yet least the Audience shou'd mistake her Raillery for her serious Opinion, there is care taken immediately to inform 'em otherwise by making her reprimand her self in these words to *Bellinda. But I shall play the fool and jest on, till I make you begin to think I am in earnest.* (Vanbrugh 1927: 23–4)

Vanbrugh is attempting to retreat into the generically protected space we have already delineated; to claim the right not to be taken seriously. For Collier, however, this only makes things worse. In his next pamphlet he quotes the exchange all over again and comments:

> Thus the Justice of God, the Court of Heaven, and the Precepts of our *Saviour* are Ridiculed! And what can make satisfaction for these horrible outrages? Not all the Blood in a Man's Veins. The Mercy that Pardons such Boldness, had need be infinite! But the *Vindicator* has taken care *that her Raillery should not be mistaken for her serious Opinion.* . . . This is an admirable defence! The Woman Blasphemes in jest, and diverts the Company with the *Bible*, and therefore all's well; and the *Poet must be commended for his Caution!* I perceive God and Religion are very Significant Things with some People! (J. Collier 1972b: 113–14)

It is an argument of some practical seriousness. Blasphemy was punishable by a fine of £10 (that is, the successful prosecution of two or three jokes would be enough to wipe out an ordinary evening's takings), and in 1701 most of the cast of *The Provok'd Wife* were in fact indicted for profanity (Krutch 1949: 170–2). Collier is accusing Vanbrugh, not merely of bad taste, but of a criminal offence. And the seriousness can be seen in the minute attention to the text: this debate was arguably the first time that a contemporary playscript was subjected to the kind of 'close reading' which it now receives in A level classes. The licensed space of comedy is being closed up, not only by what is being said, but by the whole way the discussion is being conducted.

What this newly critical discourse most immediately reflects is the fact that Collier, as a clergyman, is trained in the detailed interpretation of texts. Habits developed by studying the Bible and the Fathers are being used to read a fashionable comedy, and this is one reason for the reader's outraged response: if you read a series of jokes as if they were a sermon, then it is predictable that the sermon so constructed will prove a profane and topsy-turvy one, a satanic verse. But the reading is not *wholly* inappropriate. Lady Brute is diverting the company with the blasphemous hypothesis that the Bible might contain mistakes. The fallibility of scriptural transmission had indeed been a basis for irreligious opinions during the interregnum (Hill 1984: 198–9); and now, in the relatively liberal publishing climate of the 1690s, 'freethinking' rereadings of Scripture were once more being developed – for example, by the 'modern philosopher' Vanbrugh's Berinthia reads, Thomas Burnet (Champion 1992: 164–6). Moreover, the regime of 1642–60 had also dismantled the ecclesiastical courts and effectively instituted civil marriage (Staves 1987: 115–16); after the Restoration attempts had been made to reimpose the Church's control, but the final defeat of divine monarchy in 1688 created a climate in which matrimony, like many other institutions, could be reappraised in a secular light. Bellinda's reference to the House of Lords is not casual: a series of high-profile aristocratic divorce cases came to Parliament in the course of the 1690s, some successfully (Stone 1990: 313–22). To Collier, a High-Church clergyman and irreconcilable opponent of the entire 1688 settlement, these derogations of biblical and ecclesiastical authority were anathema: his over-reaction to Lady Brute's repartee reflects an uneasy awareness that the comic stage is not the only place where her views are gaining currency. Her rider – 'I shall play the fool and jest on, till I make you begin to think I am in earnest' – must have sounded to him less like a disclaimer than a threat.

The point here is not that *The Provok'd Wife* is a serious discussion of current issues in the manner of Ibsen or Shaw. The relative secularization of marital law doesn't really authorize the fantastic projection of English jurisprudence on to the court of heaven. And Christ's injunction to return good for evil is not really a minor doctrinal nuance which scholarly retranslation might one day emend, but the central tenet of the entire Gospel. Lady Brute is comically and parodically clutching at straws. In other words, these are not arguments but jokes; she is speaking the same comic language as Palamede or Dorimant. What has changed is the environment of that language. If the sanctity of what is profaned can no longer be seen as absolute, then the profanation can no longer be heard as simple 'raillery'. The possible presence of the heterodox contaminates the pure wit of the paradox; cheeking the headmaster, so to speak, has a quite different meaning if his authority is already under threat.

To put it crudely, the refusal of the 'foolish marriage vow' has begun to *get real*. The couples in *Marriage à-la-Mode* took to their naughtiness as naturally as ducks to water: it was as if libertinism were the accepted law of their subordinate and parodic sub-plot world. They were prevented from consummating their liaisons only by the farcical mechanics of the plot; this preserved their innocence, not only of the fact of adultery, but equally of the moral anxiety of a *refusal* of pleasure. Their fortuitous frustration permitted them to remain playful exponents of a merely possible behaviour. Lady Brute's profane musings are not generic in the same way, but are motivated by her experience of an unhappy marriage which the play presents with some social and psychological density. She is tempted to accept the advances of her lover, Constant, but not sure that she should, and not sure, either, that she wants to; at the end of the play it is still not clear what she is going to do. In other words, her predicament, without ceasing to be comic, acquires a past, a future, and a dimension of *difficult choice*. The State world of 'serious' drama is losing its monopoly on the historical and ethical; private marriages are to have their politics as well as royal ones; as a result the jokes – even if they are the same jokes – become, you could say, seriously funny.

So the dramatic writing is richer, but at the same time its jester's licence is revoked. Collier all but announces this cancellation in another of his comments on *The Provok'd Wife*, this time referring to a sceptical exchange on the subject of modesty – a value which, he says, was always respected by Euripides:

> How wretchedly do we fall short of the Decencies of Heathenism! There's nothing more ridiculous than Modesty on our *Stage*. 'Tis counted an ill-bred Quality, and almost sham'd out of Use. One would think Mankind were not the same, that Reason was to be read Backward, and Vertue and Vice had changed Place. (J. Collier 1972a: 35)

'One would think . . .': in registering his sense of travesty Collier almost reproduces the festive 'as if' which contains the 'world upside down' of comedy. But the tone denies the syntactic permissiveness; the phrase expresses outraged sarcasm; the implication is that although the immodest unanimity of these plays might make one *think* mankind not the same, in reality one *knows* this cannot be right. Mankind *is* the same; reason can only be read in one direction; virtue and vice are irreversibly fixed in their places. It is a firmly monologic frame of reception, levelling the hierarchy of genres to the single standard of truth. In this frame, it is as impermissible that the theatre should be profane as it is inconceivable that it could be sacred. It is still possible to quibble with Collier about individual cases, but to the extent that this language is accepted as valid, the carnival is over.

## 5   Reform

One reason for Lady Brute's robust attitude to her marital obligations is the attractive model offered by the recent Revolution – the deposition of James II and his replacement by William and Mary in 1688–9. This operation was an announcement by the English ruling class that it now viewed sovereignty, not as a divine institution, but as a determinable trust formed between human beings for practical purposes. As Lady Brute observes, if this argument is good between the king and the people, why not between the husband and the wife? She is perhaps still jesting, but not at random: the ideologist of the Revolution, John Locke, had tentatively endorsed this corollary himself (Locke 1963: 364), and that very unjocular feminist, Mary Astell, deployed the same analogy in *Some Reflections Upon Marriage* (1700), though, as a conservative Tory, she drew the opposite conclusion (Perry 1986: 163–5). As David Roberts suggests (D. Roberts 1989: 147), 'Bill of Rights' thinking naturally pervaded an intensifying debate about marriage in the 1690s, and the stage was not sealed off from this questioning climate. Thomas Southerne handles the predicament of a provoked wife with more argumentative seriousness than Vanbrugh in *The Wives Excuse* (1692); later and more famously, Farquhar laces the fantastical role-playing of *The Beaux' Stratagem* with fairly direct quotations from Milton on divorce. In such tentatively Whiggish moves, it is possible to see the absolutist logic of Dryden's generic structure losing control of the stage. It is hardly accidental that most of the recognized and revived masterpieces of 'Restoration' comedy – the major plays of Vanbrugh, Farquhar and Congreve – all come from the period between 1690 and 1714. The same is true of many of the writers who, like Southerne and Susannah Centlivre, are only now, in the 1980s and 1990s, re-establishing a critical and theatrical presence. Private life was acquiring a politics; the State's monopoly was broken; it is these plays, rather than the high Carolean repertoire, that really appear as 'the first modern comedies'.

An analogous break marks the theatre history of the 1690s. In 1694 the death of Queen Mary deprived the theatre of the last royal personage to take her patronage role at all seriously. In the following year, the leading members of the United Company, provoked beyond endurance by the mercenary policies of the manager, Christopher Rich, organized a walkout and set up as an actors' co-operative in the old theatre in Lincoln's Inn Fields. This divorce too was characterized by constitutionalist rhetoric. The prologues for the first night celebrated the free-born Player's emancipation from '*Egyptian* Bondage' (Congreve 1964: II, 91); and Cibber, looking back on the venture in his memoirs, portrays it as a kind of Dutch republic, with Rich playing the role of Spain (Cibber 1968: 126ff). The co-operative advertised itself to patrons – whom it desperately needed, as it had plenty of writing and performing talent but no capital – as an instance of English liberty.

So there is a superficial symbolic appropriateness in the fact that it was Collier who arose in 1698 as the arch-enemy of this dynamic and freedom-loving stage. He was an unreconciled High-Church clergyman, who had been outlawed in 1696 for absolving two Jacobite conspirators on the scaffold: as we have seen, the subtext of his attack on the theatre is an ultra-legitimist programme for the restoration of royal, episcopal, and patriarchal authority. But in fact this is little more than a local irony: the real politics of theatre reform were very different.

For what the breakaway company's rhetoric conceals is that their action reinstated the duopoly which had existed before 1682, and with it the 'zero-sum' competition. Inter-company rivalry was particularly savage during the closing years of the century, with each company, at different times, close to collapse. And the game was being played on a new pitch, from which the 'Court society' audience of the 1670s was largely absent. John Dennis explained it polemically in an essay of 1702 (Dennis 1939: 291–4): according to him, a reign of cultivated pleasure and literary humanism had given way to a reign of business and politics, and the theatres were filling up with minor gentry, *nouveaux riches* and foreign tourists. His analysis has a mythic structure which should warn us not to accept it as raw information: it could easily be matched by diatribes about the decay of taste from a century earlier or a century later. But setting aside the reactionary lament, the decade following the Revolution does appear, in more than one historical light, as the moment when London decisively ceased to be the social and cultural penumbra of the throne. Parliament took control of its own affairs, establishing party politics, triennial elections and the rudiments of cabinet government. In 1693–6, all the main financial institutions of the future British Empire were put in place: the National Debt, the Bank of England, paper money, the reformed East India Company, the Treasury, the Board of Trade, and the British monopoly on trade with the colonies. At the same time, the abandonment of State licensing of the press coincided with a flurry of journalistic enterprises and political and coffee-house clubs to form the elements of the 'bourgeois public sphere' which Jürgen Habermas dates, with provocative but plausible precision, from 1695 (Habermas 1989: 58ff). In 1698, as if in ironic Providential endorsement of these developments, Whitehall Palace, the immense rambling home of Stuart power, burned to the ground; it was not rebuilt (Carswell

1973: 48). Among the casualties was the Court's own auditorium, the Hall Theatre, but no one seems to have taken much notice: it was already an irrelevance. Fairly abruptly as these things go, theatre ceased to be even residually a part of Court culture, and had to find its place in a dynamic city which was the capital at once of a landed oligarchy and of a commercial empire. Mary Pix's 1700 comedy *The Beau Defeated* was abreast of the times, not only in its indicative title, but also in its attacks on fashionable contempt for the City – the beau monde which turns up its nose at commerce, it is implied, has simply failed to read the papers (Pix 1991: 234). Another theatrical straw in the wind is the movement of performance times from afternoon to early evening, to fit in with a working day rather than with that of a gentleman of leisure (Van Lennep 1965: lxix–lxx).

In this situation, the tensely competing companies inevitably looked for audiences beyond their traditional constituencies. Their bills confirm Dennis's sense of a drift down market as, unsure of the power of literary drama to pull the elusive crowds, the managements supplemented it with European singers, rope dancers, acrobats, impressionists and animal acts, besides exploiting the skills which their own comedy specialists had developed while moonlighting in the booths of the London fairs. By the time of Dennis's article, 'the clear direction of the theatre . . . was towards the circus. The trend around the turn of the century continued, as plays increasingly became just one element in a variety show' (Milhous 1979: 187). The plays themselves could also appear as symptoms of the same descent: Farquhar, for example, is derided as the footmen's laureate for his enormously popular *The Constant Couple* (1699) (Van Lennep 1965: 518), and superciliously allowed 'the entire happiness of pleasing the upper gallery' with *The Recruiting Officer* (1706) (Stafford-Clark 1989: 127). The implication of these gibes is twofold: that the 'low' character of the dialogue is due to the writer's respect for the 'low' part of the audience, and that this degrading collusion is the secret of the shows' success.

The Carolean audience had dissolved amid the political and financial reorganization of the metropolitan elite, and the new duopoly was seeking to break out of the diminishing zero-sum game and broaden its appeal; but at the same time this populist move was felt as a shameful lowering of – in both senses – the theatre's quality. So when, in the late 1690s, the theatre came under attack on moral grounds, it was already in a state of defensive anxiety on social grounds. A letter of 1699 gloomily catalogues the novelty acts on the season's bills and concludes:

> In short, Mr Collier may save himself the trouble of writing against the theatre; for, if these lewd practices are not laid aside, and sense and wit don't come into play again . . . the stage will be short-liv'd, and the strong Kentish man will take possession of the two play-houses, as he has already done of that in Dorset-Garden. (Van Lennep 1965: 516)

'Lewd' in that sentence doesn't mean indecent – the act at Dorset Garden was an innocent display of weightlifting – but low and uneducated. But the terminology suggests how readily the question of immorality merged with that of popularity. The *general* pressure for a 'reformation of manners' was, after all, very largely an issue of social control. Starting up around 1688–9 in broadly Low-Church circles, it interpreted the Revolution, not at all as the cue for a secularization of social relationships, but as a triumph of Protestantism over popery; accordingly, it sought to reinstate the social ethos of godly living which had become identified with the Good Old Cause and therefore marginalized after 1660 (Bahlman 1968: chapter 1). Its programme was to prompt the enforcement of existing but neglected laws against that well-rehearsed catalogue of victimless crimes which constitute disorderly conduct: blasphemy, swearing, drunkenness, Sabbath-breaking and fornication. The campaign, which soon gained the support of the throne and most of the episcopacy, targeted individual offenders – mostly lower-class offenders, as Defoe pointed out (Defoe 1927) – and also disreputable institutions, such as fairs, alehouses, gaming-houses and brothels. The attack on theatres, which literary history naturally abstracts from the wider picture, reflects their identi-fication by reformers as one member of that category of disorderly establish-ments – at exactly the historical juncture when commercial pressures were threatening to propel the stage into just such *déclassé* company.

For the writer in the theatre, the exit from this closing trap is gentility. If the theatre can establish itself as a polite amusement – whether this is demonstrated by the decorousness of its scripts or by the conduct of the audience – then it seals itself off from any degrading association with the entertainments of the gutter. This is the logic, for example, of Congreve's upward mobility. The aspirations which led him to set new standards of *literary* correctness in *The Mourning Bride* and *The Way of the World* subsequently took him out of the theatre altogether; and when he revised his plays for a collected edition in 1710, he discreetly bowdlerized them. As Peter Holland cogently points out, this was not because Collier had convinced him of the moral error of his ways, but because he wished to produce a volume whose good taste and propriety qualified it for an honourable place in a gentleman's library (P. Holland 1979: 125–37). It is a question, not of religious conviction, but of which market one is trying to make it in. The theatre he left behind was seeking, inevitably less smoothly, to manoeuvre itself in the same direction. Richard Steele catches the blend of social and ethical themes in the prologue to his programmatically reforming play, *The Conscious Lovers*:

> No more let lawless Farce uncensur'd go,
> The lewd dull Gleanings of a Smithfield Show . . .
> Redeem from long Contempt the Comic Name,
> And Judge Politely for your Countrey's Fame.
>                                   (Steele 1971: 303–4)

This language anathematizes immorality and vulgarity in the same breath. The corresponding positive proposal is that drama should, with the support of its audience, become *refined* – that it should both conform to and raise the standards of good society. This version of the drama's improvement is the theatrical branch of the cultural project undertaken by Steele and Addison in the *Guardian*, the *Tatler* and, most influentially, the *Spectator*. It was, as John Gay explained in 1711, the project of reconciling virtue and wit (Gay 1946) – that is, not only reproving the licentiousness of a socially regressive aristocracy, but at the same time elevating the taste of a socially aspirant bourgeoisie; and so uniting moralism and urbanity in a single pleasantly inclusive discourse (Eagleton 1984: chapter 1).

There was a good deal more to this than the deletion of profane jokes and unpunished fornications. At the centre of the whole transition, as many critics have pointed out, was the concept of the exemplary (Loftis 1952: 195–213). Collier objects at length to the manners of comic protagonists because he takes it for granted that since they are adorned with privilege, wit and ultimate success, they are being presented as models for imitation. Accordingly, the reforming idea, proposed most programmatically by Steele, but widely visible in comedies from the turn of the century, is that these bad examples should be replaced by good ones. Writing in 1713, Steele argues for the representation of virtuous people, not merely on the grounds of moral effect, but also as a pleasure particularly suited to the theatre. Whereas, in real life, conspicuously virtuous people are mortifying to us when we compare ourselves to them,

> in the case of the stage, envy and detraction are baffled, and none are offended, but all insensibly won by personated characters, which they neither look upon as their rivals or superiors; every man that has any degree of what is laudable in a theatrical character, is secretly pleased and encouraged in the prosecution of that virtue without fancying any man about him has more of it. (Steele 1982: 174)

What baffles detraction is that the dramatis personae are not *other people* who challenge us by being different from ourselves, but delineated characters with which we can feel ourselves to be *the same*. In other words, the reform of the moral effectuality of the theatre entails a theory of dramatic *identification*.

The theory's implications can be seen in the reception of the two big successes of what might be called *Spectator* drama – Addison's *Cato* in 1713, and Steele's *The Conscious Lovers*, which was conceived at about the same time, though it didn't reach the stage until 1722. Neither play is typical, but they were both produced according to highly conscious critical programmes, both extensively attacked and defended in periodicals and pamphlets, and both recognized, then and later, as deliberately exemplifying a redefinition of the uses of theatre.

*Cato*, despite the unsatisfactory integration of its plot material, is unmistakably unified round the project of glorifying its hero as the last and most complete exponent of Roman virtue and liberty before the onset of imperial corruption. Pope's prologue constructs a startlingly unsound classical authentication for this conception of tragedy:

> To wake the soul by tender strokes of art,
> To raise the genius, and to mend the heart,
> To make mankind in conscious virtue bold,
> Live o'er each scene, and be what they behold:
> For this the Tragic-Muse first trod the stage,
> Commanding tears to stream thro' every age.
>                                    (Addison 1914: I, 349)

This makes it very clear that the character of Cato is designed for emotional identification – that the spectators should 'be what they behold'. At the same time, the programme is extraordinarily coercive. All the words for the operations of the tragic muse are transitive verbs denoting the play's power to compel its audience, while at the same time an imagery of voluptuous emotionalism implies that the drama's authority is exerted through tenderness and tears. The theatre is to be at once imperious and erotic: virtue has co-opted, not just drama in general, but specifically the sexual model of stage–audience relations which we saw earlier. In cleansing and sentimentalizing this idea, Pope and Addison effectively disempower the feminized audience: no longer the critical and demanding virago of Dryden's grubby liaison, this susceptible maiden is swept off her feet by the commanding uprightness of the stoic hero. As another prefatory eulogist alarmingly declares, 'Unborn Cato's heave in every breast': the spectators are forcibly impregnated with virtue.

Theatrical communication ceases, on this theory, to be a matter of devices, and is imagined as simplex and irresistible. This version of effectiveness is highly visible in the drama itself. Cato quells the passions of his sons, or the rebelliousness of his troops, by his sheer presence: the dramatic form of his personal nobility is that his authority is absolutely unmediated. Exactly the same figure structures *The Conscious Lovers*. Half the plot is created by the hero's inability to question his father's will either overtly or covertly; and when the false position this gets him into almost leads to a duel with his best friend, he himself disarms the friend, literally, by the unaided force of his moral ascendancy. Both plays are full of such instances of uncontested authority: virtue appears, not only as its own reward, but also as its own executive. By such images of uncontaminated moral compulsion, the drama acts out the effect it seeks to have on its audience.

So what is to be reformed is not just the theatre's rude words or its dubiously attractive libertines, but more fundamentally its *negativity*. The

Restoration stage, as we have seen, worked on a series of codes (folly, impertinence, inversion, utopia, adultery, disguise, bad faith) which consciously and ironically declined to be positive, and proffered itself instead as a *diversion* – a term which implies not only theatrical pleasure, but also a kind of evasion, a carefully cultivated unaccountability. The mode of address is epitomized, for example, by a moment in *The Beaux' Stratagem*: arguably, the relatively schematic way the position is set out here reflects the need, in 1707, to make explicit a discursive convention which could have been taken for granted a generation earlier. Archer is *fooling* – pretending to be a servant but at the same time behaving with such gentlemanly *sprezzatura* as to render the pretence deliberately unconvincing. At the height of this untrustworthy performance, he sings a ballad about trifles. With predictable satiric innuendo, the lyric discovers trifles concealed in boudoirs, coaches, pulpits and regiments, before concluding:

> But with people's malice to trifle,
> And to set us all on a foot:
> The author of this is a trifle,
> And his song is a trifle to boot.
> (Farquhar 1976: 63)

Balefully unconvinced by the assorted claims to seriousness which throng the Town, the author disclaims any countering seriousness of denunciation by placing himself at the top of the bill of trivia. *Totus mundus agit histrionem* – the spectacle's claim to resemble the real world is founded, not on its truthfulness, but on its complicity with the real world's pretences. Reform means the abandonment of this shifty playfulness. The moralization of the stage requires that 'Virtue and Vice appear just as they ought to do' (Loftis 1952: 18) – that is, that everything should look like *what it really is*. This maxim proscribes, not merely the fashionable libertinism of the 1670s, but the reckless and offensive paradoxes of theatricality in general. Hostility to theatre is expressed, now, not in the forcible closure of the playhouse, but in the ideological closure of the play.

Indicatively, this programme is associated with a drive to raise the status of the acting profession. Whereas John Dennis, who loathed *Spectator* drama and championed Wycherley and Etherege as masters of comedy, regarded actors as hired menials and blamed the state of early Georgian play-writing on the triumvirate of ignorant players who were running Drury Lane, Steele combined his argument for an improved and improving drama with the demand for actors to be more highly paid and esteemed (Loftis 1952: 22). Colley Cibber's remarkable rise from stage buffoon to Poet Laureate is a dubious instance of such progress; and naturally he makes the same point, dreaming of a theatre in which the support and regulation of the State would raise the actor above the need to pander to the base tastes of the multitude and make him a useful and respected member of society. Despite his dizzy elevation, Cibber was too widely derided to command much respect himself. But the ideological shift is real enough: this is already the theatre which would shortly afford at least one actor – David Garrick – access to polite intellectual society.

The political content of Cibber's vision of respectability is national unity. Because drama assembles its audience in one place, it has the power to transcend the divisive scribblings of pamphleteers and inspire 'that most elevated of Human Virtues', patriotism. A wise government will subsidize and foster the means of such strengthening unanimity, and not let them get into the hands of scurrilous and opportunistic clowns (he means Fielding and Gay). The model for this benign effect is, once again, *Cato*. According to Cibber, the première, given at a high point of political factionalism, raised 'such compell'd Assent to the Conduct of a suffering Virtue, as even *demanded* two almost irreconcileable Parties to embrace, and join in their equal Applauses of it' (Cibber 1968: 196). Here again is the theme of 'compell'd Assent' – the moral force which imposes itself by sheer presence. And what is especially valuable about this power is that it is unifying: in becoming what they behold, the spectators also feel themselves to be one. At this point, the processes of moralization and gentility are being overdetermined by a third factor – the beginning of the long eighteenth-century war with France, and its ideological corollary, the pursuit of national virtue. As Steele hinted in urging his audience to judge politely for its country's fame, to countenance a disgraceful drama in London is not only immoral or vulgar, but also unpatriotic.

We can locate this national inflection by looking at what actually happens in *The Conscious Lovers*. The unchallengeable father, Mr Bevil, is a landed gentleman who wishes his son to marry Lucinda, the only daughter of a wealthy merchant named Sealand. The difficulty is that Bevil Junior is in love with Indiana, the daughter of a sea captain who is supposed to have perished and left her romantically penniless. The impasse is resolved, implausibly but inevitably, by the revelation that Sealand and the sea captain are one and the same person, and that Indiana is Lucinda's elder sister. She will therefore go up the aisle as Indiana Sealand: she comprehends in her delectable person the essential components of the eighteenth-century British State: the landed gentry, maritime trade, and overseas colonies. The son's love knew even better than the father's prudence where the prudent alliance lay. The myth is thus the one which will dominate English culture for the next two centuries – the marriage of landed and mercantile property in a new and harmonious whole, the spontaneous reconciliation of rural rootedness and bourgeois enterprise in the interests of both. This emollient project demands the magical resolution of the brackish tensions – Town and country, gentleman and citizen, style and propriety, wit and good sense – which had been at the heart of London comedy since Dekker and Middleton. All the dramatis personae are to be embraced by a single system of advantages: that is, the stage is to stop dividing its audience by location, class and gender, and produce instead a hegemonic communion. It is in the terms of this hegemony that it becomes possible to make vice and virtue appear in their native colours, because it is when the nation is unified that the colours look the same to everyone:

> The nymph with Indiana's Worth who vies,
> A Nation will behold with Bevil's eyes.
>                     (Steele 1971: 382)

The theatre's power to inculcate virtue is essentially its capacity to naturalize the new order.

# 6

# Bawdy, Manners and the English National Character

## 1 Orangemen

The voice of a new order spoke through the mouths of restored monarchists in 1983:

> excuse the cavalier in me, I know it offends but I have thought a lot of you in your cold puritan shift and come to master you like taking England back. I looked at England through a telescope from Calais thinking of your starched underthings and uncoloured face, and the smell of you, a little musty, I expect, the musty hair of a sad-eyed puritan, oh, I shall have you shuddering with love, do reply, but very sweetly, and with dignity, no cock and cunt talk, you are not a cavalier tart, are you? Oh, the modesty of a real woman it does wonders to me, I am hard as rock. (H. Barker 1983: 19–20)

In Howard Barker's play *Victory*, the Restoration is portrayed as a punitive backlash against the Puritan Commonwealth. King and courtiers are venereally diseased sexual terrorists, practising violence on the bodies of the powerless. The actress Nell Gwynn displays the erotic brutality of the new power by kissing the rotting decapitated head of a disinterred republican. Sexual 'licence' is the sign of a new freedom, a freedom that consists of allowing the Restored to take their revenge. Driven by sexual frustration, the new order behaves with an irrationality that is selfish, powerful and fulfilling. In Britain in 1983, for the audience of the Royal Court Theatre, the idea of 'freedom' was a rallying call for the Conservative party, now in government and braying with mass popularity following its successful military expedition to recover some islands in the South Atlantic that few people knew much about. Barker's violent Restoration images a vengeful Toryism, taking England back.

The violence presents the defeated with what the play's subtitle calls 'Choices in Reaction'. Resistance is not possible. Thus the central character, Bradshaw, widow of a regicide, survives by stealing from erstwhile comrades, yielding to the cavalier who desires her 'uncoloured face', and finally managing the finances and employees of the Duchess of Devonshire's household. By becoming a manager Bradshaw learns to survive as one of the most powerful social groups does. The financiers and men of property are not driven to seek instant fulfilment. They invest and bide their time. Their power goes back before the Restoration. They fought Charles I for control of money, they invited the cavaliers to return to control revolutionary elements in the Commonwealth, and they plan now to limit the power of Charles II. The violence and licence of the restored monarchy, the braying Toryism, are in fact a phase, part of a scheme organized by the men of property. These men are another version of British conservatism, and suggest another history. Theirs is not the sensational irrational pattern of conflict and backlash: it is the slow calculating rule of property and money. These are the real managers of England, the men who eventually end the rule of Charles II's brother James by inviting to the throne their own candidate, William of Orange. From him they take their name: Orangemen.

The appearance of 'Orangemen' marked a decisive change in the political and social shape of England. As a system, absolute monarchy, the last fantasy of a dead feudalism, had finally yielded to the corporate power of the propertied elite. Capitalism had officially begun. As an expression of this change, the Restoration has acquired a special notoriety within England's histories of itself – a sort of cultural punctuation mark. 'The playhouse opened by Sir William Davenant in 1661 inaugurated the epoch of classic realism in the commercial theatre.'

This quotation could come from a number of histories, but is in fact from Catherine Belsey's account of Renaissance drama called *The Subject of Tragedy*. It was one of a series of attempts to reappraise Renaissance culture using theoretical models drawn from post-structuralism, post-Freudian psychoanalysis and new theories of 'discourse' and ideology. This critical activity was going on in the mid-1980s, spanning the period in which the Thatcher government, having achieved success in its adventure overseas, turned its military attention to the domestic sphere, in particular trades unions and socialists. Part of the project of the new critical work was to show that, in the face of Thatcherite myths of economic 'realism', individualism and the property-owning democracy, the 'golden age' of English literature was great precisely because it insisted on asking unsettling questions about nature, order and the individual. And it all supposedly came to an end with the Restoration, or capitalism:

Classic realist theatre isolates the world of fiction from the world of the audience, and shows the first as an empirical replica rather than an emblematic representation of the second. The spectators recognize in the unified subjects who perform, apparently oblivious of them, within the lighted, framed space of the stage, the depiction of their own imaginary unity. (Belsey 1985: 23)

'Realism' had been a dirty word in the newly theoretical and trendy film criticism of the 1970s; it gained extra force in the political rhetoric of the 1980s. In fact the sort of picture that Belsey, and several others, draw of the realist stage, with its implication that there is no forestage, no talking out, no auditorium lighting, is pretty comprehensively wrong about the Restoration. But it is confidently accurate as a restatement of the classic image of the passive capitalist spectator, the tabloid-reading, property-owning 'democrat'.

The ready expectation that we will find this character hanging around the Restoration is something which radical Renaissance studies absorbed, unproblematically, from a much older story that English culture told of its past:

The return of a Stuart King by no means undid the work of the Civil Conflict, in so far as that work was in itself restorative and conservative; and when the selfish corruptness of Charles II and the headstrong perversity of James II had ended by bringing about another Revolution, a fresh combination of parties re-established on a still safer basis the securities won in the days of Charles I. (Ward 1875: 292)

This account of the Restoration moves us backwards from Thatcherite militarism to Victorian imperialism, from the mid-1980s to the mid-1870s. For the literary historian A. W. Ward, writing in 1875, the Restoration is already in place as a point of decadence. On one side of it there is the Puritan revolution or 'Civil Conflict' which manages to be both conservative and restorative; on the other the Orangemen who initiated a British conservatism that was – in Ward's view – balanced and moderate.

On the part of the nation at large the reaction was not against the essence of Puritanism. The Restoration, indeed, and the movements which had preceded it, implied a revulsion and a protest against the domination of an extreme and extravagant minority; but it would be a mistake to suppose the great body of it to have been hurried into the opposite extreme, and to have exchanged a fanatical observance of an unnatural code for an equally irrational lawlessness. (p. 298)

The Orangemen resist the conflict of extremes and thus beget a tradition which, in Ward's day, gave authority to the national character currently establishing its 'securities' on an imperial scale.

By 1875, Ward's picture of the Restoration as a revulsion against the fanatical extremes of an otherwise decent puritanism was an orthodox account of British history. It had been mapped out a few decades earlier by the historian Macaulay, who used a book review in 1841 to stamp on an incipient flirtation with Restoration comic dramatists: 'this part of our literature is a disgrace to our language and our national character' (Macaulay 1885: 6). What happens in the thirty years between Macaulay and Ward is that the 'national character' gets more securely sanitized. For Macaulay the drama was somehow a part of the national character, albeit 'the Nadir of national taste and morality' (p. 31); for Ward it was something foreign, imported by Charles II, imposed by a class on a nation:

> the licence and wantonness of his Court, and the literature which that Court affected, and of which it accordingly soon found a supply equal to the demand, were not the manners and the literature of the nation. Thus . . . the Restoration stage failed either to revive the old national drama, or to substitute in its place a new genuinely national growth. (Ward 1875: 298–9)

But even in the 1870s the ejection of the Restoration stage from a preferred national history was not fully secure. In 1877 the novelist George Meredith sniffily dismissed 'our so-called Comedy of Manners, or Comedy of the manners of South-sea Islanders under city veneer' (Meredith 1910: 8). Although it is the behaviour of savages it still, rather troublingly, looks like the city. That sense of something which persists in being of the nation but not National hangs around scholarly debates about Restoration drama's relationship with French or native English models. What it all meant was that if Restoration drama was indeed genuinely native then its 'licence' had to be admitted as a constituent part of the great body of the English Nation.

For the Victorian Ward the 'licence' of the Restoration amounted to treachery to 'the nobler tendencies of the national life, and to the eternal demands of moral law' (Ward 1875: 498). Fortunately, he says, by the end of the period, thanks to the clergyman Jeremy Collier and the 'wifely devotion' of Queen Mary, 'the picture of unbridled licence which had so long been offered by the palace of an English king began to fade from remembrance . . . The old Puritan feeling was not yet dead in England' (p. 509). And even as he wrote these words, some of Ward's contemporaries were reassuringly setting about the reform of the excesses of contemporary theatricality.

The 'unbridled licence' had been expressed by writers who lacked self-restraint: Lee, whose 'fire of passion' burnt 'with an impure flame', wrote bombast; poor old Otway was hastened to his death by the 'weakness of his moral nature' (p. 412). The return of the puritan feeling brings with it a proper national drama, a drama imbued with a manly spirit that is thoroughly suspicious of being loud and showy. For example, Orrery was to be commended because 'he was too clear-sighted a statesman and too thorough a soldier to incline to political declamation, and his sentiments are not as a rule displayed after a very demonstrative fashion' (p. 341). The business of running the world has no time for a demonstrative art form: 'Queen Anne herself was devoid of love for the drama . . . The main national interest of her reign was the great war in which the flag of Great Britain was borne aloft beyond the rivalry of the nations' (p. 296). The moment when drama properly interests itself in nation, with the 'notes of a patriotic spirit' being heard in plays by Farquhar and Steele, marks the end of the Restoration. It very nearly marks the end of drama itself.

For that end had come with the arrival of the moderate monarch whom the restrained men of property had invited: 'William III never showed the slightest sympathy with any of the excesses of religious or political partisanship, and, having at no time cared much for any amusement but hunting, never darkened the door of a theatre' (p. 295). Thus, in a standard version of British history, the drama that follows the decadent Restoration needs to learn to be suspicious of excess, to be realist, to accommodate itself to conservatism, to offer no threat to those men whose historical mission it was to guard the British nation from anything partisan, whether it be in politics or theatre: the men of Orange.

## 2   The Pruning Knife

The worry about Restoration 'licence' had begun a century earlier. In the opinion of that vigilant cultural guardian, Dr Johnson, the effect of Congreve's plays was 'to relax those obligations by which life ought to be regulated' (Johnson 1965: 255). The problem, once again, was excess: the *Morning Post* of October 1775 recommended that *The Way of the World* could become 'an ornament to the British stage' once Garrick, 'or some other dramatic writer, root out these poetical excrescences' (Avery 1951: 117). Where the play is an uncontrolled plant the manager needs to become a gardener: 'Congreve's imagination was naturally vivid, luxuriant, and rapid. – He heaps up, when the *impetus* is upon him, an accumulation of glitter and gawd, extravagant and mistimed' (Garrick 1791: preface). Growth and accumulation become a threat when they are not as it were properly planned: an entry in the aptly named *Public Ledger* (1765) notes that in Restoration plays 'decency and good sense were continually sacrificed to an ill-timed emanation of vivacity' (Avery 1951: 8).

In the view of the post-Collier generation, this vivacity was inevitably undisciplined, because it was the true expression of its society. Writing in 1709 the critic Steele argued that Wycherley's Horner was a 'good Representation of the Age in which that Comedy was Written', when 'Love and Wenching were the Business of Life' (Avery 1942: 144). By the end of the century Horner's drama was defined not only as the most obscene play in the language but also as utterly realistic, offering 'a more genuine representation of the loose manners, obscene language and dissolute practices of Charles the Second's reign, than in any other play whatsoever' (Avery 1942: 166). Ruling culture in the mid eighteenth century knew itself as too refined to be pleased with the previous century's sex. None of Wycherley's plays was 'fit for representation under the present regulations of the stage, regulations which the gradual refinement of the public taste has made necessary' (Avery 1944: 151). When satisfactorily regulated Restoration plays were performed, the critical response found a new interest in the conflict between threatening coarseness and modern refinement. So what was impressive about the *Old Batchelor* revival in 1776 was not the play's action but the adapter's work to 'accommodate so capital a comedy to the present taste of the town' (Avery 1951: 128), a town that displayed the power of its 'taste' by its decision to 'accommodate'.

In order to accommodate his career the actor-manager Garrick took very seriously the taste of what has to be called the Town. His regulatory activities demonstrated the precise extent of his respect for the sensibilities of an audience 'of these Times': 'There seems indeed an absolute Necessity for reforming many Plays of our most eminent Writers: For no kind of Wit ought to be received as an Excuse for Immorality, nay it becomes still more dangerous in proportion as it is more witty' (Garrick 1766: preface). That tense relationship between wit and danger creates the opportunity for a trouble-shooting literary man who wants both to respect his public and enhance his national culture: 'Without such a Reformation, our English Comedies must be reduced to a very small Number' (preface). The stock can be increased by taking a leery old text, a 'Wanton of Charles's Days', and processing it suitably for Garrick's protegée, an inexperienced new actress, so it ends up 'shewing Miss Reynolds to Advantage'. In short, after being interfered with by the manager, Wycherley's *Country Wife* lost her experience and became Garrick's *Country Girl*. The process was commended by the 1791 editor of the play: 'The usual taint of the time in which he wrote had so infected the whole mass, that Mr Garrick found himself reduced to the necessity of lopping off a limb (Horner) to save the whole from putrefaction' (Garrick 1791: preface). By mutilating the text's rotten body, Garrick made space for the innocent body he himself had trained.

Miss Reynolds, though, had a problem, in that she wasn't very good in the part. The *London Chronicle* complained in November 1766 that 'the entertainment of the Town is to be limited and confined in order to raise and establish a raw unexperienced actress' (Avery 1942: 159). A sense of innocence on stage is not produced simply by putting someone innocent on stage; furthermore, in Garrick's version the part 'has lost her original simplicity'. Something which was present in the original play, with its expressive relation to a community, seems to be missing. Later, in 1785, the part was made a success by Mrs Jordan, who 'at once displayed such consummate art, with such bewitching nature, – such excellent sense, and such innocent simplicity' (Avery 1942: 163). A theatre that had learnt to be wary of natural luxuriance had to rediscover its pleasure in displays of consummate art pretending to be simple. The taste of the Town was not moved by Miss Reynolds's inexperience, and preferred instead performers who showed they knew the rules of their art. Against the horrors of ill-timed vivacity the audience derived its pleasure from seeing rules well kept, lines delivered word-perfect, all complete and all in place.

Scandal erupted around Samuel Reddish when he stopped the last scene of *The Old Batchelor* to explain that the reason his lines were ill-learnt was because he had taken on the part at short notice, 'to strengthen the play' (Avery 1951: 130). Censure was violent and Reddish didn't go on for a second performance. His failure to do the part as already written – to deliver the pre-scribed text – became a more serious crime of disrespect when he stepped forward as a performer in his own right, severing his connection with the play-world. The moment in which the text is ruptured, when the performing body ceases to speak what is scripted for it, is a disruption of a proper hierarchy, amounting to the effrontery of a servant. Thus in her performance as Congreve's Mrs Fainall, Mrs Greville's 'indifference is intolerable, and should be noticed by her employer' (p. 118).

The actress is obliged to speak correctly the text which is culturally 'owned' by the Town; otherwise she is answerable to her employer, the manager, who produces texts which respect the taste of the Town. Defined in these terms, theatrical employment in the eighteenth century could be clearly distinguished from the old-fashioned system of personal patronage under Charles II: 'The reign of the Second Charles was favourable thus far to literature, that the Court patronized what was believed the brightest talent among the people. – Wycherley came in for a full share of this distinction: and what has seldom happened from crowned heads, Charles in person condescended to visit the poet in a severe indisposition' (Garrick 1791: preface). Wycherley, author of the most obscene play ever, also gets a royal visit: this paradoxical impropriety seemed to be evidence of what was wrong with Restoration patronage. By contrast in the eighteenth century the constantly maintained correctness of the adapted texts testified to the greater moral dignity of the Town's methods of theatrical production. Each performance observed and sustained the ongoing negotiation between Town and theatre as to the correct observation of regulations, where word-perfect actors were to deliver words made satisfactorily perfect.

This ritual of negotiation demonstrated how far the current system of theatrical production was able adequately to process dangerously licentious material. Thus, for example, a reviewer early in the next century refused to compliment the cast of Congreve's *The Double Dealer* because to have played it 'with the effect intended by the author, requires a degree of effrontery which we will not impute to any actor, particularly the females, by praising their performance' (Avery 1951: 150). The always possible effrontery, the unique problem of Restoration 'licentiousness', has a paradoxical effect: its always immanent presence means that Restoration drama provides uniquely good evidence of the production method's effectiveness in handling disorderly material. What seemed to be organic excrescence, resulting from ill-regulated Carolean patronage, required a special expertise from the eighteenth-century manager: the 'pruning knife has been handled with great discretion; so that the best humour of the piece is preserved in the Farce' (Avery 1942: 155). The play that is marked by the pruner's labour is one that has been rescued from a wasteful wildness and recuperated within a productive system. In eighteenth-century theatre, the curious usefulness of the Restoration text was that it offered the possibility of measuring how much licentious excrescence had been removed, how much labour had been productively invested.

As author-manager Garrick displayed his 'taste' – or labour power – as a productive pruner. But to be a success in a competitive business he had also to insist on his own individuality. It was this balancing act which, according to the *Morning Chronicle*, the actor Reddish muffed when he forgot his lines: 'while they were willing to applaud the man who had necessarily cleared the ground, as the Pioneer of Decency, neither hoped nor imagined that a principal figure in Congreve's group was to be annihilated by the destructive hand of a capricious and opinionated actor' (Avery 1951: 130). As a responsible, non-capricious actor, Garrick built his star status by pointedly establishing his difference from such current stars as James Quinn, who specialized in heroic masculine roles (and whose memoirs proudly enumerated his sexual conquests). Quinn's association with Wycherley's plays was one with which Garrick competed not by playing but by *not* playing roles so obviously tainted with licence. Eighteenth-century actors had a problem with their sexual status: they were attacked for licentious heterosexual behaviour, for sodomy, for effeminacy. Ideas about masculinity were, as Kristina Straub (1992) has shown, changing through the century. In Garrick's case, he distinguished himself from Quinn on the one hand and Colley Cibber's 'effeminacy' on the other. As a manager with a reforming mission he conspicuously neglected Congreve's plays; and when he did revive them, he himself acted in Congreve's only, aptly pathetic, tragedy.

When Garrick created his persona by distinguishing himself from Quinn or Cibber, he was working within the conventions of contemporary theatre journalism: reviewers defined the value of a particular performance by comparing different interpreters of the same role. Theatricality was thus neatly systematized by journalism on a scheme of contrast. The cataloguing approach was further developed in the marketing of illustrations of actors in key scenes. This all meant that the characteristics – or even the 'meaning' – of any particular performance, within a closely monitored comparison of similar performances, could be defined adequately by a fetishistic attention to gesture and costume. Performance 'meaning' here has nothing to do with conscious message or dramatic truth. Indeed, when they were dealing with what was originally a Restoration play, any approach to its message or truth might get close to its underlying licentiousness. The risky territory of 'message' can be satisfactorily avoided by developing an attitude to the theatre that concerns itself only with comparison and catalogue. A performance, like a fashion item, is measured not by its relation to an outside world but by its difference from another performance. In its dealing with Restoration drama, eighteenth-century culture had effectively constructed performance as commodity.

By showing he could provide for the Town a correctly regulated commodity, Garrick's management enacted theatre's relations with civil society. For this he was celebrated over a century later: 'He seems to have charmed all classes; the learned and the ignorant, the cultured and the vulgar; great statesmen, poets, and even the fribbles of fashion.' The words are those of another actor-manager, Henry Irving, who in June 1886 tried to delineate an actor's cultural responsibilities by describing Burbage, Betterton, Garrick and Kean (Irving 1886: 28). Following Ward and Macaulay, Irving saw the Restoration as a backlash against puritanism. Because 'fine gentlemen' wrote for the stage, characters were profligate and acting was highly artificial. Such corruption could only be ended by a great actor. Up popped Betterton to promote, and get popular support for, a nobler use of the stage. Like Garrick, Betterton was supposedly virtuous in his personal life (happily married . . .) and had a mass following. Actually, Betterton had a reputation for promiscuity and Garrick was rumoured to be sodomitical. But in Irving's story they both *had* to be virtuous since they resisted and reformed the worst excess of the Restoration. And in doing this they provided an adequately classical model for Irving's own claim to a principled high art theatre, for, as Meredith had said, 'Cultivated men and women, who do not skim the cream of life, and are attached to the duties . . . make acute and balanced observers.' Indeed, 'the middle class presents the public which . . . knows the world best' (Meredith 1910: 13). Faced in the 1880s with a licentious theatrical culture, Irving was still fighting off the ghost of the Restoration by trying to invigorate what Garrick had helped to found, and Betterton had sadly never known, bourgeois theatre.

In his cultural progenitor Irving found precisely what 1880s high art needed to claim in order to distinguish itself from commercial entertainment

– Garrick had returned 'nature' to the stage. Irving can put it that simply because he is fixed firmly on the figure of the actor-author-manager: he is temporarily forgetting that the theatre is a remorselessly social art. Garrick's contemporary audiences had a rather different view of his reforms and 'nature'. A 1772 review of his rewrite of Wycherley, *The Country Girl*, complained the central figure 'has lost her Spirit in the Transition'; and went on to say that 'it is not sufficient to make altered Plays innocent only, they should at least be pleasant too' (Avery 1942: 161). In a real-life transaction with an audience, innocence gets into a complicated relationship with pleasure. For when innocence stops being natural and pleasurable, when it draws attention to itself, it stops being innocent. So, in 1776, a review of Thomas Sheridan's pruned Congreve asked that if an indecent play had to be performed 'let it be in the naive Manner of Congreve, and not in the Puritanical punning Manner of Tuesday Night; every Indecent Idea in the Commerce of the Sexes was continually kept in the Minds of the Audience; and yet the Wit which would have atoned for them was squeezed out by the leaden Hand of Mr Sheridan' (Avery 1951: 124). A morality that gets obsessed with innocence to the exclusion of all else appears rather dirty-minded.

This is a problem, as any theatrical reformer knew, with the reality of audiences. Their capacity for indecent thoughts made them all too vulnerable to what James Beattie (1776) describes as the problem of Restoration dramatists, who 'adorn their respective reprobates with engaging qualities to seduce others into imitation' (in Avery 1944: 149). An audience had to be warned against itself; or rather, it had to learn to become a *proper audience*. 'If he would be more simple and chaste in drawing Old Foresight's character, and not imitate the action of a sailor pulling up his trowsers so often, he would not, perhaps, gain so much loud applause, but he would find more judicious approvers' (Avery 1951: 132). The actor William Parsons produced responses which disturbed the coherence of the idea of the public or 'Town', that homogeneous group of judicious approvers invoked by managers and critics. For Garrick, an audience outside this category was literally unnameable: he argued for an increase in the number of playable comedies, so they didn't pall by repetition 'or, what is worse, continue shameless in spite of publick Disapprobation' (Garrick 1766: preface). To 'continue', shamelessly, they need an audience; but that audience obviously consists of something different from a disapproving public, something that keeps breaking out into shameless loudness. So besides presenting a problem to the proper history of national culture, Restoration drama also unsettled the idea of a fixed moral identity for the public. Edmund Burke, who was to be so eloquent on the subject of the democratic decency of English public life, was very early alert to the threat of sex to civil society: Congreve's plays contained 'such Obscenity, as none can, without the greatest Danger to Virtue, listen to; the very texture and groundwork of some of his Plays is Lewdness, which poison the surer, as it is set off with the Advantage of Wit' and, for Wycherley, 'the Satyr contained in a lewd Picture, can never be so instructive as the foul Ideas it will raise' (Avery 1944: 147).

The problem specific to Restoration comedy, then, was an endemic luxuriance which couldn't be cut without removing some of the organic life. To the extent that desire and sex occupied less of its action, by contrast, Restoration tragedy lent itself more readily to a dominant culture of pathos and sentiment. Otway's *Venice Preserved* almost effortlessly entered the repertoire alongside Shakespeare. The only problem was the comic masochism of the old senator Antonio, whose scenes disappeared, came back briefly in 1716 for a royal performance, then went, with the whole character, in 1750. The main plot, a mixed sex triangle, was relatively unscathed, so that its foregrounded emotional expressivity took its place suitably alongside early-nineteenth-century melodrama. Tied to this tragic form it then later suffered from a general distaste for melodramatic emotionalism, without being able to transform itself into spectacular or naturalist theatre. Its compliance with eighteenth-century cultural values may thus be said to have assisted Restoration tragedy's slide into oblivion.

In the year when the first formally labelled melodrama was performed at Covent Garden theatre, 1802, there were three Restoration plays in the programme. Two, *Venice Preserved* and Rowe's *Tamerlane*, were tragedies which had carried constitutional or republican messages: the republican Pierre fighting Venetian corruption, a William-of-Orange Tamerlane opposed to absolutist monarchs. Later the Jacobin Holcroft's 'melodrame' was performed to great acclaim – London's politics were still affected by Revolutionary Paris. The third Restoration play was Congreve's comedy, *The Double Dealer*, a play of sex rather than power politics. It was this performance that one reviewer refused to praise because to play it 'with the effect intended by the author, requires a degree of effrontery which we will not impute to any actor' (Avery 1951: 150). The comedy offers illegitimate pleasures, a naughty disrespect. And the licentious nature of the fiction presupposes that the theatre itself is not taking seriously, indeed affronting, its public role in civil society. To do sex plays is to seduce an audience away from their proper moral identity as the 'Town', a problem which by 1802 had become urgent since audiences were by now so conspicuously of the town but not the 'Town'. The staging of Restoration comedy thus came to signify theatre's place outside public life, a sphere of entertainment purveying sexual licence as fun, naughty and irrelevant. In this respect a modern rep's publicity for an evening of 'rollicking Restoration bawdy' follows quite precisely in the noble tradition of Burke.

## 3    Arbitrary Pleasure

A utopia of gallantry was how the essayist Charles Lamb described it. What he meant was that Restoration comedy should not be expected to conform with norms and morals of everyday behaviour, and that the art-work had its own fairyland customs and practices. Lamb's antiquarian fancy was defending a cultural heritage against the assaults of contemporary early-nineteenth-century morality. His plea for tolerance was based on the comedy's harmlessness. This sounds a very moderate position, given that previous decades had seen some quite fierce defences of Restoration drama. For instance, about fifty years earlier Goldsmith had made a critique of bourgeois sentiment, which found itself troubled by Restoration wit. Against the then-fashionable 'weeping' sentimental comedy he opposed 'laughing' – 'and even low' – comedy produced by Cibber and Vanbrugh. 'Laughing' comedy had as one of its most famous authors the son of a man who had himself wielded a pruning knife: Richard B. Sheridan. After play-writing he became manager of Drury Lane and an opposition MP, but his cultural place is nowadays defined as the end point, the final flowering, of the genre of Restoration comedy, with which Sheridan's plays are an interchangeable substitute in the repertoire of modern British theatre. And flowering, final or not, is all too often, as we know, the problem: 'The flowers and fruits of the intellect abound; but it is the abundance of a jungle, not of a garden – unwholesome, bewildering, unprofitable from its very plenty, rank from its very fragrance.' The language may echo back across the decades but the date is 1827; the *Edinburgh Review* is pronouncing judgement on the whole business of Restorationism: 'No writers have injured the comedy of England . . . so deeply as Congreve and Sheridan. Both were men of wit and polished taste. Unhappily they made all their characters in their own likeness' (in L. Hunt 1840: 278).

Cultural pronouncements of death tend in practice to be the passing of death sentences: somebody wants to kill something off. By 1827 interest in Restoration comedy was more alive and well than it had been for some time. Lamb's apparently twee defence had appeared in 1822, using a concept of drama as 'escapism' or safety valve, working to return us healthy and refreshed to everyday life. But his description of that drama in effect conjures up an ideological space outside the dominant order:

> that happy breathing-place from the burthen of a perpetual moral questioning – the sanctuary and quiet Alsatia of hunted casuistry – is broken up and disenfranchised, as injurious to the interests of society. The privileges of the place are taken away by law. We dare not dally with images, or names, of wrong. We bark like foolish dogs at shadows. We dread infection from the scenic representation of disorder; and fear a painted pustule. (Lamb 1913: 230)

While Lamb assumes a commonsensical separation of the scenic and the real, he also demonstrates how easily the two are confused. That suggestion gains force, intended or not, from a similarity with the contemporary work of Mary and Percy Shelley on illusion, fantasy and subjectivity, work which was generating a model for thinking about ideology and false consciousness. Lamb's 'happy breathing-place', the 'Utopia of gallantry', could also be described as 'the oblivion of consequences – the holiday barring out of the pedant Reflection – those Saturnalia of two or three brief hours, well won from the world', and contrasted with a modern play's spectator, 'his moral vanity pampered with images of notional justice, notional beneficence, lives saved without the spectators' risk, and fortunes given away that cost the author nothing' (Lamb 1913: 237). Saturnalia are opposed to mystificatory notions; spectator risk opposed to false consciousness. This argument not only reworks Goldsmith, but it finds a close contemporary parallel in William Hone's explicitly political recovery, in 1823, of medieval clowning as a healthier cultural activity than the Church and State pieties of Regency repression.

Lamb's antiquarian fancy can, then, easily be rewritten as a political position: 'Mr Lamb has succeeded not by conforming to the *Spirit of the Age*, but in opposition to it.' This view of Lamb comes from his contemporary, the critic Hazlitt, whose own radicalism in 1825 was keen on an image of Lamb standing outside the corrupt present: 'He disdains all the vulgar artifices of authorship, all the cant of criticism, and helps to notoriety' (Hazlitt 1967b: 344, 346). In an earlier essay (1819) Hazlitt had already formulated a view of Restoration drama that anticipated Lamb's: he too saw the plays as a locus of real values that don't escape from, but are *alternative* to – critiques of – the present. Reading the plays 'we are almost transported to another world', an age 'when kings and nobles led purely ornamental lives'. Such a world contrasted with the fiercely repressive Regency of Hazlitt's time, a notorious regime which had hounded the poet Shelley from England and was to massacre working people at Peterloo in the year Hazlitt's essay appeared. The Restoration's 'happy, thoughtless, age' is defined by specific qualities which make it different from other ages, such as the Renaissance; there are specific qualities to Restoration culture: 'In thinking of Millamant, we think almost as much of her dress as of her person: it is not so with respect to Rosalind or Perdita.'

> Enviable in drawing-rooms, adorable at her toilette, fashion, like a witch, has thrown its spell around her; but if that spell were broken, her power of fascination would be gone. . . . I would rather have seen Mrs Abington's Millamant, than any Rosalind that ever appeared on the stage. Somehow this sort of acquired elegance is more a thing of costume, of air and manner. (Hazlitt 1967a: 74)

The specifically Restoration artificiality suggests an interrelationship between identity and fashion, subjectivity and social circumstances. The character of Farquhar's Lurewell 'shews, in the highest degree, the power of circumstances and example to pervert the understanding, the imagination, and even the senses' (p. 86). This insight into the power of circumstances over people has a parallel in what the sexual campaigner William Thompson said about women in 1825: their 'fictitious failings' were 'the mere results of the vicious circumstances surrounding women' (Thompson in B. Taylor 1983: 24). Thompson was a follower of the feminist Mary Wollstonecraft; he converted to the socialism of Robert Owen in the 1820s.

Against evangelical and anti-Jacobin insistence on the naturalness of woman's inferiority, Owenites argued for the perfectibility of women and the cultural construction of gender. They used ethnographic data to prove the cultural, rather than natural, basis of 'civilized' sexual customs. To a conservative view, such as that of Richard Polwhele's *Unsex'd Females* (1793), 'A woman who has broken through all religious restraints, will commonly be found ripe for every species of licentious indecorum' (in B. Taylor 1983: 15). This is answered by Hazlitt's idea of the Restoration, where Congreve's Millamant is a woman 'to whom pleasure is as familiar as the air she draws . . . and who has nothing to hope or to fear, her own caprice being the only law to herself, and rule to those about her' (Hazlitt 1967a: 73). In Hazlitt's hands the Restoration's utopia of gallantry takes its place as a possible scheme for living alongside Owenite ideals and Jacobin aspirations.

From the radical Godwin's idea that formal marriage be replaced by relations of mutual affection, through Percy Shelley's statement that enforced loveless cohabitation was a form of tyranny, to the Owenite assertion that human love finds 'its highest expression . . . in the free and unthwarted union of individuals of different [*sic*] sexes' (in B. Taylor 1983: 45): this is the thinking which frames the first period of major re-evaluation of Restoration comedy. That period reached its climax and sudden end in 1841, with Leigh Hunt's edition of Wycherley, Congreve, Vanbrugh and Farquhar. He had already, appropriately enough, edited Sheridan, whom he described as having 'a strong, a sensual, and therefore essentially coarse nature, none the less so for a veil of refined language, which was his highest notion of the dress of the heart' (L. Hunt 1840: xi, xii). These qualities recall Hazlitt's description of Farquhar, as reprinted by Hunt: 'a constant ebullition of gay, laughing invention, cordial good humour, and fine animal spirits' (Hazlitt 1967a: 85). When the comedy's licentiousness is glossed as 'animal spirits', the problematic sensuality is being defined as *natural*. To celebrate that 'ebullition' amounted to an attack on 1820s cant and mystification; the sexual is on the side of the natural and free against the social and repressive. While radicals thought that was a good thing, opponents of sexual liberation saw the sexual as a threat to society: Edmund Burke described Mary Wollstonecraft as the English equivalent of 'the revolutionary harpies of France, sprung from night and hell' (in B. Taylor 1983: 11). The great democrat's hysteria may well have been prompted by what the reforming Collier put more soberly, that 'arbitrary pleasure is more dangerous than arbitrary power.'

Hazlitt's essay intended to answer both Burke and Collier, responding to the latter that 'The stage cannot shock common decency, according to the notions that prevail of it in any age or country, because the exhibition is public' (Hazlitt 1967a: 90). Not only players – goes the argument – but preachers too make a living out of the fact that licence is a part of life. Hazlitt here draws on an uncertainty about what was denoted by the 'common' or 'public', an uncertainty that fed straight into the anxieties around changes in class power in the 1820s. By choosing to reprint Hazlitt's view in 1841, Leigh Hunt deliberately took up a position not just on morality but on Englishness, democracy and religion. His launching of texts into the public domain, as a public figure, was a form of hegemonic challenge. That challenge was met forcefully by Macaulay, whose hostile review of Hunt's edition drew down the curtain on Restoration drama once again.

The next attempt to publish Restoration texts came in the 1880s. Among the first volumes of reprinted old plays in the Mermaid series was a volume of Otway, edited by the Hon. Roden Noel. Although he was a minor poet, Noel was more famous for his fairly open avowal of a homosexuality coexisting with his married life. His reputation for matters sexual was shared by the Mermaid series editor, Havelock Ellis, a pioneer of an enlightened sexology. In a way similar to Owenite ethnography the Mermaid editions returned to and spoke about a culture which had different views on sexuality from those of late Victorian Britain. The Renaissance, together with classical Greece, offered 1880s sexuality campaigners a supply of positive images of male homosexuality. For them the identification of famous homosexually authored art-works was a step towards claiming cultural and historical importance. Just as positively it also made the space to write sexually charged prose: Viscount Falkland found his fellow undergraduate to be 'a young fellow of singular charm, exceptional good looks, wit and breeding, with the talent of a Patroclus or Pylades for romantic friendship' – Otway again, this time surrounded by other charming boys in Montague Summers's edition of his plays (Summers 1926: xviii). As a culture to be revisited, the Restoration functioned rather differently from the Renaissance. Instead of providing a galaxy of great homosexual individuals, it suggested a whole society where sexual relations were more relaxed in general, an image of possible modes of sexual being, a utopia of gallantry.

Its picture of 'equality' between women and men was what in 1913 John Palmer thought people would be shocked by. Audience hostility to the Restoration, said Palmer, was a symptom of a conservative shift in attitudes towards sexual disease and, he hints, homosexuality. Palmer's Restoration, for all his championing of the early-nineteenth-century defenders, bears the marks of early-twentieth-century sex. In the act of sex, he says, the Restoration saw nothing sacred: 'impersonal needs and instincts of sex' were separated from 'personal relations of friendship' (Palmer 1962: 42). Hazlitt's notion of animal spirits has here been dragged into, and reformulated by, the world of Nietzsche and Freud. Ten years later that pair were determinedly stalking through an account of the Restoration in which 'men and women were experimenting in social things; they were trying to rationalize human relationships. They found that, for them at least, affection and sexual desire were quite separate and they tried to organize society on that basis. Love, in which the two feelings are imaginatively fused, scarcely existed for them' (Dobrée 1924: 20). Restoration bawdy, as Bonamy Dobrée saw it, was an attempt to be honest about sex, unlike the prudery of 1920s society. The 'wild pleasures' of Etherege's comedies sprouted from a 'superabundance of animal energy' (p. 60). Hazlitt's animal spirits have here combined with the metaphor of an overflowing hydraulic system, which has come from Freudian concepts of psychic 'release'. And haunting the phrases about Wycherley's love of 'physical life' and the 'healthiness' of Dryden's virile comedy is Nietszche himself. A few years later Dobrée's sexual liberalism found a champion:

> he is a distillation of something that exists in every one of us, not merely in his eminence as a procreative animal . . . but rather of that something in us which bids us be free, to scoff at the restraints of society . . . that something which makes us wish we were fairies, to come and go as we please . . . Perhaps Casanova really was a fairy. (Dobrée 1933: 12)

Lamb's fairyland had arrived, via the eighteenth, in the twentieth century.

And the fairies turn out to be men. The freedom that art once gave to fairyland is now imagined to come from a 'natural' life which is not controlled by the 'inflamed Puritan conscience'. The native English physicality exemplified in Restoration culture challenges the nation's 'Puritan nervous system' (Palmer 1962: 27). An ideological contest between nature and conscience, echoing D. H. Lawrence's contemporary attacks on middle-class hypocrisy, takes biological form. The rule of men of property is not now opposed to absolutism or puritanism but to native Englishness, envisaged as a *natural* freedom, by definition healthy. It is also, from the example of Dobrée's virile Dryden, by definition masculine. What begins to happen in the 1920s version of Restoration is that the stress on sexual 'equality' is silently usurped by a focus that is narrowed down onto man – it is the male body which is the resource of a healthy anti-puritanism. Freedom thus defined as adventuring virility or Etherege's 'honest knavery' (Palmer 1962: 90) has something of the negative quality of 'arbitrary pleasure' or Casanova. Anti-puritan manhood starts to encompass versions of men that are decidedly unsettling: 'the same delicious creatures, with their long fair wigs, and the *creve-coeur* locks curling on the napes of their soft necks . . . their elderly faces painted young with Spanish red and white ceruse, and the frangipan exhaling from the chicken-skin gloves upon their plump white hands' (Gosse 1924: 13). These are the gallants who, according to Edmund Gosse, reappeared in London with the arrival of William of Orange (and presumably also shared his bed). Gosse's 1924 *Life of William Congreve* is an expansion of his 1888 *Memoir* – by 1924 Gosse himself had come out as a homosexual, and his Restoration gallants bear the distinct marks of 1920s nancies. The man of Orange's rule, for Gosse, spawns rather than spurns nancies. In an anti-puritan fairyland the men are also fairies.

So a woman then may live 'unhampered and free', and thus herself reveal modern hypocrisy: 'we hint, point, and suggest, where she spoke out broad words, frank and free' (Summers 1915: xxviii, xxx). The woman is Aphra Behn, as described by the great Restoration scholar, Montague Summers, in the preface to his edition of her complete plays published in 1915. It was the first of a series of Restoration editions planned by Summers and his friend, the Renaissance scholar A. H. Bullen. It was also the precursor of a series of theatrical revivals, initiated by the Stage Society's *Double Dealer* of May 1916 and then continued by Summers's own group, the Phoenix Society, from 1919 onwards. These revivals were for Summers a theatrical break-point, abandoning 'conventional nineteenth century modes of playing "old comedy" – the "School for Scandal way" as it was called' (Summers 1934: xiii). The series of editions was planned to encourage a theatrical project by increasing the range of available texts. To both Summers and Bullen the author who should begin that series was clear from the start: Aphra Behn.

We can only guess at why she was important to the male scholars. When Summers contrasts her as 'free' woman writer against a puritan present, her energy against the 'starchedness' of George III's reign, he is following a familiar model, with one difference. Freedom is not hitched onto an assumed heterosexual virility. Not only was Behn a woman but her closest male associate, John Hoyle, was convicted of a crime of sodomy. That crime is, characteristically, recounted in great detail with all Summers's consciously produced scholarly rigour – however much that very detail may offend dominant morality. Thus it is precisely scholarship's drive to know the facts which insists on an idea of the Restoration's sexual diversity. So, for Summers, the masochistic Antonio scenes of *Venice Preserved* have a dramatic integrity; they belong to a widespread Restoration interest in flagellation, and as human pictures are 'true to the uttermost, eternally true' (Summers 1926: xc). Summers's scholarship recovers a past which is stranger than Lamb's fairyland allows for. Accompanying his Restoration work he produced editions and histories of witchcraft and black magic, facing English literary culture with the diversity of its own past. And when he published with the Fortune Press, notorious for its 'deviant' and homosexual list, or with Ellis's British Society for the Study of Sex Psychology, he helped to promote cultural diversity in the present.

The 'Sex Psychology' pamphlet was a tribute to the Marquis de Sade, published in 1920. In it Summers uses the argument developed to defend Restoration licence, separating art from life and seeing the sexual as the key realism: 'According to de Sade it is only through the sexual that the world can be grasped and understood. Nor can there be a profounder truth; for the sexual, rightly understood, rightly comprehended, is deep down at the living heart of all humanity, all philosophy, wisdom, and religion' (Summers 1920: 23). The value of homosexuality (of which de Sade was, he says, the first serious secular student) is affirmed, and that leads logically into an affirmation of sado-masochistic practice: de Sade refutes 'the premise that homosexuality is unprocreative, and incidentally he points out that fertile nature destroys as well as constructs' (pp. 6–7). Summers himself agrees with Garnier's *Des Perversions Sexuelles* (1900) 'that a certain degree of sadism is normal' (p. 16), and that it is present, with male and female natures, in both sexes. By expressing opinions such as this the male theatre scholar shares with the female playwright a lack of fear of 'wantoning beyond the bounds of niggard propriety' (Summers 1915: xlix). Aphra Behn represented a 'freedom' different from that of a gallant masculinity, and hence perhaps had particular meaning for a homosexual male scholar with interests in sado-masochism to whom she owed her cultural revival.

It's a debt which modern scholarship has, however, cancelled. Summers is not mentioned in Kendall's account of the disappearance of women's plays since the Restoration. To the feminist project of reclaiming women's history, Behn's sexual 'freedom' is less important than her *professional* status, a re-arrangement of emphasis initiated by Summers's contemporary, Vita Sackville-West: 'although she might lay her scenes in brothels and bedrooms, although her language is not to be recommended to the queasy . . . Aphra Behn, in the history of English letters, is something much more than a mere harlot. . . . The importance of Aphra Behn is that she was the first woman in England to earn her living by her pen' (Sackville-West 1927: 12). This claim, though not strictly true, has power because it is a myth of origin, the beginning of women's writing.

By contrast with the other mythic woman of the Restoration, Nell Gwynn, the Aphra myth demonstrates that woman can keep her autonomy while 'she claimed equal rights with the men' (p. 13). Academic feminist criticism finds the equality imaged on stage: Behn uses Willmore and Helena, for example, who 'are as one', to explore 'modern sexual relations' (Kavenik 1991: 184, 185). By making male heroes such as Willmore 'fun-loving', she shows a belief in 'each sex's capacity for the traditional traits of both' (J. K. Gardiner 1980: 68). In its attachment to a professionally androgynous Behn a strand of North Atlantic feminism is finding its own self precisely by ignoring the historical text's 'self': in the play the 'fun-loving' Willmore is a potential rapist of Helena. The politically important work of contesting the literary canon tends to be carried out from a position which replaces sex with gender. So an account of how women's writing was destroyed by a backlash against feminism and by institutionalized misogyny conceals the fact that Behn was praised by a man in 1852, attacked by a woman, on moral grounds, in 1863 and published by a man in 1871; or that Susannah Centlivre was performed, reprinted and anthologized up to an 1872 complete edition while the obscene Wycherley had long departed the stage. Threatened by misogyny but competing manfully with bawdy, feminism's mythic Aphra takes centre stage, fighting for women in a way which was 'broad, democratic and even-handed' (Lyons and Morgan 1991: xv).

This 'democratic' Behn was a firm supporter of the Stuart monarchs, a Jacobite, holding to her 'principles' in her hostility to William of Orange. Summers, himself a Catholic priest and monarchist, calls her a 'thorough Tory', opposed by Whigs, and regrets her writing a poem for William's wife, Mary (Summers 1915: lii). The names for her 'principles' may differ, but Behn emerges consistently as a backward-looking monarchist, a supporter indeed of an 'arbitrary power'. The image of Behn the first woman writer draws together sexual independence, monarchist views and an upper-class position – Vita Sackville-West's 'born Bohemian' (and she should know). This myth of origin favours a specific form of cultural production. For, by contrast with Behn's work, we *could* celebrate the cookery books of Hannah Wolley, arguably the actual first professional woman writer, or the writings of the women sectaries and dissenters who opposed the Restoration, the Anglican Church and monarchy.

When Restoration culture is portrayed as a space of freer sexual relations, that freedom is located within a Court culture spawned by restored Stuart rule. Collier's link between arbitrary pleasure and arbitrary power remains unbroken. The 'puritan' bourgeois opposition to Restoration comedy in the eighteenth century condemned it as the licentious product of a parasitic aristocracy. The sexual libertarian defence of it makes a precise value inversion when it sets comedy in healthy opposition to dominant order – where that opposition cherishes a monarchic system residual in and 'alternative' to *bourgeois* structure. Two priests, two centuries apart: in 1720, Collier, the hero of Whig Protestantism, called for the extermination of male homosexuals; in the 1920s homosexuality and sado-masochism were defended by a monarchist Catholic, Summers.

In modern popular culture, a Restoration setting for films and novels promises sex narratives of which the licentiousness is guaranteed by the lifestyle of an old-fashioned aristocracy. 'The swashbuckling adventure opens as the beautiful Lady Panthea Vyne is forced to marry the lecherous Christian Drysdale. Miraculously, she is freed from his clutches by a mysterious masked rider calling himself the Silver Blade' (*Radio Times* blurb for *The Lady and the Highwayman*, authored by Barbara Cartland). The only other periods that offer freedom for clutches are the Regency and the 1920s. In all three periods the lifestyle of the ruling order is portrayed as enchanting, or fairylike, because it is impermanent as rule and 'outside' politics. The Restoration is thus popularly seen as a hiatus between the boring politics of the Commonwealth and eighteenth-century power-broking; the Regency as a diversion between the early Industrial Revolution and Chartist demagoguery; the 1920s as a time of gaiety after the First World War and before the General Strike and, of course, 'Depression'. Of all three the Restoration has the longest pedigree of avowed licence. This became ideologically locked into place as the wicked Other of Protestant bourgeois identity through the process by which the eighteenth-century 'Town' consolidated its cultural dominance.

The pleasures taken by arbitrary power will, according to Collier, themselves be arbitrary; a world of gallants will imagine gallantry as utopian. But for a social order which consciously opposed arbitrary power, that utopia was still attractive. When eighteenth-century rule-makers justified the need for artistic rules by reference to the seductive nature of Restoration comedy, it was this manner of proceeding which then typecast that drama as seductive. Arbitrary pleasure itself is more dangerous than arbitrary power because pleasure does not straightforwardly coincide with social structures, political or moral regimes. That's to say, the pleasures taken by an obviously retrograde rule can still have effects as pleasures. Two ways out are possible: the nineteenth century ceased performing the offending texts. The other way accommodated the pleasures, making them safely licit. When antiquarianism became institutionalized and empowered in the academy in the respectable guises of literary history or historical philology, an embargo on disapproved bits of the past was less possible. Restoration sex then re-emerged, fastidiously located as an evocation of the lifestyle of a decaying social order. The luxury and licence, and indeed drama, of that social order are themselves signs of both its impermanence and its irrelevance to the sobriety of bourgeois daily life. Restoration bawdy is now watched with a sense of nostalgia for a naughty age – lucky Lady Panthea – rather than a sense of how things might be otherwise in the future.

## 4   Modern Manners

When the director–designer team of Terry Hands and Timothy O'Brien staged *The Man of Mode* in 1971 for the Royal Shakespeare Company they discovered how things were in fact otherwise in the past: 'Restoration drama doesn't appear to have been the kind of finger twirling mannered performance we've become used to' (Waterhouse 1971: 14). Once liberated from finger twirling, *The Man of Mode* showed itself a fit companion for the familiar Shakespearean repertoire of the company: 'we found to our pleasure when we examined the play that it was not a late example of Restoration comedy, where the form is very set, but that it had affinities with Jacobean theatre; we found we were dealing with a comedy where we could sympathise with the characters and see their problems in terms of ours' (p. 14). The *Plays and Players* reviewer was more sceptical of this connection when he criticized the modern stage setting: 'There is the inescapable implication that the director knows the play won't stand firmly on its own two feet, but is important chiefly because of its appositeness to our own time' (p. 38). But the attitudes of dramatist and director to their societies were unclear: 'It is too easy and glib to claim that surfeit of sex and materialism link us to the Restoration admass' (p. 38). By 1971 the fashion for making cultural parallels was well established, but what might work for a Renaissance classic did not necessarily work for 'a post-Jacobean melodrama conceived in terms of early Restoration comedy' (p. 38). The problem, for Restoration comedy, is that classic status is not guaranteed merely by abstaining from finger twirling.

Classic here means Renaissance, and Renaissance drama is supposed, within one school of thought, to deal with universal human issues. Restoration is, by definition, that which is not Renaissance. The apparently obvious universal concerns of the earlier drama are replaced by something more parochial, Human Comedy replaced by genteel wit. The 'Restoration' described by literary criticism is a time incapable of producing a drama of high seriousness. In the narrative of Raymond Williams's *Drama in Performance*, Restoration comedy appears in a chapter called 'Plays in Transition', a watering-hole on the journey from *Antony and Cleopatra* to *The Seagull*. In its turn, that 'not-Renaissance' identity has shaped modern critical studies of Restoration drama, which tend to be predicated on the assumptions that, of itself, it is neither humanly relevant nor theatrically profound. To defend Restoration drama you have to admit both social history and theatrical pleasure into literary criticism. That's its problem. Thus Bonamy Dobrée explained the origin of tragic rant in the Restoration as the effort of verbal poetry to rival stage spectacle. Scenic pleasure is to be blamed for provoking a poetic lapse.

'Rant', like 'bombast', and indeed like 'manners', denotes theatrical excess: a dramatic language which exceeds that which is functional or necessary. These features of Restoration drama are taken to be symptoms of what its enemies usually claim about it, namely that it has no deep connection with human realities, that it turns deep emotion into posturing or depicts posturing as deep emotion. If Restoration drama were classic, like its profound forebear, it would be organically related to, nay rooted in, the whole society from which it derived. But in the Restoration 'the disintegration of the old cultural unity has plainly resulted in impoverishment.' For forty years English culture was upper class as it has been at no other time, and the drama was inferior because it couldn't even represent that culture adequately: 'it has no significant relation with the best thought of the time' (Knights 1963: 132, 133). 'We cannot study it . . . in the hope of finding clues to the attitude of a society as a whole. It is a piece broken off, one half of a split mind' (Wain 1956: 371).

Those forty upper-class years were ended by Addison. The eighteenth-century Town's act of distancing its proper 'Englishness' from a decadent aristocracy was repeated in 1841 in Macaulay's moral suppression of Lamb and Leigh Hunt, in 1875 in Ward's imperial historiography, and once again in 1937 in L. C. Knights's polemic against the High-Church Toryism which had articulated itself in 1920s defences of the Restoration. Just as Macaulay had brought back Collier to reassert Whig Protestantism after the troubled 1830s, so in 1937 Knights brought back Collier to define, in the voice of the *Scrutiny* movement, what was alien to a middling sort of democratic Englishness. The next year, in a book published by the Left Book Club, Daiches pointed to the 'respectable citizens' 'busy carrying on trade' beneath an art 'deliberately superimposed on society' (Daiches 1938: 111). The decadence of the Restoration here is something alien to the real, bourgeois England.

And the alien element is defined not just by class but by sex. The Restoration 'titillation of appetite' delights those who can't bear modern literature which 'deals sincerely and realistically with sexual relationships' (Knights 1963: 143). A critical sincerity about sex would appreciate Dorimant's 'fighter-pilot's mentality' in his relationships with women, according to the common-manly welfare state point of view of John Wain – who thus judges *Man of Mode* 'never false and unsatisfactory', indeed 'it is literature', unlike the 'rubbishy stage-fodder produced by people like Aphra Behn' (Wain 1956: 379, 382, 372). A virility which proclaims itself by pushing the Restoration to the cultural margin shows us, once again, the ideological format of the centre: a democratic class position coupled with a conservative sexual politics, a leftish suspicion not only about power but about pleasure.

For Knights, Restoration drama was inevitably doomed because it was the product of a society that was no longer whole. That organic community was destroyed for ever by the Revolution, which left a world without common values, and a drama where prose style is 'mechanical', verse has 'music-hall sentiment' and sexual attitudes have the 'stale monotony of jokes on postcards' (Knights 1963: 136, 149, 144). This concept of a seventeenth-century split, or dissociation, of cultural sensibility was derived by the Scrutineer Knights from the High-Church Tory T. S. Eliot. The commercialized waste-land of modern life is thus announced in, and celebrated by, modernity's first cultural product, Restoration drama.

The RSC team were delighted to find that, although *Man of Mode* had not been done for about 200 years, it was possible to see 'their' problems in terms of 'ours'. That moment of recognition defied all the intervening years of nineteenth-century morality. This was not, however, a new discovery, since the play had been named as one of the 'first modern comedies' just over a decade before. By categorizing Restoration comedy as 'modern' Norman Holland defended it against Knights and Wain. His defence concentrated not so much on Knights's organization of the past as on revaluing the sense of the modern. 'The special thing, the new thing about Restoration comedy is that society is regarded as less important than and irrelevant to personal, emotional relationships.' Holland discusses eleven modern comedies which show 'the conflict between "manners" (i.e., social conventions) and anti-social "natural" desires'; a 'natural' desire is 'the desire for sexual gratification' (N. Holland 1959: 224, 4, 29). The modern is the monotony of jokes on postcards for Knights; for Holland it's Horner 'carrying into actuality the conventions of *Reader's Digest* morality' (p. 75). The *Reader's Digest* is perhaps the main popular repository of a post-war Freudianism which locates what is meaningful in an openness about sexual desire, rediscovers the organic in the sexual. Knights, according to such Freudulance, stands accused, in his search for the organic, of missing the organ. A fixation with the Renaissance is thus unlikely to find the value in that which is, as Holland tells us, not-Renaissance. Defined specifically as not-Renaissance, Restoration comedy and tragedy create the need for self-consciously modern critics.

Modern critics are critics who recognize modernity. By spotting the conflict between desire and convention Holland shows himself in tune with a Freudery more modern than Knights's concerns. 'For the age of Freud and D. H. Lawrence, however, there must be a great deal of indelicacy indeed before it blots out the pleasure of understanding' (N. Holland 1959: 4). Refusing to be bound by old-fashioned prescriptions, the voice of modernity demonstrates it accepts the modern, even where that modern is violent, alienated or emptied of value. Modernity acknowledges that Restoration drama was written for a commercial theatre, and hence plays repeat stock formulas which are designed simply to sell rather than to make profound meaning: 'one may ask if viable stage plays are the place for profound and original philosophy' (Hume 1976: 190). The modern critic faces unafraid the consequences of commercialism, or repeated examples of an absence of meaning – as in *The Rover* where 'love and honour conventions serve principally to occasion extensive sword-play' (p. 284). In Hume's analysis the significance of a dramatic incident lessens in direct proportion to the number of parallels it has. This manic intertextuality might mark the birth of the modern as postmodern. No longer pining for profundity, the modern critic cynically identifies emptied significations, 'a calculated expedition into hysteria, literary, contrived, linked with no reality of the time'. Recognizing our values in theirs, the modern critic, very like the Restoration wit, won't be caught out taking seriously what is mere entertainment, 'capable of providing the theatre audience with nothing more than an agreeable sort of *frisson*' (Righter 1965: 148).

Restoration comedy needed Restoration wits; and, by finding the first modern comedies, critics and directors find themselves as modern. So what was at issue in the 1971 *Man of Mode* 'is not what the playwright's attitude was to his own time, but what the director's attitude is to our own' (Waterhouse 1971: 38). Nearly twenty years later a director of attitude brought to light for the RSC, the 1980s and feminism 'a definitive text which Behn failed to realize'. The director, John Barton, wrote additions to Behn's *The Rover*, which, by Munns's account, 'present a Hollywood, post-*Tom Jones* vision of the Restoration, all lusty wenches, big breasts, gastric noises and chamber-pots'; rewritings of which the 'very crudity seems to signal its period authenticity'. Greeted by newspapers such as the *Guardian* as feminist theatre, Barton's improvement of Behn's feminism shows that 'seventeenth-century folk were just like us – only not so fortunate. Although clad in funny costumes and speaking in quaint English, all they really wanted was racial, social and sexual equality' (Munns 1988: 17–19). Barton becomes as it were the Rover, revealing Behn's true self merely by inserting his lines into the body of her text.

RSC directors know that significance has to be rescued from finger twirling, that sexual seriousness is incompatible with mannered playing. That which is mannered was as offensive to Hands and O'Brien in 1971 as it was to Collier in 1697. In the first modern comedies 'manners' represents repressive social convention against which natural desire has to fight. Restoration comedy had in fact to be saved from its *alter ego*, Comedy of Manners. But when Palmer published *The Comedy of Manners* in 1913 he thought he was saving it from being Restoration comedy. In defences of the comedy for a century, from Lamb to Dobrée, manners had been the keyword. 'Manners' denoted a space outside the realities of everyday life, a space of playful social interaction which, because it was play, could represent what was censored from everyday life, sexual experiment. Which inevitably then returns us to Collier, whose notion of manners on the Restoration stage designated a social interaction imbued with sex, a material negotiation of the realities of desire. For Collier 'manners' was a pejorative description of a sexually occupied society; for Hands and O'Brien a sexually evacuated society was, pejoratively, 'mannered'.

When they rescued *Man of Mode* in 1971 they discovered both its modernity and its Jacobean qualities; in 1986 Barton found in *The Rover* bourgeois feminism and also John Barton. In saving Restoration plays from being mannered, modernity saves them from being Restoration. For any sense of how desire operates in a specific tightly coded society, which might be implied by 'manners', evaporates into vagueness as soon as you start using the slippery word 'modernity'. The cultural activity which formed the 'Comedy of Manners' into the first 'Modern Comedies' is thus not as much about the imaginary life of Restoration drama as the imaginary birth of the first modern critics.

## 5    Orange Women

'And it seemed to me, as one or two – I'm not saying all of them, not at all –
but one or two, saying those well-balanced lines of Mr Farquhar, they seemed
to acquire a dignity, they seemed – they seemed to lose some of their corruption' (Wertenbaker 1991: 22). Second Lieutenant Ralph Clarke, in
Timberlake Wertenbaker's play *Our Country's Good*, is justifying to his fellow
officers his rehearsals of *The Beaux' Stratagem* in an Australian convict colony.
As rehearsals proceed the convicts develop more co-operative relationships and
in particular a new sense of their own worth. Liz Morden faces hanging for a
theft she didn't commit but her sense of the uselessness of speaking in her own
defence keeps her quiet. She is finally persuaded to speak, for the good of the
play. To the Governor's hope that she will be good in her part, Liz, whose
native English is thieves' slang, replies, 'Your Excellency, I will endeavour to
speak Mr Farquhar's lines with the elegance and clarity their worth commands' (p. 83). The moment when the female convict speaks with an elegance
learnt from Farquhar is a joyous theatrical coup. Rehearsing the play has
produced Liz's sense of self-worth. When real modern prisoners rehearse the
fictional eighteenth-century prisoners rehearsing Farquhar they also develop a
changed sense of themselves, as they testify in letters printed as preface to
Wertenbaker's play. Of that prison performance the author says: 'many Education Departments of prisons are being cut – theatre comes under the Education Department – and the idea of tough punishment as justice seems to be
gaining ground in our increasingly harsh society. I hope these letters speak for
themselves and, indeed, for our world.'

.The world for which the letters speak is a world of alienation, described by
Prisoner N55463 J. (Joe) White: 'Prison is about failure normally, and how
we are reminded of it each day of every year.' That sense of a modern condition
might be recognized by L. C. Knights, whose critical position spoke very
much to that alienated world. It might also be recognized, more glamorously,
by the modern critics who, if you like, speak merely *of* that world. While
Knights rages against modernity, the moderns accommodate to it. Neither
position is capable of articulating Prisoner N55463's next sentence: 'Drama,
and self-expression in general, is a refuge and one of the only real weapons
against the hopelessness of these places.' For the modern critical engagement
with Restoration theatre is largely isolated from a theatrical practice (despite,
or because of, the RSC's forays). The procedure for studying that which is not
Renaissance drama is made possible by an academic methodology fixated on
the printed word, and thus incapable of speaking of the pleasures and material
practice of performance. Critical engagement with that which is Renaissance,
by contrast, coexists, sometimes tensely, with a largely independent theatrical
repertoire that stages Renaissance plays. For modern Restoration critics,

intellectual dignity is predicated upon an acknowledgement of the embarrassment or insignificance of theatrical pleasure. Alongside which Wertenbaker's
story of convicts transformed by doing Farquhar looks straightforwardly sentimental, an improbable fantasy in which a liberal male officer enables women
prisoners to develop self-worth by discovering the pleasures of speaking as
Farquhar's gentlewomen. But one performer of the liberal male officer's part,
Prisoner N55463, reported 'strange tricks of reality when the play and our
situation have overlapped merging the borders of the creative process and
actuality' (Wertenbaker 1991: preface).

Precisely the overlap between play and reality preoccupied those censures
which saw Restoration comedy as an offshoot of a decadent aristocratic culture.
But one of the strange tricks observed by N55463 Joe White is that it's
prisoners who find significance in prisoners finding significance in Farquhar.
The pleasure of the Restoration text ceases to be merely a reflection of the
notional pleasures of a decadent class. True to form, the comedy does incite
and enable sexual pleasure, but the sex is imaged as mutual and
transformative, while working across different layers of a power structure. The
narrative of *Our Country's Good* reorganizes the relationship to Restoration
comedy of the two terms which have done so much to shape responses to it,
pleasure and power. Its pleasures were not approved because they were products of a decadent power; but, simultaneously, that power is the only guarantee of what are *necessary* pleasures. The contradiction here comes from an idea,
restated regularly in studies of the Restoration, that theatre simply expresses,
and respects, the reality which it seems to image. But some of theatre's strange
tricks are created in the space of play and fantasy, where identifications are not
necessarily structured along class lines, where desire operates across a range of
identities. Wertenbaker's play of the convict transformed by playing Farquhar
comes out of another idea about Restoration theatre, that of an institution in
which pleasure transforms power. The idea is embodied in the myth of a
woman. It's not, however, like the Behn myth, which finds an originating
moment for a female cultural identity. It is instead a myth of transformations,
of never stabilized identity, in which a woman of low status turns actress who
then becomes a royal lover. She's not, in fact, a convict, but an orange woman,
and her name's Nell Gwynn.

Orange women sold oranges as refreshments in theatres; sometimes they
sold their bodies too. Orange women in this myth are the sexual Real Thing,
the fleshly body contrasted with the actress's artifice. 'Nan's business is fruit,
something appropriate to one's natural self as opposed to one's social front' (N.
Holland 1959: 89). The orange woman myth is a heightened instance of a
general worry about women's natural selves coming into contact with Restoration drama. A correspondent in mid-December 1776 was disturbed by the
crowds of women going to watch Congreve; in 1965 Anne Righter suggested
that Restoration tragedy, which 'flattered exactly those romantic notions and

grandiose dreams of the self . . . continued to embody a feminine as opposed to a masculine point of view' (Righter 1965: 138–9).

Through becoming an actress, Nell Gwynn the orange woman becomes a lover of Charles II. Then, in the old story, she uses her new wealth in a gesture which confirms her pre-theatrical organic worth, by founding Chelsea Hospital as a home for old soldiers. That gesture disappears from the modern Nell story, which then serves to make a tidy separation between the career of sexy actress and the public life of the nation. By contrast, the force of the original myth lies precisely in its untidiness about power and pleasure, in 'a character, to whose influence over an unprincipled voluptuary, we owe a national asylum for veteran soldiers' (Jerrold 1854: preface).

That untidy connection had its popularity in the early 1830s. Two plays about Nell Gwynn appeared in 1832 and 1833, written by dramatists concerned for their country's good. John Walker and Douglas Jerrold used the popular forms of melodrama and domestic drama to explore the antagonisms of class, capital, poverty, and the need for reform. Reform was, indeed, the buzz-word of the early 1830s (for which, see the following chapter on Melodrama). More than a decade of agitation against an unpopular monarchy was fired by the news, in 1831, of another revolution in France. That massive popular opposition to government was then headed off, in 1832, with the compromise known as the Reform Bill. In this context the evocation of the imagined glories of Charles II's reign becomes politically charged. For a decade, as we've seen, that reign had been used to describe a possibility of liberated desires: Hazlitt had conjured up 'the court, the gala day of wit and pleasure, of gallantry and Charles II!', a pleasure focused in spectacle and texture: 'what a rustling of silks and waving of plumes!' (Hazlitt 1967a: 70), which became literally embodied in one of the performances of the equestrian star, Andrew Ducrow. Plays by Susanna Centlivre had been adapted twice in 1823 and again in 1832. Jerrold himself admired the wit of Restoration comedy's dialogue, but it's the Restoration setting (rather than any pseudo-Restoration lines) that accounted for the popularity of his Nell play. As if a not-quite-impossible other world rustles with the silks, a world where power itself is different. For John Walker in 1832, Charles was a king who learnt, crucially, to mingle with his people. His play has a disguised Charles and Rochester being robbed: 'here's a situation for royalty – the levelling system with a vengeance'; and saved by Nell and 'a poor disabled old soldier, who has fought his Majesty's battles' (J. Walker n.d.: 17). Charles tells Nell about disguised royalty in Jerrold's play: 'They go sometimes unknown to shun their state, / And then 'tis manners not to know or wait' (Jerrold 1854: 75). 'Manners', that is, facilitate class mingling.

Walker's levelling system turns out more vengeful than to permit the picture of Charles to remain easily romantic. Both plays have Charles's

disguise backfiring on him: he's robbed or unable to pay a bill, called Charles
or Charley to his face and described by Nell as having 'a shallow neatness, a
sort of brassy glitter in your air that — I know not what you are, if not a pin-
maker' (Jerrold 1854: 62–3). Both plays have lower-class or criminal folk who
are more pleasurable and witty than courtiers. And both plays define the
relations of government and theatre. For Nell's staged prologue, Walker draws
on familiar eighteenth-century notions:

> For wisdom owns, that in a virtuous cause,
> The Stage has more effect than public laws. (Pause)
> The uses of the Drama are not to ape,
> But convey a moral in a pleasing shape.
> (J. Walker n. d.: 14–15)

What is pleasing about that shape is its unpredictability, for it's the very next
scene in which Charles is robbed and discovers the 'levelling system' with a
vengeance.

Charles learns more from the robbery than from the stage's moral example.
The theatre's pleasing shapes are not, eventually, pleasing for abstract moral
reasons, as Hart explains to Nell: 'would the King but condescend to mix a
little more with his people, and enjoy the pleasures of a theatre, he would not
only be much more liked, but his Majesty's Servants would be much more
thankful to him' (J. Walker n.d.: 9). As a theatre manager, Hart is interested
in money as much as government. In Jerrold's play the manager thinks about
recalling an actor who has turned highwayman: 'Get him to give the prologue,
and advertise that he will appear with his identical pistols with which he
robbed the money-broker at Finchley. Depend upon't, the pistols would do
more than the heroic verse' (Jerrold 1854: 57). The moan about heroic verse
comes deep from the Jerrold who helped found the Society of Dramatic
Authors in order to negotiate with an exploitative management, the very sort
of people who would dismiss an actor for piety, value a performer for his
pistols, or refuse to employ Nell Gwynn. Only when he learns the king likes
her does the manager want Nell. Her value is created by, and within, a
financial system in which two theatres compete for audiences and patronage.
Both Walker and Jerrold thus use an image of the Restoration theatre to
complain about the institution which developed its economic shape in the
name of reforming Restoration theatre.

The managers who value the authentic pistols over heroic verse are mocked
by a comic fruit-seller, called Orange Moll. She is the rival of that other fruit-
seller, Nell, whom she imitates and insults, and then replaces. Nell has been
pursued by an 'old' councillor, the lawyer Crowsfoot, who has hired an out of
work actor to steal her away. But Moll, wearing Nell's mask, is stolen in her

place. The narrative organizes Moll and Nell into different rooms in the same inn, where Crowsfoot confuses the identities of the women. They combine to rob him, in a scene which involves tricksy business of Nell hiding behind Moll's chair. Once Crowsfoot has left the stage, Moll embraces Nell in their new-found unity: 'Oh, Nelly, how may one woman be deceived in another!' (Jerrold 1854: 71).

Deceived substantially – as the audience knows, because Moll is played by a man. Much of the comic pleasure and sexual innuendo come precisely from the non-authentic object, the theatrically cross-dressed character. Transgression of authentic identity is the form taken by the women's comic vengeance on Crowsfoot. When he needs to escape from the tavern, Nell offers him a dress: 'What! turn woman?' 'Or be cudgelled for a man!' He chooses the dress: 'There – pull this over your head.' 'And be sure to walk pretty and tripping like one of us,' says Moll (p. 74). When comic pleasure is constituted by such topsy-turvy, the theatre refuses to participate in the clear identification of 'us'. The pleasure is produced for as long as identities cannot be firmly fixed. So in a masquerade, in Walker's play, Charles thinks he has identified Nell by her voice:

CHARLES: It is, it must be she; she's a charming creature, and come what
        come may, I will – Harkye my pretty one.
DUCHESS: (*Comes forward*) Have you so soon, sir, forgotten your vow?
CHARLES: What mean you? – it is but a masquerade, fair lady.
DUCHESS: If you have lost all sense of honour, sir, I have not – behold
        (*Unmasks*)!

(J. Walker n.d.: 33)

Throughout, the Duchess has been associated with anti-pleasure, against dance and drink. Her sexual possessiveness leads into a revelation of identity which then fixes correct social rank and ends the playing. The triumphant assertion of the theatre's image of order is secured only in the *absence* of playing; the urge towards a declared authenticity is revealed as a project that denies the shifting identities of masquerade.

The Duchess's declaration of her sexual identity ends the sexiness of a masquerade in which song and dance are imbued by desire. Sex is located not in the individual body nor even in social interaction but in theatrical play and display. Jerrold's penultimate scene has Nell preparing for her stage prologue while Dryden is 'behind admiring the big hat' (Jerrold 1854: 75). Caught up in the mechanisms of theatrical fetishism this is a very different Dryden from the dramatist defended by Lamb, Hazlitt and, later, Leigh Hunt. The re-creation of a Restoration theatre enables Walker and Jerrold not only to reflect on the political relations of monarch and people, but to construct a theatrical practice that necessarily exceeds the language of reform and realism. Sexual pleasure and theatrical pleasure are created out of one another – and they are powerfully real precisely because of their play with the real. Thus the Nell Gwynn myth tells a seductive story of power and pleasure and theatre. But the orange woman's history has to be denied, necessarily, in order to stabilize the ascendancy of the Orangemen.

# 7

# Melodrama

## 1  Managers

What happened to James Powell was perhaps typical of the way things were in 1805. He had published a play that year called *The Venetian Outlaw*. Another play of the same name, by Robert Elliston, opened at Drury Lane in May the same year. These two plays are fairly intimately connected, as Powell explains: he saw the original play in Paris, translated it and submitted it to the Drury Lane manager in 1803, then he revised it for resubmission in November 1804. But the manager never replied, and the next Powell knew was when *The Venetian Outlaw* was performed in a version credited to Elliston but in fact ripped off verbatim from Powell's first translation.

A very similar story, now called *Rugantino: or, the Bravo of Venice*, opened at Covent Garden in October 1805. This play's author, 'Monk' Lewis, already had a reputation for Gothic fiction, so when the original romance had, as he tactfully puts it, 'fallen into the hands of Mr Harris', he was asked to dramatize it. Harris was the manager of Covent Garden, and it was the established talents of his acting company which dictated the dramatic form into which Lewis 'threw' the romance. The dialogue, he says, was taken almost verbatim from the original German story, so as author he merely 'arranged its incidents'. *Incidents* had to have a major place because they would display the talents of one of Harris's principal assets, the dancer and arranger of Covent Garden pantomimes, Charles Farley. The incidents thus contain much silent action, to be accompanied by music supplied by the famous organist Thomas Busby, who had previously composed for the runaway success of 1802, *A Tale of Mystery*. When he later published the required mixture of dialogue, incident and music, Lewis thought it proper to call it 'A Grand Romantic Melo-Drame' (Lewis 1806: preface).

The process by which *The Venetian Outlaw* got onto the stage suggests a situation in which dramatic creativity is sacrificed to profit-motive. There were still only two licensed or Patent theatres in London for doing spoken drama, and they competed for audiences. Each manager was continually looking for new shows to pull in crowds. If Drury Lane had a novelty, it had to be capped by Covent Garden. Any idea with potential was exploited, at minimum cost. Which is what screwed up James Powell.

But he should not have been surprised. For decades dramatic authors had been critical of the activities of commercial theatre. Way back in the 1720s, the ending of a show had to be changed in order to comply with the 'taste of the town'. The hero of the story, a criminal, was going to be hanged as a punishment. But then the author, a beggar (of course), is summoned onto the stage by an actor, and is told that, since the performance is supposedly an 'opera', it has to end happily. The author agrees to this demand, on the basis that 'in this kind of drama, 'tis no matter how absurdly things are brought about' (Gay 1974: 158). So everything ends happily, with a marriage, a dance and a song.

This case of an altered ending is a spoof. It's the final joke of a series of satirical attacks on contemporary theatre and politics in a show called *The Beggar's Opera*, written by John Gay and staged in 1728. Gay was closely associated with a group of writers who set themselves up as critics of Hanoverian London, attacking both the policies of Prime Minister Walpole and the prevailing taste in drama. In a puff written for *The Beggar's Opera*'s opening in Dublin, Gay's friend, Jonathan Swift, claimed that the piece compared the arts of politicians to those of common robbers, and that it also exposed 'that taste for Italian music among us, which is wholly unsuitable to a Northern climate and the genius of the people, whereby we are overrun with Italian effeminacy and Italian manners' (in Fiske 1973: 97). The Italian music which was pulling in audiences was opera, most famously composed by Handel. To its critics, then as now, opera consisted of improbable stories, involving such things as last-minute reprieves, and sung words which were difficult to follow. By contrast Gay's songs had the clarity of ballads, and their tunes were often borrowed from other famous pieces of music, including opera hits. So his audience could not only understand what someone was singing, they could also recognize the tune as a deliberate parody or pastiche: the songs, in short, were functional. As an eighteenth-century commentator might put it – for instance, the theatre manager and entrepreneur Aaron Hill – 'there ought to be a *purpose* and a *point*' (in Fiske 1973: 77).

Gay has a joke about pointlessness when his Beggar announces that he has put all the fashionable opera similes into his songs. They are included for the purpose not of communicating but of showing off. The eighteenth century had a term for this effect, about which it was vigilant: a late revival of the heroic tragedy *Venice Preserved* was praised because 'None of the persons speak merely for the sake of speaking or to shew the wit and pretty thoughts of the poet. There are no mad rants, no extravagant bombast' (A. M. Taylor 1950: 182). 'Bombast' is still in our vocabulary as a negative term, enshrining a deep distrust of any performance which is extravagant or excessive. This distrust is of a piece with hostility to being improbable and speaking for the sake of speaking. They were all seen as pointless and purposeless indulgences by those who regarded themselves as serious dramatic writers. Theirs was the self-appointed task manfully to defend drama against the effeminate taste of the Town. One such defender, Colley Cibber, an actor and manager, described himself as trapped between the patronage of the Court and the 'arbitrary will, and Pleasure' of the Town (Straub 1992: 41). The Town's apparent effect on drama was to make it more sensual, extravagant and purposeless – to hand it over, as Cibber and Gay saw it, to the 'ladies'.

Even *The Beggar's Opera* got handed over: the piece was revived in 1732 by a troupe of Irish teenagers managed by a rope-dancer called, all too aptly, Signora Violante. One of the performers, who later became a major star, Peg Woffington, took three roles, including that of the hero, Macheath. That prospect of the virile hero's part being taken, so to speak, by the young woman provides a rather neat image of what was going on in the London theatres. Patent theatres supposedly had a monopoly on doing proper spoken drama, but audiences were showing a persistent predilection for looking at the non-spoken – the speechless sounds of opera, the writhing bodies of acrobatics and rope-dancing. In particular the fashion for pantomime had reached a heyday in the early 1720s. The form had started, according to John Weaver's *History of the Mimes and Pantomimes* (1728), in 1702: 'The first entertainment that appear'd on the English Stage where the Representation and the Story was carried on by Dancing, Action and Motion only, was perform'd with Grotesque Characters after the modern Italians such as Harlequin, Scaramouch etc.' (in Fiske 1973: 69). With its roots in the ancient *commedia dell'arte*, it was another 'Italian', and another primarily *musical*, form. In one of its most famous Harlequins, John Rich, it had someone who, as a theatre manager, had the opportunity to build up a pantomime repertoire. But the theatre he managed was Lincoln's Inn Fields, one of the Patents at that time, a bastion of the proper spoken. So in 1728, when he was offered a show that had been turned down by the other Patent, a show involving as much music as speaking, he accepted it. *The Beggar's Opera* opened. The show that satirized 'the taste of the town' was a huge success. With his profit, Rich, the pantomime star with a pantomime repertoire, began in 1729 to build a big new theatre at Covent Garden. Meanwhile, in the same year, spoken drama had found a new home for itself in a non-Patent theatre at Goodman's Fields. What had started to happen, rather fast, was that the old aesthetic distinction between proper drama and improper 'effeminate' entertainment, which had been institution-alized in the division between licensed Patents and the rest, now was breaking down.

There was no longer any implied connection between the theatre building and the sort of shows it did. In Renaissance London, and indeed in the Restoration, theatres had developed product identities – a building became known for specializing in a particular genre of performance. In the early 1730s theatres were functioning much more as venues – equipped spaces which could be used by entrepreneurs to put on anything which might make money (like doing a one-off gay night or live band in a heterosexual night-club). Shares in theatre management were bought, sold and quarrelled over as any other business proposition, with very little reference to artistic product. Indeed, in May 1733, the management of one of the Patents, Drury Lane, locked out the actors in an industrial dispute. When people were attempting to define 'the taste of the town' as something separate from, say, aristocratic patronage, they were reaching out for a scheme that could allocate value to – make orderly sense of – the range of different products. But aesthetic format and political affiliation were no longer necessarily connected. When he did *The Beggar's Opera*, Rich mounted a show that attacked both Italian opera and Prime Minister Walpole. But then, in 1736, Rich, as a pantomime star, was himself seen to be like Walpole:

> You wonder, perhaps, at the tricks of the stage,
> Or that pantomime miracles take with the age;
> But if you examine Court, Country, and Town,
> There's nothing but Harlequin feats will go down.
>                                   (Fielding 1967: xv)

In the free market of theatre, all that mattered was what would 'go down'.

The author of those lines about Rich was Henry Fielding, who put on a successful series of burlesques at another non-Patent theatre, the 'Little The-atre in the Hay' (Haymarket). It was one of those burlesques, *The Historical Register for the Year 1736*, another attack on Walpole, which supposedly led to the State's eventual interference in the theatrical turmoil through the Licens-ing Act. For some time, men of letters had been asking for the State to take a firmer hand as the competition and effeminacy spread ever more anarchically. They got their last-minute reprieve in 1737. The Licensing Act clarified a long-standing confusion about the responsibilities of managers in relation to the State censor that had been around since the Restoration. The 1737 Act required that all scripts be submitted to the censor in advance for licensing. It also strengthened, once again, the monopoly of the Patents on proper dramatic performance. Thus the political target of *The Beggar's Opera* seemed to have walked on, in a highly improbable twist, to protect proper drama from the degrading taste of the Town.

But, like most improbable happy endings, it didn't solve the problem. The competition between the Patents led instead to sharpened insistence on their separate identities. Covent Garden under Rich became the pantomime theatre. So, when the acting star David Garrick took over the management of Drury Lane in 1747, he wanted it to be the non-pantomime theatre. By way of manifesto, for his opening night he got the most writerly of contemporary writers, Samuel Johnson, to script him a prologue. It tells of the slow decline of Tragedy in the ages after Shakespeare, arriving at the final contemporary collapse of theatrical art: 'Exulting Folly hail'd the joyous Day, / And Pantomime, and Song, confirm'd her Sway.' At the end of the prologue, Johnson and Garrick invite the audience to become more responsible about their theatrical taste: ''Tis yours this Night to bid the Reign commence / Of rescued Nature, and reviving Sense' (Johnson 1971: 82).

Garrick had already proved himself as a rescuer of Nature. He had pioneered a more mimetically realist form of acting, with an emphasis on facial detail which seemed ideally suited to – almost made for – the intimate dimensions of Drury Lane. Having his own stage, Garrick was able to dress this acting in costumes that aspired to historical accuracy, and to light it with a new system of movable footlights and wing-lights to produce expressive variations in brightness. The spectacular elements of performance thus showed themselves to be communicating something that was not so much 'pantomime miracles' as 'Nature' and 'Sense'. Even the most slippery element, music, could be used expressively, for example in heightening the emotion when the statue comes alive at the end of Shakespeare's *Winter's Tale* – a practice which deftly enabled Garrick to supply an effect Shakespeare himself had requested. So in this way Garrick, acting as a reformer and restorer of theatrical art, could step into a public role that had already been scripted:

> Rouze, Britons, rouze, this modish Taste despise,
> And let Good Sense to its Old Standard rise;
> Frequent your luscious Pantomimes no more,
> But Shakespeare, like your Ancestors adore.
> ('Timothy Fribble', 1749, in Loftis et al. 1976: 136)

To decide to replace pantomime with Shakespeare is not only to show good sense but also to hitch this reform to patriotism.

Garrick, having resurrected Shakespeare for Drury Lane, then caught the patriotic mood in 1757 with a hit song called 'Hearts of Oak' in a show that charted the fall of pantomime. The paradox was that this show was itself a pantomime – as if Shakespeare's 'manly soul' depended for its appearance on the efforts of the 'effeminate' form. Having conceded that much to the taste of the Town, Garrick set about more reform. *His* pantomimes were to be self-consciously artistic, determinedly balletic, just as his revivals of Restoration plays were to display a conscientious avoidance of obscenity. He was, in other words, not merely a rescuer of Nature but an improver of Art. Nature and Art are not opposites here: both are purposeful and communicative, expressing the respect for innate order, the good taste and the *sense* of their manager. The opposite of both these is a theatre which is purposeless, improbable, miraculous, speaking for the sake of speaking, deliberately extravagant. When Garrick's reforms are seen, as he would wish, as progress, it's a progress towards theatre which serves Nature and Art, away from a theatre that is for its own sake. The real direction of the progress is not, however, forwards but sideways, into another theatre aesthetic. The difference between these two, equally viable, sorts of performance is summarized by a modern theatre anthropologist called Eugenio Barba. He distinguishes between performing that aims to look like reality, deliberately behaving in ways familiar from daily life, and performing that aims to mark its disconnection from reality, acting in ways that can be described as not just extra-daily, but completely outside the daily:

> the acrobats, the dancers, show us 'another body,' a body which uses techniques very different from daily ones, so different in fact as to lose all contact with them. Here it is no longer a matter of extra-daily techniques but simply of 'other techniques'. . . . pure distance: the inaccessibility of the virtuoso's body. The body's daily techniques have communication as their aim; the techniques of virtuosity aim for amazement and the transformation of the body. (Barba 1986: 138–9)

An insight into the equal validity of communication and amazement is obscured by the rivalry between the theatres of Drury Lane and Covent Garden. For Garrick's reforms, his connection with literary figures, his manifesto about Nature and Sense, and perhaps above all his 'return' to Shakespeare, all make it look as if what he is really rescuing is drama itself. Which then implies that what he is rescuing it from is not an equal-but-different form of art, but the degradation of merely commercial entertainment; theatre for the sake of sense against theatre for the sake of pence. That analysis would appear to be confirmed by the sequence of managers at Garrick's rival theatre: Covent Garden was first built by a pantomime star made good; Rich was succeeded in 1761 by his son-in-law, the great tenor John Beard, who introduced more opera into the programme; in 1767 he handed over to a syndicate which included the playwright George Colman, but sole control was finally taken in 1774 by a businessman, one Thomas Harris. It was the same man who, thirty years later, commissioned a show about a Venetian outlaw, in which the written dialogue was intended to be rather less important than the arrangement of actions to music, the 'incidents'.

The show 'Monk' Lewis arranged for Harris was to be billed as 'A Grand Romantic Melo-Drame'. Here was a new word in the English theatre scene, another import to our 'Northern climate'. Harris's eldest son, Henry, had come across it in France in about 1800. The obvious, literal translation of the French word *melodrame* was 'musical play', but that didn't really describe what Henry Harris and all the other English tourists saw. The English theatre already had plenty of shows involving music: spoken plays with occasional song and dance numbers; operas which were entirely sung; pantomimes or ballets in which there was continuous music but no speaking. The French were doing performances that combined the spoken and mimed, where the use of music was expressive and the message was conspicuously solemn and moral. Henry Harris came up with his own translation for the term: 'an entirely novel species of entertainment is performed; called melodrama – mixing, as the name implies (*mêler drame*), the drama, and *ballêt* of action; which latter, it will probably supersede' (in Reynolds 1827: II, 346).[1]

The manager's son's etymology was mistaken. But his sense of the novelty of what he had found was accurate. For in melodrama the proper purposeful drama was now mixed, inextricably, with the improper 'purposeless' form against which it was always contrasted. The distinction between communication and amazement thus became blurred. So a good writer of melodrama is happy to be an arranger of incidents. By contrast, the self-respecting dramatic author refused to move away from scripting a play into scripting incidents. James Boaden resisted the pressure to supply material designed for one of Covent Garden's dancers: 'When I refused to let him dance (though the original gave me any scope that way), it must be clear, that I relied firmly upon the simplest interest of the incident – upon momentary terror, and instant relief' (Boaden 1803: preface).

Boaden translated some of the leading French melodramatists but his way of doing it produced scripts which looked like proper eighteenth-century plays. His belief in the natural rhythms of narrative, with which it is improper to interfere, is a residue of the respect for orderly art, for good sense. His view of narrative fits with the pleasure in seeing decorum observed and hearing word-perfect lines. To disrupt an orderly action merely for the sake of showing off a dancer is just the kind of improbable, purposeless display that the businessman manager might insist on. As a literary man, Boaden was going to resist, with a whole history behind him, this outrage to his dramatic imagination. To adherents of proper drama, rescued and reformed by Garrick, this new mixed form provided a new opening for all the incoherence and pointlessness of a merely commercial entertainment. A fairly late satire on the new form found it funny precisely on these grounds: *Melodrame Mad! or the Siege of Troy* is described as 'A new Comic, Pathetic, Historic, Anachronasmatic, Ethic, Epic Melange' (Dibdin 1819).

To people like Boaden the new mixed form could be said to be 'contrary to the notion of purpose as far as our judgement is concerned, inappropriate to our powers of representation, and seemingly violent to our imagination'. It is a description that comes, not from an English dramatist, but from a German philosopher, Immanuel Kant, writing in 1790. And he was not describing melodrama but something he called the 'sublime'. The sublime is a way of perceiving things that goes beyond everyday experience and thought, a 'faculty of mind which exceeds any measure of the senses' – like amazement perhaps (quoted in J. Roberts 1988: 62). This sublime faculty of mind turns upside-down Garrick and Johnson's touchstones – it exceeds Sense, finds in Nature irregularity and formlessness. The capacity of the sublime to take spectators out of the everyday, beyond the limits of understanding, exceeding form and order, is brought about by its mixture of elements. This is how Lynda Nead summarizes it:

> Whereas the sentiment of beauty is predicated on a sense of the harmony between man and nature and the rationality and intelligibility of the world, the sublime is conceived of as a mixture of pleasure, pain and terror that forces us to recognize the limits of reason. Kant specifies this relationship in terms of framing: the beautiful is characterized by the finitude of its formal contours, as a unity contained, limited, by its borders. The sublime, on the contrary, is presented in terms of excess, of the infinite. (Nead 1992: 26)

In his being excited by the novelty and power of, precisely, the mixedness of this new foreign thing called melodrama, the businessman manager of Covent Garden in 1805 could be said to be contributing fairly profoundly to the degradation of the drama of sense and nature.

## 2   A Convulsive Noise

One of the most celebrated virtuosos of the early decades of the nineteenth century was a man called Andrew Ducrow. He was an equestrian acrobat, and his act specialized in doing such things as delivering a scene from a Shakespeare play while standing on the back of a horse that was cantering around an arena. Ducrow's audiences presumably didn't quite know whether to concentrate on the communication that was coming to them from the soliloquy of a desperate Richard III – a horse, a horse, my kingdom for a horse – or whether to be amazed by the ability of someone who could perform this while keeping his balance on the back of the very thing Richard didn't have, a moving horse.

The venue for this act was Astley's Amphitheatre, which had a circus ring in front of an enormous stage, a theatre that in its very structure seemed to hover between acrobatics and drama, amazement and communication.

When he got too old for acrobatics, Ducrow concentrated on acting. But he didn't abandon his famous recipe for good entertainment: 'cut the dialect and come to the 'osses' (in M. Baker 1978: 35) – 'ossless, he took to playing mute acting parts. One of the shows he appeared in was Barnabas Rayner's *The Dumb Man of Manchester* done at Astley's in 1837. In the play the dumb man, Tom, is wrongly accused of a murder actually committed by his brother-in-law. The only person who can clear Tom is his sister Jane. But she, who has kept secret her marriage, feels obliged to protect her husband because she fears for her child. The audience also know what Jane knows. This circumstance produces a thoroughly typical melodrama effect on the audience. The narrative moves inexorably towards what we know will be an unjust trial. That movement could be arrested by Jane telling everybody what the real truth is; but, of course, that is just what she feels she can't do. What agitates the audience, then, is a sense of frustration – an emotional effect derived from non-communication.

When Tom appears before the judge he has to use sign language to declare his innocence. In one respect the sign language is redundant, since the audience already know what is true. But the play insists on giving time to the dumb-show. For if nothing else it's a moment at which the show's star does what he is good at. But the star-turn contributes to, rather than upstages, something else that is going on. For this moment, in another highly characteristic melodrama ploy, puts its audience in a position where it doesn't so much want to know what's happened as want to see expressed *what it already knows*. Several scenes are constructed to offer the possibility of revealing, and then to delay expression of, the truth. At the end Tom–Ducrow's dumb-show is successful – the judge understands his signs, and he clears Tom. But the moment at which Tom's innocence is affirmed is not the climax of the play. It is immediately followed by the entry of his criminal brother-in-law. The acted-out confrontation between the guilty and the innocent is the real climax, marked appropriately by a theatrical shock. Tom, seeing his brother-in-law, for the first and only time makes a 'convulsive noise'.

Tom's noise works as an emotional climax because, following a series of scenes in which the truth is not expressed, is not understood, is always tantalizingly withheld, it now bursts forth unbidden with the force of convulsion. After the consistently maintained sign language, Tom's noise is less shocking as a communication of a truth than amazing as a sudden change of register. Before this, and preparing the way for it, the dramatic technique of taking non-communication to the very edge of communication is typical of much melodrama. It is given extra force here by Ducrow's mime skills. But there is a deeper, richer, connection with another form of entertainment in which Ducrow specialized, an entertainment which directs our attention to the pleasures of looking.

For about ten years previously Ducrow had been displaying his so-called 'poses plastiques', which were static impersonations. While galloping on horseback he struck attitudes as Mercury or a Roman gladiator. In time these tableaux were separated from the riding, and the stage curtain would open to reveal Ducrow motionless on a pedestal: 'He appeared first as the Hercules Farnese. With the greatest skill and precision he then gradually quitted his attitude from one gradation to another, of display of strength; but at the moment in which he presented a perfect copy of the most celebrated statues of antiquity, he suddenly became fixed as if changed to marble.' The various statues seemed 'all equally perfect and true' (in Altick 1978: 343). The acrobatic skill here is used in maintaining the stillness of the pose. That is to say, when the copy appears to be most 'perfect and true', the body is under most strain. The pleasure produced depends on the smoothness of the changes, the gradation, in conjunction with the appearance of fixedness when he stops, at once – paradoxically – flowing and marble. That paradox is a version of something deep at the heart of a great deal of performance, a tension between filling and emptying. The pose that looks 'perfect and true' slides out of your grasp, and into another perfection, and then slides again. The moment at which the copy becomes most complete, fully present, is the moment at which the performance most risks its instability and dissolution.

Ducrow was doing with his body what specialists in scenery and panoramas were doing with materials and light. For instance, in one of the key spectacular moments of *Maria Marten* (1840s), the apparently solid wall of Mrs Marten's cottage melts away as we see her dreamed image of her daughter's murder in the Red Barn. In 1820 J. R. Planché's vampire was the first figure to walk through a solid wall. On the stormy ocean of Edward Fitzball's 1826 melodrama *The Flying Dutchman*, a phantom ship appeared. The effects are produced by painted gauze, trick carpentry and, in Fitzball's case, by an oil-lighted magic lantern projecting an image on a transparent screen. That technique had been introduced to London in 1801–2 in a mechanical show called the Phantasmagoria, which gave audiences thrills by showing them 'ghosts, skeletons, and known individuals': 'the head of Dr Franklin was transformed into a skull; figures which retired with the freshness of life came back in the form of skeletons, and the retiring skeletons returned in the drapery of flesh and blood.' This was followed by 'terrific figures' which now advanced on the spectators instead of receding: 'The effect of this part of the exhibition was naturally the most impressive. The spectators were not only surprised but agitated, and many of them were of the opinion that they could have touched the figures' (in Altick 1978: 218). Later on, and more immediately contemporary with Ducrow's performance in *Dumb Man*, there was a widespread cultural interest in the mechanism of looking and the possibility of preserving what is seen. John Walker's medical treatise on *The Philosophy of the Eye* appeared in 1837, and news of Louis Daguerre's photographic invention led to a popular demand for daguerreotypes in 1839.

The great thing about daguerreotypes is that you get something for your money: it is not only remarkable, but you can buy it and take it home. For audiences of the Phantasmagoria, however, there was an agitation which is something different from surprise. It comes from feeling that you should be able to touch something which is, at the same time, a trick effect; and so, *wanting* to touch it, to verify it, but never being able to. Nineteenth-century showmen and exhibitors competed to offer sights which had to be as real as they were strange. What seems impossible to be true also seems to be fully present – and to invite itself to be authenticated, grasped, touched. Thus in the viewing arrangements of zoos and panoramas and phantasmagorias much of the excitement, or agitation, is constructed by the interplay between what you want to touch and what you can't reach. Which leads perhaps to that notorious situation in melodrama theatres where excited audiences reach out over the gap to the performance, seeking to make contact with the stage by hurling words and objects at it.

What then is giving force to *The Dumb Man*'s story of truth nearly but not quite spoken is the desire of spectators who have been worked on so that they want to affirm truth and are not able to. When the narrative ensures that Tom's sister cannot speak out on his behalf, it makes the audience want to do it for her. But they remain, of course, physically in the auditorium even if they are imaginatively on stage. Through Ducrow's performance, then, we can see a whole tradition of performing and watching which gives to that mixed thing called melodrama its characteristic effects. And the dramatists certainly learnt to work with these. Rayner has advanced well beyond the formula on which James Boaden depended: 'momentary terror, and instant relief'. The terror is less momentary and the relief not instant. Truth is shut off from communication, always in new ways slipping out of your grasp. The plotting mechanics of frustration and release produce questions about what will happen next, how truth will be revealed. These, the familiar materials of suspense, came to be the distinguishing features of melodrama as it began early in the nineteenth century.

In previous centuries, when someone wanted to suggest that drama was a serious art, it was argued that audiences became imaginatively involved with heroic characters. Thus a spectator might learn, by imitation, to aspire to the nobility of leadership or to despise the cruelty of tyranny. If this is your understanding of how drama works, you emphasize and value those dramatic devices which produce recognition of and identification with a character's concerns. But melodrama devises situations in which audiences know more than sympathetic characters, knowing, say, more than Tom knows about his sister, and hence they see but do not share a character's misunderstandings or dilemmas. The misunderstanding is important to the extent that it develops or blocks the outcome which the audience desires. The audience's involvement with the drive of the *narrative* seems more important than its involvement with the situation of any one character. From its earliest days, the first English translators of French melodrama felt that their audiences wanted action rather than lengthy exposition in dialogue. Making the main character dumb is merely a hardline implementation of this formula. For it is not the complexity of Tom's character but the shape of his narrative that grips an audience.

The fact of *Dumb Man*'s commercial success at Astley's – that half-theatre, half-circus – could be taken to indicate the debased, lower-class nature of melodrama. But that should not conceal from us another fact: in its easy assimilation of modes of performing and spectating from well outside dialogue drama, *The Dumb Man* is telling us that a new theatrical language has already come into being.

## 3   The Great Line and Claptrap

When the judge decides to believe Tom, the truth is at last seen to be communicated on stage. At that moment the audience is released from its frustration. What then follows is a *coup de théâtre* that says nothing new, but is at the same time 'amazing'. The convulsive noise does not indicate the revelation of the truth but what should properly be called its acclamation.

The moment of acclamation can be a source of theatrical excitement. To this end Robert Elliston advised an actress how to do part of his pirated text, *The Venetian Outlaw*:

> remain for a moment or two fixed, as a statue representing *horror*; then recovering *shriek* out '*He* was here – *he*' 'What saidst thou? Can it be?' – after this pause an instant – '*No, no, my eyes deceive me*' – quick – half belief half doubt – I am deceived if you don't make a great line of this. (G. Taylor 1989: 2)

Elliston's care is devoted to one of the few bits of the play he wrote himself, in order to produce the excitement of which James Powell's original translation is almost wholly innocent. The 'great line' is not created with reference to consistency of characterization or maintenance of mood but as a self-contained musical organization of pace and volume inserted at a key point in the narrative.

Many narratives of early melodrama are organized to produce a climactic speaking out, the moment of the great line. In James Kenney's *Blind Boy of Bohemia* (1807), for example, the guardian of the boy feels that the knowledge he possesses morally obliges him to disrupt a royal wedding ceremony in order to announce the boy's true parentage. The device is repeated when, at the end of the play, the wicked Prince Rodolpho tries to deny his involvement in an assassination plot until the blind boy himself produces the incriminating evidence. On the early melodrama stage, ceremonies of State and the claims of rulers are challenged by an individual who speaks out against them. This lone voice is in possession of truths which are unknown to, or more likely hidden by, authority. Set up in these terms, the moment of the great line acquires a political dimension.

In the first play to call itself a 'melo-drame', Thomas Holcroft's *Tale of Mystery* (1802), a dumb poorly dressed stranger has arrived at a country house. Although he is unknown, he gains the trust and moral support of the house-keeper. The owner of the house, Bonamo, then receives documents which incriminate this stranger. This leads to a confrontation between the owner and his housekeeper. Against his documentary evidence, and his social rank, she asserts her instinctive belief and her personal experience. And she is the one who will turn out, in a later scene, to be triumphantly right. While thunder rumbles in the distance, the female housekeeper compels the male owner to fall to his knees, in front of his own son and most trusted male friend, and repent his unjust mistake.

While most of the text of the play came from a French original by Pixérécourt, Holcroft made alterations which had the effect of downplaying references to heaven and romance, and gave prominence instead to political sentiments in line with his own radical Jacobin rationalism. It's not really surprising, therefore, to discover that in the somewhat conservative French original we won't find that repentance scene. For the housekeeper, like the blind boy, is one of the disenfranchised to whom radical melodrama not only gives a voice, but also, by summoning up the specific facilities of the stage, *amplifies* that voice with the reverberations of distant thunder. In their confron-tation with the great, the great line gives to its speakers more than truth. It gives them histrionic greatness.

For an audience who thought like Holcroft it could be taken for granted that the disenfranchised would speak truer than the gentry. Radicalism in the Regency was shaped around campaigns for universal (which is to say male) suffrage and fair taxation. And these political concerns give a shape to many melodramas (even where they don't seem to have political references). The production of Kenney's *Blind Boy* made a very big scene of Church and State ceremonial disrupted and destroyed by the individual voice. In the public sphere of Regency politics, any stage images of deceitful ceremony or upper-class legal manipulation would fairly easily trigger associations with what was called 'Old Corruption', the dominant order. Dramatic narratives shaped around confrontations between blind boy and wicked prince – individual truth and corrupt power – emerge from the same structure of feeling as demands for universal suffrage in the face of a repressive regime. A key figure in the identification and arrest of Holcroft's villain, Romaldi, is an honest miller, an artisan. He is a member of the social group from which many of the Regency radicals were drawn; and it was the same group in which many of those working in the theatres in the early days had their origins. So when those theatre workers became excited about the possibility of the great line, it had to do with the acting out of what is, in several senses, possibility.

The emotion of the moment of speaking out is something very different from the frustration experienced when the dumb man cannot speak to clear himself. Being able to acclaim the truth is the opposite of being trapped into a false truth. Melodrama may be said to construct excitement out of the possible alternation between being trapped by circumstances and being able to change them. If we want brief terminology for these two situations we could borrow from a political philosophy which had its own roots in the same period. Karl Marx said that, while people can make their own history, they cannot do it in conditions of their own choosing. Thus there is a tense relationship between *determination* and *agency*: human beings exist in conditions which are always greater than any individual, and hence set limits to, shape, 'determine', human activity; but that shaping influence doesn't cancel human ability to make change, to act as an 'agent' of history. Melodrama's excitement may be said to relate to a fantasy of *agency*, the possibility of being able single-handedly to challenge authority and change it. But, moving on from here, the politics of early melodrama ask who the agency acts for, what shapes it, in what circumstances the great line is spoken.

This question about agency, about the circumstances of the great line, may be illustrated using two speechless men who both utter wordless sounds. In Holcroft's *Tale of Mystery*, Francisco – the poorly dressed stranger – has been made dumb in a violent attack on him in the past. When interrogated in the country house he refuses to identify his attackers. In a later scene, when he himself is identified as the father of the heroine, he utters his wordless cry; and then is banished from the house. In the final act he comes face to face with the man who made him dumb, his own brother. But Francisco refuses the opportunity to avenge himself. In the closing tableau of the play, the violent brother has been hunted down and lies on the ground cradled and shielded by Francisco, while Francisco's daughter pleads for the life of her wicked uncle against the pursuing forces of law. Francisco's relationship both to his own past and to the violence done to him is fairly complicated. None of that past had been known in advance by the audience: his cry comes when he is forcibly revealed in an identity that had remained hidden. By contrast, at the end of *The Dumb Man of Manchester*, Tom, whose dumbness is 'natural', utters his convulsive noise as the response of an innocent man to a criminal. It works as an acclamation of the true identities that are clear, uncomplicated, and known by the audience from the start.

Tom had been described early on as an industrious worker, and although he is part of the work-force he is chosen to give the workers their appropriate rewards from the employer. The threat to Tom comes from a brother-in-law defined as a criminal wastrel, who is dressed as a beggar on his first appearance and automatically suspected by Tom of being a thief. Tom's dumbness aligns him with a dominant class position: the narrative of the play deploys him, on the one hand, to contribute towards a sentimentalized picture of labour relations and, on the other, to sniff out, as if instinctively, criminality in the non-industrious. Francisco's dumbness is the sign of his victimization, the scar of the habitual violence of wealth. He first appears dressed rather like Tom's brother-in-law, a beggarly stranger – although here this is coupled with a dignified demeanour and the trust of the housekeeper. As *his* story unfolds it points towards the guilt not of the non-industrious worker but of the upper-class wealthy.

Tom depends upon a perceptive judge and the law to establish his innocence. Francisco defies both the judgement and charity of an imperceptive property owner. Tom's story ends with a revelation of what the audience knew to be the case. Francisco's story ends with an unpredicted and contradictory image, of the innocent man caring for the loved guilty one in defiance of State law. Tom's muteness eloquently articulates traditional ruling assumptions about class hierarchy, beggars and judges. His convulsive noise affirms rather than challenges the dominant. Francisco's muteness speaks with difficulty about class violence and the identity between innocence and guilt. No simple noise can articulate the complex ending.

The political complexity of *Tale of Mystery* may not have been quite what the son of the manager of Covent Garden Theatre had in mind when he defined melodrama as 'mêler drame', 'mixed'. Yet it is in practice the mixed sorts of performance in *Tale of Mystery* that enabled it to achieve complexity. This contrasts with *Dumb Man*. In that play, as we have seen, Ducrow had found a home for his mime skills within the narrative of melodrama. But the play doesn't actually require those skills to be very developed, since other characters explain, or the audience already knows, what Tom is trying to say. The mime depends on or illustrates the narrative. Francisco's past life, by contrast, is not fully revealed to the audience: it is seen to torment him, pulling him forcefully between past and present, but it also remains mysterious. And because it is mysterious the audience has to cling onto its detail, registering all its changes. As a performer, Charles Farley, a choreographer and pantomimist, directed his skill less towards an accurately realist representation than to the dextrous handling of swift or contradictory emotional shifts.

Farley's acting here seems typical of its time in that it organized its performance into sequences of 'points', clearly articulated emotional pictures that establish themselves before transforming into something else – rather as Ducrow did his 'poses plastiques', but more flexibly and faster. The force of

Edmund Kean's performance as Shylock was attributed to 'the rapidity of his transitions from one tone and feeling to another . . . presenting a succession of striking pictures, and giving perpetually fresh shock of delight and surprise' (G. Taylor 1989: 34). Each picture produces response and, where they are arranged into a developing sequence, the climax has the effect of the great line, so that Kemble showing Macbeth's response to his wife's death did the 'Tomorrow' soliloquy 'rising to a climax of desperation that brought down the enthusiastic cheers of the closely packed theatre' (p. 36). The cheers are not so much a consequence of empathy with the character's desperation as an engagement with – and *by* – the rhythms of the performance. Playing a character successfully did not involve a search for coherence and unity but the creation of a succession of good pictures. And, to the extent that what was thrilling about these pictures was their transformation into one another, melodrama may once again be said to be 'mixed'.

Kemble's performance was arranged so that its audience knew what was coming. When Farley acted Francisco being interrogated about his past, he was using his body to show a character responding to memories and events which the audience had not seen. To act out a response to a supposed memory has the effect of bringing into real being, of embodying in the present, the emotional shape of events that are supposed to have happened elsewhere. The character's personal history thus insists on physically inhabiting the present. This can be seen at work in an early scene from Buckstone's *Luke the Labourer* (1826). On his arrival at Farmer Wakefield's house, Luke is surprised to see the Farmer there. For Luke, in an act of vengeance, had put the Farmer in prison for debt. In the accidental meeting, Luke's belligerent condescension rapidly changes when the Farmer accuses him of being a scoundrel. Luke begins to recall the time he was dismissed from employment. It was long in the past, but Luke feels a need to retell it: 'I never had the chance 'afore; but now it do all come fresh upon my brain, my heart do seem ready to burst wi' summut buried in it, and I cannot keep it down.' And then he recalls his wife dying of starvation: 'I saw her look at me wi' such a look as I shall never forget – she laid hold o' this hand, and, putting her long thin fingers all round it, said, "Luke, would na' the farmer give you sixpence if he thought I were dying o' want?"' As he calls attention to his own hand, it seems to bring the past into the present, for out of his own mouth comes his wife's dying speech. Luke doesn't hear the Farmer's daughter when she pleads with him to stop. After a pause he speaks again: 'I felt alone in the world. I stood looking on her white face near an hour, and did not move from the spot an inch' (Buckstone 1966: 246). The more still that the actor stands, the longer he pauses, the more intense is the feeling that the past is now present, in this very spot. But as the daughter throws herself at Luke's feet, pleading, he bursts into triumphant laughter at the sight: the daughter pleading where his dead wife was – or is – lying. And he also weeps. By the time he has got to this point, the sight of

Luke's body replaying both the sorrow of his history and the passion of his vengeance makes it very difficult to label him with a simple moral categorization.

What the Luke-actor has to do here is by no means untypical, and it brings us to an important discovery: melodrama's use of the acting body threatens to upset the common assumption that melodrama is morally simplistic. Confronted by someone acting as the 'villainous' Luke must, watching gets difficult. For a start, there is a sense that a character is not emotionally fixed, and may shift radically and unpredictably through different states. Secondly, the body seems to be not wholly governed by either the conventions or the logic of customary interpersonal exchange, and all too readily crumples under the pressure of something that is beyond control – 'I cannot keep it down.' As his emotional history starts to come out, it enacts itself through paradoxes. Luke stands alone among other people, in his own house in someone else's, in the past in the present. Melodrama, in short, is drawn towards paradox rather than simplification. We earlier met one example of it, where the story of mute Francisco leads to a violently contradictory family *tableau*, a 'picture'. Now with Luke we have an example of how a mode of acting, moving rapidly through a series of *states*, or 'points', also works to complicate simple moral categories.

Contemporary with Luke's spasms, in another theatre, Andrew Ducrow's 'poses plastiques' were also deploying the body in a succession of contrasting pictures. Both initially look similar, in that they seem to be organized as sequences of 'points'. But there is a crucial difference. In contrast to Luke's disturbing slide into an intolerable memory, when Ducrow's pictures establish themselves they offer a more comfortable pleasure. For at these points the correlation between the poser's body and a familiar classical image may be inspected. It is the *accuracy* as well as the frozen quality which is exciting. Thus while Luke's body is thrown into unpredictable tremors by his own particular history, Ducrow's body is expected to produce an accurate copy of something already known. The pleasure created by the closeness of Ducrow's imitation is very like the pleasure when people understand what dumb Tom is telling them. The same word describes both pleasures: they are realizations. Each 'pose plastique' realizes, *makes real*, for the audience a familiar image. When the image comes into place the audience realizes, *clearly recognizes*, what it copies.

When a performance is a 'realization' it defines itself as – and aspires to – accuracy of imitation. Ducrow's whole body makes itself become a complete fixed image. In working this way, however temporarily, each 'pose plastique' seems to anticipate a mode of acting in which a performance is judged to be good if it imitates accurately, sustains the imitation, and makes the imitation coherent. While Luke gets more distressing as he slides through his contradictory states, being disturbingly decentred, a different, perhaps less melodramatic, sort of performance specialized in offering what was reliable, accurate and centred.

Each 'pose plastique' aimed to produce applause for its truth. In the same way applause greeted moments of acclamation or verification. Such lines or gestures were technically known as claptraps, in that they secured (trapped) applause from the audience. What happens, when they work, is that the performance has set up the conditions in which an audience *knows* that it is meant to applaud. The ending of *Dumb Man* invites an audience to respond by organizing a simple opposition between Tom and his brother-in-law, good and evil. At the same time it allows us to forget about Jane, the wife and sister who is worried about her child. As a 'realization' it is a making real of what an audience *wants to believe* is reality. In its simplicity it becomes a truth which is, rather comfortingly, fixed, coherent, reliable. As such, the ending of *Dumb Man* offers its audience something different from Francisco's or Luke's difficult or contradictory histories. All the plays may be said to be driving towards 'truth', but much depends on how it is revealed. Where the great line or picture comes in a sequence of shocks it can produce a complex response. But a desire merely to trap the clap reduces sequence to a fixed – fetishized – moment of acclamation: cheering a truth that's been tidied up to get the cheer.

Those loud responses were culturally learnt in a tradition in which audiences commented on stage action. Boring or unpopular shows were noisily abused, popular performances were cheered. Dickens describes a melodrama at the Royal Victoria (ex-Coburg) Theatre in which the honest sentiments of 'Michael the Mendicant' were 'hailed with showers of applause' (Dickens n.d.: 176). The production of claptraps, like the production of great lines, emotionally invests the moment in which truth is 'realized'. But we have two sorts of making real, two sorts of things to recognize: the unsettling transitions that make up Luke's history or the frozen accuracy of Ducrow's statues. This hesitation between realities might in turn relate to the anxiety articulated by Dickens's wordplay on 'hailed': an anxiety not just about what was acclaimed, but about where that acclamation was coming from.

## 4 The Lady and the Sweep

The noise in the theatres visited by Dickens came from a specific social group, the 'common people'. Their presence in what were called the National, or Patent, theatres led to many complaints about rowdiness in the galleries, particularly the period after half-price entry which 'enables the most worthless and profligate to be there'. The consequence, a foreign visitor noted in 1826, is that 'the higher and more civilized classes . . . very rarely visit their national theatre. English freedom here degenerates into the rudest licence' (Booth et al. 1975: 23).

The composition of the audience at the National theatres did not produce a satisfactory image of the nation. Nor did the behaviour of 'common' visitors to national monuments. The director of the British Museum thought that 'People of a higher grade would hardly wish to come to the Museum at the same time with sailors from the dock-yards and girls whom they might bring with them.' The presence of the lower-grade folk was a threat to art and culture. Exhibits were broken, Westminster Abbey sculptures vandalized and St Paul's Cathedral is 'constantly and shamefully polluted with ordure' (Altick 1978: 445, 447). Theatres too were marked by the presence of working-class dirt. Dickens found those in the pit of the Royal Victoria 'not very clean or sweet-savoured'. The dirt, together perhaps with the class to which it was attached, represented a threat not just to art but to class harmony. A correspondent reported to the manager of the Surrey Theatre in 1827 how 'a lady in a nice white gown sat down on the very spot which a nasty sweep had just quitted, and, when she got up, the sight was most horrible, for she was a very heavy lady and had laughed a great deal during the performance' (Booth et al. 1975: 12).

Well-fed ladies who can afford to keep clean their white dresses can also afford to spend more on the theatre. Nineteenth-century theatres, as we know from the tale of the Venetian outlaw, operated as highly competitive capitalist enterprises. Managers and star performers made a great deal of money, while other theatre workers, including writers, worked for low pay in bad conditions. The managerial quest for profits can be illustrated by a story that has been told before: when the new, larger Covent Garden was opened in 1809, Kemble's management tried to recoup its investment by raising the prices in the pit. The audience that felt itself to be priced out of its cultural niche rioted for over two months, until prices were lowered. Artisan radicalism still had a loud voice in the theatre. By 1880 the very concept of the pit had been abolished in the Haymarket Theatre. The seats in what once had been the pit were now the most expensive in the house, and were called stalls. In a pit you are part of a community of bodies, liable to sweat if you laugh too much. In a stall your body is more privately contained. Those stalls were the invention of one of the most successful management teams of the century, Marie Wilton and Squire Bancroft. When Marie Wilton first went prospectively to look at the old melodrama theatre known as the Dust Hole, 'A woman looked up to our box, and seeing us staring aghast, with, I suppose, an expression of horror upon my face, first of all "took a sight" at us, and then shouted, "Now then, you three stuck-up ones, come out o'that, or I'll send this 'ere orange at your 'eds"' (Booth et al. 1975: 17). When Marie Wilton left it there were carpets and curtains. The stalls had white antimacassars, confidently free of any nasty spots. For to appreciate an antimacassar you have to sit stuck-up.

When the Bancrofts are said to be successful it means they attracted wealthier audiences into the theatre. The outcome of the 'Old Price' riots in 1809 showed that managers were still dependent on the artisan class from which theatre-goers then were mainly drawn. This dependence was broken as the numbers of theatres proliferated. In 1809 Covent Garden was a Patent theatre, licensed to perform 'serious' drama. Other theatres, the 'Minors', offered mixtures of music, song, mime and acrobatics, which they called, for want of a better word, 'burlettas' – though mêler-drames might have done. During the next couple of decades, however, that legal restriction, the Patent system, came increasingly under pressure in the competition for audiences. The proliferating Minors, methodically pirating and plagiarizing the best shows, were drawing big audiences. In their confidence they moved steadily closer to doing straight plays, with barely a pirouette in them. During the final decade of its existence – the 1830s – the Patent system was systematically flouted and more or less ignored. It was explicitly challenged at the opening of the decade, in December 1831, when, at a large meeting, the managers of the Minors argued for abolition of the Patent theatres' monopoly. The language used in this meeting was influenced by, indeed it deliberately echoed, the widespread campaign for democratic reforms which was challenging the current government. As the Minor managers argued it, the theatrical Patent amounted to the unjustified survival of an antiquated and – in particular – anti-democratic law. Putting it like that, these managers, who might elsewhere be kindred spirits with Venetian outlaws, found a radical parliamentary champion in the politician–dramatist Edward Bulwer, one of the leading proponents of the issue of political Reform. In the following year, 1832, that reform movement had its dangers defused by a compromise concession known as the Great Reform Bill. The campaigners for theatrical reform got a more satisfactory victory some time later, with the abolition in 1843 of the Patent theatres' monopoly.

When the law terminated the distinction between the two sorts of theatre, it was belatedly catching up with reality. Back in 1828 a theatre critic had raged against the confusion in the proper social arrangements of theatre:

A minor theatre is the proper region of melodrama – an entertainment to which we have no objection, provided it be found in its right place. Indeed, our sharpest tirades have been directed, not at its existence, but its introduction into temples professedly devoted to the dramatic muse. If we behold a cabbage in a tulip-bed, or a blacking-brush in a beef-steak pie, our ancient prejudices of propriety of place scout the unsightly intruders. That the stage, so rich in the works of our greatest poets, should invade the petty provinces of the minor drama, is not most praiseworthy, but intolerable; since no honour, and we suspect but little profit, can result from the spoils. (DG in Fitzball n.d.: remarks)

When that unsightly intruder melodrama appears in temples of drama it offends propriety of place as thoroughly as do the smudges of working-class dirt. But the demands of the market-place seem to be unfortunately hardened against the rules of art and discrimination of nature, woefully unmoved by the difference between a tulip and a cabbage.

On this point, however, the critical gentleman has got it wrong. Theatre managers are rather good at discrimination, and even before the market was legally opened up in 1843 some set about creating tulip beds while others made a healthy living out of cabbages. The theatrical policy of giving the public what it wanted was actually a policy of creating the public the theatre wanted. So in the London of 1850 some theatres were becoming quite smart and others very clearly bore the stain of working-class enthusiasm. In a society that was, at that time, nervous about the possible unrest of its working masses, some people began to suggest closing down the more violent theatres. But, as Charles Dickens observed, that measure would only suppress the evidence; it would not solve the problem. Dickens's own solution to the mess produced by the theatrical market-place was a cue for the re-entry of that neglected bit-part player, the dramatist: 'We had far better apply ourselves to improving the character of their amusement. It would not be exacting much, or exacting anything very difficult, to require that the pieces represented in these Theatres should have, at least, a good, plain, healthy purpose in them' (Dickens n.d.: 181). Which is to concede that, since the intruder is there to stay, it might as well be made less unsightly.

Once you connect the social unhealthiness exhibited by theatres with the artistic unhealthiness of their dramas, you have prepared the ground for saying that the mêler drames of managers need to be reformed by the work of a purposeful dramatist. It is thus perhaps no coincidence that, not long after that meeting of the Minor managers, indeed in 1832, the year of the Reform Bill itself, a number of theatre writers attempted to give their work official recognition by forming a Society of Dramatic Authors. Their main concern was that they were ripped off by managers (especially of the Patent houses), that they had no ownership in the work they produced and no real share in the profits from its performance. The highly charged language of Reform once again found its way into a theatrical dispute: the *Edinburgh Spectator* (3 March 1832) praised the dramatists' effort 'to emancipate dramatic genius from the monopoly under which it now writhes' (Nicholson 1906: 324). The emancipation of dramatic genius in effect means the emancipation of the writers of drama. To see a play as 'dramatic genius' is to insist that it is something more than a vehicle for the resident acrobat, or trained dog, or – if the dog's not available – the performing pig. Melodrama written by the emancipated dramatist stages its own seriousness as proper art. Thus, in the play *Rent Day*, at two climactic moments the action freezes into a tableau. As it does so, in front of our eyes the old device of making a 'picture' begins to bloom with a new dignity. For the stage pictures form themselves (just like Ducrow) into accurate copies of a famous pair of oil paintings by Wilkie. The play's author, Douglas Jerrold, was a leading member of the new society. He brought to it some years' experience campaigning against actor-managers, and a previous play that expressed anger about the acquisition of unearned income. He was, in short, very conscious of himself as a purposeful Author. Back in 1805, 'Monk' Lewis had been happy to present himself as an arranger of bespoke incidents to suit a resident company. In the early 1830s, Jerrold's plays present themselves as *authored*, with their emphasis on the written text and their articulation of serious reform issues: *Fifteen Years of a Drunkard's Life* (1828), *Mutiny at the Nore* (1830). Not only was the mêler-drame vanishing from the 'healthy' stage but also, when they got into print, a number of plays seem to have curtly dropped their familiar prefix.

A 'drama' is what Buckstone's play *Isabelle or, Woman's Life* was called when it was published in 1835. And he, as playwright, is described as 'Member of the Dramatic Authors' Society'. The seriousness of these labels corresponds with the play's ending, in which the leading character turns to the women in the audience and invites them to draw a moral lesson from the play. From the men it simply asks for applause, forbearing to reflect on the unattractive models of masculinity which the play produces. The story of 'Woman's Life', as Isabelle experiences it, is romantic girlhood love, marital infidelity by her husband, and motherhood in which she has been widowed or deserted. The comic action repeats jokes about masculinity in the figure of Apollo, a sometime actor who mainly earns his living posing for artists: 'In me you behold the finest model in Paris – my head, throat, and chest are perfect. Ah! if the lower part of my body but corresponded with the upper, I should be worth ten francs a-day; but my calf is too exuberant – I live too much upon beans' (Buckstone 1835: 31–2).

When he reappears in Act 3, Apollo carries on his head a tray of plaster images of classical statues. The entry of this bizarre prop is painstakingly logical. The connection between Apollo's posing career and his classical statues derives, in the first instance, from the activities of someone we have already met, Andrew Ducrow doing his poses plastiques. By joking about Apollo's physique and then by turning the statues into plaster miniatures, Buckstone – member of the Dramatic Authors' Society – has deflated the arty pretensions of Ducrow, the equestrian manager–acrobat. But the critique moves on a step. As we have noted, the end of *Isabelle* calls attention to the play's interest in gender difference. Apollo's clowning is part of, and contributes to, the demarcation of that difference. His ridiculous posing is quite specifically a masculine pretension. So when he appears with that tray the statuettes indicate what Ducrow's artiness had to conceal, that idealized statuesque masculinity is both a silly fantasy and a sellable commodity.

The pleasure in poses plastiques may be essentially masculine, but it still has effects on women. Isabelle's cousin Sophie has a lover, Andrew, who accompanies them all to Paris in Act 2. There he gets a job as a sweep, quarrels with Sophie and goes off with Apollo, who shows him an artist's studio where Andrew sees a life-size dummy and mistakes it for a real man. When Apollo appears in Andrew's village in Act 3, Andrew entertains him with all Sophie's food and brandy. They get drunk, start to quarrel, then begin to destroy the plaster images, throwing all the furniture at them: 'They laugh heartily, then waltz among the fragments, singing and shouting till they both fall insensible on the floor' (Buckstone 1835: 52). At this point Sophie enters. Masculine drunkenness, frivolity, wastefulness and destruction are placed alongside woman's housekeeping and propriety. Andrew the sweep has made a mess of his lady's home.

That gender difference is restated, in another mood, by Isabelle. While she watches on stage, her husband is nearly murdered off it. The significance of this scenic arrangement can be suggested by a quick trip to a lower-class Minor. There, the people who make things happen in a typical 'blood-and-thunder' melodrama tend to be men. Action narrative and suspense thrill are often male-centred. So when Buckstone elects to have the excitement of violence happening off-stage, and the troubled response to it on stage, he is both pointing up the masculinity of action narrative and removing it from the focus of his own audience's attention. This takes things further than the mere establishment of gender difference. It marks an artistic difference between the lower-class thriller and Buckstone's 'seriousness'.

This demarcatory zeal becomes peculiarly satisfying in the circumstances of *Isabelle*'s production at the Adelphi Theatre, for the venue specialized in taking melodrama up-market. By the lights of that theatre's cultural aspirations it is obvious that when the drunken sweep disorders the woman's space, he is there to be blamed. But playing is rarely so straightforward. There remains an attractiveness, something even joyously mucky, about the comical sweep and his theatrical friend. Sophie's entry to her shattered home has a different but not superior theatrical energy from that of the male couple waltzing in the ruins. It is as if Buckstone's play can't settle into its seriousness without being conscious of what that seriousness excludes: for if part of the play represents Buckstone 'Member of the Dramatic Author's Society' then a different part is represented by Buckstone, the leading farce actor of his day. And the part Buckstone played was that of Andrew the sweep. Thus in the confrontations between sweep and lady the farce actor's eyes watch an audience looking at the serious writer's creation. In that sort of moment melodrama itself seems to look with bemusement at its own ambitions towards health and purpose. As it spruces itself up to become drama, for ladies, it doesn't want to give up dancing in the fragments.

## 5 The Work of Mechanical Reproduction in the Age of Art

To a critic of melodrama, *Isabelle* would merely demonstrate how this sort of thing cannot, even when pretending to be drama, shake off the ghost of mêler, mixedness. It generates emotions which are in excess of or contradict its avowed purpose. The author allows his writer's status to be compromised by his role as actor. The message designed to improve the audience has to make space for hilarity shared with the audience. The play doesn't, in short, endorse wholeheartedly the distance between the Adelphi and the joyous mess, the carnival, of sweeps.

Our notional critic of melodrama might be more satisfied by an image of lower-class fun that was published in 1843, the year when the Minors were finally freed from the restrictions of Patent. This image occurs at a moment when the middle-class hero of *The Scamps of London* visits a 'low concert room in Bermondsey'. He finds he has been lured there by the villains, and he is then prevented from leaving by 'vagabonds' to whom he appeals: 'though they seem poor, doubtless possess some manly feeling, they will not tamely see me sacrificed'. But the vagabonds 'all turn aside with a sneer'. As they tie him up, they sing. The police knock to ask the meaning of the noise: 'Only a little bit of entertainment, as the old house is coming down, that's all sir' (Moncrieff n.d.: 37). With its decision that the 'old house' really is going to come down, this is a much less compromised critique of low entertainment. It was put together by a man who spent a chunk of his career purveying just such entertainment in his role as manager of that low house, the Coburg at Waterloo – a theatre with a reputation for rough audiences and bloodthirsty dramas. But the profitable dirt of the manager need not stick to the purposeful hands of the dramatist. In 1832 our author, Moncrieff, defended the dignity of the dramatist's art against exploitation by the Patent houses. A decade later his picture of treacherous singing vagabonds was on the stage at Sadlers Wells, a theatre geographically, demographically and, it hoped, culturally distant from the 'low' rooms to the south – like the Coburg – and east.

Further to the east, five years later, at the Britannia in Hoxton (near Shoreditch, due north of the Bank), one of the resident dramatists devised a rather different image of low entertainment. The theatre it was written for took seriously its relation to a working-class audience: it was designed, as Dickens tells us, so that even the poorest were not tucked away but had a good view of the stage; it attracted into itself whole families; and in return, in its later years under Sara Lane, it played a charitable role to the community. For this theatre a scene was devised which is set in a tavern in Paris; some gypsies enter and do a dance of 'a Wild and Striking Character', which everybody enjoys. An Englishman compares it to May Day festivities in England. He won't allow the French any superiority, and thinks them odd because they grumble a lot, whereas Englishmen all own a bit of property and 'they'd not like to lose their sticks & therefore stick close to the existing order of things.' The Britannia audience's response to this might be influenced by the fact that the speaker is a clown: they are thus put in a position to enjoy the wild gypsy dancing and French festivities for their own sake. And the more enjoyable the festivities are, the more ambivalent is the clown's praise of the sober English. This is a neat ruse to take us somewhere quite complex. By the clown's account the English are perfectly capable of their own festivities on May Day, but the rest of the time their lawful property-ownership restrains them – and even stops them grumbling. Taken alongside the dancing, this view promotes an image of a low, wild, even foreign, entertainment that is not precisely labelled as criminal but at the same time clearly constitutes a rather tempting challenge to law-abiding Englishness.

It was, perhaps, only the English who were sticking close to the 'existing order of things' in the year the play was written, 1848. Indeed the play itself ended up on the wrong side of the law. Although the author, George Dibdin Pitt, assured the stage censor that 'This piece does not in any way touch upon the Present Crisis', the censor was unconvinced and refused it a licence. For Pitt, who had formerly written a play in celebration of the black revolutionary, Toussaint L'Ouverture, now, with a tactlessness bordering on the insolent, had called his new piece *The Revolution at Paris*. It was a pretty provocative gesture when the real thing was coming to the boil on the mainland of Europe, and especially just across the Channel. In England the sense of crisis, which had been brewing for some years, seems to make itself felt in the anxiety which hangs around the stage's scenes of community and entertainment. Thus Moncrieff, who comes from a politics and theatre that contrast with Pitt's, portrays lower-class entertainment as a disguised form of hostility towards the middle class.

The conscious framing of the matter of entertainment in terms of social *class* itself shows the influence of political developments through the 1830s and 1840s. Earlier in the century, artisan radicalism had campaigned around suffrage and Parliamentary reform, assuming to itself a moral authority based on its own industriousness set in contrast with parasites and wastrels at either end of the social hierarchy. Its political stance was imbued with a traditional or even reactionary sense of community. But alongside this viewpoint developed an analysis which suggested that the very structure of productive work depended upon exploitation of the work-force. A community of the industrious was not possible where industry was organized on capitalist lines. Social *class* rather than moral worth was what defined a person's identity and value. The class analysis only gradually percolated into activism, but it grew in strength through the Chartist campaigns of the 1830s and 1840s. Eighteen forty-eight was not just the year the censor banned any enactment of

Revolution at Paris, it was also the year of publication of *The Communist Manifesto*.

One element of Chartism promoted physical force in class antagonism. Even in the early 1830s there were attempts to arm workers. Those who made a *class analysis* not only saw that society was irrevocably divided but assumed also that the divisions were potentially violent. George Dibdin Pitt's comic Englishman makes English orderliness a matter of joke as the play's focus slips away to locate interest in that which is non-English and marginalized, the gypsy dance. As an image of something which is *community* yet differs from property-owning Englishness, gypsies recur in plays of the 1840s. When Pitt wrote a play on Buckstone's theme, *A Woman's Life* (1844), the central figure is an elderly gypsy woman. She can't be sentimentalized by comfortably moral notions of woman's role: 'Look round on the fair estate you call your own – then tell yourself that old Bess the despised, villified beggar woman that is permitted to exist as if she were not quite human and that it were a charity not to hunt her out of life – Even she can wrest all from you – and reduce you to such a state of abject poverty – that you shall want bread.' When the squire sets his dogs on her, she kills one off-stage and re-enters 'with her hair dishevelled and grasping the bloody knife in one hand and a heart in the other. "Ha! ha! ha! – Behold! the blood of the hound."'

Old Bess watches a narrative in which the elderly squire is murdered by his nephew to get the estate: she hates the squire's family but defies the villains. At the end it emerges that the nephew is in fact her illegitimate son, by the old squire's brother who cast her off. Her hatred is a product of two linked experiences: of the damage done by an exploitative masculinity and of the thwarting of her own motherhood. This latter is expressed in the final image: she is supported wounded in her villainous son's arms and then, to save him from the scaffold, she stabs him: 'By an accursed act I gave thee life and by another take it . . . We have escaped the obloquy.' The gesture of motherhood is both fulfilled and frustrated, caring and violent; it is structured by oppositions of gypsy and landowner, old woman and villain, mother and son. It's a picture of blood-union reshaped but not reformed by social divisions, where the personal is tangled with gender, class and race difference.

If the truth is a tangle, then simple acclamation is not possible. The narrative leads its audience into something much more difficult than a polarity of good and evil. Watching becomes complex again. Buckstone's *Isabelle* pushed suspense action off-stage; in Pitt's narratives the onward drive is structurally less important than the juxtaposition of contrasted scenes which rapidly transform into one another. These transformations were made possible as a result of experiments and developments in stage technology. What comes into being on the stage, as Pitt realizes, is a new sense of place: settings may be able to multiply into a seemingly endless diversity, but at the same time the very fluidity with which one location replaces another suggests that in some sense all places interconnect. Like several of his contemporaries Pitt gives an extra spin to this by making any one location change its significance through the wild shifts between comic and serious registers. In *Woman's Life* the plan to take the old squire's corpse from its tomb, concealing it in a sedan chair, is interrupted by Toby the clown; when the others frighten him he shuts himself in the sedan chair; as they try to open it, he screams about 'ghostesses' attacking him. A very similar lurch between the really spooky and fake ghosts pops up in one of the versions of *Maria Marten*, also from the 1840s: Maria's father goes to the Red Barn to dig for his daughter's grave; he is accompanied by the fearful clown, Tim, who watches the tense digging; just after the scene's climax, Tim's partner, Anne, walks on with a sheet over her head.

In such register switches, the comic action interferes with the stage's system of signifying: one object, for instance the sedan chair, has shifting values. The serious is obviously opposite to the comic, but somehow it is also linked. Locations are diverse, but also interconnected. The technique here of visualizing things in terms of *linked opposites* had also characterized the pages of a book which we have already noted as Pitt's contemporary, *The Communist Manifesto*. The word which commonly describes its authors' mode of argument and explanation is 'dialectical'. The same word might be usefully adopted to explain the deployment of staging techniques in work like Pitt's.

From somewhere further up west, nearer the fashionable end of town, this might seem an unduly grand claim. Pitt's narrative breaks and register switches would signify to some audiences nothing more than a hack dramatist writing for an old-fashioned company. It was the very thing which a successful author, Planché, said a successful manager, Madame Vestris, avoided: 'the most scrupulous attention has been paid to all those accessories which form the peculiar charm of theatrical Representation, by perfecting the illusion of the scene, and consequently at the same time every possible chance of success has been afforded to the author' (Nagler 1952: 463). And Planché was right, for 'perfecting the illusion' led to the great theatrical hit of 1852, Boucicault's *Corsican Brothers*.

The story centres on a pair of identical twins, one living in Corsica, the other in Paris. In the first act the one in Corsica, Fabien, senses that something has happened to his brother, Louis. There are suspicious signs – the clocks have stopped at ten past nine and he feels a sharp pain in his side. He discovers at the end of the act that Louis has been killed in a duel. He is just sealing a letter to him when Louis appears, dressed like Fabien, 'but with a blood stain upon his breast; he glides across the stage, ascending gradually through the floor at the same time, and lays his hand on Fabien's left shoulder.' What happens next is that Louis waves his arm, walks through the wall and disappears:

> at the same moment the scene at the back opens and discloses a glade in
> the Forest of Fontainbleau. On one side, a young man who is wiping the

blood from his sword with a handkerchief; two seconds are near him. On the other side, Louis dei Franchi, stretched upon the ground, supported by his two seconds and a surgeon. (Boucicault 1987: 112)

The appearance of the ghost was one of the most celebrated moments of the play, so much so that the ghost theme could be purchased as sheet music. What made it exciting was a series of technical effects. In addition to the fairly regular practice of walking through a wall, a special mechanism had been elaborately contrived to enable the ghost's slow glide onto the stage. Most tricksy of all was that the same man seemed to be in three places at once. Both twins were played by Charles Kean. Here, while one sits at his desk, the other appears both as a ghost and as a picture of himself dying in the forest. They are also, simultaneously, at three different points in time: Fabien's clocks have stopped at ten past nine, the time of the duel. But this moment is also replaying precisely something which we have been told happened 300 years ago to a pair of direct ancestors. One is killed in an ambush; the other, sensing danger, is just sealing a letter to him when he hears a sigh, turns, and sees his brother standing by his side with his hand on his shoulder. The ghost waves its arm to the wall, 'the masonry seemed to obey the gesture – it opened, and the living man beheld the murder in all its harrowing identity' (p. 105).

The moment at which the murder is seen in all its 'harrowing identity' is not, on its own, an unusual melodrama event. It's the moment of sudden revelation of truth, of acclamation. What gives the Act 1 ending its peculiar effect is the sense that differences in time and place have – impossibly – vanished. It happens again at the end of Act 2. Most of that act is a flashback, set in Paris. In a sequence of short scenes it tells how Louis came to be involved in the duel. It's a story of a man's devotion to a woman, her entrapment in a dilemma, and his anger about how she is treated. As such it feels like a miniature social-problem play, with its characters trapped in a genteel sexist society which influences all their actions. The set and action together realistically evoke the recognizable environment and behaviour of a social group which would be familiar to an audience at the fashionable theatre – the Princess's – where the play was done. And time passes with regularity: the action is organized around a wager with a deadline, so people keep looking at clocks. At the end Louis is in the Forest of Fontainbleau, for the duel. As he dies, 'the back of the scene opens slowly and discovers the chamber of the first act, the clock marking the hour, ten minutes after nine; Madame dei Franchi and Fabien, looking exactly as they did before' (p. 126).

The action arrives suddenly where it has been before and, as the stage set slides open, for a moment it seems as if no time has elapsed since the end of Act 1. The present time is something we saw in the past. Which, yet again, is precisely the effect of the end of the play. Louis's murderer has found himself, five days later, in the very glade of the forest where the duel was. As he is about to leave it, Fabien appears: 'You take me for the spectre of your victim. No; I am one more terrible, more implacable. I am Fabien dei Franchi, come from the wilds of Corsica to demand of you: where is my brother?' (p. 130). He forces the murderer to a duel and kills him, saying, 'Louis! Louis! I can weep for him now.' He goes behind a tree upstage, 'then advances, with face covered by his hands, and sinks weeping upon the fallen tree. A pause. Louis dei Franchi appears, rising gradually through the earth and placing his hand on the shoulder of his brother' (p. 133).

Charles Kean's playing of the implacable revenger thrilled audiences: 'Kean's dogged, quiet, terrible walk after Wigan, with the fragment of broken sword in his relentless grasp, I shall not forget' (G. Taylor 1989: 28). But the feeling of doggedness came from more than his acting, for by arriving at a similar picture at the end of every act the narrative insists that, every time we might think we are going somewhere new, we arrive back where we started, either at ten past nine or 300 years ago. Time may seem to pass, but the clocks stand still. Despite what Fabien says, however, this effect is not to do with an ancient history. He had defined 'a strange, mysterious sympathy between us – no matter what space divides us we are still one, in feeling, in soul. Any powerful impression which the one experiences is instantly conveyed, by some invisible agency, to the senses of the other' (p. 103). In 1852 that invisible agency and its special effects had a very modern reality. The telegraph, with its rapid communication, could now suggest that space no longer divides people in the same way. The invention was one of several technical developments which were changing how urban society thought about time and place. Four years before, in 1848, Dickens described the spread of railways and the impact of their timetables: 'There was even railway time observed in clocks, as if the sun itself had given in.' The effect was not just to do with measuring time, but with a new rhythm to life: 'Crowds of people and mountains of goods, departing and arriving scores upon scores of times in every four-and-twenty hours' (Dickens 1964: 235, 236). In Boucicault's hands melodrama has been caught up in this rhythm. The interest in transformations that lead off into nightmare or buried history is replaced by an emphasis upon a time-scheme which, even as it passes, is repetition.

Repetition is what makes the murder scene thrilling. While the miniature social-problem drama of Act 2 works how Planché wanted, as the accurate representation of reality, the melodrama around it is fascinated by *repeated* representation, reproduction, of the same image. The more times it is reproduced, the more aura of mystery it has. This aura is not something ancient, as Fabien might claim, nor is it wild. It comes from the clever construction of – on one hand – the play's own timetable and – on the other – theatrical effects as made possible in what could be said to be an age of mechanical production. A phrase very like that last one is used by Walter Benjamin to describe changes in the perception of art in the modern period, an age of photography and film, what he calls an age of 'mechanical reproduction'. In the modern period some art is made to be reproducible, but for anything before that even a perfect reproduction of a work of art fails to give us 'its presence in time and space, its unique existence at the place where it happens to be.' A work of art has an authenticity, an 'aura', which cannot be reproduced, and it is that which 'withers in the age of mechanical reproduction' (Benjamin 1973: 222–3). Coinciding with the rapid developments in techniques of reproduction, Boucicault's play seems to be thrilling because of its tricks with time and space. The social-problem drama, in its unique existence and chronological development, is much less exciting than the melodrama's tricksy re-productions. It is also, perhaps, much less modern than the melodrama, which insists on the *aura of reproduction*.

That aura has a connection with the stage's demonstration of its capacity to reproduce the most intractable realities. Boucicault himself was a leading exponent of the techniques which led to the staging of boat races, horse races (with real horses, galloping), avalanches, train crashes and bursting dams. A close observer of the stage, the censor William Donne, described this new modern aesthetic: 'To touch our emotions, we need not the imaginatively true, but the physically real. The visions which our ancestors saw with the mind's eye, must be embodied for us in palpable forms' (Booth 1981: 2). When the excitement comes from the palpable, a different quality of acting as well as staging was required. Charles Kean was impressive for being 'dogged', not for being labile or fluid. His father's specialism in rapidly transforming 'points' is replaced by an awe-ful determination. Thus the key quality of the whole show was the reverse of transformation. The action returns to the same point; one brother, played by the same actor, *is* the other. We repeatedly see 'harrowing identity'. The thrill comes not from mixedness but from sameness.

The production of *The Corsican Brothers* was rather good at reproducing palpable forms because, being done at a fashionable and wealthy theatre, it could afford them. Its audience could thus be described as coming from the class that owned the means of reproduction. When the stage addressed itself to that audience, part of the pleasure of the performance came from an affirmation of that class's position. Part of Kean's acting power lay in his 'preserving a gentlemanly demeanour . . . which intensifies the passion of the part, and gives it a terrible reality' (G. Taylor 1989: 28). But it was happening on a wider scale. The *Art Journal* in 1853 lamented that the means for creating artistic illusion lagged behind other innovations: 'The scenes are still in two slides, and where they meet in the centre the most delicately painted landscape is presented to the public eye, divided by a cutting line, which is also frequently disfigured with dirt from the handling of the sceneshifters' (Booth et al. 1975: 90). Later in the century Boucicault conceived of a method of making illusion more complete, reproduction more efficient: 'The stage is a picture frame, in which is exhibited that kind of panorama where the picture being unrolled is made to move, passing before the spectator with scenic continuity' (Meisel 1983: 51). This method no longer carries the trace of working-class dirt; the hands that work the rollers are unseen. Looking forward to an illusion that doesn't show its joins, the continuity of moving pictures, the theatre contemplated its dissolution.

## NOTES

1   Henry Harris probably viewed Parisian drama with more than a tourist's eye: he was listed as having a share in the ownership of Covent Garden Theatre in 1802, he was reading submitted play-texts, and he took over as proprietor when his father retired in 1809. His note about the new drama he had discovered at Le Pont St Martin mentions that Holcroft is about to translate one of the pieces. Holcroft, as an actor at Covent Garden, had once before been instrumental in importing to England the newest thing from France, when he travelled to Paris to pirate Beaumarchais's radical *Marriage of Figaro*; Thomas Harris then organized the translation and performance of the piece. So Holcroft's presence in Paris, in contact with Henry Harris, looks like more than a chance encounter with the new drama. The attitude to this new *mêler drame* of the manager's son and the Jacobin actor may be contrasted with the opinion of the literary critic James Boaden: 'A melo-drame is an opera in prose, which is merely spoken, and in which music discharges the duty of a *valet de chambre*, because her office is simply to announce the actors' (in Wyndham 1906: II, 332).

# 8

# The Unacceptable Face of Theatre

## 1  Men of Letters

While reviewing a production of Shakespeare's *Cymbeline*, Bernard Shaw described the play as 'stagey trash of the lowest melodramatic order'. When it appears in this sort of phrase, the adjective 'melodramatic' is not being used to designate a particular dramatic genre. It functions instead as a value judgement. That won't seem strange to most modern readers, since 'melodramatic' is in wide use as a technical term for bad drama or bad acting. And it usually has several other words in tow – 'sensationalist', 'escapist', 'hack', 'stock', 'claptrap'. All of these items in the lexicon of theatrical scorn also originated at the same time.

That time is generally understood to be one of the low points in the history of English drama. It's not that no plays were being done. Indeed there were probably more performances in more theatres seen by more people than at any other period, including the present. But next to none of it seems to be either natural or proper – as if English theatre was under occupation by an alien culture:

> Melodrama did not make its way onto the boards of the patent houses without a fight. A minority of intelligent and cultivated playgoers was fully alive to the meretricious character of the repertoire, as were the critics. Opposition even became militant and organized at times, but that melodrama was preferred to the contemporary serious drama was not entirely the fault of the public. The serious drama as written during this period showed a sad decline, and the writers to whom one might naturally have looked for something better failed to rise to the occasion. (Rahill 1967: 116)

And the successful serious writer got his inspiration from France . . . In Frank Rahill's account melodrama is like an interloper taking advantage of the rightful owner's weakness, invading the theatre to inaugurate an era of drama which is neither cultivated nor serious nor, indeed, English.

That melodrama should be regularly viewed this way is a testimony to that gallant band of cultivated playgoers who so successfully publicized their struggle with the form. In his review of the huge success of 1852, Charles Kean's production of *The Corsican Brothers*, G. H. Lewes felt compelled to write about the moment when the two noble duellists break their sword-blades and fight as if with knives:

> This does not *read* as horrible, perhaps; but to see it on the stage, represented with minute ferocity of detail, and with a truth on the part of the actors, which enhances the terror, the effect is so intense, so horrible, so startling, that one gentleman indignantly exclaimed *un-English*! It was, indeed, gratuitously shocking, and Charles Kean will damage himself in the public estimation by such moral mistakes, show-ing a vulgar lust for the lowest sources of excitement – the tragedy of the shambles! But it is the fatality of melodrama to know no limit. (in Rowell 1971: 98–9)

Melodrama is, then, drama which is gratuitously violent, knows no limit, deliberately excessive; in 1990s terminology, is over-the-top. That reviewer's language in the 1850s is pretty similar to what the official drama censor said. When a play called *Rotherhithe in the Olden Time* was submitted for a licence in 1854, the censor noted a scene in which an old woman and her coachman are robbed in a churchyard. A stage direction requires that one of the robbers 'Pulls off her gown and discovers her in a short petticoat'. This combination of elements, at a lower-class theatre (the Pavilion), was not allowable:

> The Lord Chamberlain is of the opinion that a mere representation of a gross and extravagant crime should as far as his authority is concerned be always excluded from the Stage. The difference between the fair dra-matic use of a criminal incident & a mere exhibition of vulgar crimes is too obvious to necessitate any prescribed rule or instructions. (in Stephens 1980: 70)

Whereas mere exhibition is – obviously – not on, 'use' has licence.

By the early 1860s London had a new word for such 'mere exhibition'. The city was in the grip of *Sensational* Mania. Sensation plays hit the stage, shortly followed by sensation novels. A word that once simply meant the activation of the senses, in a rather private way, now designated that which was, very publicly, shocking, extraordinary, thrilling. A sensation scene is one which is constructed and performed so as to lock the viewer's attention into what was primarily sensory rather than moral–philosophical. This means that the medium normally used for expressing ideas, namely verbal language, becomes less important than non-verbal sound and visuals – those elements of performance frequently bundled together under one heading, 'effects'. In the accepted mode of talking about drama, 'effects' are to be treated as separate from acting. Thus, for example, when Henry James wrote about *Faust* at the Lyceum he advised that 'special precautions should be taken against the accessories seeming a more important part of the business than the action.' These 'accessories' include smoke, coloured lights, 'the wilderness of canvas and paint' (in Rowell 1971: 126); and if you don't keep them under control, they threaten to take over, or perhaps redefine, the drama of action.

From its earliest days melodrama dealt in scenic effects: *A Tale of Mystery* in 1802 had trees that bent in the wind; one of its most prolific early craftsmen was nicknamed after a favoured effect, 'Blue-fire Fitzball'. But the arrival of the *sensation* fad meant that all this became something more special. Thus in 1865 the management of the Princess's Theatre, where Kean had done *Corsican Brothers*, scored a great hit with Boucicault's *Arrah-na-Pogue* followed quickly by a critics' riot at the opening of Reade's *It's Never too Late to Mend*. The celebrated sensation scene in *Arrah* showed the hero escaping from a prison cell by getting out through a window and then climbing perilously up the vertical side of the prison tower. This effect was managed by lowering sections of stage-set from the flies (the concealed space above the proscenium), while the actor remained more or less in the same place. The shocking sensation scene in *It's Never too Late* showed a prisoner climbing up to a window in order to 'escape' by hanging himself from the bars. He is already half-paralysed, and collapses, dying, before he can kill himself. Boucicault's escape scene was pleasurable in two respects. An event that was highly improbable was made possible thanks to the operation of scenic machinery: the stage supplies a fantasy resolution to a grim situation. And, in doing so, the scenic panache displays the stage's reliability as an agent of fantasy: it's not so much the man but the set which is the hero of the sequence.

By contrast, the set for Reade's scene remained implacably immobile. Instead of enabling a fantasy of human prowess it showed a body so debilitated by a torturing regime that it was unable to walk through an open door, collapsing across a threshold. The set here was, in its own way, spectacular because of its precisely imitated detail – the treadmill in the prison yard worked – but what that spectacle aggressively displayed was how fantasy must be curtailed by the rules of the real. In showing that, the art of the stage appeared to have reneged on its contract with its audience. As one of the riotous critics put it, much later, in 1899, 'the stage insists that realism shall have a stopping point. Art does not countenance such horror as this' (in Barrett 1993: 12). Melodrama, that excessive form, even does realism excessively. But then it's un-English; if he had lived in Paris, our critic would have known that theatre art can countenance rather a lot of horror. For a specialist theatre of horror, the Théâtre de Grand Guignol, had opened in 1897. From 1901 onwards it was to be supplied by its most famous writer, André de Lorde, with a series of plays that turned modern technology into nightmare. Up to now, melodrama had been vividly, lucratively, aware of the horrors of technology, enacted in a succession of bursting dams, crashing trains, exploding ships. But for a theatre audience these scenes are also pleasurable for the reasons outlined above – they're the moments when the set does its acrobatics. De Lorde's plays tended to limit that pleasure, in that his technology often took a smaller form with a different relation to bodies, such as medical equipment: a father–doctor cuts open the breast of his dead daughter to implant an electric motor to restart the heart; a cuckolded doctor who cuts open the brain of his wife's lover is then overpowered by the madman he has created, and stabbed in the skull with a pair of scissors. It's now the props, rather than the set, which upstage the humans. The technology that had stretched bodies in extremes of prowess and debilitation now interferes with the integrity of the body.

This theatre of horror supplies us with yet another term for describing improper and excessive drama. For Grand Guignol, like sensationalism, like scenic 'effects', shows a stage misusing or betraying its own art, moved always to overstep each new limit or stopping point in order to excite the greatest number of people. And in these conditions emerged a new sort of professional who was unashamed of seeking the commercial rewards that came from catering for a mass audience. One of the prime exponents of the meticulously organized sensation scene was the same man who challenged the financial tyranny of theatre managers by negotiating a form of royalty payment for authors. 'Sensation is what the public wants,' said Boucicault, 'and you can't give them too much of it' (in Rahill 1967: 189). Boucicault's position had extricated itself from the problems affecting the mass-audience writer. In old 'literary' terms, the writer who merely caters for the mass compromises her dignity as writer, and thus is not a proper writer, and hence need not be given proper payment for what she produces. In market-place terms, the writer who has something people want to buy is in a position to negotiate her price, which means she can get proper payment for the job, and hence enhance her dignity.

The problem, in this particular phase of capitalist organization, was not the writer's relationship to a mass audience but the relationship to the economics of a mass audience. The melodramatic theatre was one of the places where this problem could be seen most vividly. Indeed, that economic garishness, like a fart in public, constituted some of the impropriety that was melodramatic theatre:

Heavily taxed, wholly unassisted by the State, deserted by the gentry, and quite unrecognised as a means of public instruction, the higher

English Drama has declined. Those who would live to please Mr Whelks, must please Mr Whelks to live. It is not the Manager's province to hold the Mirror up to Nature, but to Mr Whelks – the only person who acknowledges him. (Dickens n.d.: 173)

Every scene that unashamedly proffers itself as sensation sets quivering the contradictions – about money, popularity and art – that arise from capitalism's dealings with a mass audience.

So who was Joe Whelks? Dickens imagines him living in a London which in 1850 was preparing to mount a great exhibition to celebrate its imagined imperial and industrial glories. But Joe is lower-class, and *his* imagination is unlikely to be satisfied by displays of the very machines which he labours in horrible conditions to produce. Joe's imagination requires satisfaction elsewhere: 'The lower we go, the more natural it is that the best-relished provision for this should be found in dramatic entertainments; as at once the most obvious, the least troublesome, and the most real, of all escapes out of the literal world.' Since Joe needs drama as escape, however nonsensical it is, he gives himself over to it: 'now Mr Whelks concentrated all his energies into a focus, bent forward, looked straight in front of him, and held his breath' (Dickens n.d.: 172, 183).

Dickens's account of what he calls the 'Amusements of the People' suggests another of the negative words that hang around with 'melodramatic': Joe's theatre-going can be described as 'escapist'. Melodrama is escapist because it invites Joe into an impossible fiction, well distant from the hardship of daily life. But look again at how Joe watches – concentrating his energies into a focus and holding his breath – and we find another sense for 'escapist'. For Joe escapes from a world in which his body labours mechanically and repetitively for the profit of others, and he temporarily enters a space where he has control over his own energies, where even the repetition of breathing is broken as he finds focus. He escapes into another, equally impossible, fiction, of a non-alienated body.

Joe's physically engaged watching is characteristic of his class. Dickens, like several of his contemporaries, notes that the lower-class audience is not only energetic in its applause but shouts back at the stage. When G. H. Lewes said that melodrama appealed to the lowest faculties, he seems to have meant two things by 'low': lesser than the intellect, inferior to the bourgeois. A melodrama in full swing makes a noisy theatre: spectators are encouraged, through the muscular and nervous production of sound, to become part-actors in the event, as does a noisy football crowd. In a society that enforced on its prisoners regimes of silence and wholly unproductive labour, the tensile noise generated by drama is a measure of the audience's deviation from, as it were, sound morals. For this reason the theatrical censor attended especially to lower-class venues: 'It is highly desirable to elevate the tone of the drama and it is specially necessary in the case of the saloons, who have a tendency to lower the morals and excite the passions of the classes who frequent these places of resort.' Worries about 'mere exhibition', the gratuitous, 'sensation', signify a moral panic about the behaviour of lower-class audiences. This got worse during the crazes for plays about criminals – such as the eighteenth-century housebreaker Jack Sheppard (in 1839–40) or Dickens's *Oliver Twist*. When the censor stamped on an attempt to revive these plays in 1859 he was clear that the immorality of the text was intensified when 'it is performed at Theatres where the Gallery is the main resort, and the greater portion of its frequenters consists of apprentices and young persons of either sex' (in Stephens 1980: 69, 72). The assumption here – which still operates – is that a certain *low* category of person, namely the young and working-class, is not only peculiarly susceptible to forms of drama which are sensationalist, escapist, not elevated, but also responds in a *low* way, turning staged immorality into real deviation.

The censor's problem theatres were those in which, as Dickens had it, the management held the mirror up to Joe Whelks. Luckily, others knew the proper job of mirrors: 'The lighter phase of comedy, representing the more natural and less laboured school of modern life, and holding the mirror up to nature without regard to the conventionalities of the theatre, was the aim I had in view' (in Robertson 1982: 7). The man who so gracefully opposes nature to labour (and the laboured) is the actor Charles Mathews. Here he recalls his move to the Olympic when it was run by Madame Vestris in the 1830s. Under Vestris the theatre pioneered a style of elegant light comedy and witty burlesque, in which the stage setting demonstrated careful research and meticulous selection of detail, with acting that took pleasure in articulating its own restraint, its obedience to the laws of design. What was on stage at the Olympic was, in short, an exhibition of the management's taste and decorum or, as Mathews terms it, 'nature'. After Vestris died in 1856 her project was re-established by Marie Wilton, who in 1865 transformed the working-class 'Dust Hole' into the Prince of Wales' Theatre, moving, again, from labour to nature. The management, casting itself as the 'high-priest of the natural school of acting', awaited its dramatist.

That dramatist was Tom Robertson. He had already written a vehicle for E. A. Sothern, whose acting was praised as 'elegant and unobtrusive', without exaggeration, indeed 'genuine acting'. His next play was picked up by Marie Wilton, after its success in Liverpool. It opened at the Prince of Wales' in the Sensational late autumn of 1865, but *Society*, as the play was called, and its author turned their back on what was going on – sensationally – at the Princess's. As Robertson said:

> if any person should dare to place upon the stage, for the mere greed of gain, a 'sensation' scene in the likeness of the ward of a hospital, and simulate the operation of amputating the leg of the hero, or the arm of

the heroine[,] with real bandages, real tourniquets . . . and the rest of the sickening apparatus, then the newspaper critic would be *dans sans droit* to rise and hiss loudly. (in Barrett 1993: 12)

*Society* was praised for being non-sensational, for being witty and clever, for having a 'freedom' from conventional restraints, and for being English (as opposed to the sensational adaptations of French plays). The declining 'higher English Drama' had found for itself a satisfying conjunction of moderation, freedom and Englishness, the values precisely of Society.

Marie Wilton's partner, Squire Bancroft, later described Robertson's arrival as the moment at which English theatre could make its much needed 'return to Nature'. His apparently innovatory, 'natural' method was signalled in the careful use of mundane stage props and furniture as the means of expressing emotion: thus in *Caste* (1867), when George talks about his snobbish mother he expresses apprehension by 'twisting about' with a chair. This use of props sets a limit to the body's possible range of movement, since it is bound by the rules governing the accepted use of chairs and teacups. Nevertheless it is to the old tricks of melodrama that Robertson goes for doing the climax when Esther's supposed-dead husband returns. While her sister Polly softly plays the piano, Esther 'in an ecstasy' asks for her husband; she then screams and falls in his arms, while Polly plays increasingly loudly, 'then plays at random, endeavouring to hide her tears. At last strikes piano wildly, and goes off into a fit of hysterical laughter' (Robertson 1982: 181). The melodramatic use of music gives emotional weight to the action. But it differs from melodrama in 'naturalizing' the source of the music; it comes from an on-stage piano, not an off-stage band. Furthermore, the relations between the 'effect' and the actor are now arranged to give the actor dominance. Which means that the music, which had initially governed the emotional rhythm of the whole scene, breaks down as Polly uses it to hide her feelings. It works like George's chair, a stage prop. The more wildly she attempts to express herself, the more the piano changes from being a general scenic effect into a localized character effect. As such, of course, it still functions as part of the visual and aural texture of the scene. So in a paradoxical sense the breakdown of the melodrama music is itself governed by the principles of melodrama effect.

The changed relation between actor and 'effect' is, however, crucial. What disturbed critics of melodrama is that the actor seems less important than, more a function of, scenic effect. For example, much of the characterization of, say, a melodrama villain is established by the music and lighting. The whole setting feels disturbed, dark, villainous in a way which is intangible, non-human. It only becomes tangible, and thus controllable, in the *person* of the villain. If the story can get rid of him or her, all the other effects will vanish. So the melodramatic character becomes, in a sense, a stand-in for something which is otherwise too big to grasp or control. As such it provides a satisfying focus for Joe Whelks's energies. Thus, in brief, in dealing with the ungraspable and uncontrollable by means of intense focus on a stand-in, melodramatic characterization operates like a fetish.

In contrast, then, with Polly and her piano, we could put the prisoner Josephs who caused all the fuss at the Princess's by trying to hang himself. In Scene 3 of Act 2 the audience can see the separate cells of Josephs and Robinson, together with the corridor that goes between them and disappears into the distance. The set, with its elaborate galleries and staircases, was like an iron cobweb, an image of what the play calls the 'system'. Josephs begins the scene strapped to the wall in a punishment jacket, occasionally moaning; Robinson in the other cell talks to himself, angrily, and we learn he has fixed his door so he can open it. But his initiative is balanced, in many ways, by Josephs' passivity. When Josephs, out of the jacket, tries to hang himself from a window bar, he is impeded by being paralysed down one side (a result of the jacket), and finally falls to the ground lying half in and half out of his opened door. In a different play the suffering victim would eventually escape, and thus set a limit to what the villainous setting can do to a person. Here the victim's body gradually becomes like the setting: no longer fully active, attempting – in a voluntary repetition of the punishment jacket – to attach himself to, become part of, the iron web, unable to leave his cell through an open door. The absorption of person into setting makes the institutional, more-than-human cruelty, the 'system', more rather than less real. So when Robertson, the champion of realism, attacks this play, we realize that it's not so much realism but the relation of actor and setting, controllable and uncontrollable, which is the problem. And of two realist productions of late 1865, it was the comedy called *Society* rather than the melodrama called *It's Never too Late to Mend* which offered the critically preferred version.

Robertson had apparently found what Dickens wanted for the stage: class enlightenment. He claims it explicitly in a moment in *Caste* when the 'mechanic' Sam Gerridge asks Polly what the neighbours will think of her sister's liaison with a man above her:

> POLLY: They can't think. They're just like you, they've not been educated up to it.
> SAM: It all comes of your being on the stage (*Going to* POLLY).
> POLLY: It all comes of your not understanding the stage or anything else – but putty. (Robertson 1982: 147)

But the reformed stage, with its mirror towards nature, also insists on class division. Polly and Esther's scrounging parent is the target of much of the play's knowing laughter. When he fawningly claims that 'a real gentleman understands the natural emotions of the working man' (p. 140), he unwittingly vouches for the cynical perceptiveness of not only gentlemen, but gentlemen's theatre. That theatre claims to be real, and hence to know nature;

so it also knows that an unreformed working person is only interested in money, and hence that what he claims to be nature is almost certainly fake.

Indeed even as a role the scrounging father is a joke, a parody of the good old man of melodrama. This is one of several points where, despite its own melodramatic features, *Caste* insists on an audience taking pleasure in the sort of play it isn't. For its project is to continue to force the opposition that G. H. Lewes had called Drama and Melodrama, and Dickens called the higher English Drama as against the Amusements of the People. There's a note of desperation about that forced opposition in the 1850s and 1860s, for, in the absence of tragedy's combination of passion with dignity, against melodrama's emotional excitement the forms of genteel theatre could base themselves only on restraint or indeed parody of passion. By the end of the century, however, apparently serious passionate, non-melodramatic, forms had arrived from Europe. Wilde produced a symbolist treatment of desire in *Salome*, and Archer championed a stridently realist version of Ibsen. So when *Salome* was refused a licence in 1892, Wilde, with high European seriousness, attacked the censor for pandering to 'the vulgarity and hypocrisy of the English people, by licensing every low farce and vulgar melodrama' (in Stephens 1980: 113). By the end of the century melodrama drops into place as the old-fashioned form which obstructs the emergence of the serious drama of the new century. And from there it doesn't budge, so that over half-way into the new century theatre historians, caught within that forced opposition, restate it in a way which not only Archer but Robertson and even Lewes would have recognized. In his 1964 anthology, with one of those wacky melodramatic titles, *Hiss the Villain*, Michael Booth says the working classes 'demanded entertainment as relief' and that 'Their level of literacy and taste was low'; that since melodrama 'stays on the surface and never explores the depths' its distinctive features are 'character stereotypes and rigid moral distinctions'. It improved when it got more like what Robertson was writing: 'The dialogue of the better plays became less exaggerated, the characterization more credible, and the construction more skilful' (Booth 1964: 15, 10, 31).

This description, itself utterly stereotypical, leads rapidly towards more of the words on drama's negative list. Because of low rates of pay combined with insatiable demand, serious authors, we're told, wrote novels while plays were left to theatrical 'hacks'. The hack is not an author, then, so much as a compliant part of the capitalist organization of mass art. This is the attitude which Boucicault, as we've seen, did so much to complicate. But the history of melodrama prefers to keep to a fairly simple agenda. So while the term 'hack' could also be fairly adequately used of a large number of English Renaissance dramatists, it more appropriately renders the mass-produced, or 'manufactured', quality of melodrama. Which in turn leads to a way of writing about melodrama as a whole genre, with lists of typical features, with no need to differentiate particular works. The exploited hack writer thus seems to produce work that is indistinguishable, and hence undistinguished: in short, hack. A similar pressure came from the traditional organization of the stock company, where 'each performer had his own line of business and played no other' (Booth 1964: 22), and hence there was a need to produce suitable – which is to say, stock – characterization. Because it is the demand of the acting company's composition, rather than individual artistic vision, which creates characters, 'stock' comes to be a bad word meaning repetitive, unimagined and unimaginative. Lastly, since melodrama seemed only to want to please a mass audience, it organized its performances around key moments that were specifically designed to draw audience approval and applause. In 1883 a reviewer noted that *Lights o'London* was 'a direct bid for the favour of a miscellaneous audience, and does not disdain upon occasion recourse to time-honoured clap-traps' (in Rowell 1971: 210). The deliberate production of a line for applause – the claptrap – seems to be now so distant from anything that is serious, authored or meaningful that the word has come to be a synonym for nonsense.

The emergence of words such as 'hack', 'stock', 'claptrap', tells not only of subservience to the demands of mass art but also hints at melodrama's great secret. Lewes spotted it back in 1853 when he said that despite Charles Kean's real appreciation of artistic *mise-en-scène* 'there is a want perceptible through it all – the want of a poetical mind. Melodramatic effects he can reach – he falls short of poetry' (in Rowell 1971: 97). With its effects, melodrama conceals the fact it has no poetry. And that is what Henry James charged against the Lyceum *Faust*, where the blue vapours that hung around Mephistopheles were 'a very poor substitute for his giving us a moral shudder'; the show, being coarse, and cheap (metaphorically), and a *spectacular* success, could not by definition be a *dramatic* one (in Rowell 1971: 127). To watch James trying to separate Goethe's poetry from Irving's 'little mechanical artifices' is like seeing someone insist on keeping their eyes on the book rather than on the distracting spectacle. Which was precisely the activity of the audiences who attended performances by those masters of burlesque, Gilbert and Sullivan:

> I was so interested in the book that I could scarcely attend to the stage, except with my ears, and this feeling was general, for the whole audience was plunged into the mysteries of the libretto, and when the time came for turning over the leaves of the book there was such a rustling as is only equalled when musicians are following a score at an oratorio. (in Rees 1978: 176)

This is the theatre critic Clement Scott at the opening of *Iolanthe* in 1882. The Savoy Theatre, pioneer of the new theatrical electric light, had to leave its house lights undimmed so the audience could read rather than watch.

The man who is serious about Literature keeps his eyes on the book not the spectacle, disentangles poetry from effects. So when at the end of the century those who regarded themselves as Men of Letters tried to write serious work for the stage, they were all too familiar with the melodramatic heritage in which theatrical devices were the enemies of real art. That heritage forcefully asserted itself when Wilson Barrett's melodrama *The Sign of the Cross* began pulling huge crowds in January 1896. 'I have nothing that is not good to say of these entertainments' – Sydney Grundy, one of the serious new men, commented with tight-lipped heroism – 'and I rejoice that an estranged audience has returned with gusto to the theatre; but do these financial phenomena represent an advance in popular taste, do they indicate a raising of the theatrical standard?' (in Jenkins 1991: 162). When is a play not a play? When it is a financial phenomenon. Confronted by *The Sign of the Cross*, so to speak, Grundy along with other 'serious' stage writers saw renewed evidence that what was melodramatic had everything to do with gusto and popularity, and nothing to do with seriousness and standards. What the history of the *melodramatic* teaches Men of Letters is that they are correct to be suspicious of anything which is not letters. Which means that a drama that wants to be serious has to avoid effects, sensations, and unlettered people.

## 2   Men of the Theatre

In his Introduction to *The Golden Age of Melodrama* (1974) the actor and playwright Michael Kilgarriff argues:

> In the late eighteenth and early nineteenth centuries the world of letters missed the opportunity . . . to engender a new Golden Age in the British Theatre, and so the melodrama, instead of being just a passing aberration, became a century-long watershed in our dramatic culture. Had Shaw been born a hundred years earlier the story might have been very different. (Kilgarriff 1974: 23–4)

Since melodrama seems to be a hiatus in the continued rule of letters, you can't expect the criteria of the letters world to apply to it. Thus Michael Booth praises melodrama's 'refreshing lack of pretension', and brings the genre into line with a society that was watching films of angry young people in kitchen-sink settings when he assures readers that there was 'no messing around with intellectuality' (Booth 1965: 38).

Its refusal to mess around with intellectuality is the second thing (after its being melodramatic) that most people know about melodrama. Fearlessly uncomplicated, it is said to centre on a simple struggle between good and bad, ending – always – with virtue rewarded. So well established is this 'truth' about melodrama that it can be maintained even in the face of detailed evidence to the contrary. Thus in his edition of *Victorian Melodramas*, Smith (1976) explains that melodrama brought moral and emotional 'insecurities' under strict control, with characters who are 'walking clichés' inviting 'snap moral judgements' (pp. viii, ix). But among the plays he reprints is *The Factory Lad*, a story of industrial unrest and class antagonism. Its final picture has the wife of an industrial saboteur pleading for mercy, the brutal factory owner being shot, his murderer laughing hysterically and soldiers with their guns levelled at him. Not much security here. Smith, aware of this play's complexity, nudges it out of the category of melodrama and into that of late-nineteenth-century 'problem play', and thus keeps his generalizations intact.

This fairly simple fable of simplicity became newly respectable and influential with the publication of Peter Brooks's *The Melodramatic Imagination* (1985). Here the moral simplicity is connected with the conditions in which melodrama first emerged, in Revolutionary Paris of the 1790s. The Revolution had violently destroyed older systems of belief, including faith in divine order. The newly secular world then had a psychological need for a credible scheme of values. The possibility of secular moral values, their testing and triumph, were enacted in plays designed for mass illiterate audiences: melodramas. Fashionable as it became, however, Brooks's argument about an ethical project was only new to literary criticism. Theatre history had read it in 1949 in Maurice Disher's *Blood and Thunder*, which argued that melodrama sustained an idealistic myth, the human need to believe in 'Virtue Triumphant'. That belief, and thus the practice of melodrama, died in the twentieth century, a casualty of the 'vitriolic cynicism' that followed the First World War.

Where moral values have to remain clear cut, firmly either bad or good, there is – it seems – no urge towards the sort of complicated characterization that produces morally bewildered individuals who find themselves in tragic dilemmas. On these grounds Robert Heilman separates melodrama from tragedy, suggesting that, whereas the tragic hero was internally riven, the melodramatic protagonist was 'whole' (wholly good, wholly innocent). Once the form becomes defined by this somewhat abstract principle of characterization, it gets difficult to know where it begins and ends. Thus you can argue that melodrama has always been around, like air; and that most serious plays are melodramas rather than tragedies because 'we see most of the serious conflicts and crises in our everyday lives in melodramatic, rather than tragic, terms.' But while in these opening pages to his student guide to melodrama, James Smith concedes its seductiveness, he ends with a stern warning against melodrama that tangles with politics:

> Protest melodrama speaks exclusively to the converted; *The Factory Lad* was played for six nights only to an audience of workers on the seamy side of London . . . Such plays may focus discontent, fire public feeling and congratulate their audience on siding with the angels, but they

are too vehemently partisan, too shrill and facile in denunciation, to persuade the uncommitted man of even moderate intelligence that their black and white world is the grey one he knows. (Smith 1973: 10, 74)

Students of letters must learn that any genre that is committed to the contrast of black and white will be insufficiently intellectual to offer commentary on a world that we assuredly know as grey.

Someone less perturbed by the seamy might plausibly come from a different angle on the struggle between good and evil: 'probably the spirit of class war helps to explain the unnatural power with which the villain was at first endowed in the difficult art of seduction. He had an odd capability of going the whole hog without any help from the lady.' The suggestion that class war inhabits the ethics of melodrama comes from Montagu Slater's 1928 Introduction to *Maria Marten*. He goes on to celebrate the distance between this 'illiterate literature', written for illegitimate theatres, and the world of letters: 'such papers as *The Times* did not condescend to mention minor theatres at all, unless to say that they were ruining the morals of the populace just as films are accused of doing now.' Among the lettered is Dickens, with his 'smiling smug contempt' (Slater 1928: 10, 17, 18).

The Minor theatres were 'illegal . . . ; they were democratic; they were the oddest places imaginable'. Their cultural strength derived from their ability to speak for the communities in which they were situated: 'they were London theatres and provincial theatres at the same time. Each developed a style of drama suitable to its own district' – for example, the figure of the kindly Jew in Whitechapel melodramas. Writers for the Minors produced 'a kind of local journalism'. Melodrama from this angle is not, then, a hiatus in the dominant culture of letters but a high point in the decentralized culture of working communities: 'After 1780 there began to appear in different corners of London what one might call, in spite of its communist ring, "Theatres of the People"' (Slater 1928: 11, 16, 11).

That phrase 'in spite of' should read, perhaps, 'because of'. Slater was himself a Communist, and in his own novels and dramatic writing he sought to contribute to the political victory of the working class. In 1936–7 he adapted his own documentary report on a stay-down pit strike in South Wales – which was part of the campaign to build a Union of Mineworkers – into a play called *New Way Wins*, done by Left Theatre. At the same time he contributed to Unity Theatre's Living Newspaper on the London bus-workers' strike. In 1938 he wrote for the Co-operative movement's mass pageant in Wembley Stadium, *Towards Tomorrow* – where 'tomorrow' would be a time of international working-class solidarity, free of the influence of capitalist warmongers. Slater's interest in melodrama partly came out of his artistic interest in exploring and working with a very wide range of dramatic languages. But it was also, inextricably, part of a specific interest in popular theatres –

together with clowning and folk drama – which was an attempt by the left to rediscover, and commemorate, a people's history of England.

Other Communists had also found melodrama. In 1919 the Soviet People's Commissar of Education, Lunacharsky, claimed that 'Melodrama simply as theatre is superior to other dramatic genres.' In 1925 the Theatre for Young Spectators did a version of Dickens's *Tale of Two Cities*, because the director, Makariev, thought that melodrama would have a useful effect on its audience: 'In the spectator's active responses is rooted the life nerve of the stage action. . . . In the course of the performance the spectator performs complicated emotional work as he seeks the answer to the all-important questions: who is right? who is guilty? who is good? who is bad?' (Bratton et al. 1994: 192). Thus, just as Slater's editing of melodrama coexisted with his own dramatic innovations, so in the Bolshevik experiments with modernism melodrama had a place – until Stalinism did for it all.

One of the key elements, for Slater as for Makariev, is emotional engagement: 'only to read these [play]bills is enough to excite prolonged mouthwatering.' Typically, the only copy of *Maria Marten* in the British Library is a version 'which leaves out most of the story and all of its bloodthirsty charm' (Slater 1928: 9, 5). Mouthwatering and bloodthirstiness don't have a place in the smug world of letters. As another theatre historian put it: 'A modern smart audience might find something amusing in their grimaces . . . but there is plenty of evidence that the audiences of their own time were thrilled and entranced by their performances.' This is from George Speaight, whose work, although it doesn't have Slater's sharply political anger against bourgeois repression, nevertheless produces a picture of a staid dominant culture that views with distaste expressions of energy and liveliness. He warns today's smart audience about history: 'we must not see the life of this period in too lurid colours because it lacks the pampered amenities of our own age; these new men and women were not uncouth besotted animals, but human beings, lusting with life and tingling with the sharp intelligence of the Cockney' (G. Speaight 1946: 32, 24). Written while he was in the armed forces and published in 1946, *Juvenile Drama* has something of the feeling that led to the post-war Labour landslide and welfare state in its vision of new women and men looking for entertainments that reflected their own lust for life.

Now, since these entertainments preferred scenery, effects and music over mere dialogue, they are not likely to be understood by a modern literary critic 'who attends a theatre from which every broad and "theatrical" effect has been driven by a delicacy of character study'. The route to understanding is not through reading play-texts, for 'The plays themselves are, I suggest, the least important things about the early nineteenth century drama; the subject becomes a fascinating one if it is approached from the opposite direction, – from the viewpoint of the audience' (G. Speaight 1946: 31–2, 45). Approaching via the audience, the bookish value of the written play diminishes alongside the real excitement of the performance event. Such excitement is pre-eminently bodily: Speaight's spectators lusting with life, Slater's prolonged mouthwatering. Without their nostalgic and utopian colouring, Dickens was also preoccupied by being squeezed among other bodies, forcibly aware of their smell. While bodily excitement is usually part of spectating, in thinking about melodrama it becomes primary – because of the way the form both fails in the world of letters and simultaneously attracts an audience that is *mass*. Thus the study of melodrama promises to take us into a space beyond intellectual analysis, for its key features of visual excitement and the thrills of the moment are, as Booth says, 'qualities almost beyond critical recall'. For someone wanting to get beyond analysis, the motivation in writing a book about melodrama is 'to bring it back to life' (Booth 1965: 13).

It was not strictly necessary to use a book to resurrect thrill in 1965, for it was possible to get direct access to an enormous collection of playbills – the very ones Slater drooled over – at the Victoria and Albert Museum, donated by Gabrielle Enthoven. Or to visit Raymond Mander and Joe Mitchenson and see a picture of Edward Gomersal in *Mazeppa* at Astley's, or look at the Order of the Elephant worn by Kemble as Hamlet, or browse through late-eighteenth-century porcelain statues of actors, or discover images of performers on horse brasses, door knockers, plates, playing cards, ashtrays, mugs and tea towels. These various objects all tell of the thrill of the moment in much the same way as do the fanzines, mirrors and T-shirts of pop culture. As George Speaight put it in *Collecting Theatre Memorabilia* (1988), since the theatre is 'an evanescent art' it is important to find a way 'to rescue what we can of that performance so that something, at least, may survive'. That something is more than memory – it enables us to 'get near to the experience of the night of the performance'. It is, in short, a souvenir: an object emotionally charged with the residue of the thrill, no longer existing in the thrilling moment but still having a relationship with it. Put together, a collection of such objects 'has an extraordinary faculty of illuminating and evoking that half-art, half-commercial venture that can only exist when a creator and an interpreter come together with an audience' (G. Speaight 1988: 9, 10).

This hesitation between art and commerce was nearly fatal. For the theatre collection wasn't quite like the recognizably serious gatherings of, say, antiquities, books, paintings. From the point of view of letters, theatre collecting is obsessional rather than measured, random rather than discriminating. In his tribute to her on her death in 1950, James Laver said Gabrielle Enthoven 'was a great "woman of the theatre"' – not in the sense that she was an actress or stage designer, but 'she had the theatre in her blood; and for many years of her life devoted herself to amassing the collection of playbills on which her fame rests' (Laver 1952: 1). Theatre, as we should expect, is something which – unlike books or a library – can exist in the blood. Amateur dramatics, a few playscripts, a scrapbook of press cuttings – and then an accidental purchase of 200 playbills: by the early 1920s, Gabrielle Enthoven's collection was bursting out of her house.

Similarly two young actors met in 1939; found they shared, among other things, an obsession with theatre history; set up home together; started filling house and garden with objects. As collectors, Raymond Mander and Joe Mitchenson – or 'The Boys', as Sybil Thorndike called them – seemed to show no preference for medium or genre or period. Their collection is not arranged so as to give special importance to some objects over others; it shows no signs, we might say, of discrimination. Thus, when Mander and Mitchenson became known in the 1950s as authorities on the theatre, their expertise was founded not on the training of university or literary culture but on practical experience and the enthusiasm – in the blood – of the autodidact. Not so much Men of Letters, 'The Boys' went from being theatre workers to Men of the Theatre.

By 1944 The Boys wanted to leave their collection to the nation. Fifty years of campaigning later, it is contained on the top floor of a Georgian mansion surrounded by golf course, with too few staff and too little space to open to the nation's visitors. Gabrielle Enthoven had similar ambitions in 1911 when she called for 'a comprehensive theatrical section in some London Museum': to 'comprise specimens of all the different branches necessary to the working of a play from the construction of the theatre, the designing of the scenery and costumes, to the smallest workings necessary in the house' (in Laver 1952: 2). But the director of the Victoria and Albert Museum didn't want her playbills. The theatre collection's customary fate, Enthoven observed, was to be broken up and sold. While the actor Charles Mathews, Senior, collected theatre portraits, his contemporary Hans Sloane collected antiquities. Mathews's collection went eventually to the Garrick Club; Sloane's formed the basis of the British Museum. What is offered to the nation is not always what the nation wants to display.

Gabrielle Enthoven finally got the director of the Victoria and Albert Museum to accept her material in 1924, and she went with it as unpaid cataloguer. Twenty-four years later she became the first Chair of the Society for Theatre Research, formed at a meeting at the Old Vic with the aim of 'bringing together those concerned with the conservation of ephemera, theatre material generally, and with the history of the theatre, as well as the preservation of the theatres themselves' (in Rogers 1985: xiii). Agitation for a nationally housed theatre collection intensified during the 1950s, leading in 1957 to the establishment of a pressure group, the British Theatre Museum Association. The agitation took the form of letters to *The Times*, meetings with the Arts Council of Great Britain and guest appearances by leading members of the profession. The same set of names turned out to support the Mander and Mitchenson collection. It had received a grant and a building from its local public authority, Lewisham Council, but its financial appeal was publicized in a brochure with a preface by Lord Olivier and quotations from Sir John Gielgud, Dame Sybil Thorndike, Sir Peter Hall, Sir Nöel Coward, Trevor Nunn of the Royal Shakespeare Company and John Hayes, Director of the National Portrait Gallery. Although some of these were friends of The Boys, their importance for fund-raising comes from their star status: the already publicly recognized titled person urges support for 'an invaluable source of reference'. It's difficult then, in this context, to call back to mind one of those people for whom the knockers and postcards were made, the Cockney lusting with life.

Speaight's sharply intelligent Cockney is unusual: much of theatre history has a less generous version of nineteenth-century mass entertainment. For Maurice Disher, who had been writing about clowns and popular song since the early 1920s, melodrama was, as we've seen, a vehicle for sustaining a myth of moral justice. Thus the form kept its audiences naive, intellectually in 'a universal juvenility', 'making emotion do the work of thought'. Apart from ten years of political bravery in the 1830s, 'To serve democracy was less important than to entertain it' (Disher 1949: 15, 157, 159). The attack on a mystificatory form slides over into an attack on the mystified. Michael Kilgarriff suggests that melodrama was dedicated to preserving the status quo, keeping people in thrall to it. The people thus as it were enthralled have a tendency towards 'shuffling obedience'. By contrast – perhaps because he was writing for students in the heady days of the early 1970s – James Smith identified protest rather than obedience as melodrama's undoing: protest melodrama, along with leftist agitation naturally, appeals 'to men who wish to think that they are thinking while their prejudices are pampered'. And who are the pampered? The sort of people who went to the Surrey, 'workers on the seamy side of London' (Smith 1973: 75, 74).

What has happened in this history is that the excited political or intelligent Cockneys of Slater and Speaight have arrived at a place where their excitement is evidence of stupidity. In lavishing its enthusiasm on a form which makes people stupid, theatre history catches itself in a double bind. For in the effort to distinguish itself from the world of letters, it attends to what literary analysis ignores – excitement, thrill, magic. But in connecting thrill with stupidity it dooms theatre history to be unserious, trivial, non-analytical. Kilgarriff claims his *Golden Age of Melodrama* is not aimed at the 'specialist': instead his book includes press cuttings to give more of a sense of the performance event. And in order to promote performance, he abridges and mutilates the play-texts . . . to preserve the necessary *magic*; for melodrama is like a last gesture of Christian defiance against the theatrically impoverishing effect of 'rationalist hedonism'. We're now a long way from Slater's editorial work on textual variants, and The Boys' insistence on getting right the facts of theatre history.

And Slater's work is largely forgotten; Mander and Mitchenson's books not in general use. What had once been the people's drama now belongs to the non-specialist; People's Theatre mutates into amateur dramatics. The presupposition of non-specialist's melodrama is that the magic, in all its bloodthirsty charm, is well and truly lost. Which means that when you wander through the Theatre Museum, looking at figurines behind safety glass, in a building next to the Royal Opera House, in an area of London which once housed a vegetable market, where real Cockneys worked, those carefully lit objects, safe under the patronage of Men of the Theatre, glow with the allure of holy relics.

## 3   The Dream Factory

Among the most celebrated Men of the Theatre is the first actor to be honoured by the state. Henry Irving, star and manager of the Lyceum Theatre, was knighted in 1895. But entry into the ranks of the titled did not guarantee acceptance by a cultured elite. Henry James, we saw, was critical of the vulgarizing effects in the Lyceum *Faust* – effects which seemed inappropriate in more than cultural terms. Thus the *Quarterly Review* said of the 1883 *Romeo and Juliet*:

> It is by . . . the frequent sacrifice of truth and fitness to mere scenic effect, that the taste of the best class of Mr Irving's audience is revolted . . . A flagrant instance of this was the blaze of light with which Juliet's bedchamber was filled, when even the moon's light was waning, in order that the fiercely ghastly livor of the lime-light might fall upon the parting caresses of Romeo and Juliet. (in Rees 1978: 191–2)

The vulgarity of limelight comes from its being both old-fashioned and shamelessly egocentric. To ignore the moon's natural waning was to show a disrespect for realism in keeping with the lowest melodramas. Indeed by 1883, and certainly by 1887, the use of limelight at all might be seen as obstinately backward. For in 1881, in the Savoy Theatre, which he had built specially for the operas of Gilbert and Sullivan, Richard D'Oyly Carte had introduced electric light to all parts of the house. The innovation spread fairly rapidly to major theatres during the 1880s. But Irving preferred the hard-edged beam of lensed limelight, a choice which some saw as having less to do with scenic than personality effect.

> I try an' try
> To find the reason why
> A Star wants hextry light

sang Albert Chevalier, in the persona of a commonsensical limelight-man (in Rees 1978: 192). In a theatre-world vigilant for stardom, the image of Irving's cultivated idiosyncrasy was promoted by cartoons and burlesques. To one of the new men of drama, George Bernard Shaw, this was all a symptom of what needed changing: 'The history of the Lyceum, with its twenty years' steady cultivation of the actor as a personal force, and its utter neglect of the drama, is the history of the English stage during that period' (in Jenkins 1991: 257).

But the Lyceum was not the only place where the Man of Theatre's theatrics constituted neglect of drama. Melodrama, metamorphosing through sensation plays, was moving towards a form that organized itself into a sequence of grand stage pictures – the 'panoramic' – in shows with titles like *The World*. In 1900 Wilson Barrett, whose success had already depressed the 'serious' dramatists, mounted another tale of religious heroism called *Quo Vadis?*, in which Christians are pursued through a variety of precise architectural locations of ancient Rome, and Lygia is rescued from the suspenseful horns of a maddened bull. If you were against this sort of thing you called it 'episodical' as opposed to 'convincingly connective', depending 'largely upon the carpenter and the scene-painter'. But it was through the efforts of a different craftsman that *Quo Vadis?* ultimately achieved almost legendary success – the cameraman. It thus seemed as if the new technology of film enabled someone like Barrett's imaginings to be fulfilled in a fashion of which the stage was not capable. The grand panoramic pictures seem to want to become moving pictures. At least that's what a reviewer in the *New York Herald* thought in 1899:

> In the play we see merely several horses galloping on a moving platform. They make no headway, and the moving scenery behind them does not delude the spectators into the belief that they are racing . . . The only way to secure the exact sense of action for this incident in a theatre is to represent it by Mr Edison's invention. . . . The pictures on a screen . . . would be closer to realism . . . than these horses galloping nowhere at the Broadway. (in Vardac 1949: 78, 80)

He was discussing a play called *Ben Hur*.

The story of melodrama striving to get steadily more spectacular and panoramic, finally bursting off the stage to be fulfilled in film, is the story that Nicholas Vardac tells of the origins of cinema. The romantic urge of melodrama led into conflict, the story goes, with a stage that was essentially incapable of giving it satisfactory form. There were innovations in the use of trap doors beneath and flies above the stage, but these were nevertheless what Vardac calls a fraud. Then the arrival of electricity confirmed that, in its bright light, all the scenic contrivance was counterfeit. Thus the drive for more realistic scenes at the end of the century was frustrated by the limits of the stage's capability. So the popularity of stage melodrama waned: 'for the screen, paradoxical as it may seem, could present the most romantic conception in a realistic fashion, and by thus combining realism and romance was to fall natural heir to stage melodrama' (Vardac 1949: 31).

Melodrama apparently anticipates film in two respects. The one with which Vardac is most concerned is the organization of narrative. For melodrama not only aspired to panoramic scenes but also to a sense of movement within and against the expected constraints of space and time. That obsession with movement, produced perhaps by melodrama's drive to articulate the new-felt rhythms of modernity, led to experiments with suspense plots and – in particular – with fast cutting between scenes. The most famous specialist in these experiments was Boucicault, who made it possible for the viewer not only to see from a realistically impossible position – like watching from behind someone's back as they climb up a sheer fortress wall – but also to transfer with improbable speed from one place to another: in other words, to give the viewer what the camera allows them. The camera's journeying through space and place leads to the other respect in which melodrama anticipates film. When film historians write about Hollywood melodrama of the 1950s, especially the work of Minnelli or Sirk, they often note that characterization is managed by attending to the elements around a person – the look of a room, details of its furnishing and properties, clothing, jewellery. Our sense of a particular character thus derives from the *complete* picture in which we see them placed. To this sense the décor and lighting may contribute much more forcefully than the character's expression of her own feelings. This way of doing things in the dream factory of the 1950s may bring to mind G. H. Lewes's dismay at the relation between 'scenic effects' and acting in the 1850s.

While they don't always share Lewes's worry, film historians do implicitly agree with him about the mode of melodrama. In her summary of Vardac's story about the development of moving picture techniques, Christine Gledhill observes that 'Such techniques dispensed with the expression of character through dialogue.' A drama that relies on *mise-en-scène* and tableau to 'externalise the inner states of characters' (Gledhill 1987: 23) is one which breaks with *much more* than the supposed 'unities' of time, place and action. For instance, that other drama which so spectacularly broke the 'rules', Renaissance drama, still relied heavily on character expression through soliloquy or interaction. So in fact Lewes was right, in that melodrama was no longer proper drama as he knew it. Put another way round, as the film historian might, melodrama is *the form that makes the historical break* from all drama up to that point.

Melodrama can make this break because what interested it about expression was the sense of its limit or impossibility. Characters are not fully in control of their modes of expression – or, rather, they want or need to express more than language allows. If you look at this sort of representation not with the eyes of the 1850s but the 1950s, it readily drops into a new opening. What

Lewes calls 'effects' is what later writers call 'excess': 'Melodrama's recourse to gestural, visual and musical excess constitutes the expressive means of what Brooks calls the "text of muteness". Devices such as dumb show, pantomime, tableaux and spectacle reach "toward . . . meanings which cannot be generated from the language code"' (Gledhill 1987: 30). In seeking to articulate what for its characters is unsayable, or repressed, the film mobilizes the elements around them: 'The scene has no plot significance whatsoever. But the colour parallels black/black, green/green, white concrete/white lace curtains provide an extremely strong emotional resonance. . . . The desolation of the scene transfers itself onto the Bacall character' (Elsaesser 1987: 53). The new word 'excess', together with its related ideas of repression and displacement, have been provided by something which Lewes didn't know and Hollywood couldn't leave alone, *psychoanalysis*. Equipped with psychoanalysis it was thus film rather than theatre historians who found a serious shape in, and positive valuation for, that dramatic ugly duckling of the 1850s: '*Les Misérables* . . . lets through a symbolic dimension of psychic truth, with the hero in turn representing very nearly the id, the super-ego and finally the sacrificed ego of a repressed and paranoid society' (Elsaesser 1987: 49). With recognition of a changed dramatic language comes a new sense of drama's relation to society. No longer concerned with imitating daily reality, it acts instead as a dream reality. In modern dream space, magical solutions coexist with the deep anxieties which have risen to the surface. As a dream factory, Hollywood was speaking, as no self-conscious art film could, to and for the popular experience of living in 1950s North America. When a film about ordinary people is called *Imitation of Life* its form has to be, naturally, melodrama.

In the Vardac story of stage and screen, stage melodrama can't reach a mass audience because it is confined to theatres which are rich enough to afford the required spectacular effects. It only gets its audience when it is absorbed into *American* cinema, which has a unique basis in 'broad appeal'. This appeal turns out to derive from a familiar relationship to 'letters' – film melodrama being 'characterised by a dynamic use of spatial and musical categories, as opposed to intellectual or literary ones' (Elsaesser 1987: 51). There's an echo here of Henry James, censuring Irving for putting effects before poetry. And when Elsaesser goes on to argue that mass appeal movies of the thirties and forties cover up their deficiencies – flimsy plots, absence of characterization – 'by focusing to the point of exaggeration on the drive, the obsession, the *idée fixe*' (p. 57), we hear again the Man of Letters' scepticism about a form that conceals its own weakness. So despite the new medium and new approach, the popular form remains what it always was, intellectually deficient and in need, as ever, of the persons of letters, through whose efforts alone the 'stuffy kitschness', as Laura Mulvey calls it, may be transmuted into the psychoanalytically respectable 'stuff of dreams and desire' (in Bratton et al. 1994: 122).

The story of melodrama does two things for film production: gives it a point of origin in popular, or indeed 'folk', art; and validates an interest in mass-appeal art. This story operates by retelling a version of theatre history. In this version there's a crucial point at which the conditions emerged which, in Christine Gledhill's summary, 'encouraged the return of the dramatic "artist" to the theatre. At the same time a minority intelligentsia supported an "independent" theatre movement . . . while nascent cinematic entertainments competed for the popular audience' (Gledhill 1987: 26). We've heard the story before: proper character and dialogue come back after a time of occupation by an alien form. Drama returns to where it should be, with high art and literariness. Meanwhile, the people, who never should have been in the theatres in the first place, slip away to find their natural home in the cinema. Thus film history, taking what it needs from melodrama, leaves the stage form in a sort of limbo. For what Montagu Slater celebrated in 'Theatres of the People' is deemed by Men of Letters to be improperly 'theatre' and by film historians to be not really 'of the people'.

But just when you think you're cosily sorted out, the door flings open and in the blast of freezing air a man enters: ''Tis I.' Irving. Irving in the role, to be precise, that brought him to fame, Mathias in *The Bells*. The play tells of a village burgomaster, a loving family man, whose wealth secretly comes from a robbery and murder committed long ago. During the action, that murder returns to haunt him, first as the recurring sound of his victim's sleigh-bells and then as a dreamed confession of guilt to a court of law. The dream kills him, and nobody ever knows why he died. Not the action of murder, then, but the reaction to it is central. The play that opened at the Lyceum late in November 1871 – the heyday, as some say, of Victorian imperialism – concerns itself directly with what Freud taught us to call the return of the repressed, as it wreaks havoc on a series of cherished ideals – the civic dignitary, male comradeship, the man made good, the careful paterfamilias. Its climactic scene is not just a dream, but a dream in which the guilty man is subjected to a mesmerist. The arrival of mesmerism means that your mind and its secrets need never be your own.

The moment of Mathias's return is the moment Irving sets out as a star. He knew from the start what he was doing. The Lyceum did the play on his insistence; he added numerous details to enhance what drama terminology so satisfyingly might refer to as the family *business*. Above all he worked out the performance as a series of minutely constructed effects, from his own timing of speech and gesture to the arrangements of scene and lighting: Mathias is in the act of putting coke on the stove when he hears that his future son-in-law has been reading about a particular ancient murder case. Irving had the stove door hinged on its upstage side so that when the door was opened the red glow of the fire lit Mathias's face as soon as he looked up to listen. The careful realism is managed so as to produce what we might call an 'excessive' effect. When electricity was later used for the daylight outside, it was here dimmed. The insistent focus on Irving's face is perhaps what Shaw referred to as a personality cult. But it also suggests that Mathias is both controlling and controlled by his situation, that his acting is always re-enactment. That proposition has its roots deep in melodramatic tradition, but when it is so performed as to have a sort of mesmeric effect on the audience, Irving's theatre threatens to open the door into late Victorian dream-life:

> Those who remember the Lyceum setting will recall the profound feeling of eeriness produced by the comparative gloom which shrouded the members of the Court, placed well up stage. It was as if the voices of the judge and hypnotist issued from the recesses of a dark cavern. The effect was electrical. (in Mayer 1980: 26)

To be electrical you don't need electricity. To produce the blurred dream effect, Irving used gauzes and iris diaphragms on the limelight in the flies; a later production at the Savoy didn't seem so good because there was too much light. Irving's 'old-fashioned' hostility to electric light was part of the creation of the Lyceum into not so much theatrical drawing-room as dream cavern. Typically, when it did use electricity it wired it through the costumes of two performers in *Faust* (1885) so that when their swords crossed in stage fight, real electricity flashed. Performers' bodies had been wired up before, at the very electrical Savoy, when in the 1882 production of Gilbert and Sullivan's *Iolanthe* the fairies were illuminated with little lights on their dresses. But that decorative use of electricity as costume was very different from Irving's attempt to intensify action by organizing it – literally – into flashes of excitement. So too in films, when sound became available, it was as much used to enhance sensation effects – screams or gunfire – as to imitate reality. That similarity in the uses of technology directs us to look at Irving's sort of theatre from an angle that the new men of drama couldn't – or wouldn't – countenance. Far from being a backward melodramatist, the old Man of the Theatre was looking towards a possible future: as Vardac puts it, 'Henry Irving approached the staging of melodrama like a motion-picture camera in the hands of a competent artist' (Vardac 1949: 93).

A carefulness about stage pictures, however, far from being inevitably cinematic, is what one might normally expect from a skilled actor–producer, 'strengthening the weak spots in the play and in his own personality by expressive happenings in the crowd (which is also acting) and still other bare spots by expressive scene and lighting (which is also acting), he gradually makes invulnerable and fool-proof all that before was rather weak and imposs-ible' (E. G. Craig 1930: 92). That definition of the job, with its emphasis on crowd, scene and lighting, comes from someone who not only knew Irving's work but who himself helped to shape a new theatre language of the early twentieth century. The theatre designer Edward Gordon Craig was, together with Adolphe Appia, one of the pioneers of staging in which all the elements – scene and lighting design, crowd and solo performer – were conspicuously integrated into coherent visual units. While these units could be expressive or atmospheric, they in no way sought to imitate reality:

> the aim of the Theatre as a whole is to restore its art, and it should commence by banishing from the Theatre this idea of impersonation, this idea of reproducing Nature; for while impersonation is in the Theatre, the Theatre can never become free. (E. G. Craig 1980: 75)

The arch-enemy of this new theatre is thus any form of acting which is 'naturalistic'.

Craig's ideal actor is indeed a sort of puppet – what he called an *über-marionette*. To be an integrated part of a scenic unit the body must allow itself to be moulded by the design of the scene (a distant sound here of Lewes groaning). But the human body is, he says, by 'nature' disinclined to be so slavish, which is what makes the body unsuitable for theatre art. Actors thus hinder the development of theatre. The solution is to make the actor more puppet-like, to develop a form of acting which consists 'for the main part of symbolical gesture' (E. G. Craig 1980: 61). Craig's thoughts about the body and its discipline seem to link across to the explorations of rhythmic movement which the contemporary Russian director Meyerhold called bio-mechanics. But those thoughts about theatre's future are at the same time shaped by a memory of the past, a director who 'rehearsed these actors unceasingly, and tried to make good marionettes of them'. And when that director acted,

> each moment was significant . . . every sound, each movement, was in-tentional – clear cut, measured dance: nothing real – all massively artificial – yet all flashing with the light and pulse of nature. . . . the action of his face was part of all this, and was measured too; . . . this control of feature till immobility was achieved constituted a mask. (E. G. Craig 1930: 111, 78)

The actor–director who so embodies the ideal is, of course, Irving. Craig's stress on those carefully structured rhythms, Irving's 'dance', is intended as a riposte to William Archer's attack in 1883 on Irving's unrealistic speech and movement. Writing his reminiscences in 1930, Craig links Irving so directly with 'modern' practices that Archer – champion of new drama and naturalism – seems to be abandoned in a siding. And it's not just Irving himself but his practice that is hailed as modern: the craft of the actor–director is to be struck forcefully by the *idea* of a play as a theatre-piece, and then to stage it 'so that it shall strike the spectators in the same way and amaze their very faculties of eyes and ears. Especially of melodrama is this true, and melodrama is one of the best kinds of modern drama' (E. G. Craig 1930: 92). In championing melodrama Craig claims a tradition which leads to his own integrated scene and simultaneously attacks contemporary practices centred on naturalism, imitation, the predominance of the actor and *written* text.

While the idea of a theatre which is abstract, disengaged, organized only according to 'beauty', may be a by-product of the Aesthetic movement of the 1880s, in 1930 Craig was still hankering after something which had deeper force than mere staged arguments and imitations of life. The name of that force comes, again, from Irving. His acting in *The Bells* 'was, in every gesture, every half move, in the play of his shoulders, legs, head, and arms, mesmeric in the highest degree – slowly we were drawn to watch' (E. G. Craig 1930: 58). At the end of *The Bells*, while Mathias discovers how the 'dangerous faculty' of mesmerism reveals dark truths, it was in reality Irving himself who acted as mesmerist to the modern stage.

To the side of Craig's voice, there is another: 'I suggest we ought to return through theatre to . . . a means of inducing trances.' When he calls out for 'No More Masterpieces', Antonin Artaud scorns the 'foolish adherence to texts, to *written* poetry'. Instead he wants a theatre that will be able to regain a powerful social role, by reaching to an audience through their anatomies, getting beneath the fashions of taste, learnt ideas, clichés of expression. In his 'Theatre of Cruelty'

> there is continual amplification; the sounds, noises and cries are first sought for their vibratory qualities, secondly for what they represent. . . . Lighting made not only to give colour or to shed light, but containing its own force, influence and suggestiveness. . . . Following on sound and lighting there is action and action's dynamism. This is where theatre, far from imitating life, communicates whatever it can with pure forces.

Given the hostility to what is imitative or representational, and the valuing of the sensory, not to say sensational, it is unsurprising to learn that there have been, in the present, no shows that are 'worth-while in the highest sense of theatre, since the last great Romantic melodramas'. For Artaud, guru of so much contemporary drama, theatre history looks like one long decline, beginning in the Renaissance, into what is 'purely descriptive, narrative theatre, narrating psychology' (Artaud 1970: 61, 59, 62, 57). That decline was only broken, temporarily, by the one form that could show the true way to the future – melodrama.

## 4  The Living Dead

Since he rejected the imitation of life, Craig looked elsewhere for inspiration:

> my aim shall rather to be to catch some far-off glimpse of that spirit
> which we call Death – to recall beautiful things from the imaginary
> world; they say they are cold, these dead things, I do not know – they
> often seem warmer and more living than that which parades as life.
> Shades – spirits seem to me to be more beautiful, and filled with more
> vitality than men and women. (E. G. Craig 1980: 74)

Someone else who was close to Irving also found inspiration in shades: 'His
eyes were positively blazing. The red light in them was lurid, as if the flames
of hell-fire blazed behind them. His face was deathly pale, and the lines of it
were hard like drawn wires.' This particular shade has a name, Dracula, and
the man who brought him to life in 1897 was Irving's close friend and
manager, Bram Stoker. And it is to Irving's theatre that some of the psychic
effects of Stoker's tale seem to owe their origin: as the narrator, Jonathan
Harker, watches some specks in the moonlight, he hears a howling of dogs:

> Louder it seemed to ring in my ears, and the floating motes of dust to
> take new shapes to the sound as they danced in the moonlight. I felt
> myself struggling, and my half-remembered sensibilities were striving
> to answer the call. I was becoming hypnotized! (Stoker 1983: 38, 44)

When Stoker published his reminiscences of Irving in 1907, a familiar face
peers out at us: 'It was marvellous that any living man should show such eyes.
They really seemed to shine like cinders of glowing red from out the marble
face' (Stoker 1907: 35). This is Irving – recalled suddenly materializing in a
trick effect as Vanderdecken, the Flying Dutchman. But the now dead knight
bears an uncanny similarity to the undead Count.

The story of the Flying Dutchman, like that of Dracula, reaches back to the
earliest years of melodrama, the decades of Gothic. Repeated scenarios stage
the finding of what was lost, the reappearance of what was hidden, the return
of what was repressed. They are narratives of a present always haunted,
threatened by the dead who haven't died. With a remorseless persistence the
tales of a search for individual identity involve confrontation with an individual's specific worst fears. So, for instance, in the process of achieving one's great
expectations, a young gentleman must realize that he owes everything to an
old convict, and that he has – like it or not – a 'second father'. Such a moment
of discovery consists of both recognition and horror: 'He caught me, drew me
to the sofa, put me up against the cushions, and bent on one knee before me:
bringing the face that I now well remembered, and that I shuddered at, very

near to mine' (Dickens 1967: 337). Dickens's *Great Expectations* shows the force with which the ancient melodramatic shape persists into the 1860s; and that persistence is felt – by Dickens at least – as a challenge to the triviality of contemporary culture: 'The mystery of evil is as interesting to us now as it was in the time of Shakespeare; and it is downright affectation or effeminacy to say that we are never to glance into that abyss' (quoted in Hughes 1980: 28). The logic of melodrama insists that true strength is only constituted through seeking out the abyss.

In the case of the young gentleman with expectations, the discovery of the reality of his assumed adult identity requires that he re-experience the abyss of his worst childhood fears. That relation between the experience of the adult and the child is rather similarly, if more polemically, restated over a century later. As Mark Petrie falls asleep he reflects on the 'tame and domestic' terrors of adults,

> pallid compared to the fears every child lies cheek and jowl with in his dark bed . . . There is no group therapy or psychiatry or community social services for the child who must cope with the thing under the bed or in the cellar every night, the thing which leers and capers and threatens just beyond the point where vision will reach. The same lonely battle must be fought night after night and the only cure is the eventual ossification of the imaginary faculties, and this is called adulthood. (King 1976: 279)

Mark Petrie has just seen off a vampire. Thus he manages to avoid becoming one of the undead who terrorize Stephen King's *Salem's Lot*. The novel teases its readers with the proposition that when commonsensical modern adulthood denies the existence of ancient and childish horrors it only reveals its incapacity to deal with *real* evil. Real evil is what is felt in the anatomy and nervous system, deep – as Artaud might have said – beneath the cerebellum. Hence a major obstacle in dealing with vampires is the unwillingness to admit the fact of their existence. As one character remarks, when faced by something which feels like a cliché of pulp fiction, 'Life is full of melodrama.' But he speaks, naturally, with spot-on accuracy, for here is melodrama as Irving might have organized it: when Mark's parents die, the no-nonsense shine of electric light gives way to darkness broken by a glowing cross confronting a highlighted white face; when Mark's vampire smiles it looks like a 'twitching grimace – a bloody mask tragedy' (King 1976: 342, 276), and its effect, of course, is hypnotic. This is melodrama working as Irving knew it did, for his playing of Mathias 'raised the average sensual man to the disquieting consciousness of a nervous system'. The treachery of that nervous system is its ability to subvert the high seriousness of the intellect. As Archer put it, with some dismay:

The Goth is not the highest element in our composition. He lives in our nerves, whereas the Greek lives in our intellect. But since the nerves respond automatically to the stimulus of theatrical effect, whereas the intellect responds only through a voluntary effort, when Goth meets Greek in the theatre there is practically no tug of war – the Goth holds the field. (in Rowell 1971: 135, 212)

The treachery of such sensational art is that it animates everything which seriousness regards as trivial and dead. Thus when life is full of melodrama, it is full of – in several senses – the living dead.

Late Victorian society appears to have found a way to accommodate the Goth when it rewarded the player of Mathias and Mephistopheles with a knighthood. Its second theatrical knighting, which worked nicely as balance, honoured one of the pioneers of drawing-room theatre, Squire Bancroft. And whereas Irving died an idiosyncratic star, Bancroft lived long enough to become the first president of the newly formed Academy of Dramatic Art, which would steer the theatrical young towards Greekness.[1] In the two knightings, therefore, we have a neat diagram of the place of melodrama: powerful but eccentric, commercial rather than educational, out of date, culturally never here but there – ignorant audiences, idiosyncratic performing, old-fashioned movies.

But the Goth, as Archer suspected, contrives to be here all the time; indeed he seems quite unremarkable, even natural. Many people would feel cheated or dissatisfied if the action sequences or emotional confrontations in films were not accompanied by music. If you cancelled the melo from the drama *Jaws* would lose something of its bite. And those narratives which involve the perilous quest for an answer, the discovery of an awful truth, those detection stories with their ancient shape seem not so much eccentric as mainstream: we *know* that police agent Starling in *Silence of the Lambs* will have to yield up something deeply private in order to get the answer she needs from the terrifying but truth-knowing Hannibal Lecter. And when Lecter stares, penetrating, the effect is thrilling, indeed Oscar-worthy – and produced, quite simply, by working the muscles around the eyes in order to foreground the stare, in a way that would be recognized perhaps by a villain-actor from the 1830s, to create an effect that is – how shall we say? – mesmeric. For, most outrageously of all, that old idiosyncratic acting lives on in techniques that are designed to produce not mockery but engagement. So at the moment when she reaches the climax of her character's quest in *Aliens* to rescue the young girl, Newt, the editing cuts to close-up on Sigourney Weaver as she stops, pauses, slowly turns, 'realizing' – doing, in brief, a beautifully executed and very engaging display of what in, say, 1809 would have been called 'apprehension'. And she should feel apprehension for she has arrived at the place where the hideous alien creature is laying and hatching its eggs. She finds herself, literally, in an abyss. Only by facing, at last, the monstrous mother will the female warrior, with her little girl protégée, achieve her full identity, indeed find herself, as strong good mother. So too in order to prove herself as female police agent, as truth-finder, Clarice Starling must speak about and face up to what she has always run away from, the childhood memory of the screams of slaughtered lambs – which for her remains, of course, undead.

There is something cruel perhaps in forcing people to look into the abyss. Yet, as viewers know, it is absolutely necessary. In a discussion of Charles Reade's prose version of *It's Never too Late to Mend*, Winifred Hughes gives us a word for this necessary cruelty. Reade, she says, has fallen back on old stereotypes: 'these he pushes to the limit and beyond, truly shocking and disgusting the usual audience for soft-core titillation. He is left with excellent, if unsophisticated sadomasochistic fantasy, but distinctly problematical art' (Hughes 1980: 86). If Reade stands accused of cynical exploitation, Dickens presents a more worrying case, in that his public readings of his own description of Nancy's death at the hands of Sikes in *Oliver Twist* show an unconscious identification with the brutal murderer. This, it is suggested, shows the melodramatic imagination at work in respect of 'its unconscious connivance at the darker impulses and fantasies of its readers'. Those dark impulses soon acquire a familiar label: 'Melodramatic nemesis, in short, presents the dubious pleasures of what can only be called self-righteous sadism.' The moralistic vocabulary here shows that literary criticism is all too vigilantly aware of a preposterously undead Goth:

> 'melodrama' is clearly something of a liability. Despite recent attempts at its rehabilitation . . . melodrama is the mode which, along with cog-nate modes such as sentimentality and pornography, accommodates and exploits the demands of the immature and uncritical sensibility. (Prendergast 1978: 11, 12, 13)

When it slides into place alongside pornography, melodrama turns into something which civilized criticism must not so much laugh at as censor and repress. To imagine that melodrama simply deals in exaggerated fictions is to forget that dark impulses are all too real, and best left buried.

For the pleasures of, say, sado-masochism are rather less – or perhaps more – dubious than is normally allowed for, as anyone will tell you who has had dealings with vampires. For a scenario that is terrifying and cruel can at the same time be hypnotically necessary and deeply pleasurable. A sado-masochistic scene is acted out between people who have agreed conventions, so that there is a safe framework within which deep psychic memories are explored and replayed. Highly charged material is recovered, negotiated and put back again. Its cruelty is its necessity is its pleasure. 'Serious' art categorizes melodrama's repertoire of sensation, thrill and excess as escapism, which, if you have your eye on a world of duty and work, makes it trivial. Melodrama instead has its eye not on a world which is escaped from but a world which is escaped into, a world that is – for each of us – dark, ancient, childish:

> There was something about them that made me uneasy, some longing and at the same time some deadly fear. I felt in my heart a wicked, burning desire that they would kiss me with those red lips. (Stoker 1983: 37)

That moment of nearly yielding to the undead is imagined by a man who not only knew the stage work of Irving but who also championed the work on sexuality of Walt Whitman. The story of Dracula may be escapism, but into what?

In all its spectacular use of traps and flies, music and effects, melodrama is not only demonstrating its 'excess' but its sensual *necessity* – that combination of cruelty and pleasure. As one spectator put it: 'I can never forget his livid face and fixed look, in the two first Dramas. It quite haunts me.' The spectator is Queen Victoria, who had been to see that master showman Boucicault in a play called – of course – *The Vampire*. When she wanted to repeat the experience, it all vanished: a second time it was 'very trashy' (in Jenkins 1991: 8). The teasing capacity to be both haunting and trashy just about summarizes the status of the form which persists in feeling like the undead of dominant culture. Thus in the history of the English theatre, melodrama, with its spectacular attractiveness, plays the role of – as it were – lord of the flies.

## NOTES

1   It should not be forgotten here that Irving himself had hopes and plans for some sort of drama school, as Stoker 1907 describes.

# 9

# Naturalism

*Our model manager should take for standard of the people he would please an honest Englishman of the educated middle-class, akin to all that is human.*
Henry Morley, *The Journal of a London Playgoer*

## 1   Getting into Society

In 1920, when William Archer lectured on 'The Old Drama and the New', the 'New' was already a recognized movement, with a history dating back to about 1890 and a canon of playwrights which included Henry Arthur Jones, Arthur Wing Pinero, George Bernard Shaw, Granville Barker and John Galsworthy. These were 'new' dramatists not only in the sense that they happened to be contemporary, but also in the sense that they were innovators, conscious exponents of the modern.

One of the most engaging documents of this historical self-consciousness is Pinero's comedy *Trelawny of the 'Wells'*. First staged in 1898, it is set in the theatre of the early 1860s, when the 'new drama' is unknown, and a quaint but sterile traditionalism rules the stage. The subtly off-centre hero of the piece, Tom Wrench, is an unsuccessful actor and unperformed playwright who dreams of a better and more truthful drama, one which would base itself not on theatrical convention but on real people; he actually has a script in his drawer called *Life*. He is the precursor, at once heroic and comic, of the theatrical reformation which Pinero and his contemporaries felt they had themselves achieved; in *Trelawny*, the 'modern school' of play-writing contemplates, and gently romanticizes, its own genesis.

In the last act, Tom successfully gets *Life* into rehearsal, and the serio-comic victims of his ascendancy are Mr and Mrs Telfer, mid-Victorian ham actors who reigned in the old theatre of declamation and pasteboard but literally cannot find roles in this new drama of reality:

> TELFER: And so this new-fangled stuff, and these dandified people, are
>          to push us, and such as us, from our stools!
> MRS TELFER: Yes, James, just as some other new fashion will, in course
>          of time, push *them* from their stools.
>
> (Pinero 1986: 188)

William Archer quotes these lines in his 1920 lectures, and comments: 'After fifty years, Mrs Telfer's prophecy remains unfulfilled. The ideals of Tom Wrench – natural dialogue and realistic scenery – remain in the ascendant, though various attempts have been made to dethrone them' (Archer 1923: 269). With the help of Pinero's adroit myth-making, Archer can look back over two generations' ascendancy of the 'natural' and the 'realistic', confident that Tom Wrench's dramaturgy was not a mere passing fashion, but is permanently in charge. And a further generation later, in 1948, that confidence seems to be confirmed, though now somewhat bitterly, by another successful dramatist, J. B. Priestley:

> Although various breakaway experiments have been made – and I have made some myself – the theatrical tradition of our time is a naturalistic tradition, and so I have had in the main to come to terms with it. . . . Actually I have always fretted and conspired against downright naturalism. I have spent a good many of my working hours devising means to conjure audiences away from the prevailing tradition. (Priestley 1948: I, vii)

Fifty years after *Trelawny*, this restates the centrality of the 'natural' in exactly Mr Telfer's – and Archer's – language of power. This is a dramatic mode which pushes us from our stools, which resists attempts to dethrone it, and which one opposes surreptitiously by fretting and conspiring against it: it is clearly a kind of dictator. It is the 'prevailing tradition' not just in the sense that it is blandly prevalent, but in the sense that it actively prevails over other residual or possible traditions – ousts them, or incorporates them, or suppresses them. What Priestley calls naturalism, then, was the *dominant* discourse in English theatre in the first half of the twentieth century; and to understand it we need to see *how it dominated*, as well as what it was.

We can begin by returning to Pinero's play. Its real protagonist is not Tom Wrench but Rose Trelawny, an actress in a down-market theatre who leaves the profession to marry a young aristocrat named Arthur Gower. At first the marriage is not a success: oppressed by his overbearing relatives and the stifling propriety of their domestic regime, she leaves him and goes back on the stage. But then she finds that it is impossible to take up where she left off. She lacks the force she used to have, the carefree exaggeration, the trouper's indiscriminate get-up-and-do-it – in a word, she has lost her vulgarity. Without it she is of little value to the managers who used to employ her. However, her new refinement, which is disabling in the old theatre, has turned her into precisely the kind of actress Tom Wrench needs for his play. This reversal is the key to the denouement. The new Rose and the new play are evidently going to be the making of each other. The overbearing relatives, charmed by her unexpectedly well-bred manners, condescend to the extent of backing the production, and then Arthur, having secretly picked up a stage education in the provinces, arrives to join the cast and claim his bride. Just as she has become a lady without ceasing to be an actress, so he has become an actor without ceasing to be a gentleman. Rose and Arthur are reunited on the set of the first English realistic drama; theatrical and social values are reconciled.

Thus the play is quite schematically about the marriage of theatre and the social order, the 'Wells' and Cavendish Square. At first the two spheres seem to be incompatible. The theatre is too coarse and rebellious, the social order too rigidly respectable: the two of them will apparently have to lead separate lives. But then both sides find they have something to gain from these tensions: the theatre acquires a new social standing (besides locating a new source of investment capital), and the social order acquires a new flexibility and humanity. Pinero's thesis, then, turns out to be shrewder and more hard-nosed than his pleasant sentimentality might lead us to expect. It is that the emergence of the new drama is not primarily an artistic development but a sociological event: that the occasion of English naturalism is the theatre's breaking with its old plebeian and popular associations and forming a new alliance with the ruling class.

This was indeed the programme of the real theatre which Pinero is thinking of, and which we encountered in the last chapter (pp. 224–5, above): the Prince of Wales as it was managed by Marie Wilton and Squire Bancroft from 1865 to 1880. Together with their house dramatist, Tom Robertson – Tom Wrench is a lightly fictionalized portrait of him – the Bancrofts are often regarded as the immediate ancestors of the new drama of 1890–1920, and credited with exactly the reforms Pinero identifies in his play: systematic rehearsal, realistic sets, natural dialogue, understated acting.[1] Theatre historians disagree about how original they were being in pursuing these policies; but what is beyond doubt is their determination to move their theatre up the social scale – to redesign the layout, decor and pricing of the house so as to discourage the popular audience and create a modestly luxurious environment in which members of 'good society' would feel at home. In this they were decisively successful: over the last quarter of the nineteenth century the wealthy and fashionable returned to the London theatre in significant numbers, and actor-managers and dramatists, including the Bancrofts and Pinero himself, were not only entertaining the upper middle class, but also accumulating enough money and status to join it. Theatre had got into Society.

Pinero's mythic linkage of naturalism and social incorporation, then, shows an impressive historical awareness. But what is its logic? It centres on the figure of the actress who plays the heroine. At the beginning, the plot requires her to be, precisely, an actress – emotionally uninhibited, playful, changeable, diffusely expressive. The climactic scene shortly before the end, however, requires her to win over the crusty old aristocrat with her quiet dignity. This involves all the opposite physical qualities: restraint, gravity, stillness, concentrated self-assertion. Thus the performance enacts, in the charged medium of the actress's body, the transition from theatricality to civility.[2]

This powerfully theatrical move against theatricality is heavily interpreted in the play. What exactly is it that is supposed to have happened to Rose's acting? Sometimes it appears to be that her exposure to the aristocracy has made it more refined. But then it also seems to be that her unhappiness in love has made it more real. By leaving this point vague, Pinero creates an ideological image which somehow combines refinement and reality as if they formed a single quality. Tom names this potent composite, hesitantly but decisively: 'She was always a ladylike *actress* . . . but now she has developed into a – (*at a loss*) into a – Into a ladylike human being' (Pinero 1986: 171). Here 'ladylike' is the bridge by which Rose makes the tricky crossing from 'actress' to 'human being'. Her acting feels real because it is not 'actressy' – that is, it is quiet, simple, reserved, devoid of willed or unnatural emphasis. In other words, it is informed by exactly the code of physical and emotional restraint which governs behaviour in good society. Refinement – freedom from gestic and linguistic excess – has been adopted as the hallmark of the human.

The theatre's turn away from the popular audience, then, is not merely an external question of marketing, but enters deep into its representational codes. The ban on theatricality is *the same as* the ban on vulgarity, not only because theatre in the recent past has in fact tended to be a low-status occupation, but also because the two solecisms – being theatrical and being vulgar – both consist of the obtrusive presence of the signifier. The flourishes of the ham actor and the laborious vowels of the *nouveau riche* are from this point of view examples of the same thing: both gratingly draw your attention to techniques of articulation which ought to pass unnoticed. A true lady attenuates her means of expression – *refines* them, exactly – to the point where you cease to be aware of them, and feel only the unmediated presence of what Tom Wrench calls the ladylike human being. Realist theatre can be called a refined form, however gross its *objects* of representation may be, because it operates what is essentially the same regime as the lady: it discreetly effaces the historical and material character of its expressive resources in order to produce the illusion of unforced, unconstructed human presence. Getting into Society, the theatrical sign behaves like any other *arriviste*: it learns to conceal its origins.

## 2  Plays for Puritans

The story which *Trelawny* tells poetically can also be told in prose.

The Patent system of 1660, which institutionalized the patronage of London theatre by courtiers, was formally abolished in 1843. The Arts Council, which institutionalizes the support of London theatre by the State, was not set up until 1945 (see pp. 306–8, below). For exactly a century, then, theatre was a fully competitive business as it was not either earlier or later.

At first, the position of dramatists within this business was not good. The price of their product was of course free to find its market level, and since a dramatist faced competition both from other living dramatists (who were numerous) and from dead ones (who were unpaid), this level tended to be low. This made it necessary to write fast: drama was running on a policy of high turnover and minimum costs. After a while, though, this policy was progressively found to be unsatisfactory. The quality of the product was suffering to the point where the middle-class public, its expectations formed by the increasing maturity of the novel, stayed away, leaving drama at the lower end of the entertainment market. Clearly nobody was going to get rich – or respectable – in a business that was run like this.

The alternative was lower turnover and higher profits – in other words, the long run. Whereas the pre-1843 theatre was essentially a repertory set-up, with bills normally changing every few days, by 1900 every manager hoped, as a matter of course, to occupy a theatre for an entire season with a single production, and runs of a hundred nights were commonplace. What sustained these longer and longer runs was the growth of outer London. The rail network which created the commuter suburbs of the late nineteenth century also made it possible for their countless inhabitants to see a play in Town and get conveniently home afterwards. Theatre could drop the metropolitan popular audience if it could get this much bigger and more affluent suburban middle-class public.

In these circumstances, a writer who could provide the right kind of script possessed a valuable skill. The playwrights themselves realized the strength of their position, and realized, too, that it depended on stringent quality control. By the time of *Trelawny*, there was a group of established writers for the stage who were as rich and respectable as, say, successful surgeons or barristers. And like those groups, they had a professional ethos, sustained by their own working practices and validated by an increasingly ambitious critical discourse in newspapers and journals (Stephens 1992: 174–91).

This professionalization was seen as part of a wider cultural and political movement. At just this period, the general theme of reform (in the Civil Service, the armed forces, the education system) was the iniquity of amateurism and nepotism and the need to open establishments up to fair competition. In its intolerance of custom and its insistence on individual merit, this theme has a clear anti-aristocratic animus. It is not an accident that *Trelawny* achieves its happy ending by triumphing not only over the vulgarity of the 'Wells' but almost (not quite) equally over the antique hauteur of Cavendish Square. And this middle course is a homage to Tom Robertson himself, who executes exactly the same pincer movement in *Caste*, balancing the humble bride's unpleasantly low-grade father with the gentlemanly bridegroom's absurdly aristocratic mother. The 'modern movement' in the drama of 1870–1914 is visibly part of a general *embourgeoisement*, not only in the sense that drama reoriented itself towards a predominantly middle-class audience, but also that, in the process, it reorganized itself on bourgeois lines. By the end of the century, both its working relationships and its scripts were increasingly expressing the values of the new hegemony: a moralized individualism, upward mobility, technical efficiency, the work ethic.

The clearest exponent of this ideology of drama is, once again, William Archer. As we have already seen, his account of play-writing is consistently, even triumphally, progressive. In his 1920 lectures, it appears that what has happened since 1890 is that the drama, after centuries of artistic confusion, has finally become 'a pure and logical art-form'. Until this breakthrough there were two conflicting impulses informing the writing of plays – the truly dramatic principle, and an extrinsic principle which Archer variously calls passion, lyric, rhetoric, exaggeration and rhythm. The reason this anti-dramatic tendency has so many names is that Archer conceives of it negatively: it is definable only as whatever disfigures drama by getting in the way of its proper task, which is to imitate reality.

That this is the ideology of a new professionalism is made clear by the list of dramatic forms which are deselected by it. The category of the purely and logically dramatic excludes all non-Western theatre (which is too mixed up with dance and ritual to give a truthful picture of life), all Elizabethan and Jacobean drama (with the somewhat arbitrary exception of Shakespeare), and, in the modern period, almost all experiments in poetic drama (Hardy and Yeats are both dismissed as poets who are not 'born dramatists'). It also excludes experiments in staging such as those of Gordon Craig, who was probably the only Edwardian theatre practitioner of European significance, and who is not mentioned in Archer's book at all. The only English writers who appear as dramatists without qualification are the new realists: Pinero, Jones, Granville Barker, Galsworthy. Even Shaw, the dominant writer of the whole movement in terms of output and reputation, only gets in with severe and revealing reservations: he is too ready to make comic or polemical points at the expense of that consistency of character and situation which is the true dramatist's 'categorical imperative'. He is talented – perhaps more talented than several better dramatists – but he fails to concentrate on his job.

Dramatic realism, then, is a way of drawing a firm line between the proper playwrights and the others, of policing the boundaries of the profession against interlopers who might compromise the purity of the product and undermine its value. Archer is not claiming that the professionals are greater writers than the amateurs, merely that they work at the business and know what they are about as no outsider can. They form not so much a literary pantheon as a technical elite: they supply London with decent drama, rather as their contemporaries in engineering supply it with decent water, by the intelligent application of generally agreed principles. What they do may be pedestrian and unpretentious compared with the flights of the poets, but unlike such flights, it is workmanlike, stageable, and based on real life.

Conceived of like this, realism is not just a dramatic convention, it is a moral code. Archer speaks, indicatively, of 'sober imitation'; conversely, what seduces the playwright from his proper imitative path is intoxication, self-indulgence, extravagance. The dramatist proper refrains from such excesses: he uses the resources of the theatre responsibly. He accepts the wholesome disciplines of natural dialogue and consistent character, and his dramatic effects are not flashy and gratuitous but *earned* – that is, motivated and plausible. He is tempted, of course, to pile in lurid sensation like Webster, or to interrupt the action for a socialist diatribe like Shaw, but he (the true dramatist) *resists temptation*. Realist drama is the stage formula for a morality of prudence, efficiency, self-control, paying one's way – in short, for a bourgeois morality.

Realist convention is equipped for this ideological role in two particular ways. The first is the drama's moral foundation in a sort of reality principle. To accept things as they are, not as one would like them to be, is not only a formal rule of this drama, but also an explicit theme. Thus in Pinero's *The Second Mrs Tanqueray* (1893), Mr Tanqueray's vaguely utopian second marriage splits on the immovable rocks of social convention; and in Shaw's *Arms and the Man* (1894), the heroine has romantic illusions about both war and men, which the action forces her to revise. One of these examples is a tragic social drama, and the other is a parodic comedy; they have entirely different generic and political atmospheres. But their underlying dramatic formula is the same: the tempering of desire by its encounter with the recalcitrance of fact. Characters *realize* themselves by learning to be realistic about life; experience is the moral teacher. So when Archer's 'exaggerative' principle interferes with the representation of the real, allowing it to be skewed by wish fulfilment or doctored for rhetorical effect, it betrays not only the drama's artistic nature but also its ethical purpose.

Secondly, realist convention redeems theatricality. Victorian middle-class culture included a puritan strain still deeply inimical to the stage, with its artifice, eroticism and gratuitous physical display. The values of nineteenth-century Nonconformity – moral seriousness, self-restraint, sincerity – are almost definingly untheatrical ones; 'character' itself, as a moral ideal, signifies a 'uniform integrity of the self' (Auerbach 1990: 4) which is the logical opposite of the theatre's playful shifting of identities. If any theatre is to fit into this value system, it must be the realist theatre, where artifice and display are at once restrained from extravagance by the criterion of plausibility and saved from their scandalous vanity by being *put to work*. Here, autonomous theatricality is as far as possible suppressed; the theatrical sign is to appear not in its own right, but by virtue of its contribution to the task of imitating life as it really is; the essential attitude of the actor is one of deference to the non-theatrical humanity he seeks to reproduce. In short, realism is the sign that the theatre possesses that vital talisman of cultural validity, seriousness. In Oscar Wilde's reverberantly topical phrase, the realistic dramatist is the one who both acknowledges and covets the importance of being earnest (Glavin 1991: 99).

It seems that the observers who can see this configuration best are the Protestant Irish *émigrés* – Wilde himself, George Bernard Shaw, W. B. Yeats. Their position somehow afforded the right mix of insight and outsideness *vis-à-vis* the Nonconformist English middle class. Billed as 'a trivial comedy for serious people', *The Importance of Being Earnest* (1895) seizes consciously on the question of 'serious drama'. Starting (and finishing) with the conversion of the keyword 'earnest' into a silly pun, it refuses seriousness seriously, point by point, and this, as we might expect by now, also entails refusing realism, by mounting the characters on a plot whose whimsical symmetries and arbitrary motivations flaunt and enjoy their own unreality. Within a year or two, Shaw started writing his *Three Plays for Puritans*, which were eventually published together in 1901. The rationale for the title is roughly this: being constitutively in earnest, the English bourgeoisie have no idea how to play. Either they are seriously in pursuit of edification, in which case they go to church, or else they are seriously in pursuit of pleasure, in which case they go to the music-hall or worse. English drama is therefore hopelessly compromised; seeking to please everyone and offend no one, it ends up with a mixture of vapid sensuality and sentimental moralism which is both ethically and intellectually corrupting. The only exit Shaw can see from this sink of prim depravity is to bid frankly for the earnest audience – to abandon feeble pleasure-seeking, declare the theatre a place of edification, and confide in the moral seriousness and spiritual energy of the Nonconformist middle class. Hence the need to write plays for Puritans. Shaw's argument, like Wilde's play, is a complicated cross-cultural tease, but unlike the play, it sheds most of its ironies by the end: Shaw, as a self-styled 'dramatic realist', really is proposing the birth of serious English drama from the union of theatre and the Puritan tradition.

This is the seriousness which the other Ascendancy *émigré*, Yeats, calls the Accusation of Sin. Truly great literature, he says (also in 1901), is the Forgiveness of Sin, but the utilitarian muse of the nineteenth century took its dramatis personae apart like clockwork, always knowing, judging, recommending improvements. 'The Accusation of Sin produced its necessary fruit, hatred of all that was abundant, extravagant, exuberant, of all that sets sail for shipwreck, and flattery of the commonplace emotions and conventional ideals of the mob, the chief Paymaster of accusation' (Yeats 1961: 105). Yeats's terminology is deliberately extravagant: he is not only setting out the opposition but also taking sides. That does not diminish the hostile accuracy with which he nails the components of professional drama: democracy, moralism, commercial prudence. His immediate context is a discussion of Shakespeare criticism, but he could easily be talking about, say, Henry Arthur Jones's 'serious' hit of 1894, *The Case of Rebellious Susan*.[3]

Susan is Lady Susan Harabin, her rebelliousness is her determination to leave her philandering husband, and the case is handled by her uncle, who coaxes and bullies her back into the marital fold in the nick of time: 'Now, my very dear Sue. . . . It's time this pretty little escapade was ended. People are beginning to talk about you, and you've gone just as far as is possible to go without running the risk of becoming déclassé' (H. A. Jones 1982: 142). The uncle (his name, rather pointedly, is Sir Richard Kato) is a sort of domestic counter-insurgency specialist, who goes about quelling rebellious women with a mixture, adoringly noted in the stage directions, of tenderness and firmness, severity and twinkling humour. This tactical role rests on an elaborately supportive dramatic infrastructure: Sir Richard is a distinguished marital lawyer, he has the witty lines, he has an unhappy love affair in his past so that he cannot be suspected of heartlessness, he is played by the actor-manager and star of the company, Charles Wyndham, and he is opposed ideologically only by a young feminist who is obviously silly and self-deluding. Serene in the possession of this formidably stacked deck, Sir Richard is principally seen in two recurrent actions – watching other characters keenly in order to detect the feelings they are trying to conceal, and persuading them in warm and friendly tête-à-têtes that it is impossible for them to do what they want. In both these projects he always succeeds in the end: he is the reality principle incarnate.

It seems that Wyndham's role in the production was ironically similar to his role in the play. Ten months elapse between Acts I and II; during this time Lady Susan travels abroad and has, it is unambiguously clear from the published script, an affair with a man in Cairo – a token revenge, if nothing else, for the many infidelities of her husband. As actor-manager, Wyndham came to the defence at once of the heroine's purity and of the double standard, insisting on toning down the dialogue so as to leave open at least the possibility that what happened in Cairo was an innocent indiscretion (Stephens 1992: 171–2). Jones refused, but the actors cut the offending lines in performance anyway, thus withdrawing even the timid provocation the author had intended, and rendering complete the play's reverence towards 'commonplace emotions and conventional ideals'. Thus we see the play's *raisonneur*, its heroine, its producer, and its author, all being, with varying degrees of reluctance, 'realistic', in the quite brutal sense that their relationship with immediate social reality is one of unconditional surrender.

In one curiously sadistic scene, Lady Susan's lover, who has gone to New Zealand and married somebody else, has sent home pieces of his wedding cake; Lady Susan has to unwrap her piece under the keen eye of Sir Richard, pretending all the time not to be upset. The audience watch her squirming and vainly trying to move her chair out of his line of vision. This is precisely the theatre of 'hatred of all that sets sail for shipwreck': on-stage and off-stage spectators watch the weak woman with the same accusing scrutiny. With sympathy, to be sure, but still, it's her fault – she shouldn't have compromised herself. In this form, then, the idea of plays for Puritans is a highly repressive one. It is moralist, realist, professional. But its moralism is the fear of scandal; its realism is an uncritical coming to terms with whatever institutions and values are currently prevalent; its accusations are levelled at the frail and powerless. And above all, its professionalism consists of supplying the market with whatever it needs: that is the deference which underlies all the others. Jones and Wyndham are not so foolish as to expose themselves, as theatre practitioners, to the condemning and pitying gaze which they turn on their rebellious heroine: they make sure that their position remains competitive.

However, the professional-Puritan formation cuts two ways. We can sketch the other way by turning to an event at the far end, so to speak, of Archer's canonical space: the performance of Granville Barker's *Waste* in November 1907.

The play is a modern tragedy. Its protagonist, Henry Trebell, is a brilliant young politician who seems as the play opens to be on the point of obtaining real power. In classic tragic fashion, however, success arrives at the same moment as disgrace: a woman named Amy O'Connell, whom he slept with once at a weekend house party, comes to tell him that she is pregnant; then, interpreting his preoccupied and ambiguous response as a rejection, she goes off alone to a backstreet abortionist who causes her death. The scandal doesn't become public, but its reverberations destroy Trebell's standing with his new political allies. They drop him, and he shoots himself.

This bald outline is enough to show how confidently *Waste* inhabits the same conventions as *The Case of Rebellious Susan*. There is the same cast of titled or professional characters, in the same West End drawing-rooms, the same sedulously informal dialogue. Again the action is organized around an imperfectly concealed transgression which exemplifies the impossibility of evading reality; and again this realist emphasis is at the same time a form of accusation, as the apparently complete public man is detected and dismantled by the relentless course of the drama. But if the landscape is familiar, the moves within it are sharply different.

For example: *too* seriously realistic to leave his hero's political life as a vaguely evoked atmosphere of importance, Barker provides him with an entire Parliamentary crisis. It concerns the disestablishment of the Church of England. Both major parties have accepted that this measure is inevitable: the question of the hour is whether the Church is going to be disestablished by its traditional friends in the Conservative Party or by its traditional adversaries in the Liberal Party; and the question behind that is 'what's to be done with the church's money?' (H. G. Barker 1987: 166).[4] Trebell's position is subtle. He is an independent reformer who is trying to get hold of the disestablishment issue through a tactical alliance with the Conservatives. His idea is to use the money to endow a network of high-quality teacher training colleges. The deal would be that the Church could write whatever doctrinal requirements it wanted into the curriculum of these colleges, so that its money was still being applied to religious purposes; while the State would obtain the means to raise schoolteaching to the status of a properly recognized and rewarded profession.

In part, this scheme is an outrageous political sleight of hand (it depends on the Conservative rank and file failing to notice that they're supporting an immense, egalitarian extension of State power). But Trebell is not simply an opportunist. At one point, he explains to his friend Wedgecroft why he wants to carry disestablishment in this paradoxical way:

> D'you know why really I went back on the Liberals over this question? Not because they wanted the Church money for their pensions . . but because all they can see in Disestablishment is destruction. Any fool can destroy! I'm not going to let a power like the Church get loose from the State. A thirteen hundred years' tradition of service . . and all they can think of is to cut it adrift! (p. 183)

The aim, as Wedgecroft remarks, is a 'secular Church'. Trebell is an Edwardian heir of Matthew Arnold, trying to separate the dogma of the Church from its cultural role and preserve the latter alone in the form of State education.

He is not, in other words, a simply secular and progressive figure. As Trebell's crisis develops, it becomes clear that the figures he really respects are Lord Charles Cantelupe, who is the leader of the High Church group in the Conservative Party, and Amy's husband, Justin O'Connell, who is an Irish Roman Catholic and a medieval historian. Both are deeply opposed to him, but he is more drawn to them than to his worldly allies, because their attitudes are based on coherent sets of ideas, not just on spontaneous reactions and calculations of advantage – in one word, because they are serious. And it is not an accident of the story that the model for this seriousness is religion. Religious faith is interesting to Trebell, and to the play as a whole, because it provides a tradition and a frame of reference strong enough to resist currently prevailing conventions. The man with no faith, in this sense, is the acting leader of the Conservative group, Lord Horsham. He is the graceful architect of compromises who, if the play had been by Jones or Pinero, would have been the authorial exponent of its ethos: conventional but not stuffy, businesslike but never vulgar, clear-sighted without unbecoming cynicism. In Barker's context he appears as a pleasant and deeply immoral old man.

So if Barker's 'realism' is formally the same as Jones's, its orientation is opposite: it signifies not a prudential coming to terms with a coercive status quo, but a critical examination of the status quo by the light of an independent standard of truth. There are realisms of right and left, you could say. In both, the dramatic values are carried by a character who sees things as they really are; but whereas in 'right' realism this hero sees things as they are because he *accepts* them as they are, in 'left' realism the hero sees them as they are precisely because of his passionate desire to change them. This is the realism which Shaw defined in his eccentric but influential pamphlet of 1891 as 'the Quintessence of Ibsenism'. According to this theory, modern society is full of people who are being imprisoned and harmed by the institutions within which they live – marriage, patriotism, duty, respectability – but who lack the courage to break with them. To resolve this contradiction, the sufferers devise comfortingly beautiful pictures of the institutions, and convince themselves that the pictures are real. Shaw's collective term for this manœuvre is Idealism, and 'Ibsenist' drama is revolutionary, not because it directly demands social change, but because it demolishes Ideals and thus disables the psychological mechanisms which made the existing institutions look bearable. In other words, if Sir Richard Kato is realistic because he *enforces prevailing realities*, 'Ibsenism' is realistic because it *subverts prevailing illusions*.

Shaw's tract was the manifesto of a movement. Its immediate occasion was the foundation of the Independent Theatre, a small-scale non-profit-making company committed to new writing. Its opening production (in 1891) was *Ghosts*, and the famous torrent of shocked abuse it provoked from the London press partly accounts for Shaw's adversarial version of Ibsen himself. The Independent Theatre closed in 1898, but was rapidly succeeded by the Stage Society and other similar groups. 'Ibsenism' was a definite theatrical practice, playing semi-professional matinées and Sunday performances to artistically and politically progressive audiences, and trying by these means to open up a non-commercial space for new drama (Woodfield 1984).

That it was non-commercial, in fact, was one of the most important things about it. The realistic defines itself against comfortable illusions; it follows that the realities it is most of all concerned with will be the unpalatable ones, the ones which society gets along by denying. This is a theatre which does not set out to please people: quite the reverse. It is therefore incompatible in principle with the kind of management whose first priority is to maximize ticket sales. The virtual certainty that an 'Ibsenist' play will make a loss is not so much an incidental inconvenience as a point of honour: that is how the show declares that it is not a confection, not mere entertainment – in short, that it is serious. Thus, paradoxically, the values we saw emerging from the business logic of late-nineteenth-century theatre (earnestness, sober imitation) become, in this particularly intense version, anti-business values. Having made himself professional to secure his place in the West End, the dramatic realist goes one step further and rejects the West End because it compromises his professionalism.

The trouble with this honourably embattled position is that it threatens to make theatrical failure the criterion of dramatic success, a self-defeating bind which would lead the newly staged 'serious' dramatists straight back into the study. Part of Granville Barker's importance in the first decade of the twentieth century was his firm grasp of this dilemma. Equally uninterested in vapid success and heroic failure, he looked for ways of basing a commercially sustainable management on the growing audience for serious literary drama, and with J. E. Vedrenne, in a series of seasons at the Court Theatre in 1904–7, effectively invented the modern repertory system as a compromise between the tyranny of the open-ended run and the single performance of the progressive ghetto. The story of the Barker–Vedrenne management, with its mixture of creative programming and creative accounting, is well documented and too complicated to tell here (see Kennedy 1985). What matters about it immediately is that, in so far as it was a success, it brought 'Ibsenism' in from the margins and established (largely with scripts by Shaw) a 'realist' opposition within the mainstream of London theatre. It was while he was engaged in this project, as director, actor and manager, that Barker wrote *Waste*.

To see the connection, we have to take one more angle into account. In 1904, just before embarking on the Court venture, Barker had produced, with Archer, a costed proposal for a National Theatre; in 1907, as it ended, they published their scheme (Archer and Barker 1907). It envisaged, precisely, a London repertory theatre, obliged by its charter to pursue excellence before profit, and supported by an endowment large enough to enable it to do so. The Court season, improvised, precarious, hectic, was no model of the conditions which Barker felt were needed to do really good work; rather, it was the best possible sketch, under the circumstances, for a serious theatre of the future.

Trebell's visionary scam, then, is distinctly reverberant. At the end of *The Quintessence of Ibsenism*, Shaw demands an Ibsen Theatre, arguing that Ibsen is the modern equivalent of Scripture, and should be inculcated and expounded as systematically as the Bible is read in churches:

When we ask for an endowed theatre we always take the greatest pains
to assure everybody that we do not mean anything unpleasantly serious,
and that our endowed theatre will be as bright and cheery (meaning as
low and common) as the commercial theatres. As a result of which we
get no endowment. When we have the sense to profit by this lesson and
promise that our endowed theatre will be an important place, and that
it will make people of low tastes and tribal or commercial ideas horribly
uncomfortable by its efforts to bring conviction of sin to them, we shall
get endowment as easily as the religious people who are not foolishly
ashamed to ask for what they want. (Shaw 1930: 160)[5]

This is exactly the combination of identification and predation that characterizes Trebell's attitude to organized religion. His scheme to remake the national Church for the purposes of contemporary enlightenment is a projection
of his creator's scheme for a theatre of education, an 'exemplary theatre' as he
put it in a later book (H. G. Barker 1922). Although Shaw is teasing again, his
phrase is accurate: both in its imaginary expropriation of the Church and in its
own ambitious and serious realism, *Waste* proposes a theatre which will be 'an
important place'.

A place also, as Yeats would expect, of accusation, if it is really part of its
programme 'to bring conviction of sin' to its subsidized audiences. But here
again, as with the concepts of realism and professionalism, *Waste*, and the
theatre culture it represents, turn the question sharply. We can see this, for
instance, in the figure of Amy O'Connell, the woman who dies. In many ways,
she is the weak and erring woman again, caught in a far harsher light than Mrs
Tanqueray and Lady Susan and the rest of their sisters in the West End. She
is married but leads an empty social life apart from her husband; she is
flirtatious in a clever and trivial way; she is disliked by most of the other
women in the play, and the two men she is involved with, O'Connell and
Trebell, are both horrified by her miserable death but do not really mourn her.
It can seem that the play is implacable in its condemnation of her. But the
writing is different from that. In her only big scene, she appears in Trebell's
office, pregnant, frightened and resentful, a few minutes before his crucial
meeting with Lord Charles Cantelupe. He is conscientious and businesslike,
accepting his responsibilities without reservation and without enthusiasm; he
has barely time for all this, but he will have to make time, and he can; if she
will wait until after his meeting, he will give her all his attention and take
every necessary step. There is nothing in all this efficiency to meet her quite
differently centred demands: she wants it to have been love; she wants some
power over her body which has been used first by Trebell and now by the baby;
she wants an abortion – what she wants is both more and less tangible than
what he can offer. The dialogue swings the audience violently back and forth
between the two unmeeting worlds:

AMY: You might have some pity for me . . I'm so afraid.

TREBELL: (*Touched*) Indeed . . indeed, I'll take what share of this I can. (*She shrinks from him unforgivingly.*)

AMY: No, let me alone. I'm nothing to you. I'm a sick beast in danger of my life, that's all . . cancerous!

(*He is roused for the first time, roused to horror and protest.*)

TREBELL: Oh, you unhappy woman! . . if life is like death to you . .

AMY: (*Turning on him*) Don't lecture me! If you're so clever put a stop to this horror. Or you might at least say you're sorry.

TREBELL: Sorry! (*The bell on the table rings jarringly.*) Cantelupe! (*He goes to the telephone. She gets up cold and collected . . .*)

AMY: I mustn't keep you from governing the country. I'm sure you'll do it very well.

(H. G. Barker 1987: 192)

What is new about this writing is that each speaker marks the boundary, so to speak, of the other's system of values. Trebell's philosophic turn of mind displays the complexity which is invisible to Amy because she is trapped inside it; while her responses highlight the unconscious brutality which is inseparable from his competence. So that while the scene is preoccupied with morality, it cannot be moralistic because the extreme individuation of the dramatic languages has the effect of putting all the available moral categories at risk. This is another paradoxical reversal: the idea of individual character, which in Jones and Pinero provides the object of judgement, is here taken so seriously that judgement is disconcerted by the clash of values. Moral criticism mutates into a critique of moralities: if anyone is being accused of sin, it is not so much the play's fallible characters as its successful ones, those whose agreeable social world requires such cruelty for its routine maintenance.

That this different accusation was audible in 1907 is suggested by the fate of the play. Prepared as the centrepiece of a new Barker–Vedrenne season at the Savoy, it was refused a licence by the Lord Chamberlain's office and received only two private performances. Norman McKinnel, the actor who had already rehearsed the enormous role of Trebell, was forced to pull out by his commercial management, who were frightened of even an indirect connection with a banned show. A public furore ensued, during which it became clear that while every playwright of importance was opposed to the pre-censorship of scripts, the system was broadly supported by theatrical managers, for whom a licence was an effective guarantee of legal immunity and therefore a security for their investment in a new play. State censorship and private ownership turned out to form a single smoothly running system; Barker's attempt to foster non-commercial theatre in a special enclave of the profession had reached its harshly policed limits. The play was not licensed for public

performance until 1920, by which time its moment had passed. Its bitter title
acquired a special appropriateness.

*Waste*, with its single-mindedly realist technique, its intense moral seriousness, and its fierce handling of political worldliness, is more truly a 'play for
Puritans' than Shaw's own. What Barker had been doing, like his hero Trebell,
was smuggling this uncompromising material into the mainstream by forming cunning alliances with sections of the establishment. And like Trebell's
rejection, the play's suppression by that establishment was a refusal of moral
seriousness disguised as a defence of moral standards. This sleight of hand was
exposed four years later when the job of censor went to Charles Brookfield, an
adaptor of French farces whose indecency was accepted as harmless because
evidently trivial. He hated Barker's work and continued to censor his protégés.
Thus if the middle-class professional theatre demanded 'serious' plays – earnest, sincere, Puritan, realistic – it was only up to a point. There was such a
thing as being too realistic, too much a Puritan; and the penalty for this
transgression was instant return to the progressive ghetto of private performance, from which Barker had escaped with such wasted subtlety. The story
reminds us that if English dramatic naturalism now seems timid and limited
in its achievement, this is partly because the State intervened directly to stop
it from being anything more.

## 3   No Magic Casements

In this profoundly compromised sense, then, naturalism dominates drama as
the form of the theatrical profession's seriousness. At this point we can return
to J. B. Priestley in 1948, fretting and conspiring against 'downright naturalism' but also 'coming to terms with it' because it is the prevailing theatrical
tradition, and 'a play that has never found a theatre, actors, audiences, is not
really a play at all. A dramatist is a writer who works in and for the Theatre'
(Priestley 1948: I, vii). In that slightly reverent capital T, we can now
recognize the ethos of Archer's heroes, the unpretentious professionals who
serve the stage as it is. Not high-falutin artists, but honest craftsmen.

In mounting this equivocal defence, Priestley is thinking above all of his
most recent play, *The Linden Tree*. Moderately successful in the West End in
1947, it adopts naturalistic conventions without apparent reservation: from a
formal point of view you could say that here, at least, 'the theatrical tradition
of our time' has routed the fretting and conspiring.

The play is about a Professor of History in a provincial town called
Burnanley. It is his sixty-fifth birthday, and two things are happening simultaneously: his grown-up children have all come back to the family home to
mark the occasion, and the university authorities are putting pressure on him
to retire. He wants to continue his work, and the family are divided about

whether he should or not: all his ideological and emotional dilemmas are therefore neatly packed into a single weekend.

This dramatic structure exemplifies the normal procedure of the 'naturalistic tradition' – to assemble the issues in a single time and space, and at the same time to devise for that conscious and intentional conjunction a faked naturalness. The Professor's children, for example, are an anthology of possible attitudes to life: over-simplifying only slightly, we could say that his son is Money and his daughters are Socialism, Religion and Joy. The real reason why all these personages are in the same room is that they have been assembled there for a debate about the values which govern our lives together; the ostensible reason (that they have come home for a family celebration) is a pretext.

What makes such subterfuge necessary is a conflict between public and private discourses. On the one hand, Priestley is a socialist: he believes in the importance of shared values and shared social practices, and conceives of the theatre as a forum for public issues. This idea is present in the most directly thematic sense in this play, where the Professor's proposed retirement appears as a withdrawal from civic action into private contentment, and as such is eventually refused with indignation. On the other hand, the dramatic tradition whose ascendancy Priestley more or less acknowledges is one of domestic interiors, individual dilemmas, private lives. There is a tension between what is to be said and the language available for saying it; and the solution is to smuggle the public categories into the private space by disguising them as random contingencies. The opening of the play almost parodies this tactic: the housekeeper shows a visitor into the Professor's study, explaining apologetically that the sitting room ceiling has just collapsed. This cunning mishap, which keeps the sitting room out of service for the whole of the play, forces the entire cast to use the study as its social space. This ensures that the Professor conducts this domestic life in the space where he does his work, and so suspends the alienation between public and private spheres which the layout of an ordinary bourgeois home is designed to maintain.

But if at the level of conscious intention this concentration into one place is a mechanical device, the chosen mechanism has its own imaginative presence. Priestley notes more than once – it is evidently important to him – that he wrote it during the severe winter of 1946–7, when he was confined to his own study by a combination of the snow and the post-war fuel shortage. *The Linden Tree* is consciously a play of austerity, the shortages out of which it was written recorded not only in the Professor's inability to pay for the upkeep of his house, but also in the theatre's preference for a play with a small cast and a single set. Thus the whole show – its conception, its writing, its staging, its fictional situation – is consistently and as it were definingly a thing with no lavishness about it. As Priestley says, 'on the familiar "colour and glamour" of the theatre, no play could have been made out of less promising material. It opened no magic casements for anybody. It confronted our audiences with their own drab scene' (Priestley 1948: I, x).

There is a kind of sulky pride about that way of putting it which is characteristic of the ideology of naturalism. Others may indulge in the gaudy delusions of theatricality; serious playwrights confront their audience with the sober truth. But in fact the play itself is thematically preoccupied with just this opposition. Again and again in the text, Burnanley appears as a grey, shabby, gloomy town, as opposed to the colour and pleasure variously represented by the Professor's own high culture and by the luxurious lifestyle of his successful son. 'Colour and glamour' – precisely the theatrical elements which the play rejects in favour of serious talk – are repeatedly and seriously talked *about*. The show is built around what it has agreed to do without. Most uneasily, and suggestively, in this confession of the Professor's:

> I was telling my family, who don't care a damn, that we're trying to do a wonderful thing here. And so we are. But somehow not in a wonderful way. There's a kind of grey chilly hollowness inside, where there ought to be gaiety, colour, warmth, vision. Sometimes our great common enterprise seems only a noble skeleton, as if the machines had already sucked the blood and marrow out of it. (p. 475)

The great common enterprise is the 1945 Labour government, and the wonderful thing we're trying to do is to carry through a socialist revolution without violence. It is questioned in a tone of plaintive bewilderment – 'trying', 'somehow', 'kind of' – why can we not do it wonderfully? why is the commitment to the common enterprise also a commitment to drab lives, bad cooking, chilly sobriety, emotional inhibition? The wistful protest is at once political – directed against the cautious, administered welfarism of its moment – and formal – against the tight, furtive dramatic art which Priestley editorially defends.

This correspondence, between political and dramaturgic discontents, is not an accident. Schematically, we could say that Priestley's naturalism is the appropriate dramatic form of his Labourism: just as the dramatic mode is, as we have seen, the compromised and contained legacy of a bourgeois settlement in the theatre, so the ideology of the 1945 administration arguably owes its 'grey chilly hollowness inside' to its acceptance of what it inherited – the state form, the diplomatic constraints and the canons of fiscal prudence of the existing governing class. But it is also a concretely historical link. Shaw, Barker and many of their actors were members of the Fabian Society before the First World War; Lewis Casson and Sybil Thorndike (the stars of *The Linden Tree*) had ILP connections; many of the significant developments in provincial repertory theatre were influenced by local socialists (Samuel et al. 1985: 3–33). The histories of progressive naturalist theatre and middle-class Labourism overlap in complex and intimate ways. In more than a personal sense, Priestley's 'prevailing theatrical tradition' in the 1940s is twinned with his political tradition. To grasp the historical content of his uneasiness, we need to look on and beyond the margins of the immediate configuration.

There is a startling dramatization of just Priestley's problematic in a play by Sean O'Casey from the same decade, *Red Roses For Me* (1942). The play is set in Dublin at the time of the great transport strike of 1913; it could therefore be seen as a late addition to O'Casey's better known series of stagings of Irish history, such as *Juno and the Paycock* (the civil war) and *The Plough and the Stars* (the Easter Rising). But if so, it is an addition which programmatically frets against the naturalistic idiom of the earlier plays. The hero, clearly an idealized version of the young O'Casey, is both a strike leader and a poet. In the third act this figure encounters a representative group of defeated and down-and-out people on a river-bridge, and enters a sort of poetic dispute with them about whether there is any point in hoping and struggling. The dialogue already represents a well-flagged departure from realism: it makes no claim to sound like what these characters would 'really say', but offers rather to articulate what whatever they would really say would really mean – in other words, this is expressionism. But more interestingly than that, the scene is directly taking issue with naturalism, not only stylistically, but still more thematically. The poet–hero insists, against the despair of the poor, that there is no fixed and objective reality because our world is what we make it. Dublin is a bleak and bitter city but a beautiful one too; 'Meanness, spite, and common pattherns are woven thick through all her glory; but her glory's there for open eyes to see' (O'Casey 1985: 307); famously, Cathleen ni Houlihan, the legendary personi-fication of Ireland, is both a bent old woman and a radiant queen. At this point, outrageously, O'Casey hands over to his designer:

> The scene has brightened, and bright and lovely colours are being brought to them by the caress of the setting sun. The houses on the far side of the river now bow to the visible world, decked in mauve and burnished bronze; and the men that have been lounging against them now stand stalwart, looking like fine bronze statues, slashed with scarlet.
> (p. 309)

The flower-girls who have been huddling against the wall of the bridge stand up into the light in dark green robes and silver mantles. There's a song, then a dance-tune played by an unseen flute, and the poet dances with one of the girls, before the idyll is interrupted by the sound of marching feet – troops have been ordered out against the strikers.

'Gaiety, colour, warmth, vision' – the Professor's hesitant words for what is missing are here sprayed across the scene with crass literalism. Colour is particularly insistent: the lurid Maxfield Parrish palette is the schematic opposite of everyday Dublin (which, like everyday Burnanley, is grey). Thus what O'Casey is doing here is not randomly transgressing naturalist convention but pointedly negating it. All the 'extrinsic', non-imitative elements of theatre which Archer had proscribed – lyric, rhetoric, magic, music, dance, non-representational light and costume – rush on to the stage in the space of a few minutes. Of course, it is just this anxious and schematizing haste which is responsible for the scene's failure, its insubstantiality and kitsch. But that very clumsiness makes the intention clear, and revealing.

The transformation of the stage signifies derepression. The poor people on the street, crouching, lounging, huddling, are literally held down, pressed against the hard objective walls of the city, taught by experience (like Lady Susan) not to entertain desire. The hero unlocks that repression, displaying a city whose outlines are the same, but which is now, briefly, suffused with subjectivity and pleasure. The political force of the idea is indicated by the eventual arrival of the troops: it is when the mind-forged manacles are broken open that the State has to resort to the physical ones. As a myth of the role of the poet this is conventional enough; what matters for our enquiry is the way that the formula for derepression is the reassertion, against naturalism, of an autonomous theatricality. The stage, so to speak, *rebels* – shakes off its dutiful subordination to nature, and asserts its own artificial presence. The actors abandon their cramped postures, stretch themselves, and display the trained grace with which they can move; they discard their realistically shabby clothes and appear in what are obviously theatrical costumes; the lighting man drops the careful imitation of daylight and floods the place with mauve and gold. The liberation of theatricality is able to stand for political and psychological kinds of liberation; the same correspondence operates more powerfully in O'Casey's next play, *Cock-a-Doodle-Dandy* (1949), where an emotionally locked and naturalistically presented rural community is convulsed by the appearances of an enormous pantomime cock. The converse implication, which O'Casey certainly intends, is that naturalism is itself a form of repression.

In the immediate background of this proposition is Yeats. Cathleen ni Houlihan is the subject of his most uncompromisingly nationalist play (1902); the flute and dancers are almost the call-sign of the series of chamber plays which began with *At the Hawk's Well* in 1916; Cock-a-Doodle-Dandy is the raucous red cock prominent in the imagery of the most political of these plays, *The Dreaming of the Bones* (1919). The rigorous anti-naturalism of these plays can be suggested by some characteristic gestures. *At the Hawk's Well* opens with a musician's announcement:

> I call to the eye of the mind
> A well long choked up and dry . . .
> (Yeats 1982: 208)

and a few moments later one of the performers places a plain square of blue cloth on the ground, representing the well by allusion to its absent water. In *The Only Jealousy of Emer* (1919), Cuchulain in his madness is taken over by an alien spirit; his state is represented by two masks, a heroic one for his normal self, and a distorted one which the actor wears in the central section of the play. In *The Dreaming of the Bones*, a contemporary Irish activist encounters the ghosts of Diarmuid and Devorgilla, the legendary betrayers of Ireland; at the end, he says:

> A cloud floats up
> And covers all the mountain-head in a moment;
> And now it lifts and they are swept away.
>                              (Yeats 1982: 444)

The actors representing the ghosts, who have danced round the empty and plainly lit stage, walk off. In all these cases, and in the whole style they randomly stand for, the material components of the show – the masks, the music, the decor of the stage, and the performers themselves – are systematically released from the logic of imitation, to operate as symbols with their own integrity and presence. Yeats's production notes return often to the idea of proximity: it is when the audience is aware of being in the same room as the actors (precisely the awareness which naturalistic convention is designed to suppress) that the strangeness of their presentation is most intense. That the spectators should be disturbed by the unreality of what is in front of them is not (as in naturalist theatre) a solecism, but the whole point of the staging, enabling the actor, as Yeats says of his Japanese model, to inhabit, not a pictured world, but 'as it were the deeps of the mind' (Yeats 1961: 224). It is then not fortuitous that all these three plays are, thematically and precisely, rituals of derepression: the moment when the dry well floods; the curative enactment of Cuchulain's inner darkness; the encounter with the primal transgressors. Theatricality – the simultaneous presence of contingent and imaginary, actor and role, face and mask, spectators and performers – is not a distraction from the truth of the drama, but its essential condition. The appearance of spontaneity is not cultivated but scrupulously avoided; the audience's attention is arrogantly drawn to the beautiful and deliberate things which the actors are speaking and doing and wearing. (The poet, the musician, the designer, are not honest craftsmen but, precisely, high-falutin artists.) In short, theatricality is celebrated, and this shows by contrast what happens to it in the naturalistic theatre – that it is *unhappily denied*.

For Yeats, the key to his celebration was intimacy: 'As a deep of the mind can only be approached through what is most human, most delicate, we should mistrust bodily distance, mechanism, and loud noise' (p. 225). *At the Hawk's*

*Well* was written for performance in an aristocratic drawing-room, and although such conditions could hardly be the norm, the plays continue to be shaped by the ideal of a small, elite audience, and financed by patronage rather than the box office. It is instructive, then, to move across from this theatrical extreme to another contemporary one, also programmatically opposed to naturalism, but consisting precisely of bodily distance, mechanism, and loud noise:

> There we were with our gleaming megaphones, and it was a lovely summer's day, I remember, the sun beating down and the stragglers kept getting in – the workers from Earby had come over the moors and actually had had to fight their way through columns of police when they came in – bloodily – and a great cheer went up when they came in, and it was a thrilling experience to stand on the top of that truck and sing and perform, for your own people – it really was the most magnificent experience, I never will forget it – it's what theatre should be. It was what it must have been like in the time of Aeschylus in great popular theatre. (Samuel et al. 1985: 238)

This is Ewan MacColl, recalling a performance given by Red Megaphones, a Communist agitational group, in Burnley in 1932. The distance from Lady Cunard's drawing-room is immense, but the two events are surprisingly comparable. Both consciously refuse the 'prevailing' native tradition – Yeats's models were Japanese, and the thirties workers' theatre learned from the left avant-garde in Germany and Russia. Both combine stylized performance with a central role for music. Both revel in the use of a performance space which is not a custom-built theatre. Both reject naturalism in order to penetrate beyond appearances – to the archetypal ideas of Yeats's Platonism, or to the unseen workings of the capitalist system. Above all, both aspire to live in a relationship with their audiences which is entirely different from that of commercial drama. The entertainment is free; spectators have come not in order to consume a play but for a social event which would be happening anyway, which has its own energies; the show acknowledges their presence in the mobility of its arrangements and its modest running time, as well as in the foregrounding of its relationship with them as a central part of the pleasure and dynamism of the show. Despite the difference in scale, one could say that the aim in both cases is a spectacle which is not sold to customers but given to friends.

What produces these parallels, of course, is not any positive connection between the two theatrical practices, but their common situation outside the 'prevailing tradition' of what Priestley calls 'the Theatre'. Gaiety, colour, warmth and vision turn out to be the product not, as O'Casey's script gallantly hopes, of a more imaginative selection of costumes and lights, but of a different construction of the social actuality of theatre – the meeting with an audience. And it can hardly be an accident that the two cases also have in common an exceptionally decided class character. Yeats was working in an Anglo-Irish milieu which freakishly permitted him at least the fantasy of aristocratic patronage; and what MacColl means by his 'own people' is the working class, then at a high point of cultural and organizational self-definition. These two complementary amateurisms, then, confirm negatively that the naturalist English theatre, professional, serious, craftsmanlike, was deeply an institution of the middle class. Its greyness, its horror of sensuality, its ultimately inescapable abstraction, were the marks of its alienation from its audience; since its plays were commodities, and were offered, as commodities must be, to everybody and nobody.

## 4 Players

Still, a naturalist play *is* a show, whatever it says, an entertainment directed towards a real, located audience; so the determined denial of theatricality is contradictory, and the contradictions generate the energy of the form. Time and again, naturalistic characters chafe against their repression, turn out front to signal through the bars of their sealed-off world that despite the 'categorical imperatives' of verisimilitude and consistency, they know, really, where they are, and where we are. A strange series of surrogates and displacements subverts the professional closure; gives, you could say, the game away.

It surfaces, for example, in the tradition of comic characters who charmingly refuse their responsibilities. Take St John Hankin's *The Return of the Prodigal*, a Court play from 1905. The prodigal, Eustace, is the black sheep of a hypocritical business family, and his return consists of faking a critical illness at the door of the family home, and then hanging about malingering and making provocative remarks until his respectable father and brother are forced to pay him to go away. The naturalistic play represents a family's relationships, the ethics of business, and so on; but the shape of the entertainment is really determined by the playful quality of Eustace's presence on the stage. Witty, airy, devoid of self-respect, he is separated from the rest of the cast by the fact that he can say what he likes, regardless of whether it is acceptable or even true. The play begins with his arrival and ends with his departure – in other words, the device he uses to exploit his family is the fictional form of the device the dramatist uses to entertain the audience. Invention, role-playing, artistry – the denied dimensions re-infiltrate the three-walled room by means of his illicit entrance.

In a serious moment at the end, Eustace protests in passing at the very condition of the naturalist dramatis persona – being a character:

What does it matter what one *does?* It's done, and then it's over and one can forget it. The real tragedy is what one *is.* Because one can't escape from that. It's always there, the bundle of passions, weaknesses, stupidities, that one calls character, waiting to trip one up. (J. B. Marriott 1929: 528)

His formulation is interestingly illogical. Character is what one is, but also it is an enemy, waiting to trip one up. My character both is me and obstructs me. The one who is being spoken about here is Eustace-in-the-story – clever, feckless, weak-willed, and all the rest of the adjectives. But the one who is speaking is in a strange separate zone of provisional freedom, of determinability. He is Eustace-on-the-stage.

This is not Hankin's originality. Eustace's immediate ancestors are clearly Shaw's comic *raisonneurs*, such as Bluntschli in *Arms and the Man* (1894) and Dick Dudgeon in *The Devil's Disciple* (1897); and that type is itself, as Shaw himself acknowledges, the 'imperturbably impudent comedian' who was a stock figure in Victorian farce (Shaw 1971: II, 31).[6] This admission has something of the same poised impudence, as if Shaw is undermining his own claims to be regarded as a dramatic realist by coolly agreeing that he is an old-fashioned hack. Shaw's own account of that paradox tends to be couched in a style of disdainful pragmatism: too philistine to be hooked by unadorned reality, audiences need to be tickled with theatrical tricks. But this opposition between content and presentation is itself part of the naturalist system of denial. In fact, the impudent comedian is structurally central: he tends to emerge as an authorial spokesman, and it is easy to see why – it is because as the one who plays tricks, devises situations, adopts temporary roles, he is the embodiment of the play-making impulse in a formal sense, and so readily comes to embody the show's ideological impulse as well.

This logic is represented in late and schematic form, once again, by Priestley: in *An Inspector Calls* (1946), the whole action is motivated by an inquisitive intruder who appears to be a police inspector, but who ultimately turns out not to be. His investigation into the suicide of the archetypally named Eva Smith turns out to be a fictional device; a device which, moreover, is uncanny because it is not clear how the impostor possesses so much accurate information about the members of the family he tricks. This deliberate gap in the texture of the naturalism effectively declares the inspector's true identity: in his omniscience, his didactic authority, and the cunning manipulations by which he advances the dramatic action, he is clearly the playwright. Theatricality, repressed by realist convention, returns spookily as a knock at the carefully practicable door.

The device in this case is still formally comic, but the humour is squeezed out of it by the weight of authorial, not to say authoritarian, intention. This is certainly one way the structure can go: round its discontented edges, realism tends to generate author surrogates, such as the arms manufacturer in Shaw's *Major Barbara* (1905), or the doctor in T. S. Eliot's *The Cocktail Party* (1949), who after a more or less perfunctory feint at being funny, disclose angelic knowledge and apocalyptic power. But that its real home is in comedy is suggested by two prodigals a good deal less pallid than Eustace – Christy Mahon in J. M. Synge's *The Playboy of the Western World* and Captain Boyle in Sean O'Casey's *Juno and the Paycock*.

Of all the plays in the tradition we have been exploring, these are the only two whose place in the repertoire now seems entirely secure. Their first nights in Dublin (in 1907 and 1924 respectively) confirmed the Abbey Theatre as an 'important place', and their profile in Irish theatre now reminds an English observer of Shakespeare – the same rich challenge to new directors and actors, tainted by the same undertone of wearisome familiarity. One critical response to this anomalously classic status is to deny that either script is naturalistic; and certainly both writers were passing through the three-walled room on a theatrical course which took in expressionist or poetic forms as well. But it is hard to refuse the label to the densely realized interiors and intricately reconstructed colloquial idioms of both plays, without erecting a criterion of naturalism so rigorous as to exclude almost everything.

But then both plays rest on plots of central, structuring misapprehension. Christy's identity for most of the play is that of the man who killed his father (who is alive), and the dramatic shape of *Juno* is determined by the family's belief that they have come into money (which is a misunderstanding). Factual error is the ingeniously placed flaw in the naturalistic texture through which theatrical consciousness can enter. The contextual determinants of the action are a matter of social and historical realism – the mingled lawlessness and docility of Synge's Mayo community, the civil war that surrounds and penetrates the Boyles' tenement room. But the fish that swim in these waters are explicitly imaginary. And then, in harmony with that plotted suspension of the real, both protagonists exist in the comic gap between self and role. Christy is not the playboy, but a diffident kid who turns himself into one through his flailing attempts to live up to his fortuitous reputation: in a comic inversion of Eustace's gloomy insight, it doesn't matter what one *is*, one can forget it; the real matter is what one *does*, in the present, on the stage. And the Captain is not a Captain, but a sponging fantasist; the Paycock's bright feathers are a fake. At one level, the text punishes him for this failure of realism with puritan savagery, but the writing also keeps offering the actor opportunities to subvert that closure with a clown's immediacy, finding in the character's shameless fibs a boozed and shifty utopianism. Much later, as we saw, O'Casey makes his endorsement of the fantasist unconditional, and the Paycock mutates into the frankly anti-naturalist, monstrously liberating bird of *Cock-a-Doodle-Dandy*. But despite the energy of that extraordinary and underrated play, the established preference for the O'Casey of the 1920s is not incomprehensible. It is the tension between naturalistic placing and unplaced fantasy which pulls the thread taut: the unconditional supremacy of either mode induces a sort of slackening.

The thread itself, the mediating element, is comic irony. O'Casey's play is a tragedy, but it is the tragedy of Juno and her children. The Captain is immune, because unlike them he never does anything, just keeps on acting. Comparably, the playboy leaves the heroine traumatized and grieving, but he himself goes back on the road he came in from, on to the next shebeen, the next play. At its most precise and vigorous, naturalism is rescued for the theatre by the denaturing power of the audience's laughter. Theatre writing at this pitch, then, confirms by contrast Shaw's diagnosis of the English bourgeois inability to play. Only in Ireland, at one remove from the canons of earnestness which English naturalism embodied, was it possible to find a stage which was playful and important at the same time, and where, consequently, the always contradictory project of 'naturalist theatre' could momentarily be realized.

## NOTES

1  For a brief and sceptical account, see Booth 1991: 51–6. An interesting case for the Bancrofts' historical influence is made in McDonald 1984.
2  Interestingly, a closely similar performance is required for the role of Esther, the dancer who is the heroine of the best-known of Tom Robertson's own plays, *Caste* (1867).
3  The play ran for 164 nights, was published in 1897, and is conveniently available in H. A. Jones 1982: 104–61.
4  The scene in which the political situation is explained was completely rewritten in a 1926 revision of the play, and the other modern edition – the one in *Plays: one* (H. G. Barker 1993) – unfortunately uses the rewrite. I am discussing the play of 1907.
5  This chapter was added to the edition of 1913, so it does not anticipate Barker's campaign, but reflects it.
6  Shaw is thinking of plays from the 1860s and 1870s which he describes as 'forgotten' even in 1900. But there are earlier instances in plays which have been revived – for example, Sir Dudley Smooth in Edward Bulwer-Lytton's *Money* (1840) or Dazzle in Dion Boucicault's *London Assurance* (1841). And nearer home, it seems clear that another legatee of the tradition is Wilde's Algernon Moncrieff.

# 10

# Playing It Straight: Proper Drama

## 1 Modern Drama

In 1956 the relic of a past age reminisces: 'The England I left was one I remembered in 1914, and I was happy to remember it that way.' The passing of Edwardian England was being formally announced on the English stage. At that moment in 1956 the theatre seemed to have caught up with the rest of British society, which was witnessing the decay of empire, the establishment of the welfare state and above all the emergence of youth culture, with its rock'n'roll and gangs of Teddy boys in their pastiche versions of Edwardian fashion. The first performances of John Osborne's *Look Back in Anger* were taken to present 'post-war youth as it really is'. Later on, its status was quickly established as a decisive point of change, seen as 'the beginning of a revolution in the British theatre, and as the central and most immediately influential expression of the mood of its time, the mood of the "angry young man"' (Osborne 1976: 68, blurb).

The anger of the young generation was directed against a stuffy, traditionalist society, with old-fashioned values and behaviour. Up to now the commercial theatre had been taken to be a typical institution of that society, recycling plays based on worn-out formulas, set in now-dead worlds. All of that appeared to change with *Look Back in Anger*, with its attacks on the myths of Edwardian England, upper-class snobbery and repressive proprieties. Like the rest of youth culture, the play seemed to express its noise and violence against a present that felt bland, empty, without 'great causes'. It kicked back against what we would call modern alienation.

The play makes a theatrical image of this alienation when its hero, Jimmy, and his friend, Cliff, do a rehearsed music-hall routine, involving comic patter and a song. It is an ironic image of a form of popular entertainment that avoids the expression of deep and discontented emotion. Much of Jimmy's anger about modern shallowness comes from his childhood experience of the death of his father, a man who returned wounded from the Spanish Civil War, only to be rejected by the rest of his family. The defence of Spanish democracy against fascism was one of the great causes of the 1930s for which leftists in Britain volunteered to fight. In the death of his neglected father, Jimmy sees a modern embarrassment about great causes and human distress. His anger is thus a form of nostalgia about the loss of causes to fight for and the loss of a sense of humanity. 'I've an idea. Why don't we have a little game? Let's pretend we're human beings, and that we're actually alive. Just for a while. What do you say? Let's pretend we're human' (Osborne 1976: 15). Expressed that way, and put alongside his bitter music-hall routine, this nostalgia could also be said to long for a form of drama which aims to be fully human.

Jimmy's feelings about great causes, modern emptiness and acting human don't come out of the blue. Over a decade before, a director of the Festival Theatre in Cambridge, Joseph Macleod, had expressed his own dissatisfaction with modern entertainment and emptiness. He did it in a book about the Russian theatre of the 1930s. There he describes the emergence in 1927 of 'Accessible Theatre' – 'its realism bright and definite, its sense of communal history broad and fervent, overtaking at a single stroke the vague theories, the crude immediacies, of the Left-Wing theatres'. The Accessible Theatre rejected directors such as Meyerhold and Tairov, whose work could be described as modernist. In Tairov's productions, for example, life 'turned allegorical in his fingers; and that is not the attitude of a great revolutionary, nor of a great artist. It is the attitude of a man who puts ideas before sympathy, an attitude all too common among minor producers and minor poets who lead the middle-class arts in other countries.' By contrast, great stage work has always sought to increase 'humanity' in drama, and that is what proper Soviet art does: 'It would be strange if the Soviet system, in freeing the individual life, throttled the individual in culture.' Where the majority of the audiences are 'simple country folk', then 'Daring and originality were not a matter of thinking out tricks, but came from studying the world, the outlook of people, the ideas we have' (Macleod 1943: 113, 94, 63, 13, 18).

Macleod's brief history of the Estonian theatre puts in a nutshell the Accessible Theatre's advantages: 'At the independence of Estonia in 1918, the theatre started down the fashionable continental road of discontented experimentation. . . . Mass scenes were given predominance over the quiet character studies of the older generation. . . . But little by little the deeper methods of the Moscow Art Theatre won their way back, as they were doing in Soviet Russia' (Macleod 1943: 90). When it was forcibly joined to Stalin's Soviet Union – with its individual life organized into gulags – Estonia apparently learnt the values of a theatre that is deep, traditional, without tricks, anti-experimental, human.

The common word for this Accessible Theatre is naturalism. Naturalism is conceived as the form of drama which is not side-tracked by artiness. It is the dramatic expression of everything which is important about being human. Thus a few years after Jimmy Porter's plea that we act human, the Shakespeare scholar G. Wilson Knight said that 'the two most vital soul-impulses of our century' – the forces which shape our psychology, our religion and our future – are expressed in the work of one of the leading naturalist dramatists, Ibsen (Knight 1962: 115). The soul-impulses of the twentieth century are expressed by someone writing in the mid to late nineteenth century. How can this be?

It is because naturalism, as it is seen here, is not the art form of a particular period or culture. Instead it is the name given to any drama which is interested in being truthfully human. So, by this definition, it can be found surfacing at all sorts of different periods. One person sees it in the transition from medieval to Elizabethan drama, another in *commedia dell'arte* and Garrick. According to G. Wilson Knight, Ibsen's work reaches all the way back to the ancient Greece of *Oedipus Tyrannus* and Euripides. It also has links, as things usually do, with Shakespeare.

In between times, when the theatre seems more interested in art than in human beings, there are 'experimental' periods. One such is the 1930s and 1940s in England, with its experiments with documentary dramas and 'Living Newspapers', political pantomimes and revues, agitational theatre and cartoon, verse dramas and dance theatre.[1] In the standard histories of English drama all of this work is assumed to be part of the inaccessible, elitist, middle-class theatre from which audiences – and drama itself – were to be saved by the arrival of *Look Back in Anger*. For *Anger* brought back into the theatre 'All the qualities . . . qualities one had despaired of ever seeing on the stage' (Kenneth Tynan in Osborne 1976: blurb) – qualities that could be described as truth, humanness, naturalism. In a book which charts the whole of modern British drama from *Anger* – a book called *Anger and After* – J. R. Taylor makes it clear that the play was not so much an innovation as a reappearance. It was, he says, the 'biggest shock to the system of British theatre since the advent of Shaw' (J. R. Taylor 1966: 37). There, in the same theatre where Shaw was played, the Royal Court, *Anger* brings human drama – naturalism – back to the stage after the years of artiness and experiment: 'I still can't stop my sweat breaking out when I see you doing – something as ordinary as leaning over an ironing board' (Osborne 1976: 33).

The great thing about naturalism, as it is seen here, is that it doesn't *pretend* to be ordinary, it *is* ordinary. An audience hears Jimmy Porter's lines about pretending to be human as deep irony, coming from someone who has a real human presence. The rhetoric of naturalism, together with its mode of performance, have power because they claim to give us access to what is truly, ordinarily, human. One of the words that has entered the drama vocabulary from naturalist rehearsal techniques is 'subtext'. The word is often used to imply that, whatever arty peculiarity there is about the surface – the text – underneath it there is always something which is familiarly human. The notion of subtext 'has given to every actor the intellectual means to discover conflicting intentions and half-conscious awarenesses existing within the words of Shakespeare's text' (Brown 1993: 10–11). Promising such special deep insight, it is no wonder that naturalism is a regularly preferred mode for much student drama, amateur dramatics and professional theatre. By this definition of subtext, 'proper' acting is the business of finding out what's really humanly there, not messing around with deliberate artiness. 'Proper' acting does 'straight' plays, and it does them 'straight'.

In making its claim to be truly human rather than merely arty, naturalism has had a lasting impact on how people think about the history of drama. Specifically, it has contributed to the idea that *Look Back in Anger* is the point at which English drama of the modern period starts to become both serious and accessible, the moment at which drama starts saying something real again. Osborne returns us to Ibsen: in the account of many general histories, modern drama starts with nineteenth-century naturalism. But this effect on periodization is perhaps less important than the impact on thinking about dramatic practices. The opposition between humanity and artiness is completely illusory, but it is also simple, clear cut, and widely circulated – even by people who don't like naturalism.

Thus a history of left-wing British theatre between the world wars argues for a schematic battle between naturalism and modernism. In Raphael Samuel's account, the choice for or against naturalism is taken to be a symptom of the overall political divergence between the 'revolutionary' cultural work of the period of Class against Class and the 'reformist' *rapprochement* between working class and liberal bourgeoisie of the period of the Popular Front. This account flies in the face of all the evidence for the interplay between naturalist and modernist practices, but it is moved by a more urgent need to stage a sort of morality drama between wicked naturalism and virtuous modernism. That drama was being played out in the cultural debates of the period when Samuel was writing, the 1970s and 1980s, especially in film studies. When Theatre Studies A level came into being, students found their approach to drama structured around the Manichaean double-act of Stanislavsky versus Brecht. On into the postmodern world, Steven Connor does a roundup of what he calls 'postmodern performance', setting it against 'classical' theatre – which 'gives the sense of presence by making the theatre the shadowing forth of some ideal truth that lies somewhere behind or before it' (Connor 1992: 140), in other words, specifically, naturalism. Even the most perceptive of naturalism's historians is haunted by that schematic opposition. Raymond Williams contrasts the 'bitterly humane naturalism of the liberal period' with 'the kinds of despair, contempt and rejection which have multiplied since the first war'. For the modern preoccupation with violence and degradation and the kinds of drama in which it is expressed – modernism, agit-prop, symbolism, anti-naturalisms – Williams has a catch-all phrase: 'a pseudo-tough modernity which is the mark of a broken spirit' (R. Williams 1973: 395).

The mark of a broken spirit might feel the same as the loss of great causes. It's the sense of an alienated modernity against which Jimmy Porter shouts in anger. So when the play of which Jimmy is the hero is hailed as the start of modern drama in England, we have to understand correctly the relationship between the words 'modern' and 'drama'. It is a relationship of opposition. The drama doesn't express modernity, it confronts it. When naturalism is welcomed as modern drama, it is because the stage is promising to keep safe everything which is human – not broken-spirited – in an alienating age. And its definition of 'human' is the one which was invented by serious drama of the late nineteenth century.

This is why, perhaps, *Anger* allows Jimmy – an 'old puritan at heart' – to have mixed feelings about the Edwardian age: 'The old Edwardian brigade do make their brief little world look pretty tempting' (Osborne 1976: 17). The twee picture of tea-time and sunshine may be phoney, as he says, but that was also a time when people played properly at being human. That, after all, is the time where *Anger* found its model for drama.

And that nostalgic attachment to the period of Edwardian culture remains deep within English theatre. Quoted in 1993, the Director of the Royal National Theatre enthuses about what he calls 'the model play of the twentieth century'. The play in question is by Chekhov, whose work first caused a stir in England in 1912.

## 2 People Theatre

The apologist for Stalinist theatre and the historian of angry English drama are agreed on one thing: as Taylor puts it, 'a play is about people, not necessarily about ideas' (J. R. Taylor 1966: 43); or, as Macleod expresses it, 'If the audience is composed of individuals, then there is little to be gained by entertaining them with abstractions' (Macleod 1943: 63). Theory – ideas, abstraction – is the opposite of being a real person. This opposition has come, within British culture, to define two concepts which at the outset don't seem obviously linked. The first is the definition of what proper serious drama should be, and the second is the definition of what proper concerned politics should be. The story of how these two concepts come to be linked can partly be told by looking at the absorption of Chekhov into British culture.

But first we need to be clear about the place of 'people' within naturalism. 'The research that we've been doing has been . . . based really largely on the words of the people that we interviewed and talked to. And in that sense', said the director of Joint Stock, Max Stafford-Clark, in a 1977 discussion on political theatre, 'we've been a kind of sociological mirror held up to what people say, but that's really been a self-educative process for us' (*Gambit* 1977: 22). When drama is a *self*-educative process the people on which it is most centred are the performers. By following the rehearsal methods of Stanislavsky the naturalist performer becomes 'more able to sense the complex individual being whom he or she is invited to apprehend and assimilate into performance' (Brown 1993: 11). As we have seen, it is typical of naturalism that exploration of subtext will expect to find there not ideas but people, and having found them to 'assimilate' them. It is also typical that the work of 'assimilation' which began with Stanislavsky's programme of disciplined training, his 'system', has over time turned into something more relaxed, an intuitive sensitivity to 'people'. Thus Peggy Ashcroft claims that the pleasure of doing Chekhov lay in his being 'instinctive, poetical, impressionistic, and therefore one finds a Chekhov character in a much more intuitive way than in Ibsen' (McVay 1993: 97). The process of collecting, relating to and then absorbing other people seems to constitute one of naturalism's particular attractions for the performer.

Chekhov is about as culturally remote as Ibsen. The assumption that one can be especially intuitive about his work tells us how far Chekhov has been transformed into an English playwright, imbued with values that many people want to think of as typically British:

> Another quality which Chekhov and Shakespeare share, and which makes British actors feel instinctively at home in the Russian plays, is an open-handedness: neither playwright insists upon one way, or one level, of interpretation. . . . Perhaps it was a consequence of this shared sense of the inner life of the persons of a drama that neither Shakespeare nor Chekhov was confined by prescriptive ideas. . . . a freedom from stylistic restraint was theirs from moment to moment. (Brown 1993: 13)

Naturalist acting and the best naturalist writing – which includes Shakespeare, naturally – are named as the appropriate form for British actors and British culture because of open-handedness and freedom, a belief that the inner life of people is not only separate from but opposed to prescriptive ideas, reality against dogma.

When Chekhov first arrived, existing English theatre, by one contemporary account, seemed short on open-handedness: 'Western playwrights, confined within the boundary of the attainable, wage a heavy-handed polemic with social institutions and conventions.' By contrast with such dogmatic writing, 'the Russians are at grips with the deepest craving of their inward nature' (in McDonald 1993: 31). These quotations come from George Calderon, welcoming Chekhov in 1912. The arrival was opportune for all those who wanted a theatre that was free of politics. For if theatre stages deep cravings rather than heavy-handed polemic it can avoid the modern real-life drama which in 1911, for example, had taken the form of a dock strike in Liverpool and a nation-wide campaign for women's votes. Those who felt that the best drama was more properly occupied with cravings than with polemic had found a model dramatist. Thus in May 1925 a reviewer used a Chekhov play to encourage the English theatre in the direction of 'cravings': 'it must not be supposed that the play addresses itself to the intellect. It is a play of atmosphere, of mood, of those vague feelings which we English are reluctant to express and hesitate to acknowledge even to ourselves. The general atmosphere, the resultant impression of the whole, is one of the futility of life' (in Le Fleming 1993: 60). On this model, the job of proper theatre is to express those subtextual feelings, to accept the futility of life. Outside the theatre in May 1925 industrial workers were contesting the futility of life, and a year later had organized the General Strike. Inside the theatre the important issue was emotion and expression. In brief, a polemic about social institutions is seen to be necessarily distinct from the articulation of deep cravings.

That distinction was clearly set out in an attack on the playwright Miles Malleson by a fellow socialist on the grounds that in his 1929 play *Fanatics* the characters 'discuss the "sex problem" as though . . . the class struggle did not exist' (in Samuel et al. 1985: 34). In a culture that makes a separation between sex and class, inward nature and social institution – and in politically vexed times – Chekhov's work was used to enforce the idea for that culture that great drama should be the expression not of polemic but of feelings and mood. The degree of inwardness is directly connected with the degree of greatness. So when Peggy Ashcroft saw the Moscow Art Theatre's *Cherry Orchard* in 1958, she disliked the 'tremendous political emphasis' on the 'breaking of the awful old order' (McVay 1993: 90). By 1958 naturalism had taught British theatre that political emphasis is separate from deep cravings, and that great drama has to do with cravings, mood, inward nature; not class but sex, not theory but people.

The important thing about *real* people, it is often said, is that they cannot be categorized. According to this belief, a good dramatist is one who avoids creating characters whose speech can be labelled in political terms. The dramatist's business, as defined by Roger Howard in a 1977 discussion of political theatre, 'is to deal with people and to show them in the round in the important moment of their lives' (*Gambit* 1977: 26). It's salutary to recall that Joseph Macleod admired the same qualities: when the first Soviet Children's Theatre was opened by Natalie Satz: 'Her productions tended to make the usual artificial distinction between good people and bad . . . Natalie Satz was removed in 1937, and the newest Children's Theatres now show all sides of the stories they tell' (Macleod 1943: 71). Real people have several sides, enough in fact to be *round*. 'Roundness' is a special word for naturalism, one it has made its own. When Roger Howard speaks of showing characters 'in the round', two meanings are possible. One designates *place*: the open playing area, 'theatre in the round', that loose metaphoric space referred to as *platea*. The other designates *person*: a mode of fictional characterization usually opposed to caricature, an opposition formulated in E. M. Forster's account of prose fiction as round versus flat. Naturalism's effect on the language of drama has operated to transform *round* from a place-word into a person-word.

The realization that people are necessarily round is supposedly one of naturalism's innovations. Raymond Williams claims that it was difficult to perform Ibsen, Chekhov and Strindberg because what they were writing didn't deal in familiar or stock situations. Instead they tried to explore 'intense experience, often, characteristically, of a hidden or unexpressed kind. If the stock situations and responses had been there, the problem of performance would have been very much easier' (R. Williams 1991: 124). In his attempt to explain the emergence of new artistic forms and the development of cultural conventions, Williams ends up reproducing naturalism's own opposition between ideas and people. In fact he gives new force to it by introducing a word of his own. For some plays, he says, 'the description "problem play" or "thesis play" is justified. The term suggests abstraction, and abstraction is what we have. There have always been problems in drama, but in the greatest drama these are set in a body of specific experience' (R. Williams 1973: 46, 47). That emphasis on *experience*, the lived and felt, has an energy to it that comes from more than naturalism. For the category of experience played a major part in Williams's attempt in the 1970s to make a leftist critique of what he saw as the anti-human, over-abstract theoretical models of a structuralist Marxism then permeating the 'New Left'. In one of the more notorious polemics of the period – E. P. Thompson's attack on the French Marxist Louis Althusser – the respect for a humanist Marxism is identified as a specifically English, as opposed to foreign, tradition.

That tradition includes – and is partly shaped by – English culture's love-affair with the form in which intuition, craving, experience are central. In the middle of the 'New Left' decade of the 1970s, the radical teacher and director Albert Hunt contrasted the work of Trevor Griffiths with that of the majority of serious dramatists who were trying 'unsuccessfully' to break away from naturalism: Griffiths, said Hunt, uses naturalism because he wants to introduce unfamiliar ideas in a familiar form, and because 'naturalism has a powerful hold on people's imaginations.' And there is another reason: 'Naturalism is basically about the observed details of everyday life. One of Griffiths's central themes is the connexion – and sometimes collision – between political ideas and the texture of lived experience' (A. Hunt 1977: 205). These phrases echo the voice of Raymond Williams, who is there, always alongside. In the same year when Williams published his major, leftist, attack on structuralist Marxism, 1977, Griffiths himself produced a version of *The Cherry Orchard* which attempted to reclaim Chekhov from what he called the 'theatrical class sectaries' whose productions of Chekhov's work had alienated a whole generation of theatre workers. Rescued from the sectaries, Griffiths's Chekhov is 'a possible comrade'. The comrade's message to English culture of the 1970s is not, however, very different from what it was in the 1920s. Chekhov's work, once again, avoids a narrow choice between sides; political relevance is not so much argued as *felt*, 'since plays, unlike theses, require more of us than careful reflection and analysis: they demand to be *experienced* . . . with actors and audience both listening and making, which is arguably now the only truly *social* validity theatre can lay claim to in a television age' (Chekhov 1978: v–vi). Naturalism at the beginning of the twentieth century was the form which distinguished craving from polemic; when it later became political, its politics were said, characteristically, to be associated with feeling and *experience*. Thus in the 1970s a 'political' naturalism found a role for itself as the guardian of a particularly English leftism, a place where Marxism could enact itself as humanism. Opposed to abstraction, theory, structuralism, unpopular artiness, naturalism's reality was non-sectarian.

'If I develop, it might be away from naturalism. . . . but I will still be trying to re-create the reality of my experience. I would no more be non-naturalistic for its own sake than I was naturalistic for its own sake; I am concerned with both only in order to communicate what experience has meant to me' (in J. R. Taylor 1966: 146). The words are those of Arnold Wesker, 'kitchen-sink' dramatist of the late 1950s, socialist, founder of a trades union cultural centre. For Wesker, experience needs to be separated from the art form. And the art form is defined by its service to experience: 'Art is the re-creation of experience, not the copying of it' (in J. R. Taylor 1966: 146). When it is caught out at copying, art stands politically accused. The choices are mapped out for us again by Raymond Williams: 'When we speak of naturalism, we must distinguish between this passion for the whole truth, for the liberation of what can not yet be said or done, and the confident and even complacent representation of things as they are' (R. Williams 1991: 125–6). A drama which is not struggling to render 'serious experience' is a drama that exists only for itself, it's merely formal and in decay. Since naturalism has a political role to play, it needs to be suspicious of art. It wants the 'whole truth', not 'complacent representation'; it separates experience from 'formal' drama. But if a play isn't dramatic, what is it? The reviewers of Glasgow Unity's 1946 production of Robert McLeish's *Gorbals Story* offer the answer. 'What impresses most about this play is its authenticity; . . . It has no "plot" in the usual sense of the word, but is a cross-section of one way of living.' In short, the play is a 'slice of life'. As such it takes us all the way back to somewhere familiar: 'Maybe, it's unfair to bring Tchekov's name into a discussion of Robert McLeish's play . . . but it's the easiest way to fix its genre. It is a more or less plotless slice of life, and like Tchekov's slices it carries the conviction of absolute reality.' Plot smacks too much of deceitful artiness, of hidden control: 'the real point about *The Gorbals Story* is that its characters are living people and not the sort of cardboard figures which propagandists are apt to make use of' (McLeish 1985: 93, 92, 97). When we call it a slice of life, we define the play as one where the author is not trying to be arty or impose her own ideas.

One of the most influential of modern dramatists explained his creative role this way: 'I want to present living people to the audience, worthy of their interest primarily because they *are*, they exist, not because of any moral the author may draw from them.' This is Harold Pinter being quoted in John Russell Taylor's *Anger and After*. Taylor himself describes Pinter's plays as 'tiny cameos in which two or more characters are put into relation with each other and allowed simply to interact' (1966: 296). The good naturalist author doesn't interfere by plotting; he just allows people to be people. By contrast the obviousness of the construction of Wesker's *Roots* made it for Taylor a bad play: 'the same clichés recur, the same substitutes for thought, the same pointless stories endlessly, inanely repeated.' It is to be assumed that truthful speech doesn't repeat or say things twice. *Roots* is over-artificial and polemical, it amounts to 'a Zolaesque tract on the degradation of country life'. As for the characters, while they may be possible, they are not 'typical' (1966: 137–8). Wesker's dramatic art is thus bad because it deviates from what is known to be real life. And, as the apologists for naturalism tell us, a play that's good does its level best *not* to be theatrical.

Indeed, the key elements of naturalist drama, as Raymond Williams argues, don't have their roots in theatre. Its descriptive details, indeed its 'total conception of experience' (R. Williams 1991: 125), are a cultural continuation of the realist novels of the nineteenth century. Elsewhere in Europe, in different ways, that cultural continuity was disrupted by the rage and experiment of the activities called modernism. Naturalism's promise not to be theatrical – for the sake of theatre – is made to a culture for which modernism was largely outside, foreign, culturally elitist. Its declared rejection of theatricality testifies to a desire to speak seriously of general social issues without being sidetracked by artistic experiments and the quirks of a minority. To a nation whose sense of its own modern history is based on the belief that totalitarianism and propaganda, political management itself, live outside its shores, naturalism is welcomed because it puts people before ideas, theory, dogma. If, in Britain, European modernism was weakest, the continuity of an upper-class lifestyle was strongest. With its reference point in experience, as a transhistorical term, naturalism sustains unbroken from the liberal concern of the nineteenth century a sense that human beings are at the centre of a history that happens to them, changes that always come from outside. With its self-appointed identity, after the Second World War, as the guardian of liberalism, of freedom itself, the mainstream of British culture, faced by the new European avant-gardes, reacted by holding firm to an aesthetic which seemed to promise not to be experimental, partisan or abstractly political. Naturalism persists, we might say, because it promises that theatre can be serious without being – precisely by not being – either theoretical or theatrical.

## 3   Uncle Albert

A performance in Moss Side, Manchester, by the Black Theatre Cooperative in the early 1980s: the audience watch and speak back to a realist story of a family. An older male character enters the scene: one young woman in the audience says to another 'That's my Uncle Albert.' The performer was not her relative.

Another show, another response: 'At this point the play stopped because the theatre erupted in an explosion of shouts, whistles and applause . . . Literally, it was as if a real event had taken place in front of them.' Mike Phillips, a black theatre worker, suggests these responses are produced because what was occurring on stage 'forced the audience to respond as if it were part of their real lives'. Phillips uses the phrase 'emotional relevance' to define the acting: 'Clearly this can't be defined simply as putting black characters on stage and having them behave in an emotional fashion. The term . . . implies identifying and presenting on stage, events and characters whose emotional relevance to their lives strikes the audience in a direct and immediate way.' That relevance had particular force for the concerns of black plays in the late 1970s and early 1980s: 'all describe a fragmented nature and a background which has long splintered and broken apart. In front of it the characters sift through the fragments, looking for certainties. What is our true nature and how can it be assembled, is the characteristic question of this drama' (Phillips n.d. [1981]: 3–4). Questions about a community's 'true nature', its identity, are of particular relevance to any community that feels itself being culturally absorbed by a grouping that dominates and oppresses it. It is for this reason, perhaps, that several black theatre companies adopted a form of naturalism in an otherwise anti-naturalist 'alternative theatre' scene. Naturalism has political force because it claims to be able to reveal '*true*' nature.

That claim has had its most profound effect in shaping people's ideas about what proper performing is. It has produced assumptions about the relationship between acting and truth which go well beyond naturalism, leading off into philosophical questions about imitation and life and the treachery of performance.

Where it all begins is with the naturalist performer's attempt to represent truth: 'The real problem for the actor, therefore, is how to create in each performance the same believable experiences and behavior, and yet include what Stanislavsky called "the illusion of the first time".' To get this illusion Stanislavsky had developed exercises, involving relaxation, 'affective memory' (which includes the memory of real feeling), responses to imaginary objects and events. The object of such exercises is 'not that what the actor deals with is an exact parallel to the play or the character, but that when the character experiences, the actor really experiences – something'. The actor is thus more than physically engaged: 'what was most important was the use of the soul of the actor as the material for his work – the necessity for the study of the emotions and the analysis of simple and complicated feelings' (Strasberg 1989: 35, 68, 62). When naturalist acting makes the 'soul' *authentically present* it is demonstrating its great power; at the same time, it is demonstrating what its enemies, as we shall see, are most suspicious of.

This actor training programme, known as the Method, appears to offer a uniquely modern solution to the supposedly age-old problem of repeatedly *making it real*. But the notion that the problem here *is* a problem is fairly recent. It dates from a period which has learnt to think that in a person's head social rules conflict with instinctual drives, where intellect represses desire. This understanding of a person's head only became widespread after Freud and psychoanalysis. Seen from this perspective, Stanislavsky's technique takes on particular significance. 'Stanislavsky sought to replace the actor's mental, intellectual, and theorizing activities with truthfulness, experience, and behavior. He did this in order to make sure that it would not result in only verbal, mental, or formalized theatrical behavior that relates more to the director's ideas than to the actor's execution' (Strasberg 1989: 106, 173). Which is to say that if it's intellectual, it's unlikely to be true . . . plays are people, not ideas. The Method, designed initially to solve what we might call a rhetorical problem – how to produce repeated truth-effects on a stage – comes, in a culture also inhabited by psychoanalysis, to be a method for liberating the truths of the person. Defined this way, theatre exercises no longer have relevance merely to performers but can assist in dealing with all forms of intractable reality, in consciousness-raising workshops, encounter groups, and management training courses.

Despite the repeated references, the Method is not Stanislavsky's system. It is the creation of Lee Strasberg, a New Yorker who founded the US Group Theatre. His is the account of Stanislavsky given above, and it's this version of Stanislavsky that tends to predominate in the English-speaking West. Its influence, and with it Strasberg's fame, were boosted by the success of the stars trained by the Method: Marlon Brando, Jane Fonda, Dustin Hoffman, Marilyn Monroe (perhaps the finest naturalist performer of them all, since most people assume she only ever played herself, a 'dumb blonde'). The majority of acting which is consciously watched as *acting* by most people in Britain is what they see in North American movies, that's to say acting done by performers such as Strasberg's. Thus the ideals of the Method come to define what proper acting is. Furthermore, since it is done in a cultural space which is outside the director-dominated art film, or art theatre, that acting seems accessible to, and wanted by, most people.

And most would agree with Strasberg's definition of what real perform-ing is: 'Stanislavsky had located the logic of experience and of inner feeling . . . from which true drama stems' (Strasberg 1989: 46). But, while for many people this defines the norm of proper acting, there are others, natural-ism's enemies, who deeply suspect that claim to make fully present on stage the reality of spontaneous inner feeling, to give authentic existence to something as nebulous as 'soul'. These suspicions can be put into two loose groupings: a 'post-structuralist', postmodernist one that is opposed to any beliefs in a human essence or 'soul' which exists outside language or culture; and a leftist one that is opposed to an emphasis on the individual rather than society as a whole, as if 'soul' was free of system. But what's curious is that these attacks, as we shall find, are already deeply influenced by, and indeed further reproduce, naturalism's claim to deal in the real presence of 'soul'.

For Lee Strasberg a key problem in naturalism's striving for truth was 'how to create in each performance the same believable experiences . . . "the illusion of the first time"'(Strasberg 1989: 35). This could be put another way: 'a representation which is not repetition, . . . a *re*-presentation which is full presence, . . . a present which does not repeat itself'. The aim was, as we know, to replace an actor's intellectual activity with truthfulness: 'in order to make sure that it would not result in only verbal, mental or formalized theatrical behavior that relates more to the director's ideas than to the actor's execution' (Strasberg 1989: 173). This again can be put another way:

> the reconstitution of a closed space of original representation, the archi-manifestation of force or of life . . . The end of representation, but also original representation; the end of interpretation, but also an original interpretation that no master-speech, no project of mastery will have permeated and leveled in advance. A visible representation, certainly, directed against the speech which eludes sight . . . but whose visibility does not consist of a spectacle mounted by the discourse of the master.

The person putting it another way each time is Jacques Derrida (1978: 248, 238), who in an essay on Artaud's Theatre of Cruelty seeks to expose the illusory claims of naturalist – or what he calls 'classical' – theatre. Despite his intention, however, Derrida's critique seems already to have had its terms set for it, to be already permeated, by naturalism. He plays around with the words 'presence', 're-presentation' and 'repetition' (an untranslatable but useful double meaning: *répétition* means rehearsal in French). But what haunts his wordplay is the old anxiety about the relationship between repetition and the illusion of the first time. 'Presence, in order to be presence and self-presence, has always already begun to represent itself, has always already been penetrated' (p. 249). Penetration, which we could perhaps call actor training, constructs the *effect* of presence on stage. Which is to say that Uncle Albert becomes an uncle only by being penetrated. The presence and penetration could be accepted as being happily interdependent – unless you were trapped into that naturalist worry about doing it for real; and unless you wanted only to guarantee the real by the work of the performer . . . those panting assurances that it really is the first time.

Derrida criticizes the repressed, bourgeois aspects of 'classical' theatre evident in its technique: 'Repetition separates force, presence, and life from themselves. This separation is the economical and calculating gesture of that which defers itself in order to maintain itself, that which reserves expenditure and surrenders to fear' (Derrida 1978: 245). A similar critique apparently motivates the 'postmodern' theatre work of Robert Wilson: as Steven Connor says: 'What matters according to this aesthetic of impermanence is not the bourgeois-repressive qualities of memory, inheritance and repeatability, but the liberating qualities of immediacy and uniqueness' (Connor 1992: 134). The arrival of the adjective 'bourgeois' adds a new dimension to the *perceived relationship* between presence and repetition, so it is not just about truth and illusion but about the activity of capitalism itself. 'Increasingly, then, the experience of the "live" is itself being commodified, "produced", as a strategic category of the semiotic . . . The live is always in a sense the quotation of itself – never the live, always the "live"' (Connor 1992: 153). A performance that reserves expenditure rather than spends, commodifies rather than creates, is one that denies, and is lesser than, that which is spontaneous, momentary, true: a first time that really, really is a first time. Although these are still the terms of naturalism, they have produced an odd twist. For the acting techniques and skill used to produce truth effects are now seen as bourgeois, anti-spontaneous. Thus every time someone attempts to get near to it, the ideal of lifelike performance moves further away, to a new ineffable distance.

The worry about *capitalism*'s penetration of performance takes on particular urgency for leftist theatre workers. In two meetings about 'British Theatre in Crisis' in 1988, discussion was shaped around the divisions which have operated in oppositional politics and culture since at least the early 1970s: leadership versus participation, official left versus situationism, social responsibility versus anarchy. The main question is simple; Vera Gottlieb put it in 'Thatcher's Theatre': 'what can the theatre do in today's Britain?' Two assertions follow: 'Theatre illustrates and demonstrates contemporary social reality and only rarely changes it . . . In exposing contemporary issues and realities, the theatre can also explore alternatives' (Gottlieb 1988: 104). The notion of a theatre with a function, a theatre that seeks to *do* something, is one more or less born with naturalism. But there's also another respect in which naturalism was influencing the discussion. In an essay on Chekhov, Gottlieb criticized an overemphasis on individual characteristics which worked to trivialize social significance. For her the influence of Stanislavsky on British theatre might be defined as 'character exploration rather than an exploration of the *ideas* in a play' (Gottlieb 1993: 151). The formulation restates, however, what naturalism itself insists upon, that it is indeed possible to separate people and ideas. So in the Crisis talks, when an observation was made about younger writers 'who do not have the language of analysis but do have the language of protest' (NTQ Symposium 1989: 121), there's the ghost of that opposition between ideas and people, intellect and feeling. And with that opposition comes another. Naturalism, by one account, is a staging of the novelistic, always subservient to *words*. The fault of Derrida's 'classic' theatre is that it 'does nothing but illustrate a discourse', so it is not a proper stage in its own right: 'Its relation to speech is its malady' (Derrida 1978: 236). When one speaker in the Crisis talks 'urged resistance to "a culture of the image and the purely physical"' another said that if there was an aesthetic crisis in the theatre 'it was partly to do with the inability of theatre on the left to engage adequately with imagistic work' in what is a new 'image culture' of television and advertising (Lavender 1989: 212). The choice between words and images seems to be both clear cut and politically loaded: a choice between analysis and protest, leftism and anarchism. But these neat oppositions are more easily made in discussion than in performance . . .

'Talk. Use the language. Do you know what language is?' The person who has made the choice of words here is Beatie Bryant, rebelling against the monotony of her Norfolk environment in Wesker's 1959 play *Roots*. In her rages against the deadening effects of comics, radio and television, media which we could argue make life commodified, real talk is a weapon. And with real talk goes socialism. 'Socialism isn't talking all the time, it's living, it's singing, it's being interested in what go on around you' (Wesker 1964: 90, 129). But none of Beatie's statements is her own. She is quoting her London lover, Ronnie. So where we thought we had real life, we only had 'life', in quotation marks.

The story-line of the play sees her return to her family in order to prepare them for the arrival of Ronnie, who doesn't turn up but sends a letter terminating the relationship. In the last act the family have gathered to meet Ronnie. Beatie tries to stir them out of what she regards as their inertia. Her quotations from Ronnie become increasingly fervent: '*jumping on a chair thrusting her fist into the air like Ronnie, and glorying in what is the beginning of a hysteric outburst of his quotes*'. When she reaches a climax – 'I'm a socialist!' – there's a knock at the door (p. 141). Not Ronnie, but the postman with the letter. As her mother reads it out, it's obvious that Beatie ignored every suggestion Ronnie ever made. So the truth is out: as her mother says, in charging her family with ignorance Beatie is reproducing Ronnie's charges against her. This truth revelation is, however, a step towards a new truth. Beatie at the end of the play discovers the power of a voice that begins to be her own, while her family murmur in the distance. All this is in Act 3, the place where J. R. Taylor says the 'real action' begins (Ronnie's letter). But the 'real action' consists of some familiar dramatic gestures: the knock of fate, the emergence of hidden truth (both survivors into naturalism from melodrama), the shape of a predetermined sickness in Beatie's hysteria, and, of course, her accession to individual voice in a trapped world – these have the feel of classic naturalism. As such, if this is the 'real action', it's also a *repetition* of the formula of a word-based protest against a deadening capitalist world.

When Beatie shouts 'I'm a socialist!' (p. 142) the 'I' is Ronnie. On her chair, in her 'strange excitement', this is the image of a woman pathetically gripped by an ideal, subsumed in the influence of an always absent man, a presence that has, always already, been – so to speak – penetrated. But Beatie's use of Ronnie is also a way of setting herself apart from her family's inertia, a moment of possession – in which 'Beatie' (her family's Beatie) becomes a third party, neither the 'I' of her quotation nor perhaps the *strangely* excited speaker: 'I'm not a snob Beatie, I just believe in human dignity and tolerance and cooperation and equality and – '

> JIMMY: (*Jumping up in terror.*) He's a communist!
> BEATIE: I'm a socialist! (pp. 141–2)

Jimmy's gesture of terror functions to make the absent Ronnie seem closer. The more thoroughly the actor uses his Method – 'the object is imaginary; the response is real' (Strasberg 1989: 70) – the more we get a sense of the power of the strangely excited Beatie: neither quite Ronnie nor the family's 'Beatie' but what could be called a manifestation of force or of life. She is also, however, at the same time hysterical, always already 'penetrated' by Ronnie's project of mastery. The staged image thus holds in unity two opposed possibilities. This precedes what Taylor recognizes as the 'real action', the knock on the door.

Up to this point it's what Taylor calls a Zolaesque tract, with its stories inanely repeated. But Wesker wants organized inanity: '*They talk in fits and starts mainly as a sort of gossip, and they talk quickly too, enacting as though for an audience what they say. . . . The silences are important – as important as the way they speak, if we are to know them.*' Knowing them comes not from the content of speech but from the rhythms of sound and silence. Those rhythms are articulated with stage space: 'BEATIE *helps collect dishes from table and proceeds to help wash up. This is a silence that needs organizing*' (p. 92). Speech is one part of aural texture: Stan mumbling as he exits, Mrs Bryant simultaneously mumbling as she peels potatoes, then peeling to the radio, over which she and Beatie talk. Sound articulates with action: at the opening of Act 3 an empty stage, on it a table loaded with food (which will not be eaten), Beatie upstairs talking to her mother, who is in the kitchen. There are words, but no speakers; a speech which eludes sight perhaps. Is this text or image?

Debate about the really lived versus repetitive deadness shapes a disagreement about music. Beatie sings a folk song as she beats eggs; her mother likes a current pop song. Beatie quotes Ronnie: 'let me try and explain to you what he explain to me.'

> MRS BRYANT: (*On hearing a bus.*) There go the half-past-eleven bus to Diss – blust that's early. (*Puts spuds in saucepan on oven and goes to collect runner beans, which she prepares.*)
>
> BEATIE: Mother, I'm *talking* to you. Blust woman it's not often we get together and really talk, it's nearly always me listening to you telling who's dead.

She explains that her mother won't find passion in her 'third-rate' song. There's more Ronnie, then silence, out of which Mrs Bryant begins her song but she gets the tune wrong: '*BEATIE corrects her and in helping her mother she ends by singing the song, with some enthusiasm, to the end*' (pp. 114–16). Beatie's desire really to talk contrasts with her mother's immersion in the local bus timetable, caught in the 'bourgeois repressive' qualities of memory and repeatability. But Beatie's text about real life is as much dictated from outside, as much quoted, as are her mother's clichés; the rhythms of the bus service live in Mrs Bryant just as in Beatie live the rhythms of Ronnie's syntax. The two penetrated women 'really' communicate, perhaps, find a full *presence*, as it were, in *repetition* of the song, because they do it together and with enthusiasm. It is a moment won from domestic routine, which makes the work more fun, yet keeps it in place. The song itself is trivial, communicates nothing, produces no analysis. Its singing stages mother and daughter's desire to be close. Beatie's contempt for it coexists with its capacity to satisfy her needs. Intellect and feeling, theory and experience are held in dialectical unity, opposed but linked. The bourgeois repressive qualities of memory and repeatability fuse with, enable, the liberating qualities of immediacy and uniqueness.

At the end of Act 2 Beatie shares with her mother a different sort of music, Bizet's *L'Arlésienne* suite. She quotes Ronnie on socialism and asks her mother to listen: '(*She becomes breathless and excited*) Listen to it. It's simple isn't it? Can you call that squit?' 'I don't say it's all squit.' And Beatie does a dance (p. 129). Her excitement, locked onto Ronnie's and Bizet's phrases, is naive, learnt, a child impressing her mother. But Ronnie and Bizet are the only available vehicles for a woman who has no other way of acknowledging her body and desire, the all that's not squit. Mrs Bryant's response is the shape of Beatie's: 'the same clichés recur', 'memory, inheritance and repeatability', but the *rhythm* of their recurrence, their repetition, is as strong as their clichéd vacuity. The cliché is merely that: not something which conceals the 'truth' of, but something which *is*, Mrs Bryant's life. The experience produced by the stage is centred on recognition of cliché, where *cliché is truth and presence*.

The woman who saw her Uncle Albert in the Black Theatre Coop show was responding to a character who was sufficiently clichéd, typical, to invite recognition. Only within a fiction could something so rigorously typical be presented, yet it was precisely that impossible typicality which connected deeply with the woman's life. Her recognition of a character produced in the public space of play was shaped by, and invested with, the psychic energies of something privately known. It is the drama's function to produce that recognition: 'Black theatre . . . doesn't exist to describe and analyze racism or white society . . . Its proper focus is the description and interpretation of what it means to be a black person' (Phillips n.d. [1981]: 3).

That idea of a 'proper focus' for drama would constitute what its enemies think is wrong with naturalism. It claims to describe what it means to *be* a black person by staging experience, presence, individuality, real life. A fashionable trend in drama criticism would say that this is always penetrated, commodified, quoted life. But drama analysis of this sort acts the part of Ronnie's letter, showing that what seems to be really present is repetition and quotation. In performance, however, Beatie's repetition of Ronnie's ideas is a route to discovering her own being, her self-presence. Which is never not quoted as well. Thus when a naturalist performance is both an individual presence and at the same time repetitively typical, both life and 'life', it is something a person might want to call 'Uncle Albert'. Only a drama criticism that can't handle naturalism would imagine that such a person really thought she had discovered a relative's thespian double life.

# 4   Tom Browne's Schooldays

Somewhere in any consideration of naturalism you get onto 'realism'. Then you discover that realism means several things, and each time someone comes up with a new sort of realism there is usually a political motive for it. Let's see what goes on.

The start of the whole problem is that the term 'naturalism' won't stay still. Raymond Williams describes this:

> it is clear, in practice, that naturalism means several different things. In its widest sense, it is an absorbed interest in the contemporary everyday world, and a corresponding rejection or exclusion of any supposed external design or system of values. It is then an absorbed recreation of the ways in which people, within human limits, actually speak, feel, think,

behave, act. By these criteria, many of the supposed rejections of naturalism are in fact variations on it. Conventions are changed . . . because
existing conventions are no longer *true enough*, by essentially similar
criteria. (1973: 382–3)

The fact that the criteria for truth are 'similar' makes the contest between the
various rejections of naturalism even more urgent: for all these rejections –
however different – are called realism.

In the position paper drawn up for the first national conference of the
Workers' Theatre Movement (June 1932), 'the naturalistic form' was defined
as 'that form which . . . is suitable for showing things as they appear on the
surface, but does not lend itself to disclosing the reality which lies beneath.
And it is just this reality existing beneath the polite surface of capitalist
society that the Workers' Theatre must reveal' (in Samuel et al. 1985: 101).
An '*absorbed* recreation' is one deeply engaged with the life it looks at – but not
swallowed up, absorbed, by it. The model is the investigative scientist rather
than the journalist: the photograph of the surface has to be replaced by 'the X-
ray picture of society and social forces'.

With that metaphor the WTM activist, Tom Thomas, explained his term
*dialectical realism*. The realism produced by X-ray vision works 'to penetrate
the laws governing objective reality and to uncover the deeper, hidden,
mediated, not immediately perceptible network of relationships that go to
make up society'. The idea that a particular society is shaped by the action of
unseen laws and forces comes from Marxism. Their sense of something going
on away from the surface separates Marxists from, say, naturalists, who merely
offer 'passive capitulation to' – or are absorbed by – 'these phenomena of fully-
developed capitalism . . . seeing the result but not the struggles of opposing
forces'. When it is art, however, this investigative penetration must not call
attention to itself: good realism 'presents the essential element – man and his
social practice – not as an artificial product of the artist's virtuosity but as
something that emerges and grows naturally, as something not invented, but
simply discovered.' This produces trust in the reader or spectator who then
'feels confident about the direction which the events will take because of their
inner logic'. The particular inner logic of events when these remarks were
written, by the Communist Georg Lukács, was the need for a socialist transformation of a society which, by 1937–8, was threatened by the successes of
fascism. Thus realism must not only take an X-ray but also, if it wants to
depict life comprehensively, it must show from the inside how change can
happen. The realism which will then mark a 'higher stage' in artistic development has its own name: 'Socialist realism is in a position . . . both to portray
the totality of a society in its immediacy and to reveal its pattern of development' (Lukács 1977: 38; 1978: 146, 126, 129; 1963: 98–9). According to
Lukács, the term *socialist realism* was first used in 1932, the same year the

WTM urged workers' theatre to use dialectical realism to reveal the reality concealed by naturalism.

In the following year, one of the WTM groups found itself reaching for a new means to approach closer to reality, in the face of the false acting they saw around them: 'The point is we'd become interested in Stanislavsky' (in Samuel et al. 1985: 244). Later in the decade that interest was sustained by the Communist activists who organized Unity Theatre, which boasted 'the only theatre school in Britain applying the methods of Stanislavsky' (in C. Chambers 1989: 107). Thinking in terms of depth against surface, wanting a truth discovered rather than invented, anti-naturalism finds for itself a master in Stanislavsky, the guru – of course – of naturalism. Which is paradoxical; but as the paradoxes whirl around, two features remain constant. One is that, structurally, naturalism is always set in opposition to a 'realism', as bad against good; the other is that, politically, the 'realism' is always progressive, leftist, anti-capitalist. But the problem, always, is guaranteeing that the realism *is* real, whether the penetration has gone deep enough to be politically correct. Take the case of Gorky: in the Soviet Union, claims Macleod, Gorky's plays 'set the realism of the Art Theatre as Socialist Realism' (Macleod 1943: 114); but for Tom Thomas of the WTM, Gorky's *Lower Depths* was 'a classic example of bourgeois pessimism': 'While it shows the terrible degradation of the Russian working class under the Tsar, no hint is given of the revolutionary forces which . . . were preparing and organizing to overthrow the system' (in Samuel et al. 1985: 55). Such 'Sham-Left' drama is like what Lukács called *critical realism*: it is a form which is critical of capitalism while being locked within a bourgeois outlook, unable to describe the forces of change from inside. So becoming swallowed up amounts not just to being taken in, deluded, by how things look but about being taken *into*, trapped within, an outlook on things.

More problematic than Gorky was the dramatist with whom the British theatre eventually developed its famous affinity, Chekhov. Not only did his plays challenge the attitudes of dominant theatre but they also seemed to move beyond naturalism into a realism in which the events were 'emblems and generalizations about life at large', totality perhaps. The human figure is seen to be subservient to 'the atmosphere in which it is plunged' (in McDonald 1993: 38–9). *Atmosphere* – with its sense of human life beyond human control – is a key feature of Chekhovian naturalism.

> FIRST CHARACTER AT TABLE: (*Drearily*) I'm tired of waiting for breakfast.
> (*Takes pistol and shoots himself.*)
> SERVANT: (*Enters hurriedly*) The canary has committed suicide in the soup.
> (*Takes poison and dies.*)
> SECOND CHARACTER AT TABLE: (*Mournfully*) The soup is spoilt. (*Stabs himself with carving-knife.*)

This atmospheric scene is set in 'A *dismal room in a gloomy farmhouse somewhere in a bleak part of Russia. . . . Several people sit shivering at a bare table. The door opens with a crash. Enter a small procession of characters representing the Playwrights of Gloom*' (in Samuel et al. 1985: 199, 198). The first named playwright in the procession is Chekhov.

The Playwrights of Gloom were the invention of one of the ideologists of the Workers' Theatre Movement, Huntly Carter, quoted in Ness Edwards's 1930 book *The Workers' Theatre*. The Scottish playwright Joe Corrie gave them a different name when he described his changed feelings towards dramatists he once loved, Ibsen, O'Neill, O'Casey: 'the present chaos of the world has made me a bit tired of my dramatists. Their work, though powerful enough to make good drama, is not sufficiently vital. . . . Their work is grey with tragic hopelessness, and, as the Bolshevists would say, they are "defeatists".' The problem with Playwrights of Gloom is that they make good drama but not good politics; stagecraft, atmosphere even, are a bogey that distracts from purpose. Writing in the 'present chaos' of June 1932, the same month as the first Workers' Theatre conference, Corrie expected a big change soon:

I believe the first great dramatist in this country will not spring from the footlights, but from the ranks of the unemployed, or employed oppressed. His work will not be 'perfect stage' (that bogey), but it will embrace something greater than has ever been done. He will be more of an economist than a dramatist, he will be blind to the footlights, and will be looking instead into the future. (Corrie 1985: 184)

Half a century into that future, a dramatist described how his generation of playwrights were united by 'an almost unhealthy obsession with explaining things, and, particularly, with explaining those big public events which have created our contemporary world'. Again, since it 'seeks merely to produce a replica of observed reality', naturalism won't do. Nor will its mirror image: 'If agit-prop reveals the objective at the expense of the subjective, then naturalism is at the opposite end of the pole.' The terms begin to slither around in a familiar way. Naturalism, as a revealer of subjectivity, has ended up in the opposite place from where Macleod had it in 1943: 'there develop at the same time naturalism (a photographic copying of superficial details) and the rebellious "subjectivity" of expressionism, surrealism, etc.' (Macleod 1943: 14). And just as Macleod suggests that the way out of this unsatisfactory opposition between subjectivity and objectivity is socialist realism, so, forty years on, the way out is realism again, with a slightly adapted name: 'social realism provides a kind of dialectical synthesis between the super-subjectivism of naturalism and the super-objectivism of agit-prop' (Edgar 1982: 969). The author who has decided on this 'dialectical synthesis' – or middle way – is David Edgar. Whether he and his generation were what

Corrie anticipated, there is something of an eye to the future which has led to the economical slimming down whereby socialist realism must, being realistic, become *social realism*.

The sorts of 'explaining' plays which Edgar has in mind might be exemplified in his own account of the rise of English fascism in *Destiny* (1976). With its reference points in recognizable public events, its gradually interconnecting private stories, a thirty-year time span and choric prologues, the form of the play is that of a modern chronicle, depicting the state of the nation. As such, it became popular with Edgar's generation of theatrical explainers. But it didn't begin with them. Wesker's *Chicken Soup with Barley* (1958) moves a family from 1936 through to 1956. At the end of the first scene the Jews of the East End take to the streets to stop the fascists marching: 'Sarah, wait for me – Sarah! Hey, wait for me!' (*He follows her, banner streaming. The voices outside grow to a crescendo.*) 'They shall not pass, they shall not pass, THEY SHALL NOT PASS!' (Wesker 1964: 24–5). Edgar's agit-prop and naturalism correspond to the two 'levels' that J. R. Taylor finds in Wesker's play: 'Personally, the play seems to be about recurrent patterns of behaviour from generation to generation: socially, it is about the working classes' loss of sense of purpose with the arrival of a socialist government and the Welfare State' (J. R. Taylor 1966: 132). The social, agit-prop's streaming banner, and the personal, naturalism's subjective dependence of the man on his wife: both combine together, in a dialectical synthesis perhaps, to tell a story of the loss of purpose which comes with the arrival of socialism.

What preoccupies these explaining plays is that THEY do – after all – pass. In Brenton and Hare's *Brassneck* (1973) an economic elite avoids defeat, managing its survival in power and wealth through personal deals, secret fraud, customary violence. At a picnic with members of the local hunt a Tory ex-minister has horse-shit put down his neck by one of the local gentry, who in turn is punished by the loss of his drainage contract in Cardiff. That horse-shit is not strictly necessary to a mere explanation. It is a deliberately shocking disclosure of the conduct of upper-class society. Indeed, disclosure rather than explanation is the mode of the stage's rhetoric. One scene is set in 'A *Masonic Lodge. Pillars, desks, ashlars etc. . . . Authentic*'. After the initiation ceremony, the new brother is warned of the penalty of 'having your throat cut across should you improperly disclose the secrets of Masonry' (Brenton and Hare 1974: 18, 22). Like the moment when the doctor reads from the scientific text on venereal disease in Brieux's *Damaged Goods* (with foreword by Charlotte Shaw, 1914), the dramatic thrill of the Masonic ritual derives not from its function as explanation but from its penetration, through 'authentic' public enactment, into that which should properly be hidden. In its final scene *Brassneck* summarizes its own action as a striptease: '*A girl comes on wearing Mayor's robes. She starts stripping off. Underneath she toys with Masonic aprons. Then strips down to a bowler hat and away. . . . Round the stripper's middle is a rubber tube which she detaches and wraps round her upper arm. . . . The naked* STRIPPER *fixes, then raises her hypodermic. Fanfare. End of strip'* (pp. 101–2). There, with the wealthy, heroin-dealing crowd toasting 'The last days of capitalism', the play ends. In the chronicle of modern times, the scientific insistence of the X-ray develops, through an inner logic, into the obsessional disclosures of the voyeur's lens.

The toast to dying capitalism is proposed by Sidney Bagley, the knife-carrying fixer who as a child bullied his younger brother, who himself ends up a Eurocrat. The Bagley children manage to be survivors, but their different careers are shaped, inevitably, by their natures, unchanged since childhood. They are joined by Tom Browne, a man we first met as an 'independent communist', who also has a family history:

> you know I want to get into public life. Set myself to work. . . . I used to think I would spend the whole of my life in draughty halls, pamphleteering, be a crank with a megaphone at the factory gate, be locked in smoke-filled attic rooms, endlessly discussing, dotting the I's – that's what happened to my father – romantic – dies cursing his friends for minor misinterpretations of the exact meaning of revolution – that mustn't happen to us, Harry. If that happens to us, God help England. And working people. (p. 27)

What Tom Browne learns from his early days, what he learns from his labour movement forebears – men like Joe Corrie perhaps – is a hatred of defeatism. At the end Tom finds his sense of purpose among the wealthy: 'I was a communist in my youth. Now I'm looking for revenge. A revenge on everything I believed in. Count me in' (p. 100). The abrasive effect of this sort of play's realism comes, as it does for all the realisms, from the relentless inner logic that here moves from Communism to vengeance. The growing up of Tom Browne, and those like him, is a repeated story. These chronicles meticulously count him in because they recognize the logic of economic forces in the state of modern Britain. In getting Tom Browne to learn his vengeance the new dramatists of the 1970s espoused a realism which claimed to be that of an economist rather than that of a stagey playwright. Social realism defines the reality of England through its Tom Brownes and Bagleys. Social realism is thus real precisely to the extent that it is not socialist, dislikes defeatism, and aims bigger than draughty halls and smoke-filled rooms. But, as we know, social realism, like all the other realisms, is itself a version of naturalism. So, when it starts to invent people like Tom Browne, naturalism, with a kind of inner logic of its own, as it were swears its revenge on socialism in the name of something which in the Tory 1980s was called, by other economically minded people besides dramatists, *new realism*.

The place of stagey naturalism in relation to new realism was demonstrated in a production that converted an ancient chronicle of England into a modern chronicle. When the English Shakespeare Company did their post-Falklands *Henry V*, the modern dress created a feel of up-to-date war technology. The French scenes, however, had the Edwardian costume and dappled lighting effects of a 'classic' British theatre Chekhov production. The contrast between old-fashioned and new societies was figured as a clash between the stagey, but forever lost, and the real, nastily here and now. The real is not there to be comfortably enjoyed; just as Tom Browne's growing up from his schooldays was not a pretty sight, so this production of *Henry V* didn't present the spectacle of post-Falklands Britain as something in which one might wish to rejoice. The abrasiveness, as in all similar cases, comes from the urgency of the desire to make an audience face the real reality of modern life. The search for a form that will be 'true enough' is most frequently pursued by a left that needs to demonstrate, in the face of a dominant order, that it has a grip on what is a remorselessly contemporary real: 'The obsession with the past . . . has been a wondrously agreeable and oh-so-English world to dwell in but is de-modemed from the virtual-reality Britain digitalised into shape in the past decade.' That decade was just coming into being with the modern-army *Henry V*, but, whereas there the past was figured as an old if agreeable staginess, the missing words from the quotation above define it more precisely: 'the past that permeates Labour Oxfordism (including the Ruskin and History Workshop variants)'. (The author is Denis MacShane, Labour MP for Rotherham, writing in *New Statesman and Society* (1994: 20) on Tony Blair's accession to leadership of the Labour Party.) When its political outlook gets caught up in the drive for a really real account of the reality of present and past, the left finds itself organized by an inner logic which insists that any realism which is not new is not realistic.

## 5   Dear, Wonderful Woman

In the preface to his version, Trevor Griffiths says: '*The Cherry Orchard* has *always* seemed to me to be dealing not only with the subjective pain of property-loss but also and more importantly with its objective *necessity*' (Chekhov 1978: vi). When naturalism is thought of as a form that deals with the necessity of change it lands us with Tom Browne, between an agreeable, always lost past and a disagreeable, vengefully real present. Politically, a communal, even Communist, possibility yields to a triumphant individual-ism. But alongside this remorseless inner logic naturalist drama seems simul-taneously to promise access to something different. In the preface to his play *Piano*, based on a film on Chekhovian themes, Trevor Griffiths quotes from Raymond Williams writing about nineteenth-century realism: 'it was a way of seeing the world in which it was possible to experience the quality of a whole way of life through the qualities of individual men and women. Thus, a personal breakdown was a genuinely social fact, and a social breakdown was lived and known in direct personal experience' (in Griffiths 1990: preface). Naturalism has its power, for many people, because it can put them in touch with *wholeness*.

That quality of wholeness has a particular feeling, and construction, on stage.

> *He sits, still wearing Sashenka's hat, as if drained by the passage from irony to mania.* SOPHIA *finds it difficult to look anywhere.* ANNA *sits detached, ironically watchful; whistles a snatch of 'Una Furtiva Lacrima'. Silence.* YASHA *enters suddenly with a tray of drinks,* TRILETSKI *turns him around and heads him back off. A train whistles in the distance.* SOPHIA *looks around her, trying to speak; can't.*

The action is organized to inhibit the selective focus on any one individual or relationship as they are held in temporary stasis. The non-spoken noises and fidgety movement pull the attention to and fro across the scenic space. The train whistle in the distance creates distance, space beyond sight. The image of 'empty' stasis is serviced by a sound effect which mimics, and thus defines, the 'meaningless' noise activity; what thus builds up is a sense of something layered, self-referential, as it were, deep. The country-house society of *Piano* deals with its crises through its unspoken interrelations: 'PLATONOV *sighs his exasperation. Glares across at* TRILETSKI. SHCHERBUK *dins relentlessly on.* TRILETSKI *grins nervously at* PLATONOV, *who softens to a chuckle. The company moves to laughter, another crisis negotiated.*' What is not spoken is displaced onto the scenic space, which organizes itself around them to produce metaphoric relations of which they have no knowledge. Platonov meets again his previous – now married – lover Sophia, and tells of his last farewell to her. Finishing, he

> (*. . . turns slowly in the swing to face the table.* SOPHIA *bangs her glass down, heads off for the house, in tears, a napkin to her mouth.*)

SASHENKA: (*In tears herself*) Oh God, what have you done now, Mishenka? Must you hurt *everybody* . . . ?

> (*A rocket blasts into the sky from behind the house, bursts above them, washes them in a strange pink glow. They stare up at the night.*)

ANNA: (*Calling, from terrace*) Enough, my friends. Everyone to the river. Magic time!

> (*Black.*)

SASHENKA: (*Calling from the blackness*) See, Misha, see. Look how beautiful they are . . .

> (*The first of a series of brilliant flare-like explosions convulsing their settled world order.* SOPHIA *moves quickly through empty space, a lamp in her*

*hand, spectral in the weird off-white glow.* PLATONOV *appears in her wake: he wears a long off-white open burberry, mid-calf, like a Long Rider's coat.*)

PLATONOV: . . . Wait. Listen. For Christ's sake, woman, hear me out. Please . . .

(*She stops, half turns. He gulps for air. They stare at each other across the ghostly space.*)

Dear, wonderful woman . . . My life's gone, I know it, but yours? What's become of *you*?

(Griffiths 1990: 17, 38, 45)

The lighting effects, introduced as fireworks, image a necessary unsettling; characters have props and costumes to make them ghost-like in a space ready to receive them as ghosts. Without making any explicit intellectual analysis, the scenic effect gives the sense of a knowing overview. This kind of scenic writing derives its lasting theatrical attraction from a capacity to show 'wholeness'. It thus offers something unavailable in other genres and media: 'Should *Piano* prove to be about anything at all, I suspect it may prove, like its illustrious forebears, to be about just this felt sense of break-down and deadlock; and thus perhaps, in a nicely perverse irony, about what it's like to be living in our own post-capitalist, post-socialist, post-realist, post-modern times' (Griffiths 1990: preface). Naturalism's theatrical vocabu-lary promises a 'felt sense' of the breakdown by which other art forms are shaped; and in doing so it compensates for its own necessary insistence that neither socialism nor realism are true enough by offering an experience of wholeness.

That wholeness, sustained across scenic space, finds a body for itself. 'Dear, wonderful woman . . . My life's gone, I know it, but yours? What's become of *you?*' Or, said earlier, by another: 'Sarah, wait for me.' Platonov and Harry Kahn share in the faith that emanates from their founding father: 'The idea of absolution had in many of his plays been bound up with the idea of a woman.' The remark is about Ibsen, from early in Williams's *Drama from Ibsen to Brecht*. By the end Williams has traced the shape of naturalism into 1950s Britain and *Look Back in Anger*, where 'the woman is made the bearer of society.' When an individual man rages against a frustrating society, woman – as bearer of society's 'continuing life' – becomes a symbol: 'the woman is seen as the society which traps and swallows a particular self' (R. Williams 1973: 50, 369). Jimmy Porter has to come to realize that some sort of absolution can come from Alison. His lesson is well learnt by the men who find themselves raging against a frustrating society in the 1980s: 'It's wonderful being a woman because you have that knack of knowing what's going on. Men just don't seem to have it. What is it? A sort of instinct?' By the 1980s, on the serious 'art' stage, that sort of speech was very likely to be heard as so sentimental that it is comic: 'ISOBEL *is for the first time able to smile to herself.*' One of Isobel's especial problems as a woman – as she is conceived, so to speak, by David Hare's *The Secret Rapture* (1988) – is that men thrust admiration or devotion upon her: 'Is it the same for all women? People get a fix. You do nothing, absolutely nothing. You're just chatting, you're just walking round the room. And then suddenly, for no reason, they're looking at you as if you're away to the races!' (Hare 1990: 6, 24–5). It's his fix upon her that causes her former lover, Irwin, to kill her.

As a male dramatist demonstratively alert to feminism, Hare uses his male characters to show the destructive effects of fixing on, objectifying, women. As his play opens, the scenic space teases at the object status of woman:

> *The curtain goes up on almost complete darkness, then a door opens at the back and a dim and indirect light is thrown from the corridor.* MARION, *in her late thirties, brisk, dark-haired, wearing a business suit, stands a moment, nervous, awed, in the doorway. She moves into the room which you can just detect is dominated by a large double bed, in which a man is lying, covered with a sheet reaching up over his face.* MARION *stops a moment by the bed, looking down. She then turns to go back towards the door.*
> ISOBEL: Marion?
>     (MARION *lets out a scream, not having realized that* ISOBEL *was sitting in a chair at the end of the bed.*)
>
>                                                       (p. 1)

We can see the covered man, but not Isobel. An imagined, and suggested, connection between the entering woman and the dead man is interrupted by Isobel's voice. We are invited to work hard visually, only to discover that the field of vision is made partial, decentred by sound. The lit, walking woman is not the one in control of the scene. There is already – always? – another woman within the whole scenic space. Later that space works, in its wholeness, to express the individual woman's experience. At the end of Act 1, 'ISOBEL *and* IRWIN *are left alone in the empty room.* ISOBEL *is turned away from him, he behind her.*'

> IRWIN: Isobel, please. Just look at me. Please. (*She doesn't turn.*) . . . I love you. I want you. There's not a moment when I don't want you.
>     (ISOBEL *stands quite still, not turning. The sound of the guns.*)
> ISOBEL: The guns are getting nearer. God, will nobody leave us in peace?
>     (*The lights fade.*)
>
>                                                      (p. 45)

The empty room receives the woman's stillness, her own emptiness; the sound effect of the distant guns extends the space into a fictional distance, and slides into metaphoric invocation of her entrapment. The woman's emotional state, not the man's, is filled out visually and aurally into the whole space.

The woman who walked through that door at the start is Isobel's sister; the body on the bed their father. Their mother died in childbirth. The play begins from the premise that paternal authority is dead. The sisters have to make their own lives, in the memory of the father. Thus Isobel cares for her alcoholic stepmother, which wrecks her business career, and she dies. Marion, a Tory junior minister, maintains her position, survives. Her stepmother's sentimental belief in her relationship with Irwin contributes to Isobel's death. That element of the action speaks for the male dramatist's own distrust about sentimentality towards women. They can be hard politicians as well as carers. But when Isobel is dead, the Tory sister admits: 'It's all obscure. It frightens me. What people want. . . . My memory of childhood is of watching and always pretending. I don't have the right equipment. I can't interpret what people feel' (p. 82). Her Tory politics connect with her failure in naturalism's speciality, interpreting the *felt*. It's naturalism's role not only to 'reveal' this but to specify its necessity. Just before this moment Marion tells us of her mother's death in childbirth: there, where the inevitable history starts, naturalism puts an absent mother. Dead in childbirth she is thus fixed as self-sacrificial bearer. Without such qualities the successful sister is only a partial woman. She ends the play alone, centre stage: 'Isobel, why don't you come home?' (p. 83). In enacting the voice of new realism, naturalism finds itself longing for an appropriate womanhood: caring, unsuccessful, tragic.

That secret rapture becomes a response to, a way of coping with, the very thing which created it, naturalism's inner logic. In David Edgar's 1983 chronicle of the state of the nation, *Maydays*, the ending finds its positive values only in a male Russian dissident and some Greenham women.[2] One of them addresses a 'Tom Browne' character, a man who has moved to the right:

> what we are all trying to do, in our many different ways, can only be accounted for by something in the nature of our species which resents, rejects and ultimately will resist a world that is demonstrably and in this case dramatically wrong and mad and unjust and unfair. And I wonder, Martin, if you ever really felt like that. Or, if you did, if you can still remember. (Edgar 1989: 146)

Within the male-authored chronicle, the fictional woman embodies the nature that of itself will reject defeatism; she will remember across history what it really *felt* like.

And she remembers it for the man: 'She also stirred for me memories of Storyville, New Orleans.' Richard Schechner, theatre director and writer, is here describing Phoebe Legere's work on his production of Genet's *The Balcony* in 1979:

She composed a score . . . that took the revolution seriously – except that it was not a military revolution organized and fought mostly by men according to rules of combat that are culturally masculine, but a revolution of consciousness and song led by women. . . . Legere involved herself deeply in Chantal: a Chantal who was not a symbol of someone else's revolution, but the main actor in her own.

The methods by which the acting was to be done are made clear: another actress 'built her characterization from memories of her own childhood'. The stage directions, treated as the property of those staging the play, produced a problem: 'once rehearsals began in New York, the creakiness of scene 6 became plain. The streets of Manhattan gave the lie to Genet's vision of revolutionary action.' The production method not only referred itself to the truth of a real world but offered to uncover the concealed truths in the play: 'the Chief ripped off Irma's wig, smeared her lipstick, revealing her, for one pathetic moment, as an early-middle-aged drag queen.' Through the production method – or should we say Method – naturalism absorbed Genet's theatre into itself, with the aid of a woman who connected the male director's theatrical whorehouse with his memories of the real, whose presence transformed Chantal from symbol to reality, making a revolution that has ceased to be possible for men. All this 'wouldn't have been there if Legere hadn't auditioned in February. I took an opportunity that walked in the door' (Schechner 1982: 92, 94, 91, 86, 92). Making real the illusion of the first time, the woman comes in from outside, through a doorframe built by that specialist in verisimilitude, naturalism. The man of the 1980s merely – passively – takes what is opportune.

In a previous generation, in 1962 – sometime between the Wolfenden Report and homosexual law reform – Wilson Knight used Ibsen to fantasize a positive image of an unmanly man: 'His highest value we may perhaps define as the bisexual integration from which the plays are composed. Ibsen is as much in his women as in his men and *Hedda Gabler* an emotional autobiography' (Knight 1962: 109). Naturalism, with its secret raptures, has become perhaps the emotional autobiography of a culture. And, as Franco Moretti says, 'the forms with which we picture historical moments to ourselves are crucial for the fashioning of our identity' (Moretti 1988: 344). Naturalism tells us now what concerned serious drama should feel like: the whole scenic space imbued with feeling, truths revealed beneath the surface of an irresponsible and violent society, progress made possible in the authentic experience called woman. Moretti moves on, rapidly, to talk of 'mass literature':

Once avant-garde literature abandoned plot, the void was inevitably filled by a parallel literary system – mass literature . . . The appeal of mass literature is that 'it tells stories', and we all need stories . . . in this century, narrative forms capable of dealing with the great structures and transformations of social life more often than not have belonged to the various genres of mass literature. (p. 344)

Side-stepping avant-gardes and modernisms, naturalism proffers itself not as art form but as the shape of experience, a slice of the life of whole societies, respectful of the bearers of social reality. So it is oddly appropriate that those who are committed to stage naturalism actually have a fantasy of its necessary departure from the theatre, out into 'mass' culture: 'The largest audience for drama . . . is in the cinema and on television, and in many countries these are explicitly popular forms where the theatre is self-consciously, even willingly, a minority form.' Whereas film studies found its own origin in a somewhat recalcitrant melodrama, naturalism suicidally throws itself into the mass-art embrace of film. For, it seems, film and television offer 'certain real solutions' to problems of form where drama can't. So, looking out through the stage door in 1968, Raymond Williams concludes 'there can be little doubt, when the critical history of the next half-century of drama comes to be written, that the majority of its examples will be taken from these new forms' (1973: 399–400). Following the lead of its great theorist, naturalism's new realists urge the political responsibility of writing for television, and produce theatre scripts which do not so much imitate the surface of life as the surface of film: *'The set parts and we are on the lawn at the back of the house. There is a little garden furniture, seemingly at random'* (Hare 1990: 9). The 'we' has all the disembodied fluency of the camera's eye.

Except that behind the camera there is a system of cranes and trolleys. Indeed, the more virtually real it is, the more it is programmed. To discover the apparently random furniture takes a good deal of stage machinery. That machinery, and the budgets which command it, tend to be available only in film and television studios, and well-funded theatres. Naturalism in the 1980s turned its back, like Tom Browne, on draughty halls. Its commitment to the emotional wholeness of scenic space needs a large stage with a technology that can make randomness convincing. The form that tells its necessary stories of wholeness and defeat can afford the cost of being a slice of life. Enacting both its distance from minority experiment and its respect for lived experience, naturalism finds its appropriate cultural home in the theatre called National.

## NOTES

1    For more information on the range of dramatic performance being developed in the 1930s and 1940s, see C. Chambers 1989 on Unity Theatre, Dawson 1985 on Merseyside Unity, Goorney 1981 on Theatre Workshop, Sidnell 1984 on Group Theatre, Stourac and McCreery 1986 on agitational drama, Wallis 1994a and

Wallis 1995 on Popular Front pageantry. Scripts and documents are reprinted in Samuel et al. 1985, but the introductory overview is highly misleading.

2   Greenham women were activists campaigning against nuclear weapons. They camped for several years in the 1980s outside a military base at Greenham, near Newbury, where there were cruise missiles with nuclear warheads. Greenham became a focus for imaginative and heroic anti-nuclear protests, usually by women alone, during the militaristic years of Margaret Thatcher's government.

# 11

# Post-war Theatre and the State

## 1  A People's Civilization

The theatre of post-war Britain is a creature of the State. The Arts Council of Great Britain was set up in 1945 and given £235,000 to spend in its first year on subsidizing 'the fine arts' – visual art, music, opera, ballet, and drama.[1] By 1984, when the Council published its major policy review document *The Glory of the Garden*, its grant had risen to £100 million, of which about a quarter was being spent on drama. By this time, eighty-two theatre companies had the status of Arts Council 'revenue clients' – that is, they depended on regular State subsidies to bridge the gap between their normal costs and their normal income. Virtually all the significant theatres in the country were – and still are – on this list: the National Theatre, the Royal Shakespeare Company, the English Stage Company at the Royal Court, the other venues for new writing such as the Bush and the Traverse, all the repertory theatres in Wales, Scotland and the English provinces, and about thirty touring companies. Most of these theatres had come into existence since 1945 on the basis that subsidy was available, and most would fold if it were withdrawn. The West End continues to operate as an enclave of private enterprise, but even here there are many kinds of indirect dependence: West End managements frequently take over shows which have first proved their commercial potential in a subsidized theatre, and for their own independent productions draw on writers, directors, actors and technicians who have acquired their expertise by working in the public sector. Government funding is built into the financial and physical structure of theatre as a whole. It is a decisively new situation for British drama, and one which proved surprisingly resistant to the free-market ideology of the Thatcher years: despite various incidents of cutting and squeezing since 1979, this particular example of State intervention has so far (1995) survived substantially intact.

State theatre, in other words, is a minor component of the post-war welfare state; and like the major ones, it has its origins in the war itself. The Arts Council was not a new invention in 1945, but a peacetime renaming and reauthorizing of the Council for the Encouragement of Music and the Arts (CEMA), which had been set up in 1940 under the joint patronage of the Board of Education and the Ministry of Information (Baldry 1981: chapter 1). CEMA was explicitly a wartime expedient: its purpose was to promote substitutes for private cultural activities which had been disrupted by the war, and to contribute in whatever way it could to the maintenance of civilian morale. These modest aims were then enthusiastically interpreted by many of the administrators and artists involved: considering their art as having been requisitioned for a great common purpose, they set themselves to bring the best in British culture to the people as a whole, and made a point of touring to venues and audiences which had never seen literary drama, or heard classical music, even in peacetime. Thus, almost inadvertently, the national emergency offered the theatre a social role and a source of support which normal times had failed to afford it; and it was naturally keen to hold on to these ideological and material advantages once the emergency was over. The relevant politicians and civil servants agreed, for an assortment of reasons – because the institution already existed; because they were very effectively lobbied by CEMA's Chairman, John Maynard Keynes; because the amount of money involved was very small by the standards of the massive general transfer of resources from private to public expenditure which the war had entailed; and because the wartime activities of ENSA (Entertainments National Service Association), CEMA, the BBC and the film industry had established a description of the arts as a sort of national asset, which the State might reasonably be expected to foster.

So paying for the arts was a consensual government policy, and the consensus was still in place in much the same terms in 1949, when Parliament voted to empower the Chancellor of the Exchequer to release, when appropriate, £1 million for the building of a National Theatre. The debates surrounding this decision were almost comically devoid of controversy, and at the heart of the unanimity was the idea that the theatre would be, as the chairman of the pressure group, Viscount Esher, had put it, 'the first artistic venture of our new, young, educated democracy' (Elsom and Tomalin 1978: 85). Ironically, this ambiguous populism was especially audible in the House of Lords:

Perhaps Britain can show, with the coming-of-age of her working classes, that they can emulate, and must emulate, the standards and quality and example given them by their parents and guardians, her old aristocracy. By the building of a National Theatre on the Thames side we shall, I hope, make a real contribution towards the ideal of a people's civilisation. (Lord Jowitt, the Lord Chancellor, *Parliamentary Debates* 1949: 987)

That last phrase, oxymoronic in the ears of its noble audience, suavely covers a latent ideological divergence; the happy passengers on the bandwagon were not all making the same assumptions about its destination. The most striking early indicator of this tension is the case of Covent Garden. By the time CEMA became the Arts Council, a few weeks after the end of the war, it was already committed to a plan to rescue the Royal Opera House, which was leased to Mecca Cafés as a dance hall, and develop it as the home of an opera and ballet company of international standing. This ambitious project was unthinkable without generous and continuing public funding; from the very beginning, then, it was understood to have first call on the Council's government grant.[2] The Arts Council and the Board of the Royal Opera House were administrative twins, growing up together, shaping one another's development, and linked in the most practical way by a discreetly nepotistic system of interlocking membership (Hutchison 1982: 27–43).

Thus the dominant paradigm for State culture was sharply at odds with the populist ideology of its wartime prehistory. Shoe-string Shakespeare in works canteens gave way, symbolically, to lavish visual and musical settings for the international stars of the new jet-age opera circuit. Of course, there was no automatic reason why the Council could not support both kinds of practice; up to a point it did, and does. But there was no doubt about which model had the decisive influence. The structural centrality of Covent Garden – the Council's 'flagship', or, in a later cliché, the 'jewel in its crown' – signified the precedence of the large-scale over the small-scale, the fixed over the touring, the metropolitan over the provincial. And underlying all these distinctions, it signified a *class* determination of the politics of subsidy. Not that opera is an inherently patrician art form; in principle, its links with popular theatrical tradition are stronger and richer than those of most modern play-writing. But Covent Garden, in its genesis, its pricing, and the criteria of excellence which informed its rise to international status, distinctively expressed the values of the social elite which supplied at once its management and the dominant part of its audience. This was not the organ of 'a people's civilisation'.

An alternative model was by no means unthinkable; in fact it existed. In August 1945, a month after the launch of the Arts Council, Joan Littlewood's touring group, Theatre Workshop, opened at a school in Kendal. Its manifesto was speaking a language not wholly different from the Lord Chancellor's:

The great theatres of all times have been popular theatres which reflected the dreams and struggles of the people. The theatre of Aeschylus and Sophocles, of Shakespeare and Ben Jonson, of the Commedia dell'Arte and Molière derived their inspiration, their language, their art from the people.

We want a theatre with a living language, a theatre which is not afraid of the sound of its own voice and which will comment as fearlessly on Society as did Ben Jonson and Aristophanes. (Goorney 1981: 41–2)

This mixture of popular expression and classic drama sounds almost like a realization of the official formula, and the company's opening repertoire exactly bore it out: a new ballad-play by Ewan MacColl, a *commedia* show based on a script by Molière, and a poetic drama by Lorca. Its early venues – mostly civic halls in the north of England – also represented a continuation of the populism of CEMA. It was an artistic venture for the new democracy, a sketch for a National Theatre; and a decade later it was beginning to function as such, when it took *Volpone* and *Arden of Faversham* to the Théâtre des Nations festival in Paris, and was hailed as the authentic representative of British theatre. Covent Garden's Arts Council grant at this point was £250,000; Theatre Workshop's was £500.[3]

Thus in 1960, when a serious lobby got under way to persuade the Chancellor of the Exchequer to implement the dormant 1949 National Theatre Act, its politically ecumenical make-up concealed the fact that a political decision had effectively been taken already – a decision not about the scale and timing of the project, which would be argued about for years, but about its character. If we identify this decision, schematically, as the choice of a Royal Opera model and the rejection of a Theatre Workshop model, we can grasp its implications in somewhat more theoretical terms.

Why *does* the State – not the State in the abstract, but the post-war British State – pay out money to help people put on plays? Why not just leave it to the operations of supply and demand, like other kinds of art (for example, novels) or other kinds of performance (for example, ice-skating)?

The Royal Opera answer to these questions has to do with an idea which is no less conspicuous in the Lord Chancellor's remarks than that of 'the people': the idea of 'quality'. Drama cannot be left to the market because the market promotes what most people want to buy, and since good taste is the prerogative of an elite – the aristocratic 'parents and guardians' of the culture – the effect of *laissez-faire* would be to sink the theatre in vulgarity. If individual aristocrats were rich enough to act as patrons, then the State would not be required, but 'unfortunately in the conditions of today, Maecenas is dead, and I do not see any new Maecenas arising, unless it is the people themselves.'[4] The public purse, socialistically distended, compensates for the sad state of the private ones: the new Renaissance patron is a civil servant.[5] In this model, then, the role of the State is to protect the quality of drama from the cultural ill effects of social and economic egalitarianism.

In the Theatre Workshop model, on the contrary, the objection to a free market in drama is that it necessarily offers it for sale to the highest bidders. The effect of *laissez-faire* is therefore a theatre which reflects only the values, interests and world-view of the rich. This is bad not only for the rest of us, since we find our lives and concerns unrepresented or distorted on the stage, but also for the theatre itself, which becomes cramped and attenuated if it is cut off from the popular sources of its vitality. In this model, then, the role of the State is to protect the quality of drama from the cultural ill effects of social and economic inequality.

These models, which somehow coexist within the frail consensual ideology of the 'people's civilization', are fundamentally opposed versions not only of theatre but also of the State. The contradiction is very much that of the post-war Labour administration which was the matrix of both. As Raymond Williams pointed out, looking back from 1977,

> The major transfer of further kinds of power to an increasingly central-ized state after the war was partly a function of the needs of the capitalist system itself, but it was partly also the realization of the programme of the British left. This is a dreadful truth. Of course the National Coal Board is not the army, British Rail is not the Special Branch. But to the extent that a generation believed that you could transfer the responsi-bility of popular power to that state, with those organs, it would be fair for any subsequent period to conclude that it must have been mad. (1978: 416)

The hope that State patronage of drama would produce a counter-hegemonic 'people's theatre' is a precise if politically minor instance of that madness. It derived plausibility from the fact that the enfranchisement, the political and cultural *arrival*, of the people, was not just window dressing, but really part of the ideology of the party which was carrying the programme through, as well as of many of the artists who were making use of the resources that became available. It 'must have been mad' in the sense that, as we have seen, the Theatre Workshop model was never seriously on offer: the *dominant* practice of the Arts Council was always a function of the cultural needs of the existing ruling class. But even so, the contradiction survived into the developing system as, if nothing else, an interesting unease.

After another long postponement following its Parliamentary victory in 1949, the National Theatre finally took shape in the early 1960s, and for adventitious reasons it ended up as a duopoly: the National Theatre itself, which opened at the Old Vic in the autumn of 1963, and the Royal Shake-speare Company, which had been created in 1960–1 when the Shakespeare Memorial Theatre, Stratford-upon-Avon, opened a second house at the Aldwych Theatre in London and was granted a Royal Charter. The total Arts

Council grant was growing fairly rapidly at this point (it was increased by 46 per cent in 1966, following the incoming Labour Government's White Paper of 1965), and the ambitious new companies were well placed to benefit. Around 1970, their status began to be marked by an Arts Council habit of using the phrase 'national companies' as a collective term for its four biggest clients – the RSC, the National, the Royal Opera House and the English National Opera. In 1976 the National acquired a conspicuous and demanding new building, and the RSC did the same in 1982; these monumental assets (and liabilities) effectively ratified the 'national' status of both companies. The importance of the label can be seen in *The Glory of the Garden*, which defines the English Stage Company at the Royal Court as a 'non-national drama company' (Arts Council 1984: 27), and requires it to seek supplementary funding from the relevant local authorities. Since the Royal Court had been the acknowledged centre for new English play-writing since 1956, this discrimination makes it clear that 'national' is not an innocently descriptive term. A 'national company' is one whose situation is metaphysically deemed to be ubiquitous rather than local, whose primacy is a parameter, rather than a component, of Arts Council policy, and whose grant is routinely about ten times bigger than that of the next largest organization. Theatre had, so to speak, secured its Royal Opera Houses.

The big two were of course widely attacked for soaking up millions when many smaller groups were in difficulties for lack of a few thousand. But it seems unlikely that the sums worked in that way. While the 'national companies' were being built up, the rest of the drama budget rose more or less in step, and many of the best-known fringe groups were in fact set up during this period.[6] The Arts Council's overall commitment to drama, which in the late 1950s had dropped to about 7 per cent of its total grant-in-aid, came out of the 1970s at around 29 per cent. 'Non-national' companies may have resented having to subsist on the crumbs that fell from the top table, but if the table had not been put there, there would have been almost no loaf. With partial justification, the national institutions argued that they were not the exploiters of other subsidized drama, but its leading advocates. And it is around the issue of this leadership that the important contradictions operate – not in a zero-sum competition for money between one company and another, but in the structure of State theatre as a whole.

It is obviously a hierarchy. The NT and the RSC form the centre, and transitory and homeless touring groups the outer 'fringe'. In between, subtly competing for relative centrality, come the Royal Court, the big-city reps, the London club theatres, and the more established touring companies. This concentric arrangement functions as a sort of promotion ladder, each group recruiting writers, directors, actors and occasionally entire companies who have succeeded on the rung below. One progresses, as it were, from a merely local or sectional audience in the direction of a national stage where one will be addressing, not just the neighbourhood, the region, the avant-garde, or the constituency defined by political or ethnic identity, but *the public*. The 'national' theatre audience – this is the most ideologically forceful sense of the category – is taken to be an unconditional one: not anyone in particular, but everybody in general.

This neutral collective is what the 1940s founders meant by 'the people'; it is that universal constituency to which 'national' drama addresses itself, which confers recognition and authorizes subsidy; it is the Public in whose interests the State is juridically presumed to act. And it is, crucially, a fiction. In reality, the audience was constructed in quite sociologically specific ways. As Alan Sinfield has argued in detail in relation to the RSC (Sinfield 1985), national theatre emerged, not coincidentally, at the same historical juncture as the amorphous youth culture of the 1960s, produced by post-war affluence in general and, in particular, the dramatic expansion of higher education after the Robbins Report of 1963.[7] The effect of this constituency was that State theatre's populist language mutated rapidly into a rhetoric of the 'young' audience, which in practice mostly meant an audience of the expanding middle-class intelligentsia. This class reorientation was confirmed by the logic of the companies' market situation. Large-scale, high-cost and politically exposed, they needed to be able to predict ratios of audience to capacity with great accuracy; and one of the ways they achieved this was by marketing via the mailing list, the outer circle of regular patrons who get advance notice and priority booking for each season. This is a highly cost-effective way of selling tickets, but it has naturally tended to establish a regular audience of 'theatre-goers', predominantly middle class and home counties – in other words, a slight redefinition of the audience of the old West End. As with education itself, the principal beneficiaries of enhanced public provision were those social groups which possessed some private cultural capital already. This was not the audience that the leading practitioners particularly wanted: in the early 1970s, at least, the artistic directors of both the big companies were making policy statements with a distinctly radical and egalitarian tinge.[8] But it was the audience they had.

This contradictory situation has its architectural monument in the 'national' stages themselves: the Olivier at the National Theatre, and the RSC's main stage at the Barbican. Both these spaces were imagined as forums for public drama: Edward Bond, in an uncharacteristic moment of optimism, described the Olivier stage as a place 'like a public square or the meeting of several roads or a playing field or a factory floor or a place of assembly and debate' (Bond 1978); the unbroken arc of tiered seating round the focal point is intended to recall the amphitheatre at Epidaurus, the festive meeting place of an entire political society. And at the Barbican, the out-front thrust of the forestage is meant to combine with the overhanging galleries to provide a modern equivalent of Shakespeare's wooden 'O', in which 'the audience is embracing the actor' (Burrows 1982). Both designs connote a big, self-present, participatory crowd, with the actor performing in the midst of the collective. But in both cases this is an illusion: there are virtually no seats upstage of the very front of the acting area, the real spatial relationship is end-on, and the layout is dictated by the demands of the spectator as individual customer (comfort and good sightlines). It is indicative, to say the least, that both stages first demonstrated their full potential in spectacular musicals; *Guys and Dolls* at the Olivier, and *Les Misérables* at the Barbican. Representatively, the major national auditoria combine the *practice* of quality entertainment with the *idea* of public drama. In both, the design provides for consumers but pretends that they are participants: as a result of this duplicity the audience's 'embrace' is a constrained and nervous one.

Another symptom of the tension is the tendency of State theatre to split in two. Just as the theatrical scene as a whole divides, like the Edinburgh Festival, into official and fringe, mainstream and alternative, so the National Theatre sprouted first the Young Vic and then the Cottesloe, while the RSC has proliferated alternative spaces – the Arts Theatre, Theatregoround, the Place, the Other Place, the Warehouse, the Swan, the Pit. This recurrent splittage is certainly an ironic comment on main house claims to totality: the show on the big stage plays to 'the people', but somehow always there are also the other people, round the corner in the studio. However, it also reflects a more specific irony of the structure. The alternative space is often to the left, roughly speaking, of the official one: it stands for young artists, new writing, formal experiment, offences against prevailing canons of taste, a politically radical tendency. In fact it is because the company believes that these things are valuable that the alternative space is set up. This is where the Theatre Workshop model of State drama continues a somewhat bracketed existence, in the interstices of the 'Opera House'; where, in poor theatre, rough theatre, open stages, engagement with ethnic and sexual and class difference, the idea of a democratic theatrical culture is pursued. But then what is implied by the relative sizes of the polarized spaces, and by the marketing calculations which inform their programming, is that the 'other place' is a minority theatre, catering for the tastes of an avant-garde, of the connoisseurs of experiment who find the repertoire in the main house a bit banal. Thus the alternative strand of the theatre's activities is located both above and below the mainstream – above, because it appears as a coterie art which deserves to be subsidized for the sake of an inherent excellence which is not widely appreciated; and below, because it is intended to pose a demotic, popular challenge to the aesthetics of official drama, and to appeal to a less acculturated clientele.[9] This double location precisely reproduces the rationale of State drama as a whole: the other place is, so to speak, the subsidized theatre's subsidized theatre. The vision of a theatre which plays to all the people seems to get deferred through an endless sequence of minorities: the public, that finally validating constituency, remains elusive.

## 2 Athenian Summer

The context of national theatre has been national decline. The State which set up the Arts Council was a world empire emerging victorious from an immense war which had, in fact, broken the economic and strategic basis of its power. By 1949, India was independent, and the superpower system of the next forty years was already in place. Viscount Esher, whose family had been involved in the campaign for a National Theatre since the high imperialist era before 1914, put the best possible shine on this irony:

> [Power and wealth] have passed to those two remote monsters who live to the East and West of Europe. Their way of life, though very different one from the other, has no real appeal to us. But I am convinced that Shakespeare's countrymen are about to enjoy an Athenian summer of great interest and charm. (*Parliamentary Debates* 1949: 998)

The idea is elegantly autumnal: England hands over its big guns to the new empires, and retires to the country to grow old gracefully among its books and pictures. Only the note of timid xenophobia hints that the loss of power and wealth might cut deeper than that. Over the years when the cultural institutions of post-war drama were emerging, it became apparent, as it clearly had not been in 1949, quite how much power and wealth were going to be lost. The English Stage Company was formed in 1956, the year of British imperialism's disgrace at Suez; by the time the national companies were set up a decade later, there was little left of the Empire except rebellious remnants overseas and hardening racism at home; and when the National opened in 1976, the revolution in the oil trade had already tipped the British economy into crisis. Symptomatically, the new theatre was soon involved in two industrial disputes, one with its technicians, and one with the Theatre Writers' Union. Esher's tranquil separation between power and wealth on the one hand and culture on the other proved difficult to sustain: the outlook for the Athenian summer was changeable.

The most obvious dramatic formula for national decline is nostalgia. Anyone who has seen much State drama in this period recognizes that discursive space: the ruminative monologue half-detached from the action, the note of historical loss. Billy Rice in *The Entertainer*, 1957:

> They were graceful, they had mystery and dignity. Why when a woman got out of a cab, she descended. Descended. And you put your hand out to her smartly to help her down . . . (Osborne 1957: 33)

Anna in *Old Times*, 1971:

> innocent girls, innocent secretaries, and then the night to come, and
> goodness knows what excitement in store, I mean the sheer expectation
> of it all, the looking-forwardness of it all, and so poor, but to be poor and
> young, a girl, in London then . . . (Pinter 1981: 14)

Jerry in *Road*, 1986:

> And the way you stood, you know, and you had a cigarette. You even lit
> a cigarette different then. There was some way, I can't do it now. Good
> thing too, if I could I'd cry me flipping heart out. That's why I never
> wear Brylcreem these days. I can't. (Cartwright 1986: 13)

It is a personal note, certainly: the speakers remember the sexual freshness of
their youth. But it isn't about individual experience. The courting days are
located in history: Billy Rice looks back to Edwardian England, Anna to the
poor and hopeful London of the late 1940s, and Jerry to the 1950s, the period
which is also, ironically, the disenchanted present time of *The Entertainer*. And
what they all recall is not particular events, but prevailing codes – the way
things were done then. The code generalizes the memory and so makes it
possible to share it with the audience, but it is also the very object of the
retrospective longing. In those days, 'you' had a role, you knew who you were
meant to be; nowadays, I'm not sure. The audience substantiates this image of
a lost cultural wholeness through its recognition of the coded fragments that
are offered: cabs, austerity, Brylcreem. Sitting in our seats, all together but
mutually invisible, we experience our community through the past which we
share with the speaker, and our separation through identification with the
same speaker's present lostness. So our shared identity is definingly retrospective. This is nostalgia in a precise sense: the past appears as home, the present
as exile.

This is how the theatre might be expected to entertain Shakespeare's
countrymen in their Athenian summer, and certainly its attractive power
should not be underestimated. Arguably it *was* underestimated, for example,
by Theatre Workshop, in the case of their best-known show, *Oh What a Lovely
War* (1963). Self-consciously working class in its style and point of view, it
presented the 1914–18 war as an enormous criminal enterprise in which the
European ruling classes sacrificed millions of lives in defence of their own
prejudices and profits. Transferred to the West End, this carefully researched
piece of communist propaganda became a commercial hit on the strength of its
stylish period feel, its catchy old tunes, and, above all, the warm feeling of
humanity with which the audience could deplore together the pointlessness of
these battles long ago – overlooking the play's divisive insistence not on their

pointlessness but on their *point*. The appetite for the unifying magic of the past turned out to be capable of swallowing a great deal.

But the effect is precarious as well as powerful. The magic is located, not really in the evoked past, but in its relation with the yearning present; it therefore registers not only the communal memories but equally, in the same breath, the loss of community. The collective apprehends itself *as lost*. The gentleness of the rose-tinted retrospect can then turn, without discontinuity, into acrid, cynical rejection – looking back in anger. At that point, the cynicism corrodes even the idealized past, which appears as a cruel fraud. So there is a constant tendency for collective nostalgia to slide into self-mockery: Osborne, Pinter and Cartwright more or less clearly place their lost England as an illusion, and it is parodied in countless other plays, ranging from Alan Bennett's wry irony in *Forty Years On* (1968) to Steven Berkoff's violent sarcasm in *Decadence* (1981).

The sarcastic end of the range is concisely illustrated by the opening of Howard Barker's *The Hang of the Gaol*, staged in one of the RSC studios in 1978. The gaol has burnt down, and the Governor and his lady stand in the blackened wreckage:

GOVERNOR: My lovely ringing corridors of English iron. Struck sparks
    off the heels of warders' boots.
LADY: Probably what started it.
GOVERNOR: My girders bearing in their grace the criminals' sleep . . .
LADY: Glass and concrete next time.

(H. Barker 1982: 9)

The lament for lost heritage, sketched in with confidence that the audience will recognize it instantly, is rendered grotesque by its object: you used to know your role in the less than idyllic sense that you were either a con or a screw; present alienation takes the form of no longer being able to find one's cell. This is not an isolated effect. The gaol, which is called Middenhurst (Parkhurst/Middlemarch/dungheap), offers itself as a vague metaphor: the play is a vision of England as a chaotic bureaucratic enquiry taking place in the ruins of a Victorian prison. Thus both sides of the nostalgic structure of feeling are consciously degraded: the Governor's blowsy poetry appeals from a corrupt and ruinous present to a corrupt and tyrannical past. The prevailing tone of the writing is at once vituperative and blasé: the implicit judgement could be summarized as 'this society is a shambles, and that's fine with me.' Thus nostalgia, ironized, mutates into denunciation, and becomes the formula for what is almost the official genre of national decline: the bad-state-of-the-nation play.

One of the most ambitious of these – and one which failed spectacularly and interestingly – is John Arden and Margaretta D'Arcy's Arthurian epic *The*

*Island of the Mighty* (1972). Its sixth-century setting seems at first to remove it completely from the terrain of nostalgia, but the historical scene soon looks familiar. Arthur is presented as a post-imperial reactionary, struggling to sustain Roman methods of control in a society to which they are irrelevant, and the entire action is set in the twilight of even his ascendancy, when his great victories against the Saxons are already a twenty-year-old memory, and the heavy cavalry which made them possible are 'old men / Strapped up with hooks of iron' (Arden and D'Arcy 1974: 98). The island of the ironically majestic title is disintegrating into little principalities divided by sovereignty, ethnicity and religion; we see Arthur fighting Galloway Picts and English invaders with the unreliable assistance of semi-autonomous rulers in Strath-clyde and Dunedin. Thus the play demystifies the contemporary United Kingdom in two ways – by a historical placing (these bloody events are its origins) and by a transhistorical analogy (this political order, like our own, is sustained by the cultural scraps of a lost empire).

So it was a contradictory project for a 'national company'; and when the RSC accepted the play for abridged main stage production at the Aldwych in 1972, the contradictions surfaced in unexpected form. About a fortnight before the opening, the authors watched the first run-through, and were dismayed by what they felt was a basic misinterpretation of their script. They had been imagining a style of production which would be a mixture of Brecht, English medieval theatre, and the mythic open air drama they had recently seen in Bengal – 'the style of the staging was simple and direct, the main emphasis was always towards a strong and vivid story-telling, and where the plot became too diffuse for "dramatization", the action was hurried forward by means of rapid verse-narrative, songs, and instrumental music' (D'Arcy's preface, Arden and D'Arcy 1974: 20).

By these lights, the decor and music of the RSC's production seemed picturesque and atmospheric in ways which blunted the narrative drive, and the acting style distorted by a concern for psychological depth which weak-ened the emphasis on action and, in particular, built Arthur up into a tragic protagonist whose point of view therefore acquired an arbitrary authority. For the Ardens these issues were a matter not just of taste but of political meaning: they maintained that the RSC had given their play 'an imperialistic effect' (letter to the *Guardian*, 5 December 1972). They asked for a company meeting to discuss their objections; the director decided against this; the Ardens interpreted his refusal as a violation of their contractual rights as writers, and declared the matter to be an industrial dispute. Hence the unusual spectacle, which rapidly became more famous than the play itself, of two distinguished writers picketing the opening performances of their own work.

The immediate theatre politics of all this are quite revealing of the con-ditions of national drama, but to understand them we must first consider what was going on in the play. Its plot is strange and complex, but it is not

hopelessly simplistic to see it as centring on a grand opposition between the
rationalistic neo-Roman regime of Arthur himself and the alternative secret
sovereignty which comes in the course of the action to be represented by his
dangerous young wife, Gwenhwyvar. This opposition is reproduced at every
level of the imagined society: it is Roman/Celtic, but also Christian/pagan,
male/female, regimental/guerrilla, reason/magic, centre/margin, uniformity/
difference. These polarities are further articulated by providing each of the
conflicting factions with a professional bard: Arthur's is Merlin, whose
language is reflective, courtly and controlled; and Gwenhwyvar's is Aneurin,
who impudently rejects the approved genres and metres in favour of a rough-
edged ballad idiom which circulates anonymously among the poor. This
dimension of the show extends the list of opposed principles into literature,
aligning the dominant Arthurian system with the official and authorial, and
the suppressed tradition with the popular and collective.

Now in one way, it is obvious that the female–popular side of this opposition represents, point by point, the values of the semi-political 'counter-
culture' of 1972. To that extent, the Ardens, with their explicit commitments
to feminism, to community action, and to anti-imperialism in Ireland, India
and Vietnam, were remaking their myth by discovering, as Arden flatly said,
that Arthur had changed sides (Page 1985: 50): where romantic versions had
encouraged identification with the hero-king, this one, if anything, took the
part of his enemies. This makes immediate sense of the charge that the
production was 'imperialist': by playing Arthur and Merlin for empathy, and
staging the social milieu for atmosphere and exoticism, the RSC had allegedly
cancelled the Ardens' revisionism and reinstalled Arthurian values at the
centre of the drama. Moreover, it was appropriate, if not inevitable, that the
company would do exactly this. Roman, Christian, male, regimental, reason,
centre, uniformity, official, authorial – the terms of the Arthurian half of the
opposition are precisely the terms on which a large metropolitan State theatre
exists, committed as this one is by its very name both to the United Kingdom
and to its official bard. Not that there was anything stopping the RSC doing
plays which represented the British State as ineffectual or repressive or super-
annuated: it could and had, as its Artistic Director pointed out when the storm
broke. But what it could not do, according to the Ardens' critique, was to get
*outside* the British State and adopt a formally and politically *other* standpoint.
Indissolubly wedded to the post-imperial centre, it produced historical drama
in a style appropriate to decline: sombre, introverted, heavy with ironic
consciousness.

However, only in the heat of the moment, only on the pavement outside the
Aldwych, could this appear as a simple case of an anti-imperialist show
deviously censored by agents of the State. The Ardens' own position was more
contradictory than that. For one thing, their insistence on their right as
authors to control the interpretation of their play sat awkwardly with their

implicit identification with Aneurin, who teaches his songs to travelling brigands and lets them wander the roads unsigned. Confrontational as it was, their stand was based on their having accepted the 'Arthurian' character of the RSC, and consequently having formal and determinable rights within that official structure. The counter-cultural partisanship of the show is to that extent a piece of wishful thinking. It belongs, itself, already, to the imperial culture, and the writing is too theatrically intelligent not to acknowledge that; the script – independently of any production – *is* imperialistic in the sense that the pagan values, however sympathetically presented, are structurally secondary, coming into focus, in a familiar colonialist manner, only as the 'other' of the official centre. This was the reason, of course, why it was possible for the style of the performance to have such a drastic effect on the import of the play. The text was already ambiguous: if the director was indeed looking for a tragic evocation of the fall of imperial civilization, then he did not need to rewrite the script to find it, only to emphasize some elements rather than others.

In any case, the dramatization of the 'other' tradition is sympathetic only in a very qualified sense. The secret sovereignty of Gwenhwyvar is a doubly repressed myth: it persists in the folklore of the powerless, and it is also, literally, the skeleton in the royal cupboard. Its return is apocalyptic, confounding high and low, ancient and modern, Christian and pagan. The accumulated energy is released in fragmentation and madness: the explosion is not convincingly an alternative to the sclerotic order it shatters, rather a reaction to it. There may be a fleeting image of a politically emancipated life, but it is at once soaked in blood. In staging this futureless revolution, the play is surprisingly typical: the same thing happens to Arden's own Serjeant Musgrave (1959), and to the heroine of his radio play *Pearl* (1978);[10] comparably futile cataclysms form the climactic moments of Howard Brenton's plays *The Churchill Play* (1974) and *Weapons of Happiness* (1976). This recurrent pattern is not simply a reflex of subjective political pessimism. Rather, the point is that the various outbreaks signify, as stage events, a sort of absolute negation of prevailing conditions, a statement of unconditional immediacy; and this would be compromised by the mediations which any measure of practical success would entail. Futility is the sign of total refusal; as with the stage rhetoric of nostalgia, it is as lost, and *only* as lost, that the community realizes itself.

So despite its feminist and populist utopianism, the subversive gesture is also intensely reactionary: a reaching back, beyond the failing rationalities of the post-imperial rearguard, to a darker principle, preliterate, visceral, rooted in myth and kinship, promising renewal by its very archaism, but issuing in irrational violence. The buried past, impiously recovered, impacts upon the present not as a unifying heritage but as terror.

*The Island of the Mighty* actually ends on just this note: Aneurin sings a heretical ballad of Lazarus in which the dead man returns with a message from the corpses he has met:

> And when the big boots
> Dance on the grave
> It is the corpses
> They will raise
> For you went and you buried them
> With all the life inside
> That they could not live
> When they were alive.
> We are going to come back
> And we are going to take hold
> So hideous and bloody greedy
> We take hold of the whole world!
> (Arden and D'Arcy 1974: 235)

With this festive and horrific image, the play, despite its truculent idiosyncrasy, fits into an identifiable genre of 1970s drama. Earlier the same year, Howard Brenton's seminal *Hitler Dances*, worked out with Max Stafford-Clark at the Traverse, revolved round the image of a dead German soldier brought back up to life in a children's game; the same relationship, between the animated corpse and the naughty child, was naturalized in Brenton's less experimental *Weapons of Happiness*, which was the first new play in the new National Theatre, in 1976. Later, Howard Barker's *Victory* (Joint Stock, 1983) begins with a dead regicide being dug up by agents of the Restoration in 1660; the body is carted about, horror-comic fashion, in increasingly random bits as the play proceeds. In the immediate background of all these grotesqueries, clearly, are the devoured and recycled corpses of Edward Bond's *Early Morning* and *Lear*. Nostalgia finds its ironic metaphor in exhumation; decisively, 'living in an old country' is staged, not as Lord Esher's autumnal fullness, but as a struggle with the unappeased past – ghosts, zombies, things that are neither living nor dead.

Many of these figures come out of a conscious impulse which could loosely be called Artaudian. The violent travestying of Englishness is linked to the rejection of a perceived English theatrical tradition of verbal fluency and physical constraint: the monstrous images are an attempt to force out a stage language which will reverberate in the nerves and guts of the audience. We will be returning to this project in the next section; what is more striking here is that the same logic informs the work of the most verbal and cerebral writer of state-of-the-nation drama: David Edgar.

First performed in 1976, Edgar's *Destiny* is about an imaginary neo-Nazi party called Nation Forward fighting a West Midlands by-election. Most of the twenty-odd characters are involved in one or another of the political parties contesting the election, and between them they dramatize the socio-political factors which lead people to support or to oppose fascism in contemporary Britain. This schematism tends to give the performance the form of an illustrated talk, constructing the audience as a group of students in pursuit of objective understanding, and so depoliticizing the theatrical occasion despite the intensely political nature of the theme. The strain of this contradiction is occasionally felt in the language of the dialogue. Here, for instance, are the NF leaders coming to an understanding with a representative capitalist:

> — The army?
> — Can contain, perhaps. They can't destroy.
> — We also combat international capital.
> — We also need protection.
> — If it means control?
> — You scratch us, we'll scratch you.
> — You'd sacrifice the 'free' of enterprise?
> — Yes, to preserve the privacy of property.
>                              (Edgar 1987: 401–2)

This is an opinion, about the relationship between capitalism and the far right, pretending to be a conversation. The writing addresses not so much a public as a disembodied mind.

What releases the play from this attenuated expository convention is, by and large, the affective repertoire of the right itself. At the beginning and ending of the play the set is dominated by 'a large, dark painting of the putting down of the Indian Mutiny'; at several moments the argument is punctuated by the imperial verse of Kipling or Laurence Binyon, or Edgar's pastiche of it; there is a famous shock-effect when a crypto-Nazi group ceremonially unveils a portrait of Hitler. At all these moments, the play is quoting iconography from the object of its analysis to generate the theatrical energies which the analysis itself doesn't command. More subtly, the language of exposition is transgressed by one of the officer-class fascists, Major Rolfe, who is conceived of as someone who actually lives the soiled grandeur of the imagery. For example, he has a monologue about the death of his son, shot by a young sniper in Belfast:

> And on the plane, I realised, I had more time for him, the 12-year-old boy killer in the Divis Flats, the dark child with his Russian rifle, far more time for him, than they. The Generals. The Ministers. Assured us that the sun would never set. The Generals, could not prevent my son, in his high morning, his sun going down. . . . (*He is crying.*) The sun has set. And we should not remember. We should not look back, but

should, instead, think only of the morning. (*He looks at the crumpled flag.*) His fault. He turned his back. (*The tears stop.* ROLFE *raises the flag, holding it in a high salute.*) We need an iron dawn. (pp. 377–8)

Here the theatre language acquires a sudden density. The flag, the tears, the gesture; the outrageous conflation of personal bereavement and national decline; the fragments of archaic rhetoric and the alogical jumps of feeling between them – these compacted elements move the audience out of the lecture hall and into momentary participation in a ritual of atavistic nationalism, a deviant remembrance day. The point is not at all that Rolfe is 'convincing' as the lay figures of the exposition fail tó be: with his poetic idiom, his messianic violence, and his daring sympathy with the enemy, he is a fairly unlikely figure. It's that his formal, intransigent code of speech and action is what communicates Nation Forward's meaning on the stage. Just because his opinions are so flatly unacceptable, they open up a space beyond opinion: this consistently thoughtful show finds its dramatic centre in a nostalgia so extreme that it is barely sane.

It's ironically relevant to this paradox that *Destiny* was the key point on its author's professional advance from the fringe towards the national centre. Before its production, Edgar had written about a dozen plays, which had all been done by touring groups, club theatres or the studios of provincial reps, and published, if at all, in small left-wing imprints. He wrote *Destiny* for the Birmingham Rep, with whom he already had a working connection: it clearly made sense as a show about the politics and society of the Midlands. Birmingham decided not to do it, and after some debate it found a home, geographically close by but institutionally remote, in the RSC's Other Place at Stratford, whence it transferred to London in 1977. In a textbook example of the close relationship between national theatre and mainstream publishing, the script was at once brought out by Methuen, first as a 'Methuen New Theatrescript' (1976), then as a 'Methuen Modern Play' (1978), and eventually as the work of a 'Methuen World Dramatist' (1987). Almost accidentally, it had become a 'national' drama.

In this context, the significance of Nation Forward is not a simple reflection of that of its real life counterpart; it is more structurally a *perverse image of national identity*. This comes to the surface explicitly in a monologue by the Tory candidate, Crosby, after he has visited the Nation Forward campaign office:

And it was very strange, talking to these people; thought, oh, no, these can't be, with their grisly xenophobia, they can't, or are they, our creation. Demons. Alter-ego. Somehow. And I remembered, being small, the Coronation, and the climbing of Mount Everest, a kind of homely patriotism, sort of, harmless, slightly precious self-content.

A dainty, water-colour world, you know. And then, their monstrous chauvinism. Dark, desire, for something . . . Kind of, something dark and nasty in the soul. (*Pause*) Felt out of time. . . . I'm scared. (pp. 366–7)

In a way, the play invites identification with this dismay: the Coronation and Mount Everest are coded fragments of community in the manner we have already encountered. But equally, the writing places it as a laughable political incapacity. The 'homely patriotism' had kept itself innocent by denying the 'dark and nasty' forces on which it actually depended, and now, as racism and class warfare reassert themselves undisguised, there is an undertone of glee at the spoiling of the water-colour world. Not that the play's opposition to the National Front is at all ambivalent: Edgar's political commitment is solid. And of course, there are good reasons for developing an empathy with the other side. But the staging of reactionary national feeling is not just tactical in that sense. Rather, it is seeking to appropriate the far right, dialectically, for revolutionary theatre. Nation Forward, after all, is founded on the proposition that the British State has failed, that its constitutional leaders have lost all honesty and conviction, that catastrophic national decline is not reversible under the existing dispensation, and that a war between order and subversion has to all intents and purposes already begun. This is a radical analysis: it is in effect Edgar's own. But it is not one which can be coherently conducted in a 'national' theatre, because the theatre is sponsored by that same despised State, and because, as we've seen, the institution, its audience, and its discourses are built on a consensual conception of the public which the analysis fundamentally rejects. So the play proceeds by indirection. The National Front is not its subject so much as its stalking-horse, the positive form of its cultural and political negation. To an extent that the writing itself doesn't wholly command, the show wants to *be* as evil, as unacceptable, as that. It is inviting the audience to grasp the nation as the neo-fascist characters grasp it – to draw different conclusions in the end, certainly, but first, really to see that dark picture.

Parody of communal nostalgia; revision of national myth; festive exhumation; dialectical reworking of reactionary nationalism – the common theme in all these variants of national theatre can be named in one word: irony. Across wide differences of style and focus, what is consistent is that State-sponsored theatre's relation to the national community it is supposed to serve and express is oblique, left-handed, avoiding affirmation. The national institutions cannot quite place the actors, even virtually, before 'the people': the ideological fragmentation attendant on the loss of national power and wealth means that Shakespeare's countrymen are somehow not there.

This appears, for example, in the way so many of the plays we have been considering return as if compulsively to the memory of the Second World

War. Arden provides a sixth-century equivalent for the mythology of 1940. Edgar stages a crucial exchange in *Destiny* at a Remembrance Day ceremony. Brenton digs up Hitler and Churchill. Even in the bizarrely isolated world of Barker's gaol, characters attempt to orient themselves by memories of V-1s and Dunkirk. The significations attached to the war are various – heroism, barbarity, service, real or faked national unity, erotic energy, unconditional evil. Whichever way the associations are turned, they combine to accord the war a unique cultural *authority*. That was the last time, it seems, for good or ill, when the nation was a positive entity, when a national utterance could be unironic; so everything since then has had to locate itself in relation to that primal moment of definition. The writer most closely identified with this ambiguous and specific strain of nostalgia is David Hare; his first play for the National Theatre, *Plenty* (1978), is in many ways the most economical instance of the bad-state-of-the-nation genre, displaying the whole theme through the painful disintegration of one character from 1946 through to 1962 as she fails to recapture the fullness of being she once had as a courier for Special Operations in occupied France. The play presents a post-war world in which nothing which has been won is as real as fighting for it was; its emotional tone is one of inconsolable grief. The title of Hare's most recent 'national' play, *The Absence of War* (1993), refers to the same emptiness; it doesn't in this case have very much to do with the action, which is a rather thin dramatization of the 1992 election, but as if in deference to a generic obligation, the play, written to complete a bad-state-of-the-nation trilogy, begins and ends on Remembrance Day at the Cenotaph.

This habit of remembrance is itself a further irony: consciously or unconsciously, State theatre is revisiting what is, as we saw, the moment of its own administrative birth. The pioneers of CEMA, looking ahead to a post-war future when British theatre would achieve great things thanks to the patronage of a democratic State, can hardly have expected that the future theatre would spend so much of its time looking back, in sorrow or anger or derision, to the moment of that hope.

### 3   Talking About Theatre

Arden, Bond, Barker, Brenton, Edgar, Hare – with the possible exception of Hare, these are not the paradigmatic State theatre writers. Arden has not worked in the subsidized mainstream since 1972; Barker has never had more than a toehold in the 'national companies'; the rest fluctuate between the main stages, the studios and the fringe. All of them exacerbate the tensions we have been exploring by their conscious position on the socialist or anarchist left. If we want to see a 'normal' representative of national drama, we should look at someone like Peter Shaffer, who wrote himself into the history of the National

Theatre with three enormously successful plays in successive decades. In the 1960s *The Royal Hunt of the Sun* was the National's first new play; in the 1970s *Equus* was rumoured to be the most popular new play ever, with productions in most of the theatre capitals of the world; in the 1980s *Amadeus* was critically acclaimed and turned into a globally successful film. If the aim of subsidized theatre is to combine quality with wide access, then this is what success looks like.

To a striking extent, the three plays were variants on a common pattern. An ageing narrator, characterized by an attractive but crippling self-awareness, greets the audience and tells them about his encounter with his opposite, a young, radiant figure who has been destroyed. This other is a kind of god – Atahuallpa, the Inca in *Royal Hunt*, is the earthly form of the Sun; Alan, the boy in *Equus*, is the ecstatic celebrant in a demented cult of the horse; and Mozart in *Amadeus* is the sacred vessel of his genius. The narrator is aware of the divinity, but unsure whether to believe in it or not: just as the god character is identified by his implacable certainty, so the narrator is defined as human by his doubt. The narrator is more intelligent and articulate than the god, but he envies the god his divine genuineness, and he is guilty because he believes himself to be responsible for the god's destruction.[11]

The formula for the 'god' side of this opposition is conspicuous theatricality. Apart from Atahuallpa, the Incas have no lines, but communicate through masks, stylized movements and musical cries; similarly in *Equus* the horses are played non-naturalistically by actors who are required to suggest, in dance-like movement and portentous non-verbal sound, their divinity in the imagination of the boy; the staging of *Amadeus* involves an illuminated up-stage 'Light Box' which offers a visual correlative for the amplified playing of Mozart's music. In every case the written script frankly presents itself as incomplete, calling on the director and the designer to actualize the unarticulated heart of its imagery. So the inventiveness of the *mise-en-scène* does not integrate with the language in the manner of poetic drama; rather, the drab and prosaic verbal idiom is simply interrupted by an incompatible mode of expression. The effect of this discontinuity is to thematize the non-verbal resources of the stage: the masks, music and movement are not just theatrical signs, they are also *the sign of theatricality as such*.

But then the catch is that the theatricality which is thus signified is for that reason not exactly a part of the play; rather, it is an object which the play denotes. The primary dramatic medium, unmistakably, is the ironic and companionable speech of the narrator – he is the one with a virtual monopoly on direct address to the audience, and it is his narrative that shapes and paces the action. He agonizes about his own mediocrity and failure of vision, but actually we find this doubly reassuring: it means that he is an ordinary fallible person like us, and also that he can be trusted because he has no illusions about himself. However much he is put in the shade, then, by the theophanic glamour upstage, it can never shake his power over the performance, because we are in that same shade, sitting in the darkened auditorium with our coats on our knees, aware that we cannot sing and dance and create like those people. He is well in with us – our representative among the aliens. In short, the play constructs theatricality as abnormal and irrational, and then defines itself, against theatricality and with the audience, in the terms of normality and rationality. Admittedly, this rational discourse is able to entertain the possibility that the irrational is superior to itself. But that only confirms how thoroughly rational it is.

This is a drama, in other words, which conceives of theatre in terms learnt from Artaud – ritual, madness, darkness, cruelty – but which does not execute that conception. Rather, it contemplates it from the viewpoint of its actual English middle-class audience – secular, thoughtful, user-friendly. This duality can be read, for example, in the way that the particular metaphor for dark otherness is determined by cultural fashion: in 1964, as Britain rapidly shed its overseas possessions, *Royal Hunt* had an anti-colonialist alibi; by *Equus* in 1973, after R. D. Laing had become a household name, the politics became those of anti-psychiatry; and in 1980, the Thatcherite springtime, *Amadeus* located its idea of subversive energy in the figure of the unconditionally creative individual, slighted by a hidebound establishment. Each time, the image of anti-discursive strangeness is actually rather familiar, because its components are already present in the discourse of the quality press. Total theatricality – the Artaudian, the unspeakable – remains safely and specifically something which can be talked about.

It is as if there is a latent drama locked up inside the actual one, which would if released *get at* the audience in some absolutely immediate way; but then the narrator interposes his self-deprecating consciousness and mediates that 'cruelty', so that the spectators, the mailing-list subscribers on whom the theatre depends, get no more than they have bargained for. But of course that narrative – *first* the pure event, *then* the adulteration – is itself a fiction. In reality, the idea of theatricality takes on its air of absolute immediacy only because it is projected out of the language of mediation and compromise. That is why the marks of theatricality are completely wordless – decor, mime, music. They are constituted by their opposition to talk; they are not a real alternative to the liberal discourse, but its complement. A dramaturgy of the word adopts non-verbal action as its compensatory myth; 'drama' dreams of 'theatre'.

Here is the typicality which underpins Shaffer's success in the subsidized theatre. It links him, for example, with the very embodiment of the myth of 'theatre', Peter Brook. A founding associate director of the RSC, Brook did a series of productions in the first decade of the national companies – *King Lear*, the Theatre of Cruelty season, the *Marat-Sade*, *US*, Seneca's *Oedipus*, and *A Midsummer Night's Dream* – which rapidly acquired compulsory status on anybody's syllabus of modern English theatre studies.[12] This canonization was not a reflection of uncritical acclaim: with the exception of the fabulously successful *Dream*, all these shows met with mixed receptions. Rather, it was that in their European theatre literacy (drawing on Brecht, Artaud, Grotowski, Meyerhold), and their audacious use of space and rhythm, they were unmistakably recognizable as *properly theatre*, and so became symbols of the rights of live performance in the era of increasing subsidy. Here, resisting the dominance of mechanically reproducible media – print, film, recording – was a form to which '*the* audience (as opposed to *an* audience) [was] really necessary' (Milne 1964). It is not surprising, then, that 'getting at the audience' is the connecting thread which runs through the whole series of productions. The *Marat-Sade* ended with an orgiastic riot in which its madmen-actors attacked their stage spectators and, apparently imminently, their real ones too; *Oedipus* tethered its chorus to the pillars of the Old Vic auditorium; the cast of the *Dream* spilled off the stage at the end to shake hands in the stalls.

*US* can be taken as the paradigmatic instance of this artistic aggression. Most of the time, it looked like an agit-prop play about the war in Vietnam, using songs, sketches, cartoon images and so on to denounce American imperialism. But its overall impact suggested, in the end, a curious lack of interest in the densely researched history which it presented; what really preoccupied it, as its punning title suggested, was the problem of its own legitimacy. What about 'us'? What can we know or feel or do about these remote atrocities from which we are so profoundly protected? How can they be real to us? At this level, the show slipped its political occasion and closed on the familiar question of theatricality: how to get beyond mere talk. In yet another famously disturbing ending, Brook had an actor release several butterflies from a box; they flew up towards the lights so you could see they were really alive; then the actor took out another butterfly (actually a model) and set fire to it. The power of this tiny outrage to illuminate the politics of Southeast Asia was limited; the point was, after much exuberantly staged imagery of violence and burning, to make the audience think it was in the presence of the real thing. Not something described, but something happening (nearly). This intention had been articulated, a few moments earlier, in the show's other legendary moment, a speech of unqualified rage and hatred delivered by Brook's discovery Glenda Jackson:

I WANT IT TO GET WORSE! I want it to come HERE! . . . I would like to smell the running bowels of fear, over the English Sunday morning smell of gin and the roasting joint, and hyacinth. I would like to see an English dog playing on an English lawn with part of a burned hand. I would like to see a gas grenade go off at an English flower show, and nice English ladies crawling in each others' sick. And all this I would like to be photographed and filmed so that someone a long way off, safe in his chair, could watch us in our indignity! . . . I want it. You want it. They want it. Like lust, it goes on because we want it. And as with lust, we suspect most of all those who shout loudest, 'No!' (*She collapses.*) (*US* 1968: 183)

The rage is directed at those who sit safe in their chairs, remote from the literal violence of history, and also from the repressed violence of their own desire – that is, at the audience. The actress says that she does not want to be contemplating these things, she wants to be *in* them. But the language continues to imprison her in the spectatorial role she hates: 'I would like to smell . . .', 'I would like to see . . .' She collapses, in the end, because her contradiction is unsustainable. Despite the incomparably greater daring of the stage language, this is still the dilemma of the psychiatrist who wants to be mad, the cerebral talker who wants to be the visceral actor. English drama (the stress on Englishness is interestingly obsessive in the quotation) entertains a utopia of total theatre which is at once generated and rendered unattainable by its actual habit of reasonable speech.

Since the *Dream*, Brook has on the whole pursued exits from this dilemma in a thoroughgoingly international context: his organization, the Centre for International Theatre Creation, is funded from private bequests, not a national government; it is based in Paris, but has also sought to play in deliberately exotic locations; its ensemble is multinational and its shows often polyglot. This chosen exile contributes to his mythic status: permanently elsewhere, he allegorizes the absent theatricality of the national stage.

In the native theatre, though, 'Glenda's speech' has enjoyed a pervasive afterlife. Anyone who has been in many of the 'other places' will recognize this register:

Anyhow there's this kid, growing in her womb all the time, science tells us they feel the tension, I mean the great heartbeat revs up, the umbilicus twitches, the placenta turns, and all on a diet of 1,800 calories a day and no redress for strange cravings. Anyhow there she is hoping the little bastard'll turn blue and suffocate in her blood or whatever, a fall on the stone steps maybe, as gin baths or quinine are out of the question. (*Lay By*, Traverse, Edinburgh, 1971; Brenton et al. 1972: 52)

Of your brain, turned over a fire! With your guts fed to the pigs! Your arseholes gnawed by my dogs! I will hold your bloody hearts, today! Today! Up to the sun as it sets, and your blood will run down my throat, and I will drink you, get pissed on you! And vomit on you and drink more of you! (*The Romans in Britain*, National Theatre, 1980; Brenton 1980: 40) we'll send him a Christmas cake juiced up with cyanide / lots of sherry to help disguise the acrid taste that burns his guts / she'll scream in pain / they'll wait as death starts digging inside their brain / or, excuse me, what's the time? hydrochloric acid in his eyes / he screams / then in the dark / a fine needle penetrates his heart / he didn't see it / so in his dying breath he cannot identify Mr Death (*Decadence*, New End, Hampstead, 1981; Berkoff 1982: 11)

These speeches have very different immediate occasions: the first is an official narrative voice, its brutality connoting professional cool; the second expresses the powerless rage of a Briton experiencing Roman colonization; the third is a 'decadent' verbal performance with which the speaker is trying to turn his girlfriend on. But the same stage language is audible in all of them; and also in other styles, such as the ethical Grand Guignol of Edward Bond or the relentless linguistic obscenity of Howard Barker. It is an odd genre, character-ized by provocative cruelty, by gratuitous physical detail (an insistence on smells, sensations, dismembered bits of people), and by moral neutrality: the tone varies between passionate enthusiasm and flip indifference, but either way it withholds any implication of condemnation or disgust. Whatever particular authorial intention informs this or that instance of it, the genre as a whole speaks a cult of bodily immediacy. *This* at least, it declares, in its unflinching harshness, its clogged materiality, its indefensible eroticism, is not going to be mere talk. The words are contorted by their unrealizable desire to be things.

It's a language which wants its object to be corporeally, coercively present; it wants it to get worse, it wants it to come here. But whereas in *US*, in 1966, this longing had a specific political and cultural content, in the repetitions of the 1970s and 1980s it audibly hardens into a style, an undifferentiated pursuit of impact as such.[13] And the hysteria encoded in the confrontational grossness of the imagery is a trace of the fear that in spite of everything 'it' *isn't* here − that the drama remains, like Salieri, incurably secondary. For what is stopping drama from getting at the audience is not really, of course, a mere lack of verbal forcefulness. If that were all, the obstacles would have been swept away many times in the blood-dimmed tide of rhetoric. The barrier which persists, immune to the frustrated rages it provokes, is the institution-ally given relationship between the audience and the stage. Caged by the programme of State-sponsored enlightenment which constitutes them, the wild creatures of the theatre divert us with their passionate rattling of the bars.

Escaping from the cage, then, means changing the relationship with the audience, and this solution has been diversely sought by theatre practitioners in the 1970s and 1980s. Outside the centralized State system I have described, though often partly funded with Arts Council money, companies have estab-lished themselves by abandoning the project of addressing 'everybody', and forming relationships instead with specific publics constituted by youth, gender, sexual orientation, ethnicity or locality. These specifications rely on an attribution of 'community': the difference which marks out the particular audience is understood to confer on it a shared identity which the play both belongs to and dramatizes. The object of the exercise is not to contribute to a transcultural dramatic canon, but to substantiate, locally and immediately, the distinctive interests of the group. The performance does not take its spectators for granted, but constructs them, so to speak, *as* something – as gay, as Asian, as neighbours. If one trace of such an event should then be a script which official culture can recognize as what is called a 'good play', that is an accident, unplanned and perhaps even unwanted: what counts is the event, the interaction.

The effect of this move, in principle and at best, is that the problematic which I have called 'getting at the audience' magically dissolves. The rhetorical violence of the effort to break down the barrier between stage and audience is calmed by the fact that the stage has been set up in the audience's own space; the gap is not bridged so much as not produced in the first place; the dramatic language defers to the cultural character of the audience because that is its criterion of significant form. There is no need for the images to insist, viscerally or exotically, on their material reality, because they are materialized naturally, as it were, by the recognition of the community.

But the condition of this regeneration is what Ann Jellicoe, in her book *Community Plays*, startlingly calls a 'good community' (Jellicoe 1987: 45–6) – that is, on the whole, one whose members are actively in touch with one another, and in which group identity is quite strong and internal tensions (of class for example) quite weak. In so far as these good things do not obtain, it is part of the drama's mission to foster them; and its success, in the end, is measured by how far it has done that. Jellicoe is talking about the towns and villages in Dorset which were the scene of her own spectacular development of large-scale amateur community drama; but a similar logic applies to the differently constituted 'communities' addressed by Women's Theatre Group, Gay Sweatshop, Temba, Tara Arts and so on. The idea of the good community shapes the spectacle, whether as its base, as its goal, or – since any subcultural formation must in a certain sense be an emergent one – as a mixture of the two.

So what distinguishes these outposts of the State system is not, as one might suppose, exclusivity. Very few of them are so particularist as to be incomprehensible to non-members of the community; if anything, most are more generally accessible than the 'national' drama whose universalist orientation masks, as we saw, its address to its own culturally distinct fraction. Rather, these forms are marked off from the mainstream by their underlying gesture of *affirmation*: instead of taking up the usual ironic stance within-and-against the national framework, they commit themselves to subgroups which they are, in every sense, *for*. The structuring negativity of the centre finds its counter, or more inertly its compensation, in the positivity of the margins: the bad-state-of-the-nation play is answered by the good-community play. In general terms, the strengths and weaknesses of this route are fairly evident – on the one hand, the practical engagement with social living, the assertion of marginalized identities, the capacity for euphoria; and on the other, the pieties, the suppression of contradiction, the respect for communally sanctioned banality. But these are issues which can be developed – this is just the project's distinction – only in particular.

## 4    Show Business

In late 1976, within a few weeks of the state opening of the National Theatre on the South Bank and the first performances of *Destiny* in Stratford-upon-Avon, another national theatrical statement was being made in the West End. Alf Garnett, the reactionary working-class anti-hero of the sitcom *Till Death Us Do Part*, had come to the conclusion that the national rot had gone far enough, and that there was nothing for it but to break out of the confines of the small screen, hire a theatre, and give the public the benefit of his views on the issues of the day. In homage to a hero of the trendy left who died in the month the show opened, it was called *The Thoughts of Chairman Alf*. The prickly sarcasm of the title was typical of its moment: this was the time of Callaghan's administration, characterized by wage militancy, racial tension, a Conservative opposition moving rapidly to the right, and, within the theatre, an increasingly confident socialist fringe. The implication of Alf's intervention was that the stage should not be given over to college-educated Communists.

For this was another bad-state-of-the-nation show. From behind a table untidily draped with the Union Jack (much like those at the meetings of Nation Forward), Alf delivered an outline history of the country's long decline from the great days of Henry VIII, whose achievements in keeping women in their place and making everybody be C of E appeared as a mark at which subsequent legislators had aimed in vain. The narrative was pervaded by nostalgia for a vague past in which the East End was a real community, Britain ruled the world, there were no coons around and West Ham won the FA Cup most of the time. At the heart of this idyll, as we have come to expect, was the war, conceived of as the time when the whole country, heroically united behind Winnie (boiler-suited on bomb sites with V-sign and cigar), made mincemeat of the Jerries with some marginal tactical support from the Yanks. Thus all the mythic and retrospective preoccupations of national drama reappeared in the broad effects and exuberantly caricatured clichés of a comic one-man show: if *Plenty* was the quality press, this was the tabloid version.

But then the event was an extremely complex one. From a commercial point of view, it was based on the character's TV success – a notoriety which had its own well-known ambivalence. Alf Garnett had been developed during the liberal consensus of the late sixties as a satire on working-class Conservatism by a left-of-centre cockney scriptwriter, Johnny Speight, and a London Jewish actor, Warren Mitchell. The resulting series combined domestic sitcom and anti-racist polemic in a way which secured it a large and culturally heterogeneous audience, and made Alf Garnett himself more famous than either of his creators. He became an ambiguous figure in two different senses. One was that he began to function, within the signifying systems of the mass media, as a real person, capable of making guest appearances, being interviewed and so on. And the other was that he became fashionable, quotable, and even lovable to an extent which disconcerted the original liberal intentions of his inventors. The man who appeared on the stage in 1976 was thus a hybrid: he was an unemployed worker in Wapping, who was known only to his relatives and neighbours, and whose irrational opinions could be grasped, in naturalistic fashion, as symptoms of his limited perspective; but he was also a media celebrity with an acknowledged representative role in national life.

This complexity was reflected in the show's performing context. It began at the Theatre Royal, Stratford East, the home since 1954 of Theatre Workshop. It wasn't a TW production – the company had effectively come to an end in 1974 – but both Speight and Mitchell had connections with Stratford, and this genesis linked the show to the populism and the left-wing commitment of the Littlewood tradition. Then, after a brief transfer to the Criterion, it moved to the Whitehall, where it followed the last Brian Rix farce, which closed in January 1977. The Whitehall at the time was being managed by Paul Raymond, an impresario of exceptional vulgarity who had made money out of sex shows in the aftermath of the abolition of theatrical censorship in 1968. What attracted Raymond to Garnett was that the box-office risks were underwritten by a TV reputation; what attracted Garnett to Raymond was a special licence which permitted drinking and smoking in the auditorium, thus catering for proper men instead of your normal West End middle-class pooftahs.[14]

The audience, in other words, was assembled by means which had very little in common with the mailing-list system of the subsidized theatres. Certainly the theatre-going intelligentsia was well represented, but there was also a constituency for which this was a celebrity appearance rather than a play (that is, seeing *The Thoughts of Chairman Alf* was rather like seeing Ken Dodd or Barry Humphries), and a still less theatrical clientele for whom the connection – as in Christmas pantomime – was the television tie-in. With its jokily political pretext, the show formally treated this miscellaneous audience as representative of the nation: the evening's alibi, so to speak, was a public meeting. A version of the elusive 'general public' had been put together by departing from the State theatre establishment in several directions at once – towards a terminally neglected community theatre in the East End, towards the most nakedly commercial side of the West End and towards the mass media.

As far as the character was concerned, the effect of this newly public space was that it authorized fantasy. Whereas in the formally naturalistic world of the sitcom his unreasonable subjectivity had always been checked – by the resistance of his family, and by the unanswerable put-down which is administered by the plot at the end of the half-hour – here, in the virtual reality of the solo performance, developments were guided only by his freewheeling consciousness and the bottle of scotch which he got through in the course of the evening. The fantasies were abjectly silly – Alf getting a medal for saving the Queen's life, Alf leaving George Best flat-footed down the right wing. But one of these Walter Mitty personae was that of a star of the music hall – Alf as the unacknowledged source of all Max Miller's material. And this one, of course, was literally being acted out: Alf *was* appearing as an already famous comedian, dominating the stage, managing the laughter, doing music-hall songs and routines, handling hecklers. So the audience were accomplices in his wish fulfilment; the show substantiated what the TV series had inevitably short-circuited – the character's raging inner life.

The result was that the comic format was troubled by indecent extremes of emotion. In one sketch, Alf outlines a scheme for transferring wives in the way football clubs transfer players: breaking the prison of marriage 'till death us do part', the manager-husband can put the out-of-touch wife on a free transfer, or, if there are funds available, trade up to a higher level of talent. The routine leads into an ultra-sentimental performance of the music-hall's hymn to uxoriousness, 'My Dear Old Dutch'. In another, he imagines being one of the Queen's dogs, lapping champagne, lying around on silken cushions and only doing occasional light tasks like licking Her feet or biting cabinet ministers' ankles. Rather that (a long way down the bottle, as his self-assertiveness dissolves into self-pity) than spend his life working his arse off in a factory which has now, in any case, thrown him on the scrap heap. In sequences like this, the show went well beyond the satirical picking off of Alf's politically incorrect opinions, and made parody into a form of analysis, rooting the reactionary chauvinism in resentment, and the resentment, in turn, in a class-specific historical experience of entrapment and loss.

It was a minor and eccentric theatrical event. But the stylistic freedom and richness of implication with which it reproduced the motifs of the official 'national' drama of its time are suggestive. What enabled it to do so much, with such lightness, was its hybrid condition – it was television *and* theatre, committed *and* commercial drama, middle-class naturalism *and* working-class entertainment. Too much a unique configuration to be influential, it nevertheless anticipated at least one significant escape route from the narrowing institutions of State theatre.

What it was generically, after all, was stand-up comedy; and in 1977 the reorientation of this traditional form was just starting to happen. The political marriage of club stand-up and punk, which Trevor Griffiths had imagined in his uneasily naturalistic play *Comedians* in 1975, was arguably celebrated in 1979, when the Comedy Store opened in Soho, dominated initially by Alexei Sayle. Several of the early comics there were ex-actors, and brought to the microphone some of the techniques and preoccupations of community and socialist theatre groups.[15] But the primary performance model was not drama of any kind; rather, it was a cross between old-fashioned English variety and rock music. From the point of view of the theatre, the important thing about both these sources was that they are *commercial* popular forms, defining a field of theatrical energy clearly outside the whole system of subsidized drama. In deliberate opposition to the bureaucratically mediated rationales of the Arts Council,[16] comedy offered a beguilingly unpretentious relationship between performing artist and public – the punters want to be entertained, if they laugh you're paid, and if they don't you're dead. This defiantly simple-minded formula was never a complete account of the project: there was a pronounced anti-racist and anti-sexist agenda, a strand of violent audience provocation, a special respect for surrealist risk-taking, and so on. But the space was cleared for these experiments by the basic choice of the persona of the showman rather than the artist: the idea was to travel light by jettisoning the ideological baggage of the post-war arts settlement, refusing, with relief, the duty to raise standards, foster appreciation, or contribute to the quality of civilization. Like Chairman Alf, though with a different audience and a different (younger) popular cultural repertoire, the Comedy Store group used stand-up to mobilize low art against the State-sponsored hegemony of the high.[17]

Unlike Chairman Alf, this enterprise *was* influential, founding a genre which took over wide swathes of the touring circuits and the Edinburgh Festival fringe in the mid-1980s, as well as very significant sectors of television light entertainment. Its success had to do with its show-business ethos in both senses. For one thing, its immediacy – improvisation, direct address, a real-time relationship with the audience – meant that it inhabited effortlessly the theatricality which we saw official theatre pursuing in vain. Here was a stage convention with no problems about 'getting at' its audience: it was drawing them in, inviting them to talk back, getting in fights with them – nobody could say that this was anything but 'live', and at a time when both stadium rock and national theatre had become more technologized and remote, audiences responded enthusiastically. But there was also a simple *business* logic, in that a single performer with a suitcase of props has an irreducible competitive edge over a play with a cast and a set. In part at least, alternative cabaret owed its freshness, its euphoric rejection of the mediations of the arts bureaucracies, to its canny decision to be cheap.

As the dates irresistibly suggest, this was a political question. The Comedy Store opened in the same month as the Thatcher government; what it was pioneering was both ideologically and economically an entertainment form for hard times. Not that the expected bonfire of Arts Council commitments actually happened: as we saw earlier, the budget continued to expand, if only because the new government's rhetoric of rolling back the State was in conflict with its need for mechanisms of patronage. But certainly the screw was turned on conspicuously left-wing groups, of which several were cut altogether, and others neutralized by the changes in structure and policy needed to secure continued funding from an increasingly politicized arts establishment. And more generally, the project of a socialist or libertarian theatrical *culture* looked more and more tenuous as the right-wing populist bandwagon rolled on.[18] If the system of State theatre had been constraining before, it was now actively corrupting; escape into the low-cost, low-profit private space of cabaret could look like a rational route.

It was also a retreat, though. The content of the alternative comedian's performance was essentially a single voice. Angry, parodically inadequate, grotesque, mocking, self-mocking, or all these things by turns, each new voice was always very highly characterized, since it was its distinctiveness, even its oddity, which constituted its forcefulness. Politically, then, what the act was doing was assailing the prevailing order of things by constructing an isolated character from whose peculiar point of view the order appeared absurd – in other words, an eccentric. The form was thus an index of cultural defeat in the sense that it confined itself, inescapably, to the language of marginal protest. Whereas 7:84 or Monstrous Regiment undertook to *replace* the hegemonic account of social reality with a whole different story (and risked becoming stiff and pretentious because of that labour), Jim Barclay or Ben Elton denounced or guyed the *existing* story from a position of wittily staged powerlessness (and gained a new authenticity – and a new audience – by agreeing not to claim authority).

Moreover, the turn from an ossified, scripted public stage to the verve and immediacy of the solo performer was clearly not only a response to Thatcherism; it also replicated its themes – anti-intellectualism, individualism, free competition, hostility to collective planning. Spontaneous and entrepreneurial, its radical energy started decaying at once: from the beginning, there were *cognoscenti* declaring that *real* 'alternative' comedy was already finished. This was partly the competitiveness of fashion; and of course it was part of the vigour of the whole development that it was fashionable. But as with the music which shared its venues and values, the price of its edgy, stylish contemporaneity was obsolescence. And in any case, the lament for a lost edge was not simply a fashionable pose. The scene really did go off the boil – not because of anyone's relative lack of talent or principle, but because the logic of the entertainment market to which the performers had entrusted themselves was to stabilize the composition of the audience. As the genre acquired its own public, its own TV slots, its own classification in *Time Out*, it was placed as a specialism. The stars of this incorporated circuit were faster, funnier and more daring than Chairman Alf, but they couldn't have access to his enlivening hybridity.

If the reorientation of stand-up could be understood as left-wing theatre's fraught love affair with show business, the same structure of feeling acquired literary dramatic form in the Royal Court's best-known hit of the decade, Caryl Churchill's *Serious Money* (1987). A comedy of the Thatcherite City in consciously graceless doggerel verse, it shares some obvious surface features with the alternative circuit: exuberant linguistic obscenity, surreal parody, rock music rhythms, an anti-elitist romance of street-wise style. But it is not in any direct sense a theatrical appropriation of cabaret. Formally, the play came out of the tradition, associated with Joint Stock Theatre, the director Max Stafford-Clark and Churchill herself, of scripted drama based on direct social research and group improvisation (Ritchie 1987). The analogy with cabaret is more to do with the play's specific complexity of attitude.

At one point in the parodically labyrinthine plot, the corporate raider Billy Corman has a conference with a PR consultant about his personal image. His adversary in a takeover battle is conspicuously nice, and Corman naively thinks that he can be made to look even nicer by spending enough on presentation. The consultant explains that niceness is out of his range, so he has to settle for glamorous wickedness. Corman, an utterly unprincipled money-making machine, thinks he must be wicked enough already, but discovers that things are not that simple:

> There's ugly greedy and sexy greedy, you dope.
> At the moment you're ugly which is no hope.
> If you stay ugly, god knows what your fate is.
> But sexy greedy *is* the late eighties.
> (Churchill 1987: 92)

The tone of that – knowing, weightlessly ironic, morally sophisticated without moral conviction – *is*, you could say, *Serious Money*. The play presents Big Bang (the derestriction of the London money market) as a festive turning loose of greed: however strongly it registers the attendant exploitation, it cannot help, theatrically, warming to the collapse of inhibitions, the sexual rush of energy. Its one-liners sketch an intoxicating directness of appetite. A young market-maker says: 'I never dream. (I never sleep.)' A trader concludes a scene with a banker: 'You don't seem to get it. You're sitting in my chair. Walk.' The heroine, a stockbroker's daughter who is slumming it on the floor of LIFFE,[19] brings a long tradition of English middle-class drama to an end with the line, 'Daddy, you're trading like a cunt.' These bright, hard cartoon characters are unmistakably. *liberated* – and if the word suggests the values of the sixties rather than the eighties, so does their repertoire of pleasures, which consist of sex, drugs and dealing. Their ruthlessness is not a real obstruction to radical theatre's identification with radical trading: it only confirms the completeness of their liberation, as the Royal Court's traditional targets (the English establishment, class distinction, evasive moralism, the censorship of desire) are gleefully trashed by these unexpected and powerful allies. Jimmy Porter has finally stopped whinging and acquired some clout.

The phenomenon was not unique: almost exactly the same analysis could be made of the National Theatre's equally ambivalent 'Fleet Street comedy' *Pravda*, staged in 1985. But *Serious Money* was the most confident statement: in its coked-up, stuttering pace and its zigzag moves between parody, documentary and tub-thumping crudity, its style has a freedom and ease which make most British post-war theatre writing look tense with self-doubt. It can therefore be taken as the representative instance of State theatre in decline. Like Chairman Alf, it offered a comically grandiose diagnosis of the condition of England (the main action is the fraudulent takeover of a company called Albion) which sent up the ambitions of national drama. And like him too, it assembled an intriguingly hybrid public for its West End transfer, mixing the ordinary Royal Court constituency with the tourist audience for a hyped hit and a specialist contingent from the City itself. Both shows, in their sharply different contexts, created a provisional space, outside the closure of Arts Council culture, by a partial, contradictory surrender to the commercial values the Council had been set up to reprove or transcend.

## NOTES

1  All unreferenced figures about levels of subsidy are taken from the Annual Reports of the Arts Council of Great Britain.

2  In 1946 the Chancellor of the Exchequer, Hugh Dalton, promised to 'see to it that . . . Opera is not let down'. The letter, which was addressed to the Chairman of the Covent Garden Board and copied to the Chairman of the Arts Council, is reproduced in Pick 1983: 158.

3  See Goorney 1981: 149–52, 214. Unable to afford freight charges, the company took the set across the Channel as hand-luggage.

4  Maecenas was the legendary millionaire in the reign of the Emperor Augustus who was the patron of Horace and Virgil. The Lord Chancellor assumes that his listeners know that – which is itself a mark of the cultural roots of this version of subsidy.

5  For Charles Landstone, meeting Keynes was 'my first real contact with the genuine patron of the arts, big enough to suit his actions to his belief' (Minihan 1977: 218n).

6  For example: Portable Theatre and Red Ladder, 1968; 7:84, 1971; Women's Theatre Group, 1973; Joint Stock, 1974; Monstrous Regiment and Gay Sweatshop, 1975.

7  The 1965 White Paper transferred political oversight of the Arts Council from the Treasury to the Department of Education, a symbolic recognition of the connection between the two kinds of State cultural expansion.

8  In the course of a controversy which will be discussed later, Trevor Nunn described the RSC as a 'basically left-wing organisation' (letter to *The Times*, 5 December 1972). He was believed at least by the Conservative MP for Stratford, who resigned from the RSC Board. And in the same era, compare Peter Hall's style as the new director at the National (Elsom and Tomalin 1978: 251–2).

9  One attempt to negotiate these contradictions is sympathetically described in Chambers 1980: 7–14.

10  *Pearl* is among other things an allegorical version of the events surrounding *The Island of the Mighty* itself.

11  *The Royal Hunt of the Sun* slightly complicates the pattern by splitting the ageing narrator into two – Pizarro, who loved and destroyed Atahuallpa, and Martin, who loved Pizarro, went on the expedition to Peru as a boy, and now recalls the story forty years later.

12  See D. Williams 1988, and its eight-page bibliography.

13  The dates suggest the name of the style in question: this is theatre punk.

14  It would be hard to find another subject which united the views of Paul Raymond, Alf Garnett, Johnny Speight and Bertolt Brecht.

15  For example, Jim Barclay from 7:84, Tony Allen from Rough Theatre (Wilmut and Rosengard 1989: 24–30).

16  Itself one of the targets of Sayle's tireless abuse: 'They fucking love me down the Arts Council, you know . . . down Piccadilly with the ponchos and the Lapsang Suchong, you know . . . they say, "Here's a working-class half-wit . . . *let's patronize him!*" ' (Wilmut and Rosengard 1989: 24).

17  The continuity includes the impresario: in 1980 several Comedy Store performers set up a second venue, the Comic Strip, so called because (like the Whitehall) it was a Paul Raymond joint.

18  The damage can be measured by comparing John McGrath's two books on popular left-wing theatre (1981 and 1990). Both are lectures delivered at Cambridge University, the first in the spring of 1979 and the second in the autumn of 1988. The self-confidence and energy of the first make the bitterness and exhaustion of the second painful to read.

19  The London International Financial Futures Exchange, a section of the market known for lacking both social kudos and economic usefulness. The programme for the show included lengthy explanations of these seductive in-jokes, rather in the manner of Elizabethan cony-catching pamphlets.

# 12

# Drama in the Age of Television

## 1 The Voice of the Living Newspaper

Buried up to her waist, the woman has her life organized into a series of tiny social routines and meticulous conversational clichés. Since her predicament is displayed on a *stage*, these gestures and speech have a tendency to turn into empty formalities, becoming disconnected from natural function. But the precise observation of these empty formalities enables Winnie to cope with her continued existence in a landscape that has all the appearance of being post-holocaust: desert, deserted, something which Samuel Beckett might invent; an image from the depth of the cold war, 1961. The unseen and unknown device which buries her deeper might be the engine of something random, discouraging and superhuman. In the face of it she keeps herself going with the remembered gestures and phrases of a lost culture and social existence. Trapped within a remorseless present, her routines gradually fail. 'One loses', as she says, 'one's classics' (Beckett 1963: 164).

Winnie's attempt to hang on to her classics and her proprieties makes a striking contrast with her silent male companion, who is named – naturally – Willie. He occasionally reads out bits from a newspaper, looks at sexually explicit photos and blows his nose on the same handkerchief he wears on his head. Of the two it is the woman who seeks to manage her attenuated existence through the articulation of as it were irrelevant social rituals and chatter: 'That is what I find so wonderful, a part remains, of one's classics, to help one through the day' (p. 164). Eleven years later, in a play by John McGrath, the woman is in the civic version of vacant public space, sitting on a park bench; the man is a stranger, pursuing the girlfriend whom he has beaten up but still loves. Neither character can sustain communication, each is disturbed. The violence of his story triggers her compulsion to recite newspaper headlines and stories: 'Wellbourne Mining Horror Tunnel Collapse. Late last night the main tunnel and several minor tubes at Welbourne [*sic*] Dorset colliery collapsed crushing many Stop Rescue work continues hampered by lack of correct equipment Stop' (McGrath 1972: vi). As she says, and the other buried woman might agree, 'Events do catch up with one so' (p. vi).

McGrath's play gives a clinical name to the woman's psychological condition: schizophrenia. In 1972 that condition was attracting an interest that spread beyond the clinic in that, as an illness, it seemed to dramatize the discrepancy between received, dominant concepts about human society and the human reality which would not fit itself into those concepts. Seen this way, schizophrenia was less a madness than an articulation of the true reality of society. McGrath's woman character is set at a distance by, alienated from, the dominant on account of her sex. Her consequent suffering and bewilderment find a voice for themselves in the disaster stories of newspapers. In a society which doesn't allow her a voice she can't help but speak the text which is daily pushed at her. She has to speak that text in order to articulate a voiceless suffering; at the same time, she is trapped into the fabric of that text. She is, as the play's title ambiguously puts it, *Plugged into History*.

The picture of a person speaking newspaper language comes, as much as does schizophrenia, from social concerns of the time. Through the 1960s there had been debate about the effects on people not only of newspapers but also of advertising and television. The anxiety that fuelled this debate had been developing since the 1930s when a particular form of opposition to capitalism had blamed it for reducing the quality of life, turning people into passive consumers, mechanizing human relations, and, above all, replacing what was traditionally communal and interactive with a mass culture, a culture endlessly technologically reproduced and imposed from above. Threatened with a loss of their classics, the critics of mass culture tended to characterize the modern as something mechanical, non-creative, reproduced, objectifying. Self-consciously 'modern' plays of the 1960s have characters who speak in a language acquired from newspapers: not thinking but thought for, passively caught up in events, not a person but a number, 'one'.

Capitalism had other opponents in the 1930s for whom technology and indeed modernity were no threat. In 1937 the Communist-aligned Unity Theatre did a show about the London Transport bus-workers' strike. The play aimed to give its audiences a history and explanation of the strikers' cause. So, alongside emotional enactments of working conditions and political arguments, the stage also offered information and statistics. As a Member of Parliament rises to speak against the strike, his voice is drowned by that of a loudspeaker which lists the companies he owns or manages. The loudspeaker is referred to as the Voice of the Living Newspaper, a key presence in theatre shows which aimed to document events of the present moment. That voice had

come to London's Unity from the State-sponsored Federal Theatre Project
in the United States, and from Erwin Piscator's innovative explorations in
how to stage history in the politically polarized Germany of the late 1920s.
In a Living Newspaper show the stage's claim is to be able to educate an
audience by giving them the true facts of a crisis, in counter-balance to the
lies of a capitalist-owned press. Those true facts were offered by means of, and
with all the authority of, modern technology: location film, photographs,
audio records. These non-human means, set against the lies of the oppressors,
were far from anti-human. The electronically amplified Voice of the
Living Newspaper was, in 1937, an active agent in a continuing political
struggle.

The woman on that park bench in 1972 finds herself compelled, by history,
to be the voice of a living newspaper. But the true facts spoken by her
headlines tell a story about the speaker rather than about the news events:

> When I read my papers, I feel plugged in to history. I feel the course of
> events coursing through my veins. I feel taken over, crushed, by many,
> many men. I feel occupied, a house squatted in, defiled. I feel like a
> deserted ball-room being defecated in by a halted army. . . . I become a
> human news-tape, mile after mile of me, torn out, ripped off, aban-
> doned. (McGrath 1972: ix)

The human news-tape has lost sense of herself as person, has become empty
space occupied by men. The casualty depends on her fix from a history that
guarantees always to be alien from her own life: 'I need pain. It stops me
suffering' (p. ix). The voice of the living newspaper is the voice of an addict,
volunteering to be occupied by a world in which she has no control. Things
had seriously changed since that other voice struggled for control in 1937.
Between them had come the development of a post-war world in which, once
rationing was over, new communications technology seemed to spread into
more people's lives than ever before. Newspapers, radio and television promised to give a mass of people nearly instant access to news events and information. Reality was no longer simply reported but also recorded, not just seen
by others but seen for itself, 'as it is', as it were.

In this post-war world, drama had for the first time to articulate itself in a
culture where reality was both televised and televisable. Measured by a technology that efficiently records the real, drama's mode of production seems
excessive and redundant, fictional and unnecessary, like a deserted ballroom
full of shit. Self-consciously 'modern' drama in the late 1950s, and through the
1960s, enacts the way in which it is occupied by modernity. Plugging itself
into history not like a recorder but like an addict, its very excess and
fictionality enable it to articulate what the new voice of the mass newspaper
can't or won't speak. Insecurely placed in a high speed, mobile modernity,

'modern' drama dreams up bodies inexplicably buried in earth, habitually fixed to an unspecified park bench, caught in the routine repetitions of domestic existence, and indeed on a stage which defines itself as simultaneously without function and impossible to leave. Unable to guarantee its truths in a mass-communicating modernity, 'modern' drama invents voices which speak in half-remembered quotations, unconsciously learnt clichés, conversational proprieties that reproduce themselves in a self-generating pattern of reflexes, and indeed in a lament over lost expressivity which is simultaneously a joke about its impossibility. In the modern world of news, modern drama performs life as repetition.

This sense of bodies and voices caught up in meaningless but necessary routines is characteristic of the work of the playwright whose name alone signalled for a whole generation the specific feel of 'modern' drama: Harold Pinter. In his first full-length play, from 1958, two strangers arrive at a seaside boarding-house and take away its sole resident. The couple who run the boarding-house, Meg and Petey, are locked into a set of daily routines the humdrum nature of which is expressed in their attenuated speech and minimal activity:

> *(She takes the socks etc. back to the sideboard drawer.)*
> MEG: I'm going to wake that boy.
> PETEY: There's a new show coming to the Palace.
> MEG: On the pier?
> PETEY: No. The Palace, in the town.
> MEG: Stanley could have been in it, if it was on the pier.
> PETEY: This is a straight show.
> MEG: What do you mean?
> PETEY: No dancing or singing.
> MEG: What do they do then?
> PETEY: They just talk.

> (Pinter 1960: 13)

Without knowing it, Petey defines the sort of play he's in; and it's clearly different from an end-of-the-pier show. There's an archness not shared by the characters, for whom talk is just talk. Petey, we would not be surprised to note, shuts himself from the world by reading a newspaper. Meg's routine proprieties have been acquired from a mass culture, which is seen to have the effect of making her speech and action feel like things done out of learnt habit rather than as self-expression and initiative. After the violence of the strangers' visit, life returns to this norm. Contemporaries praised Pinter's dialogue for its 'realism', as if the drama's power could be measured by the accuracy of its copy of everyday reality; theatre-goers started hearing Pinteresque phrases in conversations on the top deck of buses.

Yet the fascination exercised by this play, *The Birthday Party*, derives much more forcefully from its refusal of drama's potential to copy or articulate a recognizable reality. At the high point of suspense, the stage is blacked out: the action can no longer be seen or made sense of. Furthermore that action, following from the appearance of the strangers, is never given a motive. There is no explanation for the interest of the strangers, Goldberg and McCann, in the lodger, Stanley. Sufficient is done, however, to induce speculation. In 1958, the year when racial tension exploded in race riots in Nottingham and Notting Hill, Pinter's story has a Jew and an Irishman arbitrarily pick on a boarding-house lodger in a typical English seaside town. This selection of detail ought to imply some significance but the play refuses to supply any of the machinery, such as a logical causality or reference to reality, which might work to confirm that significance. The play enacts its own method in the figure of the Jew who keeps inventing always true, but always different, life histories for himself. The images on stage may be said to be in excess of available explanation. We may not know why the strangers want Stanley, but we do see what happens to him:

> (*Stanley concentrates, his mouth opens, he attempts to speak, fails and emits sounds from his throat.*)
> STANLEY: Uh-gug . . . uh-gug . . . eeehhh-gag . . . (*On the breath.*) Caah Caah . . . Caah . . .
> (*They watch him. He draws a long breath which shudders down his body. He concentrates.*)
> GOLDBERG: Well, Stanny boy, what do you say, eh?
> (*They watch. He concentrates. His head lowers, his chin draws into his chest, he crouches.*)
> STANLEY: Uh-gughh . . . uh-gughhh . . .
>
> (Pinter 1960: 85)

A mass communication society stares at a nightmare inversion of itself crystallized in that gibbering figure. Where all reality is recorded and recordable, Pinter's play acts out a refusal to offer explanation or causality. Much of its characteristic feeling, and much of its dramatic business, are produced by the play's attempt to display its own distance from the activity of telling a logical story, or tracing a connected sequence of events, or constructing what some people now call a 'grand narrative'. The grand narrative offers a historical overview in which one event connects to another, and so makes sense of what might be experienced as fragmentary while it happens. In Pinter's hands drama became 'modern' by staging its inability to explain, insisting on the limits of accessible meaning.

A couple of years later Beckett was to have a joke about drama's relationship to knowledge and information. The buried Winnie recalls a time when two people suddenly appeared in her landscape. One of them, a woman, looked at her: 'What's the idea of you, she says, what are you meant to mean?' (Beckett 1963: 156). The trick of asking the audience's question about itself is a feature of modernist art. In Beckett's non-realist stage image – with its playful division of Winnie and Willie, female and male, voice and body, repetitions and silence, routine and emptiness – there is an imaging of what modernity might feel like. Pinter's play shares with Beckett's a sceptical attitude to knowledge and information, but it makes no space to ask the question 'What are you meant to mean?' The fine balance of comedy and tragic loss of Winnie's happy days is tilted into the ironic cruelty of Stanley's birthday party. That boarding-house setting belongs in a recognizably real world in a way that a post-holocaustic landscape does not; which in turn perhaps motivates people to discover realism in the dialogue. These features pull the play away from the project that, in other respects, Pinter shares with Beckett. In their situation and habits, Meg and Petey seem to be representative members of the British lower middle class. In their mode of speech and action, they – and their class – are offered by the play as objects of mockery. So if Beckett might be said to make jokes with philosophical modernism, Pinter by contrast might be said to make jokes against modern society.

The voice which modern English drama finds for itself, in a televised world, is one which may speculate about the limits of knowledge; but it also finds itself in angry confrontation with those social groups who are content to absorb the effects of mass culture. There's a difference between experiencing life as a human news-tape, and passively accepting a role as a deserted ballroom in which people shit. A key element of that mass culture is transformed in *The Birthday Party* into a stage image that is both inexplicable and yet deeply engaging. The image aggressively confronts an audience with the most common, mass produced, source of knowledge functioning in a way which is anti-social, irresponsible, fiercely unknowable. While waiting for the moment of the violence he will inflict on Stanley, McCann systematically tears into strips a newspaper. Part of that image's deep fascination comes from its suggestiveness as a metaphor for the stage's relation to mass culture.

## 2    Theatre of Cruelty

Crumpled newspapers signified, aptly enough, the garden in which lay the murder victims in Howard Brenton's 1969 play *Christie in Love*. The police constable digging for bodies slowly recites limericks. The female corpse is a naked shop-window dummy; the police are what we'd call cardboard creations – recognizable media stereotypes – yet given to spasms of sudden unpredictable violence. Alongside all of these, Christie and his murderous love have to be played, Brenton says, 'believable', played for 'real'. The contrast here reworks the sort of relationship that exists between Meg's cliché-ridden patter and the violence done to Stanley. Instead of the attenuated speech that was mistaken for realism, Brenton's verbal text consists of a pastiche of theatrical styles and conspicuously fake explanations. The violence, though, is not inexplicable: it is caused by Christie's desire. That desire is felt to be the only real thing in an obviously stagey world. As the play develops, the audience, sitting around and close to that crumpled newspaper graveyard, are faced by an insistence upon the nature and presence, the 'reality', of that desire.

By operating in this way the play intends an assault upon the values and proprieties of its audience. That assault is made to feel like a necessary laying bare of what decorum or the 'establishment' wishes to conceal. In the previous year, 1968, that establishment had itself brought to an end centuries of institutionalized concealment when it abolished official censorship of the theatre. To that gesture the theatre had responded with a literal-minded insistence on laying bare. The theatre critic Kenneth Tynan put together a revue, called *Oh! Calcutta!*, containing scenes of sex and nudity which seemed designed to test the limits of the new tolerance. It became something of a commercial hit in 1970. Meanwhile back in 1968, in what would have been called the 'underground', a fringe show at the Ambiance Basement staged its sense of theatre's new relationship to its audience in this state of 'freedom'. When they came in to Ed Berman's *The Nudist Campers Grow and Grow* the audience were offered fig leaves; at the end of the show they were invited to throw off their clothes and join the nudists on stage.

The invitation was aggressive because it dared the audience to take personal risk in order to affirm the values they supposedly assented to. By contrast, in the imported North American musical *Hair* (1968), nudity stood for freedom, the show celebrated the love and peace values of contemporary counter-culture and managed to assimilate anti-Vietnam protest to the age of Aquarius – but none of it invited physical risk from the audience. *Hair* was a greater success than *Oh! Calcutta!*, perhaps precisely because it worked to make easy what Ed Berman's show had made so difficult: as the glossy theatre monthly *Plays and Players* noted, with satisfaction, 'it brought the *underground* out into the *boulevard*.'[1] What enabled that comforting cultural meeting was precisely the very thing which the establishment once supposedly viewed with distaste. Such shows as *Hair*, said *Plays and Players*, 'testify to the continuing commercial power of the naked body' (*Plays and Players* 1973: 39). That power presumably came not from the sort of challenge mounted by Ed Berman, who remained in the Basement, but from the boulevard's capacity to assimilate the underground. So it is an acceptable naughtiness, freedom without risk. The nudity remains on the stage, offering all its promise to an audience naughtily aware that through the proscenium frame they look at the permissiveness of the age. Not so much permissiveness itself, perhaps, as the spectacle of permissiveness.

If nudity's commercial success depended on keeping intact the traditional way of watching theatre, the impulse really to lay bare led, necessarily, to a disruption of that viewing arrangement. Brenton's nude in *Christie* is itself neither special nor shocking; it's a dummy. What is more disturbingly laid bare is a necrophiliac desire which is made more emphatically violent by breaking familiar rules: it is done physically close to the audience, in a story which brazenly enacts its repudiation of realist convention. Early 1970s fringe theatre became notorious for its disruption of the traditional relationship between audience and performance. This disruption was deliberately organized as trespass, transgression, offence. When naked performers crawled over an audience they intended to test the limits of that audience's tolerance and permissiveness. The assault aimed to upset the assumed proprieties of an everyday life cushioned within the clichés and consumerism of mass culture. That sort of everyday life was targeted by a theatre that consciously differentiated itself, a theatre that defined itself, in its physicality, as real life. Put in these terms the early 1970s assaults on audiences may be seen as a more aggressive version of theatre's understanding of its relationship with mass culture.

For by this date there was, in general, a new emphasis shaping thoughts about culture: 'We were trying to smash the apparently water-tight division between the private and the public man – the outer man whose behaviour is bound by the photographic rules of everyday life . . . and the inner man whose anarchy and poetry is usually expressed only in his words.' The passive rule-bound mass-culture person had developed an interior which was the inverse of the exterior: buried within each individual was the opposite of rules, anarchy, and the opposite of cliché, poetry. The rules of the outside are challenged by the truth which is inside, and the voice of that truth sounds anarchic, poetic, non-rational, mad. Thus, for the so-called anti-psychiatry of R. D. Laing, the schizophrenic articulates a truth which is concealed by the norms of public life. The message that is carried by madness's truth says that everyday norms are imposed on human beings, and the imposition does violence to them. In terms of this message, the development of mass consumerist culture doesn't merely corrupt people's tastes and modes of living so much as actively suppress the human being's full self. This is the point at which two major modern theories meet: a Marxist analysis of how capitalism turns human beings into objects finds shared ground with a psychoanalytic stress on how individuals learn the repression of desire. These ideas were most famously set out in the works of Herbert Marcuse and Wilhelm Reich. They were eagerly seized by English counter-culture, which thus began a productive engagement with contemporary European thought. In the books of Marcuse and Reich there could be found the story of a capitalism which required passive rule-bound subjects, individuals tamed within family units organized for the inculcation of dominant middle-class values. 'Bourgeois' became a multi-layered term of abuse. In its relation with mass-culture, or shall we now say 'bourgeois', existence the job of 'modern' drama turned from imaging the rule-bound limits of knowledge to a more aggressive discovery of the non-rule-bound – the smashing of the division between public and private. As the theatre director Peter Brook put it:

> Today, it is hard to see how a vital theatre and a necessary one can be other than out of tune with society – not seeking to celebrate the accepted values, but to challenge them. Yet the artist is not there to indict, nor to lecture, nor to harangue, and least of all to teach. . . . He challenges the audience truly when he is the spike in the side of an audience that is determined to challenge itself. (1968: 52, 134)

Peter Brook's account of theatre as challenge was published four years after he came to notoriety with his 'Theatre of Cruelty' season, with Charles Marowitz, in 1964. The title of that season performed homage to the French theorist Antonin Artaud who, in Brook's words, wanted 'A theatre working like the plague, by intoxication, by infection, by analogy, by magic; a theatre in which the play, the event itself, stands in place of a text.' And 'an audience that would drop all its defences, that would allow itself to be perforated, shocked, startled, and raped, so that at the same time it could be filled with a powerful new charge' (Brook 1968: 49, 53). The artist's 'spike' turns out to be rather penis-shaped, as the theatre, turgid with blood, thrusts into its audience. Those who turned up for the first performance of the Theatre of Cruelty season 'came to see an "experimental" evening': Brook's quote marks pick out what was at this period the particular codeword for anything new. 'The programme began with Artaud's three-minute play, *The Spurt of Blood*, made more Artaud than Artaud because his dialogue was entirely replaced by screams' (Brook 1968: 129–30).

Artaud's violence implied a strategy for smashing the public, and of course rule-bound, behaviour of an audience. That implication had already been turned into a performance training by the Polish practitioner Jerzy Grotowski.

> In Grotowski's terminology, the actor allows a role to 'penetrate' him; . . . 'Auto-penetration' by the role is related to exposure: the actor does not hesitate to show himself exactly as he is, for he realizes that the secret of the role demands his opening himself up, disclosing his own secrets. . . . the actor invokes, lays bare what lies in every man – and what daily life covers up. (Brook 1968: 59–60)

Conceived as both plague and laying bare, the theatre finds for itself a language which stands, so to speak, in opposition to a 'daily life' defined as rule-making, objectifying, repressive. On its mission to mess up its tidy bourgeois niche, 'modern' drama at the end of the 1960s turned itself towards Europe, defined itself as event rather than 'text', and constituted itself as 'happening', 'performance art' and 'cruelty'.

In 1968 Peter Brook had said that 'from the arresting words "Theatre of Cruelty" comes a groping towards a theatre, more violent, less rational, more extreme, less verbal, more dangerous. There is a joy in violent shocks. The only trouble with violent shocks is that they wear off. What follows a shock?' (Brook 1968: 54). The answer, in the immediate term, was another shock. In 1970 a collectively written piece called *Lay By* tested the limits of the new permissiveness, that naughty freedom packaged by *Oh! Calcutta!* The idea for the play came from a news item about a sex attack in a lay-by. The authors wrote their individual responses to the story. These responses were in turn stitched together into a show that stages images of childhood violence, adolescent drug-taking, the manufacture of pornography. The scenes are designed to put pressure on the spectators by the device of sharing their space and time: the stage temporarily became the setting for a series of real sexually explicit poses, pornographic photos were distributed among the audience, an actress took time shooting up with simulated heroin. While pornography and drug addiction are pretended, they happen in real time and space. Thus the show has the audience encounter not only the representation of these activities, as in a newspaper report for instance, but also a sense of their presence.

The scene which most disturbed audiences, however, was not the realistically enacted sex photography but the more metaphorical final image. The play ends in a hospital where naked corpses are washed in blood, dumped in a bin and made into strawberry jam.

> The intention of the last scene was to show what happens to the people after death – their reputations, the very knowledge about them as people. That knowledge is ground down. It's pulped. So we thought simply that we would find a visual device to show them being pulped, and we'd lay over it every conceivable bland statement that you can get about 'the nature of our terrible world'. . . . I like what it does to the audience, the last scene. It gives them a 'for us' or 'against us' feel. It presses the statement as hard home as it can. . . . We have alienated permanently a section of the British theatre-going public. People fainted, passed out and dropped over the back of the rostra at the Traverse. (Ford 1971: 83)

The force of this scene comes not from shared time and space but from a violence done to the proprieties of representation, the mixing of blood and jam, the aggressive emptying of sympathetic expressions. Cut up and patched together from divers sources, in its format the play enacts its distaste, not just for cliché, but also for the conventions of narrative, stylistic coherence, the pretence that a text can be expressive. There's no narrative logic governing the order of scenes; the audience is not offered the means of understanding usually provided by a clear sequence of causes and results. Words and images that might initially seem to be natural communication are replayed so they become artificial: making inadequate the language for talking about the horrors that the cut-up job insists on showing.

The play's 'cruelty' to its audience consisted of its making strange what the audience might take for granted combined with making present what is nasty or taboo: ideological demystification on one hand and on the other shocking confrontation. When in 1975 he reviewed 'Five Years of Experimental and Fringe Theatre in Britain' Peter Ansorge tried to describe this double quality in *Lay By*. In order to do so, he quoted the performance artist Jeff Nuttall's account of one of his own spectacles, 'a fake disembowelling in Better Books basement', clearly another underground event:

It was certainly a razor's edge between public ritual and private ceremony. At that time we were never quite sure whether what we were doing in happenings was demonstration or personal therapy. Frequently a savagery that began as satire, depicting, say, a politician engaged in some fantastic foulness, changed midway to sadistic participation on the part of the artist, as he expressed himself in the mood of the piece.

Ansorge continues: 'I think the borderline between a "savagery that began as satire" and "sadistic participation on the part of the artist" is not clearly defined in *Lay By*' (Ansorge 1975: 53). Ansorge's experience of *Lay By* is haunted by the sort of dramatic event which the late 1960s referred to as a 'happening'. The shape and imagery of the event blurred private and public, making 'rituals' that took place in real space and time, no longer playing to an audience so much as playing with them.

At the Royal Court's *Come Together* event in 1969: 'the Ken Campbell Roadshow spread chocolate cake and eggs across the laps of their clientele . . . Carlyle Reedy, a high priestess of happenings, opened a coffin which contained an enormous dead fish and proceeded with the aquatic burial rites' (Ansorge 1975: 38). Hovering dubiously between childhood regression, a custard-pie fight and Artaudian infection, the chocolate cake insists rather awkwardly on its own unmetaphoric self. The happening *disallows interpretation* of the very activities which are staged as if they require it. An alternative response might be, as the title of the 1971 Pip Simmons show suggests, *Do It!* The show, based on the student attack on the Chicago Democratic Convention in 1968, pressed its audience to choose between guards and protestors: 'one of the actors screamed "Come on! You can't all be pigs!" and about thirty people joined the actors running through the audience. It was like a madhouse' (quoted in Ansorge 1975: 33).

Using a similar strategy – 'to evoke a direct response from the audience' – they were treated as slave-owners in *The George Jackson Black and White Minstrel Show* (1973): 'Towards the end of the first half a slave auction was held. The minstrels ran through the audience begging to be bought. . . . The interval was spent with some of the audience with the slaves they had bought chained to their wrists' (Ansorge 1975: 34). The show as it were locked its audience into an invidious role which would persist for as long as they remained submissive. It could only be ended by active repudiation, like making a madhouse. Ansorge connects the theatrical rationale here to Marcuse's description of 'the power of the imagination' in *One Dimensional Man*. Theatre generates a madhouse in specific opposition to a familiar version of modern society: 'the Pip Simmons Group were unequalled in the English underground between 1968 and 1973 in evoking a "one-dimensional" society, based upon second-hand experiences and ideas often fostered by comic books and the television screen.' In a society which makes ideas banal, drama makes interpretation unavailable. What it urges you to do is to express emotion not think politics: '*Do It!* was certainly not a protest play . . . Rather it caught the image of a society during a potential moment of breakdown and, above all, the hysteria of its youth reflected in the rhythms, power and even obscenities of the language and music' (Ansorge 1975: 35, 33). Marcuse's analysis of the one-dimensionalism produced by capitalism presides over a crucial fudge, as it were: hysteria or protest; hysteria as protest. Like having your cake or/and eating it.

The performance which is undecided as to whether it is 'demonstration' or 'personal therapy' is one which lays itself bare in order that the audience also do so: 'Grotowski's actors offer their performance as a ceremony for those who wish to assist: the actor invokes, lays bare what lies in every man.' The block to the actor's search for 'his own freedom', as Brook sees it, is the director, who 'cannot help projecting his own state of mind on to the stage' (Brook 1968: 60, 61). In this logic, the performer finds freedom by centring her work on herself. Thus in her reflections on the female nude and exploitation, Roberta Graham produced a series of self-portraits: 'it makes sense to use your own image if you are expressing your own emotions; using models in very intimate work isn't being very honest.' Her next show, with the rather Christie-like title *In the Slaughterhouse of Love* (1983), maintained the intimacy in that she performed with her personal partner, whose arm she cut, then licked his blood: 'It was designed to make people . . . ask how far they were able to push a fantasy into a real-life situation, without denying the fact that it could be dangerous' (Hughes-Hallett 1992: 24, 25).

Grotowski's exercises work through the body to enable the performer to invoke a reality which takes its force not from a director's project but from the performer's own psychic engagement. That engagement is shown in the performing body; its display of muscular and nervous tensions becomes a guarantee of the reality of what's happening. And where real blood is shed the performance refuses the safety of fantasy, becoming more real-life than an audience might want. Access to this risky reality is made possible by performance alone in a culture which transforms everything, including bodies, into commodity. Thus there's a pressure on the body to keep coming up with viable guarantees of the real: 'Schrick begins to daub runny gobs of paint over his penis and head . . . then he starts to paint with his head whilst giving birth to an extraordinary vocabulary of invented words and sounds, squeaking and chattering like some psychotic undergoing crisis.' As in shamanic rituals, which are a key reference point for so much of this work, the performer becomes psychically transformed by what he or she has set in motion: 'Scribbles on the walls mark the ferocity of Schrick's physicality . . . becoming softer and more plaintive he returns to his former self and regards the audience quizzically as if uncertain what else to do' (Caton 1989: 28).[2]

The audience take their cue and applaud. But the performer's quizzical look is one which refuses to be answerable for any planned significance in the event. The more messy the paint is, the more unartistic its use, the truer is the sense of psychic ferocity. Any respect for learnt rules or interpretation would constitute a block to the expressive freedom. The performance collapses any distance between itself and audience; there is no offered position from which to spectate: 'Schrick's world darkens under the frenzy of his interaction with the audience – he grabs certain individuals and hugs them or immerses them into the ritual paint action' (Caton 1989: 28). The ritual or ceremony assumes a readiness to be smeared with paint or cake, to be psychically transported, as its precondition for experiencing whatever reality is found. The performance enters no contract with its audience to make meanings, to entertain, to give messages, to instruct how it's to be watched. It is left to the audience to decide on their relationship to what they feel to be dangerous, or to decide on their need to be present at something which feels pointless. Defined as ceremonies, these events find analogies for themselves in the case studies of anthropology rather more than theatre history. They are known generically by labels that have nothing to do with the words 'drama' and 'theatre' – 'performance art', 'performance' or, most revealingly of all, 'live art'.

When she is neither the vehicle for a director's project nor the medium for delivering a message, the emphasis falls on the performer's own presence. 'Presence' became a keyword in new drama practices of the 1990s. Grotowski's actor training exercises met with theatre anthropology's interest in non-Western forms – such as Kathakali dance and Noh theatre, forms in which the body's physical expertise gives to the performer's whole being a sense of specialness, a 'presence'. Contemporary training in stage presence teaches an actor to respond with and through the body rather than with the mind. Exercises might concentrate on what it feels like physically to be water or fire, how one moves in the space of the colour red. These skills were learned in the

Jacques Lecoq School in Paris by many British performers, including most famously, in 1994–5, members of the Theatre de Complicite.

Founded in 1983, Complicite have been credited with revolutionizing British theatre. Their name has been glossed as 'collusion between celebrants' (Ratcliffe 1994), the performer as celebrant rather than vehicle for author or director, celebrating and colluding with the physical skills of others. One of Complicite's exercises has actors moving around as a shoal of fish, constantly changing leaders, where each leadership emerges not out of design but from the collusive physical sensibility. By the mid-1990s Complicite's was the accepted language of new theatre. They had shows on in London's West End – *The Street of Crocodiles, The Three Lives of Lucie Cabrol* – the sponsorship of Sainsbury's and teaching residencies in any drama school that aimed to put itself at the cultural cutting-edge. In a programme note for a National Theatre show in 1991 they were celebrated for directing British theatre away from its customary intellectualism towards a new physicality. In making this argument, that note displays an ignorance of decades of physical performing and, more damagingly, a ready willingness to separate the physical and intellectual. Discovered to be acceptably new on these terms, what must now be called neither 'happening' nor 'live art' but 'physical theatre' finds itself swimming like a shoal of its fish, wondering who might really be leading.

The physical event now, as when it was done in the 1960s, could be said to balance on 'a razor's edge between public ritual and private ceremony'. Jeff Nuttall's performances worked to explore the feasibility of separating public from private: for ceremony's shape and rhythms work on audience members to incorporate them into a participant group. Nuttall's sense of *interrelation* between public and private is modified by Ansorge's commentary into a *choice* between them. So that his account of *Lay By*, for instance, suggests that the obvious private concerns of the authors, their 'sadistic participation', betray their adherence to a moral nihilism. To condemn public theatrical language by revealing its private roots is to be suspicious of the private. That suspicion inhabits Peter Brook's attack on the misuse of Artaud which has 'led to a naive belief that emotional commitment and unhesitating self-exposure are all that really count. . . . There is now a form of sincere acting which consists of living everything through the body. It is a kind of naturalism' (Brook 1968: 117). This is really an attack on sloppy acting. It is not an engagement with the interpenetration of private and public, the ceremonies of authenticity, staged by 'performance art'. But at the same time it's a demonstration of the extent to which the dramatic language which is spoken by performance art gets absorbed into, and modified by, a mode of thinking which sets up the private as a distortion of public art.

Public art itself is at the centre of Howard Barker's radio play about a fictional Venetian painter, *Scenes from an Execution* (1984). Galactia is commissioned to depict a victorious battle: 'Sometimes you have to admit they get things right, the bureaucrats; for all their corrupt deliberations, they pick an artist who might just **tell the truth**.' Her commitment to truth leads her to walk out of a funeral of a fellow painter: 'A dead painter, claimed. The dissenting voice, drowned in compliments. . . . And yet a frightful liar. Couldn't put a brush to paper without lying.' Her own work turns out to be so shocking that she is imprisoned, until the Doge of Venice discovers how the State may comfort itself with art: 'To have said this work could not be absorbed by the spirit of the Republic would be to belittle the Republic, and our barbarian neighbours would have jeered at us. So we absorb all, and in absorbing it we show our greater majesty. It offends today, but we look harder and we know, it will not offend tomorrow' (H. Barker 1990a: 270, 275, 301). The Doge learns to govern along lines formulated by another Italian, famous for his analysis of the modern prince:

> the supremacy of a social group manifests itself in two ways, as 'domination' and as 'intellectual and moral leadership' . . . A social group can, and indeed must, already exercise 'leadership' before winning governmental power . . . it subsequently becomes dominant when it exercises power, but even if it holds it firmly in its grasp, it must continue to 'lead' as well. (Gramsci 1971: 57)

By being felt to lead, it obtains the consent of those over whom it rules, and thereby maintains what Gramsci calls 'hegemony'. The Doge knows that his regime can sustain the confidence of its rule by being comfortable with what may intend to offend it.

Galactia's contempt for a dissenting voice which allows itself to be drowned in compliments is an echo of her dramatist's attack on 'cultural managers' who 'will demonstrate the frivolity, the absence of concentration, the impatience, the dictatorship of television habits over the minds of the audience, but never the appetite for challenge, truth, or discrimination.' Barker's own writing is, he says, shaped by 'a culture now obsessively concerned with dissemination of statistics and facts which themselves do nothing to stimulate change' (H. Barker 1989: 17, 50). This sense of culture grows out of a belief that knowledge is becoming 'an informational commodity', and that 'society exists and progresses only if the messages circulating within it are rich in information and easy to decode.' These words are from one of the gurus of late 1980s society, Jean-François Lyotard, who shares that anxiety about drowning in compliments:

> By becoming kitsch, art panders to the confusion which reigns in the 'taste' of the patrons. Artists, gallery owners, critics, and public wallow together in the 'anything goes', and the epoch is one of slackening. But this realism of the 'anything goes' is in fact that of money; in the absence

of aesthetic criteria, it remains possible and useful to assess the value of works of art according to the profits they yield.

Lyotard's remarks are part of his attempt to answer the question 'What is Postmodernism?' He suggests that

> The postmodern would be that which, in the modern, puts forward the unpresentable in presentation itself; that which denies itself the solace of good forms, the consensus of a taste which would make it possible to share collectively the nostalgia for the unattainable; that which searches for new presentations, not in order to enjoy them but in order to impart a stronger sense of the unpresentable. (Lyotard 1984: 5, 76, 81)

That refusal to accept and produce consensus of taste, the 'endless drizzle of false collectivity', defines Howard Barker's artistic project:

> The audience experiences the play individually and not collectively. . . . If it is prepared, the audience will not struggle for permanent coherence, which is associated with the narrative of naturalism, but experience the play moment by moment, truth by truth, contradiction by contradiction. The breaking of false dramatic disciplines frees people into imagination. . . . The real end of drama in this period must be not the reproduction of reality . . . but what might be, what is **imaginable**. (H. Barker 1989: 13, 36)

This project produced in 1989, the bicentennial of the French Revolution, a play – *Golgo* – which imagined a group of aristocrats playing their version of Christ's death at Golgotha while outside the park gates stands the crowd.

> WHATTO: It's
> > After All
> > An
> > Entertainment
> > Death
> > And then to find this. To have to tolerate this. Cavorting and. No, it spoils the. Naturally he. Within the obvious constraints of. Expressed his chagrin. (*He emits a long and terrible cry.*) This cry goes unrecorded in the gospels. (*He repeats it.*) This cry has only now been excavated. (*And again*) This cry –
> CHORUS: **He knows our cries better than anyone!**
> > **He knows the sound of our despair!**
> > **The scale of agony he practised daily**
> > **And wrung notes from misery of such rare intensity!**

LUNATIC: I danced!
　I danced!
　And few could tear their eyes from me!
　(*The assembly stands, laughing as an audience laughs at a street performer.*
　*This laughter is orchestrated, rhythmic and consciously flat. During the*
　*laughter,* WHATTO *dances a mockery of* CHRIST. *He stops suddenly.*)

(H. Barker 1990b: 72)

Barker describes this sort of writing: 'A theatre of Catastrophe, like the tragic theatre, insists on the limits of tolerance as its territory. It inhabits the area of maximum risk, both to the imagination and invention of its author, and to the comfort of its audience' (Barker 1989: 53). Coherent meaning has to be dissolved, elements of the drama have to be dislocated, only to be recombined within the individualized perception of each audience member. Meaning is not authorized, so that Whatto slides in and out of being 'Christ' and the Chorus is placed within neither truth nor ignorance; imparting a sense of the unpresentable. Drama excavates the cry that the Gospels don't repeat, 'Tragedy restores pain to the individual' (p. 13), while collective laughter is mechanical and mass carnival is always outside the gates.

The aristocrats cope with historical inevitability by expressing their fantasies and desires, by acting. In Barker's drama the emphasis on the centrality of the actor, on truth and on the necessity for the audience's resentment or pain all seems to connect Theatre of Catastrophe to Theatre of Cruelty: Barker wants an audience 'stirred at a subconscious level by the sheer volume of imagined life' (p. 82), working a bit like intoxication, plague, the sheer volume of imagined death perhaps. Both Theatres try to remove drama from the obligation to show life as it is lived, from sharing the role of other media in an information culture. Both distrust that culture which opposes, in Barker's phrase, 'challenge, truth or discrimination', an opposition which Denys Thompson and F. R. Leavis called in 1964 *Discrimination and Popular Culture.* The antagonism between individual truth and degraded mass culture replaces the political hostility between left and right: the 'imperative to enlighten, amuse, and stimulate good thoughts of a collective nature (family, nation, party, community) clings to the carnival mania of the left and the moral crusade of the right' (p. 54). Barker seems to speak for a generation of 'Cruelty' and 'performance art' when he declares that 'In a culture now so rampantly populist that the cultural distinctions of right and left have evaporated, the public have a right of access to a theatre which is neither brief nor relentlessly uplifting, but which insists on complexity and pain, and the beauty that can only be created from the spectacle of pain' (p. 55). The problem with the spectacle of pain is that, if it is spectacle, it is in some respect organized to be performance. Whatto's repetition of the cry that was unrecorded in the Gospels becomes less painfully authentic each time it is repeated.

The dramatic project is always open to accommodation by those like the Doge of Venice: 'It offends today, but we look harder and we know, it will not offend tomorrow.'

The Doge and his fellows had in fact already been at work before 'modern' drama hurled its cruelty at 'false collectivity'. Barker's views remind David Ian Rabey of 'Nietzsche's identification of the herd instinct' (H. Barker 1989: 74). The phrase Peter Ansorge uses of Pip Simmons's work – 'moral nihilism' – also leads back to Nietzsche. But let's allow the guru to take us there: 'Modernity, in whatever age it appears, cannot exist without a shattering of belief and without discovery of the "lack of reality" of reality.' And what does this 'lack of reality' signify? 'The phrase is of course akin to what Nietzsche calls nihilism' (Lyotard 1984: 77). The year that *Golgo* was performed, 1989, was also another anniversary, marking ten years since the Thatcher government had come to power. That particular form of modernity had insisted on the 'lack of reality' of several realities. Those Doges justified their dismantling of the welfare state on the basis that charity harmed individual development, or as Barker might put it 'to be kind to the weak might stunt the ability of the weak to develop their own strategy' (H. Barker 1989: 74). There is, said Thatcherism, no such thing as society, merely a collection of individuals. By locking it outside its gates, *Golgo*, like Thatcherism, turns away from the very thing which in effect shapes its aesthetic and political strategy, mass culture.

## 3   The Fun Palace

In the final scene of John Arden's *Workhouse Donkey* (1963) demonstrators chant outside the auditorium and some force open the doors: *'They are carrying bottles, and placards with such slogans as "All fine art is a hearty fart", "Paint me, paint my dog", "You can't gild a mucky lily", "If the people scrawl, put glazed tiles on the wall", and so on'* (Arden 1964: 126). They are supporters of Charlie Butterthwaite, who has been removed from political power in the town. His former allies and enemies, Labour councillors and Conservative opposition, have gathered on May Day for the opening of a new art gallery. The stage is set with paintings hung on screens and a champagne reception. The building housing the gallery used to be an upper-class sex club, the Copacabana.

During the demonstrators' commotion Butterthwaite enters at the back of the stage and sits on a table, helping himself to champagne and cake. He begins to review his political downfall:

I was the grand commander of the whole of my universe. Now all that's left me is the generalship of these. I need to assume a different order o' raiment. (*He pulls the baize tablecloth to him and arranges it like a shawl.*)

Three times three, but all that's left is paper.
(*He pulls down a paper chain and hangs it round his neck.*)
Three times three is nine, but the old cocked hat's bashed in. So here's
a replacement.
(*He picks up a ring of flowers that has been garnishing the buffet and puts it on
his head.*)
. . . In my rejection I have spoken to this people. I will rejoice despite
them. I will divide Dewsbury and mete out the valley of Bradford;
Pudsey is mine, Huddersfield is mine, Rotherham also is the strength of
my head, Osset is my lawgiver, Black Barnsley is my washpot

(Arden 1964: 129)

The religious pastiche turns Butterthwaite not into Christ but into the figure
of parody itself, of topsy-turvy, transgressive, mess. Dionysos comes to
Yorkshire.

In his Author's Preface Arden says: 'the theatre must be catholic. But it
never will be catholic if we do not grant pride of place to the old essential
attributes of Dionysus':

> noise
> disorder
> drunkenness
> lasciviousness
> nudity
> generosity
> corruption
> fertility
> and
> ease.
>
> (Arden 1964: 9)

He outlines an idea of theatre in which a play such as *The Workhouse Donkey*
might last 'six or seven or thirteen hours'. with the audience coming and going
as they please: 'A theatre presenting such an entertainment would, of course,
need to offer rival attractions as well, and would in fact take on some of the
characteristics of a fairground or amusement park' (p. 8). He then notes that
Joan Littlewood has proposed a similar idea. Littlewood was the director, and
co-founder, of Theatre Workshop, a company most famous for pioneering a
mode of work in which the actors worked together as an ensemble, developing
the shape and sound of scenes through improvisation and shared research.
What emerged on stage had at its core a sense of the performers' spontaneity,
marked not only by the irruptions of song and dance but by a feeling of a free
relationship to anything pre-written or practised. It was noisy, generous and

risky. When Joan Littlewood thought of extending her work beyond her theatre into 'fun palaces for the people', this was the sort of fun she had in mind.

The people she had in mind were working-class. People's fun, and its relation to 'hearty fart' fine art, pushed its way into public awareness in what turned out to be a seminal conference of the National Union of Teachers in 1960. The title of the conference, 'Popular Culture and Personal Relationship', points in two directions at once: back to that worry about the corrupting effect of mass media on individual morality and taste; and forward to a recognition of the existence of a culture that might be described as popular rather than high art. One of the books to emerge, in 1964, in response to the conference we've met before, *Discrimination and Popular Culture*; the other was *The Popular Arts*, by Stuart Hall and Paddy Whannel. That second book makes a crucial theoretical distinction between a depersonalized mass art and a popular art which has its roots in folk culture: 'The typical "art" of the mass media today is not a continuity from, but *a corruption of*, popular art' (Hall and Whannel 1964: 68). This distinction escapes from the pessimistic nostalgia for a lost organic culture by a simple step: it sees popular art as current and, hence, as an already existing possible alternative to mass culture. That sense of an alternative, even of a contest, had already been formulated in one of the period's most influential texts on culture, Raymond Williams's *The Long Revolution*, which appeared in 1961. Williams defined culture as a 'whole way of life' and attempted to describe its historical transformation: 'This deeper cultural revolution is a large part of our most significant living experience, and is being interpreted and indeed fought out, in very complex ways, in the world of art and ideas' (R. Williams 1975: 12). The 'whole way of life' of popular culture might include popular film, football, rock music, teenage magazines, all the sorts of cultural phenomena that were studied at the Centre for Contemporary Cultural Studies established at Birmingham University in 1964. It might also include a sense of a lived but forgotten history, 'a mainstream tradition of guizers, carnival and subversive folk art which was the heritage of the working class' (Coult and Kershaw 1983: 19). Arden's mythic Dionysos is backed by the placards of street protest. Both unruly elements may be described as people's fun.

The proposal for fun palaces was part of a cultural fight which was perceived to be still continuing on the same lines in 1983 when Tony Coult wrote his introduction to a history of Welfare State International, a theatre group founded in 1968:

> In modern technocratic states, at war within themselves socially and morally, communal images and myths are highly likely to be empty relics of past organic culture, or state propaganda designed to subdue popular expression and action. The filling of that vacuum in human

social needs is therefore left to artists. (Coult and Kershaw 1983: 12)

The use of communal images and myths to tame popular expression is a recognized method by which a dominant class organizes consent to its rule within the domain of civil society. Charlie Butterthwaite sings a song about it. His adviser, Blomax, describes Napoleon Bonaparte's power based on wealth and weapons; then Butterthwaite adds:

> But I am not the same as that:
> I bow to the public voice.
> My best endeavours are bent thereto
> As befits the people's choice
> (Arden 1964: 30)

In the narrative of the play Butterthwaite sees as his main enemy Colonel Feng, a policeman brought in from outside the region to organize a cleanup of the town's corruption. Butterthwaite aligns himself on the side of pleasure in a contest with law; in doing so he maintains his own corrupt political power. By the end both Butterthwaite and Feng have lost power, marginalized by an alliance between Labour and Conservative councillors. Butterthwaite is thus perhaps, like Howard Barker's individual, beyond left and right.

The Labour Mayor explains his presence at the Tory-funded art gallery: 'Not to be construed as an official occasion but purely as a social courtesy in recognition of cultural attainment.' A particular form of 'culture' – fine art – enables the political compromise which retains a grip on wealth and power. Against this culture are placed the Dionysos mess of Butterthwaite, with its obvious energy, and the blank verse of Feng, which in its *gravitas* has a different sort of force: 'I said that I / Derived authority from my high office not / From the jerk and whirl of irrelevant faction' (Arden 1964: 120, 125). The conventional opposition of left and right is replaced by a cultural opposition – fine art versus fun – which is itself grounded in a sort of bodily opposition between polite sterility and personal force. Feng and Butterthwaite are enemies but alike, powerful, selfish, individuals versus a compromised crowd. Feng has to realize he can't exist outside that crowd, Butterthwaite depends on a popular support which he also manipulates. The relations between these various positions are opposed but linked, dialectically organized. Thus, while Barker blurs what's popular with what's populist, Arden enacts a cultural diversity, making a play where the notion of the popular is both powerful and disingenuous, and where the cultural works to organize consent.

The effect of *The Workhouse Donkey* on its critics was, said Arden, to baffle them and make them mad. For the Chichester Festival audience the whole theatrical space suddenly got risky as fake protestors hammered at real doors

into a real auditorium. The organization of Dionysiac fun threatened to mess
up the tidy separation between performance and non-performance space. And
when the performance talks to the audience about its relationship to them, it
suddenly changes tack away from being an apparent imitation of reality
towards a more metaphorical, insinuating, tone of voice:

> The first day of May is the day of Art and Beauty,
> The dust of Sweetman thrust into the eye-balls of you all
> For to wash you white and whiter than the whitewash on the wall.
> But out in the dark back lane
> The great grey cat still waits by the mouse's hole.
>
> (Arden 1964: 119)

The pleasure in Art and Beauty amounts to a collective cultural mystification,
organized by a wealthy Tory councillor. But there is something else, says the
speech, that we ought to be conscious of: the great grey cat. The stage's
metaphors, its dialectical switchback, all unsettle easy comprehension; but
they also madden moral complacence, finding the dark spaces underneath the
whitewash.

The stage urges its audience into a more complex response, shifting them
away from easy, but false, securities. That sort of working on and with an
audience could be construed as 'education through theatre':

> Not theatre in the sense of putting on plays, although this later became
> part of it, but theatre in the sense of setting up concrete situations
> through which people could learn, directly and by experience, how to
> handle and use concepts that, in the abstract, had seemed complex and
> mystifying. (A. Hunt 1976: 41)

The educationalist envisages participation more conscious and chosen than
that of the *Workhouse Donkey* audience. But in each case theatre intends to work
directly on people's experiences in order to alter their relations to accepted
truths, such as Art and Beauty. When Arden's friend Albert Hunt became a
teacher at Bradford Art College, he began to experiment with theatre as a
mode of concrete learning, where the 'education industry' conditions us 'to
accept as normal a number of highly questionable assumptions'. But he
rejected the 'missionary' role of literature teaching, which he associated with
Leavis and Thompson, as a solution to a deadening society: 'A man whose
"sensibilities" and "capacities for living" have been largely shaped by reading
books can only assume that people who don't share his commitment to
literature will be in danger of having their responsiveness of feelings destroyed.' This sense of a culture in which not everybody shares a commitment
to literature, and particularly where students are culturally placed differently

from their teachers, echoed the concerns of the National Union of Teachers' conference of 1960. An awareness of cultural differences carried a perception that there was another power struggle going on somewhere besides that in labour relations, namely in education. Hunt argues that pupils learn that their lives are controlled by other people, and that the education system, with its uniforms and routines, is itself theatrical:

> Until we begin to understand that the education system itself works in terms of theatre to communicate a particular experience of society, we won't get very far in saying what the role of theatre – *our* theatre, not the education system's – can be in contributing to the true aim of education, that of giving pupils understanding, control, and the power to make decisions about changing their environment. (A. Hunt 1976: 18, 17–18, 121)

A theatrical learning situation explicitly draws on the pupils' culture by using the roles and structure of children's games. Hunt used 'grandmother's footsteps' to work on a classroom scene: 'the game we had played had unearthed several levels of paradox. Behind the masks, the children became a well-drilled, subversive, and slightly cruel army. The art master, the authoritarian believer in straight lines, became a man trying to cling to some sense of reality' (p. 28). The game has two effects: it stimulates physical energy and it enables something familiar to be grasped in a new way. When they played the events of the Cuban missile crisis as a Hollywood movie, Hunt's company 'saw the imaginative reawakening as a necessary first step towards regaining control of that situation'. The situation itself had the world hanging for a few days in 1962 on the brink of nuclear holocaust. Playing aims to grasp control over what is, literally, deadening:

> We'd dreamed up a practical situation and then acted to bring it into being. And the existence of that situation had made possible more acts of imagination; which in turn gave us weapons with which to assault the mystifications of a society intent on hiding its true identity behind a curtain of jargon. (p. 164)

*Games* thus became one of the key elements of modern drama practice. Clive Barker's *Theatre Games*, published in 1972, acknowledges the influence of Joan Littlewood's methods, and in its turn shaped the rehearsals of many younger directors. But it is more than a rehearsal method: 'I drew the analogy with children playing in the streets. When they play, say, cowboys and Indians around street corners, they're totally absorbed in their game. They fire bullets at each other and to them the bullets are real' (A. Hunt 1976: 68). The child is not a cowboy, but in the game is not not a cowboy. Such playing raises the question of 'what was meant by acting, of the relationship of the actor himself to the part he was playing':

> In the Nixon show, for example [*The Fears and Miseries of Nixon's Reich*, first performed in February 1974], one performer, Chris Vine, pretends to be Nixon, pretending first to be Marilyn Monroe, then Tony Curtis. Throughout all these switches, Chris Vine remains himself, playing with a Yorkshire accent. But the megalomaniac look in his eyes, and the thrust-out chin is Nixon's. And the wiggle of the hips is Monroe's. (p. 101)

This enactment of history and politics differs considerably from so-called documentary theatre, much of which 'might as well have been pamphlets': 'to us, theatre arose from contradiction – between what you said you were doing, and what you were actually doing, between what people saw, and what they were told they were seeing, between the real performer, physically *there*, and the parts he said he was playing' (p. 103). Free from the supposedly natural assumptions of real life, by 'demonstrating the importance of play, the theatre is also demonstrating an alternative way of looking at social processes' (p. 124). The play is serious precisely because it is *play*.

The images in this theatre are neither documents nor imitations of life, but metaphors: 'an image of the Vietnam war as a circus. . . . a circus band of clowns, which turned into soldiers machine-gunned in battle; a President Johnson who popped out of a huge tea-chest, like a jack-in-the-box' (A. Hunt 1976: 80–1). The metaphors are shaped by the performers' private imagination energetically re-engaging with the common currency of popular culture. Those two elements produced their fusion in a Welfare State International event in Bracknell in 1982:

> If you have, as we did, a procession of bike boys with Donald Quixotty, you're dealing with young men with dreams, but you're also dealing with all the films that've been around, be it 'Easy Rider' or 'Mad Max II'. It doesn't matter, so long as you can use the imagery in a positive way to release energy for good. (Coult and Kershaw 1983: 24)

The game which enables performers to demystify their world also draws its energy from staging their dreams. That release is crucial to Clive Barker's theory of games: 'One's development as an actor is . . . inseparably bound up with a growing understanding of oneself and one's fellow men through personal and social relationships. To restrict the concept of education to a short period of learning facts and skills . . . is to inhibit the processes of learning' (C. Barker 1977: 52). Games supply the self-learning which is omitted from education and thus come to occupy the space of therapy, personal development, discovery through role-play. *That* space is somewhere different from the production of theatrical metaphor and political demystification. Where demystification had depended upon participation and engagement, there is now a danger, warns Hunt, that 'the theatre will accept the role of yet another teaching aid . . . at best, sugar on the pill, and, at worst, yet another form of oppression' (A. Hunt 1976: 122). The link between drama and teaching, the practice now widely known as theatre-in-education, is one of the major innovations of modern theatre. It grew out of the same cultural battleground as did the interest in games. In Hunt's metaphoric theatre, games and popular idioms had held the performer's psychic investment in tension with a political project. But, as games drifted towards personal therapy, and theatre-in-education settled into animated civics lessons, the sense of a contestatory practice began to dissolve.

In the 'happening' the spectator confronts a world of private imagery generated by a personal response to society; in the show that uses popular idiom the spectator recognizes images that are in general social circulation. Recognition is instant rather than exploratory; not a painful encounter, a bewilderment, but a way of making sense, of intellectually fixing. It's like a cartoon.

> At the time, we actually invented looking straight in the audience's face and telling them what we were talking about. We called it 'presentationism' – sort of here we are, entertainers, but theatre as well. . . . Peter Brook used to come and say, 'Where did you get that style from?' As if I owed him something! And I told him our influences were working-class entertainers. . . . Theatre then was all about sitting down and standing up and walking out of french windows. We were the first rock'n'roll theatre group. (in Itzin 1980: 14)

The person speaking is Ronald Muldoon, who founded Cartoon Archetypal Slogan Theatre (CAST) in 1965 after becoming dissatisfied with the Communist-affiliated Unity Theatre. CAST polemically separated itself from what it defined as narrowly political agit-prop and alienated its associates on the Trotskyite left. In making space to be theatre as well, the cartoon insists on the political force of quoting and so taking control over other modes of theatre. CAST's *Muggins' Awakening*: 'took the piss out of the new wave of theatre, like burning the butterflies in [Peter Brook's] *US*' (in Itzin 1980: 17). The capacity to quote, and indeed inhabit, other modes of theatre has a force which is compatible with, or is even produced by, looking the audience straight in the face. In the late 1970s the Birmingham-based Banner Theatre of Actuality toured a show, commissioned by the National Union of Public Employees, about cuts in the public services. Banner's technique was to interview the affected workers and photograph them in their workplaces, then retell their words, alongside the photo, on stage. *Dr Healey's Casebook* (Healey was Chancellor of the Exchequer) intercut these documentary accounts with *commedia dell'arte*-inspired scenes, in which a masked civil servant recited gibberish, based on the words 'cut' and 'chop', while a Healey figure slid between being a manic surgeon and a bullfighter. Banner said they had been told by a regional arts authority that the *commedia* scenes were a mistake. The authority could live with a compassionate, even left-wing documentary, but the promiscuous capacity to inhabit other modes became a strain on patronage.

Aristocratic patrons on a shooting party are liable to get nastier. Lord Crask and Lady Phosphate, English owners of Scottish land, are hunting grouse. They sing (as one does):

LADY PHOSPHATE:    How I wish that I could paint –
        For the people are so quaint
        I said so at our ceilidh
        To dear Benjamin Disraeli.
        Mr Landseer showed the way –
        He gets commissions every day –
        The Silvery Tay.
LORD CRASK:    The Stag at Bay [etc.]

Later *'They become more serious. Turn their guns on the audience.'*

LORD CRASK:    But although we think you're quaint
        Don't forget to pay your rent,
        And if you should want your land,
        We'll cut off your grasping hand.
                (McGrath 1977: 20, 21)

As cartoons the aristocrats invite recognition of the conjunction of wealth, brutality and stupidity. But their double-act and song take longer than is necessary merely for recognition. The length of the act itself becomes oppressive, not so much in pointing guns but in the confident occupation of the stage. The shapes of the jokes and song are culturally recognizable. They are not to be taken to express 'real' feelings but a social–cultural attitude, towards Scotland, towards the audience. In Bertolt Brecht's theory of drama, there is a name given to a moment of action which suddenly clinches and clarifies a specific set of social relations. Brecht calls it the *gestus*. Our aristocrats' routine might thus be called a cultural *gestus*, in that it performs an attitude in which culture speaks clearly as class and nation.

The English and their administrators oppress the Scots whom they define as savages. An under-factor reports to his boss the number of illegal stills in Strathnaver: 'The whole thing smacks of a terrible degeneracy in the character of these aboriginals.' They barter on a land-sale, then sing, to the tune of 'Bonnie Dundee':

> Your barbarous customs, though they may be old
> To civilised people hold horrors untold –
> What value a culture that cannot be sold?
>
> (pp. 8, 9)

An audience that knows 'Bonnie Dundee' will recognize the altered words, most audiences will recognize the shape of the bartering sequence, and an anti-racist audience will recognize the language about aboriginals. The play's action demonstrates how a dominant group encodes its texts, and the audience are invited simultaneously from their own position to decode. The activity of encoding–decoding works not only politically, as demystification, but also shapes a theatrical experience. The audience enacts its political attitude (by decoding against the oppressor) and in doing so comes into an identity, pleasurably finds 'itself' by finding a decoding position. That amounts, in John McGrath's opinion, to the most important function of political theatre, 'the creation of a counter-culture based on the working class, which will grow in richness and confidence until it eventually displaces the dominant bourgeois culture of late capitalism' (in Itzin 1980: 126). Or, as the Doge of Venice might have put it, the creation of a counter-hegemony forceful enough to displace the ruling hegemony.

In a later scene of this Scottish play, called *The Cheviot, the Stag and the Black, Black Oil*, done in 1973 by McGrath's company, 7:84, the audience are expected to be confident enough to talk back. '*Enter* BILL *as Sturdy Highlander . . . He does elaborate pantomime double take at Red Indian painted on the set*': he then asks the audience to warn him if any Indians approach, by shouting 'Walla Walla wooskie', and he makes them practise until they do it 'with gusto'. Only then does he return to the narrative. This scene doesn't quote pantomime, it acts it out. Thus while recognition or decoding may have produced resistance to the incipient racism here, the pantomime shape promises pleasure that comes from joining in, finding a voice. An accepted feature of the pantomime is that the performer is and is not a character: they shout for Bill so that he will show them his Sturdy Highlander enactment. When he comes out of the pantomime fiction Bill gains the authority of a truth-speaker: 'in time, the Red Indians were reduced to the same state as our fathers after Culloden – defeated, hunted, treated like the scum of the earth, their culture polluted and torn out with slow deliberation.' Then another performer, Doli, reads a poem in Gaelic. The feeling of seriousness is generated by a display of real commitment to a people's culture: Bill as Bill shares an anger about Culloden, Doli enacts Doli's competence in Gaelic. As performers they are responsible not just for presenting a show, but also for researching and constructing it. Which makes them almost not performers: in the published text, 'it has not been possible to separate "Liz" – Elizabeth Maclennan – from what she says, or "Doli" – Dolina Maclennan – from what she sings. If other actors decide to perform the piece, they should try to create the same identification with what they say and do – something quite different from normal actor's learning of lines' (McGrath 1977: 15, 17, 4).

After one scene, '*all go off except* ALEX, *who comes to the mike and talks to the audience as himself.* ALEX: What was really going on?' The performer who speaks as himself tells the reality. Throughout the show there is a contrast between false dominant media images of Scotland and a true people's culture, with the performers enacting their – already existing – ability to distinguish Landseer's fiction from real Gaelic. This is evidence that they are not passive subjects who have merely learnt lines written for them by a mass media culture. At the end of the play the audience is asked to take up a similar position against passive subjection: 'Have we learnt anything from the Clearances?' (McGrath 1977: 11, 33).

That 'we' is crucial. For the performer's authority comes not from an ability to speak truth but from identification with a truth that needs speaking. That means speaking *from* and *with* the oppressed rather than speaking for them. Those performance protocols connect with wider issues around participatory as against representative democracy which in the 1970s led to campaigns for democratizing the structure of trades unions, questions about the adequacy of Parliamentary rule, self-organization by the oppressed. Performances which contested ruling hegemony looked for authorization, clearance perhaps, from their audiences. To this end they developed a stage language which went further than the appeal to 'our' fathers, 'our' history: characters recognized friends in the audience, plays opened out to include the auditorium in scenes of trades union meeting or public assembly, the invention of the post-show discussion facilitated a real meeting of cast and audience. Those meetings of common interest produce a feeling that the play derives its being from the audience. What, as researchers, the 7:84 performers had found, and articulated, was something that existed prior to the play: the history of the audience, or rather, to use the keyword, community.

'Community drama' is a label that comes from the drive to find a participatory – indeed organic – theatrical practice. Many of the debates around community drama – who does what for, with, from whom – are shaped by that history. Performances of an authentic 'us' work to empower: 'The community may be strengthening itself in the present by representing its past' (Kershaw 1992: 194). But when you find 'us' you don't necessarily need to fight 'them': 'Politics are divisive. We strongly feel that the humanising effect of our work is far more productive than stirring up political confrontation' (Jellicoe 1987: 122). The opposition between divisive politics and humanizing drama recalls the ambiguity of theatre game, between demystification and therapy. In much community drama the game is seen as a way of helping the non-actor to act. What is acted may be a local history, a problem of community relations, the community's ability to make performance. But when Albert Hunt had organized a game of the October Revolution in Bradford, he produced a combination of fun and metaphor which contested the rule of an oppressive culture.

Hunt's students became dissatisfied with metaphor and fun. Those working on the television course wanted to learn how to make 'real' television, programmes looking like those on the BBC or Yorkshire TV. The learning of reality techniques led to 'the diminution of imaginative ideas', and the students' commitment expressed itself in 'derivative documentaries about terraced houses and motorways' (A. Hunt 1976: 136–7). The effect of the mass medium was not to make the students alienated and bewildered but to teach them the shape of proper concern. Television offered pictures of the real alongside of which game, metaphor, Dionysos all appeared false. If theatre was to be a fun palace, the real resided in a terraced house.

## 4  'How They're Connected up'

Talking about the success of her play *Serious Money* (1987), Caryl Churchill said that many of the audience 'just enjoy seeing the world they know depicted. . . . Quite a lot of people . . . who didn't know much about the City have been entertained and invigorated by the energy of it, but also appalled by what goes on.' The play was written after workshops and group research into aspects of the City, while simultaneously various real financial scandals occurred. The action shows people who are greedy, deceitful and violent, whose behaviour appals. But their energy also invigorates. And many of the invigorated themselves worked in the institutions depicted in the play. The method of group research and devising; the committed theatre workers; the value placed on 'energy' – all produced a satire which worked also, *for its targets*, as a community drama. 'I believe that some of the multinational companies have booked blocks of seats for their employees . . . Two different banks did at the Court. They booked a whole evening' (Churchill 1988: 16, 15).

For its author 'The piece seemed to be about events having causes' (p. 14). A similar concern with money, effects and causes characterized one of her earliest plays, *Owners* (1972): 'it's to do with the whole thing of western capitalistic individualism, puritanism, and everything which comes out of Christianity' (Churchill 1973: I). In his review Martin Esslin spoke of 'a parable about property owning' (Esslin 1973: 42). That word 'parable' points back to Brecht's effort to give concrete form to abstract ideas and issues, in a series of works that had an influence on Edward Bond: 'I am not content just to show those power struggles. What I want to show is why those power struggles happen' (Bond 1985: 8). Showing why things happen, how events

have causes, is a project that characterizes a mode of drama in which Churchill
places her play *Softcops*: 'it's a "this is how it happened" play' (Churchill 1984:
10).

Not everybody agrees that it's possible to say how it happened. 'The myth
of a single linear reality doesn't hold true.' Forced Entertainment's blurb for
their show *200% and Bloody Thirsty* describes them 'struggling to orient
ourselves in the midst of our pasts and presents, assembling and re-assembling
our contradictory experiences of the world' (Forced Entertainment 1986).
Unlike the urge to find causes for events, the struggle to orient yourself where
there is no single, linear reality is doomed to be endless: 'The purely personal
and private expression is found next to and among, received elements from
mass culture. The inevitable language through which we discuss our identities
and aspirations is made up of images, texts and genres, half remembered from
television, adverts, music and film.' The entertainers show themselves to be
forced by the linguistic and desiring structures of mass culture, trapped into
pop star imitations, the learnt rhythms of chat shows, the tropes of romantic
Hollywood. Popular culture is already inhabited by, is indistinguishable from,
mass culture. 'New' theatre of the mid-1980s had learnt its lessons from
courses on post-structuralist linguistics and psychoanalysis. It stages a human
subject that achieves identity by learning to enter a field of agreed language
usage, replaying in its fantasies images that are always culturally derived: as
much spoken *by* language as an always incomplete speaker *of* it . . . We recall
perhaps the anguish of a woman on a park bench parroting the headlines of
crisis. And, back behind her, two tramps: 'All the dead voices.' 'They all speak
together.' 'Each one to itself' (Beckett 1965: 62–3).

In Dogs in Honey's *Architecture for Babies* (1991) 'the preoccupation is not
with reality itself but with its reflection in a culture dominated by the mass
media' (Armitstead 1991). In a chat show format the performers make films
for their unborn children: 'Each performer eventually speaks to camera in an
intimate message to posterity. Each is shown on screen, each mimes giving
birth and answers basic questions about identity' (Hoyle 1991). The device of
the authentic speech recurs: in the 'post-holocaust' *Sons of Bitumen* (1989) an
actor 'walks up to a microphone and begins to explain with a mixture of
aggression and bashfulness how he has always hated theatre, how "doing this"
on a £5,000 Arts Council grant is better than being on the dole' (Armitstead
1989). Delivered at a microphone the personal testimony is always both
confession and cabaret, enacting the desire and maybe impossibility 'to speak
clearly of our lives' in 'words that are not quite our own' (Forced Entertainment 1986). The safely ironized anxiety about being a real person in mass
culture found its form in *Sons of Bitumen*'s pastiche of a soul number about
zodiac signs: telling about yourself is both necessary and already cliché-ridden.

The comedy of the soul number works like that of the share dealing in
*Serious Money*: the audience recognize the formal shape together with its

dislocation from context and real effect. The stage exhibits its skill at pretend-ing. No audience would want to be caught tapping its feet to that soul number. By contrast, 'You should be able to dance to *Job Rocking*.' In his preface to his verse play about a job club Benjamin Zephaniah explains 'we are in the age of rap . . . but I still have to emphasise that we are not putting words on to music but making music with words, creating a theatre of rhythm' (Zephaniah 1989: 144). The visual quotations and pastiche invite recognition of machismo and wealth, but the verbal rhythms are shared in a way which is less cognitive than physiological, just as rhythm moves a body into dance. The primary pleasure thus comes from a sense of in-corporation, almost becoming one body with, the utterance and hence the project of the performer. The roots of performance poetry go back to a practice of theatre as story-telling. The story, like the poem, has its own rhythms – of syntax and structure – in which an audience becomes incorporated, becoming a body of listeners in a shape felt physiologically almost before it is known intellectu-ally. That story-telling theatre was rediscovered in the 1970s by the group Shared Experience, and from his contact with them Noel Greig developed a series of plays which could all be done by solo narrator/performer.

In Greig's *Plague of Innocence* (1988) Sarah watches television:

> Sarah spat at the screen
> remembering the days
> when you could turn the blasted thing off,
> not now
> now New Dawn announced itself

The play is set in a future Britain, recognizable and totalitarian. The regime uses a health crisis around HIV and AIDS as a means of labelling and quarantining its opponents. Central power operates ideological control by policing education, constant broadcast of TV and the interrogation of dreams. But Sarah discovers that the people with HIV and AIDS isolated in the hospital 'were not condemned, / inevitably, / to death'; she begins to steal vaccine, reserved for the privileged, and to send it to the quarantine lands. One night her messenger doesn't come so Sarah decides to go herself:

> its only a small thing
> but something I can do,
> and she wrapped a batch of bottles
> in her mother's old worn scarf
> went out of the door
> went out of Sheffield
> went out into history
> (Greig 1989: 9, 28, 39)

She sets off for Eyam, the village that once isolated its own plague, now used by the Primo of England as a heroic example of self-quarantining. As the play opens, the Primo has come to Eyam to make a speech, watched by TV, troops and the deviants of a totalitarian society. The narrative then moves backwards to explain how the various people have come to be there now. Stories of individuals, personal histories, begin to cross over and connect up, making sense of a larger history. That sense of history is felt in the structure of the play which moves back in fictional time even as the real time of performance goes forward. What happens next in the narrative is always what happened before. A discovered past, not an imagined future, is the subject. The play ends where it began, three seconds before the end of the century.

The act of Sarah going out into history is constituted by the statement that she 'went out into history': Sarah is spoken about by a performer who doesn't try to 'be' Sarah but to tell a story in which Sarah figures. Much as a street accident is described in Brecht's 'Street Scene' (Brecht 1964), the performer recounts a history, only part of which focuses attention on an image of Sarah. She is an enactment which is engaging, recurrent and temporary. The performer's reference point is not in a fictional character's psyche, nor in real political commitment, but in a story that is to be told. And, in contrast with performances which enact anxiety about second-hand language or the impossible reality of personal confession, this story is sayable. The very act of saying itself makes present the tense relation of personal and public:

> And here's the Primo of England
> proclaiming:
> New England
> reborn
> in the new dawn
> of a new century
>
> Rejoice
>
> Well who dared not?
> Rejoicing was official
>
> And then the silence
> born of those last three seconds
> beating on the brink of a new age
> (p. 2)

Recognizable public words – new dawn, rejoice – associate themselves with Prime Minister Thatcher; but there's also the uncertain metaphoric fiction of a 'last three seconds'. A public history and a very precise, totally fictional moment: yet that fiction, in the rhythms of the syntax, its pauses and changing intonations, works in 'reality', biologically, on a listener, 'beating on the brink'. In those rhythms the performer speaks from different places – as a fiction, the Primo, and as it were from nowhere, 'the silence'. The story of Sarah spitting at her TV brings Sarah into being, makes her action present, articulates the person as history. That articulation becomes politically loaded as it tells insistently of a regime that spreads ignorance and superstition. Speaking a different history becomes an act of resistance, and the audience that is incorporated by the rhythms of that story, tracing its connections, is itself thus placed as resistant to a hegemonic power, poised as it were at the end of the century.

'New technology has destroyed the structure not only of our society but also of our subjective selves. So we had better learn how to rationally guide this change.' In 1978 Edward Bond asks for a new sort of staging: 'we need to set our scenes in public places, where history is formed, classes clash and whole societies move. Otherwise we're not writing about the events that most affect us and shape our future.' History is not just a past but an attitude to the future. Like Greig, Bond responds to 'new technology' with a 'subversive' theatre: 'unless a story has a beginning, a middle and an end its events can't be fully understood and it can't lead to an action that results in change. Telling such a story, describing history, needs a new sort of acting.' The new acting requires that 'an interpretation (of the situation, not the character) must be applied to an emotion, and it is this concept or interpretation or idea that is acted. This relates the character to the social event so that he becomes its story teller' (Bond 1978: 8, 9). He called this 'theatre acting': 'it shows the social role, how society exists in the character' (Stuart 1991: 176).

The stress is on *showing*. Thus Bond's plays contain 'theatre events', incidents which 'can't be captured by the story but must be examined for themselves in relation to the story'. The audience is positioned by the tensions not between characters but between story and what can't be contained. The tension becomes focused upon the effort, often made urgent by staged violence, to fix meaning. 'We cannot incorporate the story into the events to give them meaning. At the most the story will point to cause and effect – but not to give meaning, purpose, and value. The story does not give the stages of the story meaning' (Stuart 1991: 173). At the end of Act 1 of Bond's reworking of the Lear story, soldiers arrive at the house of the Gravedigger's Boy, looking for Lear. The Boy's wife, Cordelia, has been hanging out sheets to dry; the Boy comes on with a body found down the well:

> (SOLDIER E *shoots him. He staggers upstage towards the sheets. His head is down. He clutches a sheet and pulls it from the line.* CORDELIA *stands behind it. Her head is down and she covers her face with her hands.* SOLDIER D *is preparing to rape her. The* BOY *turns slowly away and as he*

*does so the sheet folds round him. For a second he stands in silence with the white sheet draped round him. Only his head is seen. It is pushed back in shock and his eyes and mouth are open. He stands rigid. Suddenly a huge red stain spreads on the sheet.)*

SERGEANT: Kill the pigs.

(Bond 1972: 29–30)

The violent effect has coherent, explicable causes, but it is larger than those causes in the sense that it triggers a range of metaphoric associations that exceed any simple account of what is happening. The sign of the orderly home becomes winding sheet, a baby in swaddling, a ghost, the evidence of a consummated marriage, or rape: all of these and not definitely any one of them.

The pigs squeal and Cordelia is taken to the house. Soldier E re-enters:

*(There is blood on* SOLDIER E's *face, neck, hands, clothes and boots. In the house* CORDELIA *gives a high, short gasp.)*

SOLDIER E: *(Muttering contentedly)* An' I'll 'ave 'er reekin' a pig blood. Somethin' t' write 'ome t' tell mother.

*(The* CARPENTER *follows him on. He carries his tool pack. He takes a cold chisel from it.)*

*(Sees* CARPENTER.) Yes? *(A fraction later he calls towards the house.)* Sarge!

*(The* CARPENTER *kills him with a blow from the cold chisel.)*

(p. 31)

The tool becomes a weapon in an act of violence that is necessary, both subjectively and as part of a process. The feeling of process is created by proliferating images that exceed the logic of cause and effect, confound emotional neatness. Cordelia's voice echoes the pigs' squeals; pig blood on the Soldier images her rape; he is turned on by the prospect of fucking in blood even as he thinks of his mother; we struggle to think Cordelia's rape in a space separate from dying pigs. The audience is subjectively engaged, by a process that expresses more than characters' subjectivity.

Later on the Gravedigger's Boy returns as a ghost to accompany Lear. As a ghost he ages, and becomes more frightened. Even ghosts can't be outside the biological process of history. He is killed a second time, by pigs:

*(The* GHOST's *head falls back. It is dead. It drops at* LEAR's *feet. The calls and pig squeals stop.)*

LEAR: I see my life, a black tree by a pool. The branches are covered with tears. The tears are shining with light. The wind blows the tears in the sky. And my tears fall down on me.

(p. 86)

Lear had to take part of the guilt for the first death of the Boy. At the second death Lear can accept the Boy's loss – violent, unnecessary, pathetic – as a historical process. Which enables him then to image his own life, seeing 'tears' and 'me' as somehow outside the 'I' who speaks: an emotion narrated as much as felt, and felt in being narrated. There's a similar feeling when Val returns after Frank has murdered her at the end of Caryl Churchill's *Fen* (1983):

> There's so much happening. There's all those people and I know about them. There's a girl who died. I saw you put me in the wardrobe, I was up by the ceiling, I watched. I could have gone but I wanted to stay with you and I found myself coming back in.

She is pressed in upon not by newspaper stories of disaster but by history as necessity: 'The girl, I'll try and tell you about her and keep the others out. A lot of children died that winter and she's still white and weak . . . I can't keep them out. Her baby died starving. She died starving. Who?' (Churchill 1986: 95–6).

The death of a baby from starvation is a private family tragedy caused by public economic privation. Val's murder is self-willed, frustrated, socially produced. She wants to live with her lover Frank but misses her daughters; with him she feels guilty, with them she feels trapped. He won't run away with her, because he won't leave his work, but he hates his employer. Val is blamed by women who are themselves trapped. The play stages the links between the tough agricultural working conditions of fenland women and their family lives; individuals fantasize their personal history of survival and in turn transfer the brutalities of that history to others. The interconnection of the macro-economic and the familial is produced by doubling of parts and fast cutting between short scenes, acted out in a space that is neither wholly private nor public: the first production design set the fenland field in a room. In another play, *Softcops*, the effect is that

> things whose existence in their present form one might take for granted – you suddenly see how they're connected up and why they are like they are and what effects of control it can have on you that they are like they are. For me to some extent the possibility of . . . being free from that control is helped by understanding how it works. (Churchill 1984: 10)

*Fen* opens with a Japanese businessman sentimentally evoking the history of the rich earth which his company now owns; it ends with a dead woman seeing casualties from the past and present of that land. The play shows how they're connected up. The murdered Val can see into other people's lives: Becky having a dream of escape from her violent stepmother. And Becky is suddenly there on stage, saying to her stepmother, 'You're not here.' Nell crosses on stilts: 'I was walking out on the fen. The sun spoke to me. It said,

"Turn back, turn back." I said, "I won't turn back for you or anyone."' Shirley irons the field, remembering what unhappiness was like. A boy scarecrow from the past is there, speaking a line recalled by Val's grandmother. Then Val's mother appears: 'My mother wanted to be a singer. That's why she'd never sing. MAY *is there. She sings*' (Churchill 1986: 97–8). This is not wholly dream space: Frank is still there. It's not wholly history, nor the present. It's a space in which there's possibility. For a moment one of these women, up to their necks, as it were, in the rich earth they work, can sing.

Like the ghosts in Bond's *Lear*, these ghosts are a history and a present reality. Bond's drama is asking 'in the middle of all the economic relationships, how does one's human subjectivity find itself?' (Bond 1985: 8). Churchill wants to show how things are connected up – a bit like the effect of Greig's story-telling. These plays understand human suffering to be explicable, but not diminished, by reference to the history of human society; plays which tell a rather grand, if painful, narrative. To understand those connections produces, for Churchill, the possibility of being free. Or as Bond puts it: 'Lear's new world is strange and so at first he can only grope painfully and awkwardly. Lear is old by then, but most of the play's audiences will be younger. It might seem to them that the truth is always ground for pessimism when it is discovered, but one soon comes to see it as an opportunity' (Bond 1972: xiii).

Dead Val's new world of opportunity can only exist as the world of play. Past and present coexist, living and dead speak together, the field is a room: one thing can, at the same moment, be another; which is one definition of acting. And acting is always physically present, biologically real for its audience. Nell on stilts is the image of a historical fenland woman *and* the thrill of this actress walking on stilts; May – impossibly – sings. When, in the space of play, we see how real things connect up, there is something inescapable about those connections. They set limits to – determine perhaps – human life. But the moment of seeing those connections becomes a vision of the possibility of being freed, of making another history. When the Primo arrives in Eyam, the ghosts of the historical plague-dead return to walk with the living, defiant, 'towards the guns'. Only possible within the play-world, but in the play-world real. The history from which we can't escape is real, but so too, held there in play, equally real, is the desire to be free. Three seconds before the end of the century, before the end of the show, that desire is acted:

> and a soldier remembers
> what it was once like
> to be touched
> without fear
> to touch
> without loathing

and he lowers his gun
for a moment
(Greig 1989: 48)


## NOTES

1   In his review of *Hair* Charles Marowitz noted both these elements: the director, Tom O'Horgan, was associated with the 'alternative' North American company, La Mama; it was an anti-war piece which could be linked with another 'experimental' show, Living Theatre's *Paradise Now*. On the other hand, the nudity scene was 'the tool of the publicists' (Marowitz 1968: 55). Certainly *Hair*'s London opening was put back, from July until September, in order to coincide very precisely with the final ending of censorship: the Lord Chamberlain's job was officially abolished on 26 July, with a two-month retirement period; *Hair* opened 27 September. By August 1969 London was full of the publicity for the New York opening of *Oh! Calcutta!*, billed in the *Observer* as 'the most blatant simulation of the sex act', and Thames Television had done a programme asking if theatre and other arts were getting 'out of control'. *Oh! Calcutta!* finally opened in London nearly a year later, on 27 July 1970, almost exactly two years since the official abolition of censorship.

2   Egon Shrick is not an English performer. His work is not well known outside west Germany. I have selected him as an example of this sort of performance work for two reasons: it is a good example of such work, of which there are similar examples from Britain; secondly the activity of finding and describing an 'unknown', especially non-British, performer is typical of the spirit of much writing about 'live art'. Caton (1989) describes tracking down Shrick, spending all night 'sharing his art' and resolving next day to 'promote' his work in England. The performance artist is also a journalist and a promoter of others: the combination of these roles, and the establishment of an international community around this performance practice, are again typical of the cultural activity of 'live art'.

# Chronological List of Plays by Performance Date

| | |
|---|---|
| 15th century | York Corpus Christi play |
| | Chester Corpus Christi play |
| | *The Castle of Perseverance* |
| | N-town play |
| | Towneley play |
| | Croxton *Play of the Sacrament* |
| | *Mary Magdalen* |
| 1496–7 | Medwall *Fulgens and Lucres* |
| 1520 | Skelton *Magnyfycence* |
| 1538 | Bale *King Johan* |
| 1538 | Bale *The Temptation of Our Lord* |
| 1540 | *Godly Queen Hester* |
| 1553 | *Respublica* |
| 1587–8 | Marlowe *Tamburlaine I* |
| *c.*1590 | *Thomas of Woodstock* |
| *c.*1591 | Shakespeare *1 Henry VI* |
| 1592 | Marlowe *Dr Faustus* |
| 1592–3 | Shakespeare *Richard III* |
| 1596–7 | Shakespeare *The Merchant of Venice* |
| 1598–9 | Shakespeare *The Merry Wives of Windsor* |
| 1599 | Shakespeare *Henry V* |
| 1599 | Shakespeare *Julius Caesar* |
| 1601 | Shakespeare *Hamlet* |
| 1602–3 | Shakespeare *Othello* |
| 1603–4 | Shakespeare *Measure For Measure* |
| 1605–6 | Shakespeare *King Lear* |

| | |
|---|---|
| 1606 | Shakespeare *Macbeth* |
| 1606 | Tourneur (?) *The Revenger's Tragedy* |
| 1607 | Beaumont *The Knight of the Burning Pestle* |
| 1607 | Heywood *The Rape of Lucrece* |
| 1610 | Jonson *The Alchemist* |
| 1610–11 | Shakespeare *The Tempest* |
| 1611 | Beaumont and Fletcher *A King and No King* |
| 1611 | Shakespeare *The Winter's Tale* |
| 1614 | Webster *The Duchess of Malfi* |
| *c.*1621–2 | Middleton *Women Beware Women* |
| 1624 | Middleton *A Game at Chess* |
| 1626 | Massinger *The Roman Actor* |
| 1631 | Shirley *The Traitor* |
| 1634 | Milton *A Masque Presented at Ludlow Castle* |
| 1634 | Shirley *The Triumph of Peace* |
| 1637 | Suckling *Aglaura* |
| 1638 | Brome *The Antipodes* |
| 1641 | Brome *A Jovial Crew* |
| 1667 | Dryden *Secret Love* |
| 1668 | Dryden *An Evening's Love* |
| 1668 | Sedley *The Mulberry Garden* |
| 1671 | Dryden *Marriage à-la-Mode* |
| 1671 | *The Reformation* |
| 1675 | Wycherley *The Country Wife* |
| 1676 | Etherege *The Man of Mode* |
| 1676 | Shadwell *The Virtuoso* |
| 1680 | Otway *The Soldier's Fortune* |
| 1682 | Behn *The False Count* |
| 1682 | Otway *Venice Preserved* |
| 1692 | Southerne *The Wives Excuse* |
| 1696 | Cibber *Love's Last Shift* |
| 1696 | Vanbrugh *The Relapse* |
| 1697 | Congreve *The Mourning Bride* |
| 1697 | Vanbrugh *The Provok'd Wife* |
| 1699 | Farquhar *The Constant Couple* |
| 1700 | Congreve *The Way of the World* |
| 1700 | Pix *The Beau Defeated* |
| 1706 | Farquhar *The Recruiting Officer* |
| 1707 | Farquhar *The Beaux' Stratagem* |
| 1713 | Addison *Cato* |
| 1722 | Steele *The Conscious Lovers* |
| 1728 | Gay *The Beggar's Opera* |
| 1736 | Fielding *The Historical Register for the Year 1736* |

| | |
|---|---|
| 1757 | Garrick *Harlequin's Invasion* |
| 1766 | Garrick *The Country Girl* |
| 1802 | Holcroft *A Tale of Mystery* |
| 1805 | Elliston *The Venetian Outlaw* |
| 1805 | Lewis *Rugantino or the Bravo of Venice* |
| 1805 | Powell *The Venetian Outlaw* |
| 1807 | Kenney *The Blind Boy of Bohemia* |
| 1819 | Dibdin *Melodrame Mad!* |
| 1820 | Planché *The Vampire* |
| 1826 | Buckstone *Luke the Labourer* |
| 1826 | Fitzball *The Flying Dutchman* |
| 1828 | Jerrold *Fifteen Years of a Drunkard's Life* |
| 1830 | Jerrold *Mutiny at the Nore* |
| 1832 | Walker *The Factory Lad* |
| 1832 | Walker *Nell Gwynne* |
| 1833 | Jerrold *Nell Gwynne* |
| 1834 | Buckstone *Isabelle* |
| 1837 | Rayner *The Dumb Man of Manchester* |
| 1840s | *Maria Marten* |
| 1840 | Bulwer *Money* |
| 1843 | Jerrold *Rent Day* |
| 1843 | Moncrieff *The Scamps of London* |
| 1844 | Pitt *A Woman's Life* |
| 1846 | Pitt *Toussaint L'Ouverture* |
| 1848 | Pitt *The Revolution at Paris* |
| 1852 | Boucicault *The Corsican Brothers* |
| 1852 | Boucicault *The Vampire* |
| 1854 | Elphinstone *Rotherhithe in the Olden Time* |
| 1865 | Boucicault *Arrah-na-Pogue* |
| 1865 | Reade *It's Never too Late to Mend* |
| 1865 | Robertson *Society* |
| 1867 | Robertson *Caste* |
| 1871 | Lewis *The Bells* |
| 1882 | Gilbert and Sullivan *Iolanthe* |
| 1883 | Shakespeare/Irving *Romeo and Juliet* |
| 1885 | Goethe/Irving *Faust* |
| 1891 | Ibsen *Ghosts* (in English translation) |
| 1892 | Wilde *Salome* |
| 1893 | Pinero *The Second Mrs Tanqueray* |
| 1894 | Jones *The Case of Rebellious Susan* |
| 1894 | Shaw *Arms and the Man* |
| 1895 | Wilde *The Importance of Being Earnest* |
| 1896 | Barrett *The Sign of the Cross* |

| 1897 | Shaw *The Devil's Disciple* |
| 1898 | Pinero *Trelawny of the 'Wells'* |
| 1900 | Barrett *Quo Vadis?* |
| 1901 | Shaw *Three Plays for Puritans* |
| 1902 | Yeats *Cathleen ni Houlihan* |
| 1905 | Hankin *The Return of the Prodigal* |
| 1905 | Shaw *Major Barbara* |
| 1907 | Granville Barker *Waste* |
| 1907 | Synge *The Playboy of the Western World* |
| 1916 | Yeats *At the Hawk's Well* |
| 1919 | Yeats *The Dreaming of the Bones* |
| 1919 | Yeats *The Only Jealousy of Emer* |
| 1924 | O'Casey *Juno and the Paycock* |
| 1926 | O'Casey *The Plough and the Stars* |
| 1929 | Malleson *The Fanatics* |
| 1937 | Allen et al. *Busmen* |
| 1937 | Slater *New Way Wins* |
| 1938 | Slater *Towards Tomorrow* |
| 1942 | O'Casey *Red Roses For Me* |
| 1946 | McLeish *The Gorbals Story* |
| 1946 | Merseyside Unity *The Second Shepherds Play* |
| 1946 | Priestley *An Inspector Calls* |
| 1947 | Priestley *The Linden Tree* |
| 1949 | Eliot *The Cocktail Party* |
| 1949 | O'Casey *Cock-a-Doodle-Dandy* |
| 1955 | Beckett *Waiting for Godot* |
| 1956 | Osborne *Look Back in Anger* |
| 1957 | Britten *Noyes Fludde* |
| 1957 | Osborne *The Entertainer* |
| 1958 | Pinter *The Birthday Party* |
| 1958 | Wesker *Chicken Soup with Barley* |
| 1959 | Arden *Serjeant Musgrave's Dance* |
| 1959 | Wesker *Roots* |
| 1961 | Beckett *Happy Days* |
| 1963 | Arden *The Workhouse Donkey* |
| 1963 | Theatre Workshop *Oh What A Lovely War* |
| 1964 | Britten *Curlew River* |
| 1964 | Brook 'Theatre of Cruelty' season |
| 1964 | Shaffer *The Royal Hunt of the Sun* |
| 1966 | *US* |
| 1968 | Bennett *Forty Years On* |
| 1968 | Berman *The Nudist Campers Grow and Grow* |
| 1968 | Bond *Early Morning* |

# References

Addison, J. 1914: *Cato*. In A. C. Guthkelch (ed.), *Miscellaneous Works*, vol. I, London: G. Bell and Sons.

Allen, D. 1993: *The Cherry Orchard*: a new English version by Trevor Griffiths. In Miles, P. 1993.

Altick, R. D. 1978: *The Shows of London*. Cambridge, Mass.: Belknap Press.

Ansorge, P. 1975: *Disrupting the Spectacle: five years of experimental and fringe theatre in Britain*. London: Pitman.

Archer, W. 1923: *The Old Drama and the New*. London: Heinemann.

Archer, W. and Barker, H. G. 1907: *A National Theatre: schemes & estimates*. London: Duckworth.

Arden, J. 1960: *Serjeant Musgrave's Dance*. London: Methuen.

Arden, J. 1964: *The Workhouse Donkey*. London: Methuen.

Arden, J. 1979: *Pearl*. London: Methuen.

Arden, J. with D'Arcy, M. 1974: *The Island of the Mighty*. London: Methuen.

Aristotle 1965: *On the Art of Poetry*. In T. S. Dorsch (ed.), *Classical Literary Criticism*, Harmondsworth: Penguin.

Armitstead, C. 1989: Sons of bitumen. *Financial Times*, 30 June.

Armitstead, C. 1991: Barclays new stages. *Financial Times*, 21 June.

Artaud, A. 1970: *The Theatre and its Double*. Trans. V. Corti. London: Calder & Boyars.

Arts Council of Great Britain 1945–: *Annual Reports*.

Arts Council of Great Britain 1984: *The Glory of the Garden*.

Auerbach, N. 1990: *Private Theatricals: the lives of the Victorians*. Cambridge, Mass.: Harvard University Press.

Avery, E. L. 1942: *The Country Wife* in the eighteenth century. *Research Studies of the State College of Washington*, 10.

Avery, E. L. 1944: The reputation of Wycherley's comedies as stage plays in the eighteenth century. *Research Studies of the State College of Washington*, 12.

Avery, E. L. 1951: *Congreve's Plays on the Eighteenth Century Stage*. New York: MLA of America.

Baer, M. 1992: *Theatre and Disorder in Late Georgian London*. Oxford: Oxford University Press.

Bahlman, D. W. R. 1968: *The Moral Revolution of 1688*. Hamden, Conn.: Archon Books.

Baker, D. C. et al. (eds) 1982: *The Late Medieval Religious Plays of Bodleian MSS Digby 133 and E Museo 160*. Oxford: Oxford University Press for the Early English Text Society.

Baker, M. 1978: *The Rise of the Victorian Actor*. London: Croom Helm.

Bakhtin, M. 1984: *Rabelais and his World*. Trans. H. Iswolsky. Bloomington: Indiana University Press.

Baldry, H. 1981: *The Case for the Arts*. London: Secker and Warburg.

Bale, J. 1986: *The Complete Plays of John Bale*. Ed. P. Happé. 2 vols. Cambridge: D. S. Brewer.

Barba, E. 1986: *Beyond the Floating Islands*. New York: PAJ Publications.

Barber, C. L. 1959: *Shakespeare's Festive Comedy: a study of dramatic form and its relation to social custom*. Princeton: Princeton University Press.

Barish, J. A. 1981: *The Anti-theatrical Prejudice*. Berkeley: University of California Press.

Barker, C. 1977: *Theatre Games: a new approach to drama training*. London: Eyre Methuen.

Barker, F. 1984: *The Tremulous Private Body: essays on subjection*. London: Methuen.

Barker, H. 1982: *The Hang of the Gaol*. London: John Calder.

Barker, H. 1983: *Victory: choices in reaction*. London: John Calder Ltd.

Barker, H. 1989: *Arguments for a Theatre*. London: John Calder.

Barker, H. 1990a: *Collected Plays*. vol. I. London: John Calder.

Barker, H. 1990b: *Golgo*. London: John Calder.

Barker, H. G. 1969: *The Exemplary Theatre*. Reprint. New York: Benjamin Blom.

Barker, H. G. 1974: From *Henry V* to *Hamlet*. In *Prefaces to Shakespeare*, vol. VI, London: Batsford.

Barker, H. G. 1987: *Plays by Harley Granville Barker*. Ed. Dennis Kennedy. Cambridge: Cambridge University Press.

Barker, H. G. 1993: *Plays: one*. London: Methuen.

Barker, H. G. and Harrison, G. B. 1934: *A Companion to Shakespeare Studies*. Cambridge: Cambridge University Press.

Barrett, D. 1993: *It's Never too Late to Mend* (1865) and prison conditions in nineteenth century England. *Theatre Research International*, 18(1).

Barthes, R. 1986: The death of the author. In *The Rustle of Language*, Oxford: Basil Blackwell, 49–55.

Bates, R. 1936: *The Olive Field*. London: Jonathan Cape.

Beadle, R. (ed.) 1982: *The York Plays*. London: Edward Arnold.

Beadle, R. (ed.) 1994: *The Cambridge Companion to Medieval English Theatre*. Cambridge: Cambridge University Press.

Beadle, R. and King, P. M. (eds) 1984: *York Mystery Plays: a selection in modern spelling*. Oxford: Clarendon Press.

Beaumont, F. 1969: *The Knight of the Burning Pestle*. Ed. M. Hattaway. London: Ernest Benn.

Beaumont, F. and Fletcher, J. 1964: *A King and No King*. Ed. R. K. Turner, Jr., London: Edward Arnold.

Beckett, S. 1963: *Happy Days*. London: Faber & Faber.

Beckett, S. 1965: *Waiting for Godot*. London: Faber & Faber.

Beckwith, S. 1992: Ritual, church and theatre: medieval dramas of the sacramental body. In D. Aers (ed.), *Culture and History 1350–1600*, Hemel Hempstead: Harvester Wheatsheaf, 65–90.

Behn, A. 1967: *The False Count*. In M. Summers (ed.), *Works*, vol. III, reissue, New York: Benjamin Blom, 95–176.

Bell, M. forthcoming: Booksellers without an author, 1627–1685. In G. Taylor (ed.), *Thomas Middleton and Early Modern Textual Culture*, Oxford: Oxford University Press.

Belsey, C. 1985: *The Subject of Tragedy*. London: Methuen.

Benjamin, W. 1973: *Illuminations*. London: Fontana.

Bennett, A. 1969: *Forty Years On*. London: Faber.

Bentley, G. E. 1941–68: *The Jacobean and Caroline Stage*. 6 vols. Oxford: Clarendon Press.

Benzie, W. 1983: *Dr F. J. Furnivall: Victorian scholar adventurer*. Norman, Oklahoma: Pilgrim Books.

Bergman, G. W. 1977: *Lighting in the Theatre*. Stockholm/Totowa N. J.: Almqvist and Wiksell/Rowman and Littlefield.

Berkoff, S. 1982: *Decadence and Greek*. London: John Calder.

Boaden, J. 1803: *The Voice of Nature*. London: James Ridgway.

Bond, E. 1972: *Lear*. London: Methuen.

Bond, E. 1977: *Plays: one (Early Morning; Saved; Narrow Road to the Deep North)*. London: Methuen.

Bond, E. 1978: Us, our drama and the National Theatre. *Plays and Players*, October, pp. 8–9.

Bond, E. 1985: Edward Bond – British secret playwright. Interviewed by M. Hay, *Plays and Players*, April.

Booth, M. R. 1964: *Hiss the Villain*. London: Eyre & Spottiswoode.

Booth, M. R. 1965: *English Melodrama*. London: H. Jenkins.

Booth, M. R. et al. (eds) 1975: *The Revels History of Drama in English*. vol. VI, *1750–1880*. London: Methuen.

Booth, M. R. 1981: *Victorian Spectacular Theatre 1850–1910*. London: Routledge & Kegan Paul.

Booth, M. R. 1991: *Theatre in the Victorian Age*. Cambridge: Cambridge University Press.

Boucicault, D. 1987: *Selected Plays*. Washington: Catholic University of America Press.

Bradley, A. C. 1965: *Shakespearean Tragedy*. Paperback edition. London: Macmillan.

Bratton, J. et al. 1994: *Melodrama: stage picture screen*. London: British Film Institute.

Braunmuller, A. R. and Hattaway, M. (eds) 1990: *The Cambridge Companion to English Renaissance Drama*. Cambridge: Cambridge University Press.

Brecht, B. 1964: The street scene (1938). In J. Willett (ed.), *Brecht on Theatre*, New York: Hill and Wang.

Brenton, H. 1970: *Christie in Love and Other Plays*. London: Methuen.

Brenton, H. 1974: *The Churchill Play*. London: Methuen.

Brenton, H. 1976: *Weapons of Happiness*. London: Methuen.

Brenton, H. 1980: *The Romans in Britain*. London: Eyre Methuen.

Brenton, H. 1982: *Hitler Dances*. London: Methuen.

Brenton, H. and Hare, D. 1974: *Brassneck*. London: Eyre Methuen.

Brenton, H. and Hare, D. 1985: *Pravda*. London: Methuen.

Brenton, H. et al. 1972: *Lay By*. London: Calder and Boyars.

Bridges Adams, W. 1954: *The Lost Leader*. London: Sedgwick and Jackson.

Brome, R. 1873: *The Weeding of Covent Garden*. In *Dramatic Works*, vol. II, London: John Pearson.

Brome, R. 1966: *The Antipodes*. Ed. A. Haaker. London: Edward Arnold.

Brome, R. 1968: *A Jovial Crew*. Ed. A. Haaker. London: Edward Arnold.

Brook, P. 1968: *The Empty Space*. London: MacGibbon & Kee.

Brooks, H. 1935: Some Notes on Dryden, Cowley, and Shadwell. *Notes and Queries*, 168, 94–5.

Brooks, P. 1985: *The Melodramatic Imagination*. New York: Columbia University Press.

Brown, J. R. 1993: Chekhov on the British stage: differences. In Miles, P. 1993.

Bruster, D. 1992: *Drama and the Market in the Age of Shakespeare*. Cambridge: Cambridge University Press.

Buckstone, J. B. 1835: *Isabelle or, Woman's Life*. London: Sherwood, Gilbert & Piper.

Buckstone, J. B. 1966: *Luke the Labourer; or, The Lost Son*. In J. O. Bailey (ed.), *British Plays of the Nineteenth Century*, New York: Odyssey Press.

Burrows, J. 1982: The Barbican. *Plays and Players*, June, p. 43.

Butler, M. 1987: *Theatre and Crisis 1632–1642*. Cambridge: Cambridge University Press.

Carswell, J. 1973: *From Revolution to Revolution: England 1688–1776*. London: Routledge Kegan Paul.

Cartwright, J. 1986: *Road*. London: Methuen/Royal Court.

Caton, S. 1989: A profile of Egon Shrick. *Performance*, 59.

Caudwell, C. 1946: *Illusion and Reality*. London: Lawrence & Wishart.

Cawley, A. C. et al. (eds) 1983: *The Revels History of Drama in English*. vol. I, *Medieval Drama*. London: Methuen.

Chambers, C. 1980: *Other Spaces: new theatre and the RSC*. London: Methuen/TQ.

Chambers, C. 1989: *The Story of Unity Theatre*. London: Lawrence & Wishart.

Chambers, E. K. 1923: *The Elizabethan Stage*. 4 vols. Oxford: Clarendon Press.

Chambers, E. K. 1963: *The Medieval Stage*. 2 vols. London: Oxford University Press.

Champion, J. A. I. 1992: *The Pillars of Priestcraft Shaken: the Church of England and its enemies 1660–1730*. Cambridge: Cambridge University Press.

Chekhov, A. 1978: *The Cherry Orchard*. A new English version by Trevor Griffiths. London: Pluto Press.

Churchill, C. 1973: Caryl Churchill . . . talks to p + p. Interview with Steve Gooch, *Plays and Players*, January.

Churchill, C. 1984: A fair cop. Interview with Lynne Truss, *Plays and Players*, January.

Churchill, C. 1986: *Softcops & Fen*. London: Methuen.

Churchill, C. 1987: *Serious Money*. London: Methuen/Royal Court.

Churchill, C. 1988: The common imagination and the individual voice. Interview by G. Cousin, *New Theatre Quarterly*, 13.

Cibber, C. 1968: *An Apology for the Life of Colley Cibber*. Ed. B. R. S. Fone. Ann Arbor: University of Michigan Press.

Clopper, L. 1978: The history and development of the Chester Cycle. *MP*, 75, 219–46.

Coleridge, S. T. 1987: *Lectures 1808–1819: on literature*. Ed. R. A. Foakes. 2 vols. London: Routledge Kegan Paul.

Colletti, T. 1990: Reading REED: history and the records of early English drama. In L. Patterson (ed.), *Literary Practice and Social Change in Britain, 1380–1530*, Berkeley: California University Press.

Collier, J. 1972a: *A Short View of the Profaneness and Immorality of the English Stage*. Reprint. New York: Garland Publishing.

Collier, J. 1972b: *A Defence of the Short View of the Profaneness and Immorality of the English Stage*. Reprint. New York: Garland Publishing.

Collier, J. P. 1831: *The History of English Dramatic Poetry to the Time of Shakespeare*. London: John Murray.

Congreve, W. 1964: *Complete Works*. Ed. M. Summers. Reprint. New York: Russell and Russell.

Connor, S. 1992: *Postmodernist Culture: an introduction to theories of the contemporary*. Oxford: Blackwell.

Corrie, J. 1985: *Plays, Poems and Theatre Writings*. Ed. L. Mackenney. Edinburgh: 7:84 Publications.

Coult, T. and Kershaw, B. 1983: *Engineers of the Imagination: the welfare state handbook*. London: Methuen.

Craig, E. G. 1930: *Henry Irving*. London: J. M. Dent & Sons.

Craig, E. G. 1980: *On the Art of the Theatre*. London: Heinemann.

Craig, E. G. 1983: *Craig on Theatre*. Ed. J. Michael Walton. London: Methuen.

Craig, H. 1955: *English Religious Drama of the Middle Ages*. Oxford: Clarendon Press.

Cross, C. 1976: *Church and People 1450–1660: the triumph of the laity in the English Church*. London: Fontana.

Crowley, T. 1989: *The Politics of Discourse*. Basingstoke: Macmillan Education Ltd.

Daiches, D. 1938: *Literature and Society*. London: Victor Gollancz Ltd.

Davenport, W. A. 1982: *Fifteenth-Century English Drama: the early moral plays and their literary relations*. Cambridge: D. S. Brewer.

Davidson, C. (ed.) 1981: *A Middle English Treatise on the Playing of Miracles*. Washington D.C.: University Press of America.

Davis, N. (ed.) 1970: *Non-Cycle Plays and Fragments*. Oxford: Oxford University Press for the Early English Text Society.

Dawson, J. 1985: *Left Theatre: Merseyside Unity Theatre*. Liverpool: Merseyside Writers.

Deelman, C. 1964: *The Great Shakespeare Jubilee*. London: Michael Joseph.

Defoe, D. 1927: The poor man's plea (1698). In *The Shortest Way With Dissenters and Other Pamphlets*, Oxford: Basil Blackwell.

De Grazia, M. 1991: *Shakespeare Verbatim: the reproduction of authenticity and the 1790 apparatus*. Oxford: Oxford University Press.

Dennis, J. 1939: A large account of the taste in poetry (1702). In E. N. Hooker (ed.), *Critical Works*, vol. I, Baltimore: Johns Hopkins University Press, 279–95.

Derrida, J. 1978: 'The Theater of Cruelty and the closure of representation. In *Writing and Difference*. Trans. A. Bass. London: Routledge & Kegan Paul.

Dibdin, T. 1819: *Melodrame Mad! or the Siege of Troy*. London: J. Miller.

Dickens, C. n.d.: The amusements of the people. In *Miscellaneous Papers*, introd. B. W. Matz, London: Cassell and Co.

Dickens, C. 1964: *Dombey and Son*. New York: Signet Classics.

Dickens, C. 1967: *Great Expectations*. Harmondsworth: Penguin.

Disher, M. W. 1949: *Blood and Thunder*. London: Frederick Muller.

Dobrée, B. 1924: *Restoration Comedy 1660–1720*. Oxford: Oxford University Press.

Dobrée, B. 1933: *Giacomo Casanova, Chevalier de Seingalt*. London: Peter Davies.

Dobson, M. 1992: *The Making of the National Poet: Shakespeare, adaptation and authorship, 1660–1769*. Oxford: Oxford University Press.

Donohue, J. 1975: *Theatre in the Age of Kean*. Oxford: Basil Blackwell.

Dowden, E. 1892: *Shakspere: a critical study of his mind and art*. 10th edition. London: Kegan Paul, Trench, Trübner and Co.

Drake, F. 1736: *Eboracum: or, the history and antiquities of the city of York*. London: William Bowyer.

Drake, N. 1817: *Shakespeare and His Times*. 2 vols. London.

Dryden, J. 1966: *Works*. vol. IX. Berkeley and Los Angeles: University of California Press.

Dryden, J. 1970a: *Selected Criticism*. Ed. J. Kinsley and G. Parfitt. Oxford: Oxford University Press.

Dryden, J. 1970b: *Works*. vol. X. Berkeley and Los Angeles: University of California Press.

Dryden, J. 1978: *Dryden: a selection*. Ed. J. Congleton. London: Methuen.

Dryden, J. 1987: *The Oxford Authors: John Dryden*. Ed. K. Walker. Oxford: Oxford University Press.

Dugdale, W. 1656: *The Antiquities of Warwickshire Illustrated*. London: Thomas Warren.

Eagleton, T. 1984: *The Function of Criticism*. London: Verso.

Eccles, C. 1990: *The Rose Theatre*. London: Nick Hern Books.

Eccles, M. (ed.) 1969: *The Castell of Perseverance*. In *The Macro Plays*, Oxford: Oxford University Press for the Early English Text Society, 1–111.

Edgar, D. 1982: Viewpoint: politics and performance. *TLS*, 10 September.

Edgar, D. 1987: *Plays: one*. London: Methuen.

Edgar, D. 1989: *Maydays*. London: Methuen Drama.

Edwards, P. et al. 1981: *The Revels History of Drama in English*. vol. IV, *1613–1660*. London: Methuen.

Egan, M. (ed.) 1972: *Ibsen: the critical heritage*. London: Routledge Kegan Paul.

Elias, N. 1983: *The Court Society*. Trans. E. Jephcott. Oxford: Basil Blackwell.

Eliot, T. S. 1951: *Selected Essays*. 3rd edition. London: Faber and Faber.

Elliston, R. 1805: *The Venetian Outlaw*. London: C & R Baldwin.

Elsaesser, T. 1987: Tales of sound and fury: observations on the family melodrama. Reprinted in Gledhill, C. 1987.

Elsom, J. and Tomalin, N. 1978: *The History of the National Theatre*. London: Cape.

Esslin, M. 1973: Review of *Owners*. *Plays and Players*, February.

Etherege, G. 1966: *The Man of Mode*. Ed. W. B. Carnochan. Regents Restoration Drama Series. Lincoln, Nebraska: University of Nebraska Press.

Farquhar, G. 1976: *The Beaux' Stratagem*. Ed. M. Cordner. London: Ernest Benn.

Fielding, H. 1967: *The Historical Register for the Year 1736*. Ed. W. H. Appleton. London: Edward Arnold.

Fiske, R. 1973: *English Theatre Music in the Eighteenth Century*. Oxford: Oxford University Press.

Fitzball, E. n.d.: *The Inchcape Bell*. London: J. Cumberland.

Forced Entertainment 1986: *200% and Bloody Thirsty*. Publicity document.

Ford, J. 1971: Getting the carp out of the mud. *Plays and Players*, November.

Foulkes, R. (ed.) 1986: *Shakespeare and the Victorian Stage*. Cambridge: Cambridge University Press.

Fox, A. 1989: *Politics and Literature in the Reigns of Henry VII and Henry VIII*. Oxford: Basil Blackwell.

Frazer, J. 1890: *The Golden Bough: a study in comparative religion*. 2 vols. London: Macmillan.

*Gambit* 1977: *Gambit* discussion: political theatre. *Gambit: International Theatre Review*. 8(31).

Gardiner, H. C. 1967: *Mysteries' End: an investigation of the last days of the medieval religious stage*. Reprint. New York: Archon Books.

Gardiner, J. K. 1980: Aphra Behn – sexuality and self-respect. *Women's Studies*, 7, 67–78.

Garrick, D. 1766: *The Country Girl*. London: Becket & de Hondt.

Garrick, D. 1791: *The Country Girl*. Bell's British Theatre. vol. 7. London.

Gay, J. 1946: *The Present State of Wit* (1711), Augustan Reprint Society, series I, no. 3.

Gay, J. 1974: *The Beggar's Opera and Other Eighteenth Century Plays*. London: Dent.

Gibson, G. M. 1989: *The Theater of Devotion*. Chicago: University of Chicago Press.

Gibson, R. (ed.) 1990: *Secondary School Shakespeare: classroom practice*. Cambridge: Cambridge Institute of Education.

Glavin, J. 1991: Caught in the act: or, the prosing of Juliet. In J. I. Marsden (ed.), *The Appropriation of Shakespeare: post-Renaissance reconstructions of the works and the myth*, London: Harvester, 93–110.

Gledhill, C. 1987: *Home is Where the Heart is: studies in melodrama and the woman's film*. London: British Film Institute.

Goorney, H. 1981: *The Theatre Workshop Story*. London: Eyre Methuen.

Gosse, E. 1924: *The Life of William Congreve*. London: William Heinemann.

Gottlieb, V. 1988: Thatcher's theatre – or, after *Equus*. *New Theatre Quarterly*, 14.

Gottlieb, V. 1993: The dwindling scale: the politics of British Chekhov. In Miles, P. 1993.

Grady, H. 1991: *The Modernist Shakespeare: critical texts in a material world*. Oxford: Oxford University Press.

Gramsci, A. 1971: *Selections from the Prison Notebooks*. Ed. Q. Hoare and G. Nowell Smith. London: Lawrence & Wishart.

Greg, W. W. (ed.) 1904: *A New Enterlude of Godly Queene Hester*. Louvain: A. Uystpruyst.

Greg, W. W. (ed.) 1952: *Respublica*. Oxford: Oxford University Press for the Early English Text Society.

Greig, N. 1989: *Plague of Innocence*. Unpublished play.

Griffiths, T. 1990: *Piano*. London: Faber & Faber Ltd.

Griswold, W. 1986: *Renaissance Revivals: city comedy and revenge tragedy in the London theatre 1576–1980*. Chicago: University of Chicago Press.

Gurr, A. 1987: *Playgoing in Shakespeare's London*. Cambridge: Cambridge University Press.

Habermas, J. 1989: *The Structural Transformation of the Public Sphere*. Trans. T. Burger. Cambridge: Polity Press.

Hall, S. and Whannel, P. 1964: *The Popular Arts*. London: Hutchinson Educational.

Halliwell-Phillipps, J. O. 1840: *The Harrowing of Hell, a Miracle Play*. London: John Russell Smith.

Halliwell-Phillipps, J. O. 1841: *Ludus Coventriae*. London: Shakespeare Society.

Hardison, O. B. Jr. 1965: *Christian Rite and Christian Drama in the Middle Ages*. Baltimore: Johns Hopkins University Press.

Hare, D. 1990: *The Secret Rapture*. London: Faber & Faber.

Hattaway, M. 1982: *Elizabethan Popular Theatre*. London: Routledge Kegan Paul.

Hawkins, H. 1972: *Likenesses of Truth in Elizabethan and Restoration Drama*. Oxford: Oxford University Press.

Hazlitt, W. 1931: *Lectures on the Dramatic Literature of the Age of Elizabeth*. In P. P. Howe (ed.), *Works*, vol. VI, London: J. M. Dent.

Hazlitt, W. 1967a: Lecture VI: on Wycherley, Congreve, Vanbrugh, and Farquhar. In *Lectures on the English Comic Writers*. London: Dent.

Hazlitt, W. 1967b: *The Spirit of the Age*. London: Dent.

Heywood, T. 1888: *The Rape of Lucrece*. In A. Wilson Verity (ed.), *Thomas Heywood*, London: Vizetelly & Co.

Hill, C. 1984: Irreligion in the 'Puritan' revolution. In J. F. McGregor and B. Reay (eds), *Radical Religion in the English Revolution*, Oxford: Oxford University Press.

Holcroft, T. 1802: *A Tale of Mystery*. London: R. Phillips.

Holland, N. 1959: *The First Modern Comedies: the significance of Etherege, Wycherley, and Congreve*. Cambridge, Mass.: Harvard University Press.

Holland, P. 1979: *The Ornament of Action: text and performance in Restoration Comedy*. Cambridge: Cambridge University Press.

Hone, W. 1823: *Ancient Mysteries Described, Especially the English Miracle Plays*. London: William Hone.

Hoyle, M. 1991: Architecture for babies. *The Times*, 21 June.

Hughes, W. 1980: *The Maniac in the Cellar: sensation novels of the 1860s*. Princeton: Princeton University Press.

Hughes-Hallett, L. 1992: The battlefields of love: insights into the work of Roberta Graham. *Performance*, 65/66.

Hume, R. 1976: *The Development of English Drama in the Late Seventeenth Century*. Oxford: Clarendon Press.

Hume, R. D. 1980: *The London Theatre World 1660–1800*. London: Feffer and Simons.

Hunt, A. 1976: *Hopes for Great Happenings: alternatives in education and theatre*. London: Eyre Methuen.

Hunt, A. 1977: A theatre of ideas. In P. Barker (ed.), *Arts in Society*, Glasgow: Fontana.

Hunt, L. 1840: *The Dramatic Works of Richard Brinsley Sheridan*. London: E. Moxon.

Hunter, G. K. and Hunter, S. K. (eds) 1969: *John Webster: a critical anthology*. Harmondsworth. Penguin.

Hunter, J. 1836: Preface *The Towneley Mysteries*. Durham: Surtees Society.

Hurd, R. 1911: *Hurd's Letters on Chivalry and Romance with the Third Elizabethan Dialogue*. Ed. E. J. Morley. London: Henry Frowde.

Hutchison, R. 1982: *The Politics of the Arts Council*. London: Sinclair Browne.

Irving, H. 1886: *English Actors: their characteristics and their methods*. Oxford: Clarendon Press.

Itzin, C. 1980: *Stages in the Revolution: political theatre in Britain since 1968*. London: Eyre Methuen.

James, M. 1986: Ritual, drama and social body in the late medieval English town. In *Society, Politics and Culture: studies in early modern England*. Cambridge: Cambridge University Press, 16–47.

Jameson, F. 1972: *The Prison-House of Language*. N.J.: Princeton University Press.

Jellicoe, A. 1987: *Community Plays: how to put them on*. London: Methuen.

Jenkins, A. 1991: *The Making of Victorian Drama*. Cambridge: Cambridge University Press.

Jerrold, D. 1854: *Comedies and Dramas*. London: Bradbury & Evans.

Johnson, S. 1965: Life of Congreve. In R. Montagu (ed.), *The Lives of the English Poets*, London: The Folio Society.

Johnson, S. 1971: *The Complete English Poems*. Harmondsworth: Penguin.

Johnston, A. F. and Rogerson, M. (eds) 1979: *Records of Early English Drama: York*. 2 vols. Toronto: University of Toronto Press.

Jones, H. A. 1895: *The Renascence of the English Drama*. London: Macmillan.

Jones, H. A. 1982: *Plays by Henry Arthur Jones*. Ed. R. Jackson. Cambridge: Cambridge University Press.

Jones, S. 1899: *The Actor and his Art*. London: Downey and Co.

Kavenik, F. 1991: Aphra Behn: the playwright as 'breeches part'. In M. A. Schofield and C. Macheski (eds), *Curtain Calls: British and American women and the theater, 1660–1820*, Athens, Ohio: Ohio University Press.

Kendall 1988: *Love and Thunder: plays by women in the age of Queen Anne*. London: Methuen Drama.

Kennedy, D. 1985: *Granville Barker and the Dream of Theatre*. Cambridge: Cambridge University Press.

Kenney, J. 1808: *The Blind Boy of Bohemia*. London: Longman, Hurst, Rees & Orme.

Kershaw, B. 1992: *The Politics of Performance: radical theatre as cultural intervention*. London: Routledge.

Kilgarriff, M. 1974: *The Golden Age of Melodrama*. London: Wolfe Publishing.

King, S. 1976: *Salem's Lot*. London: Hodder & Stoughton.

Knight, G. W. 1962: *Ibsen*. Edinburgh: Oliver & Boyd.

Knights, L. C. 1963: Restoration Comedy: the reality and the myth. In *Explorations*, London: Chatto & Windus.

Kolve, V. A. 1966: *The Play Called Corpus Christi*. Stanford: Stanford University Press.

Krutch, J. W. 1949: *Comedy and Conscience after the Restoration*. Second edition. New York: Columbia University Press.

Lamb, C. 1913: On the artificial comedy of the last century. In A. Hamilton Thompson (ed.), *Essays of Elia*, Cambridge: Cambridge University Press.

Lamb, C. 1980: *Lamb as Critic*. Ed. R. Park. London: Routledge Kegan Paul.

Lancashire, I. 1977: Medieval drama. In A. G. Rigg (ed.), *Editing Medieval Texts English, French and Latin Written in England*, New York and London: Garland Publishing.

Lavender, A. 1989: Theatre in Crisis: conference report, December 1988. *New Theatre Quarterly*, 19.

Laver, J. 1952: Gabrielle Enthoven, O. B. E., and the Enthoven Theatre Collection. In M. St. Clare Byrne (ed.), *Studies in English Theatre History in Memory of Gabrielle Enthoven, O.B.E. First President of the Society for Theatre Research, 1948–1950*. London: Society for Theatre Research.

Lawrence, W. J. 1935: *Those Nut-Cracking Elizabethans*. London: Argonaut Press.

Le Fleming, S. 1993: Coping with the outlandish: the English response to Chekhov's plays 1911–1926. In Miles, P. 1993.

Levin, B. 1985: When mystery was an open book. *The Times*, April. Reprinted in *Making of the Mysteries*, 1985.

Lewes, G. 1875: *On Actors and the Art of Acting*. London.

Lewes, G. 1964: *Literary Criticism of George Henry Lewes*. Ed. A. R. Kaminsky. Lincoln, Nebraska: University of Nebraska Press.

Lewis, M. 1806: *Rugantino: or, the Bravo of Venice*. London: J. F. Hughes.

Locke, J. 1963: *Two Treatises of Government*. Ed. P. Laslett. Second edition. Cambridge: Cambridge University Press.

Loftis, J. 1952: *Steele at Drury Lane*. Berkeley: University of California Press.

Loftis, J. et al. (eds) 1976: *The Revels History of Drama in English*. vol. V, *1660–1750*. London: Methuen.

Lozar, P. 1976: The 'Prologue' to the ordinances of the York Corpus Christi Guild. *Allegorica*, 1, 94–113.

Lukács, G. 1963: *The Meaning of Contemporary Realism*. London: Merlin Press.

Lukács, G. 1977: Realism in the balance. In R. Taylor (ed.), *Aesthetics and Politics*, London: Verso.

Lukács, G. 1978: Narrate or describe? In *Writer and Critic*, London: Merlin Press.

Lyons, P. and Morgan, F. (eds) 1991: *Female Playwrights of the Restoration*. London: J. M. Dent & Sons.

Lyotard, J-F. 1984: *The Postmodern Condition: a report on knowledge*. Trans. G. Bennington and B. Massumi. Manchester: Manchester University Press.

Macaulay, T. B. 1885: Comic dramatists of the Restoration. In *Lord Macaulay's Essays and Lays of Ancient Rome*, London: Longmans, Green, and Co.

Macleod, J. 1943: *The New Soviet Theatre*. London: George Allen & Unwin Ltd.

MacShane, D. 1994: in *New Statesman and Society*, 22 July.

*Making of the Mysteries, The* 1985: London: Channel Four Television.

Marowitz, C. 1968: Review of *Hair*. *Plays and Players*, November.

Marriott, J. B. (ed.) 1929: *Great Modern British Plays*. London: Harrap.

Marriott, W. 1838: *A Collection of English Miracle-Plays or Mysteries*. Basel.

Massinger, P. 1887–9: *The Roman Actor*. In A. Symons (ed.), *Philip Massinger*, 2 vols, London: T. Fisher Unwin.

Mayer, D. 1980: *Henry Irving and 'The Bells'*. Manchester: Manchester University Press.

Mazer, C. M. 1981: *Shakespeare Refashioned: Elizabethan plays on Edwardian stages*. Ann Arbor, Michigan: UMI Research Press.

McDonald, J. 1984: New actors for the new drama. In J. Redmond (ed.), *Themes in Drama*, vol. VI, *Drama and the Actor*, Cambridge: Cambridge University Press, 121–40.

McDonald, J. 1993: Chekhov, naturalism and the drama of dissent: productions of

Chekhov's plays in Britain before 1914. In Miles, P. 1993.

McGrath, J. 1972: *Plugged into History. Plays and Players*, November.

McGrath, J. 1977: *The Cheviot, the Stag and the Black, Black Oil*. Isle of Skye: West Highland Publishing Co.

McGrath, J. 1981: *A Good Night Out*. London: Methuen.

McGrath, J. 1990: *The Bone Won't Break*. London: Methuen.

McLeish, R. 1985: *The Gorbals Story*. Ed. L. Mackenney. Edinburgh: 7:84 Publications.

McLuskie, K. 1989: *Renaissance Dramatists*. New York and London: Harvester Wheatsheaf.

McNeir, W. F. 1951: The Corpus Christi Passion Plays as dramatic art. *Studies in Philology*, 48, 601–28.

McVay, G. 1993: Peggy Ashcroft and Chekhov. In Miles, P. 1993.

Medcalf, S. (ed.) 1981: *The Context of English Literature: the later Middle Ages*. London: Methuen.

Medwall, H. 1980: *The Plays of Henry Medwall*. Ed. A. H. Nelson. Cambridge: D. S. Brewer.

Meisel, M. 1983: *Realizations: narrative, pictorial and theatrical arts of nineteenth-century England*. Princeton: Princeton University Press.

Meredith, G. 1910: *An Essay on Comedy and the Uses of the Comic Spirit*. In *Miscellaneous Prose*, New York: Charles Scribner's Sons.

Middleton, T. 1975: *Women Beware Women*. Ed. J. R. Mulryne. London: Methuen.

Miles, P. 1993: *Chekhov on the British Stage*. Cambridge: Cambridge University Press.

Milhous, J. 1979: *Thomas Betterton and the Management of Lincoln's Inn Fields*. Carbondale: University of South Illinois Press.

Milne, T. 1964: Reflections on *The Screens. Encore*, July/August. Reprinted in Williams, D. 1988, p. 57.

Minihan, J. 1977: *The Nationalization of Culture*. London: Hamish Hamilton.

Moncrieff, W. T. n.d.: *The Scamps of London or, the Cross Roads of Life*. London: T. H. Lacy.

Moretti, F. 1988: The spell of indecision. In C. Nelson and L. Grossberg (eds), *Marxism and the Interpretation of Culture*, Basingstoke: Macmillan Educational.

Morgann, M. 1972: *Shakespearian Criticism*. Ed. D. A. Fineman. Oxford: Oxford University Press.

Morley, H. 1974: *The Journal of a London Playgoer*. Reprint. Leicester: Leicester University Press.

Mullaney, S. 1988: *The Place of the Stage*. Chicago: University of Chicago Press.

Munns, J. 1988: Barton and Behn's *The Rover*; or, the text transpos'd. *Restoration and Eighteenth Century Theatre Research*, 3(2).

Nagler, A. M. 1952: *A Source Book in Theatrical History*. New York: Dover Publications.

National Curriculum 1989: *English for Ages 5 to 16: proposals of the Secretaries of State for Education and Science and for Wales*. London: Department of Education and Science and Welsh Office.

Nead, L. 1992: *The Female Nude*. London: Routledge.

Nicholson, W. 1906: *The Struggle for a Free Stage in London*. London: Archibald Constable & Co.

Nicoll, A. 1980: *The Garrick Stage: theatres and audiences in the eighteenth century*. Manchester: Manchester University Press.

NTQ Symposium 1989: Theatre in Thatcher's Britain: organizing the opposition. *New Theatre Quarterly*, 18.

O'Casey, S. 1985: *Seven Plays*. Ed. R. Ayling. London: Macmillan.

O'Connor, M. F. 1987: Theatre of the empire: 'Shakespeare's England' at Earl's Court, 1912. In J. E. Howard and M. F. O'Connor (eds), *Shakespeare Reproduced*, London: Methuen, 68–98.

Ormerod, G. 1819: *The History of the County Palatine and City of Chester*. London: Lockington.

Osborne, J. 1957: *The Entertainer*. London: Faber.

Osborne, J. 1976: *Look Back in Anger*. London: Faber & Faber.

Otway, T. 1932: *Works*. Ed. J. C. Ghosh. 2 vols. Oxford: Oxford University Press.

Page, M. (ed.) 1985: *Arden on File*. London: Methuen.

Palmer, J. 1962: *The Comedy of Manners*. New York: Russell.

*Parliamentary Debates* (Lords) 1949: 5th ser. 160.

Percy, T. 1765: *Reliques of Ancient English Poetry*. 3 vols. London: J. Dodsley.

Perry, R. 1986: *The Celebrated Mary Astell: an early English feminist*. Chicago: University of Chicago Press.

Phillips, M. n.d. [1981]: Black theatre in Britain. *Platform*, 3.

Phythian-Adams, C. 1972: Ceremony and the citizen: the communal year at Coventry 1450–1550. In P. Clark and P. Slack (eds), *Crisis and Order in English Towns 1500–1700*, London: Routledge and Kegan Paul, 57–85.

Pick, J. 1983: *The West End: mismanagement and snobbery*. Eastbourne: John Offord.

Pinero, A. W. 1986: *Plays*. Ed. G. Rowell. Cambridge: Cambridge University Press.

Pinter, H. 1960: *The Birthday Party*. London: Methuen.

Pinter, H. 1981: *Plays: four*. London: Methuen.

Pitt, G. D. 1844: *A Woman's Life and Trials of the Heart – or the Witch and the Spectre*. Play on fiche in *Nineteenth Century English and American Plays*. New Canaan, Conn.: Readex.

Pitt, G. D. 1848: *The Revolution at Paris*. Play on fiche in *Nineteenth Century English and American Plays*. New Canaan, Conn.: Readex.

Pix, M. 1991: *The Beau Defeated*. In P. Lyons and F. Morgan (eds), *Female Playwrights of the Restoration: five comedies*, London: Dent, 161–234.

*Plays and Players* 1973: photo-feature on nudity in the theatre (section of an article on London's long-running shows), January.

Poel, W. 1968: *Shakespeare in the Theatre*. Reprint. New York: Benjamin Blom.

Powell, J. 1805: *The Venetian Outlaw, his Country's Friend*. London: M. Allen.

Prendergast, C. 1978: *Balzac: fiction and melodrama*. London: Edward Arnold.

Priestley, J. B. 1948: *Plays*. 3 vols. London: Heinemann.

Rahill, F. 1967: *The World of Melodrama*. University Park: Pennsylvania State University Press.

Ratcliffe, M. 1994: Collusion between celebrants. In programme for *Street of Crocodiles*, London: Royal National Theatre.

Rayner, B. n.d.: *The Dumb Man of Manchester*. London: T. H. Lacy.

Reade, C. 1986: *Plays*. Ed. M. Hammet. Cambridge: Cambridge University Press.

Rees, T. 1978: *Theatre Lighting in the Age of Gas*. London: Society for Theatre Research.

*Reformation, The* 1986: Augustan Reprint Society, nos. 237–8.

*Retrospective Review* 1820: Mysteries, moralities, and the other early drama. London, vol. I.

Reynolds, F. 1827: *The Life and Times of Frederick Reynolds*. 2 vols. London: Henry Colburn.

Righter, A. 1965: Heroic tragedy. In J. R. Brown and R. Harris (eds), *Restoration Drama*, London: Edward Arnold.

Ritchie, R. (ed.) 1987: *The Joint Stock Book*. London: Methuen.

Roberts, D. 1989: *The Ladies: female patronage of Restoration drama 1660–1700*. Oxford: Clarendon Press.

Roberts, J. 1988: *German Philosophy: an introduction*. Cambridge: Polity Press.

Robertson, T. W. 1982: *Plays*. Ed. W. Tydeman. Cambridge: Cambridge University Press.

Rogers, J. S. 1985: *Stage by Stage: the making of the Theatre Museum*. London: HMSO.

Rossiter, A. P. 1950: *English Drama from the Early Times to the Elizabethans*. London: Hutchinson.

Rowell, G. 1971: *Victorian Dramatic Criticism*. London: Methuen.

Sackville-West, V. 1927: *Aphra Behn, the Incomparable Astrea*. London: Gerald Howe.

Samuel, R. et al. 1985: *Theatres of the Left 1880–1935*. London: Routledge Kegan Paul.

Schechner, R. 1982: Genet's *The Balcony*: a 1981 perspective on a 1979/80 production. *Modern Drama*, 25(1).

Schechner, R. 1983: *Performative Circumstances from the Avant Garde to Ramlila*. Calcutta: Seagull Books.

Sedley, C. 1928: *The Mulberry Garden*. In V. De Sola Pinto (ed.), *Poetical and Dramatic Works*, vol. I, London: Constable, 99–186.

Sellar, W. C. and Yeatman, R. J. 1975: *1066 And All That*. Paperback edition. London: Methuen.

Shadwell, T. 1966: *The Virtuoso*. London: Edward Arnold.

Shaffer, P. 1964: *The Royal Hunt of the Sun*. London: Hamish Hamilton.

Shaffer, P. 1973: *Equus*. London: André Deutsch.

Shaffer, P. 1980: *Amadeus*. London: André Deutsch.

Shakespeare, W. 1964: *Macbeth*. Ed. K. Muir. London: Methuen.

Shakespeare, W. 1982: *Hamlet*. Ed. H. Jenkins. London and New York: Methuen.

Sharp, T. 1825: *A Dissertation on the Pageants or Dramatic Mysteries Anciently Performed at Coventry*. Coventry: Merridew.

Shaw, G. B. 1930: *The Quintessence of Ibsenism*. In *The Works of Bernard Shaw*, vol. 19, London: Constable, 3–161.

Shaw, G. B. 1971: *Three Plays for Puritans*. In *Collected Plays with their Prefaces*, vol. 2, London: Bodley Head.

Shirley, J. 1888: *The Triumph of Peace*. In E. Gosse (ed.), *James Shirley*, London: T. Fisher Unwin.

Shirley, J. 1965: *The Traitor*. Ed. J. S. Carter. London: Edward Arnold.

Sidnell, M. 1984: *Dances of Death: the Group Theatre of London in the thirties*. London: Faber & Faber.

Sinfield, A. 1985: Royal Shakespeare. In J. Dollimore and A. Sinfield (eds), *Political Shakespeare*, Manchester: Manchester University Press, 158–81.

Slater, M. 1928: Introduction. In *Two Classic Melodramas: Maria Marten and Sweeney Todd*, London: Gerald Howe.

Smith, J. L. 1973: *Melodrama*. London: Methuen.

Smith, J. L. 1976: *Victorian Melodramas*. London: Dent.

Southern, R. 1957: *The Medieval Theatre in the Round*. London: Faber.

Speaight, G. 1946: *Juvenile Drama: the history of English toy theatre*. London: Macdonald & Co.

Speaight, G. 1988: *Collecting Theatre Memorabilia*. Ashbourne: Morland Publishing Co.

Speaight, R. 1954: *William Poel and the Elizabethan Revival*. London: Heinemann.

Spector, S. (ed.) 1991: *The N-Town Play*. 2 vols. Oxford: Oxford University Press for the Early English Text Society.

Stafford-Clark, M. 1989: *Letters to George*. London: Nick Hern Books.

Staves, S. 1987: *Players' Sceptres: fictions of authority in the Restoration*. Lincoln, Nebraska: University of Nebraska Press.

Steele, R. 1962: *The Theatre 1720*. Ed. J. Loftis. Oxford: Clarendon Press.

Steele, R. 1971: *The Conscious Lovers*. In Shirley Strum Kenny (ed.), *The Plays of Richard Steele*, Oxford: Oxford University Press, 297–382.

Steele, R. 1982: *The Guardian*. Ed. John Calhoun Stephens. Lexington: University Press of Kentucky.

Stephens, J. R. 1980: *The Censorship of English Drama 1824–1903*. Cambridge: Cambridge University Press.

Stephens, J. R. 1992: *The Profession of the Playwright: British Theatre 1800–1900*. Cambridge: Cambridge University Press.

Stoker, B. 1907: *Personal Reminiscences of Henry Irving*. London: William Heinemann.

Stoker, B. 1983: *Dracula*. Oxford: Oxford University Press.

Stokes, J. 1972: *Resistible Theatres*. London: Elek.

Stone, L. 1990: *Road to Divorce: England 1530–1987*. Oxford: Oxford University Press.

Stourac, R. and McCreery, K. 1986: *Theatre as a Weapon: workers' theatre in the Soviet Union, Germany and Britain 1917–1934*. London: Routledge & Kegan Paul.

Strasberg, L. 1989: *A Dream of Passion: the development of the method*. London: Methuen Drama.

Straub, K. 1992: *Sexual Suspects: eighteenth century players and sexual ideology*. Princeton: Princeton University Press.

Strutt, J. 1775: *A Compleat View of the Manners, Customs, Arms, Habits, etc. of the Inhabitants of England*. 3 vols. London.

Strutt, J. 1801: *Glig-Gamena Angel-Deod., or the Sports and Pastimes of the People of England*. London.

Stuart, I. 1991: Answering the dead: Edward Bond's *Jackets*, 1989–90. *New Theatre Quarterly*, 26.

Styan, J. L. 1977: *The Shakespeare Revolution*. Cambridge: Cambridge University Press.

Styan, J. L. 1986: *Restoration Comedy in Performance*. Cambridge: Cambridge University Press.

Summers, M. 1915: *The Works of Aphra Behn*. London: W. Heinemann.

Summers, M. 1920: *The Marquis de Sade: a study in algolagnia*. London: Bentley Bros.

Summers, M. 1926: *The Complete Works of Thomas Otway*. Bloomsbury: The Nonesuch Press.

Summers, M. 1934: *The Restoration Theatre*. London: Kegan Paul, Trench, Trubner & Co.

Taylor, A. M. 1950: *Next to Shakespeare: Otway's 'Venice Preserv'd' and 'The Orphan' and their history on the London stage*. Durham, North Carolina: Duke University Press.

Taylor, B. 1983: *Eve and the New Jerusalem: socialism and feminism in the nineteenth century*. London: Virago Press.

Taylor, G. 1989: *Players and Performances in the Victorian Theatre*. Manchester: Manchester University Press.

Taylor, G. 1990: *Reinventing Shakespeare: a cultural history from the Restoration to the present*. London: Hogarth Press.

Taylor, J. R. 1966: *Anger and After*. Harmondsworth: Penguin.

*The Theatre* 1880: nos 1 and 2 (n.s.).

Theatre Workshop 1965: *Oh What A Lovely War*. London: Methuen.

Thomas, D. (ed.) 1989: *Restoration and Georgian England 1660–1788*. Theatre in Europe: A Documentary History. Cambridge: Cambridge University Press.

Tiddy, R. J. E. 1923: *The Mummers' Play*, with memoir of Tiddy. Oxford: Clarendon Press.

Tillyard, E. M. W. 1943: *The Elizabethan World Picture*. London: Chatto and Windus.

Trussler, S. 1994: *The Cambridge Illustrated History of British Theatre*. Cambridge: Cambridge University Press.

Twycross, M. 1983: 'Transvestism' in the mystery plays. *Medieval English Theatre*, 5(2).

*US: the book of the Royal Shakespeare Company production* 1968: London: Calder and Boyars.

Van Lennep, W. (ed.) 1965: *The London Stage 1660–1800*. part I, 1660–1700. Carbondale: South Illinois University Press.

Vanbrugh, J. 1927: A short vindication of *The Relapse* and *The Provok'd Wife*. In B. Dobrée and G. Webb (eds), *Complete Works*, vol. IV, London: Nonesuch Press, 193–216.

Vanbrugh, J. 1989: *Four Comedies*. Ed. M. Cordner. Harmondsworth: Penguin.

Vardac, N. 1949: *From Stage to Screen: theatrical method from Garrick to Griffith*. Cambridge, Mass.: Harvard University Press.

Vickers, B. (ed.) 1979: *Shakespeare: the critical heritage*, vol. V, 1765–1774. London: Routledge Kegan Paul.

Wain, J. 1956: Restoration comedy and its modern critics. *Essays in Criticism*, 6(4).

Walker, A. 1964: Edward Capell and his edition of Shakespeare. In P. Alexander (ed.), *Studies in Shakespeare*, Oxford: Oxford University Press, 132–48.

Walker, J. n.d.: *Nell Gwynne*. London: J. Duncombe & Co.

Wallis, M. 1994a: Pageantry and the Popular Front: ideological production in the 'thirties. *New Theatre Quarterly*, 38.

Wallis, M. 1994b: 'To be, or not to be' – What are the questions? In I. Clarke (ed.), *Hamlet. Essays*, Loughborough: Loughborough Theatre Texts.

Wallis, M. 1995: The Popular Front pageant: its emergence and decline. *New Theatre Quarterly*, 41.

Ward, A. W. 1875: *A History of English Dramatic Literature*. vol. III. London: Macmillan.

Warton, T. 1774–81: *The History of English Poetry from the Close of the Eleventh to the*

*Commencement of the Eighteenth Century.* 3 vols. London.

Waterhouse, R. 1971: A case of Restoration. *Plays and Players*, November.

Weimann, R. 1987: *Shakespeare and the Popular Tradition in the Theater.* Ed. R. Schwartz. Baltimore: Johns Hopkins University Press.

Wertenbaker, T. 1991: *Our Country's Good.* London: Methuen.

Wesker, A. 1964: *The Wesker Trilogy.* Harmondsworth: Penguin.

West, A. 1975: *Crisis and Criticism, and Selected Literary Essays.* London: Lawrence & Wishart.

White, A. 1993: *Carnival, Hysteria and Writing: collected essays and autobiography.* Oxford: Clarendon Press.

White, P. W. 1993: *Theatre and Reformation.* Cambridge: Cambridge University Press.

Wickham, G. 1963: *Early English Stages 1300 to 1660*, vol. II, part I. London: Routledge and Kegan Paul.

Williams, D. (ed.) 1988: *Peter Brook: a theatrical casebook.* London: Methuen.

Williams, R. 1991: *Drama in Performance.* Milton Keynes: Open University Press.

Williams, R. 1973: *Drama from Ibsen to Brecht.* Harmondsworth: Penguin.

Williams, R. 1975: *The Long Revolution.* Harmondsworth: Penguin.

Williams, R. 1978: *Politics and Letters.* London: Verso.

Wilmut, R. and Rosengard, P. 1989: *Didn't You Kill My Mother-in-Law?* London: Methuen.

Womack, P. 1992: Imagining communities. In D. Aers (ed.), *Culture and History 1350–1600*, Hemel Hempstead: Harvester Wheatsheaf, 91–146.

Woodfield, J. 1984: *English Theatre in Transition 1881–1914.* London: Croom Helm.

Wyndham, H. S. 1906: *The Annals of Covent Garden Theatre from 1732 to 1897.* 2 vols. London: Chatto & Windus.

Yeats, W. B. 1961: *Essays and Introductions.* London: Macmillan.

Yeats, W. B. 1982: *Collected Plays.* Paperback edition. London: Macmillan.

Young, K. 1933: *The Drama of the Medieval Church.* 2 vols. Oxford: Clarendon Press.

Zephaniah, B. 1989: *Job Rocking.* In Y. Brewster (ed.), *Black Plays: two.* London: Methuen.

# Index of Proper Names

# Index of Keywords